W9-DHG-891

W.H. Auden
A Legacy

Edited by

David Garrett Izzo

LOCUST HILL PRESS
West Cornwall, CT

Library of Congress Cataloging-in-Publication Data

W.H. Auden : a legacy / edited by David Garrett Izzo.
    p.   cm. -- (Locust Hill literary studies ; no. 31)
    Includes bibliographical references and index.
    ISBN 0-933951-94-9 (lib. bdg. : acid-free paper)
    1. Auden, W.H. (Wystan Hugh), 1907-1973--Criticism and
interpretation. I. Izzo, David Garrett. II. Series.

PR6001.U4 Z885 2001
811'.52--dc21

                  2001050308

"As I Walked Out One Evening", copyright 1940 & renewed 1968 by W.H. Auden, "The More Loving One", copyright © 1957 by W.H. Auden, "A Lullaby", "Twelve Songs", copyright 1937 and renewed 1965 by W.H. Auden, "Letter to Lord Byron", copyright 1937 by W.H. Auden, "Journey", "Spain 1937", copyright 1940 & renewed 1968 by W.H. Auden, "A Voyage", from W.H. AUDEN: COLLECTED POEMS by W.H. Auden, copyright © 1976 by Edward Mendelson, William Meredith and Monroe K. Spears, Executors of the Estate of W.H. Auden. Used by permission of Random House, Inc.

Pp. 441–485 *passim*: From COLLECTED POEMS by James Merrill, copyright © 2001 by the Estate of James Merrill. Used by permission of Alfred A. Knopf, a division of Random House, Inc.

Printed on acid-free, 250-year-life paper
Manufactured in the United States of America

To my wife, Carol Ann Corrody,

To my friend the novelist/essayist Richard Stern
and to his friend the poet and gay activist Edgar
Bowers, who left his body on 4 February 2000.

Acknowledgments

Tom Bechtle, the kid from Long Island who had a dream; Edward Mendelson, who keeps Auden's dream alive; Martin Blank: the Truly Strong Man; to my mother who passed away on 19 January 2001; to Don Bachardy who graciously spoke to Jim Fisher for Jim's essay; the Vedanta Society of Southern California; my brother Paul, Rosemary, and P.J.; Lo Corrody and David Corrody; Bill Corrody, Yong, Mary Ann, Lauren, and Billy; Mark, Lucille, and Dan Fink; and especially to the contributors, without whom I am the editor of nothing.

Contents

Introduction

W.H. Auden was a great poet, but he represents much more and left us much more than just his verse. Yes, he was the first or second most important twentieth-century poet in English (the other hierarchical choice being T.S. Eliot). And now that the twentieth century has ended, Auden must make his presence felt in the twenty-first century. It is time to know again that Auden was a poet plus. He leaves a legacy of influence that certainly includes his verse but does not preclude the adventures of his life, the plays he wrote (which are under-appreciated), the brilliant essays of literary criticism and philosophy, the gestalt of being first the *enfant terrible* of British poetry in the 1930s, and later the expatriate who grew into his furrowed face of Martian canals that said: "Look at me; I have lived enough for more than one lifetime." (And who is to say, as per Isherwood's beliefs as a neo-Hindu mystic, that this isn't true?) Indeed, now and in the future, more lifetimes than just those of the past century can look forward to appreciating him.

This anthology by no means ignores Auden-as-poet, but rather acknowledges that the poet-Auden has received his deservedly just due from previous studies, most notably those by his literary executor and *the* preeminent Auden scholar, Edward Mendelson. Rather, this collection is both an appreciation and scholarly study, with a group of informal articles about Auden as man and icon, and more essays about Auden as a major figure for academic appreciation. He is man and artist, and of late has been somewhat betwixt and between legend and museum piece. He is still remembered and appreciated for what he *was*, but both the world at large and the academy need to be reminded of who he *is*!

Modern verse would not be the same if Auden had not chosen to write his own. Modern sensibility would not be the same if he hadn't lived. He coined the phrase *The Age of Anxiety* after World War II, and it aptly described the second half of his century. Before

World War II he was revered as the "coming man" who was the de facto leader and inspiration to a generation of anti-heroic rebellious artists who would be emulated in the succeeding generations. Britain's "angry young men" of the 1950s were the first lineal descendents. Today's hero was the anti-hero of Auden's era—the sensitive man who came to grips with the turmoil of his inner and outer worlds. This assessment of Auden's stature is not overstated. *The Modern Library* featured him in a volume titled *Makers of the Modern World*—and one need only see the company he keeps in this volume to validate that he belongs with the best and brightest in every human endeavor that shaped the century so recently ended.

All but three of the twenty-five essays included herein were written for this volume, and the three reprinted articles deserve the second look. Auden still makes the features page in newspapers, and this volume leads off with Jim Ross's 1999 article about Auden for the *Saint Petersburg Sun-Times* (which will also serve as an introduction of sorts to readers now just learning about Auden). Poet J.D. McClatchy explains Auden's legacy as poet in an interview from the Auden Society Newsletter. One of our most esteemed men of letters and fiction writers, Richard Stern, writes movingly of the influence of the poet Auden on his young life and then of meeting Auden later. Auden loved to teach and believed this to be one of his roles and goals as a poet—to teach through parable; in this regard Stephen Gale shows, by teaching an Auden poem to his English class, how Auden teaches still. Auden as teacher is the subject of the editor's interview with John Duguid, who was the poet's adolescent student in England at The Downs preparatory school in the mid 1930s. Rod Jellema recalls Auden the gentleman who chose to defer to an older fellow named J.R.R. Tolkien. Dennis Paddie takes on the "cool distance" of Auden's gay spirituality.

The formal essays then begin to insert themselves (with an essay on Gerald Heard excepted) and look at Auden's life and work in more or less chronological order.

James Young considers the very early influence of D.H. Lawrence on Auden. Chris Hopkins looks at a still-young Auden and his relationship with one his earliest supporters, Naomi Mitchison. Then there are two articles on a fellow named Gerald Heard. The first is a general introduction to one of the most important yet unknown influences of the twentieth century, and in the second Paul Eros draws the specific correlation of Heard to Auden.

Adrienne Hacker-Daniels, a scholar of rhetoric, meets head-on Auden's most challenging work, *The Orators*, and analyzes the connection to Ciceronian/Roman rhetoric and Auden's epic. The under-appreciated Auden-Isherwood plays are given their due in two essays: Owen Brady sees *The Dog Beneath the Skin* as a performance vehicle with an analysis of the combination of words and staging that delivered the full message of a British society in terminal decay. Richard and Janis Londraville examine the early plays and the connections of Auden to W.B. Yeats.

Letters from Iceland provides the fulcrum upon which Robert L. Caserio makes his case for Auden's place among gay modernists. Rory McTurk, an Icelandic scholar and linguist, analyzes the poem *Journey to Iceland*, its translation into Icelandic, which he then translates literally into English, after which he annotates the people and history contained therein. Peter C. Grosvenor writes about one of the watershed events of the later 1930s, the Spanish Civil War, and Auden's participation as well as his poem "Spain." Auden and Isherwood made a *Journey to a War* (Sino-Japanese in 1938), and Douglas Kerr writes about what they found and the book that resulted.

In 1939 Auden landed in America and returned to the church; Brian Conniff talks about Auden's re-conversion and the influence of theologian Paul Tillich. James Fisher sees the Christopher Isherwood-Don Bachardy play, *A Meeting by the River*, as a logical extension of the Auden-Isherwood plays, and his essay includes an interview with Bachardy.

There has been some debate by critics as to whether or not Auden was a "modernist" poet; Jay Ladin considers this question by defining both modernism and Auden. The fact that Auden was a librettist is less known, and here Robert Stanley looks at the Auden-Kallman translation of Mozart's *The Magic Flute*. Auden as a man-child never lost his love for children's literature; one will read of Auden's ideas concerning Fairy-Tales, Quests, and Sagas. Then, as an ultimate consideration of Auden's influence on another poet, Piotr Gwiadza explains how James Merrill composed his own verse epic sagas and featured Auden as the central character. Lastly, Roger Lathbury looks back at the essays that precede his.

In sum: This volume is about W.H. Auden's legacy; hence, it is not about his past, but his future.

Contributors

David Garrett Izzo (Editor) is a former writer and editor from New York City who became an educator in 1985. He is the author of the novel *A Change of Heart: An Historical Fiction of British Authors, 1929–1933*. His non-fiction studies are *Aldous Huxley and W.H. Auden: On Language*, *Christopher Isherwood: His Era, His Gang, and the Legacy of the Truly Strong Man*, and *The Writings of Richard Stern: The Education of an Intellectual Everyman*. He wrote, performed, and published the one-man play, *The American World of Stephen Vincent Benet*. He is the editor of and contributor to *Advocates and Activists Who Shaped the Twentieth Century: With an Emphasis on the Period Between the Wars*, and co-editor of and contributor to *Thornton Wilder: New Essays*. David has also published essays on Auden, Isherwood, Huxley, Benet, Gerald Heard, AE (George Russell), Conrad Aiken, Thornton Wilder, Archibald MacLeish, Vachel Lindsay, Carl Sandburg, Lew Sarett, Scott Nearing, Paul Rosenfeld, Genevieve Taggard, Sara Teasdale, and Elinor Wylie.

Owen E. Brady is Associate Professor of Humanities at Clarkson University, Potsdam, NY. His teaching and research focus primarily on dramatic literature and performance. He has published numerous articles and theatrical reviews on drama from ancient Greece, Renaissance England, and contemporary Canada and the United States. His critical work on Thornton Wilder, Theodore Ward, Amiri Baraka, David Rabe, and Richard Boleslavsky have appeared in such publications as the editor's volumes *Thornton Wilder: New Essays* and *Advocates and Activists Who Shaped the Twentieth Century: With an Emphasis on the Period Between the Wars* as well as *Callaloo*, Prentice-Hall's *Twentieth Century Views* series, *War, Literature and the Arts*, and *Theatre Journal*.

Robert L. Caserio chairs the Department of English at Temple University. He is the author of *The Novel in England 1900–1950:*

Theory and History (Twayne-Simon & Schuster-Macmillan, 1999). His previous essay on Auden, "Auden's New Citizenship," appeared in *Raritan*.

Brian Conniff is the Chair of English and Associate Professor at the University of Dayton. He is the author of *The Lyric and Modern Poetry: Olson, Creeley, Bunting* and is in progress with two books: *The Sacred and the Poetic: W.H. Auden's Encounter with Theology*, and *Before the Law: Race, Morality and Violence in Contemporary American Prison Writing*. Conniff is on the Board of Directors of the Conference for Christianity and Literature.

Paul Eros is a D.Phil. candidate at Corpus Christi College, University of Oxford. He is currently writing a monograph on Gerald Heard. His research interests include Aldous Huxley, P.G. Wodehouse, pacifism between the wars, and literary dandyism. An avid fan of the automobile, he's most happy when tooling about Oxfordshire in his 1968 Morris Minor.

James Fisher, Professor of Theater at Wabash College in Indiana, has authored five books, including *The Theater of Tony Kushner, Living Past Hope* (Routledge, 2001), and has published articles and reviews in numerous periodicals (including the editor's *Advocates and Activists Who Shaped the Twentieth Century: With an Emphasis on the Period Between the Wars* and *Thornton Wilder: New Essays*). He has held several research fellowships, edits *The Puppetry Yearbook*, and is book review editor of the *Journal of Dramatic Theory and Criticism*. Fisher was 1999–2000 McLain-McTurnan-Arnold Research Scholar at Wabash and was named "Indiana Theater Person of the Year" by the Indiana Theater Association in 1997. He is currently completing books on Edward Gordon Craig and Stephen Sondheim.

Stephen Gale received his B.A. from Duke, his M.A. from the University of California at Los Angeles and his Ph.D. from the University of Southern California. He has taught at UCLA, USC, the University of Puerto Rico, the University of Liberia (as a Fulbright Professor), the University of Florida, and Missouri Southern State College (where he was head of the Department of English). Currently, he is the holder of the University Endowed Chair in the Humanities at Kentucky State University. Gale was the founding President of the Harold Pinter Society. He is the author of nineteen scholarly books (including *Butter's Going Up: An Analysis of Harold Pinter's Work; Harold Pinter: An Annotated Bibliography; Harold Pinter: Critical Approaches; Critical Essays on Harold Pinter; The Films of Harold Pinter: Collected Essays; Encyclopedia of American Humorists; Encyclopedia of British Humorists;* three volumes on S.J. Perelman; and two on West African folktales. He has also published well over one hundred articles and book chapters. In addition, he is the founding co-editor of a book *series (The Harold Pinter Review: Annual Essays)* and the General Editor of Garland's "Critical Essays on Humor" series. Presently he is completing a monograph, *Harold Pinter: The Screenplays,* and working on a novel and a screenplay.

Peter C. Grosvenor graduated in Political Theory and Government from the University College of Swansea. He was subsequently awarded an M.Sc. in International Relations and a Ph.D. in Government from the London School of Economics. He is currently an Assistant Professor of Political Science at Pacific Lutheran University in Tacoma, Washington.

Piotr Gwiazda has recently completed a dissertation on James Merrill and W.H. Auden at New York University. His essays and papers have appeared *in XCP: Cross Cultural Poetics, Texas Studies in Language and Literature, The Explicator,* and other journals. He teaches at the University of Miami, Florida.

Adrienne Hacker-Daniels is an Assistant Professor in the Department of Communication & Theatre at Illinois College, Jacksonville, Illinois. She has written essays on Thornton Wilder (for the editor's *Thornton Wilder: New* Essays, 1999), Hallie Flanagan and Maurice Schwartz (for the editor's forthcoming *Advocates and Activists Who Shaped the Twentieth Century: With an Emphasis on the Period between the Wars*), and Gertrude Stein, and she is completing a manuscript on eloquence in the plays of Thornton Wilder. Her main area of research is examining the rhetorical dimensions of literary—or, as Auden would say, verbal—artifacts.

Chris Hopkins is a Senior Lecturer in English Studies at Sheffield Hallam University. He works mainly on British writing between the Wars and Anglo-Welsh writing. He has published on these topics in journals including *Critical Survey, Literature and History, Focus on Robert Graves and His Contemporaries, Notes and Queries, The Journal of Gender Studies, The Review of Irish Studies, The Review* *of Contemporary Fiction, English Language Notes* and *Style*. He has contributed chapters to several books on the 1930s, including three in editor's *Advocates and Activists Who Shaped the Twentieth Century: With an Emphasis on the Period between the Wars.* He has published *Thinking About Texts: An Introduction to English Studies* (Palgrave, 2001).

Rod Jellema is Professor Emeritus of English at the University of Maryland, where he directed the Creative Writing Program. Jellema is the author of three books of poetry: *Something Tugging the Line* (1973), *The Lost Faces* (1978), and *The Eighth Day: New and Selected Poems* (1985). He was twice the recipient of a National Endowment for the Arts Fellowship for poetry. A graduate of Calvin College and of the University of Edinburgh, Scotland (Ph.D.), he edited *Christian Letters to a Post-Christian World: Essays by Dorothy Sayers* (1972) and was the General Editor *of Contemporary Writers in Christian Perspective* (32 monographs, 1966–73). His work in selecting, translating, and introducing two collections of Frisian poetry was awarded the Columbia University Translation Prize and Friesland's annual literary award, the Pieter Jelles Prize. Jellema and his wife now spend much of each year in Old San Juan, Puerto Rico, writing. He has just completed a new book of poems, *Travel Advisory.*

Douglas Kerr studied at the universities of Cambridge and Warwick, and is currently Associate Professor of English at the University of Hong Kong. He has written on the literature of the First World War, including *Wilfred Owen's Voices* (Clarendon Press, 1993), and on colonial discourse analysis and the literary representation of the East in English. He is now completing a book on George Orwell, which will examine the ways in which Orwell's writing is shaped by his engagement with Asia and empire.

Jay Ladin teaches literature at Princeton University, where he received his Ph.D. His criticism appears regularly in *Parnassus: Poetry in Review.*

Roger Lathbury is a Professor of English at George Mason University in Fairfax, Virginia, where he has taught since 1973. The author of two volumes of poetry, a novel, an editing workbook, several critical articles, and a study of *The Great Gatsby*, he has, since

1983, run Orchises Press, one of the nation's premier independent publishers, which specializes in poetry and non-fiction.

Janis and Richard Londraville are noted for their publications about John Quinn, W.B. Yeats, Jeanne Robert Foster, and their circle. Their work has appeared in many journals, including *Yeats Annual, Yeats: An Annual of Critical and Textual Studies, The Journal of Modern Literature, Paideuma, The Independent Shavian, English Literature in Transition, English, The Journal of the William Morris Society, Eire Ireland,* and *Irish America.* They published *Too Long a Sacrifice: The Letters of Maud Gonne* and *John Quinn* with Susquehanna University Press in 1999, and their biography of Jeanne Robert Foster, *"Dear Yeats," "Dear Pound," "Dear Ford": Jeanne Robert Foster and Her Circle of Friends,* was published by Syracuse University Press in 2001. Janis Londraville's *On Poetry, Painting, and Politics: The Letters of May Morris and John Quinn* (Susquehanna University Press) was published in 1997. They also contributed to the editor's *Advocates and Activists Who Shaped the Twentieth Century: With an Emphasis on the Period Between the Wars* and *Thornton Wilder: New Essays.*

Richard Londraville has lectured on Yeats's *Last Poems* at the Yeats International Summer School in Sligo, Ireland, and at Trinity College, Dublin. He has held visiting professorships at the University of Hiroshima and Taipei Normal University, Taiwan (where he produced Yeats's Cuchulain cycle in the style of Chinese Opera). He is Professor Emeritus of Literature at the Sate University of New York at Potsdam.

Janis Londraville is a fellow at the Center for Independent Scholars of the Associated Colleges of the Saint Lawrence Valley and holds a guest appointment to the English Department at SUNY Potsdam.

J.D. McClatchy is an esteemed poet with a number of well-received volumes and he is the editor of the *Yale Review.*

Rory McTurk, M.A. (Oxford), B.Philol. (Iceland), Ph.D. (National University of Ireland), has taught at the Universities of Lund and Copenhagen, at University College Dublin, and at the University of Leeds, where since 1994 he has been a Reader in Icelandic Studies. He is the author of *Studies in Ragnars saga loðbrókar and Its Major Scandinavian Analogues* (Oxford, 1991) and of numerous articles on the interrelationship of the Icelandic, Irish, Anglo-Irish and Old and Middle English literary and folk traditions. Since 1991 he has been an editor of the Saga-Book of the Viking Society for Northern Research, of which he was President from 1994 to 1996, and in 1998–99 he was Visiting Professor of English at Vanderbilt University, Nashville, Tennessee.

Dennis Paddie has been a poet, gay activist and local character in Central Texas since the days of "flower power" when he was the "high priest" of Austin's hippie community.

Jim Ross has been a reporter for the *St. Petersburg Sun-Times* since 1989. He graduated from Northwestern University, where he studied journalism. Ross lives in Ocala, Florida with his wife and two children.

Robert Stanley (Ph.D., University of North Carolina at Chapel Hill) teaches French and German at the University of Tennessee at Chattanooga. His research interests include twentieth-century French literature, in particular the French Catholic novelists, especially Julien Green and François Mauriac. He contributed the chapter on Julien Green *to The Contemporary Novel in Franc*e, ed. William Thompson (Gainesville: University of Florida Press, 1995). His interest in opera, particularly the operas of Mozart, inspired his interest in the study of the Auden-Kallman translation of *Die Zauberflöte*, Mozart's last opera.

Richard Stern is one of America's most distinguished Men of Letters as an award-winning writer of novels, short stories, and essays as well as a professor at the University of Chicago from 1955 to 2001. His novels include *Golk, Europe: Or Up and Down with Baggish and Schreiber, In any Case, Stitch, Other Men's Daughters, Natural Shocks, A Father's Words,* and the recently published *Pacific Tremors.* Stern is considered a master of the short story, and his stories are collected in the volume *Noble Rot.* His essays written up to 1989 are collected in *One Person and Another.* His longest essay, the book *A Sistermony,* concerning the death of his sister Ruth, won the Heartland Prize as best non-fiction book of 1995.

James A. Young is Emeritus Professor and Chair of the Division of Administrative and Media Studies at Central Pennsylvania College in Summerdale, PA. He completed bachelor's, master's, and Ph.D. degrees at Ohio University, the University of Toledo, and

Case Western Reserve University respectively and is also Professor Emeritus of History at Edinboro University in Pennsylvania. Professor Young has written on a wide range of political, historical, and literary matters, has produced the multimedia program "Workin' on the Railroad" (2001), and has published fictional work as well. He lives in Harrisburg, PA. He also contributed to the editor's *Advocates and Activists Who Shaped the Twentieth Century: With an Emphasis on the Period Between the Wars*.

Chronology

1907 Wystan Hugh Auden is born on 21 February in York, England.

1908 His family moves to Birmingham where Auden's father, a physician, is appointed School Medical Officer for the City and a Professor of Public Health at the University.

1915 Attends St. Edmund's School until 1920 where he first meets Christopher Isherwood.

1920 Attends Gresham's School until 1925 and begins reading Freud.

1925 Attends Oxford until 1928.

1928 In the summer, his Oxford classmate and friend, Stephen Spender, purchases a hand press in order to print forty-five copies of Auden's *Poems.* In August he begins a year's stay in Berlin, which will change his life.

1930 Becomes a school master at Larchfield Academy in Scotland. In September, the publisher Faber and Faber, under the auspices of T.S. Eliot, publishes *Poems.*

1932 Faber publishes *The Orators*, and Auden begins teaching at The Downs Preparatory School, Colwal, and begins a period of great happiness, as the school is progressive and he becomes an influence on both pupils and parents.

1933 On a summer night Auden has the mystical experience of *agape*, the transcendental love for all existence. This is also a life-changing experience. In November his play *The Dance of Death* is published.

1935 The Auden-Isherwood play *The Dog Beneath the Skin* is published and then produced by The Group Theatre on 15 January 1936. Auden marries Erika Mann in order to provide her with a British passport. After leaving The Downs School at the end of summer, Auden begins six months of work with the GPO film unit as a writer and assistant director, as well as performing other tasks.

1936 Auden visits Iceland with Oxford classmate and fellow poet Louis MacNeice. The second Auden-Isherwood play, *The Ascent of F6*, is published and produced by The Group Theatre 26 February 1937. In October, Auden publishes new verse in *Look, Stranger*. American edition is published in 1937 with the title *On This Island*.

1937 From January to March, Auden visits Spain during the Civil War, supporting the Republican Government. In May his poem "Spain," is published with all royalties for medical aid to the Republicans. In August *Letters from Iceland*, co-written with MacNeice, is published.

1938 In January Auden goes to China with Isherwood to record their impressions of the Sino-Japanese War for their book *Journey to a War*. Visits America and decides to move there. In October the third and last play with Isherwood, *On the Frontier*, is published and produced by The Group Theatre in November.

1939 In January Auden and Isherwood leave for America. Auden lives in New York City; Isherwood goes to Los Angeles. *Journey to a War* is published in March. Auden meets Chester Kallman, who is at first his lover, then his lifetime—but platonic—companion.

1940 *Another Time* is published. In the fall Auden begins teaching for a year at the New School for Social Research in Manhattan. Also in the fall he returns to the Anglican Church.

1941 *The Double Man* is published (English title: *New Year Letter*). An operetta, *Paul Bunyan*, libretto by Auden, music by Benjamin Britten, is performed at Columbia University on 5 May. In the fall he begins a year of teaching at the University of Michigan.

1942 Begins three years of teaching at Swarthmore and adds Bryn Mawr in 1943–45. In the summers he stays on Fire Island, NY.

1944 *For the Time Being* is published.

1945 *The Collected Poetry* is published. From April to August, Auden goes to Germany and other parts of Europe as civilian research chief in uniform with a rank of major in the Morale

Division of the U.S. Strategic Bombing survey; visits England for the first time since he left in 1939.

1946   In the spring he teaches at Bennington College in Vermont and becomes an American citizen. In the fall he returns to the New School to teach Shakespeare.

1947   Spring, at Barnard College, he teaches as an Associate in Religion. *The Age of Anxiety* is published and wins a Pulitzer Prize.

1948   In the fall he teaches at the New School.

1949   Spends springs and summers from 1949 to 1957 in Ischia, Italy.

1950   A prose work, *The Enchafed Flood*, is published, and is based on his 1949 Page-Barbour Lectures at the University of Virginia.

1951   *Nones* published. Stravinsky's Opera, *The Rake's Progress*, is produced in Vienna with a libretto by Auden and Kallman.

1952   In spring term Auden is a research professor at Smith College.

1955   *The Shield of Achilles* is published.

1956   Auden is elected Professor of Poetry at Oxford for a term of five years. In each year he gives three public lectures. His first, *Making, Knowing and Judging* is published.

1958   In the spring he buys and moves into house in Kirchstetten, Austria and will spend every spring and summer there until his death.

1960   *Homage to Clio* is published.

1961   An opera composed by Hans Werner Henze, *Elegy for Young Lovers*, and with a libretto by Auden-Kallman, is performed in Stuttgart, Germany.

1962   *The Dyer's Hand* (essays) is published.

1964   Returns to Iceland. Six months in Germany as an artist-in-residence sponsored by the Ford Foundation.

1965   *About the House* is published.

1966   *The Bassarids*, music by Henze, libretto by Auden-Kallman, is performed in Salzburg, Germany. *Collected Shorter Poems 1927–1957* is published.

1968   *Collected Longer Poems* and *Secondary Worlds* (essays) are published.

1969 *City Without Walls* is published.

1970 *A Certain World*, a commonplace anthology with Auden's commentary, is published.

1971 *Academic Graffiti* is published.

1972 *Epistle to a Godson* is published. In October, Auden returns to Oxford to live in a cottage at Christ Church.

1973 *Love's Labors Lost*, music by Nicholas Nabakov, libretto by Auden-Kallman, is performed in Brussels. Auden dies in his sleep some time on 28–29 September. He is buried in Kirschstetten on 4 October.

Impressions of Auden

For Auden, Love Has No Ending

Jim Ross

Ross is a feature reporter for Florida's Saint Petersburg Sun-Times. This article from 1999 recorded how Auden the poet was still getting a hearing by way of movies and television.[1]

W.H. Auden once wrote "O let me not deceive you, You cannot conquer time," yet, indeed the late poet has done just that, and in felicitous fashion.

This remarkable poet's verse, never more true than in the first half of the century, now resonates anew at the century's close in a seemingly unlikely forum: the popular media.

Tuesdays with Morrie is the story of an old professor who draws on personal experiences to teach a former student about life. To drive home one point, though, the instructor simply refers to another man's words.

"Love each other," Morrie Schwartz said, "or perish."

Schwartz was paraphrasing "September 1, 1939," a work from his favorite poet, W.H. Auden. The former student, journalist, Mitch Albom, mentioned the lesson in his best-selling book that he wrote about his final visits with his old mentor. (Since 11 September 2001, this poem has been a feature in many articles about the tragic events of that day.)

TV producers, though surely aware that poetry rarely appears in prime-time programming, decided to prominently feature the poem in their adaptation of *Tuesdays*. So when millions of ABC viewers tuned in earlier this month, they saw Jack Lemmon, portraying the title character, emotionally reading a stanza from Au-

---

[1]Reprinted with permission of the *Saint Petersburg Sun-Times*, Sunday, December 19, 1999.

den's classic verse. The TV script included the full, correct line to which Schwartz had alluded.

ABC isn't the only electronic media outlet to believe that Auden (1907–1973) wrote poems worth mentioning today. Though Auden's work isn't the only poetry recited on big and little screens, it certainly is getting its share of exposure these days with prominent mentions in *Tuesdays*, films such as *Four Weddings and a Funeral* and *Before Sunrise*, and the popular TV show *Felicity*.

The trend seems to intrigue viewers, many of whom are hearing Auden's words for the first time, or at least the first time since high school or college. The exposure has also sparked strong sales of Auden's work.

This makes more than booksellers pleased. Scholars are happy that, through the safe portal of popular culture, a new audience has found the poetry that they treasure.

Wystan Hugh Auden was a son of the English middle class who moved to the United States in 1939, when he was 32. He came of age as an artist during the 1930s, which he called a "low dishonest decade" because of the political cowardice and apathy he witnessed.[2]

Violence, hatred, and the appeasement of Hitler would lead to World War II, and the world seemed an uncertain place. Against this background, Auden wrote movingly about love, loss and fear. His poems were deep and rich, varied in style and tempo. But the language was largely accessible.

It also was universal. Auden was gay, yet his love poems speak to all couples. Auden was absorbed in the present, yet his verse rings true to people for whom the 1930s, '40s and '50s are the stuff of history books.

During Auden's day, many critics counted him among the most diverse, witty and technically masterful modern poets. Today, that reputation is reaching new heights.

But why resurrect his poems during the late 1990s?

---

[2] A target of Auden's accusation of cowardice was himself. He had written a poem, "Spain," in which he exhorted others to fight in Spain's civil war against fascism. In it, he said that the war was a case where "necessary murder" was a reality. Yet, he did not go and fight. He was called to task for writing such a poem by George Orwell, who did go and fight and was wounded in Spain. Auden agreed and later banned the poem from future collections and went on record that he should never have written it.

Perhaps because they "are so transportable. They'll sort of go anywhere with you," said Marsha Bryant, who teaches English at the University of Florida and has written a book about Auden.

Or, as literary critic and Auden expert Katherine Bucknell puts it, Auden "really could hit a bull's-eye again and again and again." A few words from Auden can capture a moment, a feeling better than any screenwriter's dialogue or camera operator's clever work ever could.

The artist no doubt would have sanctioned these modern uses of his work: Auden believed that people should read poetry aloud, and that art should be an integral part of community life.

If that means his work is heard in family rooms and movie houses, so be it.

"He wasn't interested in speaking to other poets," Bucknell said. Auden and his contemporaries "felt the importance of having their work be accessible to the whole of the population. "

Perhaps the best-known Auden citation came in *Four Weddings and a Funeral*, which starred Hugh Grant. When a character dies, his grieving partner recites Auden's "Funeral Blues" to conclude the eulogy.

> He was my North, my South, my East and West,
> My working week and my Sunday rest,
> My noon, my midnight, my talk, my song;
> I thought that love would last forever: I was wrong.

The poem's beauty, and actor John Hannah's emotional delivery, created perhaps the film's most memorable scene. The Auden recitation also provided an easy, non-intimidating way for viewers to hear, understand and enjoy a classic work.[3]

The combination proved explosive: Tens of thousands of people were inspired to seek out the poem.

"My phone kept ringing off the hook," recalled Edward Mendelson, a Columbia University professor and leading Auden scholar who also serves as literary executor of Auden's estate.

A publisher quickly capitalized on the interest, issuing a small, affordable collection of Auden poetry. To date, the book has sold 70,000 copies in the United States; in the United Kingdom, where

---

[3]An irony of the poem's dirge-like reading in the film is that Auden wrote it originally as lyrics for a much livelier interpretation in a cabaret act by Hedli Anderson, the wife of his good friend and fellow poet, Louis MacNeice.

movie stills were used on the book jacket to remind buyers where they had heard "Funeral Blues," sales stand at 200,000.

Mendelson said such sales were "unheard of for a book of poems."

In 1995, one year after *Four Weddings* was released, Auden's work returned to the big screen in *Before Sunrise*.

Ethan Hawke's slacker character, cynical about life and relationships, falls in love with a woman while touring Vienna, the city where Auden died. The lovers pause at dawn, knowing they will soon go their separate ways.

They feel time's inexorable power, just as Auden did nearly 60 years before them, when he wrote of two lovers whose bliss was interrupted when the city blocks "began to whirr and chime."

The poem is "As I Walked Out One Evening." Hawke's character recited the verse:

> In headaches and in worry
> Vaguely life leaks away
> And Time will have its fancy
> To-morrow or to-day.

Bryant, the professor, thought of that passage recently when she was stressed out about the work piling up on her desk.

"It is part of my daily life. Hardly a week goes by when there's not a situation that reminds me of a line from Auden's poems," she said. "Auden wrote memorable lines. That's why they show up in headlines and movies."

Auden scholars need not be the only ones who feel that way. In an essay, Bucknell observed that people will recall, over and over, a song they hear on the car radio or in a play.

"Why not beguile your ears with poetry that offers something more?" She asked.

Felicity fans received an Auden lesson during the past TV season, though they may not have known it.

The title character is a college student who, at that point in the plot line, wondered whether the classmate she loved would ever reciprocate. Felicity's pen pal, with whom she communicates by audio letter, observes that Felicity's dilemma reminds her of a poem. "If equal affection cannot be, / Let the more loving one be me."

The lines are from "The More Loving One," Auden's reflection about one of his own relationships. The TV script did not identify the author.

Auden thought of poetry "as one person communicating to another," Mendelson said. But, like all great literature, the message in "The More Loving One" might give comfort, and hope, to anyone stuck in a similar spot.

Auden's verse is also cited, or alluded to, in newspaper headlines and speeches. Bryant noticed many Auden references in news accounts about Bosnia, and she recalled that President Clinton read from "In Memory of W.B. Yeats" ("In the deserts of the heart / Let the healing fountain start") when talking about the Oklahoma City bombing.

Neither Auden nor any other great poet is likely to become a ubiquitous source for popular culture. It concerns itself with the here and now, leaving scant room, or reason, to regularly feature another day's verse.

But beautiful writing endures, and neither time nor cultural change can render it obsolete. Whether found on the shelves of the library, or the shelves of the nearest video store, Auden's poetry can still guide us.

Mendelson considers Auden "the first poet writing in English who felt at home in the twentieth century."

Today, with that century over, Auden seems as welcome, and welcoming as ever in this new one.

Auden's Influence:
An Interview

J.D. McClatchy

J.D. McClatchy is a critically praised poet and the editor of the Yale Review. *Here he speaks of Auden's influence and legacy.*[1]

What period of Auden's career has most influenced you?

At a time—in my twenties—when I should have been attracted to the early poems, in their obliquity and spiky glamour, I was instead sitting for lessons to Stevens, who must have scratched the same itch over my angel wing with a more precise fingernail. By the time I could read more intelligently, the late poems had their garrulous appeal; I liked their tone, their having been written under the stoic motto: hold on hold off. But it was his middle period that struck me most forcefully. The poems of the 1940s and 1950s, the work of the American Auden, these exerted the sway I fell under, or tried breathlessly to rise to. They were the work of a writer who literally entertained ideas. Nietzsche, an avatar, once defined maturity as the ability "to recover the seriousness one has as a child at play." He meant, I suppose, the quality of attention and of imagination—utterly free, utterly absorbed. For me, then and now, those poems brim with perfectly chosen details, with phrases that can upend a lifetime's complacencies, with further mysteries posing as fresh solutions.

Which particular poems do you like best, or find most useful to you as a poet, and why? And have your choices changed over the years?

From the start, "The Shield of Achilles" and "In Praise of Limestone" have been touchstones for me. Among longer poems, I re-

---

[1]Reprinted with permission from the W.H. Auden Society Newsletter, November 1999.

turn most often to "Bucolics," "Horae Canonicae," and "Thanks-giving for a Habitat." None of these poems, though, do I find "useful" to me as a writer—however essential they are to my life as a reader. What I have "taken" from Auden has been more general, or more technical. The occasional stanza scheme, a model for handling syllabics, that sort of thing. Most of all the exhilarat-ing example of his discursive mode; his sense that poems are not decorative, but diagnostic, not self-full effusions or mystical anec-dotes, but practical investigations of the psyche and the culture. *The Collected Poems* hasn't been a hornbook so much as a pan-theon—some cool vaulted marble temple I can stroll through, admiring the shrines, wondering at the shaft of light slowly cir-cling through the giant hole at the top. He's a presence, a pressure, an example of what can be done, not what to do. And because I consider him to be the greatest poet of this [the twentieth] cen-tury—my century—I'm instinctively drawn to his formulations of experience. He looked under more rocks than any of his peers; with the exception of Proust, he was more honest about the heart's duplicities than anyone; and he used his capacious intelligence to create a wondrously kaleidoscopic mythology of modern life.

What technical or stylistic innovations do you find most helpful in Au-den's work and why?

There are lessons I've learned, but don't yet feel ready to try. A certain eccentric boldness of phrasing, for instance. Auden's word-play is of a high order, and thankfully has nothing to do with puns or catchy enjambments.

Your poems often display great formal mastery. What is it like to write in form after Auden?

Intimidating. But no more so than to be writing after a Larkin or Merrill, a Hecht or Wilbur. I think there's been a minor resurgence of interest in formal poetry—or perhaps I should say a greater tol-erance, or awareness of its expressive possibilities that the domi-nant aesthetic of the last forty years had denied. Myself, I find it difficult to start a poem, or to move much beyond the scattering of phrases and a strong impulse that is the start of most any poem, without its filings being drawn into some sort of form by an in-stinctive magnet. Form's what affirms, said James Merrill, and I'd agree. I like what it prompts and what it authorizes. By the way, one unsightly blemish on the face of the new respect accorded formal poetry has been the so-called New Formalists, whose work by and large is wooden. Their emphasis is all exoskeletal. There's no guts, no heart.

Have you been influenced by Auden's public persona (both in England and America)?

I hope not. I mean, I like a good martini, but I was never for a moment attracted to the slovenly, drug-addled, tyrannical, distracted Auden of popular legend—except as a legend, rather like his iconic, Navajo-elder face. And I'm unworthy of the private Auden who was so considerate and generous, so disciplined and productive. But the way he construed the writer's life has been a model. Or at least a sanction. He only considered himself a "poet" when he was writing poems. There was nothing bardic about him. He was a man of letters for whom criticism, journalism, song lyrics, record jacket copy … anything went. With the amount of prose I write, and the opera libretti, I suppose you could say I share his temperament—or at least the sense of the writer's pleasures and responsibilities.

When you are in the process of writing a poem that does not explicitly address Auden, are you conscious of Auden's influence on your work?

I've only written one poem explicitly addressed to Auden. It's called "Auden's OED"—a set of books, as it happens, that is shelved near my desk, a gift some years ago from James Merrill, who'd in turn had it from Chester Kallman. But I don't want to be coy about this. There are certainly other poems that implicitly—or I should say, a little less explicitly—address Auden, or at least his concerns in certain poems. In my book, *The Rest of the Way*, there's a poem called "The Shield of Herakles." It takes as its premise the shield described in Hesiod, as Auden's poem on Achilles takes its lead from Homer. As I've already said, "The Shield of Achilles" is a favorite of mine, so an obvious way to pay homage to the poem—that is, to read it even more carefully—was to imitate it. To imitate Auden doesn't mean to copy him. My poem doesn't— couldn't!—sound with his grace or authority, but it segues from the shield's details to both autobiography and a kind of political discourse ("Machine-made Armageddons—tanks / Or missile shields in outer space— / Threaten always to turn against / The false-hearted power they excite. / What draws attack is self-defense / A target for the arrow's flight"). And in my collection *Ten*

Commandments, the poem "Under Hydra" is an effort to make the sort of gesture Auden's "Under Sirius" (and James Merrill's "Under Mars," itself a nod to Auden's poem) does. If I were forced to admit it, I'd say that the phrasing of "Under Hydra" owes whatever crispness, even abruptness, it has to Auden's characteristic tone. As for all the other poems I've written, no, I wasn't conscious of Auden while composing them. At times like that, you're so engrossed in getting something out *and* down that you're only aware of its unconscious sources much after the fact. Auden's influence on my work, frankly, would be more easily spotted and evaluated by someone other than me.

What has Auden made possible for younger poets?

As I've already said, a sense of what can be done in the art, and for the art. His genius for synthesizing vast amounts of information, for linking in his poems otherwise disparate spheres, for using literature as an instrument of discovery—these are all there to be drawn on by young poets. Do they? There are so many competing flashes of energy in our image-glutted society that Auden's high lonely beacon may be obscured by glitzier rhetorics, from kiss-and-tell surrealism to empty-headed L=A=N=G=U=A=G=E scrolls. Better poets, even as tyros, would read their Auden and agree with Proust, who wrote in a letter, *"L'Art est un perpetuel sacrifice de sentiment à la vérité."* [Art is a perpetual sacrifice of sentiment to truth.]

What, if anything, was available to Auden as a poet, as a member of the twenties generation, that is not available to you, as a member of a younger generation?

An outside stage of worldwide calamities—the collapse of traditional attitudes after the Great War, the Depression, the Second World War, the Holocaust ... the works. The horrible events of more recent times—Cambodian massacres or African famines—always seem to be happening too far away from one's possible involvement. The only comparable event in the life of my generation—barring the Vietnam war protests, and the civil rights struggle in the States—has been the AIDS crisis, a viciously destructive horror that raised all sorts of moral questions. [This changed on 11 September 2001.] But it doesn't move at newsreel speed, and hasn't prompted the kind of poetry of events that the first half of the century did. I also think that Auden moved to New York at just the right time. Contrary to old misunderstandings, the 1950s were an exciting, adventurous time for culture in New York. Auden petered out just as the mind did—eek! The '70s were a low point in the history of civilization, and the recovery from it all has been only a chilly post-modernism. No, Auden lived, as the Chinese say, in interesting times. And it drew his work continually toward a serious meditation on the wages of history.

What difference do you think it makes in the way Auden wrote poetry and the way you wrote poetry that he was English and you American?

Every English writer seems hobbled by his struggle to disengage himself from the ridiculous class system that's bred in the bone there, but I couldn't begin to calculate here the array of pressures from apologetics to pranks, it occasioned in Auden's work. Auden had a better education for a poet than most Americans are offered. As it happens, I was schooled by Jesuits and had a rigorous training in the classics. But that's rare nowadays. Being English (excuse my trading on silly stereotypes, but your question allows me elbow room), he had the advantage of a kind of verbal fluency that must have made his work in prose less of a burden to him. Then, when he arrived in America, his Englishness had a double advantage, making him at once more curious about the spectacles and freedoms of his new country and more skeptical of his self-proclaimed superiorities. Unlike Yeats or Frost, he wrote all his life as if from exile. On the other hand, I've always detected a tiny bit of squeamishness in Auden, and that's something I have myself been troubled with. My work deals with sensuality—indeed, with sexuality—more directly. Of course, the closet having collapsed, it's easier to write about one's homosexuality now than it was for Auden—though he may not have wanted to explore more than he did. It doesn't rank high on my list of preferred subjects either. Still ... it was a crucial part of his life and could only be dealt with in code.

What is your perception of the public place that Auden now occupies? He is probably not as influential and imposing a figure today as he was in his lifetime, but what role do you think he still plays in shaping the contemporary poetic climate?

Yes, during his lifetime his presence—the authority of his opinions more than the specific of his line—must have been daunting. You can tell from the hushed testimony of other poets—Elizabeth

Bishop say. With the next generation, a direct stylistic influence is more overt. In Hecht or Merrill, Auden is a prominent ghost in the machine. And the poets he chose as Yale Youngers were all Audenesque in their first books—Wright and Rich and Hollander and Merwin. In my generation, as you rightly suspect, most poets have looked elsewhere—and often to younger models, to Plath, say, or Merwin. That may in part be due to the fact Auden is not taught in schools or universities. Always considered a British poet, he is excluded from courses. Eliot holds court still in the curriculum, and American professors jump to Pound or Williams or Moore or Frost. None of these poets has as complex a body of work, and this too may make the professoriate hesitate. Still, students have the distinct thrill of finding Auden on their own, and secret treasures, postponed pleasures, are the most captivating. This is less true in England than in America. Auden's hand is quite visibly on the shoulder of many younger poets there from James Fenton to Glyn Maxwell. Here, things are less obvious. On the other hand, the appreciation of Auden's achievements is a thriving cottage industry—biographies, critical studies and commentaries abound. But these sorts of books appeal more to the scholar than the poet. I fear among younger American poets, from William Logan to Rachel Wetzston, Auden will continue to be passed on samizdat-style. That may just be the way he'd prefer it.

With Auden

Richard Stern

Richard Stern of the University of Chicago is one of America's most criti-
cally praised (and awarded) writers of fiction and essays and is now an
esteemed elder statesman and man of letters in that title's truest sense.
Here he recalls the influence of Auden on a young Stern when he was a
recent college graduate in 1947 and then later meeting Auden in the mid-
1960s.[1]

1. September 1947. New York City.

I have a new B.A. degree from Chapel Hill and a mother who
doesn't like to see it going to waste. Six dawns a week, she rouses
me with anti-inspirations; my come-backs are unspoken. "You
won't find a job on your back." *Michelangelo did the Sistine Chapel*
on his. "You know who catches the worm." *Who's fishing?* "Jobs go
to go-getters." *I don't want to go anywhere but Paris.* She has never
held a paying job. I am her non-paying one, and know there'll be
no peace until I am out the door.

I walk or bus downtown. Subways are for go-getters. For four
wartime years, I rode them every school day, rousing the threats
and curses of women whose silk stockings the loose struts of my
book bag ripped while my nose was buried in *The Ring and the*
Book and the *Dialogues of Hylas and Philonius.*

Up and down Fifth, Madison, Park, and Lexington, I walk in
and out of buildings whose tenants' names I study on lobby direc-
tories. Now and then, I elevator up to advertising agencies and
publishers, fill out job forms, and, if a personnel officer is bored,
have an interview. I talk about my honors B.A. in English, my job

---

[1]Stern's essay was written for this volume and was previewed in the
Fall 2000 issue of the *Antioch Review.*

experience in shoe and jewelry stores (sweeping and polishing, wrapping, running an addressograph), Wall Street (a bonded messenger—attesting to my trustworthiness), on Vermont farms (haying, weeding, milking, to show I'm competent in pastoral as well as urban activity). I've published poems, editorials for the *Daily Tar Heel* [the then and still student newspaper of UNC-Chapel Hill], am, in short, accomplished, experienced, worldly wise, hard-working, and willing to improve their operations—"a quick learner"— for—I manage to get out —five thousand dollars a year.

This figure has been supplied by my Chapel Hill girlfriend, Jo B. With the $2300 a year she is making back in her hometown (pre-Disney Orlando), it would enable us to live in the way she wants to live. She and I exchange daily multi-page letters, and until my mother's chilly intervention, telephoned each other twice a week. Now Jo, terrified by mother's voice, never calls, and I call only when my father remembers that I'm still his dependent and slips me a few dollars (which I change into quarters to call from a pay phone in the Hotel Bolivar around the corner). Jo has the ring I won in a game of Casino from Great Uncle Herman. Its tiny diamond sits in the navel of a gold nude. Jo is saving for a more neutral setting; the ring stands for a sort of engagement of which my parents know zilch.

A cousin gets me an interview with the editor of *Coronet Magazine*, Larry Spivak (not yet the founder-host of *Meet the Press*). In his small office, Spivak, a little, suspicious-looking fellow in shirtsleeves, eyes me over spectacles which sit on his hawk beak.

"Understand you wanna be a writer."

"I am one."

"Good for you," he says. "Now get some experience. Nothing's more important for a writer than experience." I disagree but say nothing. "Get a job in a coal mine. A cannery. Both." "I could do research there or anywhere else you send me." Changing gear, he asks me what sort of salary I had in mind. Assessing the office, I lower Jo's figure a thousand dollars. He looks down through the eyeglasses, then, what the hell, turns avuncular. "There's no one in this city or any other I know that'd pay you half that much. Get experience, write a hundred stories, then see what happens." Eyes lowered to desk-work, he holds out his hand, "So long." I shake it, say "Thank you" and wish him a short painful life.

That evening my father is sympathetic, my mother puzzled and suspicious. "There may be no job in publishing or advertising.

You better think about business." *Business* is a sacred word and concept. Her brothers left school in their teens to go into it. First employed by their Uncle Gustave Veit, the founder-president of York Mfg., they have gone out on their own and, like him, succeeded. *Business* is the family *Tao*.

A year ago, Momma sat daily at Uncle Gus's deathbed. She fetched, fed, and consoled the old man but would not give him what he daily begged for, poison to end his suffering. "His last smile was for your Phi Beta Kappa key." How she wishes Uncle Gus were here to guide me now. Failing that, she calls Bert, her older brother, an ex-cotton goods salesman, living off his annuities. Bert makes calls, the last to tell her that I have an appointment with important men at Consolidated Retail Stores; he hopes that I won't be a wiseacre and tell them I want to make five thousand simoleons a year.

On Seventh Avenue, I dodge whirling racks of suits and go up four stories in a funereal elevator to a smoke-clouded office where two beef-colored faces behind cigars give me the once over. One face tops a small, the other a huge body. "You're Boit Veit's nephew?" This from big beef.

"Yes."

"That's good."

Small beef: "We gotta store in Evansville, Indiana. Bon Marché. Ed Schneider—your uncle knows his dad—'s the manager, he needs help dere."

Big beef: "Toity-five a week to start, trainin' you couldn't buy. He wants you should start Monday."

I've never been west of Newark. My mother, relieved, even proud, is now also apprehensive. Nervously, frantically, she packs and repacks my bags while shedding advice: Don't be impatient, don't lose your temper, get plenty of sleep, drink milk.

A reservation is made for the first plane ride of my life.

I arrive in Evansville at dusk, am met by Schneider, a short, dark, pleasant-looking-and acting man in his late thirties who, after carrying my bags to the hotel room he's reserved for me, drives me home for a meal which his marooned-looking wife has cooked. "Tomorrow Joannie will drive you around till you find a room. Then come down to the store and start learning the ropes."

The meal in the white leathery house is good; he and Joannie are sympathetic and kind. Only not my kind. Nor is Evansville my kind of town, this my kind of life. In the hotel room, on what is probably the loneliest, most unhappy night I'd spent since I was a little boy, I take out of my bag the only link I have to the life I want, the *Collected Poems of W.H. Auden*. It's the only book I've brought with me. I read it that night, as I will read it every single night of the six weeks I spend in Evansville, and as I've read few books since, with almost desperate need.

I see the book now, the black on white cover, the Random House logo, the generous spacing of the poems on the page. I still know several hundred lines I never tried to memorize: *"To throw away the key and walk away, / Not abrupt exile, the neighbors asking why...." "Our hunting fathers told the story / Of the sadness of the creatures / Pitied the limits and the lack / Set in their furnished features;/ Saw in the lion's intolerant look, / Behind the quarry's dying glare, / love raging...." "Lay your sleeping head my love? Human on faithless arm." "A shilling life will give you all the facts: / How Father beat him, how he ran away, / What were the struggles of his youth? / what acts made him the greatest figure of his day"; "Consider this, and in our time, / As the hawk sees it or the helmeted airman"; "That day, far other than that day / They gave the prizes to the ruined boys"; "Sir, no man's enemy, forgiving all / But will its negative inversion, be prodigal / Send to us power and light, a sovereign touch / Curing the intolerable neural itch"; "Doom is dark and deeper than any sea dingle / Upon what man it fall ..."; "Let me tell you a little story / About Miss Edith Gee; / She lived at Clevedon Terrace / At number 83."*

The sound of these poems was deeper than any instruction, but I was endlessly instructed by them. From Miss Gee's story I "learned" that cancer originated in suppressed desire; from "Freud," I learned about the historical component of illness; from "Spain," the stakes of the past and the future in the Spanish Civil War. I learned that old masters like Brueghel were never wrong, and that suffering and great events like the fall of Icarus took place when nobody was noticing. Everywhere, I learned about the viciousness of the old guard, the hunting fathers and befurred tourists constellated at reserved tables in snowy resorts while the devil's agents spread rumors and disasters around the ports and in the eyes of stoats. I imbibed the meters of chic brilliance, the semantics of assonance, the rhythms of civility and passion. Auden was a world every bit as intricate as Evansville, more intact, more concentrated, more insistent, but more, a novel individual, one who made no promises, only poured delight. Underneath the poems, his voice said that there wasn't any class but intelligence, no requirement but sensibility. The poems were gifts; they were yours and you were part of others who read them. With them you weren't lonely. The mind that made them was your friend.

At Bon Marché, I learned other things. A three-story, not unhandsome brick building, it stood on Main Street (though I don't remember if this was the street's name), near other stores, including the town's fanciest, DeJong's. The street looked like those in Andy Hardy movies and there was a certain charm about it, a charm about my being on it.

There was less charm in the work. The first day, Edgar gave me a book on retail merchandising, as boring a tome as I'd ever laid eyes on. The matter therein was fleshed out in the counters, the cash registers, the saleswomen, the sweaters, dresses, stockings, shoes, bras, panties, coats, accessories displayed in the glass cases or mounted in racks. At six, every morning (and a few Sunday mornings), Edgar and I went over the day's receipts, matched them against orders, then discussed returns, slow movers, new orders, seasonal fashions. In our arms, we carried merchandise from desired to undesired spots and packed up the least desirable items for return.

During the week, I worked in different parts of the store: *Packaging* (I wrapped dresses, suits, shoes); *Advertising*, where "Cele," the charmingly goofy copy writer showed me what to stress in our newspaper and radio ads; *Windows*, where Kolya, a—now that I think of it—Yeltsian-looking window-dresser, showed me the display tricks of his art; and *Sales*, where various salespeople, young and old, instructed me in the ins and outs of their specialties. Tying my tie and putting a jacket over my sleeveless yellow sweater, I floor-walked up and down the aisles, greeting and joking, though I don't believe that I could have radiated much confidence, let alone delight. One day, the homunculus who was president of hundreds of Consolidated Retail Stores appeared on the floor, fingered the yellow sweater, and told me, "Sonny, never wear this garment on the floor again." The word "preppy" did not then exist, but what it stood for was, I'm sure, the loathsome suggestion of the yellow sweater.

Sales days were a revelation. From the faces bunched behind the glass and then from the almost abstractedly insane drive past me toward the garments whose price reductions Cele had featured in her ads, I understood what a mob could do, what revolution might be like, what Goebbels and Hitler manipulated, what the class Auden hated built their fortresses against.

No, my days in the store weren't good ones. Nor was home life much better. I had a room in the rickety bungalow of Ev and Ginny Metcalfe on Walnut Street. I was the only boarder; Ginny was kind, maternal. A huge woman with very short iron-gray hair, she told me about her operations. "The doctors mapped out my whole back." (It was quite a back.) Mac, a laconic, kindly man, drove a taxi at night and slept much of the day. He'd had a bar in Chicago and Ginny said that there'd been trouble up there; he'd had to leave. I knew "The Killers" and was as alert as Nick Adams had been to those who might come looking for Mac, but no one came near the house the six weeks I lived there.

Ginny and I were closest at breakfast, which she cooked for me until calls to Jo left me without the fifty cents a day it cost. I read the Evansville paper while Ginny put the perfectly fried eggs and bacon on the plate with a rack of toast, and a dish of fresh butter and strawberry jam. There was orange juice with bits of fruitmeat in it and wonderful coffee with fresh cream and sugar. (I weighed a hundred pounds less than I do now, and back then, people didn't diet.) I read Ginny the newspaper's poem of the day, quatrains often by Edgar Guest. She told me that she'd reread and meditate about it for hours. If Auden was my link to the highlife, these poems were Ginny's to hers. Though the structure of their sentiment went deeply against my grain, I was grateful that these poems existed to enrich Ginny's life. The few seconds it took to read them to her every morning were special to both of us.

My rent was fifteen dollars a week. If it hadn't been for the calls to Jo, I could have made it on the thirty-five-dollar salary. (There were no tax withdrawals that I recall—although I know that Beardsley Ruml had invented the Pay-As-You-Go system during WW II. If there were, I don't remember what they were. I did know that every single dollar counted for me.

Despite this unprincely salary, I seemed to be regarded as a person of standing in Evansville. When I opened a bank account, I was treated with a respect I'd never encountered. Then, too, some of the salesgirls seemed interested in me, and I played to the interest. There were miscalculations: one evening, one girl with whom I habitually flirted introduced me to a husband. Since I hadn't noticed her ring finger, I was amazed. Another girl, whom I persuaded to stay late one evening to help with inventory chores, made it clear that her erotic geography was also circumscribed by that finger.

I had no money to take girls to a movie, let alone dinner, so I had no dates. On Jo's urging, I wrote my parents to send on the war bonds—about two hundred dollars' worth—into which for several years most of my pre-Evansville earnings and birthday money had gone. Grumbling and suspicious, my mother sent them on. They were to pay for my getaway.

It was Auden's father-in-law, Thomas Mann,[2] who got me fired. In the Evansville Public Library, I read *The Magic Mountain* every working day after my fifteen-minute, sixty-cent lunch in the drugstore and again, after my dollar-thirty meatloaf, mashed potatoes, and string beans in a diner gloomier and emptier than Edward Hopper's. I lost myself in the snowy alpine clinic among uproarious arguments of Settimbrini and Naphta, the speculations of the great doctor, Hofrat Behrens, the sex-boggling lisp of Claudia Chuchat, the ups and downs of the fever charts. It was so wonderful I could hardly bear to stop reading, and every day, I was later getting back to work. The week after Thanksgiving, Edgar called me into his office and told me it was clear that the retail life should not be mine. I would be happier doing something connected with writing. He understood; he himself had read the dirty parts of *Ulysses*. He wished me well, and if there was anything he or Joannie could do for me, let him know. I'd just finished *The Magic Mountain*. Like Hans Castorp going back into the world, it was time for me to leave.

II. Chicago, Winter 1965.

In his room at the Quadrangle Club, I find Auden rummaging and fuming. "I thought this was a club. They tell me they don't serve liquor before five p.m." I tell him about the Baptist roots of the institution. Meanwhile, he's found a bottle of gin in his bag and two glasses in the bathroom. He plops into the other armchair, drapes stockinged feet over the arm and talks in his crowded, nasal, amiable oxcamese of his peripatetic life. "Only way I can live. A tour every two years. In a month, I'll have my fifty-ninth birthday in an Oregon hotel room."

---

[2]In the late 1930s Auden "married" Thomas Mann's daughter, Erika, so she could get out of Germany. Paper only, both remained legally married to the other until the end of their lives.

I'd seen hundreds of pictures but had never laid eyes on the living man. In the flesh, the famous face looked as if it's survived a terrible siege. A pox that strikes only the rarest sinner had pitted, trenched, puffed, bewarted, and empurpled the white face-flab. The lips too were loose, large, somehow unintegrated. It took minutes to get used to this bizarre topography. Meanwhile, talk, drink, and amiability flowed. The man was immediately direct, decent, unposed, and, if not exactly warm, eager for talk.

We talk of Shelton. He wants to meet my friend Arthur Heiserman whose *Skelton and Satire* he admires. Then Anglo-Saxon: he condemns Pound for getting the accent wrong in "Seafarer." Yeats, Brecht, and Claudel—the three poets were bad men, mistreaters of women. He muses over his old friend MacNeice who "caught a cold and died [in 1957]," his Austrian house—the first he's ever owned—what poets can and can't alter from life: "If Joan rhymes better than Mary, call her Joan, but you can't change nos to yesses." "It's hard to be a religious poet in English. Nothing rhymes with God." I start to tell him what the first *Collected Poems* had meant to me eighteen years ago, but it's clear that such stories are familiar and without intellectual or, in this case, emotional interest.

At the reading, I sit in the front row next to the political scientist Hans Morgenthau, whose English is good but not good enough to understand Auden's. I myself miss a third of what I hear. The meters, however, are clear, and since he reads from his translations of Icelandic sagas, this goes a long way.

Afterwards, a small party at Heiserman's. Erich Heller, an Auden friend, has, despite the zero-degree cold, come from Northwestern [University]. He talks of his trip to the Greek monastery where the only females around are insects. He befriended a monk who takes him aside and begs an enormous favor: will Heller please, for God's sake, send him from America, a carton of *Milky Ways*. Auden, in the slippers he carries, listens, gabs, laughs, drinks. It looks as if he could go on for hours. Heller leaves, and we follow, but our car gets stuck in ice ridges. Out comes Auden in slippers, scarf around his neck. The image of him pushing at the car is the most memorable of the visit, although it is matched by one the next day.

At noon, he comes alone into the Quadrangle Club. I leave my companions and sit with him. We talk about his time in Spain— he'd just wanted to drive a car, but they didn't need him, and he came home. He'd driven Tawney's car during the Great Strike of

1926 and said the driving was what it was all about. "I just liked driving cars." His name? "From Odin, surely." (I remember an early picture of a white-blonde boy with untroubled skin and flabless face.) Would there ever be a plaque on his St. Mark's Place House? "There should be," he said. "Trotsky lived and edited *Pravda* there." He was off in an hour and I had a class. I got up and shook his hand. He said, "Thank you so much for sitting with me."

The "thank you" I had for him was so deep, I nearly broke down.

III. Vienna, September 1973.

I give a little talk to the Vienna PEN. My host, the fiction writer Peter von Tramin, works in a bank but apparently has time to read and keep up with world literature. On the way out, I notice that Auden is giving a reading there in a couple of weeks. "I wish I could stay for it." Peter says that he'll let me know how it turns out.

Back in Chicago, I read how it turns out. After the reading, Auden went back to his hotel, had a heart attack and died.

Coda. Stanford, November 1999.

For the past fifteen or so years, I end a course in the great modernists writers of the twentieth century with the poem that's said to be the last Auden wrote, days or weeks before his death in the Vienna hotel room. It's called "Archaeology." One thread of the course is that the twentieth century has been the archaeologizing, anthropologizing century, not only digging up the remains of cultures in the Schliemann tradition but seeing in what would once have been called primitive, strange, or alien societies complexities of organization and intelligence equivalent to our own. Auden has subtilized and expanded this notion, turning words, à la Rilke, from one grammatical function to another and ending with the note that surfaces again and again in his poems.

The coda of the poem reads:

> From Archaeology
> One moral, at least, may be drawn,
> to wit, that all
>
> our school text-books lie.
> What they call history
> is nothing to vaunt of,
>
> Being made, as it is,
> By the criminal in us:
> Goodness is timeless.

W.H. Auden's "Musée des Beaux Arts" and the Stranded Mother

Stephen Gale

Gale, an esteemed writer and educator, recollects how an Auden poem influenced a discussion concerning an event in contemporary life.

An experience that I had teaching W.H. Auden's "Musée des Beaux Arts" illustrates the potential effect that exposure to literature can have on an individual or even a whole classroom full of students. Many years ago, when I was teaching at the University of Florida, I attended a Danforth Associates Meeting. One of the Associates was the Dean of the College of Business, and during our conversation about what we teach, he said that he wished that he could include the teaching of ethics in some of his business classes. My response was that I could not imagine an English literature course in which ethics were *not* part of the curriculum.

Like most English teachers, over the years I have had numerous experiences in which a former student returns to tell me that he or she has been accepted to dental school or medical or the equivalent as a result of some things that were taught in my class, or an accountant confesses that, in retrospect and in spite of his or her many protestations to the contrary, the literature requirement actually makes sense. Still, instances that prove the theory that literature can have a deep importance in and an impact on our lives, which was the sub-text in my conversation with the business school dean, while manifested less frequently, make a greater and more lasting impression on me than "How taking a literature class helped me get a better job."

I include Auden's poem "Musée des Beaux Arts" in a number of the classes that I teach, but the particular event that demonstrated the way in which literature can influence our day-to-day lives occurred in an "Introduction to Literature" course that I taught at Missouri Southern State College. "Musée des Beaux Arts" was inspired by the poet's visit to the Museum of Fine Arts in Brussels and is about the poet's understanding of the place of suffering in human life as depicted in the paintings of the old masters.

In class we discuss the imagery, word choice, and particularly the structure of the poem, which opens with the statement that "About suffering they were never wrong? The Old Masters." In the first stanza the poet then uses examples from several paintings to demonstrate his contention that the painters recognized both the ubiquitous presence of human suffering and the fact that it occurs in the midst of ordinary life (the children skating happily while the "aged" wait for "miraculous birth," the coexistence of "dreadful martyrdom" and dogs and the torturer's horse, which lead lives oblivious to the suffering that surrounds them).

What is of great import to some witnesses may go unnoticed by those around them. In the second stanza Auden uses Pieter Brueghel's painting of the mythical fall of Icarus—the son of Daedalus who fell into the ocean and drowned after flying so high on artificial wings that the wax melted when he allowed ambition to take him too near the sun—as a specific example of his thesis. Based on their discussion of these elements, the class generally concludes that "Musée des Beaux Arts" depicts suffering as a normal component in human life, one that is too often overlooked when it does not have an immediate impact on the viewer or individual not directly involved, who thus continues going about his or her life unconcernedly (as represented by the plowman and those who sailed on the "expensive delicate ship").

In the follow-up discussion we talk about how we as individuals respond to the suffering that surrounds us, in our own country and in our everyday lives (sickness, poverty, death), and so on. This normally leads to commentary on what we can do to help alleviate suffering from the world, and how we have to make personal decisions about what and how much, if anything, we can do.

At the beginning of the class two days after our discussion of "Musée des Beaux Arts," one of the young men in the class raised his hand and asked if he could make a comment about the poem. He proceeded to tell us how that morning, about a mile from school where there are no buildings, he noticed a car parked by the side of the road. A little farther on, about halfway between the traffic light and the school, he had seen a young mother walking along, carrying an infant in one arm and a gas can in the other. The young man said he had not stopped to help the woman but rather had continued on to school.

When asked by a consternated classmate why he had not stopped, he replied that he was running late on his way to school; if he had stopped and offered assistance he would have been late to our class. The important thing that he wanted to make clear, though, was that he had *noticed* her, something which he admitted he was sure he would not have done if it had not been for our discussion of Auden's "Musée des Beaux Arts" earlier in the week.

This admission had a great impact upon the other class members who talked for quite a while about the ramifications evident in the incident, and it certainly focused our attention on the concept of sensitivity; apparently the other students in the class profited from seeing the event through their peer's eyes and from being compelled to confront the relevance of human concerns that he raised as they might come into play in their own lives.

It was gratifying to see a real-life application of an in-class subject, especially since it was so close to our consideration of the subject, and that literature and the applications were so clearly linked. It was nice, too, that we were provided with the opportunity to extend our discussion. More importantly, although not a sensational major victory, this event was a significant one for it illustrated the taking of a necessary first step. While more obvious ethical maturity was still in the student's future, it is seldom that the effect of literature can be seen so quickly, and there is no doubt that exposure to Auden's poem potentially changed at least one student's life by helping to foster his sense of empathy and thereby shaping his identity. In other words, taking a literature class in which one read a poem by an English writer about ancient paintings that hang in a museum in Belgium may not have helped him get a better job, but it helped him see that humanity (and poetry) transcends borders, and that poems can teach as parables, as Auden intended.

The Student and the Master:
A Pupil's Recollections of the Poet,
W.H. Auden

David Garrett Izzo

Stephen Gale's preceding essay talks about teaching an Auden poem. In this interview, a former preparatory school student of Auden's, John Duguid, recalls Auden teaching him.[1]

Before he became the poet/angstmeister of *The Age of Anxiety*, W.H. (Wystan Hugh) Auden (1907–1973) did what many post-college, pre-fame writers have done—he taught English, first to adolescents, and later to college students. And he loved it. In his autobiographical *Letter to Lord Byron* (1937), Auden summarizes his teaching career as a teacher in British preparatory schools:

> Today it's a profession that seems grand to
> Those whose alternative's an office stool.
> For budding authors, it's become the rule.
> The Head's M.A., a Bishop is a patron,
> The assistant staff is highly qualified.
> Health is the care of an experienced matron,
> The arts are taught by ladies from outside;
> The food is wholesome and the grounds are wide;
> The aim is training character and poise
> With special coaching for the backward boys.
> It's pleasant as it's easy to secure
> The hero worship of the immature.

Known as Uncle Wiz, his adolescent charges did, indeed, become enraptured with their flamboyant, anything-but-donnish, teacher. Auden's amiable eccentricities—chain-smoking, loud

---

[1]Reprinted with permission from *The Carolina Quarterly*, Summer 1996.

garrulousness, play-acting, odd clothes (Flemish hats and an umbrella in all weather used as a pointer), fun-oriented, innovative, yet demanding teaching methods—were a welcome change from the usual British, stiff-upper-lip stuffiness. Former students remember him fondly even after sixty years. One is Chapel Hill's John Duguid, a retired New York advertising executive via England and The Downs school 1934–37. Here then are some memories of a student and his master:

Duguid: First of all, one must make clear that in Britain it was expected that a child of the middle class—my father was a doctor—would be sent away to a boarding school; it did not mean, as some people think here, that it was for troublesome children. As for Auden, that phrase, *anything-but-donnish* is quite accurate. I would say that we all adored the man and he related so well to us because he could talk to us on our level and not sound condescending; he could josh with us which normally was not encouraged because masters were a little more formal, keeping their dignity, although The Downs unlike other schools was not too heavy on that.

Izzo: The Downs, from all accounts, was very progressive.

Duguid: Yes, a very liberal school [mildly Quaker] with an innovative Headmaster, Geoffrey Hoyland. I look back on this over the years and I realize what a good thing it was because he believed that boys should be encouraged to try their hand at certain cultural things: music, art, and poetry, of course, in *The Badger* [the school's literary magazine] because they might have a latent talent that couldn't be brought out in any other way, certainly not at other boarding schools of that era where sport was the only thing that mattered which was antithetical to Hoyland's vision and philosophy.

Izzo: That vision was one that Auden greatly appreciated as his student days were quite the opposite; he and many of his contemporaries, Christopher Isherwood, Stephen Spender, George Orwell, Cecil Day-Lewis, et al., thought those years were ones where students were herded into a mass inculcation of right-wing pseudo-fascist conformity. Auden's reaction to them was a lifelong socio-political liberalism, and he was determined not to be such a teacher as those he had had. From your experiences of other schools, how justified was this pejorative estimation of public schools and Auden's rebellion from them?

Duguid: Absolutely justified! He was at Oxford at a time [1926–29] when there was a very strong social consciousness which you saw with people like Auden, Spender, etc. Auden was never actually a communist [which was very *in* during the '30s] but he did have very strong feelings for the underprivileged and though as a child one cannot fully understand the political situation, I could see the liberalism in this rumpled, crumpled creature, always untidy and reeking with nicotine, who would not have fitted in to your average school.

Izzo: That description of him is shared by so many of his other students. Auden was inclined to be extraordinary rather than ordinary and in his first teaching position, Larchfield, which was a more conventional school, he felt somewhat an outsider and was never as comfortable there as he was to be at The Downs. At Larchfield, even his reputation as a writer was disparaged for its leftward tilt.

Duguid: Conversely, I know that when my parents were considering sending me to The Downs, they spoke somewhat in awe of him, "Oh, W.H. Auden is one of the teachers there." At the time it didn't mean anything to me. And though he was too independent to be in the traditional mold, I would imagine, his being an intelligent human being with a certain self-defensiveness which we all have, that he probably did try to conform a little, but it was so against his nature that he didn't know how to be anything but what he was.

Izzo: But, he did love to teach.

Duguid: Yes, he did.

Izzo: So much so that all of his close contemporaries have said that his years at The Downs were the happiest time of his life equaled only by his first two years in the United States (1939–40) after leaving England on the eve of World War II.

Duguid: For which he was wrongly excoriated, although I can understand why he was so, and was not entirely surprised by it.

Izzo: He, Aldous Huxley, Isherwood, and Gerald Heard were lambasted as deserters. Circumstances were not quite so simple as that and would entail an entire discussion of its own.

Returning to Auden, the master, many popular teachers are such because they retain a childishness into adulthood which students recognize. Auden said of himself that because he was the youngest child, the youngest grandchild and always the youngest—and most precocious—child in his class, this had given him, "the lifelong conviction that, in any company, I am the youngest person present."

Duguid: I would say that is so; I think that boyishness was typical of the man and, looking back, one probably could see that he was, perhaps, rather a child who never did grow up.

Izzo: According to many accounts he did not, and it could be said that the subsequent sadness and depressions he suffered in adulthood may have been from the conflict of having had, by his recollection, an almost ideal childhood, the nurturing of which could never be matched by adult relationships. That he was very close to and enormously influenced by his mother is evidenced by the fact that right into his last years he would judge a situation and say, "Mother would/would not approve." Consequently, the boyishness he brought to teaching was, in a sense, an extension of his childhood and the approval of his students was a reasonable substitute for his mother's.

Let's talk about the teacher/student relationship in a boarding school then which was different from Britain today and perhaps always different from the U.S. Students called their teachers "masters" with the implied meaning acted upon much more so than Americans can imagine. Contrary to the typical student/teacher arrangement here, where it is the rare teacher who becomes involved in all aspects of the student's life, what was the master's role?

Duguid: They had to teach, of course, and then supervise, in shifts with colleagues, all activities outside of class, making sure students were on time and present at meals, sports, chapel—where, by the way, Auden sang in the choir—etc. There had to be more structure because we lived there so everything we did was their responsibility including games in the field. Speaking of games, I do have this memory of Auden's concern for us because he did try to get involved with them, not by playing, but to supervise, even though it wasn't his inclination. He made an attempt up to a point; he didn't just say no or act indifferently.

Izzo: Which, in fact, must have required an effort, having hated games as a student himself.

Duguid: That was obvious because Auden was just so clumsy beyond words; he seemed built in a kind of a stocky, untidy way, but it was difficult to know because he wore such crumpled clothes that you thought he got them out of a thrift shop. They didn't fit at all and were only to keep him warm and covered up. *This* master was never interested in the sartorial side of teaching as the other masters were.

Izzo: In general, by all accounts, personal grooming was a low priority.

Duguid: Indeed, and it may have gone back to the cold showers we were all subjected to, students and masters alike. It was most horrifying. Can you imagine on a day like this [mid-thirties, cloudy] in a bathroom with all the windows open, and cold water. All you could do was dash in and out so you didn't really clean yourself thoroughly, if at all, because it was just too damn cold; as long as you went in and got wet and shivered demonstrably, it was acceptable.

Izzo: Even at age 65, Auden wrote about it with such contempt as a psychotic ritual; he couldn't believe anyone could be subjected to that as a matter of almost national policy.

Duguid: And I don't know why it was done at The Downs which was really not a harsh insensitive place. I suppose it was traditional and was thought to mount a certain fortitude. Certainly we were not caned as was done at other schools although there was Mr. Cox who, if you did something naughty and you were wearing shorts which we did all year 'round, would lift up one side of them and give you a great slap with his big hand which we actually didn't think was too awful and rather normal.

Izzo: In thinking about normal, we have mentioned Mr. Auden's nonconformity; how else was that manifested?

Duguid: He would be one of the gang, not stand-offish, and attend meals with us. I can remember one breakfast that is very vivid in my mind. Mail was delivered and he opened a large manila-type envelope in front of us—very unusual for a master to do—and inside were a number of book jackets of the same design but in different color combinations for the play *The Ascent of F6* which was to be coming out [1936].

Izzo: This was the second play he wrote with Christopher Isherwood featuring a mountaineering theme and a T.E. Lawrence-ish antihero, both as parables for 1930s world politics.

Duguid: Yes, none of which I understood at the time and, of course, I didn't really know he was Auden the famous person. You don't at that age; he was just your teacher—either you liked him or you didn't—and we did. In any case, he spread the book jackets out and asked us all at this refectory-type table—I happened to be sitting next to him—"Which one do you like?" and I said "I like that one," and he said, "We'll take that for the one we'll use."

Izzo: Was that usual or unusual for a master to do?

Duguid: Very unusual because a master wouldn't normally get the boys involved in his personal stuff at all. Other masters were much more distant and didn't relate to the boys, like that Mr. Cox I mentioned. They were not harsh disciplinarians but they were austere which was what we were used to. Auden was not like that; he jollied us along, that was his way.

Izzo: I would think that it was very encouraging for students to feel that they had in some way participated in his work. Even if not fully understanding Auden's celebrity, you knew he was a man who had written a book and was asking all of you to be involved in the preparation of that book.

Duguid: Yes, it was, and then, of course, as boys do, we went right on to some other topic, mostly one boy making remarks about another—"you did, you didn't, you did, you didn't"—that sort of thing which we might not have done in front of a different master. And he might join in the fun. Of course, never unpleasantly; he was never tactless.

Izzo: In fact, he was much more sensitive to children than he ever was with adults, towards whom he could be quite acerbic.

Duguid: Well, they were the ones who had conflicted with his childhood—it wasn't the children; it was the grownups. As natural as he was though, I'm sure that he must have had some learning to do in dealing with us; it couldn't have come automatically. My own guess is that Geoffrey Hoyland, who was a very strong, firm man, an athlete, would make suggestions. Auden was wise enough to hear his employer in order to stay on.

Izzo: In that process of learning, he did bend tradition, shaping his own teaching style, writing articles about education and sharing his ideas with other teachers. In the 1950s, Dorothy Farnan, a Brooklyn, NY, high school English teacher and a good friend of Auden, asked him for some ideas and he responded with a curriculum adapted from his Downs' days. Ms. Farnan used them to great success and later became the Chairwoman of her school's English Dept.
    What do you remember of him in the classroom?

Duguid: That he certainly was different, always joking and encouraging us to talk and answer questions; he wasn't the type of person to simply teach in a dogmatic manner. In those days English literature and grammar were not separated; they were just one topic and you had to learn your parts of grammar and read various books, usually by rote. Instead, he kind of jollied you along; you weren't just reading something [as with other teachers] and if you got some amusement, well it didn't matter. *He* was interested in making *you* interested; he'd talk at you quite a bit and, as I said, we were like a gang.

Izzo: Yes, for this era the idea of groups was very popular and certainly Auden was an exponent even so far as writing his plays for The Group Theatre. The "Auden Gang" of poets/writers was given large play in literary circles although this was more by attribution than their own declaration.

Duguid: That carried over into his class. This was his way of doing things. Other masters would just stand in front of the class and write things on the blackboard and use a pointer and say this is what this means and you'd have to memorize and later in the term there'd be an exam, but you weren't expected to ask too much.

Izzo: In that sense Auden was more like today's teachers who are encouraged to have children participate. He wanted their parents to join in also. In 1932, he wrote a chapter on "Writing" for a book called *An Outline for Boys and Girls and Their Parents* which was meant as a guide to help adults be more involved with their children's education. Moreover, he didn't believe in inundating children with literature; he felt that since it was written by adults for adults how could you expect a child to understand it? In 1935 he published an anthology, *The Poet's Tongue* (with colleague John Garrett) which had poems, not his own, that he believed were more suitable for children.

Duguid: I agree with him about literature. I think that's one reason I've never really cottoned on to Shakespeare, which is a terrible admission, because in school I felt it was a duty.

Izzo: Being an English teacher, I can confirm that the majority of students feel this way. On the other hand, you are very fond of poetry. Tell us about the school publication that Auden initiated at The Downs. Hoyland wanted the children to write well technically but also to tap into any latent talent for creative writing, and Auden thought they'd be more enthused if they had a publication to write for that others would see.

Duguid: The magazine was *The Badger* which was the school's symbol with the idea of the badger's industriousness; the school's motto was *We build!* I remember one thing I had in it which was a poem called "The Bells" and I was immensely proud of it. The fact that *he* had selected it and there it was in print, I would never have dreamed of. I didn't know how people got in print. I suppose I thought books came into being *deus ex machina*, something magical. I had no idea about printing press and writing. Here I saw something for the very first time, a very personal thing and it happened to have been picked by the master who was such a nice teacher and suddenly it appeared in this forest green little book that had in the front of it an impressionistic wood cut of geometric shapes and shadows. Maybe there was even a badger somewhere in there. In any case, I know that Auden believed we would learn much more about poetry by writing it than just reading it. Maybe that's what gave me a love of poetry. I do have quite a bit of it in the house. Unlike Shakespeare, I really like poetry and relate to it. Maybe he sowed the seeds. I remember taking it home to my parents with great pride and they were very proud of me too. Today, they say, "hands-on," and it was typical of The Downs where we were also encouraged to play violins, paint, sculpt in wood and stone which, when I look back on it now, I can't imagine that they had left a lot of chisels and mallets in the hands of kids our age. It was a question of exposing the children to the arts to see if they had a natural interest and, if so, they could continue. That was Geoffrey Hoyland's philosophy and for its time was quite unusual.

Nature, in fact, also accounted for The Downs being located in a lovely countryside: lush, green, gentle, rolling fields, farms— something like this (Chapel Hill). Auden composed a poem about it, "The Malverns." The site was selected because the school's founder, old Sir George [Cadbury, of the chocolate fortune] lived nearby and wanted it to be a very outdoors sort of school.

Izzo: How "outdoors" was it?

Duguid: Oh, my goodness, there were always windows open; it was so damned cold. We slept in the main dormitory which was kind of free standing with a few steps connecting it to the main building; it had windows all the way around and even in winter we had those windows open.

Izzo: A lack of warmth seems to have been the idea in those days.

Duguid: Yes, it was thought to be terribly healthy when the fact of the matter is we had constant colds, chilblains and coughs in a way that people don't have over here.

Izzo: Auden recalls all of this as a ludicrous absurdity. His take on it was that instead of breeding strength and fortitude it bred that famous, masochistic British reserve (i.e., T.E. Lawrence) which was a form of pre-conditioning for Empire serving. Auden was not one to adhere to this. He never forgot the cold baths and the year before he died wrote about them with still-felt horror. He, himself, much enjoyed languishing in a *warm* bath which one would certainly not do in a cold one.

Duguid: So do I, and it has always seemed a luxury.

Addendum

Auden's years at Larchfield and The Downs (1930–1936) were not only a period of sweet contentment, but were, for many literary critics, the most artistically fruitful of his long career as a poet/writer. His first two volumes of poems came out to great acclaim as groundbreaking, followed by his prose masterpiece of obscurantism, *The Orators*, and three of his four plays: *The Dance of Death* (alone), *The Dog Beneath the Skin*, and *The Ascent of F6* (with Isherwood). One can easily surmise the correlation between his happiness and his art. Still, the best proof is in the master's own words where he describes his one and only mystical exposure to the vision of *agape*—the love of one's neighbor as of God—and it happened at The Downs:

> One fine summer night in June 1933 I was sitting on a lawn after dinner with three colleagues, two women and one man. We liked each other well enough but we were certainly not intimate friends, nor had any one of us a sexual interest in one another. Incidentally, we had not drunk any alcohol. We were talking casually about everyday matters when, quite suddenly and unexpectedly, something happened. I felt myself invaded by a power which, though I consented to it, was irresistible and certainly not mine. For the first time in my life I knew exactly— because, thanks to the power, I was doing it—what it means to love one's neighbor as oneself. I was also certain, though the conversation continued to be perfectly ordinary, that my three colleagues were having the same experience. (In the case of one them, I was later able to confirm this.) My personal feelings towards them were unchanged—they were still colleagues, not intimate friends—but I felt their existence as themselves to be of infinite value and I rejoiced in it.
>
> I recalled with shame the many occasions on which I had been spiteful, snobbish, selfish, but the immediate joy was greater than the shame, for I knew that, so long as I was possessed by this spirit, it would be literally impossible for me deliberately to hurt another human being.

Certainly, at The Downs, as far as Mr. Duguid and his fellow students were concerned, he never did.

Auden on Tolkien:
The Book That Isn't,
and the House That Brought It Down

Rod Jellema

Although Auden was the renowned poet, when it came to his elders he maintained a deferential respect. In this case the elder was J.R.R. Tolkien, and the result was an article that was never written.

In the spring of 1966, popular interest in the writings of J.R.R. Tolkien was at its height. Much to his annoyance, the aging Oxford philologist had become a cult figure among the young. Mushroom-eating, costumed, Middle-earth-inspired "Tolkien Societies" had sprung up everywhere. And just at that time W.H. Auden stopped writing a booklet he had contracted to write, a critical appraisal of Tolkien's work. He stopped work because Tolkien himself insisted that he stop. And the main factor that deprived the world of a sustained 48 pages of Auden on Tolkien, it now seems certain, was a single sentence spoken by Auden. Ironically, it was the year of the publication of Auden's *About the House,* and the doomed sentence was, of all things, a sentence about J.R.R. Tolkien's house.

As editor of the series of critical monographs for which Auden was writing, I thought Auden on Tolkien a perfect matchup. It was not just his stature as a poet. His critical work in matters medieval and Anglo-Saxon and Scandinavian, not to mention his published insights into myth and fantasy and Christian theology, gave him all the expertise an editor could wish for. He knew well the base from which Tolkien was working. He had published review essays on Tolkien's works as they appeared, was in fact one of the first reviewers to recommend these books as major achievements of historical imagination. His interest in Tolkien was keen enough so that he came to contract for the book through his own initiative, not mine: he deflected my proposal that he write on T.S. Eliot ("Everything as a good man has been written about his work that can be written") with his own. He would like to tackle Tolkien. Perfect, I thought.

A few months after the contract was signed, Auden told me (backstage at the Library of Congress, where he had just given a reading) that he could not finish the book. Professor Tolkien (who was always referred to under his academic title by Auden, a former student) had asked him not to, and that was that. Auden looked pained, but determined to yield. Within the next few days a small flurry of letters caught up with me—letters passed among Auden, Tolkien, Roger Verhulst of Eerdmans Publishing, and myself. The surprising thrust of Tolkien's letters was that Auden did not know him or his work. He included in a letter to Roger Verhulst an excerpt from the letter he had written Auden which raised a larger, more general objection:

> I regret very much to hear that you [Auden] have contracted to write a book about me. It does meet with my strong disapproval. I regard such things as premature impertinences; and unless undertaken by an intimate friend, or with consultation of the subject (for which I have at present no time), I cannot believe that they have a usefulness to justify the distaste and irritation given to the victim.

But then, for publisher's and editor's eyes and not for Auden's, he narrowed and intensified his objection. "I feel obliged to comment that he does not know me," Tolkien wrote Verhulst. He went on to say that he did not want "the distraction of comment or analysis which cannot in the nature of the case be well-informed." He was still on that theme when he wrote to me a month later, responding to my attempt to reassure him about Auden's approach:

> I do not ask that any such article should be "respectful", but that it should at least be accurate.... To produce an article that does not misrepresent biographical facts or my opinions would require a person having an intimate knowledge of both, if it was to be written without troubling me.

I found Tolkien's attitude toward Auden surprising. A much honored modernist poet and critic who stays at the plow in a former professor's obscure field, medieval literature and languages, is certainly a credit to that professor. Then, too, Auden and Tolkien shared religious beliefs deep and ancient enough to seem nearly subversive. (We now know that Auden had written Tolkien a decade earlier to thank him for helping Auden to see more clearly "how to write a 'Christian' piece of literature without making it obvious or 'pi' [exaggeratedly pious].") In addition to a BBC broadcast praising Tolkien's work and several reviews, Auden had contributed a paper on language to a *festschrift* in honor of his old professor, and had later dedicated a poem, "A Short Ode to a Philologist," to him. Such things might have assured Tolkien that Auden's book was going to be well-informed and accurate, and nothing like an impertinence.

The kind of gratitude we might expect Tolkien to feel toward Auden does, in fact, flow out and into print exactly one year later. The *Shenandoah Review* in 1967, as part of a *festschrift* for Auden's sixtieth birthday, published a poem in Old English, with a modern translation, written by Tolkien and dedicated to Auden. Auden wrote to thank him, not only for that poem but also in praise of another that Tolkien had contributed, "Frodo's Dreme." Auden's praise, Tolkien replied, "really made me wag my tail. I hope we can meet again soon."

The somewhat puzzling rift between these men from February through April of 1966 was not so much about Auden's credentials as about something he had said, or was reported to have said, about Tolkien's house. The Eerdmans' office and I, trying to put things back on track, kept bumping into what we called among ourselves "the house thing." Tolkien's stern letter to Auden, now in print in *The Letters of J.R.R. Tolkien*, makes a vague reference to "reports" that had displeased Tolkien about Auden's visit to a meeting of a Tolkien Society in Brooklyn. We had not seen that part of the letter. But even so we surmised that something more was nettling Tolkien. Here is some more of what we did see in Tolkien's letter to Verhulst, March 9th, 1966. After quoting the paragraph from his letter to Auden, Tolkien wrote:

> I owe Mr. Auden a debt of gratitude for the generosity with which he has supported and encouraged me since the first appearance of *The Lord of the Rings*. At the same time I feel obliged to comment that he does not know me.

On the word *me* Tolkien placed a handwritten footnote:

> We have of course met, perhaps half a dozen times in 40 years, but we have not had any private or personal exchange of views, in talk or in writing.

That sets a curiously exacting requirement for writers of 48-page essays. But Tolkien goes on:

> It is possibly unfair to judge him by the press reports (possibly garbled) about me and my views at a meeting on [sic] the so-called Tolkien Society. They at any rate, as reported, show him to be entirely mistaken about my views on the topics he touched on.

The "press reports" turned out to be reports in the London papers of an off-handed little item in the *New Yorker* about a meeting of the Tolkien Society in Brooklyn to which Auden, arriving late, addressed a few remarks. What was briefly quoted said really nothing about Tolkien's "views" or biography or "opinions." Auden was reported to have said *(New Yorker,* January 15, 1966) that Professor Tolkien "lives in a hideous house—I can't tell you how awful it is—with hideous pictures on the walls."

That this was the offending piece, and that it was the major irritant in Tolkien's outcry against the projected book, was made clear in Tolkien's second letter about Auden to Roger Verhulst (April 8th):

> Judging by Mr. Auden's remarks as reported in the New Yorker, "The Elvish Mode," I do not think his discussion would have been either valuable or understanding, unless he had been willing to consult me personally: a distraction for which ... I have no time at present.

We had no idea whether Auden knew that Tolkien had seen the insulting remark. We had no evidence that Auden himself had seen what the *New Yorker* alleged he had said. Because he was known to be a gracious person, our last hope was that he would, if he knew the problem, explain or apologize. We were giving some credence to the rumor that Auden had been drinking heavily just before that meeting. With the approval of Cal Bulthuis, the editor at Eerdmans, I breached good manners and the privacy of Tolkien's correspondence by quoting to Auden what Tolkien had written us about him. But Auden did not respond. What he had said that night at the Library of Congress was still true. The book was well along, he said, but "if Professor Tolkien does not wish it to be written, it shall not be written."

There's an epilogue to this strange, sad tale that worked itself out over the next few years. There are on record three reports of visits to Tolkien's house in the following year, and each of them reveals how sensitive Tolkien was about the subject of the house, and how deeply Auden's reputed remark had wounded him.

Clyde Kilby, an American professor who spent the summer of 1966 helping Tolkien sort and file the enormous collection of papers that were to become *The Silmarillion*, reports that on his first day with the Tolkiens they told him of their "anger" with W.H. Auden, "especially his comment [about] the Tolkien home."

> Mrs. Tolkien invited me to come and sit in the same chair Auden had occupied when visiting them and see if I thought the house looked hideous. I readily confessed that it was a nicer house than I had ever lived in myself.

Some time near the end of that year, Tolkien gave an interview to Richard Plotz, the founder of the Tolkien Society of America. Tolkien, showing at the time signs of irritability, had been surprisingly cordial in a long and informative letter to Plotz (September 1965). Plotz, a high school student who was featured in the *New Yorker* piece as the host of the infamous meeting, certainly was more responsible than Auden for whatever in the proceedings was offensive to Tolkien in reflecting his "views" and "opinions."

But the interview at 76 Sandfield Road went well. Whether Plotz was given the chair test given to Kilby is unknown, but in reporting his visit to Tolkien's house in *Seventeen* magazine, the "Thain" of the Tolkien Society of America went out of his way to tell his readers about "the nice pictures on the wall, a comfortable, attractive home."

A few months later, in February of 1967, Tolkien wrote a seven-page letter to a pair of journalists who had interviewed him for the *Daily Telegraph Magazine*. In the course of an amazingly thorough and minutely picky set of corrections to their first draft, Tolkien apologized for having received them in what they had described in that draft as "the cramped garage that he uses as a study."

> If you wonder why I received you, two courteous and charming people, in such a hole, may I say that my house has no reception room but my wife's sitting room, filled with her personal belongings. This was contemptuously described in the New Yorker (by a visitor), and we both suffered ridicule (and worse: commiseration) when this was quoted in the London papers. Since then she has refused to admit anybody but personal friends to the room.

A final rounding out of "the house thing" was brought about by the publication of Tolkien's *Letters* in 1981. He reveals himself in his correspondence of this time to be a harried, pestered, far-too-meticulous man; he was angered by, and somewhat paranoid about, American publishers and copyright questions; the flood of questions he received about Middle-earth and about his relations with other writers drew testy, often uncharitable responses. He seemed sometimes on the verge of derangement. Understandably, the public ridicule of his "hideous" house, amplified at Oxford, where his sudden fame as a popular figure made his reputation go down, not up, seemed part of a barrage that he was not handling well.

W.H. Auden may have felt some concern about Tolkien's mental stress. The Tolkien letters reveal, what I could not have known at the time, that Auden was told directly about "the house thing." Six days after my letter to Auden, in which I tried to tip him off, Tolkien himself wrote to Auden (April 8, 1966):

> If my letter to you of February 23rd was a little tart, I must confess that this was caused by the article in the New Yorker purporting to report the meeting of the Tolkien Society in New York and your remarks about me.... In case you have missed it I enclose a copy. It is ... unfortunate that the general Press, with its usual slant towards sneering, fastened on your remarks about my house and pictures. This was the main item in reports in English papers and exposed my wife and myself to a certain amount of ridicule.

My letter went unanswered, but Auden did respond to Tolkien's. However, according to Humphrey Carpenter (*W.H. Auden: A Biography*), his reply made no explanation or apology for his remarks, and in fact made no reference to the matter. My own efforts to purchase Auden's manuscript for the Eerdmans' vault, with the understanding that Auden could set the conditions for its eventual release, was gently vetoed by Auden, who responded through his agent that he "did not want to do anything about it until after Tolkien's death." Meanwhile Tolkien was gradually letting the matter drop—which may be all that Auden was hoping for. As the tone of Tolkien's general correspondence relaxed and softened, he also moved on to write the *festschrift* poem for Auden's sixtieth birthday.

Upon the death of Auden in 1973 at age 66, Tolkien (then 79, and three years removed from the house on Sandfield Road) answered some questions about Auden for Robert Boyers, editor of the journal *Salmagundi*. He placed Auden "as one of my great friends." Among other comments were these:

> [H]is interest in Old English Poetry ... was mainly due to his own natural talents and the possession of an "open ear" among the majority of the deaf.... His support of me and interest in my work has been one of my chief encouragements. He gave me very good reviews, notices and letters from the beginning when it was by no means a popular thing to do. He was, in fact, sneered at for it.

Almost certainly the manuscript of the little book, whatever its stage of completion, was quietly destroyed by Auden.

Notes

All quotations from W.H. Auden are from unpublished letters, copyright 2000 by the Estate of W.H. Auden; reprinted by permission. Quotations from J.R.R. Tolkien's letters to Roger Verhulst and to Rod Jellema are copyright 2000 by the Estate of J.R.R. Tolkien, reprinted by permission.

Some parts of J.R.R. Tolkien's letters to Roger Verhulst, and Clyde Kilby's comment on the Tolkien house, first appeared in Clyde Kilby, *Tolkien and the Silmarillion.*

All other quotations from J.R.R. Tolkien are from *The Letters of J.R.R. Tolkien,* selected and edited by Humphrey Carpenter.

The series for which Auden was contracted to write his critical booklet was *Contemporary Writers in Christian Perspective,* a series of critical monographs published by Eerdmans between 1966 and 1972.

Cool Distance:
W.H. Auden's "Gay" Version
of Christian Spirituality

Dennis Paddie

The pre-Oxford Auden was raised by his pious mother, and he was also dutifully pious. His school friend Robert Medley recalls offending Auden when Medley disparaged Christianity. Auden, both pre- and post-Oxford, loved to sing in choirs (see herein "The Student and the Master") and bang out hymns on the piano. Consequently, Auden's "conversion" to Christianity in America (see herein Conniff and Paddie) was really a re-conversion.

This impressionistic essay, written by a Gay Christian, takes a look at Auden's place as a fellow Gay Christian who inspired the author to seek his own spirituality.

The poetry of W.H. Auden speaks from the first generation in the world to benefit from the real science of psychoanalysis in the modern milieu of the early twentieth century, a milieu that tied art to revolutionary, scientific and surreal, even Da-Da, necessities, and the first generation that went mad about the movies. Auden and Co. were top-drawer intellectuals, such as those who inhabited with her, Virginia Woolf's twilight. Auden's poetry shares the enthusiasm of the first generation to valorize demotic music and art. And finally Auden's poetry is the emblem and the cipher of the predispositions of the first generation to give the world again, after a two-thousand year hiatus, the fires of the Greek passion, fires that burn so brightly in C.P. Cavafy, a Greek—and gay—poet Auden greatly admired.

Auden's poetry declaims itself from the battlements of these trends, but he himself was cool and distant to the "gay" struggle. Auden was never a "gay" poet. He left that prescient, political

consciousness to the Vedantist, Christopher Isherwood. As Isherwood said, "One is not born with a non-conformist conscience for
nothing."

But Auden, despite his ever-so-slight brush with an atheistic
Communism, his early interest in Freudian psychoanalysis, his
"Germanism," was a non-conformist, yet conforming High Church
Englishman all of his life, forsaking the church only for his brief
interlude of the 1930s. New York, his choice of turf, loves
aristocrats. Auden was, by birth, a high, ministerial son of an M.D.
bourgeois missionary, but by individual talent, he was a prince.
Naturally, he settled in Manhattan.

Between the age of phrenology and of the invention of racism
along with the other grotesque classification systems of the late
nineteenth century and our own time, lies an unexplored idea, an
aesthetic point-of-view. This is "The Poetry of the Invert," and this
poetry is the very model for a culture that bred an art that coun-
tered oppression. Auden, while understanding this oppression,
and because of his Modernist tastes, which submitted homosexual
love to "analysis," related to the world from the august position of
the civil poet. As a reward for his discretion, he is permitted
participation in the high culture and remains free of all classification, all typification because of his dissimulation in the "straight"
world.

Yet, within Auden's non-declaration, "Lullaby" is secretly a
"gay" lyric and one of the finest expressions of the meaning of
physical love from any age. And the meaning of the poem was
available to all. This must have been the higher octave in Auden's
reasoning with regard to his false stance concerning his own way
of loving.

Although gay people have overcome the stigmatizing, spiritual norms of Judeo-Christian doctrine on the one hand, and the
social typifications of homosexuality in secular civilization,
Socrates and Hadrian would be tagged as sex-criminals today,
along with the frank homosexuals Caravaggio and Leonardo, and
probably Michelangelo, despite the myth of the latter's Neo-Pla-
tonic chastity. The denial of one's homosexuality by creating a
compensatory personality for the public was not invented by Auden. In fact, the phenomenon is one of the basic elements of Gay
History and the poetry of the invert.

But a *gay* poet must know the history of the last two thousand
years and what it means, in particular, with regard to the issue of
the masks of sexuality. For the classical ages ended for us in the

two-thousand-year era of the fiat of the auto-da-fe. The gay poet must remember, in present skin, that the American JAG Corps hauled homosexuals back into Hitler's camps to serve out sentences handed down from the Third Reich. These memories and all others like them reify the category of suffering to which a conscious, gay artist pays primary political and aesthetic allegiance. They also determine what the art he produces will be and do in the world.

For the gay poet not only remembers, he *affirms* the history of gay oppression as philosophically and existentially real. And recognizing and reconstructing his history has brought him to this point to the gay phenomenon, its history and art, as a primary cultural paradigm in all of Western Civilization. In a short step, then, he sets that paradigm into a critique of our present world. To articulate and to practice this view is to resist the elements of the social bargains which still inculcate and still promote the oppression of the paradigm of Love's primacy over all, a principle attested to, universally, by the world's sages, and particularly by Jesus of Nazareth.

Auden never made these transpositions in his interpretation of the role he would play as a poet. Admittedly, such transpositions were part of the "role-in-the-making," as described. Nonetheless, he remained, politically and formally and therefore spiritually, detached from the vision of the two-thousand-year persecution of his kind. In that, despite his position in the world, he never publicly moved beyond the Camp persona and its world-view.

Isherwood says that Camp is a *faux* silly take on a serious subject that makes fun of the subject but not the subject's seriousness, like Baroque art on redemption and opera on human passion. Camp is a bitterly humorous reaction to the serious accusations made against gays by the Judeo-Christian tradition. To affirm our existence we disguised it for centuries in the Camp code, using one thing, like the pronoun, "she" to stand for another, like the pronoun "he," and this is a recapitulation of the process of metaphor. This use of metaphor as a social tool can be added to Isherwood's definition.

Auden's pose *was* Camp.

However, if, even in the conceits of Camp, we can presume no more than our own existence; and as inverted poetry and its paired twin, our historical, homosexual experience, then that is enough. Auden's spirituality, gleaned from the poet's legend and verse, reflects that Camp view and pose.

Gay people share existence in the world with both the kind and the cruel Other. Our fate, historically, in the West, even in Greece, at times, has been to be persecuted, by kind and cruel alike. All the while we have attempted to solve life's puzzle and then, following the dictates of the heart, desire, common wisdom and moral taste, sought to love, and by loving, to be good.

In the realm of the personal, from which the common and philosophical view of this situation must be drawn, persecution begins in childhood as a multi-form evil. The child whose kind has been typified, de-humanized, and targeted, is existence as it is. And from that pit, one's earliest solutions about one's self are rigo-rized by the truth that cruelty exists. But the abused child also learns that pity and love give life back to the battered heart. That child also learns the meaning of joy as liberation.

The abuse of gay people does not totally define us, of course, as it does no abused individual, however much it defines gay cul-ture and the poetry of the invert. However, in the flames of the auto-da-fe, from the pillory, from the concentration camp, upon the throne, in well-fed, lusty 'burbs, at Muscle Beach, amongst warriors, fairies and young bucks, all who were and are gay, who are and were able to speak, testify to a common, primary perspec-tive, born of persecuted love.

A line of Auden's gives life to the abstract of this gestalt:

We must love one another or die.

This perspective and the vision inflected by Auden's utterance are a critique of life as it is now actually lived in Western civiliza-tion. It is the spoken word of a functioning category of being with vital knowledge for the general milieu. Vision is always, in part, critique. And being possessed of the perspective under examina-tion and of the existential tasks of a primary homosexual poet, one is in possession of the same tasks as Auden: to love and to be good. This is a metaphysical gift; for studying Auden one studies one's own soul.

In Auden's introduction to Rae Dalven's translation of Cavafy's verse, he asks the question, "What happens to the boys?" ... after their assignations with the poet. In his introduction to *The Protestant Mystics*, where he comments upon Dame Juliana of Norwich as an exemplar of a purely English spiritual tradition which merges pre- and-post Christian ages into one heritage, Auden renders for us the four stages of divinely transcendent experiences as they endure in the English tradition, and remembered especially as exemplary in the life of Dame Juliana: 1. The Vision of Dame Kind (spiritual love nature), 2. The Vision of the Beloved (spiritual love of another person), 3. The Vision of Agape (spiritual love of all existence), 4. The Vision of God.

As presented in his remarks in the forewords of these two books, Auden's spirituality oscillates between two poles: 1. simple human love ("What happens to the boys?"), and 2. the concern for a method of approaching the divine. This is the classic dichotomy. It encompasses the entire Classico-Christian tradition. Despite the tradition's prejudices toward corporeal existence as against the opportunity for a putative paradise after death, we have examined substance, age to Aristotelian age, with an artistic eye to describe—incessantly. Can we call this a permanent fixture in Western civilization, "Scientific Christianity"? Auden's work and life seem to suggest that we can. The presence of the concern in his poetry elevates that poetry above ordinary verse and makes of the man a seeker of truth. This is another of his metaphysical gifts to us.

He must have been clear about all of these various themes and facts in western intellectual and religious life when he introduced us to the Protestant mystics, and when he revealed something of his own inner, religio-sexual life in his concern for Cavafy's catamites. Gossip contends that he was similarly concerned with the promiscuity of his choice of Beloved, Chester Kallman, and its affect upon the beloved soul. His tenderness is exemplary:

> Lay your sleeping head, my Love,
> Human on my faithless arm....
> Guardian angels see you to rest....
> Nights of insult let you pass
> Watched by every human love.

The concern for the fate of those with whom one has had the experience of same-sex desire, fulfillment, and mutual love is the concern of the Lover for the Beloved, the platonic model that still rules male love, gay *and* straight, today. It is also the concern of Christ for us all, in our tradition.

It is in this physical milieu, the substantial medium of sexual love alone that one who is homosexual, queer, gay, an invert, a third-sexer, can experience metaphor as form. The substantial experience of Love is necessary in order for us to come to manhood and to Lawrence Durrell's "great inkling," which is the sense/ intuition of the existence of higher octaves of consciousness and of true, eternal Love. Then we enter into a reality in which Love is neither straight nor gay, nor exclusively chaste nor exclusively, permissively promiscuous, nor even, finally, *physical.*

All of humanity oscillates, in devotion and action between these two poles: 1. that of the existential realization of self, modern always as the crisis of self, and 2. that of a particular and emphatic awareness of the divine, which always implies an eternity that is ours as both a transpersonal quality and as a person. Therefore, Auden's "gay" spirituality, oscillating as it does between love for the individual and the divine as inspired by the individual, is human spirituality informed of, as opposed to defined by, gay experience.

Not that a specifically "gay" spirituality does not exist, as witness *The Epic of Gilgamesh*, the institution of The Sacred Theban Band in early Greece, Socrates's oration upon Love in *The Symposium* at the peak of Athenian culture, and Hadrian's passion for Antinoos in later classical times. But what we have in Auden, but only as a sub-text, is the implication of a fully *Christian* awareness at the dawn of the modern era, an awareness that understood the ancient honor of the love of man for man that had been unjustly, barbarously, fatally persecuted for almost two millenia. In the subtext of his work what we have is the interpolation of this divine realization into a lesson for all of humanity constructed upon the highest principles of our civilization. But he doesn't label in the written text that the sources of his great lessons result from homosexual eroticism, and yet, even though his choice of words renders the public text as gender-neutral equivocations, the emotions felt in the subtext were, indeed, gay.

He did discover the higher notes of liberation from human suffering by love in realizing his nature and its history, however privately, and participated in the prophecy of what was to come for gays at the end of the Millennium. But he did so on the other side of the divide in history which created the modern gay movement. Nonetheless, the discovery of love is always a positive value, whether or not one is capable of shouldering the political and social burdens implied in that discovery.

The "gay" poet, struggling against oppression, represents a whole category of being, a history and a role in history and a responsibility to history. He is called upon by his position in that history to resolve tragedy in the manner of the saint and the hero. Powerful without limit, with the overtones of a Classical, Christian, Humanist and Modernist core to work from, his sensibility rises from the fate of the male body. The male form and its fate are the source of compassion and of eros for the male homosexual poet.

The attempt to pose for one's self an identity independent of the oppressive public definition of the quality and reality of his eros and compassion and the need to resolve the ontic problems of a persecuted history are the roots of the homosexual spirituality that became the blooming rose. Let's say that *resolving* the tragedy of our history and coming into full possession of our own Western tradition are the stem, and that *accepting* that we are the heirs of great intellectual and spiritual wealth is the leaf. Then finally we can say that *acting* from the heart of the Gospels by loving one another and trying to be good is the flower.

The metahistorical reality symbolized by the rose in Western civilization gives us a clue to the possible foundations of Auden's re-conversion to Christianity. (He had been quite fervent growing up before his temporary lapse.) It is not surprising that he re-converted. All of his life Auden had accepted the facts of his redemption as a privileged member of imperial English society, even as a lapsed high-church Christian. "No trouble when I found I was queer, published in the right places at the right time," he once said. Pretty rosy!

The facts of his biography, his tilt toward science and psychology, his sympathies with Socialist-Communist politics, and his pacifism in the face of a fascist reality he had once fleetingly eroticized, but then helped to articulate the threat of to England, do not violate his class identity. Even his life in America after abandoning England in 1939, and his American citizenship do not violate his position in the world as an upper-caste Englishman. And one rather doubts that he was ever anything but a believer in God, despite his heart-felt, intellectually rigorized and brilliant poses of the modern monster child in the 1930s. The child and the youth die hard in the man. But in Auden, neither ever did. Even his aged, frumpy, soiled affectations, his habitual insouciances were those of a public-school boy.

Auden had faced the moral analysis of imperial society in the thirties as a kind of secular, yet still spiritual trial. From there, he found his way to an affirmation of the contribution of Christian society to humanity, despite the undeniable facts of the fates of homosexuals at the hands of official and heretical Christianity. The struggle to be recognized as human is Christ's will for us in the modern world as it is for all oppressed peoples according to Liberation Theology. One can believe that Auden knew this. One can believe he also knew that the *being* of gay people provides a question that fuels one of the basic arguments of Western civilization: "Do we exist?"

For Auden, the trip out of Edwardian England to the acceptances of the late sixties was a long one. Although he never clearly stated his personal doctrine, his personal perspective upon gay history and oppression, we know that his homosexuality defined his sexual interest in his existence, his identity and his interpretation of his existence as well. This awareness makes him a forerunner of the contemporary gay sensibility.

We would not have arrived here without Auden's "Lay Your Sleeping Head, My Love."

The poet's life and the life of every gay person, of course, really means that there is an innate sweetness in life that transcends physicality. This shared sweetness means that pleasure is a human right regardless of the human configurations seeking this right. It also means that homosexual passion is a powerful, adolescently motivated eros. Eros means that homosexual pleasure, in the body, historically a category of Christian anathema, is, in the spirit, an acceptable sacrifice, before God, and that this sacrifice, which *all* are required to make, is human.

Auden's donation is a real place in which to locate that power and mystery and to practice that love, an existential ground, a position in an ordered universe and, most importantly, an ironic take upon the circumstances of that position in the great ontology.

He had enjoyed himself immensely in that milieu, in that position no matter how much he had probably suffered. Everything suffers. And when the chips were down, Auden, as a person imbued with the spirit of our position in the human drama, had spoken beautiful, great and sublime words to the public that read his verse in every epoch of his career, not as an inverted victim of his homosexuality but as a supreme citizen of the world.

This cosmopolitan spirit, shared throughout the gay world, has been stiffened by AIDS into an even greater awareness of who we are and what our responsibilities might be beyond a simple sexual identity and its prerogatives. We all act as we can, but we understand what it is that we have inherited from an Auden. One can learn a great deal from Auden that has nothing to do with po-etry.

In an informal colloquy at his apartment in New York, Richard Howard, the gay poet and critic, said that all of the major poets, who were or are homosexual, eventually become recluses, renun-ciates or outlaws. The statement is a good rule of thumb for exam-ining the poetry of the invert. A turning away from the world happens naturally as anyone ages or responds to the morbidities of disease and depression and death. As ideas, institutions, nations and empires endure, they change and wear away almost like phys-ical substance. *Do* gay poets wear out and turn away more pro-foundly?

Howard had misread the factual history of Auden's life. The three stereotypes—recluses, renunciates, outlaws—dramatize the existence of the poetry of the invert and characterize the art of an epoch. Auden was unique. In the various revolutions that had by turns on the wheel of fortune liberated and enslaved humankind, in the transit from the old world into the modern one, he is, liter-ally, a participating theorist, despite his mythic, fiercely anti-social messiness and his final unknown silent introspections on his sex-uality.

He was a primary figure in the transfiguration of the gay man into person and citizen. That might seem a grim task, but his life, in fact, embodies the high hilarity of the Camp figure inside the gay circle, a figure known to the world as the poet of the age but to his friends as "Lulu" or "Fifi" or whomever he became in the cir-cle.

This "inside" understanding is part the general turning away from the public, literary and social forms of the Victorian and Ed-wardian periods by the Lost Generation, to which Auden and his crowd were the teen-agers. World War I had converted all that had gone before the bright lights of the twentieth century into a quaint past that was not remote but only yesterday to the Chap-lins, Swansons, Garbos, Pickfords and Fairbanks of the new cin-ema world.

W.H. Auden, Christopher Isherwood, Stephen Spender, et al., were the youth of the world to their time, the dialectics of the friendships among them part of the lore of the day. They were stars, but Oxford-Cambridge left-liberal politics shaped their mo-tivations and their personal dramas drastically, despite their love affairs, escapades, literary successes and failures. And their political and artistic performances before the passing scene and panorama of the thirties were brilliant. This brilliance is their distilled essence. And it is the fountainhead of Auden's spiritual personality. It remains luminous at these cooling distances from the vortices into tumult that he and they and their world hurled themselves.

The youth of Isherwood and Auden evokes the figures of Achilles and Patroclus. Their friendship formed them as artists and in their mutual devotion one recalls a tribe of Amazonian Indians, in which boys take lovers assuming that the relationships will last a lifetime. In feathers and beads and loincloths, as young men, who had been out into the world, two of them walk the banks of a river with bows and arrows, fishing. One says, "Without him I would have gone down to death, many times."

The famous photograph in the train station documents the image that then stood for sophisticated youth. The photograph also illustrates a remark Auden made as the two friends returned from another excursion abroad and another political crisis. Auden quotes Ilya Ehrenburg on the Russian Revolution: "You did not live in our time. Read about us and be sorry."

By the time this author's generation was fully aware of who he was, Auden had become the naked ideologue that one suspects he always was with his Oxonian education and genius. The poetry of his maturity was formal and cool to the white-hot issues of his youth, and this verse was effortlessly discursive, always one of his tendencies, especially in his more private verse, and best of all, in terms of a dissemination of his homoerotic sub-text, he was widely read. I can hardly find the young revolutionary in the old semi-recluse, but he was there. The proof of that is in his Christian conversion in which the rebel brings his life home and full-circle. And to everyone's consternation the later Auden became an ideologue and this time a *religious* one.

But really, Auden had accepted his sub-lunary lot—just a queer poet in the world, even within all of his ideological, philological, Christo-psychological, mythological, ethnological fine feather. He was the foremost poet in English. And as just that poet, he had had, it seems, a first-class, mystically Christic experience on a summer night in 1933 that predated, yet made inevitable, his subsequent re-conversion. (See in this volume the end of "The Student and the Master" for Auden's description of this experience.)

But despite his Christianity, Auden was hagiogrified as an existential saint by the great world. But, along with Sartre, Heidegger, and a host of others, he was also a despairing figure, an apostle of doom. Not because of anything he said but because of his face. That face, in youth, never beautiful but tenderly affecting, had turned into a roadmap of the indulgences of his old age. It served to caution one of his own "notions and me tendencies," to quote Scobie from *The Alexandria Quartet*.

The image of the face is Hogarthian and is as bleak as despair itself. It shows us that time is real, as real as the spirit, that the downbeat and the rhythm of the universal dance tax the flesh with effort and compels one to a need for comfort, whether chemical or conjugal. The habitual expression that the face wore spoke of thwarted passion. The face seemed always to speak of a lifetime of unhappy loves. He seemed like a Moses unable to claim Canaan for himself.

One learns from Auden's face to prefer aging honestly rather than to try to remain falsely young.

The aesthetic tragedy is, however, in the right hands, a comedy. "Eat, drink and be merry, for tomorrow we die," is not a tragic statement. It is *high* comedy. And I think that its stated and implied truths held for Auden. The Epicurean tone to his discourse is unmistakable throughout the years before and after his re-conversion. And since Christian Humanism is a crazy type of Epicureanism, fanciful in its metaphysics, Auden's conversion was not discontinuous with his past. Instead of the banquet of the world, he turned to Christ's table and never lost his sense of humor. Cavafy's bitter, wistful take on his experience did not seep into Auden's work either. And once inside the church, he continued to express his Humanist biases without ecclesiastical contradiction.

The whole life taken together, then, reforms the idea of necessity of the poetry of the invert. Auden is a civil poet throughout, never a radical one. Even his concern with libretti for opera is civil action, however distant from the hot surfaces of youth and cool to the touch of the memories of his lustful days.

His devotion to poetry provided him with the interface for his age. But it is the complex Buddhist concept of the fullness of the void that finally and best describes Auden's gay spirituality. He was his world, and mastering metaphor was the preoccupation of his entire lifetime. And metaphor, as we know, is not so simple as the common understanding has it. If metaphor is all that we may know of the divine through representations to ourselves of symbolic actuality, its practice as verse becomes a spiritual, a metaphysical art.

"Mah Deah! What have you done to it?" Auden exclaimed, circa 1936, to Isherwood, within earshot of the straight world, at a rehearsal for *The Ascent of F6*. (He had just returned to London, posthaste, from the Spanish Civil War, where he had been no Orwell who had fought and been wounded.) It seemed that he thought Isherwood had modified the spiritual questing in the play for a more secular version.

He had returned from Civil-war torn Spain to his internal spiritual sanctuary away from politics and writing. Over time he came to believe that art could not have an effect beyond its own orbits. Such resignation, almost always, in ordered lives, precedes fundamental change. Therefore, a re-conversion was in the cards for him.

If "gay" culture is culture itself, then the phenomenon of homosexuality has had a profound influence upon the classification systems of the times in which we live, an influence out of proportion with the actual number of homosexuals in the Western world. The concept of the poetry of the invert is only one example of this influence. But it must be said that we are in the province of the masculine dialectic. And in a masculine culture, the influence and prevalence of homosexuality is virtually subliminal. And to the degree that poetry, in this publicly perceived context, is seen to be, and is considered to be, an effeminate and effeminizing process, the influence is negative. And to the further degree that art is taken as a sub-pre-unconscious function of the human psyche, the poetry of the invert vitiates the forces it incarnates. The extreme internality of modern art mimics autism, automatism and schizophrenia and functions at a disadvantage to the discourse necessary to the re-establishment of artistic canons that might reinvent contemporary poetry and art and transform them into whatever shape, personal, local, national, or international, into instruments of the Gods.

A smaller canon of poems that realizes and renders Auden in the role of the civil poet rather than an inverted one and as a wise doctor of the spirit of humanity, would include, but not exclusively, "September 1, 1939," "Lullaby," and its unforgettable first line, "Lay your sleeping head, my love," etc., "In Praise of Limestone," "In Memory of William Butler Yeats," "Caliban to the Audience," "Musée des Beaux Arts," "Precious Five," and "Under Which Lyre."

Each of these poems is in itself a singular proof that Auden, in the age of the poetry of the invert, was a civil poet, concerned in the public forum of his day with the ideas and the fate of the world over and above his own plight and always, always, trying to love and to be good.

He is a Modernist artist of the first water. His greatness lies in his choice of the role he would play as a poet in his time. To understand what his choice means we posit the existence of a new interpretation of modern art created by the Gay minority as a culture of oppression. It was Auden's refusal to take onto himself the mantle of this oppression that defines his spiritual and political stance with regard to his homosexuality. This is a contradiction in present light, and yet one applauds the poet's refusal.

Can we divine from the contradiction the nature of his conversion to Christianity? Contradiction and refusal had defined his love for Chester Kallman. Perhaps the reality of his experience as a homosexual did not measure up to his poetry. His loyalties, therefore, were elsewhere, and the enigma of his loyalties made him into a great artist. And metaphysical pain, probably induced by sexual wounds, led him back to the Christian tendernesses of his childhood.

When his last and posthumously published volume of verse, *Thank You, Fog*, was published in 1973, this author was honestly puzzled at what seemed, at first, the befuddled devotions of an old man.

Considering here what his gay spirituality might have been, it seems that the "Fog" in question can be correlated with the medieval, mystical notion of "The Cloud of Unknowing." In this last note from the poet's life does he give us a clue to the quality of the mystical experience which returned him to mainline Christianity?

Was the mentalized, neurotic intellectual artist, tempted by all of the complaints and habits of inversion as Auden surely was, finally relieved of all knowing before he disappeared into a gentle fog of release from the world? Was he waking into more and brighter light, rewarded with prize, peace and glory for artistic valor, even before he died?

Essays on Auden's Influence,
His Life, His Work,
and His Legacy

W.H. Auden and D.H. Lawrence:
A Journey of Ideas

James A. Young

*While at Oxford Auden fell under the spell of D.H. Lawrence the ideo-
logue and temporarily embraced Lawrence's philosophy of the "blood"
and the intuitions inspired by the blood as a guide to his life and work.*

W.H. Auden's indebtedness to the influence of a large number of
persons has been well documented and has evoked considerable
commentary. Some, such as Randall Jarrell, have on that basis
taken Auden to task for his "rapidly-shifting beliefs" (Jarrell,
"Changes"); and, Richard Hoggart calls Auden "something of an
intellectual Jackdaw, picking up bright pebbles of ideas" (Hoggart,
8). These views are fundamentally inaccurate, but there is no
doubt that the omnivorous Auden considered the theories and
perceptions of a wide range of leading thinkers and that they
made an impact upon him. One of these influences was D.H.
Lawrence, who affected the early Auden's thought and work in
several ways and whose concerns remained those of Auden
throughout his life.

That D.H. Lawrence influenced the young Auden is not sur-
prising. Lawrence intrigued many, including Auden and Aldous
Huxley in the U.K., Ernest Hemingway and William Carlos
Williams in the U.S., as well as other progressives elsewhere
(Hemingway, 95; Mariani, 167, 246, 360). A precise catalog of
Lawrentian impacts upon Auden is impossible, for the fields in
which both worked over a period of years were cultivated by
many others who held similar views. Auden's physician father,
George A., studied and used Freudian psychological methods in
his practice and provided his son's first exposure to the new psychology of the individual. Auden showed an early interest in this
area and was struck by Lawrence's call for less intellectualizing

about life and for more natural living—to feel more blood first before applying the brain. In this vein, Lawrence's character Paul
Morel, in *Sons and Lovers* (1913), voices the belief that "one should
feel inside oneself for right and wrong" (Lawrence, *Sons*, 298),
rather than seek moral guidance from philosophers, churchmen,
and convention. Paul's mother, moreover, sees that "Anything that
is natural is pleased to be itself," even as she withholds her approval of such a basis for living (Lawrence, *Sons*, 186) and seeks,
with destructive consequences, to mould her sons, whom she loves
more than her natural-living, Lawrentian husband. Nor would she
have admired Lawrence's Tom Brangwen of *The Rainbow* (1915),
who rejects the "cold, unliving purposes" of the intellectual life in
favor of the natural, bodily, instinctive life that he shares in kind
with his stepdaughter Anna, who intuitively avoids thinking in
order "to save herself" (Lawrence, *Rainbow*, 74–75, 86). Such notions appealed to a broad section of the cultural left, for various
reasons—and, in certain misguided interpretations, to the fascist
right as well.

   In addition, for Lawrence, consciousness leads to mechanized
evil, self-consciousness to nothingness; and, "He yearned for the
separateness of an individual isolation somehow in conjunction
with another human being—a woman—but not dependent upon
that person ..." (Oates, 23). For a young man such as Auden, who
was—among other characteristics—a gay man in a convention-
ridden, straight society, the notions of living one's natural way
and of confronting the problem of isolation vis-à-vis others held
enormous appeal. Many others, including Sigmund Freud and the
American psychologist Homer Lane—another important influence
on Auden—confronted the same problems, so one cannot be certain of where a Lawrentian influence left off and that of a
Lawrence or Lane or another began. By Auden's own account, as
in *Letter to Lord Byron* (1936), "Part came from Lane, and part from
D.H. Lawrence" (Auden, *English*, 195), but Lawrence's influence
impacted earlier and apparently lasted longer than did that of
many others—even if the impact resulted, as it did for Auden, in a
subsequent reversal and renunciation of Lawrence.

   Before the end of the 1920s, Auden came to see the "life-wish"
as the desire for separation from the family and from literary predecessors, which is to say from the closed systems of the family
and of conventionality, including in the latter case the conventional morality of Freud (Mendelson, 40, 42). At this point, the unconventional Lawrence remains a touchstone, and Auden advo-

cates "the liberation of impulse, the wisdom of desire" and the movement of the rhythms of nature as guiding principles (Wright, 47; Mendelson, 47). One must, Auden holds, lose inhibitions imposed by society, by the tyranny of the dead, as depicted in his *Paid on Both Sides,* a play written in 1928 which contains the additional Lawrentian theme of the negative role of women, chiefly of mothers upon their sons (Auden, *English,* 1–17).

While rhetorically and methodologically rebellious, Auden remained, like Lawrence, within bourgeois parameters. His was to be a rebellion along the lines of the psychologist Homer Lane and the poet Baudelaire, not a revolution as imagined by Marx and led by Lenin. Auden, who sought—again, like Lawrence—to approach life scientifically (Isherwood, "Notes," 10), focused upon the psychology of the individual, even as he diagnosed the whole of English society as sick (Hoggart, 19; Wright, 48). While living in Berlin in 1928–29, the young poet enjoyed a lifestyle that tempted him to believe that human evolution was leading toward a separation of mind and body, in which state the mind will occupy itself with "the incommunicable privacy of abstract thought" while the body may be left to sexual coupling and other physical pleasures (Mendelson, 65). Although Auden soon realized that the mind requires more than isolation, the Lawrentian separation between upper and lower nerve centers, between thinking and nature, remains with Auden into the 1930s and is still accompanied by his concern about the individual's separation from society.

Both individuals, Lawrence and Auden, lived as middle-class professionals in a society dominated by the conventions of the middle classes, whom the two found terribly wanting. Lawrence wrote "How Beastly the Bourgeois Is" and characterized him as "... like a fungus, living on the remains of bygone life" and asserting "Touch him and you'll find he's all gone inside / just like an old mushroom, all wormy inside, and hollow/" (Lawrence, *Poems,* 430–31). Auden, similarly, weighs in for "the destruction of error," including those who wish "... to enforce / Conformity with the orthodox bone, / With organized fear ...," even if the destruction requires "... death, death of the grain, our death/" (Auden, *English,* XXIV, 40). Yet, the enemy, even when depicted as the rich, are not condemned for exploitation or for idle consumption; rather, Auden rakes them for their sickness, as evidenced by their conformity and their anxiety (Wright, 53). He also dismisses them on the basis of age.

For Lawrence, as for the young Auden, the unnatural life and bourgeois society and the burden of the past combine to frustrate the young and the natural. Even his character Tom Brangwen becomes too old for Lawrence. Faced by his stepdaughter's decision to marry, Brangwen cannot bear it, becomes infuriated at this signification that he is old: He becomes "… ugly, unnatural, in his inability to yield place. How hideous this greedy middle-age, which must stand in the way of life, like a large demon" (Lawrence, *Rainbow*, 106). Similarly, Auden in September 1932 instructs the older generation that

> Your son may be a hero
> Carry a great big gun
> Your son may be a hero
> But you will not be one
> Go down with your world that has had its day.
> (Auden, *English*, IX, 125)

In a similar vein, the opposite-sex parent is portrayed as "the Enemy," a giantess, early in Auden's *The Orators* (1932) and the perpetuator of a deadly family feud in *Paid on Both Sides* (1928), both in a manner that suggests the stereotype of mothers who at bottom receive gratification by sacrificing their sons to war. In any event, the older generation clings to its ways and its power over the young, even to the latter's destruction. Memory, then, as ingrained cultural influence, is death (Greenberg, 29), for it prevents the young from attaining the balance required to usher in an era of loving and living naturally.

The young, Auden asserts in Poem XXIV (Auden, *English*, 37–40), view contemporary British society as decadent and seriously ill, psychologically. The theme is repeated early in *The Orators* when the Prize Day speaker asks, "What do you think of England, this country of ours where nobody is well?" The monologue continues, depicting in categories consistent with those of sinners in Dante's *Purgatorio* "… three main groups" of imperfect lovers: "… those who have been guilty in their life of excessive love towards themselves or their neighbors, those guilty of defective love toward God and those guilty of perverted love." In elaborating upon these categories, Auden's speaker, as John Fuller demonstrates amply (Fuller, *Guide*, 55–56), adheres to theories of Homer Lane, who associated various physical symptoms with corresponding personality traits and behaviors, a position consistent with Lawrence's views. Yet, by the time Auden completed *The Orators*, he no longer considered the work an argument *for* Lawrence's ideas but a satirical refutation of some of these ideas, particularly "The cult of the Leader" as he had seen what this could lead to in Hitler's Berlin.

To the logically subsequent question of What to do?, Auden's "Argument" section of *The Orators*, like Lawrence, looks for a leader, a Truly Strong Man who will provide the Way Out, a leader to die for, if need be. "Argument" also remains faithful to Lawrence's division of the psyche into four centers as the speaker prayerfully seeks protection against "the drought that withers the lower centers," i.e., the physical and natural impulses. Returning to the Leader—the masculine singular pronoun capitalized, as in a deity but also suggestive of Der Führer and Il Duce—the monologue in Part III of "Argument" slips into stream-of-consciousness wherein the Leader disappears. The Way Out will await another day.

Educational reform has long served as the focus of the would-be reformer, and Auden and Lawrence were no exceptions. In the "Statement" section of *The Orators*, Auden seems (in part III) to endorse Lawrence's insistence that the sexes remain segregated because "The nice clean intimacy which we now so admire between the sexes is sterilizing. It makes neuters" and spoils any future "deep, magical sex-life" (Lawrence, *Fantasia*, 84). As Fuller, again, demonstrates, Auden also remains attached to Lawrence's theories on the opposites which comprise the final paragraph of the section and which—right/left, sun/moon, light/dark—are consistent with Lawrentian cosmological dualism as well as W.B. Yeats's antinomies, which he borrowed from the ancient Hindu Vedas (Fuller, *Guide*, 61; Lawrence, *Fantasia*, Ch. 13). It is, however, in the "Journal of the Airman" that Auden and Lawrence come nearest in ideas as the result of a spiritual relationship suggested in the first Ode of Book III.

"Journal of the Airman" implies much and sows considerable confusion. Posed again is the question of leadership, but raised as well is the problem of individual human relationships to the whole of society. "Much more research needed into the crucial problem—group organization (the real parts)," states the Airman in the section "After Victory." The nebulous Enemy is still at work confounding those who seek to balance mind and body, society and the individual. At some junctures Auden approaches Lawrence's apparent disparagement of women: "Self-regard ... like haemophilia is a sex-linked disease. Man is the sufferer, woman the carrier." One cannot evaluate a woman according to her specific attributes, for he says: "Not so fast: wait till you see her son" (Auden, *English*, 73). This seems little different from Lawrence's "old serpent-advised Eve" and his "And then, oh, young husband of the next generation, prepare for the daughter's revenge" (Lawrence, *Articles*, 197). Yet the Airman faces other concerns as well.

A major concern of the Airman is, again, the problem of the Leader. The Airman himself is a leader, as demonstrated by his strategies and tactics, which resemble military considerations. He decides, as he prepares for his final encounter and envies "the simple life of the gut," that traditional acts of heroism will not effectively resist the enemy, that the only effective resistance lies in "self-destruction, the sacrifice of all resistance, reducing him [the Enemy] to the state of a man trying to walk on a frictionless surface." The odes that compose Book III begin with a dream that associates the death of Lawrence with the narrator's coming out from under morphine following an operation; and in Ode IV the hero-worship often associated with Lawrence is ridiculed, as are the working class, the upper class, and various named political leaders and groups. "This is the season of the change of heart," the ode proclaims. In the same vein, as *The Orators* nears the end, Ode VI predicts "Our necessary defeat" and that light will "… disarm/Illumine, and not kill" (Auden, *English*, 93–110). The breach with Lawrence would seem to have opened.

Auden's later treatment of Lawrence indicates the younger man's growing distance from his one-time mentor. No longer, argues Edward Mendelson, did Auden share the enthusiasm of Lawrence, Yeats, and Ezra Pound for "the grand, lofty violence of a lofty hero" (Mendelson, 20), although some did pose the question of whether the Airman was a Fascist (Wright, 59–60; Fraser, "Career," 82). Auden, however, added the concluding Odes as a deliberate postscript to point out that the material preceding them is not to be taken seriously but as satire. In a review of B.H. Liddell Hart's biography of T.E. Lawrence published in the spring of 1934, Auden expresses admiration, not for the man of exceptional deeds and blind action, but for the man like T.E. Lawrence who understood that "… action and reason are inseparable" because they complement each other. This view breaks with D.H. Lawrence's view, echoed by Auden in 1930, that "the mind is the dead end of life" (quoted in Mendelson, 134). Yet in the next paragraph Auden cites approvingly the view of D.H. Lawrence that the Western conception of romantic love is a poor (and neurotic) substitute for human rootedness in life (Auden, *English*, 321). Moreover, Auden may have been aware that, some perceptions aside, Lawrence saw that those who acted simply out of defiance had lost the Way Out: "... *doing it on purpose* is just as unpleasant and hurtful as repression, just as much a sign of secret fear" (Lawrence, *Articles*, 103). If the parting of ways with Lawrence had begun in 1931–32, Auden still kept his predecessor in full view as late as 1934, but would shortly after forsake him altogether.

When Auden wrote the *Letter to Lord Byron* (1936) he seemed to have rejected much of Lawrence, and he said so. Auden makes an early reference to Lawrence that is ambiguous but which implies that Lawrence wrote all that he actually had to say very early, implying perhaps that Lawrence failed to develop after an early stage. In Part II the gloves come off, and Auden refers to "D.H. Lawrence hocus pocus," but in a way that indicates that the author feels Lawrence's residual influence. Still, Auden continues, noting that Byron's (the Romantic) hero could "... know instinctively what's done, and do it," but that such a natural life has been prevented by industrial capitalism and its "more efficient modes of stealing" (Auden, *English*, 173, 176–77). This surely breaks away from Lawrence—but does it? In the year of his death (1930), Lawrence published *Assorted Articles*, a short collection of pieces that he had written for periodicals. Among the articles are several that deal with the socio-economic situation of the time, and one, "The State of Funk," in which Lawrence asserts that "... people want to be more decent, more good-hearted than our social system of money and grab allows them to be." Of course, he would not have been Lawrence if he had not followed with the contention that the same holds true of sexual feelings, "only worse" (Lawrence, *Articles*, 99). Nonetheless, the significant similarities between Auden and Lawrence remain obvious well into the 1930s.

It is reasonable to believe, then, that D.H. Lawrence's influence upon Auden was considerable and was lasting. Carlo Izzo includes Lawrence among the nine components of "the armature" upon which Auden built his work (Izzo, 136). And this seems appropriate, for the chief concerns of Auden—the divisions of mind and body, thought and action, and the individual and society— arose within a context heavily dependent upon Lawrence and remained Auden's focus into middle age, although he would address these concerns by looking at new influences—Gerald Heard and Paul Tillich among others (Fenton, 10). Eventually shedding Lawrence's "hocus pocus," i.e., the four centers of the psyche, the radical division of mind and body, blood feelings, the isolated individual, Auden nevertheless acknowledges the Lawrentian component well into his long career—after his move to the United States in 1939 (Mendelson, *Later*, Ch. 1)—and, in a sense, retains it to the end.

Works Cited

Auden, W.H. *The English Auden: Poems, Essays and Dramatic Writings, 1927–1939.* Edited by Edward Mendelson. London and Boston: Faber and Faber, 1977.

Fenton, James. "Auden at Home." *New York Review of Books*, April 27, 2000. <http://www.nybooks.com/nyrev/WWWfeatdisplay.cgi?200 00427008F@p3>

Fraser, G.S. "The Career of W.H. Auden." In *Auden: A Collection of Critical Essays*, edited by Monroe K. Spears. Englewood Cliffs, NJ: Prentice-Hall, 1964. 80–104.

Fuller, John. *A Reader's Guide to W.H. Auden.* New York: Farrar, Straus, and Giroux, 1970.

Greenberg, Herbert. *Quest for the Necessary: W.H. Auden and the Dilemma of the Divided Consciousness.* Cambridge, MA: Harvard UP, 1968.

Hemingway, Ernest. *True at First Light.* New York: Scribner, 1999.

Hoggart, Richard. *W.H. Auden.* London: Longmans, Green, and Co., 1961 (1957).

Isherwood, Christopher. "Some Notes on Auden's Early Poetry." In *Auden: A Collection of Critical Essays*, edited by Monroe K. Spears. Englewood Cliffs, NJ: Prentice-Hall, 1964. 10–14.

Izzo, Carlo. "The Poetry of W.H. Auden." In *Auden: A Collection of Critical Essays*, edited by Monroe K. Spears. Englewood Cliffs, NJ: Prentice-Hall, 1964. 125–41.

Jarrell, Randall. "Changes in Attitude and Rhetoric in Auden's Poetry." *The Southern Review* 7 (1941): 326–49.

Lawrence, D.H. *Assorted Articles.* Freeport, NY: Books for Libraries Press, 1968 (1930).

———. *The Complete Poems of D.H. Lawrence.* Edited by Vivian de Sola Pinto and Warren Roberts. New York: Viking Press, 1964.

———. *Fantasia of the Unconscious.* London: Heinemann, 1961 (1922).

———. *The Rainbow.* Ware, UK: Wordsworth Classics, 1995 (1915).

———. *Sons and Lovers*. Cambridge: Cambridge UP, 1992 (1913).

Mariani, Paul. *William Carlos Williams: A New World Naked*. New York: W.W. Norton, 1981.

Mendelson, Edward. *Early Auden*. New York: Farrar, Straus, and Giroux, 1981.

———. *Later Auden*. New York: Farrar, Straus, and Giroux, 1999.

Oates, Joyce Carol. *The Hostile Sun: The Poetry of D.H. Lawrence*. Los Angeles: Black Sparrow Press, 1973.

Wright, George T. *W.H. Auden*. Rev. ed. New York: Twayne, 1981.

W.H. Auden and Naomi Mitchison

Christopher Hopkins

Very early in his career Auden met writer Naomi Mitchison, and she had an impact on his verse and thinking that would influence the English Auden of the 1930s and—by artistic evolution—the later Auden as well. This essay mentions Gerald Heard, who became an even greater influence on Auden and is the subject of the subsequent two essays.

Mitchison wrote in the dedication to her 1939 novel *The Blood of the Martyrs* that "books are never written only and entirely by their authors. There are always others who have helped shape them." This essay is about the ways in which Auden and Mitchison helped to shape each other's work in a brief but intense period between 1928 and 1930. It will look at the ways in which Mitchison and Auden influenced each other in the period where they had the most to do with each other, at their common ground and divergences, and at the texts they produced, debated and exchanged at that time: poetry, reviews, a children's book and letters. It may thus add something to our knowledge of how Auden and Mitchison asserted and constructed their identities as writers at this period at the very beginning of the 1930s.

W.H. Auden quickly became the representative poet of the 1930s even as the decade developed its literary identity. Moreover, this representative status, though often challenged and disputed, still retains a firm grip on canonical memory. Thus, Samuel Hynes's *The Auden Generation* (1976), the first modern critical work to see Auden as the figurehead of a generation, is still, and rightly, an essential work for scholars of the writing of the 1930s. If writers such as Adrian Caesar in *Dividing Lines* (1992) have argued that poetry was a diverse field, not entirely dominated by the upper-middle-class leftists of whom Auden was representative, nor by their aesthetics, and if Valentine Cunningham in *British Writers of the 1930s* (1986) has argued that one of Auden's chief advantages was his skill as a self-publicist, this has not removed Auden from a central position in 1930s writing. It is certainly true that Auden and a circle of friends and acquaintances with access to literary and cultural institutions did help each other's careers in a whole range of ways, but this is part of the literary history of the 1930s—part of what and how writing in that decade in Britain worked—rather than just a regrettable manipulation of reputation. The "Auden Generation" sobriquet is not simply a later framework imposed on the period to tidy it up for critical consumption. Naomi Mitchison was one of Auden's contemporaries who helped to construct him as the representative of a younger generation of writers. And, of course, members of these loose series of groupings were not automatically destined for success, and neither were they a seamless whole with already established elites. They did have considerable "cultural capital" on which to draw, but this did not mean that they did not represent a new voice in British culture. At the same time, it would be a mistake to see such a circle as anything like a closed group or one with an entirely cohesive set of values or tastes. Agreements and disputes within these circles may tell us something about the literary possibilities and cultural politics of the period.

Naomi Haldane Mitchison—she was the daughter and sister of esteemed British scientists—had already established something of a reputation by the start of Auden's career. In 1920 Naomi had published a play, *Barley, Honey and Wine*, set in the country of Marob, an imagined Scythian culture later to be the setting of one of her best-known novels, *The Corn King and the Spring Queen*. In 1923 she published her first novel, *The Conquered*, set during the Roman conquest of Gaul. The novel was very well received, reviewers remarking on its ability to represent a past period as if it had the reality and complexity of contemporary life. It was the beginning of an extraordinarily productive writing career, not only as a novelist, but as a short story writer, poet, polemicist, and writer of occasional pieces of all kinds.

Naomi was also known as a political activist in a number of fields. Thus, in the 1920s she had published articles or stories in several liberal and feminist journals concerned with the position of women: *The Woman's Leader*, *The Journal of the Divorce Law Reform Union* and *The Liberal Woman's News* (Benton, 177). By 1925 Naomi and her husband Dick had agreed to an open marriage in which neither partner was to be bound by ideas of ownership; both partners had a number of relationships with other partners over the years, while also remaining committed to their marriage. Naomi had also begun to contribute to various causes: she helped organize a birth-control clinic in North Kensington and took part in her first political demonstration, a march in London in 1921 urging "Peace with Ireland." Her commitment to feminist—and family—issues continued into the early 1930s with articles such as "Comments on Birth-Control," "Child-rearing Services Some Day," "How to Educate Children," "Breaking Up the Home," and "Comment on the Basis of the Sexology Group" (Benton, 179). She enjoyed having the freedom to write and to express her developing radical views.

In 1931 her astonishing historical novel, *The Corn King and the Spring Queen* was published to excellent reviews. "A triumph of the historical imagination," said *The Birmingham Post* (26 May 1931; cited in Calder, 100); "a great English novel" said the novelist Winifred Holtby in *The News Chronicle* (4 June 1931). However, as one of Mitchison's biographers, Jill Benton, has pointed out, most reviewers did not pick up the feminist force of the novel, focusing on the King instead of the Queen (Benton, 69). The novel, drawing on Naomi's intense reading and intertwining of *The Golden Bough*, of classical history, and of Marx's *Capital*, concerns the lives of two important figures in the life of Marob: Tarrik, the Corn King, and Erif Der, the Spring Queen. Erif Der ("Red Fire") is undoubtedly the protagonist of the novel. She is born into a culture in which her role is unquestionable: chosen as Spring Queen, she must celebrate the rituals that ensure good harvests and survival for her people. But caught between the ambitions of her father and her husband, the Corn King, she is driven to disrupt that given culture. Her baby is killed in this power feud: she cuts her father's throat during a corn ritual and then cannot bring herself to perform the ritual of fertility with the Corn King. She is cursed and driven out of Marob; she travels through the late Hellenic world, seeking some way of life in which she can be not just a role, but herself. She is accompanied only by her brother, the artist Berris Der, who seeks in his own way a life where he can express himself. Erif Der founds a new mystery religion in Alexandria and finally returns home to Marob—but the novel leaves her fate there problematic, ending with a coda centered on the next Corn King, Klint-Tisamenos and the daughter of Berris Der, Erif Gold. Perhaps the ending is indicative of an uncertainty about how Erif Der could now organize an independent life in the cleansed and attractive, but still primitivist, culture of Marob. Despite, or rather *through*, its ancient and exotic settings, the novel explores both the losses and gains of entry into modernity—where identity is not given but won. Her novel was exactly the type of fantasy-with-a-philosophy that Auden appreciated. (See David Garrett Izzo's "W.H. Auden on Fairy-Tales, Quests, and Sagas" in this volume.)

The novel uses Frazer's and Marx's ideas of historical phases and social organization to explore a range of ways in which cultures have regarded and organized feminine and masculine power. (Oddly enough, in 1930 Auden went to teach at Larchfield Academy in Scotland, where Sir James Frazer had been a pupil.) Erif Der, in being exiled from her "primitive" Scythian homeland to neighboring states in different stages of development, becomes conscious of the possibilities of different ways of imagining societies. Though the novel gives a full sense of the deep satisfaction of belonging to an apparently organic culture such as Marob's, where individual identity and role are one, it is also clear that this "primitivism" is not recoverable. It is a model of a deeply communitarian, if patriarchal, belonging, but not an end-point: the quest which Reif Der embarks on is for a social being in which individual and collective identities are both realizable. This perhaps went beyond what was possible in the modernity of capitalism—seeking both belonging and separate being. As we shall see, this kind of quest was one in which Auden's writing of this period was also interested. Indeed, many of Mitchison's interests were ones she and Auden could share, though without complete agreement.

Naomi Mitchison was certainly a writer who helped Auden early on in his career, and took an interest in him throughout his life. He, at least during the 1930s, also took a close interest in Mitchison's writing, and they had some interesting exchanges of views. Mitchison first heard of Auden before he was well established. In 1928 Auden had left Oxford with a third-class degree (a result which surprised Auden and many of his friends). He had then gone to live in Berlin for a year, taking up his father's offer to pay him an allowance until his twenty-third birthday. By August 1929 this period had come to an end ("I loved my time in Germany," wrote Auden; quoted in Carpenter 104), and Auden had to make plans for earning a living. At first he returned to live with his parents in Harborne, a suburb of Birmingham. This was far from satisfactory, as Humphrey Carpenter suggests in his quotation from a slightly later letter from Auden to his former mentor, John Layard: "the unemployed young university graduate is unlikely to starve, but he will have to live at home, ask for his pocket-money, and endure the mutely resentful anxiety of his parents" (108). Auden's response was, indeed, to ask his friends if they could help him find employment. Margaret Gardiner (a friend of Layard's) told him of Flora Benenson, a friend's sister, who was looking for a tutor for her son in London. In the summer of 1929 Auden took up the post, which involved living in Flora Benenson's London house, together with her invalid husband Colonel Solo-mon and their son Peter Benenson, age eight. Auden in his turn did his best to help other aspiring literary friends. Carpenter tells how Auden, having learned that Flora Benenson ran a publishing house, and was seeking a translator for Baudelaire's *Journaux Intimes*, recommended Christopher Isherwood on the basis of his excellent French. In fact, Isherwood had no particular expertise, but he did carry out the commission, with, according to Carpenter, only "a few howlers in the published text" (109). Soon Auden was seeking something more substantial and satisfactory in the way of employment. He had recently been introduced to Naomi Mitchison by Richard Crossman, a friend from Oxford. (Crossman would later edit *Oxford and the Groups* [1934], to which Auden contributed the essay "The Group Movement and the Middle Class.") Crossman had suggested that Mitchison include some of Auden's poetry in a new magazine of which she was editor, *The Realist*. Unfortunately the periodical folded after one issue, before any of Auden's work could be published. Now he wrote to her, inquiring, "Do you by any chance know of a job for me? Anything from nursing to burglary. Is it possible to get into a publishing firm in any capacity?" (quoted in Carpenter, 109). Mitchison knew of nothing permanent, but helped both Auden and herself by engaging him as a Latin tutor to her son Murdoch, age twelve, who needed some coaching after an illness. Though this was something of a makeshift post, Auden did the job conscientiously and successfully, coming to the Mitchison's house in Hammer-smith two or three times a week. From a long-term point of view, the temporary job not only gave him some further experience of teaching on which to draw when he shortly afterward began applying for school teaching posts, but also confirmed Naomi's good opinion of him, leading to some literary opportunities.

The first of these came when Naomi had a chance to review Auden's first volume of poetry, *Poems*, in *Weekend Review* in Octo-ber 1930. The review is supportive of Auden and "his generation," but far from uncritical. Mitchison first of all carefully marks a di-

vide between those whom she classes as the "post-war generation": "still children, almost undisturbed, in 1918" and "we older
ones" (Haffenden, 81). This distinction is an important part of her
response to Auden, for it allows her both to be simultaneously
critical and to encourage her readers (imagined as mature and discriminating) to try to understand "the Auden generation" as a phenomenon. Thus she confesses to being "puzzled and excited" by
Poems, comparing this to the similar reactions of "the wise" to the
London post-impressionist exhibition of 1910. This aligns the review reader with those who are prepared to be open to the new,
but are not merely automatic consumers of the fashionable. The
encouragement of the discriminating reader of Auden then allows
Mitchison to criticize faults in the poems, without being off-
putting. In fact, the reader imagined here is virtuous because he
can deal with the raw and mixed nature of these young people's
poems, and the poems themselves are of value because they *are*
raw and mixed.

Auden's faults include being "wantonly obscure": "passages
in the middle ... seem as if they could only be understood by a
psycho-analyst," poems VIII and IX "are quite unintelligible." At
the same time, this failure immediately to yield up meaning is part
of the excitement of this verse: there are "startling lines which, if
only one could somehow shake oneself and catch the meaning,
might light up like rockets."[1] More positively, what these poems
do show is Auden's command of technique: his "very satisfying
consonant rhymes" and his ability to "do much what he likes over
rhythms." And they also show a deep—if not a rational or analytical—sense of the *zeitgeist* through their modern terms and images
and through their rhythms and rhymes.

Curiously, the poems are "signs of the times" though, not only
in their modernity, but through their recovery of primitive virtues:

> The whole poem ["Locksley Hall"] has a young, strong, rebel-
> lious he-quality, and, indeed, that is a thing that strikes one over

---

[1]*Editor's note:* Auden's "obscurity," in fact, highlighted the very argument of Mitchison's review: the differences between her generation and
Auden's. His poems were certainly obscure to an uninformed majority,
but to his immediate gang—Isherwood, Spender, Day Lewis, and a very
few others—the poems were parables evoking the plight of Auden's generation. See the studies of Edward Mendelson, and the editor's study,
*Christopher Isherwood: His Era, His Gang, and the Legacy of the Truly Strong
Man* (Columbia: South Carolina UP, 2001).

and over again in the poems. They may be romantic, may be obscure, but they have the curious archaic maleness which seems
to me to fit in with three things: the fifth century before Plato
came and muddled it, the heroic age in Iceland and the modern
youth movement in Germany.

Auden's first poems are signs of a cultural renewal: they have
a directness that is not intellectual, but physical, youthful. Part of
this primitivist, mythical association, the Icelandic saga reference
in particular, sounds as if it might come from Auden himself (who
was, of course, particularly interested in the sagas at this period).
Other aspects might draw on Mitchison's own reputation and interests as an historical novelist—she had published several novels
set in the ancient world, and was currently working on her great
epic novel about gender, fertility and social organization in different cultures, *The Corn King and the Spring Queen*. Readers who
knew her work are perhaps here being invited to see Auden as
sharing some of her virtues and interests. In fact, Mitchison is establishing Auden as part of tradition in several ways: he is "at ease
with English words, ancient and modern," he is part of a cycle of
renewal that can be seen in different parts of European history,
and he is like recent avant-garde artists—puzzling at first, but with
a value which will soon become classical.

Nevertheless, despite these strategies for creating a sympathetic response to Auden, this is not quite merely "Naomi Mitchison Advertises a New Generation," as John Haffenden calls it (81).
While the "wanton obscurity" has its appeals, the deeper sense of
the time needs to be made rational. The archaic maleness needs to
be translated more directly into action, into, in short, a more
socially responsible aesthetic. Thus, Mitchison picks out Auden's
"Locksley Hall" for particular attention: it is the "only completely
intelligible poem, a protest and a call to action." And the review
ends with a quite clear suggestion to Auden about the direction he
should take: readers are advised to "hope that Auden will go on
and keep unmuddled—for I am almost sure his ideas are clear,
though he chooses to express them at present in unexplained
symbols, perhaps too economically." If Mitchison is supporting
Auden, and carefully shaping her arguments to position her
readers so that they will too, she is also trying to shape Auden.

The next thing that Mitchison was able to do for Auden (and
he for her) was to invite him to contribute to an unusual children's
book project she was working on for Victor Gollancz. Titled *A
Short Outline for Boys and Girls and Their Parents*, this was intended

to offer intelligent, approachable commentary on current cultural
issues—social, scientific and artistic—for families of a left/liberal
tendency. It was to consist of a series of essays, written by
Mitchison's circle, including her husband Dick, Margaret Cole,
Hugh Gaitskill, Olaf Stapledon, John Pilley, and Gerald Heard,
who in fact was a great influence on Auden in general and
Auden's article in particular as concerns Heard's philosophy of a
continually evolving integrated world consciousness. Naomi
asked Auden to write an essay called, simply, "Writing" (this
should not be confused with the later and wholly different essay
called "Writing" printed in *Selected Essays* in 1956).

It is an interesting piece, in which Auden takes his mission of
writing clearly for a (partly) young, intelligent readership seriously. As Edward Mendelson points out in *Early Auden* (1981),
"critics have ignored this remarkable essay perhaps on the
assumption that anything written for [such] a volume ... must be
too trivial to bother with" (15). But, in fact, "Auden used this
unpromising setting to publish a manifesto of his (and Heard's)
private ideology" (15). He sets out to give a complete theory not
just of literature, but of writing in a wider sense. This theory is
rooted in ideas about language, beginning with speech and
moving through the following headings:[2]

> Speech
> Meaning
> Language and Words
> Inflection
> Writing
> Spoken and Written Language
> Verse Forms
> Different Kinds of Writing
> Why People Write Books
> How People Write Books
> Why People Read Books
> Books and Life

Auden's attitudes to language here show signs of a particularly
1930s interest in the collective—and shows few signs of the obscurity noted by Mitchison in her review, though it does show an
interest in primitivism, anthropology and cultural phases akin to

---

[2]*Editor's note:* See the editor's study, *Aldous Huxley and W.H. Auden:
On Language,* Locust Hill Press, 1998.

hers. Language was, he argues, at first essentially expressive. It showed:

> The feelings of the speaker; feelings about something happening to him (the prick of the pin), or attitudes towards other things in the world (the other hungry dog; the darling baby), or ... as a help to doing something of his own kind (pulling the boat in). (Quoted in *The English Auden*, 303).

The last kind of co-operative expression is privileged by Auden: other animals can use the other two kinds of expression, but "the last is peculiar to the most highly organised" (303). Auden argues from a variety of scientific examples that connection and co-operation are the world's natural state:

> Nucleus and cell, cell and organ, organs and the human individual, individual and family, nation and world, always groups linked up with larger groups, each group unique, different from others, but without meaning except in its connections with the others.

(This sentence comes more or less directly from Heard's ideas.) However, humanity has fallen from this world of connections, with the growth of consciousness: "man became self-conscious; he began to feel, I am I, and you are not I; we are shut inside ourselves and apart from each other" (303). Language grew as a "bridge over the gulf," a way of recovering wholeness. Some language is imitative (through onomatopoiea, for example), but most, says Auden, is not, a disconnectedness which paradoxically makes language work more authentically: "in fact, most of the power of words comes from their *not* being like what they stand for" (*English Auden*, 305). By not corresponding simply to a single entity, language has more resonance—a space and applicability that the imagination must work on.

Writing develops from speech eventually, again motivated by "man's growing sense of personal loneliness, of the need for group communication" (305). However, speech and writing are distinguished by different perceptions of loneliness:

> while speech begins with the feeling of separateness in space, of I-here-in-this-chair and you-there-in-that-chair, writing begins from the sense of separateness in time, of "I'm here today, but I shall be dead to-morrow, and you will be active in my place and how can I speak to you?" (305–6)

This new mode of communication leads in due course to the recording of oral forms such as stories and also to the invention of new forms, particularly of record-keeping and genres designed for more abstract kinds of knowledge. Printing leads to the wider dissemination of all kinds of written material, with, says Auden, mixed effects. He claims that vocabulary increases with print culture, so that language choices become more complex, resulting in poorer language use:

> Education in the use of language becomes more and more necessary. At present nobody gets such an education. The speech of a peasant is generally better i.e. more vivid, better able to say what he wants to say, than the speech of the average University graduate.... It is not the language which is to blame, but our skill in using it. (307)

Poetry is partly an antidote to this, as it restores authenticity—particularly emotional effect—which has a collective impact on readers or hearers:

> When a poet is writing verse, the feeling, as it were, excites the words and makes them fall into a definite group, going through definite dancing movements, just as feeling excites the different members of a crowd and makes them act together. (307)

Reading, whether of poetry or prose, widens experience and thus overcomes isolation. However, reading can ironically become a substitute for experience; it is dangerous "when we get frightened of real people and find books safer company; they are a rehearsal for living, not living itself. Swots and 'bookish' people have stage fright" (311). The essay ends with a section on "Books and Life" which develops this point much further and into an analysis of culture and society which returns to Auden's ideas about language and isolation. In a healthy society, there is a good deal of "common interest." Great writing particularly arises in societies that have this common purpose:

> Homer, Dante, Shakespeare.... There is something common to all three: the small size of the society and the unity of interests. Whenever a society is united ... it has a great outburst of writing.... Being made one, like the sailors pulling the rope, it has all the power. (311)

This resembles in some respects a Marxist cultural analysis (of the kind which began to be developed by British leftists a little later into the decade, particularly after the Soviet Writers' Congress of 1934). It has something of the same concerns: how are culture and society related, and how can historical change help us to understand their relations? Though the term "ideology" is not used, perhaps the idea is that Homer, Dante and Shakespeare were able to express the concerns of their societies in ways that did authentically represent at least some of the interests of all classes in that culture.

Now, however, there is a social fragmentation that makes it difficult for writers to represent anything like social reality successfully. Indeed, there is an over-production of writing which is a hysterical response to its own current ineffectiveness:

> But whenever society breaks up into classes, sects, townspeople and peasants, rich and poor, literature suffers. There is writing for the gentle and writing for the simple, for the highbrow and for the lowbrow; the latter gets cruder and coarse, the former more and more refined. And so, today, writing gets shut up in a circle of clever people writing about themselves for themselves, or ekes out an underworld existence, cheap and nasty. Talent does not die out, but it can't make itself understood. Since the underlying reason for writing is to bridge the gulf between one person and another, as the sense of loneliness increases, more and more books are written by more and more people, most of them with little or no talent. Forests are cut down, rivers of ink absorbed, but the lust to write is still unsatisfied. What is going to happen? If it were only a question of writing, it wouldn't matter; but it is an index of our health. It's not only our books, but our lives, that are going to pot. (311–12)

Mendelson suggests that Auden's "complaint is political only in the broadest terms" (*Early Auden*, 18) and that "where the rest of the book advocates a practical communism, Auden's essay implies the fraternal visionary communism (or collective consciousness) he was imagining in some of his writings at this time" (18). But, in fact, the idealism is not that unusual for 1930s cultural analysis, nor are the broad and wide social perspectives of the piece. However, the interest in language *is* distinctive. Certainly, it is a serious and interesting essay expressed in very clear terms. It seems likely that the interest in the collective, the co-operative and their loss can be related to Mitchison's similar interests at this time, and particularly to the sense of cultural development—and loss— which she was exploring in *The Corn King and the Spring Queen*.

An Outline was brought out by Victor Gollancz, the leftist publisher, in 1932. Though clearly intended to reach the next generation before they had settled into unthinkingly conservative positions, it is unclear whether the contributors expected the reaction that the book received. A number of Anglican clergy, including several bishops, together with the Headmasters of both Eton and Harrow, protested against the book in a letter sent to the major newspapers. First, they objected that a book for young people made no mention at all of Christianity. Furthermore, two related aspects of the book had touched a nerve: its discussion of the family and its sympathetic portrayal of the Soviet Union. An essay by Charles Skepper, "The Family or One Way of Keeping Together," explored the idea that the traditional family unit might be a form of social organization that had damaging effects, and argued for other possibilities:

> Marriage laws and the unequal treatment of women are therefore only likely to disappear if and when we devise other means of bringing up children which will do the job as well as the family does. (*Outline*, 492; cited in Benton, 83)

The essay referred to Soviet childcare centers as a successful innovation. The Anglican letter regarded this as an attack on the family and marriage as the essential, natural and divinely-approved social forms. Many liberal and left figures defended the book, including Gollancz himself, George Bernard Shaw, Harold Laski, Rebecca West, C.E.M Joad and, most particularly, the feminist Lady Rhondda.

Lady Rhondda supported the book in her periodical *Time and Tide*. She suggested that it might be worth at least examining the benefits of the different kinds of social organization being tried in Soviet Russia, and observed the unthinking conservatism of the open letter, which did not include a single female signatory. However, this kind of defense was, of course, unlikely to win over the strand of public opinion to which the writers of the letter spoke. Some have thought that the book might have sold well if it had not been for this controversy. "It should have been a success" wrote Mitchison in one of her autobiographical books, *You May Well Ask* (1979, 170). However, this seems difficult to judge: perhaps some of the types of liberal parents who might have purchased a left-leaning Gollancz book for their offspring were put off. No one reacted specifically to Auden's essay. Auden's own view was that the controversy was a good thing, and that the book should have been even more forthrightly anti-religious: "I agree with the Bishops that Xrist [Christ] should not have been omitted. Why not attacked [?]" (letter to Mitchison, 18 October 1932; quoted in Carpenter, 133). Humphrey Carpenter observes that, despite this statement, Auden's views on religion were far from clear at this time (133). Indeed, he would return to the church of his youth after he came to America in 1939.

The essay was the last formal publication to which Mitchison helped Auden. However, their correspondence at this time picks up interestingly on some of the joint interests and discussions that seem to inform the points at which their published writing touches. These reflect Mitchison's sense in her published review that Auden's obscurity was at fault:

> And of course, he was being extremely obscure, putting in private references all the time. He became better about this later on, but always demanded a bit of hard work and education, especially in the classics, from his readers. Rather an adolescent attitude. (Mitchison, *You May Well Ask*, 120)

Auden sometimes provided explanation for his poetry in letters to Naomi, including his "marginal notes" to *The Orators* in a letter of August 1931. Edward Mendelson comments in *Early Auden* that this is Auden's "clearest account of the poems" (97; discussion 100–103). The notes explained that "in a sense the work is my memorial to Lawrence; i.e. the theme is the failure of the romantic conception of personality" (Mitchison, *You May Well Ask*, 120). The mention by Auden of "Heredity-Matrilineal descent and initiations" again suggests their shared interests in anthropological ideas that Gerald Heard had become famous for writing about since 1929 (see Heard essay).

For his part, Auden made some comments about *The Corn King and the Spring Queen*:

> Some of the scenes in the Prawn King and the String Queen were hotter than anything I've read. My dear, how do you get away with it?
>
> I liked *The Corn King* very much indeed. I do wish though you would do a contemporary setting sometime. What is this curious psychological sturk of yours against it? I always feel in reading your work that you are only using those silly old Greeks as a symbol. (Mitchison, *You May Well Ask*, 121)

Auden's comment may have had some influence: Mitchison's next novel, *We Have Been Warned*, did have a contemporary setting. Though not published until 1935, Naomi was already writing this novel during 1930. In fact, Auden's other comment about her treatment of sex is also very much relevant to the history of some severe difficulties Mitchison had with *We Have Been Warned*. The novel was finished by 1933, but publishers, including Jonathan

Cape, Victor Gollancz, and John Lane, were unwilling to publish it as it stood, fearing—or not wishing to court—prosecution for obscenity. Mitchison later suggested that it was precisely the contemporary setting that made the treatment of sex a problem for the publishers:

> In some of the stories in *The Delicate Fire* there is, I would have thought, far more overt sex than in *We Have Been Warned*, but apparently it's all right when people wear wolfskins and togas. (Mitchison, *You May Well Ask*, 179)

After *We Have Been Warned*, Mitchison went back to the historical novel, later observing—partly perhaps in response to comments like Auden's about the use of the Greeks as symbols that:

> dropped historical novels for a time, because of interest in present-day social problems and education. Then re-started because it seems better sometimes to look in a mirror for what one is trying to see." (*Literature Online*, Mitchison entry)

Mitchison and Auden lost touch in more ways than one after he went to the U.S. in 1939. Auden moved on almost as soon as he reached the U.S. from the kind of direct social responsibility that Mitchison had wanted him to embrace more fully in her 1930 review. Thus Auden wrote in *The Prolific and the Devourer*, on which he was working during 1939:

> Artists and politicians would get along better in a time of crisis like the present if the latter would only realise that the political history of the world would have been the same if not a poem had been written, not a picture painted, nor a bar of music composed. (Carpenter, 255–56)

Nearly thirty years later, Mitchison wrote a piece about this period when she and Auden were in close contact, published in *Shenandoah* in 1967. It adds some detail that confirms the general account of their literary relationship, but it also suggests some different emphases. One notes that here it is Auden who is the supreme judge of poetry (unlike the Mitchison as patron suggested in the 1930 review), that there is some antagonism as well as co-operation between the generations, and that it is Auden who is committed to political purpose, rather than being led toward greater social awareness and clarity:

> He and his friends were rather fierce with us older writers.... Sometimes I argued rather timidly about the apparent content of Wystan's poems:

> All of the women and most of the men
> Will work with their hands and not think again.

But I was always overwhelmed. He and his friends were always certain—or at least put it across to us—that they knew best about everything.

It was all mixed up with politics. They were all more or less communists at a period when that was the done thing to be.... Some of them occasionally took a corner too quick and landed into fascism, at least temporarily. (Mitchison, "Young Auden," 14)

Or is it rather that this species of enthusiastic communism is and was associated by the Labour Party Mitchison with a lack of authentic social purpose and clarity? At the end of the article, Mitchison returns to "the judgement of the future," an idea she had used in her 1930 review to try to introduce the young Auden into literary tradition:

I don't know what the judgement of the future will be on Wystan Auden. I can't find myself reading him these days, not like I used to, though he may take another jump into what for me would be memorability. But perhaps the man who wrote "Paid on Both Sides" should never have gone to America. Yet if he hadn't done that he would never have written "September 1, 1939." But then when he follows that poem by cutting out the most essential verse in his *Collected Poems*? I don't know. But I did know then very clearly that his first book was a major poetic event. (Mitchison, "Young Auden," 15)

Auden seems to have been quite irritated when he read this brief piece. Mendelson quotes from a letter Auden wrote to Mitchison after reading the article but apparently did not send:

The reason (artistic) I left England and went to US was precisely to *stop* me writing poems like "Sept. 1st, 1939," the most dishonest poem I have ever written. A hangover from the U.K. It takes time to cure oneself. (Mendelson, *Early Auden*, 330)[3]

Perhaps here Auden asserts finally that he does *not* want to be the poet envisaged in Naomi's 1930 review. Nevertheless, he had at the time certainly been interested in her view of what the poet

---

[3]*Editor's note:* Auden considered this poem and his 1937 poem "Spain" as "dishonest" because he believed he had written them as propaganda and did not actually "feel" the emotions that he wished to manipulate readers into feeling, and to act in ways he himself would not have acted.

should be doing, as well as in her own—in fact quite individual—interpretation of political relevance. And there seems little doubt that at this period both writers had at least been willing to try out authorial identities suggested by each other. As Mitchison wrote in 1967, this was not simply a matter of supporting one's friends, but more fundamentally of allowing new literary possibilities to at least have a chance of reaching a wider public:

> When Wystan's first book came out I decided to do something I've never done before or since and never for anybody else. I made up my mind that the first review must be a good one.... If I left it to the professionals they might well overlook the first book by a new and very different poet.... It was something I would never do out of simple friendship, fond as I was of Wystan, but I did think that this book must be given its maximum chance of being seen by and influencing the people to whom poetry matters. (Mitchison, "Young Auden," 15)

Works Cited

Auden, W.H. *The English Auden: Poems, Essays and Dramatic Writings 1927–1939.* Edited by Edward Mendelson. London: Faber and Faber, 1977.

———. *Selected Essays.* London: Faber and Faber, 1956.

Benton, Jill Kathryn. *Naomi Mitchison.* London: Pandora, 1990.

Calder, Jenni. *The Nine Lives of Naomi Mitchison.* London: Virago Press, 1997.

Carpenter, Humphrey. *W.H. Auden—A Biography.* London: Unwin, 1983 (revised from 1981 edition).

Haffenden, John. *W.H. Auden: The Critical Heritage.* London: Routledge and Kegan Paul, 1983.

Mendelson, Edward. *Early Auden.* London: Faber and Faber, 1981.

Mitchison, Naomi. "Young Auden." *Shenandoah* 18 (Winter 1967): 12–15.

——— *You May Well Ask: A Memoir 1920–1940.* London: Victor Gollancz, 1979.

———. *Literature Online.* www.lion.chadwyck.com.

The Incredible Gerald Heard and "This Thing"

David Garrett Izzo

In proportion to how great his influence was compared to his present anonymity, Gerald Heard may be one of the most neglected figures of the twentieth century. He met Auden in the early 1930s, and Auden was forever after writing verse and essays about how man's true purpose on earth was to understand the nature of evolving consciousness. Even Auden scholar and literary executor Edward Mendelson has suggested that he underestimated Heard's influence in his study Early Auden *and later gave Heard his due in* Later Auden. *This essay gives an overview of Gerald Heard and his impact on our world. Paul Eros will follow this segment with a more detailed account of Heard's influence on Auden.*

W.H. Auden's great friend Christopher Isherwood is having a revival. The Huntington Library in California just acquired his papers; three books about him have appeared in the last two years, and his centenary is in 2004. Interest in him, his work, and his associates—including Auden—is on the upswing, which brings us to Gerald Heard, or as he is more commonly known these days— *Gerald who?* The answer is that he was one of the most influential intellectual personas of this century, and number one in proportion to how unknown he is now.

So, who was this fellow with whom Isherwood would start a gossip session by asking, "And now what has Gerald Heard?" After which Herr Isseyvoo's brilliant friend would disseminate the latest from his eclectic contemporaries starting with news from the Hollywood Hills Vedanta Society, to his own very best friend Aldous Huxley's misadventures as a screenwriter, to Maria Huxley's most recent high-speed car ride in the California desert, to the daily letters received from esteemed intellectuals and artists from all over America and Europe. These included W.S.

Maugham, Igor Stravinsky, George Bernard Shaw, Huston Smith, Joseph Campbell, Alan Watts, Arthur Waley, John Gielgud, Lewis Mumford, J.B. Rhine, Ray Bradbury, Ethel Barrymore, Dave Brubeck, Henry Miller, Vincent Sheean, Ivan Tors, Bill Wilson (founder of Alcoholics Anonymous with which Heard had an important—and until now anonymous—connection), and dozens of think-tank planners among philosophers, theologians, and artists who wanted to hear Heard talk about "this thing." (These letters are collected at UCLA.)

Heard, who was so compelling a personality that he became a character in four novels by Huxley, Maugham, and Isherwood, was sought out to teach his utopian vision of a better world based on what he called "intentional living." This would be a complex systemic overhaul of society in all aspects that nonetheless has a simple underlying premise. One must abnegate the willful ego and replace it with a selfless mystical consciousness that surrenders to what Huxley, borrowing from Leibniz first and Heard second, called a divinely-inspired Perennial Philosophy, or as Heard would say, "this thing." Heard preferred a euphemism for saying God so as not to scare away the wary among new recruits who, while still reeling from their rebellions against traditional Judeo-Christianity, still needed *some* thing to believe in, so it might as well be *this* thing.

Today, one finds the gloss of "this thing" in the guise of *cool* pop mysticism that gives the public facilely feel-good facsimiles of pseudo-mysticism. The public eats up *The Sixth Sense, The Green Mile, Touched by an Angel, Unsolved Mysteries,* 1–800-PSYCHIC, etc., ad infinitum, because many feel a need for a temporary vicarious transcendence that does not take too much effort. And for those willing to put in a short-attention-span effort, there are also pop mystic millionaires such as Deepak Chopra selling diluted versions of "this thing" as mind candy for the less discerning.

Meanwhile, Heard, a spokesperson for the *real* thing, is virtually unknown even though he was one of the preeminent precursors of the New Age. What might he think of today's pop mysticism? He believed that Wisdom works in mysterious ways. One never knows how and why wisdom gets where it needs to go. If one starts with Chopra, this is better than not starting at all. It might even lead to Heard. What might also lead to Heard is his association with the creator of the deservedly omnipresent Twelve-Step program used worldwide that comes from the same "intentional living" philosophy Heard advocated. Heard would publish his own step-by-step manual, *Training for the Life of the Spirit* in 1942. That Bill Wilson, who as "Bill W." of AA is credited with writing the Twelve Steps, became friends with Heard and Huxley is almost unknown and not mentioned at all in the two Huxley biographies or in Isherwood's diaries. Yet there are numerous letters from Wilson and his wife Lois to Heard that are written in the most cordial and familiar terms as good friends to a good friend.

Today, many of the people Heard influenced are remembered while he is not. Yet, without Heard, and his theories of an evolving consciousness and how to live within it and nurture it, there would not have been quite the same W.H. Auden, Huxley, Isherwood, and the many others who then influenced so many more. As an example, one can start with Isherwood.

In 1939 Isherwood left Auden in New York to see Heard in California because he wanted to talk to another pacifist. He did not return, and Auden never fully recovered from his best friend's exit. Thus, indirectly, Heard affected Auden, whose future poetry would feature a hybrid of existentialist and Christian mysticism to match—or compete with—Isherwood's Eastern mysticism. (Indeed, Auden was just adapting Heard's ideas that influenced his British years.) In Hollywood, Heard introduced Isherwood to the wisdom of Vedanta as taught by Swami Prabhavananda, the subject of Isherwood's last book, *My Guru and His Disciple*. Both Heard and Isherwood then became sources for Maugham's much-read, soul-searching novel *The Razor's Edge* in 1944. In the late 1940s and early 1950s, Isherwood and Swami Prabhavananda translated the *Bhagavad-Gita* and Patanjali's *How to Know God*, while Swami Nikhilananda of the New York Vedanta Society did the same for the *Upanishads*. These versions would sell voluminously, particularly in the late 1960s through 1970s, and have an impact on many people. An early reader was J.D. Salinger who studied with Nikhilananda and retreated from public life. He also corresponded with the Hollywood Vedanta Society. Books such as these spurred an interest in Eastern philosophy that led to a first wave of pop mysticism that included *Kung Fu*, *Billy Jack*, *One Flew Over the Cuckoo's Nest*, and *Jonathan Livingston Seagull*. The Isherwood-Prabhavananda-Nikhilananda translations were among the original sourcebooks that influenced the present New Age era and the many Chopra-esque imitations of them. Madonna reads Chopra and becomes an Eastern philosopher. (Chopra recently and egregiously borrowed the title *How to Know God* for a book of his own.

Anyone who claims to know what he knows and *mean* it would be familiar with the earlier book and show some respect for his antecedents. For example, a psychologist—pop or otherwise—would not use one of Freud or Jung's titles.)

Another late 1960s best-selling handbook was Huxley's novel *Island*, his own manual for Intentional Living with concepts Huxley shared with Heard. After Huxley left his body in 1963, Heard called him, in a tribute, "The Poignant Prophet," in which Heard modestly gave his best friend credit for many ideas that were originally his own, but that Huxley also came to believe in.

Then there is the philosopher Michael Polanyi who was in England in the 1930s when Heard was as well known as Huxley, perhaps more so. Heard had a very popular weekly BBC radio program, *This Surprising World*, where he translated the latest in science, philosophy, and related disciplines for the educated lay listener. Polanyi's *Personal Knowledge* (1958), and his later writings, all seminal forerunners to Post-Modernism, owe a debt to ideas Heard began formulating thirty years before, ideas that always came back to "this thing" as the core of all understanding.

The same thing that Isherwood couldn't resist, which would transform his life from one of a frantic tearing-down in Europe to a Vedantic building-up in America where he became Vedanta's—and the Perennial Philosophy's—primary spokesperson as well as a gay-activist icon. The latter role was greatly enhanced by the serenity inherent in the former. Without Heard, Isherwood stays in New York with Auden, and their futures would have been very different. Without Heard, many lives would be different.

This is Isherwood on Heard in a 1972 interview in the *Paris Review*:

> He was one of the most astounding people I ever met. He was a wonderful mythmaker. It was something approximate to knowing Jung. He saw the archetypes that govern life to an extraordinary extent, and he knew an immense amount of what was going on in the world, all the really important advances on different scientific fronts, and how they related to each other; and he had taken in the whole area of mysticism and reconciled this with his other areas of knowledge. And he was Irish and had the extraordinary gift of talk. An absolute spellbinder, and yet extraordinarily little known. He was the sort of person who, if you asked: "What do you think of Vietnam" would answer, "I suppose you know, of course, Holdstein's great work on the Soldier ant ..." and then go into a tremendous dissertation and about fifteen minutes later you would realize that this was a very

appropriate way to answer the question. By that time, you'd be
so awfully interested in what he was saying that you'd forgotten
what your question was. But if you did remember, then you saw
that he did in fact answer the question. He gave very definite
answers, yet at the same time contrived not to be dogmatic....

Concerning Jung: As H.F. Heard, Gerald Heard wrote fiction,
mysteries, and bizarre tales in a mode that one might have imagined Jung trying if he had been so inclined. Particular charmers
among Sherlock Holmes fans are three mysteries about a Mr. My-
croft (the name of Sherlock's older brother), an aged beekeeper in
retirement and amateur detective who seems to be Holmes incog-
nito. Also as Jung, Heard referred to "this thing" as a beneficent
power's sponsoring of an evolving universal consciousness. Heard
rejected what he called the "drum and trumpet" approach to history. Man's manifest actions are not his important history, as these
actions are merely the symptomatic and often misguided byprod-
ucts of a more substantial search, which is to find his inner, ego-
less Self and reintegrate it within the universal consciousness from
which it originally came:

> What we now can see in history, the clue to the sequence and
> process is, then, this: *The Emergence of Man*. All his acts and
> achievements, however contradictory they must appear when
> only viewed by themselves, can be co-ordinated and understood
> if we realize that they are shadows cast on the outer world by the
> changing shape of his spirit, projections and symptoms of a slow
> inner evolution of mind whereby it has stage by stage taken its
> present form. As in the Paleontological record of the rocks we
> have learnt to recognize as stages toward our present form, types
> which, till the idea of evolution was grasped, were thought
> wholly distinct, so now we can see the stable "superstitions,"
> magical Aeon, the Heroic Age of violent strife, and our present
> individualised age as connected, successive, inevitable phases of
> a single evolutionary process—evolution being carried on now
> in the mind as it was once carried on in the body. (*The Emergence
> of Man*, 1931)

Rather nouveau even now, let alone in 1931. And he was a
spellbinder as Isherwood said, leaving behind audio, of hundreds
of lectures given all over the United States and now collected at
UCLA with titles such as: "Meaning in the World of History,"
"Faith in the Modern World" (1952), "Is Progress Possible?" (1955),
"Psychology and Religion in the World of Tomorrow," "Art and
the Artist" (1956), "Ethics" (1957), "Mysticism as a Means of

Integration with the Cosmos" (1958), "The Possible Value of LSD in a Therapy of Growth" (1960).

LSD?

Ah, yes, LSD ... and mescaline with Huxley that prompted Huxley's epiphany *The Doors of Perception* in 1954, which would also be widely read in the 1960s and from which Jim Morrison got the name for his band. (Huxley got his title from William Blake.) Therein is a clue to the current neglect of Heard. When he and Huxley experimented with these drugs beginning in 1953 under the supervision of Dr. Humphrey Osmond, they were legal, and Huxley and Heard were attempting to learn if these drugs could enlarge consciousness and benefit society. The negative stigma that came later did not yet exist. Even the ultimately mainstream *Saturday Evening Post* featured this front-page-headline article by Huxley on October 13, 1958: "Drugs That Shape Men's Minds." Later, when the drugs turned into "bad trips" in the 1960s and were banned, Huxley and Heard's good intentions were seen by some as pseudo-scientific intellectual quackery. Huxley's reputation persevered in spite of this, as he was, after all, the writer of *Brave New World*, that high school and college staple.

Heard did not have such a book to fall back on; indeed, one of his books, *The Riddle of the Flying Saucers* (1950), which claimed they existed (and which Heard may have meant to be a tongue-in-cheek exposé) did not help when the drug issue came up. Consequently, his reputation and vision would eventually dissipate into the mist rather than into his mysticism. He left his body in 1973 remembered only—albeit very fondly—by the circle he started with; and, as they left their bodies—Auden also in 1973, Prabhavananda in 1976, Isherwood in 1986, etc.—there were very few voices left to remember his real achievements, rather than UFOs and LSD. Gerald Heard and the story of how he arrived at "this thing" deserve better.

While Henry Fitzgerald Heard's family home was in Ireland, he was born in London on 6 October 1889. His background was distinguished. John Heard of Wiltshire arrived in Ireland with Walter Raleigh in 1579. Gerald's father, Henry James Heard, was a priest in the Church of England and had been given a post in London just prior to his son's birth, after which Gerald's youth was spent in both Ireland and London. He originally intended to follow his father into the clergy; however, according to Michael Barrie, Heard's amanuensis during his life and then his executor:

such a probing mind as his, consumed with curiosity and with such a vast spread of interests, had been on a collision course with doubt as to many of the doctrines of Christianity from the time he was in his teens. The crash came at last in 1916. The result was a nervous breakdown. After a long illness, Heard recovered to find that the young man who had wanted to be a priest-missionary had become a scientific materialist with a strong sense of social responsibility and equally strong conviction that the world *could* be tidied up, that justice could and *must* prevail, and that it was his duty to dedicate his life and efforts to a frontal attack on the obstacles to these ends. The next few years, then, found him active in such things as agricultural cooperatives, progressive education, prison visiting, and social reform.

An imposing factor acting on Heard was his self-awareness that he was gay, which, in the early 1900s and with the Oscar Wilde case still a hovering albatross, was not only "the love that dare not speak its name," but also a love that was illegal. This would have been a rather difficult conflict to deal with as a priest, so Heard crashed from the pressure of being expected to follow his father. He then recreated himself around "this thing."

In 1916, Theosophy, with its eastern leanings, was at its height, and the Irish poet, AE, who as George Russell was an agricultural economist, was a mystic follower of Vedanta replete with visions reproduced in his poetry and unique paintings. These were influences on a young Heard that would move him toward the Perennial Philosophy, which asserts that there is an absolute underlying truth in human consciousness that has a mystical basis and that this truth exists in the mystic aspects of all religions, beginning with seminal Hinduism. In 1944 Huxley would synthesize the essence of the Perennial Philosophy into four tenets of an all-inclusive Minimum Working Hypothesis, which was first published in his introduction to the Isherwood-Prabhavananda translation of the *Bhagavad-Gita*.

Heard became secretary to Horace Plunkett, who founded the Irish Agricultural Cooperative Movement. Through Plunkett, Heard met leading intellectual figures such as AE, G.B. Shaw (who likely shared his socialist views), and W.B. Yeats, another aspiring mystic who added Celtic nuances to his Yeatsian adaptation of Vedantic cosmology. Indeed, in 1938, Yeats would publish his own translation of the *Upanishads*. Through these contacts Heard would meet H.G. Wells and the Huxley brothers, Aldous and Julian, the latter an eminent scientist following in the path of his grandfather, T.H. Huxley, Darwin's advocate.

Heard's eclectic interests and mellifluous voice turned him into a popular lecturer. He served on the council of The London Society of Psychical Research, an interest that would later lead him to the paranormal studies of J.B. Rhine at Duke University. 1929 would be a pivotal year for Heard on three counts:

(1) His study, *The Ascent of Humanity*, won a major prize from The British Academy and placed Heard among the intellectual leaders in England. This book was the first of many to interpret man's true history to be an ascent into a higher consciousness, a rise that cannot be measured in lifetimes but in eons.

(2) Heard met Auden just before Auden became *Auden*, and Isherwood recalls them huddling for hours with the poet enraptured with Heard's theories of a mystically evolving universe. With Heard as an initial catalyst, Auden's verse was thereafter variations on man's place in the psychic evolution. Yet Heard's great influence on Auden has been, until recently, either ignored completely or, at best, Heard is just a footnote as more of an acquaintance than as an important mentor. In the last two years, two books, this writer's *Aldous Huxley & W.H. Auden: On Language* (1998), and Auden scholar-executor Edward Mendelson's *Later Auden* (1999), have given Heard his due credit.

(3) Heard met Huxley. Both were voracious readers of the esoteric. A year later, when Huxley's first best friend and intellectual stimulus, D.H. Lawrence, left his body, Heard replaced Lawrence in both roles.

After the acclaim for *The Ascent of Humanity*, more books followed in rapid order, all elaborating with intricately complex and assiduously researched detail the integration of man and consciousness. Among them were *The Social Substance of Religion* (1931), in which Heard refers to scientists and scientific studies that Polanyi would reiterate in 1958 to make a very similar case. Then came the previously quoted *The Emergence of Man* (1931), followed by *This Surprising World* (1932), derived from his BBC radio program. In *The Source of Civilization* (1935), Heard introduced his concept of "foetilization." This is the inherent aspect in the human psyche that retains the child-like power of wonder that compels certain humans to discover, create, and continue the progress of evolving consciousness. Later Polanyi posited the same idea as the basis of his theories concerning collective subjectivity. With *Pain, Sex, and Time* (1939) (and not at all about what it sounds like),

Heard explored the important evolution of mind-body-hand-tool coordination in human progress in very similar terms as those Polanyi employed twenty years later. (As concerns Polanyi there seems to be a pattern here; nonetheless, in a perpetual continuum, as Heard believed, the unfolding of knowledge is a shared, communal process. The Heard-Polanyi connection also features this adjunctive item from the small-world department: William H. Poteat, theologian and professor emeritus from Duke, was an early adherent and supporter of Polanyi; his father, William McNeill Poteat, also a theologian and professor, was an early supporter of Heard in America). Books by Heard of non-fiction and fiction followed year after year until Heard's last book in 1963, *The Five Ages of Man*. By then, few were reading him and by then all of his books were out of print, so it is a bit difficult to see how prescient he was. (One *can* find them on the internet through used book cooperatives and in major university libraries.)

In the early 1930s Heard cemented his friendship with Aldous Huxley after Huxley fell into a severe depression caused by a prolonged writing block. Sybille Bedford, Huxley's friend and biographer, recalled that "Gerald Heard was very good to them [Aldous, Maria, and son Matthew], popping in and out almost daily, reassuring Maria. To him Aldous was able to talk." In 1936, after Heard helped Huxley recover, Huxley's block unblocked and Heard became Miller, the priest-seer of good will—and good humor—in the novel *Eyeless in Gaza*. The duo became ardent pacifists as leaders in H.R.L. Sheppard's Peace Pledge Union. They frequently gave speeches together in England and in 1937 took their plea for pacifism to the United States and decided to remain there. One of their stops was at Professor Rhine's E.S.P. laboratory at Duke. Huxley and Heard were always intrigued by any means that sought as its end an enlargement of consciousness.

Heard and Huxley ended up in Hollywood, California, and Huxley again fictionalized Heard as Mr. Propter, another priest-seer, in Huxley's 1939 novel about a Hearst-like figure, *After Many a Summer Dies the Swan*. Heard, with his endless curiosity, visited the Vedanta center and befriended Swami Prabhavananda. (For more information on the Vedanta movement in America, see the chapter on same in Laurence Veysey's book *The Communal Experience*, 1973.) The Swami taught him a 2,500-year-old Vedantic cosmology that, to Heard's delight, seemed to say what he had been saying for years: that there are essential, timeless truths within consciousness and that these truths would be revealed to those who would learn to remove their egos. He gave his revelatory news to Huxley, who also met Swami. Isherwood arrived, searching for *some* thing, and Heard gave him *this* thing. Isherwood was shocked to find that the Gerald of London, an almost dandy of sartorial splendor, had grown a straggly beard to match his new asceticism. From Isherwood's diaries he wrote that while he doesn't quite remember the exact words of their first California meeting, the sense was this:

> "Well, Gerald—so you're really doing all those things we heard about—meditating, and studying yoga...."
>
> "Yes, Christopher, I really am."
>
> "And you believe in it? You think it's worthwhile? "
>
> "For me, it's the only thing that matters in the world."
>
> Yes, he really believed. I could see that. Other people believed in mystical religion—but I had always been able to dismiss them as cranks, simpletons or sex maniacs, creatures of another breed. Gerald was different. He was one of us [gay]. He spoke the same language. He accepted the same values. He might be theatrical, affected, vain, eccentric, but he certainly wasn't crazy.
>
> But if—and this was a terribly disturbing thought—if Gerald *was* sane, then I couldn't afford to ignore his ideas.... Gerald, I could see at once, was expecting that I should. He had the air of having waited for my arrival. Very few people, he hinted—he hadn't forgotten how to flatter—could come to "this thing" (his favorite way of referring to the subject).

As Isherwood said, Heard could be a spellbinder. Heard began teaching Isherwood what he had learned. Then when Heard thought Isherwood was ready, he introduced him to the Swami to whom Isherwood would be devoted for the rest of both of their lives. Heard, with the zeal of the recently converted, began meditating for two-hour stretches three times a day; this soon moderated to a more reasonable duration. Huxley and Heard, with Isherwood as editor, began contributing to the Vedanta Society's bimonthly periodical, *Vedanta and The West*, with articles that gave them an outlet for long-held philosophical musings. Among many of Heard's essays were "Vedanta as the Scientific Approach to Religion," and "The Philosophia Perennis," and of many by Huxley, "Seven Meditations," and "Action and Contemplation." From *Vedanta and the West* over one hundred essays would later be collected in *Vedanta for the Western World* (1946), and *Vedanta for Modern Man* (1950). In the former Isherwood wrote a brilliant introduction explaining the core of Vedanta cosmology in accessible language. Both of these books reached a wider audience and wider influence than the periodical, which was limited to members.

The Hollywood center became the "in" place for many artists and intellectuals. Garbo wanted to be a monk. When told there were no female monks, but nuns, she replied, "Well, then I'll wear pants." The dramatist John van Druten, another British expatriate, also joined up. (Among his plays were *I Remember Mama* and his adaptation of Isherwood's *Berlin Stories*, *I Am a Camera*, that later became the musical *Cabaret* in 1967.) Krishnamurti visited. Superman attended; that is, the first actor to play him on film, Kirk Alyn. Huxley and Heard frequently lectured at the temple, drawing more interest to Vedanta and the Perennial Philosophy. During a world full of war, people wanted to find some hope for the future of man's survival. A timeless mind-centered cosmology seemed a possible answer. When the Isherwood-Prabhavananda translation of the *Gita* appeared in 1944, the *New York Times* said it was "a book for every soldier and everybody who loves a soldier."

Over time, Heard and Huxley, while enamored with Vedanta as an intellectual philosophy that they were happy to write articles about and give lectures on, were not at all inclined to defer to Swami as their Guru as Isherwood was. Nor did they have any tolerance whatsoever for participating in rituals such as collective prayer, group meditation, meals, etc. By 1941, Heard and Huxley rarely attended functions other than lectures at the center. Heard wrote the Swami a letter explaining that their reluctance was a matter of an intellectual difference of opinion as to how different personalities might approach the same universal truths.

Heard decided to make a formidable leap of faith and built, with his own funds, Trabuco College, south of Hollywood at a time when "south" meant empty. By all accounts the 300-acre site was suitably isolated within a natural beauty ideal for its serene intentions: how to develop consciousness. Briefly, Huxley kept some distance from Heard; perhaps thinking that Gerald's real difference with Swami was that *he* wanted to be the guru instead of following one. Huxley was waiting to see how Trabuco, called a college, but really an intellectual retreat for the spiritually inclined, would develop. By 1942, however, Huxley began visiting Trabuco, and his concerns were ameliorated, if not erased, by the ambience. Maria Huxley wrote: "Aldous says Gerald has the whole thing, ways of life as well as philosophy, very clearly worked out ... and that people here find it extremely stimulating." Maria also describes a certain amount of meal-taking and hymn-writing that seem at odds with Heard's differences with Swami and might suggest that Huxley wasn't that far off in his initial estimation. Isherwood, in his diaries, wrote:

> It seemed to me a new cult, Heardism, was being born ... such however, was far from Gerald's intention. However much he might enjoy the limelight, the prestige of leader, I am sure that his intentions were sincerely democratic. He spoke repeatedly of Trabuco as a "club for mystics"—nonsectarian, non dogmatic, strictly experimental, a clearinghouse for individual religious experience and ideas.

Among the visitors in 1944 was one of America's earliest advocates of nonsectarian equality, Bill Wilson, the founder of Alcoholics Anonymous. Wilson recognized that the twelve-step program was a logical adjunct to the Perennial Philosophy. He always said his personal revelation came to him in a vision that belonged to a greater universal truth. The Perennial Philosophy, in his estimation, was the basis of this truth. Wilson's wife Lois recalls that Heard "became a lifelong personal friend and admirer of AA" and that Huxley considered Wilson "the greatest social architect of the century."

Heard's experiences during the first two Trabuco years were synthesized in his 1942 book *Training for the Life of the Spirit*. Part one has twelve steps; part two has fourteen. All of the steps are expressed in three of four pages each of direct prose that is far more accessible to a general audience than Heard's earlier books aimed at academics and scientists. In fact, it resembles many of the contemporary self-help books that are now commonplace. It also resembles the 1953 Alcoholics Anonymous publication *Twelve Steps and Twelve Traditions* that is the more recognized antecedent to today's books. In Southern California old-timers from the Heard era have bruited about for years that Heard contributed to this book's philosophy and may even have helped to write it or, indeed, written it completely. To add some mystery to this possible equation, in Ernest Kurtz's history of AA, *Not God*, 1975, the dedication is to an anonymous "G.H."

While Heard was at Trabuco, Huxley, Isherwood and Prabhavananda were busy with their own projects. In 1941 Huxley published *Grey Eminence*, about France's Father Joseph who started as a mystic but then became corrupted as Richelieu's advisor. This framework gave Huxley ample latitude to think out loud about the Perennial Philosophy. 1944 and 1945 became landmark years for the cause of mystical writing. In 1944 there was Maugham's *The*

Razor's Edge (the title from the Katha-Upanishad), which is about a seeker of truth who finds it in Vedanta; and while the protagonist Larry Darrell has often been thought to be Isherwood, he is Heard. Then came Isherwood and Swami's translation of the *Gita*. This has Huxley's introduction promoting the Perennial Philosophy about which Heard had previously written an article for *Vedanta and the West*. In this introduction Huxley first states his Minimum Working Hypothesis (see pp. 103–4).

Also in 1944 appreared Huxley's novel *Time Must Have a Stop*, which is his parable on the Perennial Philosophy, and Heard's *Preface to Prayer*, which was an influence on Dr. Bob (Smith), the co-founder with Bill Wilson of AA. In 1945 Huxley's anthology, *The Perennial Philosophy*, quoted numerous mystics in all disciplines to demonstrate the essential sameness of the inner truths arrived at by divers hands across time and continents who could not have communicated with each other. The quotations are further elucidated by Huxley's commentary. Last was American poet Witter Bynner's very popular translation of Lao Tse's *The Way of Life*. (Buddhism, the Tao, Zen are derivations from Vedanta; all four, as well as the mystical offshoots of Islam, Judaism, Christianity, et al., fit under the umbrella of the Perennial Philosophy.) Mysticism, with these inroads into the mainstream, was now not quite so esoteric. With its popularity at a height that would not be repeated until the 1960s, Heard, in contrast to Huxley and Isherwood, was willing to tour the U.S. and give hundreds of lectures on "intentional living" and would continue to do so into the early 1960s. He became a spokesperson of great popularity in intellectual, academic, progressively theological, and artistic circles, and received voluminous correspondence from figures in these circles. While Huxley, Maugham, and to a lesser degree Isherwood, were better known to the general public, Heard was still the hub of their collective wheel among the cognoscenti.

By 1947, despite Heard's efforts to think otherwise, the practical exigencies and expenses of running an institution began to overtake Trabuco's spiritual mission. Heard reluctantly gave up Trabuco but generously donated the entire college and property to the Vedanta Society in Hollywood after which it became the Ramakrishna Monastery that is still functioning today. Heard did not regard this as a setback. He saw Trabuco as having been an enlightened enterprise of great benefit to those who visited and whose influence would now be passed on to the world at large.

Trabuco College, even though many great minds visited and shared there, is now as unknown as Heard.

Heard's own influence continued, at least until the start of the bland Eisenhower-era 1950s, which had started with McCarthyism putting fear into the unenlightened masses. Anything left of center became suspect, with intellectuals and artists easy targets. The lowbrow masses were reminded of the American inclination to be wary of highbrows. Then came flying saucers—possibly flown by communists. (Wish it were true that this is present-day facetiousness, but some people really believed it.) Heard's *The Riddle of the Flying Saucers: Is Another World Watching?* was published in 1950. This was one of the first UFO books to appear after a number of "sightings" beginning in 1947 that became part of UFO folklore. Roswell and other notable UFO legends have now become myths in books, TV, and films, which, while not yet making UFOs an incontrovertible reality, have jumped them a little past the strictly lunatic fringe they were in 1950. Even Heard's friends groaned to each other that his book would bring negative attention to him, them, and the causes they believed in. And Heard certainly defended his book in response to questions and letters he received about it.

24. XI. 52

Dear Mrs. Ford—

Thank you for your letter of the 10th. Certainly, *Is Another World Watching* was *not* written with "tongue in cheek." Study the evidence.... I have only quoted sincere observers.... Look at the articles in *Life* especially the ones re the Radar of the flying saucer sightings for hours on separate nights....

In the same letter, Heard charmingly says yes to a request to sign his book, if Mrs. Ford would send it to him with an SASE marked "to await return" so that she can, as he writes, assist the "secretaryless writer" to distinguish it from "a mountain of mail & so have pity & help an overworked elderly journalist."

The UFO period coincided with the experiments in "psychedelics" with Huxley, among others. (One of the others would be Timothy Leary whom Huxley would, in a letter, call an "ass" for craving publicity that discredited what was supposed to be scientific study.) Neither "saucers" nor "psychedelics" were Heard's primary interest, but he became associated with both and this somewhat obscured his more important advocacy of intentional living guided by the Perennial Philosophy. Moreover, in the 1950s interest in mysticism declined. Heard remained a popular figure but to a diminishing circle. In 1955, he was still highly regarded enough to secure a Bollingen Prize that allowed him to research and write his last book, *The Five Ages of Man*. On publication in 1963 the Los Angeles *Times* writer Robert Kirsch said that it was "the most important work to date of this challenging and brilliant philosopher, a volume which in scope and daring might be the Novum Organum of the 20th Century."

In 1962 Isherwood "fictionalized" Heard as the delightful Augustus Parr in *Down There on a Visit*. After Huxley died in 1963, Heard's health declined, and until he left his body in 1973, his last years were spent in a semi-coma. Consequently, he missed participating in the resurgence of interest in mysticism in the 1960s. Had he been able, he might have reminded the new seekers of his important role with the seekers of the previous generation. He could not, and his work and reputation have languished in an obscurity interrupted occasionally by scholars who sometimes reference him but only as an adjunct to Huxley, Isherwood, Auden or Maugham, all of whom owe a good deal more to Heard than he does to them. In 1996 Isherwood's *Diaries* from 1939 to 1960 were published, and there is a good deal of Heard reported on, sometimes with verbatim conversations included. Isherwood, who didn't spare people his judgments for posterity, was otherwise very kind to Heard, who is an even more charming combination of brilliance and blarney in Isherwood's accounts than in any of Heard's novelized reincarnations. He is in fiction and non-fiction a *character* and a *mensch*.

When one reads him today, his work, so outré seventy, sixty, fifty and forty years ago, sounds au courant and cutting-edge still. Even without his books, his philosophy was, and remains, in proportion to its impact on others, one of the most neglected influences on thought in the 20th century. This phrase, in other contexts, is tossed around lightly. In Heard's case, not only is the phrase not hyperbole, it's probably an understatement.

The Minimum Working Hypothesis

Huxley and Heard arrived at the following four tenets after reading the mystical writers East and West. These writers said the same things in their various ways and with a remarkable consistency that the four tenets summarize.

First: The phenomenal world of matter and of individualized consciousness—the world of things and animals and even gods— is the manifestation of a Divine Ground within which all partial realities have their being, and apart from which they would be non-existent.

Second: human beings are capable not merely of knowing *about* the Divine Ground by inference; they can also realize its existence by a direct intuition [i.e., meditation, dreams, visions] superior to discursive reasoning. This immediate knowledge unites knower with that which is known.

Third: man possesses a double nature, a phenomenal ego and an eternal Self, which is the inner man, the spirit, the spark of divinity within the soul. It is possible for a man, if he so desires, to identify himself with the spirit and therefore with the Divine Ground, which is of the same or like nature with the spirit.

Fourth: man's life on earth has only one end and purpose: to identify himself with his eternal Self and so come to unitive knowledge of the Divine Ground.

A Prevision of Agape:
Gerald Heard's Importance to Auden

Paul Eros

Eros, of Oxford, has looked closely at Gerald Heard's written philosophy of an evolving consciousness and has correlated Heard's ideas with the emergence of the early Auden, who took these ideas and evolved with them into the later Auden.

On 27 November 1931, Roger Fry wrote to G.L. Dickinson to recommend Gerald Heard's new book, *The Social Substance of Religion*, having found it "full of moving and inspiring suggestions" which "almost ought to have been written in poetry" (*Letters*, 665). Fry's observation is somewhat ironic, considering Dickinson knew Heard and had written the very favorable introduction to Heard's 1929 book *The Ascent of Humanity*. However, Fry's belief in the poetic potential of Heard's work is fascinating when one considers the importance of Heard's ideas to W.H. Auden, who would make great use of not only Heard's "suggestions," but would quite often rework what Edward Mendelson describes as Heard's "woozy sentences" (*Early Auden*, 26n) into poetry; as Mendelson writes, Heard "provided Auden with a cluster of phrases and implications that he applied in his own way" (*Early Auden*, 25). Auden was first introduced to Heard by Naomi Mitchison in 1929. At the time of their meeting, Heard was then the literary editor of a short-lived review, *The Realist*, whose editorial board boasted such names as Julian Huxley, Arnold Bennett, H.G. Wells, Rebecca West, and Mitchison's brother Jack. Mitchison, already close friends with Auden, approached Arnold Bennett with some of his poetry, and the two arranged with Heard to publish a selection of his poems in *The Realist*. The journal, however, went bankrupt before Auden's poems were published (Benton, 62). From their first meeting, Auden grew to regard Heard as a sort of guru. Auden most openly admits his respect for Heard in a poetic fragment (first published by Lucy McDiarmid in 1978) entitled "In The Year of My Youth...." Harold Nicolson notes the subject of the uncompleted poem in his diary entry of 4 August 1933: "The idea," Nicolson writes, "is Heard as Virgil guiding him through modern life" (*Diaries*, 153). But while Heard's importance to Auden has been widely recognized, there has been little critical attention given to Heard's ideas and their place in Auden's poetry. For example, Edward Mendelson attributes Auden's conception of agape, of harmony within a given group of individuals, to the ideas of Gerald Heard. Furthermore, Heard's own thoughts on psychology and human evolution show a similarity of minds and thought between the two. Beyond these brief comparisons, there has been little said about Heard and Auden. Just who was Gerald Heard? And why was he important enough to play Virgil to Auden's Dante?

Although little more than a shadowy figure lurking in the footnotes today, Gerald Heard (1889–1971) was a ubiquitous and popular figure in the 1930s. Aldous Huxley, for example, would be enabled to embrace both pacifism and mysticism under his guidance; Christopher Isherwood would be introduced to Vedantism by him; William Somerset Maugham would find inspiration, incorporating his thought into the mystically-inclined Larry Darrell in *The Razor's Edge*; and to E.M. Forster, Heard was quite simply "one of the most penetrating minds in England" (Woolf, *Diary*, 54n). First and foremost, Heard was a journalist and radio broadcaster. He was most famous for hosting a radio program of new scientific advances and ideas entitled "This Surprising World"; an unsigned *TLS* review of his 1937 book *Science Front 1936* describes him as "one of the most intelligent and vital of the BBC's regular speakers" (382) while yet another review of his 1936 book *Exploring the Stratosphere* accords Heard a "notable place" "among popularisers of current scientific work" (547).

Heard was most famous for his vision of a utopian future made possible by advances in psychology. Heard attributed modern social ills to a fundamental misunderstanding of human nature, namely that we are entirely self-sufficient individuals. Writing in *Time and Tide* in 1935, Heard objected to the "Hobbesian outlook" (rev. of Leon and Huxley, 1907) of modern political and social thinkers, that "man is an individual, his communities only constructs of and for his personal convenience and that therefore you had only to satisfy his individual needs for him to become wholly amenable" (rev. of Harrison and Osterly, 1545). Heard instead argued that "individual mutual self-interest is not enough" ("Religion," 115). As he wrote in 1932, society was not held together "by each constituent coldly calculating his profit and loss in the arrangement" but rather "through subconscious forces" ("Religion," 115). Psychology could demonstrate an underlying subconscious bond between all individuals, a corporate mind that enabled us to be sociable. By applying psychological thought to history, Heard constructed what he called an "outline of the evolution of consciousness" in his 1929 book *The Ascent of Humanity* (21). Heard argued that our earliest prehistoric ancestors were not self-interested, but rather possessed of a tribal sense which precluded "any consciousness of individual separateness" (23) from the group. As Heard writes, the "first human unit is the group, not the individual" (*Ascent*, 14).

Heard called this tribal sense "co-consciousness," a level of consciousness below self-awareness in which each individual constituent was only part of a larger whole. In this "co-conscious" state, Heard posited that each constituent of a community was in "constant telepathic communication with the rest of the group" (15). Heard cites W.H.R. Rivers' anthropological work *Instinct and the Subconscious* as evidence of "co-conscious" behavior in modern tribal cultures. The Melanesians, Heard explains, associate without any verbal communication, able to arrive at decisions as if by instinct. As an example, Heard describes Rivers' account of how the tribe could man a boat without any prior discussion, as though possessed of a common consciousness. However, at some point in history, this "co-consciousness" dissolved. In his 1932 essay "The History of Ideas, or How We Got Separate" (published alongside Auden's "Writing" essay in Naomi Mitchison's *Outline for Boys and Girls and Their Parents*), Heard asserts that paleolithic humans, who "did not think of themselves as self-conscious, separate individuals" (430), could scarcely help but feel a unity with all life; "their ideas of their own aliveness and the aliveness of animals," Heard writes, "were not divided" (430). "At that stage," continues Heard, "we took things very much for granted and assumed that everyone and everything was very like oneself" (445). However, growing human knowledge brought about an evolutionary advance in our consciousness. The psychological homogeneity of our ancestors eroded as humans became increasingly better able to understand and control the world they lived in. In the Neolithic period, humans began to exercise a mastery over their world, learning such arts as agriculture, pottery and making tools. Such advances were only possible by what Heard called a "power of separating" (433), the power to regard the world objectively. Despite the material benefits afforded by this new-found power to dissect and study, it ultimately brought about the dissolution of our original sense of unity. To illustrate this point, Heard compares the cave art of the Neolithic with that of the Paleolithic era. The paintings of the Paleolithic, argues Heard, were not so much "works of art, but works of magic" (428). Feeling that "the world is emotionally tied up with him" (429), the Paleolithic artist would represent scenes of hunting, believing in a unity between the act of drawing and successful hunting. However, by the Neolithic period, Heard remarks that a change in artistic style betrays a significant shift in consciousness:

> Those little pictures that the New Stone Age men made, and have no beauty like the pictures of their predecessors drew, show that men's ideas have become so clear, and have broken up what they see into such distinct parts, that the old vague sense of unity is gone, and instead of it men have a new power of taking things to pieces and of feeling themselves detached. (433)

It was at the moment when individuals became conscious of their detachment from the world that the tribal "co-consciousness" vanished; as Heard argues in his 1935 book *The Source of Civilization*, our "inherent power of co-operation" was lost at the "period in [our] psychic evolution when [we] attained self-consciousness" (*Source*, 224). Heard attributes this loss to the development of a self-conscious awareness which created "a fissure and specialisation" (*Substance*, 30) in our unified undifferentiated psyche, a divide which elevated our self-awareness at the expense of our "co-consciousness." Heard would write that, psychically, "we are divided against ourselves" (*Substance*, 42) by a "threshold," or a "'limen' … that now divides the subconscious and conscious mind so completely that the conscious mind can generally have not direct knowledge of the subconscious" ("Religion," 145). In *The Ascent of Humanity*, Heard explains that, like the primitives, the Melanesians were not "blinded to that wider field of illumination by the dazzling 'spotlight' of individual self-consciousness" (*Ascent*, 50); "no 'limen' has risen," writes Heard, "to shut off this way to the larger whole"(*Ascent*, 50). Heard felt it was imperative to break down the bulkhead between the subconscious and conscious mind if we were to enjoy a true sense of community with others. Within our subconscious mind, Heard argued, "that original nature of man remains, though denied vision" (*Substance*, 27).

Despite being isolated by the conscious mind, the subconscious mind is "still the source of all human energy" (*Substance*, 27). This blind, innate social power of our ancestors somehow percolates through our conscious minds, and is visible in our perpetual attempts to find unity with one another through love or friendship. Heard also attributed the origin of human civilization to the machinations of this subconscious force; he described civilization in 1931 as "the precipitation of the unconscious social habits of man" (*Substance*, 42), and asserted more succinctly in 1935 that "Civilization *is* self-consciousness" (*Source*, 87). Society is more than a convenient "profit and loss" arrangement, but an unconscious expression of our innate sociability. "The individual and society," concludes Heard, "make a psychic reciprocation" (*Substance*, 25) which cannot be ignored for the convenience of an economic theory. It was therefore essential to develop a deliberate technique of making this subconscious force readily accessible to self-conscious individuals.

Looking to prehistoric civilizations, Heard attempted to identify how early civilizations and religions provided a means of crossing the "threshold," conjoining the independent conscious mind with our greater subconscious social instincts. In 1932, Heard wrote a four-part series in *Time and Tide* entitled *Religion and the Problems of a Modern Society*, in which he discussed how religious experience had worked to alleviate the sudden isolation felt by our first self-conscious ancestors. "Religious communion" enabled each individual to feel a "direct sense of the union with their community and through it with eternal life" ("Religion," 145). United "in a like minded group," Heard believed that the limen in our consciousness could be surmounted, enabling "the individual ... to recover his symbiotic relationship with his fellows," and providing the "social satisfaction of coming together as a congregation" (*Source*, 15). Heard is essentially describing a state of agape in which the individual participant experiences a life that is "supra-personal and unlimited," achieving what Heard calls "at-one-ment" ("Religion," 145) with his or her community.

A mistaken belief in the solidarity of the individual made the religion of experience, that primitive agape, increasingly impossible. The earliest religion, argues Heard, was primarily "an exercise which gave men direct experience of the common, immediate external life" ("Religion," 145). However, as individualism grew stronger, the religion of experience developed "into rites which were intended to assure those individuals after death" (145). In his

1935 book *The Source of Civilization*, Heard would extol the merits of pre-historic fertility religion, which he believed

> rouses the individual from his growing preoccupation with his
> calculated personal economic concerns ... throws him back into
> the stream of life and chokes, at least for a moment, the growing
> anxiety rising from his fellow and his narrow concern as to what
> is going to happen to this precarious perishable self, which is all
> that now is fully real to each. (*Source*, 204)

However, once religion became "infected with the very thing it exists to cure—Individualism" ("Religion," 145), it only served to further their isolation by stressing personal salvation instead of promoting group unity. With the failure of religion, Heard sought a new means of uniting our divided consciousness.

Heard argued in 1932 that "the essential requirement ... and ... chief need of society ... is to find access to a force which will give individuals the power to act socially" ("Religion," 145). He often wrote about developing a "deliberate technique" to tap the subconscious "social and greater self" (*Source*, 17), or a "psychic hygiene" ("Religion," 115) which would enable each individual to "re-mend the fissure in his own psyche and so see himself and his community, it and Life, and Life and the universe as one" (*Source*, 20). Our earliest self-conscious ancestors were able to cross over that limen quite easily, having been recently "condensed" out of a natural co-consciousness. However, Heard asserted that, "in a self-conscious age," any attempt "to explore the subconscious, cross the limen, and make the vital contact that exists beyond the individual self-consciousness" had to be made "deliberately, self-consciously" (*Source* 17). The first step in Heard's solution was to recognize that individualism was not the correct paradigm for human relations. He argued that we had to understand our "vast psychic evolution" (*Ascent* 12), and appreciate that individuality is only a "growing pain or birth-pang" of a "larger consciousness" (*Ascent* 11). Just as individuality had "condensed" (12) out of the earlier "co-consciousness," so too would a larger consciousness spring forth from self-consciousness. The "intensity and isolation" of individualism was to be considered "a very late and passing consequence of man's psychological evolution at its acutest" (*Ascent*, 11). Heard believed that we were on the cusp of a new phase of psychic evolution, made possible by our growing understanding of psychology. Beyond co-consciousness and self-consciousness awaited what Heard called "superconsciousness" (*Ascent*, 6), a state in which we would be simultaneously self-aware and aware

of our subconscious extra-individuality. This evolution would occur naturally in the fullness of time, but its arrival could be sped
up with our help. A better understanding of our own psychology
would facilitate "a swift transition between the complete insensi-
tiveness of the absolute individual and the new collective being"
(*Ascent*, 11). Heard proposed a combination of psychological
analysis and mystical experience as a means to achieve this
transition. By means of psychological analysis, Heard believed we
could understand and apprehend the deep-seated forces which
motivated us. By meditation, Heard argued, our subconscious
"social habits" could be raised from the depths of the subconscious
mind and into the conscious mind.

Heard believed that group meditation was essential to breaking down the barriers both in our minds and between each other.
In *The Ascent of Humanity*, Heard describes the self-transcendence
afforded by group meditation:

> Individuals, psychology suggests and the spirit of man ap-
> proves, grow by fusion. When two or three are gathered together
> in the spirit of the future it begins to dominate them, to break
> down their isolation, to confer new powers, and finally to deliver
> them into a new unity as real as their former separation. (*Ascent*,
> 12)

Heard was initially skeptical of mysticism as a means to his
end, writing in *The Ascent of Humanity* that it "has been charged,
and it has not cleared itself of the accusation, of wish-solution,"
but believed there was some hope that the mysticism could quell
the self-regarding instinct of individuals; "the usual survival-
prompting wish," argues Heard, "resents the mystic emphasis on
the necessary dissolution of individuality a little less violently than
it resents extinction" (*Ascent*, 12). By the early 1930s, however,
Heard had begun to regard mystical experience as the key to social
renewal. In "Religion and the Problems of Modern Society," Heard
argued that, in meditation, self-conscious individuals could
achieve "an experience of precipitated power" and come to feel a
"direct sense of the union with their community" ("Religion," 146).
In his 1935 essay "The Significance of The New Pacifism," Heard
asserts that "small like minded groups ... meeting once a week for
meditation" contained "the powers essential to curing conflict in
the self, in society, and between humanity" (*New Pacifism*, 21). The
only limit to group meditation was the "absurdly small"
("Religion," 146) size of the group. While Heard believed the experience of communion could be "obtained by any group of like-

minded people," he also remarks that "the dozen seems to be the number which give best results" (146). In "The Significance of the New Pacifism," Heard would reiterate that "queer but distinctive limitation" ("New Pacifism," 21) that an effective group could not exceed twelve members. Heard was searching for a wide-scale solution to the problem of group organization, and did not propose that the world be divided into small groups. Instead, Heard envisioned a society in which group meditation would reassure individuals of their greater supra-personal unity before they returned to their daily lives. Having been reassured of their unity with all life, individuals could then return to a larger community, confident in their role as part of a larger whole. Such a technique, Heard believed, would enable individuals to "to live a life of unlimited liability with their companions" ("New Pacifism," 18) rather than regarding human society as a construct of enlightened self-interest. By meditation, Heard believed we could effectively lay the foundations of a new society, "a true co-operative commonwealth based surely on psychology" (18).

In his early poetry, Auden gives much consideration to the existence of an almost insurmountable barrier dividing our sub-conscious social instincts from our self-conscious rational mind. Auden's 1928 poem "The Secret Agent" deals overtly with the question of crossing this border into potentially hostile territory and tapping the pent-up energy it contains. According to Edward Mendelson, the "frontier" motif in Auden's poetry began in 1927. Auden's "frontier," Mendelson explains, represents "a watershed or divide isolating the mind from the cycles of unconscious nature" (*Early Auden*, 31). The poem reads well as a statement about the divide between the conscious and subconscious mind. However, Mendelson remarks, the border in "The Secret Agent" presents a new possibility, that of "using a barrier to produce energy rather than restrict it" (*Early Auden*, 35). In the opening line of the poem, the speaker reflects that "control of the passes" is "the key / To this new district" ("Secret," 1–2). Some means to establish regular communication between these realms is suggested. In Edward Callan's schema, the secret agent can be identified as a representation of the Ego, a "frontier creature," one who "tries to mediate between the world and the Id" (Callan, 6). The secret agent emblematizes the relationship between the conscious and subconscious; all communication is covert, and our conscious mind sees only glimpses of the strange world beyond. The speaker reflects that there is "easy power" ("Secret," 5) to be had at this border, remarking that it is a "fine site for a dam" (6). A dam is a liminal space which would control, rather than restrict, communication between two realms. The image of the dam fits neatly within Heard's and Auden's belief in bridging the gap between the subconscious and conscious mind; in fact, in 1935, Heard would argue that our subconscious, inner nature is something we must "trust and *tap*" (*Source*, 27, my emphasis). However, by the conclusion of the poem, we see that there is no hope of harnessing this energy. The speaker is "Woken by water / Running away in the dark" ("Secret," 10–11), suggesting that this potential energy trickles away unharnessed. Further, the speaker remarks that no one tries to communicate with this realm. At the end of the second stanza, he tells us "the bridges were still unbuilt and trouble coming" (8). The foreshadowed, nameless crisis can only be averted by establishing communication with that part of the mind we cordon off.

In his 1932 fragment "In the Year of My Youth ...," Auden borrows heavily from Heard's *Social Substance of Religion* in order to discuss the social implications of this psychic rift. The speaker of the poem, led through modern London by his friend Sampson (a model of Gerald Heard), observes men and women who live like automatons, working but without purpose or satisfaction. Sampson attributes this to a division between motivation and "executive" power. The speaker of the poem questions Sampson about this division:

> "What did you mean when you mentioned the limen?"
> I asked. "The barrier," he answered, "which divides
> That which must will from that which can perceive,
> Desire from Data; the watershed between
> The lonely unstable mad executives
> We recognize in Banks and restaurants as our friends
> And that lost country across which
> Dreams have made furtive flights at night
> To reconnoitre but have never landed
> Where dwells the unprogressive blind society
> Possessing no argument but the absolute veto.
> ("Youth," II. 150–60)

In her commentary on this fragment, Lucy McDiarmid acknowledges that Auden borrows the word "executive" from Heard's 1932 book *The Social Substance of Religion*. Heard uses the word to describe the rational, conscious mind which sees only what it can use. In Auden's poem, the executive mind is personified by those "lonely unstable mad" individuals, those we "recognize in Banks," their reason and personal greed emblematized by their economic ambitions. McDiarmid also notes that his use of the word "unstable" is a direct reference to *The Social Substance of Religion*, where Heard attributes tangible human achievement to the "growth of the outer, executive, unstable side of man's nature" (*Substance*, 30). The outer side of our nature is unstable because it changes and grows as we learn and develop. Heard goes on to say that our inner nature is "unadapting, unalterable" (30); "the subconscious," he writes, "is completely resistant to change in its circumstances, and remains unaltered by the outward economic modification of its environment" (25–26). By "denying [the subconscious mind] those expressions natural to it," our condition is one of "profound distress" (25); while advancing outwardly, we have no inner conception of what it is we work toward. Unaware of the potential for real unity that exists within us, we work to further isolate ourselves from one another by listening to the demands of the "surface mind" (25). Writing in 1935, Heard would again use the word "unstable" to describe a society that "advances economically" without matching this outward growth "proportionately [with] self-conscious knowledge of its inner nature" (*Source, 136*). Heard would conclude in a *Time and Tide* review of 1935 that "there is the psychological man as well as economic man, and without satisfying those two sides, man is deranged" (rev. of Leon and Huxley, 1908). The problem for both Heard and Auden was that the subconscious mind, the realm of "desire" which ultimately governs our social behavior, was isolated and ignored, while the conscious mind, the world of "data," was made invincible. Auden, who describes the subconscious mind as "possessing no argument but the absolute veto," is simply reworking Heard's conception of the subconscious, "possessed of an absolute veto but shut off with equal absoluteness from the argument" (*Substance*, 30). Like Heard, Auden believes we must rediscover that "lost country" which still exercises its blind influence over our actions, and consciously channel the energy it offers.

Auden's "Writing" essay (published alongside Heard's "History of Ideas" in Mitchison's *Outline* in 1932) shows how closely his conception of the subconscious social self resembles Heard's. For example, consider how Auden's discussion of prehistoric "co-consciousness" and of the birth of individualism are identical. Auden writes about the "continuously present group life" ("Writing," 43) of our pre-individual ancestors that preceded language, and, like Heard, Auden posited that this "continuously present" group sense was akin to a kind of telepathy. As evidence, Auden cites Rivers' example of the Melanesian; "There was no discussion as to who should stroke or steer," writes Auden; "All found their places as we should say by instinct" (40). This connection has been noted before by Katherine Bucknell, who in her commentary on Auden's essay remarks that "the fact Auden does not give the exact source of the story suggests that he may have been recalling it from Heard's telling in *The Ascent of Humanity*" (40n). Auden's familiarity with Heard's *Ascent* is further supported by his argument for the dissolution of this co-consciousness and the birth of self-consciousness. "At sometime or other in human history," writes Auden, "man became self conscious, he began to feel, I am I, and You are Not I; we are shut inside ourselves and apart from each other" (40). Self-consciousness, as in Heard's scheme, meant that each individual constituent of a society became aware of him or herself as an individual entity first, and a part of the group second; Auden describes this initial state of self-awareness in which each constituent of a society perceived itself as "an individual thing, different from other things, but without meaning except in its connection with other things" (40). Ultimately, Auden argues, individual autonomy supplanted this feeling of unity entirely. As Auden writes, "a part begins to work not only as if it were a whole (which it is) but as if there were no larger wholes" (40). "The more this feeling grew," argues Auden, there was an increasingly greater need "to bridge over the gulf, to recover the sense of being as much part of life as the cells in his body are part of him" (40). Whereas Heard argues that civilization was constructed as an artificial means of reassuring the "part" that it was part of a "larger whole," Auden suggests that the more fundamental development of language was developed by self-conscious individuals as a means to recover the lost sense of co-consciousness. The origin of language, argues Auden, goes back to the noises of excitement made during intensely social activities enjoyed by a co-conscious group. Before the loss of our co-conscious unity, Auden writes, when early humans were "doing things together in a group, such [as] hunting; when feeling was strongest, ... the group had made noises, grunts, howls, grimaces" (40). "If he made the noise," Auden asks, "could he not recover the feeling?" (40). By using language, individuals attempted to "bridge" the rift between the individual self and a larger whole. Auden describes language as "a tunnel under which the currents of feeling can pass unseen" (40–41). David Izzo, in his *W.H. Auden and Aldous Huxley: On Lan-*

guage, explains Auden's conception of the duality of language, which exists in the "individual mind *in part*" but also within "a collective unconscious that unites each individual—a world mind" (Izzo, 4). Auden illustrates this concept by highlighting the numerous unconscious "currents" which are to be found in a simple conversation between two strangers on a train:

> Man. Its very cold for this time of year
> Girl. Yes it would be warmer if the sun were to come out.
> What is really going on is something quite different, something like this
> Man. What a nice looking girl you are. I hope you don't mind my speaking to you like this but I should like to know if your voice is as pretty as your hat. Journeys are dull aren't they unless one finds someone nice to talk to. I expect you have your difficulties too, like me. We all have. Let's be friends.
> Girl. You look nice but a girl has to be careful. You can never tell what men will be like if you encourage them too much. I hate trains too. Have you ever been in love. What was she like. Alright. We'll try and see how we get on.
>
> ("Writing," 41)

Auden acknowledges that language has a purely literal quality. The "sense" of language, which Auden characterizes as "fat stock prices on the radio," is literal and indisputable; "sense" communicates pure data. But beneath this surface level, there are greater forces at work. The numerous undercurrents in a simple conversation demonstrate the presence of an unconscious social force. The quirky punctuation of Auden's subconscious conversation further suggests a mind ungoverned by the conscious mind, which imposes order and grammar on the information it receives from the subconscious. Language is a bridge between the two, the act of communication briefly connecting our individual mind to a greater whole. Language not only proves the existence of this subconscious social mind, but also presents a means by which self-conscious individuals can access it.

In the early 1930s, Auden began to look seriously for a means of uniting these two realms more concretely. The solution he suggested owes much to Gerald Heard's theories on group meditation and agape. In his 1934 essay "The Group Movement and The Middle Classes," Auden discusses the potential for "a group of very moderate size, probably not larger than twelve" in which it would be possible for an individual to "lose himself, for his death instincts to be neutralized in the same way as those of the separate cells of the metazoa neutralize each other in the body" ("Group," 98). Auden's cellular imagery is a recapitulation of his argument in "Writing" that early individuals sought some means to "recover the sense of being as much a part of life as the cells in his body are a part of him" ("Writing," 40). Auden's reflection that group activities can suspend the individual's "death instinct" is identical to Heard's description of group meditation. Heard claims that religion potentially has the power to demonstrate to each individual that "he is eternal, if he dares to step out of his individuality into the common life that flows about him sustaining him" ("Religion," 145). Once our self-regarding instinct is checked, Auden argues, we can experience real unity with one another.

Auden's 1933 poem "A Summer's Night," and his later commentary on the experience of agape in *The Protestant Mystics*, shows the influence of Heard on his thoughts on meditation. In "A Summer's Night," the speaker of the poem, sitting "equal with colleagues in a ring," finds himself possessed of a feeling of unity between them. The image of the ring appears in Heard's *Social Substance of Religion* in reference to early Christian agape. Heard believed that a "small group of about a dozen" had come together regularly and "formed an inward-looking group—perhaps a ring" (*Substance*, 213). So assembled, Heard argued, early Christians merged in a common "psychic field" (213) which reassured them of their bond to one another. Writing "The Protestant Mystics" in 1963, Auden would describe how on that summer night in 1933 he had "quite suddenly and unexpectedly" found himself "invaded by a power" which made it possible for him to know "what it means to love one's neighbour as oneself" (*Forewords and Afterwords*, 69). Auden has successfully stepped outside himself into the larger life, and transcended his fear of individual death; as he writes in "A Summer's Night," at the height of his experience "Fear gave his watch no look" and "Death put down his book" ("Summer," 4). The individual's sense of self-preservation and fears of death vanish with this experience of a greater eternal life of which he or she is a part. This experience, however, he knows to be fleeting: "I also knew that the power would, of course, withdraw sooner or later and that, when it did, my greeds and self-regard would return" (*Forewords and Afterwords*, 69). However, the memory of the experience stays with him, and "more difficult for [him] to deceive [him]self" (70) when he behaves greedily or selfishly toward others. Like Heard, Auden believed the vision of agape would provide individuals with an intense feeling of their place within a larger whole. And although that experience would fade, the memory of it would remind them that their individual autonomy is illusory. The self-regarding instinct would return, as Auden admits, but the memory of the experience would make it impossible to believe in the insolubility of the individual, and reaffirm communal ties.

For the rest of Auden's career as a poet and also as a philosopher via his essays, the impetus of Heard's early influence that conditioned a search for consciousness in Auden would remain, steadfastly, the dominating concern of Auden's life and art.

Works Cited

Auden, W.H. "The Group Movement and The Middle Classes." In *Oxford and the Groups*, edited by R.H.S. Crossman. Oxford: Blackwell, 1934. 98.

———. "The Protestant Mystics." *Forewords and Afterwords*. London: Faber and Faber, 1973. 49–78.

———. "The Secret Agent." *W.H. Auden: Collected Poems*. Edited by Edward Mendelson. London: Faber and Faber, 1976. 41.

———. "A Summer's Night." *W.H. Auden: Collected Poems*. Edited by Edward Mendelson. London: Faber and Faber, 1976. 103.

Benton, Jill. *Naomi Mitchison: A Century of Experiment in Life and Letters*. London: Pandora, 1990.

Bucknell, Katherine. "Auden's Writing Essay." In *W.H. Auden: 'The Map of All my Youth,'* edited by Katherine Bucknell and Nicholas Jenkins. Oxford: Clarendon Press, 1990.

Callan, Edward. *Auden: A Carnival of Intellect*. Oxford: Oxford UP, 1983.

Fry, Roger. "To G. L. Dickinson," 27 November 1931, letter 675 of *The Letters of Roger Fry*, Vol. 2. London: Chatto and Windus, 1972. 665.

Heard, Gerald. *The Ascent of Humanity*. London: Jonathan Cape, 1929.

———. "The History of Ideas, or How We Got Separate." In *An Outline for Boys and Girls and Their Parents*, edited by Naomi Mitchison. London: Gollancz, 1932. 417–59.

———. "Men and Books." Rev. of *Ancient Art and Social Ritual* by Jane Harrison and *The Sacred Dance*, by W.O. Osterley. *Time and Tide*, 26 October 1935: 1545–46.

———. "Men and Books." Rev. of *Ethics of Power* by Philip Leon and *We Europeans* by J. Huxley et al. *Time and Tide*, 21 December 1935: 1907–8.

————. "Religion and the Problems of Modern Society." *Time and Tide*, 30 January 1932: 115–16; 6 February 1932: 145–46; 13 February 1932: 168; 20 February 1932: 197–98.

————. "The Significance of the New Pacifism." In *The New Pacifism*, edited by Gerald K. Hibbert. London: Allenson, 1936. 13–22.

————. *The Social Substance of Religion*. London: Allen and Unwin, 1931.

————. *The Source of Civilization*. London: Jonathan Cape, 1935.

Izzo, David. *Aldous Huxley and W.H. Auden: On Language*. West Cornwall, CT: Locust Hill Press, 1998.

McDiarmid, Lucy. "W.H. Auden's 'In the Year of My Youth …'" *Review of English Studies* N.S. 29 (1978): 267–312.

Mendelson, Edward. *Early Auden*. London: Faber and Faber, 1981.

————. *Later Auden*. London: Faber and Faber, 1999.

Nicholson, Harold. *Diaries and Letters, 1930–1939*. Edited by Nigel Nicolson. London: Collins, 1966.

Rev. of *Exploring the Stratosphere*, by Gerald Heard. *Times Literary Supplement*, 27 June 1936: 547.

Rev. of *Science Front 1936*, by Gerald Heard. *Times Literary Supplement*, 15 May 1937: 382–83.

Woolf, Virginia. Diary entry of 1 February 1932. *The Diary of Virginia Woolf*. Edited by Anne Oliver Bell. Vol. IV. London: Hogarth Press, 1982.

Understanding W.H. Auden's *The Orators*: Understanding Ciceronian Rhetoric

Adrienne Hacker-Daniels

The Orators *has long been considered Auden's most inscrutable long work. Recently, its supposed opaque density has been subject to a more discernible elucidation including the editor's study of Christopher Isherwood, which asserts that there is a code to be found in an Isherwood-Auden schema related to their "mythified" interpretation of their public school days as neo-saga—at least as concerned the content. Then there is the structure and presentation of* The Orators, *which reflects the classical training of British students in Roman rhetoric. Hacker-Daniels—a professor of rhetoric—makes a strong case that Auden's epic is not only neo-saga but also neo-classical.*

W.H. Auden poses an interesting paradox as a literary figure during the 1930s—a period in which poetry, drama and fiction oftentimes served as mouthpieces for the promulgation of ideas contemporaneous with particular social, political and economic upheavals—and in which that same poetry, drama and fiction promised, at the very least, an accessible, communicative path toward passion, knowledge and outright persuasion. As a poet whose cachet has included Marxism,[1] H.W. Hausermann characterizes Auden's initial poetic ventures as "a protest against tradition and the belief in tradition, against the unquestioned authority of 'less noble men;' against the idea of war, against private and civic degeneracy, against selfish individualism, public inertia,

---

[1]See Peter E. Firchow, "Private Faces in Public Places: Auden's *The Orators*," *PMLA* 92 (1977): 256.

sloth and despair."[2] The political ideology becomes inextricably tied to a new, rather novel, solipsistic use of language which is evident in Auden's early works, and which Hausermann claims "is extremely obscure, but of an obscurity connected not with recondite meanings of a learned character; it is on the contrary caused by the absence of intellectual significance and by the density of an almost animal emotion."[3] Notwithstanding the lack of magnanimity afforded Auden, a reluctant, albeit small and qualifiable concession would not be totally off the mark.

As a poet of political tendentiousness, Auden is peculiarly "autistic"[4]—a volitional autism—but autistic nevertheless, insofar as the language traverses an augmented and densely layered poeticization, which ultimately devolves into a privatization of thought—writing so abstrusely, that he appears to be keeping any publicly accessible meaning "at bay." Writing on Auden's poetry, Randall Jarrell said, "our political or humanitarian interests may make us wish to make our poetry accessible to large groups; it is better to try to make the groups accessible to the poetry, to trans-

---

[2]H.W. Hausermann, "Left-Wing Poetry," *English Studies* 21 (1939): 206.

[3]Ibid., 208.

[4]See n. 13, "Part Two: The Poet," in David Garrett Izzo, *Aldous Huxley & W.H. Auden: On Language* (West Cornwall, CT: Locust Hill Press, 1998), 92. Izzo explains Auden's fascination with the autistic through the work of Dr. Bruno Bettelheim. Although researchers have thankfully jettisoned Bettelheim's theories of autism's *etiology*, the predominant modes of semantic operationalization have remained fairly constant. Izzo quotes Auden from his essay, "Children, Autistic," *A Certain World*, pp. 72–73: "For anybody interested in language, the linguistic behavior of autistic children is of the greatest interest and significance" (72). Izzo compares the autistic's language with the linguistic behavior of the motion picture character Nell of the same name. Although Izzo is right in saying that, "for the autistic child and Nell, sound symbols are invented after experience; it just happens that their unique experiences were cut off from any other world but their own," Nell is more idioglossic than autistic, resulting from, among other variables, phonological concerns which have a different causality and weightiness. Two representative dictionary definitions define *idioglossia* as a psychiatric term which means "defective speech characterized by a succession of meaningless sounds," and as "a condition in which the affected person pronounces his words so badly as to seem to speak a language of his own."

late the interests into political or humanitarian activity."[5] Jarrell claims that the disjunctive argument propounded by the political poets of the 1930s was ill conceived as a false dilemma fallacy. That is, if poetry is not rendered accessible to "the People," it is "decadent escapism."[6] In fact, Jarrell punctuates the point through his vilification of MacLeish's notion of poetry as "public speech."[7]

As writers in the 1930s, both Auden and Gertrude Stein struggled with the disaffection accorded their respective solipsistic and autistic approaches. As one of maniacal, but oftentimes short-lived, opinion, Auden liked Stein's work, extolling it in 1926; within a few months she was tripe.[8] In *Early Auden*, Edward Mendelson observes, "the glut of gerunds and participles in both poem and journal results from Auden's early enthusiasm for Gertrude Stein, but his theory of perception is virtually the same as Wordsworth's."[9] But a greater, more important parallel is both writers' preoccupation with the instantiation of language in poetic form[10] and the concomitant hermeneutical dimensions of poetic diction as quintessentially rhetorical in markedly classical[11]—albeit ostensibly modernistic—ways. Scholars have examined the myriad ways in which the literary artifact is rhetorical. As a macro-rhetorical approach, one can circumnavigate the world of the poem through an examination of the tropes and schemes. Another approach broadens the journey as a micro-rhetorical approach through an examination of larger contextual considerations—i.e., how does the poem respond to our quotidian contingencies and

---

[5]Randall Jarrell, "Changes of Attitude and Rhetoric in Auden's Poetry," *The Southern Review* 7.2 (1941–42): 349.

[6]Ibid., 349.

[7]Ibid., 349.

[8]Humphrey Carpenter, *W.H. Auden: A Biography* (Boston: Houghton Mifflin Company, 1981), 66.

[9]Edward Mendelson, *Early Auden* (New York: The Viking Press, 1981), 69.

[10]See Rainer Emig, *W.H. Auden: Towards a Postmodern Poetics* (New York: St. Martin's Press, 2000), 66; and John Fuller, *W.H. Auden: A Commentary* (Princeton: Princeton University Press, 1998), 97.

[11]See Kathy Eden, *Hermeneutics and the Rhetorical Tradition* (New Haven: Yale University Press, 1997).

exigencies—highlighting the import of language as public discourse—as acts of speech?

Auden and Stein have written substantively and illuminatingly on this issue. Stein published a piece entitled "Forensics" in 1931, and in 1923, a piece entitled "Practice of Oratory." In her introductory comment to "Practice of Oratory," Ulla Dydo suggests that an impetus for this work could be correspondence from Mabel Weeks regarding a possible lecture tour and that the piece itself "is a rehearsal for how to begin a speech, a lecture, an address."[12] Stein's education in the American schools in the last 25 years of the nineteenth century is indebted to William McGuffey's pedagogical philosophy in which the McGuffey Eclectic Reader was an American mainstay for the teaching of—among other skills, "articulation, inflection, accent and emphasis, and cultivation and management of voice."[13]

In her introduction to Auden's essay "Writing,"[14] Katherine Bucknell[15] claims that "'Writing' is centrally concerned with the relation between the writer and the society in which he lives, and it marks the birth in Auden of a self-conscious desire to communicate with his audience."[16] Bucknell continues by arguing for Auden's redemptive motive insofar as "after the obscurity of *The Orators* (completed late in 1931), Auden now wished to be understood, perhaps remembered, and even loved by his readers,"[17] accomplishing what she parses as a "kind of communicative ease."[18] And Gertrude Stein, too, found a redemptive quality in her 1932 volume *The Autobiography of Alice B. Toklas*. As Richard Bridgman

---

[12]Gertrude Stein, *A Gertrude Stein Reader*, ed. and introd. Ulla E. Dydo (Evanston, IL: Northwestern University Press, 1993), 443.

[13]Dydo, 443.

[14]"Writing" or "The Pattern Between People," was originally published in *An Outline For Boys & Girls and Their Parents*, ed. Naomi Mitchison (London: Victor Gollancz Ltd., 1932), 853–68.

[15]Katherine Bucknell, "Auden's 'Writing' Essay," in W.H. Auden, *'The Map of All My Youth,'* ed. Katherine Bucknell and Nicholas Jenkins (Oxford: Clarendon Press, 1990), 17–34. This is the original manuscript minus the deletions which appear in the Mitchison volume.

[16]Bucknell, 17.

[17]Ibid., 17–18.

[18]Ibid., 18.

says, "After twenty-eight years of enigmatic utterances, Gertrude Stein at last chose to speak in a voice of singular clarity."[19]

In Auden's essay "Writing"[20] in the section entitled "Writing," he asserts the relationship between the written and spoken word:

> Writing and speech are like two tributary streams, rising at different sources, flowing apart for a time until they unite to form a large river... The urge to write like the urge to speak came from man's growing sense of personal loneliness, of the need for group communication. But while speech begins with the feeling of separateness in space, of I-here-in-this-chair and You-there-in-that-chair, writing begins from the sense of separateness in time of "I'm here today, but I shall be dead to-morrow and you will be alive in my place and how can I speak to you."[21]

In the section of "Writing" entitled "Spoken and Written Language," Auden says:

> Generally speaking, the feeling/meaning is transmitted with extraordinary accuracy, as the gestures and the tone of voice which go with the words are remembered also. With a statement in writing it is often impossible after a time to decide exactly what the author meant.[22]

And in the last section entitled "Summary," Auden says:

> I am inclined to think we read too much; that if literature is to revive, most of us will have to stop learning to read and write and stop moving from place to place, and let literature start again by oral tradition.[23]

In his Introduction to "The Poet's Tongue" (1935) Auden further illumines the importance of the spoken word:

> Of the many definitions of poetry, the simplest is still the best: "memorable speech": That is to say, it must move our emotions, or excite our intellect, for only that which is moving or exciting is memorable, and the stimulus is the audible spoken word and ca-

----

[19]Richard Bridgman, *Gertrude Stein in Pieces* (New York: Oxford University Press, 1970), 206.

[20]W.H. Auden, "Writing," in *'The Map of All My Youth,'* ed. Katherine Bucknell and Nicholas Jenkins (Oxford: Clarendon Press, 1990), 39–54.

[21]Ibid., 43.

[22]Ibid., 44.

[23]Ibid., 54.

dence, to which in all its power of suggestion and incantation we must surrender, as we do when talking to an intimate friend.[24]

Auden articulates what should be the province of the poet's intent:

> The propagandist, whether moral or political, complains that the writer should use his powers over words to persuade people to a particular course of action, instead of fiddling while Rome burns. But Poetry is not concerned with telling people what to do, but with extending our knowledge of good and evil, perhaps making the necessity for action more urgent and its nature more clear, but only leading us to the point where it is possible for us to make a rational and moral choice.[25]

Auden ostensibly abides by the classical distinctions between poetry and rhetoric; however, from a neo-Aristotelian perspective, the only genre Auden seems to suggest is outside the purview of the poetic intent, and the one made indirect reference to, is deliberative rhetoric—speechmaking within a civic, legislative arena, the intent of which is exhortation and dissuasion—arguing for the expedience or inexpediency of implementing a particular course of action for social/political good. Irrefutably, the aforementioned quote does not make the other two genres of rhetoric, epideictic and forensic discourse, *personae non grata*, but clearly welcomes forensic and epideictic modes as residing in the poetic domicile.

Regardless of the genre of rhetorical discourse, all speechmaking employs the five Aristotelian canons of rhetoric: invention (*inventio*), arrangement (*taxis*), style (*lexis*), memory (*memoria*), and delivery (*hypokrisis*). Invention, comprised of the three modes of proof (*pistis*): logos, pathos and ethos; arrangement—the proper ordering of the statements; style—the choice of words and sentence structure; memory—the mnemonic strategies; and delivery—the presentation.[26] Interestingly, in his *Poetics*, Aristotle refers us to the *Rhetoric* for a complete discussion of thought (*dianoia*), one of the six components of the drama. And although diction, another of the components of drama, is broached in the *Poetics*, its treatment is adumbrated compared with the fuller,

---

[24]W.H. Auden, "Introduction to 'The Poet's Tongue,'" in *The English Auden*, ed. Edward Mendelson (New York: Random House, 1977), 327.

[25]Ibid., 329.

[26]See G.M.A. Grube, *The Greek and Roman Critics* (London: Methuen & Co. Ltd., 1965), particularly 70–102, for an excellent summary of Aristotelian poetics and rhetoric.

more pellucid treatment in the *Rhetoric*. In assessing the relationship between the two arts of rhetoric and poetics, G.M.A. Grube says:

> "Rhetoric" was for the ancients the art of speech and writing generally, and Aristotle makes very clear that this is the subject of his treatise when he introduces it by saying that rhetoric is an art which all men practice since all men engage in argument, criticism, accusation and defense, some at random, some with conscious method. In the Poetics, he referred us to the Rhetoric for a study of how to express thought in words, even in poetry. It is true that the study of language, because of its origins, was slanted to oratory, and that the orator remained the practitioner of the art of prose as the tragedian was, for Aristotle, the poet, so that prose is discussed in oratorical terms, but this should not mislead us; a great deal of "rhetorical" theory, in Aristotle as in other critics, is equally applicable not only to the art of writing prose but to poetry as well.[27]

The intertwined relationship between rhetoric and poetics can be traced back to the sophistic movement. In his book *The Sophists*, W.K.C. Guthrie discusses the broadly based meaning of the term sophist and the kind of artistic "multitasking" in which they engaged:

> Probably it assumed that a sophistes would be a teacher. This accords with the fact that the name was often applied to poets, for in Greek eyes practical instruction and moral advice constituted the main function of the poet ... the great dramatist of the fifth century, both tragic and comic, certainly regarded themselves as having an educational mission... Euripides himself, challenged to state the grounds on which a poet deserves admiration, replies "For him wit and good advice, and because he makes men better citizens."[28]

Guthrie's account provides evidence that not only were poets the first sophists, but that they served an important pedagogical and didactic function in Athenian society.

W.H. Auden's poetry, particularly *The Orators*,[29] would benefit from an interpretation through a rhetorical prism. Although sev-

---

[27]Ibid., 92.

[28]W.K.C. Guthrie, *The Sophists* (Cambridge: Cambridge University Press, 1971), 29–30.

[29]W.H. Auden, *The Orators* (New York: Random House, 1967). All quotations are taken from this edition.

eral scholars have acknowledged both the micro-rhetorical[30] and macro-rhetorical tenets in Auden's poetry,[31] the one that has seemed most elusive is the one that bears emphatic resemblance to, and owes unadulterated allegiance to, oratorical discourse, and to a major progenitor of rhetorical theory and oratorical practice— the Roman orator and theorist Marcus Tullius Cicero (106–43 B.C.E.).[32] Looking at *The Orators* through this prism allows for militating against the notion that the poetic-rhetorical devices devolve into "infractions" of sorts, which ultimately impede the communication. And given the presumed diminished communicative status, one could too easily and erroneously conclude that Auden is perspicacious without perspicuity, engaging a density of idiom which obfuscates meaning and compromises any semblance of connection with audience. As expressed by Peter Firchow, "the early Auden's language is to a marked degree an in-group dialect, intentionally designed to be incomprehensible to outsiders."[33]

Auden's unique challenges as a poet are rhetorical challenges: who is his public, who is his audience, and what is his attitude toward his subject? In the very perceptive essay "W.H. Auden: The Search for a Public," David Daiches discusses Auden's challenges in the poet's first volume, *Poems.*

> On the whole, these poems give the impression of a man of genuine poetic gifts and possessing to a quite uncanny extent the power to do new things with words, who is not quite sure what he wants to say, and who is even less decided about whom he wants to speak to. The latter problem, we feel, is the more ur-

---

[30]Scholars who highlight the micro-rhetorical tendencies in Auden's poetry have examined the semantic impenetrability, noting constructs such as *parataxis* (see Jarrell, 337), *periphrasis* (see Jarrell, 342), and *polysyndeton* (see Elizabeth Rice Turpin, "Rhetoric and Rhythm in Twentieth-Century Sonnets By Hopkins, Auden, Frost, Cummings, Thomas, and Merrill Moore," diss., Texas A & M University, 1972, 163.

[31]See, for example, Rainer Emig, *W.H. Auden: Towards a Postmodern Poetics* (London: Macmillan Press Ltd., 2000); Frederick Buell, *W.H. Auden as a Social Poet* (Ithaca: Cornell University Press, 1973); Trevor Davison, "The Method of Auden's 'The Orators,'" *The Durham University Journal* n.s. 32.3 (1971): 167–78.

[32]Cicero was certainly the progeniture of the sophists—particularly Isocrates, as well as Aristotle.

[33]Peter E. Firchow, "Private Faces in Public Places: Auden's *The Orators,*" *PMLA* 92 (1977): 258.

gent: once he finds his audience—either a real or an ideal audience; it does not matter which, for the problem is simply to give consistency to his symbolism and coherence to his attitude—he will be able to speak more clearly[34].

For Daiches, the challenge of pinpointing attitudinal and audience loci is intensified in Auden's *The Orators*. The dedication to Stephen Spender engenders the first clue: "Private faces in public places / Are wiser and nicer / Than public faces in private places."[35] Auden's predilection is indubitably toward communicating to the many and not the few; however, upon first blush he seems hard pressed to engage an idea couched in a compatible lexicon which is genuinely archetypal. As effective oratorical discourse, adaptations are made, but Auden expresses the "between a rock and a hard place" syndrome vis-à-vis audience adaptation, in his "Summary" section of his essay "Writing":

> Man writes and reads because he is lonely and wants to be reunited with a group. Writing must do two things. It must affect the whole group and the way in which it affects it must be valuable, assisting the group towards a completer and more discriminating life. The larger the group the harder to unite it and the cruder the feelings which do. But it is impossible for people now to exist in small groups only.[36]

Auden's struggle to create the proper relationship between idea and audience is rooted primarily in his attempts at reconciling poetic and rhetorical/oratorical propensities. The poet concerns himself with the universal, the orator with the particular. Arguably, *The Orators* exemplifies that reconciliation more than any of his other works. The irony of offering up oratory—particularly Roman oratory—as a primary influence for Auden is inescapable. Auden wrote an essay entitled "The Fall of Rome" (1966) which was originally commissioned by *Life* magazine, but ultimately rejected for publication. Appearing for the first time in "'In Solitude for Company': W.H. Auden After 1940," Auden expresses his obloquy toward classical Rome:

> By heredity and temperament, I think of the Romans with distaste. The only classical Latin poet I really like is Horace. I find

---

[34]David Daiches, "W.H. Auden: The Search For a Public," *Poetry: A Magazine of Verse* 54 (1939): 151.

[35]Ibid., 152.

[36]Auden, "Writing," 53.

their architecture, even in ruins, as oppressive and inhuman as the steel-and-glass buildings of to-day. I prefer "the rolling English road" made by "the rolling English drunkard" to the brutal straight line of the Roman road or the thru-way. One reason why I like Italy and the Italians so much is that, aside from their unfortunate addiction to rhetoric, I cannot imagine a people less like the Romans of antiquity.[37]

Notwithstanding Auden's expressed and unapologetic disdain for rhetoric and its Roman progenitors, *The Orators* generates interesting parallels between Britain of the 1930s and its classical counterpart of the Roman Republic; between the oratorical practices of Britain and those of the Roman Republic (at once both important and impotent) and the Ciceronian conflation of the canons of invention (*inventio*) and style (*elocutio*), allowing for the metaphor as a mode of proof within the canon of invention—a modern conceptualization of the metaphorical construct with roots in classical rhetorical theory.[38] In spite of Auden's attitudes toward rhetoric, John Fuller has exactingly alembicated the essence of *The Orators* and its Roman influences:

> It is "an English study", then, in a number of senses: it is a portrait of a culture sketched both by social and political allusion, it is a self-referential display of literary and verbal forms, and it is a quasi-anthropological analysis of a variety of socially embedded rites of initiation, conflict and sympathetic magic. The orators are compulsive verbalisers, all with some apprehension of the malaise, some with a felt need for spiritual leadership; but all bound by their own social and psychological conditioning, and all doomed to failure. The Ciceronian political ideal, mirrored in the British educational and diplomatic system, may have provided an ironical justification for the work's final structure, with parallels to be found between *De Oratore*, on the orator's training (*inventio, dispositio* and *elocutio*), and Book I (Address, Argument, Statement); between *Brutus* and Book II; and between *Orator*, partly autobiographical and concerned with the ideal orator, and Book III. For Cicero the orator was a statesman, but Auden is looking to see how a writer/schoolmaster might be politically effective in a world where the

---

[37]W.H. Auden, *'In Solitude for Company': W.H. Auden After 1940*, ed. Katherine Bucknell and Nicholas Jenkins (Oxford: Clarendon Press, 1995), 120.

[38]See, for example, Patricia Bizzell and Bruce Herzberg, *The Rhetorical Tradition* (Boston: Bedford Books of St. Martin's Press, 1990), 149.

existing orators are corrupt. By his virtuoso range of parody and stylistic allusion, Auden shows that he is as much concerned with rhetoric as with individual or social psychology; and of course the whole work shows a sustained interest in education.[39]

Although the nexus generated by Fuller is fruitful and on the mark, that same nexus does not end with the aforementioned Ciceronian treatises. It will be argued that besides *De Oratore* (55 B.C.E.), *Brutus* (46 B.C.E.), and (*Orator*) (46 B.C.E.), *De Inventione* (84 B.C.E.) serves an important role in illuminating the macro-rhetorical dimensions of Auden's *The Orators.*

Oratory and rhetorical theory played a pivotal role in Roman education and literature[40] and "to Cicero, oratory was the highest form of literature":[41]

> Oratory was, of all forms of literature, the most congenial to the Roman temperament, and it is only in Roman times that Isocrates' theory of education as "learning to speak well on great subjects" came into his own, when rhetorical and higher education became synonymous terms. Rhetoric now claimed all literature as its province and poetry came to be looked upon as rhetoric in verse.[42]

As Cicero's progenitor, we can look to Isocrates (436–338 B.C.E.) who bridged the gap between philosophy and rhetoric in the sophistic tradition, and for whom the education of the individual within the rhetorical tradition was the best training ground for "talented men to become ethical and effective political leaders."[43] Unlike the first sophists who—with their itinerant lifestyles—set up temporary shingles in one town and then another and charged fees for their expertise, Isocrates set up his own school and tried to instill some rigor in the program of study, thereby engendering an ennobling rather than an ignoble pedagogical experience.[44] This, too, was Cicero's intent.

---

[39]John Fuller, *W.H. Auden: A Commentary* (Princeton: Princeton University Press, 1998), 86–87.

[40]*The Cambridge History of Classical Literature,* eds. E.J. Kenney and W.V. Clausen (Cambridge: Cambridge University Press, 1982), 2:233.

[41]Grube, 163.

[42]Ibid., 163.

[43]Bizzell and Herzberg, 25.

[44]Ibid., 25.

Auden's situating of Book I of *The Orators* within a rhetorical paradigm is relevant to the understanding of Auden's poetic-rhetorical reconciliations both in terms of subject and style. And as George Kennedy suggests in *The Art of Rhetoric in the Roman World*, "with the arrival of the empire the opportunities for persuasion in oratory decreased,"[45] and while oratorical opportunities dwindled, poetry flourished. Kennedy explains this seeming paradox as follows:

> Poetry can criticize without exacerbating. It can present evils of tyranny to a tyrant or the virtues freedom to a despot as long as it gives the impression of aiming primarily at literary distinction and preserves its innate ambiguity and universality.... But at a time when political oratory grew silent, the poets continued to teach, to charm, and to move with the techniques of both the old and the new rhetoric.[46]

In 60 B.C.E., with the formation of the First Triumvirate, Cicero found himself in a most unenviable and portentous place.[47] To Caesar, he was an enemy, to Crassus, he was contemptible, and to Pompey, he was loathsome.[48] In light of his *First Catilinarian*, a charge was made against Cicero that he "caused the execution without trial of Roman citizens involved in the Catilinarian conspiracy.[49] Among other untoward circumstances for Rome, and for Cicero, politically and personally, in spite of the disintegration of the Triumvirate in 53 B.C.E., the once flourishing Republic was in shambles.[50] With Caesar's victory in 49 B.C.E., Rome was a bona fide dictatorship.[51] And as Gotoff says, "the talents even of a consummate orator were superfluous."[52] With the assassination of Caesar in 44 B.C.E., while on Italy's east coast, Cicero heard "that the Senate was to reconvene and attempt to reassert its author-

---

[45]George Kennedy, *The Art of Rhetoric in the Roman World* (Princeton: Princeton University Press, 1972), 387.

[46]Ibid., 387.

[47]Harold C. Gotoff, *Cicero's Elegant Style/An Analysis of the Pro Archia* (Urbana: University of Illinois Press, 1979), 14.

[48]Ibid., 14–15.

[49]Ibid., 15.

[50]Ibid., 16.

[51]Ibid., 16.

[52]Ibid., 16.

ity."[53] Cicero returned to Rome, eminently prepared to speak against Marc Antony, Caesar's successor, and on December 7, 43 B.C.E., he was murdered on the order of Marc Antony.[54] In his excellent book *Controlling Laughter: Political Humor in the Late Roman Republic*, Anthony Corbeill claims that it was Cicero's use of humor, particularly in his *Second Phillipic*, that might have precipitated his own death:[55]

> This speech, filled with humorous abuse redolent of the period before the civil war, attests to Cicero's attempts to reestablish himself as a public representative of traditional Republican values. His bitter private jests about Antonius not being slain on the Ides resemble earlier jokes in which he desires the death of a political foe.... Antonius eventually gave Cicero's *Phillipics* as the reason for proscribing the orator and nailing his head and hands to the speaker's rostrum in the forum.[56]

Cicero seems to have been politically circumspect when he should have exercised boldness, and almost feckless when prudence should have been the order of the day. In terms of Cicero's legacy, Gotoff states,

> Cicero is criticized for his vanity and the lack of political insight which prevented him from fully understanding the realities of the situation at Rome. He is criticized for accommodation and cowardice in the 50's, when he silenced himself in the face of the extra-constitutional power of the Triumvirate. But, in the end, when he saw a faint ray of hope that the Republic might be revived, he rejected caution and spoke out with vehemence and effectiveness.... He was a central and often dominating participant for nearly forty years in the complex and not infrequently political system at Rome. If at the end his principles or his convictions led him to associate himself with the losing side, he shared that error with many Roman political insiders; and the evidence does not support the view that in his adherence to the Senatorial side he was blind to the weakness, insincerity, and corruption of other advocates of that cause.[57]

---

[53]Ibid., 17.

[54]Ibid., 17.

[55]Anthony Corbeill, *Controlling Laughter: Political Humor in the Late Roman Republic* (Princeton: Princeton University Press, 1996), 217.

[56]Ibid., 215–16.

[57]Gotoff, 17–18; see also *The Cambridge History of Classical Literature*, 233.

In his foreword to the 1966 revised edition of *The Orators*, Auden says, "the central theme of *The Orators* seems to be Hero-worship, and we all know what that can lead to politically."[58] James Ramsay MacDonald's political career[59] in Britain parallels Cicero's in several significant ways. Like Cicero, MacDonald was a political leader of great longevity and import. And although Cicero did not champion the cause of the working class, according to Neal Wood in his superb book, *Cicero's Social and Political Thought*, in theory, he argued for

> the principles of natural law and justice, and of universal moral equality; a patriotic and dedicated republicanism; a vigorous advocacy of liberty, impassioned rejection of tyranny, and persuasive justification of tyrannicide; a firm belief in constitutionalism, the rule of law, and the mixed constitution; a strong faith in the sanctity of private property, in the importance of its accumulation, and the opinion that the primary purpose of state and law was the preservation of property and property differentials; a conception of proportionate social and political equality, entailing a hierarchy of differential rights and duties; a vague ideal of rule by a "natural aristocracy"; and a moderate and enlightened religious and epistemological skepticism.[60]

Cicero, like MacDonald, worked diligently to try to correct the ills in the late Republic and England respectively. According to Wood, Cicero advanced the causal argument that "social and political ills arise from the irrationality of human beings," and that through his writings, he attempted "to purify their psyches by revealing to them their false beliefs and by persuading them to follow the principles of rational conduct and civic virtue that he so convincingly expounds."[61] But all of the wisdom and eloquence was to no avail.[62] He was, according to Wood, ultimately ineffec-

---

[58]Auden, *The Orators*, vii–viii.

[59]See the discussion of MacDonald in Stan Smith, "Loyalty and Interest: Auden, Modernism, and the Politics of Pedagogy," *Textual Practice* 4.1 (1990): 68.

[60]Neal Wood, *Cicero's Social and Political Thought* (Berkeley: University of California Press, 1988), 4.

[61]Ibid., 212.

[62]Ibid., 212.

tual in "prescribing an effective therapy"[63] for the "malady of the ruling class."[64]

As an antiwar Socialist, MacDonald seemed to have been seduced, according to Robert Garner, "by the trappings of office and the eager courting of the Establishment."[65] In the end, his career was "marked by controversy and tragedy. His name, for many, is synonymous with betrayal."[66] In 1931, he formed a National Government which, according to Garner, "became in all but name a Conservative Administration."[67] There was seemingly no forgiveness for his desertion, and as Garner suggests, although his reputation would have stayed intact had he retained his position as Labor leader, "for MacDonald, however, this option was equally unacceptable because he would then have been forced to attack the very economy measures which he thought were in the national interest."[68] MacDonald found himself on the horns of a dilemma with respect to the economic crisis. An integral part of the malaise was economic, and the tempered voice of John Maynard Keynes seemed to have fallen on deaf ears—at least MacDonald's. Although, as Robert Heilbroner[69] suggests, Keynes' notion of a managed capitalism,[70] or the "'socialization' of investment"[71] might seem "misguided," he does offer up his plaudits to the economist:

> One might quibble with Keynes's theories, with his diagnosis and with his cure—although, in justice, it must be said that no more thoughtful theory, no profounder diagnosis, and no more convincing cure was propounded by those who insisted that Keynes was only a mischievous meddler with a system that worked well enough. But no one could gainsay his aim: the creation of a capitalist economy in which unemployment—the

---

[63]Ibid., 213.

[64]Ibid., 213.

[65]Robert Garner, "James Ramsay MacDonald," in *Modern British Statesmen 1867–1945*, ed. Richard Kelly and John Cantrell (Manchester: Manchester University Press, 1997), 144.

[66]Ibid., 144.

[67]Ibid., 153.

[68]Ibid., 155.

[69]Robert L. Heilbroner, *The Worldly Philosophers*, rev. 7th ed. (New York: Touchstone, 1999).

[70]Ibid., 278.

[71]Ibid., 279.

greatest and gravest threat to its continuance—would be largely eliminated.[72]

In a biography of MacDonald, David Marquand argues that MacDonald's fatal mistake was his very rejection of Keynes's advice,[73] given his ill-conceived and ill-fated attempts at parity. Keynes believed that the key to turning around the economic crisis was devaluing of the currency and reducing unemployment. MacDonald chose "to follow a middle way between the harsh orthodoxies of the past and the still untried doctrines of the future,"[74] and "it was the most tragic, as well as the most disastrous mistake of MacDonald's life."[75]

One can surmise that Auden understood the far-reaching implications of rhetoric and economics in the political arena and possessed awareness of Keynes's role in the doomed British economic recovery. Keynes, in fact, backed Auden's and Isherwood's play *On the Frontier*[76] and provided assistance in other arenas as well. After dinner with Auden in Cambridge in 1938,[77] Keynes reflected on the evening:

> He was most charming, intelligent, straightforward, youthful, a sort of senior undergraduate; altogether delightful, but but but— his finger nails are eaten to the bones with dirt and wet, one of the worst cases ever, like a preparatory schoolboy. So the infantilism is not altogether put on. It was most disconcerting. For all other impressions so favourable. But these horrid fingers cannot lie. They must be believed. I talked to him about F.6 [*The Ascent of F.6*, the play he had written with Christopher Isherwood]. He has re-written the last part and would like us to look at it again.[78]

Auden's ambivalence about rhetoric and its role in the political arena appears almost luminously. In spite of rhetoric's place as the

---

[72]Ibid., 279–80.

[73]David Marquand, *James Ramsay MacDonald* (London: Jonathan Cape, 1977), 614.

[74]Ibid., 613.

[75]Ibid., 614.

[76]Edward Mendelson, *Early Auden* (New York: Viking Press, 1981), 268.

[77]Edward Mendelson, *Later Auden* (New York: Farrar, Straus and Giroux, 1999), 45.

[78]Robert Skidelsky, *John Maynard Keynes*, vol. 2 (New York: Allen Lane, 1992), 628.

backbone of education, literature and culture, including the socio-political arena, rhetoric is—to this very day—sorely misunder-stood as an *ersatz* of sorts for the "real thing." What that real thing is no one seems to know, but the bifurcation seems to be made be-tween action and words (rhetoric), and the concomitant allegation that the main stuff of a politician's vocation is articulating ideas that have no basis in reality, i.e., whose words belie reality, and reflect selfish pursuits bereft of any common good, and which are—in the end—futile. However, this is really a perversion of the affirmation of the sophistic notion of human knowledge as exem-plified in the words of Protagoras: "Of all things the measure is man, of things that are that they are, and of things that are not that they are not."[79] All knowledge is context bound and reflective upon human limitations as expressed in the treatise *Dissoi Logoi*, which argues that "the assignment of a particular value depends on social and historical circumstances,"[80] with multifarious soci-etal manifestations, including economics and diplomacy.[81]

In spite of the tragic outcome, like Cicero, MacDonald was considered one of the preeminent orators of his time.[82] Marquand even attributes his physical deterioration in the 1930s in part to his psychological malaise—an observation that might not have gone unnoticed by Auden who was profoundly influenced by the work of Georg Groddeck in his *The Book of The It*,[83] and more directly, the work of Homer Lane and John Layard, espousing the notion that illnesses of the psyche engender physical malady.[84] The issue does not seem to be so much one of the corrupted orator, as the ineffectual orator who will necessarily find himself in a "catch-22."

The subject and style of Book I of *The Orators* is irrefutably rhetorical, the main influences being Cicero's *De Inventione* and *De Oratore*. The structure suggests speechmaking with a beginning, a middle and an end. The scene is the Larchfield School where Au-

---

[79]Bizzell and Herzberg, 23.

[80]Ibid., 23.

[81]Ibid., 23

[82]Marquand, 791.

[83]Georg Groddeck, *The Book of the It* (New York: Vintage Books, 1961).

[84]See the excellent discussion of the Groddeck, Lane, Layard influ-ences in Firchow.

den was a teacher from March 1930 through the summer of 1932,[85] and according to Stan Smith, *The Orators* espouses a vilification of "the bad faith at the heart of 'the best modern ways' of contemporary pedagogy."[86] The pedagogy does not excise the evils of oratory, but rather exercises it, so that "'persuading people' is the orator's aim, and 'management by flattery' and the exploitation of loyalty are skills practiced, and taught in the world of *The Orators* (as well as in the British Public schools)."[87] According to Grube, the Ciceronian curriculum was a "thorough general training in philosophy (including logic, ethics, and psychology), in political science, history and law, with a stiff Honour course in the art of speech in both Latin and Greek."[88] This is precisely Plato's indictment of rhetoric in his dialogue *Gorgias* (386 B.C.E.), in which he claims, through the arguments of Socrates, that rhetoric *is* flattery and serves as no pathway to truth.[89] Cicero, too was concerned with rhetoric's role in society, where, in his *De Inventione*, his most immature work which was "hardly more than an elaborate notebook in which he recorded the dictation of his teacher,"[90] Cicero articulates his concerns regarding the relationship between wisdom and eloquence:

> I have often seriously debated with myself whether men and communities have received more good or evil from oratory and a consuming devotion to eloquence. For when I ponder the troubles in our commonwealth, and run over in my mind the ancient misfortunes of mighty cities, I see that no little part of the disasters was brought about by men of eloquence. When, on the other hand, I begin to search in the records of literature for events which occurred before the period which our generation can remember, I find that many cities have been founded, that the flames of a multitude of wars have been extinguished, and that the strongest alliances and most sacred friendships have been formed not only by the use of the reason but also more easily by the help of eloquence. For my own part, after long thought, I

---

[85]Stan Smith, "Loyalty and Interest: Auden, Modernism, and the Politics of Pedagogy," *Textual Practice* 4.1 (1990): 54.

[86]Ibid., 56.

[87]Ibid., 58.

[88]Grube, 171.

[89]Bizzell and Herzberg, 72.

[90]Cicero, *De Inventione*, intro., trans. H.M. Hubbell (Cambridge: Harvard Univerity Press), vii.

have been led by reason itself to hold this opinion first and fore-most, that wisdom without eloquence does too little for the good of the states, but that eloquence without wisdom is generally highly disadvantageous and is never helpful. Therefore if anyone neglects the study of philosophy and moral conduct, which is the highest and most honourable of pursuits, and devotes his whole energy to the practice of oratory, his civic life is nurtured into something useless to himself and harmful to his country; but the man who equips himself with the weapons of eloquence, not to be able to attack the welfare of his country but to defend it, he, I think, will be a citizen most helpful and most devoted both to his own interests and those of his community. Moreover, if we wish to consider the origin of this thing we call eloquence—whether it be an art, a study, a skill, or a gift of nature—we shall find that it arose from most honourable causes and continued on its way from the best of reasons.[91]

Cicero advances the notion that "in the greatest undertakings of peace and war, [eloquence] served the highest interests of mankind. But when a certain agreeableness of manner—a de-praved imitation of virtue—acquired the power of eloquence un-accompanied by any consideration of moral duty, then low cun-ning supported by talent grew accustomed to corrupt cities and undermined the lives of men."[92]

Monroe Spears argues for a double irony in "Address for a Prize-Day," with the movement from irony and absurdity to seri-ousness and back to absurdity and irony.[93] The second part of Book I, according to Spears, "deals with the search for a hero, re-deemer, savior; and its chief effect is to ridicule both the search for a political leader (and the adolescent hero-worshipper upon which it is based) and the search for a secular savior and redeemer."[94] John Fuller sees "Argument" as "an adolescent day-dream about the elusive Leader, and the sanctimonious prayers which he in-spires."[95] According to Fuller, Part III of Book I entitled "State-

---

[91]Ibid. , I. 1–2

[92]Ibid., I. 3–4

[93]Monroe K. Spears, *The Poetry of W.H. Auden*, (New York: Oxford University Press, 1963), 48.

[94]Ibid., 49.

[95]John Fuller, *W.H. Auden: A Commentary* (Princeton: Princeton University Press, 1998), 90.

ment" is a "display of prophetic fatalism,"[96] with a cataloguing of many different individuals. As Davison explains:

> The quality of "statement" is obvious in the method of cataloguing derived from St. John Pearse's *Anabase*. "Statement" contains one list of variously talented individuals, a second list in which examples of good fortune are set against examples of bad, a shorter list which seems to have the function of stressing man's animal origin, and finally a list of predictions, some serious and pessimistic, others flippant, the whole being interspersed by expressions of the cyclical nature of existence.[97]

A few of the talented individuals showcase their verbal aptitude, like the eloquent one who "persuades committees of the value of spending," and "one announces weddings in a solemn voice."[98]

In the fourth part of Book I, "Letter to a Wound," Auden writes a letter to his wound, which is a metaphor for both his psychological illness and a recent surgery for a rectal fissure. Fuller claims that "the wound enables the writer to understand various other forms of perverted love...."[99] Mendelson argues for a relationship between "Address for a Prize-Day" and "Letter to a Wound," in which both parts are "spoken by individual leaders, [and] have confident brisk styles that parody the manner of relatively mature speakers—the patronizing and authoritative tone used in a meeting-hall and that used by a relaxed, experienced and dispassionate lover."[100] For Mendelson, the "potential solipsism of 'Statement' yields the absolute solipsism of 'Letter to a Wound.'"[101] So the public, "speechified" rhetoric which manifests itself in an oratorical mode has given way to a more private rhetoric, which manifests itself in the epistolary mode.[102]

Given its serious-parodistic tone, Book I is a genuine instantiation of Auden's ambivalence about language. And although Cicero believed, like Isocrates, that language and concomitant speech are the cachet of a civilized people and a civilized society, they were

[96]Ibid., 90.

[97]Davison, 173.

[98]*The Orators*, 22.

[99]Fuller, 98.

[100]Mendelson, "The Coherence of Auden's *The Orators*," 123.

[101]Ibid., 122.

[102]Emig, 65–67.

equally aware of its deficiencies and exploitations in the hands of the morally corrupt, which occurred primarily with the untoward bifurcation between rhetoric and philosophy, and wisdom and eloquence. Clearly, Auden too is doubtful of language's role in promoting good and militating against the corruption of power. The paradox of Book I of *The Orators* coalescing tenets of *De Inventione*, Cicero's most immature work, and *De Oratore*, Cicero's most mature work[103] ought not go unnoticed. In the prefatory note to *The Collected Poetry* (1945), Auden comments that *The Orators* is "The fair notion fatally injured," as W.H. Sellers says, "by youthful incompetence or impatience."[104]

For Spears, all four sections of Book I, "The Initiates," represent four of the "common forms of expository prose that English studies would be likely to deal with in school: oration or public speech, argument, statement or scientific exposition, letter or informal style."[105]

One can also conceive of Book I of *The Orators* as exemplifying the Ciceronian notion of *stasis*. *Stasis*, originating in Hellenistic rhetoric with Hermagoras, applied originally to judicial oratory, with Cicero's subsequent application of *stasis* to deliberative and demonstrative oratory.[106] Simultaneous with Auden's experimentation with genres: epideictic (demonstrative), judicial (forensic) and deliberative (political),[107] he is experimenting with *stasis*, thought to be the most important rhetorical development in the two centuries following Aristotle's death.[108]

In *De Inventione*, Cicero states that in pursuit of examining a case, one must look at the *quaestio* (the question), the *ratio* (the excuse or reason), the *indicatio* (the point for the judge's decision), and the *firmamentum* (the foundation or supporting argument).[109] The first two words of Book I, "The Initiates," "Address for a

---

[103]Bizzell and Herzberg, 195–97.

[104]W.H. Sellers, "New Light On Auden's *The Orators*," *PMLA* 82 (1967): 455.

[105]Spears, 49.

[106]Kennedy, 117.

[107]Cicero, *De Inventione*, I. 7.

[108]Bizzell and Herzberg, 30.

[109]Cicero, *De Inventione*, I.18.

Prize-Day," are "Commemoration. Commemoration,"[110] suggesting an epideictic (demonstrative) thrust and tone. The question
posed is "Not what does it mean to them, there, then. What does it
mean to us, here, now?"[111] Epideictic discourse is of the present
tense, the objective of which is to praise or blame. Auden is laying
blame squarely on the shoulders of the educators for the inadequate training given to the students[112]. The section is punctuated
by the interrogative, "What do you think about England, this
country of ours where nobody is well?"[113] In the next section of
"Address for a Prize-Day," Auden offers a corrective to the
malaise with an analeptic of sorts. Most scholars acknowledge the
influences of D.H. Lawrence in his *Fantasia of the Unconscious* and
Dante's *Purgatorio*, with the latter's categories of sinners: the excessive lovers of self, the defective lovers, and the perverted lovers.[114]
One can also view this section as a pastiche of the myth of the
charioteer in Plato's *Phaedrus*, in which the schoolmaster instructs
the students using the allegory of the three lovers. In the *Phaedrus*
"the relationship between Socrates and Phaedrus enacts this ideal
pedagogy"[115] where "the student should take care to choose a
teacher who will raise the student to the teacher's higher level, and
the teacher should take care to choose a student who will not drag
the teacher down."[116]

---

[110]*The Orators*, 7.

[111]Ibid., 7.

[112]See the excellent essay by Trevor Davison, "The Method of Auden's
'The Orators,'" *The Durham University Journal* n.s. 32.3 (1971), which excels
at examining both the macro- and micro-rhetorical dimensions. Davison
sees Auden castigating the school system as articulated by Auden in his
essay "Honour," in which schoolmasters make appeals to honor and
loyalty, in which "the whole of our moral life was based on fear, on fear of
the community, not to mention the temptation it offered to the natural
informer, and fear is not a healthy basis. It makes one furtive and
dishonest and unadventurous. The best reason I have for opposing Fascism is that at school I lived in a Fascist state" (17). The essay "Honour"
appears in *The Old School*, ed. Graham Greene (London: Jonathan Cape,
1934), 9–20.

[113]*The Orators*, 8.

[114]See, for example, Edward Mendelson, "The Coherence of Auden's
The Orators," *ELH* 35 (1968): 114–33.

[115]Bizzell and Herzberg, 59.

[116]Ibid., 58–59.

Book II, entitled "Journal of an Airman," embodies tenets of Cicero's treatise *Brutus*. According to Kennedy, Cicero had affection for Brutus, and although their dual interests in political dispositions and philosophy converged, Cicero was unsuccessful in changing Brutus' literary tastes.[117] Besides being a sweeping history of eloquence in Rome,[118] *Brutus* is a commentary on what was known as the Atticist-Asianist controversy, as well as a lament of sorts for oratory and its imminent demise,[119] for "as the Empire was consolidated, political oratory, that had been the lifeblood of Cicero, lost importance; forensic speeches rarely swayed wide emotions, and there was more and more call for flattering panegyric. The consequent loss of prestige sustained by oratory was called its decay and corruption; and the phenomenon aroused widespread speculation."[120] Cicero was attacked as conforming to an Asiatic style of oratory, characterized by inflation and emptiness, while the Atticists were characterized by conciseness and wholeness.[121] Undergirding all of Roman oratory, as has been already shown, is the educational system, and as Amy Richlin discusses in her article, "Gender and Rhetoric: Producing Manhood in the Schools," in Roman society, oratory was a male-dominated activity, with "the rhetorical schools and performance halls as a locus of gender construction, a place where manhood is contested, defended, defined, and even produced."[122] Richlin continues the discussion by explaining the notion of oratorical cultivations as a crucial rite of passage:

> But freeborn Roman boys, each year on the day of the Liberalia (March 17), were brought by their fathers to the forum, clad for the first time in the *toga virilis*, in a *rite de passage* that may have included a physical inspection of the boy's genitalia; the day, then, links the male body with place, dress and male bonding. Indeed, apprenticeship to a great orator was an important factor

[117]Kennedy, 246.

[118]Grube, 179.

[119]*The Cambridge History of Classical Literature*, 45.

[120]Ibid., 45.

[121]See the excellent essay by Amy Richlin, "Gender and Rhetoric: Producing Manhood in the Schools," in *Roman Eloquence: Rhetoric in Society and Literature*, ed. William J. Dominik (London: Routledge, 1997), 106.

[122]Ibid., 90.

in this Roman *rite de passage*. It was known as the *tirocinium fori*
("recruitment for the forum").... Whatever the process was really
like, we have some attestations that it was charged with emotions and sentiments similar to those we attach to boarding
school or summer camp, and that it involved a strong hierarchical bonding between seniors and juniors.[123]

And as Richlin points out, Cicero alludes to this *sine qua non* male
mentorship in the *Brutus* (304–12), with a begrudging commenda-
tion in *Brutus* (210–11) to the women who taught their sons to
speak well.[124] But part and parcel of the Atticist-Asianist controversy previously discussed was the fact that the Asianist style of
oratory, and the man who embodied the Asianist style, became associated with effeminacy and a diminished physical excellence as
well.[125] In *Brutus*, Cicero defends the Asianist style, with Cicero
and Hortensius, and not Brutus and Calvus as the true heroes of
Roman oratory.[126]

As Fuller explains, "Book II, 'Journal of an Airman,' contains
the central action of the whole work."[127] Auden provided an explanation of the work to Naomi Mitchison in August 1931: "I am
now writing the second half, which is the situation seen from
within the Hero.... The flying symbolism is I imagine fairly obvious. The chief strands are his Uncle (Heredity-Matrilineal descent
and initiations), belief in a universal conspiracy (the secret society
mind), kleptomania (the worm in the root)."[128] According to
Spears, "Journal of an Airman" shows the initiate as a man
"dedicated to the overthrow of the society represented by the ora-
tor-initiates of the first book."[129] According to Kennedy, given "the
note of political despair [which] recurs throughout the *Brutus*,"[130]
some scholars suggest "that one of Cicero's objectives was to incite
Brutus to rid Rome of Caesar."[131] Spears characterizes him as

---

[123]Ibid., 92–93.

[124]Ibid., 93.

[125]Ibid., 106.

[126]Ibid., 107.

[127]Fuller, 99.

[128]Ibid., 99.

[129]Spears, 50.

[130]Kennedy, 247.

[131]Ibid., 247.

something of a romantic figure[132] whose actions might correspond to the flourishes of the Asianist oratorical style. The flying symbolism, as manifested in the "flying tricksters," based on the work of anthropologist John Layard, involved rites dealing with "the reanimation of the dead," and characteristics including homosexuality.[133] The issues of sexuality and rites of passage are evident in both the *Brutus* and "Journal of an Airman."

In Book III of *The Orators*, entitled "Odes," Auden hearkens back to a fundamental Ciceronian question: what constitutes an ideal orator? Like "Odes," and *The Orators* as a whole, the *Orator*, written in 46 B.C.E., is an apologia on behalf of his oratorical career.[134] The *Orator* is a vehement and unequivocal defense of the Asianist style, which had been highly criticized by the Atticists. Auden's "Odes" too seem to be a modernist's—or even post-modernist's—refutation of the Atticists' charges against the Asianists, among whom Cicero was the most vociferous, and he is credited with the creation of the artistic Latin prose.[135] Of the five canons of rhetoric, the one that is at the heart of the *Orator*, is style (*elocutio*).[136] And the aspect of style bridging the *Orator* and Book III of *The Orators* is the trope of the metaphor.

As Spears explains, the five odes and epilogue of Book III are "the public utterances (as odes traditionally are) of the ambivalent bourgeois schoolmaster who is committed to the overthrow of what the school stands for."[137] A savior is needed who can restore "social and spiritual health."[138] But the locus of the sanguine and salutary won't be found with the ideal orator, for as Spears says in light of his reading of the first ode, "the dreamer wakes, and the only orator is a beggar in the courtyard."[139] According to the *Compact Edition of the Oxford English Dictionary*, the modern conception of an ode is "a rimed (rarely unrimed) lyric, often in the form of an

---

[132]Spears, 50.

[133]Fuller, 100.

[134]Cicero, *Orator*, trans., intro. H.M. Hubbell (Cambridge: Harvard University Press, 1942), 297.

[135]Ibid., 298.

[136]Kennedy, 257.

[137]Spears, 53.

[138]Fuller, 113.

[139]Spears, 53.

address; generally dignified or exalted in subject, feeling, and style, but sometimes (in earlier use) simple and familiar (though less so than a song)." Auden's odes seem to suggest another rapprochement between the Atticist and the Asianist styles. And the "address" is a hybridization of the judicial, and epideictic deliberative genres, as well as the three styles: plain, middle and grand.[140]

A fruitful gateway point in understanding Auden's attempts at a rapprochement between the poetic and the rhetorical in *The Orators* is the work of Kenneth Burke, considered one of the preeminent critics of the twentieth century. In a book review of Burke's *The Philosophy of Literary Form*, which Auden entitled "A Grammar of Assent," Auden—although praiseworthy of Burke's illumined understanding of poetry—says:

> It is the siege mentality, I think, that makes Mr. Burke overdo the division between the semantic and the poetic, that makes him emphasize, quite rightly, the role of synecdoche in the poetic, but because it is shared by the semantic vocabulary, ignore an equally important function of words namely the way in which they recover the Possible from the Actual.[141]

The Burkean influence on Auden was not left untested by the critics. In his essay "Changes of Attitude and Rhetoric in Auden's Poetry,"[142] Randall Jarrell expresses his indebtedness to one of Burke's books, *Attitudes Towards History*. However, indebtedness is also manifest in attributing to Auden's poetry a dependence on perspective by incongruity. In Burke's 1935 work *Permanence & Change*, Part II, chapter 3 explains the incongruity as metaphor: "Indeed, the metaphor always has about it precisely this revealing of hitherto unsuspected connectives which we may note in the progression of a dream. It appeals by exemplifying relationships between objects which our customary rational vocabulary has ignored."[143] In the *Orator*, Cicero discusses the metaphor and its relationship to the three styles, and ultimately what makes an eloquent speaker:

[140]Cicero, *Orator*, 90–92.

[141]W.H. Auden, "The Grammar Of Assent," *New Republic*, 14 July 1941, 59.

[142]Randall Jarrell, "Changes of Attitude and Rhetoric in Auden's Poetry," *The Southern Review* 7.2 (1941–42): 326–49.

[143]Kenneth Burke, *Permanence & Change* (Los Altos, CA: Hermes Publications, 1954), 90.

He in fact is eloquent who can discuss commonplace matters simply, lofty subjects impressively, and topics ranging between in a tempered style. You will say, "There never was such a man." I grant it; for I am arguing for my ideal, not what I have actually seen, and I return to that Platonic Idea of which I had spoken; though we do not see it, still it is possible to grasp it with the mind.... He, then, will be an eloquent speaker—to repeat my former definition—who can discuss trivial matters in a plain style, matters of moderate significance in the tempered style, and weighty affairs in the grand manner.[144]

In his foreword to *The Orators*, Auden credits Charles Baudelaire's *Intimate Journals*[145] as one of his sources serving as a "stimulus to writing *Journal of an Airman*."[146] In *Permanence & Change*, Burke quotes M. Jean Royere who "noted the great prevalence of metonymy and 'systematic catachreses;'" and "discusses Baudelaire's 'systematic use of the most illogical figure of speech, the catachresis (or mixed metaphor), which might be called the metaphor and hyperbole in one.'"[147] And although Aristotle, according to Cicero, notes the "catachresis" as a misuse of terms,[148] Aristotle did acknowledge the epistemological dimensions of the metaphorical construct. And as a poet, how could Auden not have embraced this idea?

Auden's poetry has been a fascination to the medical community—not too surprising given his exposure to medicine and his interest in science.[149] Dr. Oliver Sacks, author of—among other noted works—*Awakenings* and *An Anthropologist on Mars*, and who has studied the relationship between autism and creativity, befriended Auden in the last few years of the poet's life and offered up the following paean:

---

[144]Cicero, *Orator*, 100–101.

[145]Auden wrote the "Introduction" to the Christopher Isherwood translation of *Intimate Journals* (Hollywood: Marcel Rodd, 1947), 13–28.

[146]Auden, *The Orators*, vii.

[147]Burke, *Permanence & Change*, 116.

[148]Cicero, *Orator*, 94.

[149]See W.H. Auden, "A Literary Transference," *The Southern Review* 6 (1940–41): 78–86; "Until my sixteenth year I read no poetry. Brought up in a family which was more scientific than literary, I had been the sole autocratic inhabitant of a dream country of lead mines, narrow-gauge tramways, and overshot waterwheels" (78).

That afternoon sensitized me to the concept of cosiness, and
amongst other things, drew my attention to something which
runs through all his poems, but which I had never properly seen
before then; his delight in the cosiness of language itself, the fit-
ting-together of words and ideas, the way in which phrase is fitted into phrase, the way in which every word is embodied, en-
cysted, nested cosily in its right and proper place, where it belongs at home in the body of the poem.[150]

Although conventional wisdom would claim that the poetry is
comprised of semantic and syntactic infractions, Dr. Sacks recognized the "commensurateness," the correspondence between word
and idea usually reserved for the scientific mind and scientific discourse, but then again, Auden, as the son of a physician, had "a
deep love and understanding of doctors and medicine—he would,
I am sure, himself have been one of our greatest physicians, had he
not felt 'elected' or 'ordained' (other favourite words!) from his
earliest years, for the wider destiny of a poet and genius."[151] Not
unlike a post-modernist like Auden, Cicero acknowledged the
shifting of semantic sands from one social, historical, and cultural
context to another. The ideal orator must locate the proper genre
and style, and manifest that proper balance between wisdom and
eloquence.

For Cicero, speech is a divine faculty,[152] and bereft of it, one is
left without human reason. Wood summarizes this relationship between *ratio* and *oratorio*:

> Language and its constituent elements are the raw materials of
> reason, the means by which reason is expressed and articulated,
> whether internally through thought and ratiocination or exter-
> nally through the written and spoken word.[153]

Presumably our entire epistemic derives from our ability to reason,
where the predominant *telos* is truth.[154] Cicero argues that the soul

---

[150]Dr. Oliver Sacks, "Dear Mr. A," in *W.H. Auden: A Tribute*, ed.
Stephen Spender (London: Weidenfeld and Nicholson, 1975), 189.

[151]Ibid., 191. Gertrude Stein too was a formal student of medicine,
having almost completed a medical degree at Johns Hopkins University
and whose language too seems ineluctably influencd by science and
medicine.

[152]Wood, 81.

[153]Ibid., 81.

[154]Ibid., 81.

consists of a rational part and an irrational part. The rational part is reason centered, with a cachet of peace and tranquillity.[155] The irrational part is hostile to reason, with a cachet of passions: anger, recklessness, desire, delight, fear and grief.[156] An individual, to maintain his virtue, must harness the irrational part—always entropic, determined to overtake reason.[157] Cicero propounds the notion that the guiding force toward irrationality is our desire for pleasure—which can be both good and evil.[158] And as Wood states, "The unrestrained pursuit of pleasure, however, in the forms of sensual gratification, self-aggrandizement, avarice, and the lust for power, are mainly responsible for the evil of the world. Anyone succumbing to these pleasures suffers from a disordered or diseased psyche, an unnatural and intemperate soul."[159] The list seems to comport with Auden's interest in the Seven Deadly Sins,[160] as instantiated in *The Orators*. Wood suggests that Cicero's entire life "can be said to have been dedicated to remedying what he takes to be the widespread malady afflicting his countrymen which he holds responsible for the serious troubles besetting the late Roman Republic."[161]

At the conclusion of *The Orators*, the scales seem to tip on the side of pessimism, with a distorted and perverted eloquence winning out over wisdom. But, then again, for Auden, as it was for Cicero, our only hope for *humanitas* resides in our ability to communicate.[162]

---

[155]Ibid., 83.

[156]Ibid., 83.

[157]Ibid., 83.

[158]Ibid., 86.

[159]Ibid., 86.

[160]See, for example, Fuller, 122.

[161]Wood, 87.

[162]See Neal Wood, *Communism and British Intellectuals* (New York: Columbia University Press, 1959), for a brilliant discussion of the relationship between British politics of the 1930s and poetry. Wood makes some very astute comments about Auden. See particularly 105–6; 110–11.

Chorus and Character
in Auden and Isherwood's
The Dog Beneath the Skin:
A Poetic Shaggy Dog Story
for a Revolutionary Theater

Owen E. Brady

The Auden and Isherwood plays have been mistakenly relegated to the category of 1930s agitation propaganda that doesn't wear well after that decade. Not so. The Dog Beneath the Skin *is a madcap and disturbing look at the fallacies of middle class life that are not so different now than in 1935. Brady asserts that the words are in a partnership with a choice of stage manifestations that make the visual at least an equal partner with the audible and give the audience a head-turning theatrical experience.*

In the 1930s, Auden collaborated with Christopher Isherwood to produce three plays for The Group Theatre in London: *The Dog Beneath the Skin*, *The Ascent of F6*, and *On the Frontier*. Auden and Isherwood attempted to synthesize a number of theoretical ideas about the nature of poetic drama borrowed eclectically from Eliot in England and numerous continental practitioners such as Cocteau, Copeau, Obey and Brecht. Like Eliot, they searched for the most effective way to revitalize British theater and to use it to create a response to the dangerous social, political, and psychological forces operating within Europe and England. As early as 1929, Auden pondered in his journal how to enlist poetry in the doubly revolutionary quest: "Do I want poetry in a play or is Cocteau right: 'There is a poetry of the theater, but not in it'?" (Sidnell, 64). In the plays for The Group Theatre, he and Isherwood clearly opted for Cocteau's idea of using the plastic elements of theater, not just the verbal text, as part of the "poetry of the theatre." Of the three plays crafted for The Group Theatre, *Dog Beneath the Skin*

151

stands out as the most theatrically poetic and socially revolutionary. It is a volatile, perhaps even unstable, combination of elements, a sort of theatrical Molotov cocktail to explode political illusions and destroy commercial forms.[1] An energetic, virtuoso text, it borrows freely from a variety of sources: romantic comedy, cabaret, popular songs, opera, Brecht's and Eliot's poetic choruses, theatricalism, and expressionism. And to pull this mélange together, it requires an actor to play his role in a shaggy dog costume. The play's stylistic brilliance attempted to open British theatre to invigorating influences that would move it into the current of modern drama. At the same time, through a theatrical experience radically different from West End commercialism, it hoped to open the eyes of its bourgeois British audience to the danger of its own personal and social self-delusions and in so doing create the possibility of a more humane society.[2]

Dog Beneath the Skin, then, has a two-part agenda. First, it is an all-out theatrical assault on commercial British theater, especially middle-class romantic comedy. Second, it wants to expose the dangers of the comfortable British bourgeois assumptions behind that form. The radical mixing of theatrical forms seems intended to produce a kind poetry of the theater that produces an uncertain

---

[1]Critics differ on *Dog Beneath the Skin* as an effective didactic piece of revolutionary theater. Frederick Buell, for example, argues that the virtuosity is a kind of artistic exhibitionism Auden uses "to dazzle his audience first and only secondarily confront them with the moral that all this dazzle ostensibly serves"(Buell, 135). Michael Sidnell surveys theatrical critics' responses to the initial 1936 production and finds that both left and right-leaning reviewers were mixed as to the specific ideology the play supported (Sidnell, 16–64). The play's intellectual stance may best be described as skeptical and consciousness-raising rather than ideological. As George Wright notes about Auden's poetry, *Dog Beneath the Skin* uses various theories, like those of Marx and Freud, to provide multiple perspectives on an issue, not as solutions to a social problem (Wright, 60–61).

[2]While *Dog Beneath the Skin* employs numerous avant-garde elements, Auden and Isherwood mixed them with popular forms in an attempt to attract a broad-based audience. In pursing their theatrical and social agenda, they borrowed from Eliot's ideas about the audience for poetic drama. Like Eliot they wanted a middle class audience which, like the Elizabethan, "wanted *entertainment* of a crude sort, but which would *stand* a good deal of poetry" (Eliot, 70). And like Eliot, they wanted to re-create an audience-community of shared belief to save the modern world.

laughter creating ironic insight that destabilizes smug certainties.[3]
It is a consciousness-raising experience intended to shake up the
audience and to reconstitute them as a community rooted in a
transnational humanism nurtured by social scientific paradigms,
in particular Marx and Freud. Focusing on the relationship between a few non-realistic elements—the chorus and the dog character—and the romantic comic form in *Dog Beneath the Skin* shows
how Auden and Isherwood aim poetically to undermine and explode romantic comic bourgeois illusions about England that seem
to insulate it from the madness afflicting 1930s continental Europe.

   To facilitate an examination of how Auden and Isherwood
fulfill their agenda, a capsule description of the play's dramatic elements may be useful before looking more closely at their dynamic
juxtaposition, which creates the audience's uncertain laughter,
anxiety, and cognitive dissonance. Auden and Isherwood use a
relatively simple romantic comic plot and dramatic action. *Dog Beneath the Skin* theatrically represents a journey from innocence to
experience. Through a quest story, the play portrays the transformation of the hero, Alan Norman, from a naïve true believer in the
idyllic virtues of Britain to a more mature critic of its underlying
corruption. Leaving his idyllic rural home, Pressan Ambo, Alan
journeys to the continent in the company of a faithful village dog
to seek the lost aristocratic heir whom all hope will restore
"beauty" and " a sense of duty" (199) and restore the old, badly
needed, communal unity and harmony.[4] If successful, he is
promised the hand of Iris Crewe, the beautiful daughter of the

---

   [3]George Wright observes that Auden is "fundamentally a poet of
doubt, of uncertainty, of insecurity, of hesitations, second thoughts, quali-
fications—in short, of anxiety" (Wright, 155). *Dog Beneath the Skin* seems
designed to achieve these same poetic effects through theatrical as well as
literary means.

   [4]All references to *Dog Beneath the Skin* are from the text edited by
Edward Mendelson *in W.H. Auden and Christopher Isherwood: Plays and
Other Dramatic Writings by W.H. Auden, 1928–38*. There is a certain degree
of indeterminacy when talking about this play since it was a collaborative
effort, not just between Auden and Isherwood, but also between the authors and Rupert Doone, the director of its first production, who asked for
modifications in the original script. In particular, the play has been published and produced with different endings. Mendelson courageously
sorts through its permutations and constructs a very useful edition. He
discusses these issues in the textual notes included in the volume mentioned above.

aristocratic family. On the continent, Alan finds oppression, violence, and powerful distractions that have caused his heroic predecessors to fail. Saved from dangerous entanglements on the continent by the faithful dog who finally reveals himself as Sir Francis Crewe, the lost heir, Alan and heir return to Pressan Ambo to find the idyllic Britain of popular belief as corrupt below the surface as the continent. Alan finds Iris betrothed to a politician and munitions maker; the heir is killed by a deranged woman; and Alan exits sadder, wiser, and committed to confronting unreality to promote change.

While the plot and action seem simple enough, the play's experimental combination of theatrical techniques complicates the audience's experience emotionally and intellectually. Alan's journey is a theatrically varied learning experience for him as well as for an audience conditioned by cup-and-saucer realism and romantic comedy. The absurdly violent expressionistic scenes, parodic songs in various genres, and the stinging irreverence of cabaret satire conspire to alter perceptions. Moreover, Auden and Isherwood's innovative use of choruses and the dog character create special perspectives for re-seeing social reality.

A variety of techniques and structural patterns "cue" the audience to be alert to the harsh underlying reality behind the comedy, establishing a perspective from which the audience can continuously and repeatedly view and evaluate the romantic comic form and the false ideals that support it. The choruses, the comic dogskin disguise, and the hidden heir inside it serve to engage as well as provide critical distance for the audience. Through these theatrical devices, Auden and Isherwood predict and focus on the transformation of Alan Norman, the naïve hero. The perspective of the chorus becomes an informing historical and poetic intelligence. It represents "the place" toward which both Alan, the nominal hero, and the audience itself move, the final state of their consciousness, an ironically transformed vision of the idyllic Pressan Ambo. They prepare for "When the green field comes off like a lid / Revealing what was much better hid: / Unpleasant" (194). Remaining on stage throughout much of the action, the choral group is a continuous reminder, even when silent, of the wider consciousness with which Alan and the audience are intended to merge by play's end.

While the lyric and narrative choruses establish a seriousness in theme and tone, they also frame the episodic romantic quest for the lost heir within a poetic, panoramic perspective that reveals a horrible, hidden reality. To create an unsettling anxiety, this choral knowledge is presented, then masked. Auden and Isherwood delay the full impact of the discovery by creating laughter that is uncertain and anxious. For the audience, the play becomes a process of discovery of what is already known but repressed. Then, through highly unconventional theatrical means—a suddenly altered use of the chorus and a multi-dimensional dog character—Auden and Isherwood bring the romantic comic plot to a climax that drives home what the middle class audience has known but repressed about themselves and their idyllic Britannia.

The quest story's incidents set on the continent contrast sharply in their satiric, expressionistic style and tone with the romantic comedy setting of Pressan Ambo, Britain, but the chorus functions to establish an underlying similarity. In Alan's quixotic search for the lost heir, the biting satiric laughter of the continental incident is double-edged. It slashes at the absurd cruelties of continental Europe but also nicks the laughing audience because the chorus has suggested their similarity with the objects of their derision. While the episodic continental journey is filled with absurd, expressionistic representations of the madhouse horrors of the continent, "Ostnia and Westand, in post-war Europe"(206), the chorus reminds us, "Do not comfort yourself with the reflection: 'How very unEnglish'" (212). And it warns the audience in a scientific metaphor, calling attention to the audience's "complacent" (212) self-image of social health and the reality of a spreading corruption: "like an air-bubble under a microscope-slide, the film of poverty is expanding / And soon it will reach your treasure and your gentlemanly behaviour. / Observe, therefore, and be more prepared than our hero" (212). The choral knowledge is comically masked but borne out when Alan and the faithful dog, unable to find the trail of Pressan Ambo's lost heir in Ostnia's court, leave the royal palace. The blood-thirsty but saccharinely sentimental King of Ostnia, who has nostalgic, romanticized memories of England, commands his band to play "something suitable, to honor our guests." The audience may laugh, but also wince as the band strikes up "Rule, Britannia!" The familiar nationalistic anthem glorifying Britain's imperial power is now commanded by an inhuman, foolish autocrat, and mocks the audience's own nostalgia for a romantic comic idyll (217). Thus, the choral poetry enriches the dramatic action, producing a complex poetic effect.

Alan and the dog continue their quest for the lost Sir Francis in Ostnia's Red Light District, a landscape where souls have sought powerful deflections and intoxicating substances, sexual pleasures and drugs, to escape the harsh reality of industrial urban capitalism. The chorus grounds the middle class audience in a hard reality, taking them imaginatively from "a square of Georgian houses" to a place where "chimney's fume gently above us like rifles recently fired" (218). Calling on the audience to use its imagination, the chorus confronts the audience with a metaphoric mirror for "Full as a theatre is the foul thoroughfare: some sitting like sacks, some slackly standing, / Their faces grey in the glimmering gaslight: their eyeballs drugged like / a dead rabbit's" (218). Though the bordellos and opium dens and their singing proprietors, presented in comic expressionistic terms, seem antithetical to middle class *mores*, the discovery of Sorbo Lamb, one of Alan's predecessors in the quest for the lost heir, connects the Red Light District with the audience's own fantasy Britannia. Like the earlier scene in the Ostnian court, this scene ends with familiar music as the seedy proprietors of middle class iniquity sing a bouncing ditty about their former patrons to the gay tones of the penny whistle and concertina. The audience must smile in the face of a refrain that dwells on the death. Like Sorbo Lamb, those who trade consciousness of harsh social reality for escapist pleasure suffer the same fate: "Death's Black Maria took them all away" (224). Thus the dramatic action validates the choral insight in a way that is both whimsically familiar and lugubriously uncomfortable.[5]

As the journey continues, the chorus provides a link between Ostnia and Westland, a seemingly different and hostile land. Like Ostnia, Westland is a "land ruled by fear." In Ostnia, the King's fear generates paranoid violence, while in Westland the fascist Leader uses fear to stir the citizens to violence. It is a place where "private terrors" breed brutality in human conduct," and the fearful citizen may unleash his violence in "a splendid career in the

---

[5]This *danse macabre* sequence is a signature of Auden and The Group Theatre. At the request of Rupert Doone, the artistic leader of The Group Theatre, Auden wrote a mixed form performance piece called *The Dance of Death*, produced to modest acclaim in 1933. Sidnell in his excellent critical study of The Group Theatre, *Dances of Death: The Group Theatre of London in the Thirties*, notes that the *danse macabre* was The Group's metaphor for the bourgeoisie's pursuit of illusory pleasures even as it was dying. Like *Dog Beneath the Skin*, *The Dance of Death* was an experiment to use workers' theater agitprop techniques to transform a middle class audience (Sidnell, 68).

public services" (224). In linking Ostnia and Westland, Auden and Isherwood forward their proposition that nationalistic differences mask a pandemic corruption of civilization. With this imaginative elimination of borders, the comic insanity of Westland, governed by a Leader full of volkish sentimentality, paranoia, and violence, cannot easily be dismissed merely as a cultural difference. Presenting the Leader only as a disembodied electronic voice, Auden and Isherwood satirize Hitler but refuse to locate the combination of nostalgic, nationalistic sentimentality in a specific figure. Indeed, it is the deadly combination already seen in Ostnia's King. In the Leader's mawkish speech to calm the asylum inmates, who threaten to harm each other, the audience may also hear notes that associate Westland's bucolic idyll with their own romantic comedy Britannia. The Leader's electronic voice conjures up a fairy tale world of peace and innocence filled with "meadows and mountains ... flushed with the sunset glow" where "a young mother looked down at her suckling babe with ineffable Westland tenderness" and "down the street came the returning cattle, all their bells a-chiming in a sweet symphony, followed by the peasants, so honest, so thrifty, so frugal, wedded to the dear Westland earth in an eternal, holy marriage" (228–29). To direct the inmates' paranoid violence toward others, he creates national difference alluding to a hostile, militaristic neighboring country. The obvious allusion to Hitler was undoubtedly a palpable hit with the audience, but their own complicity is an unsettling undertone.

Alan laughs as he escapes the ludicrous fascist insanity in Westland. But the laugh, borne of relief to be free of this foreign insanity, masks the underlying similarity between German and British versions of the nationalist myth which sanctions social brutality. The chorus in its long, measured lines, however, nags at the audience's consciousness, complicating the laughter by linking England with the seemingly dissimilar Westland asylum. Alan and the dog travel in a Pullman car on "just such a train" as those that stop at familiar London stations. In fact the chorus begins the scene by calling out "Paddington. King's Cross. Euston. Liverpool Street" (234), dislocating the audience from Westland and re-locating them in a familiar English cityscape. The theatricalism used to stage the train scenes also functions to eliminate realistic details, allowing the train to be an "everytrain," a mainliner that has a pan-European origin and terminus.[6]

As Alan's quest continues, the local settings become less specific and, thus, more widely applicable, as the chorus makes clear. Escaping by train, Alan and the dog encounter the international financier Grabstein, another representative of the sentimentalist justifying his violence. This time the economic violence of capitalism is justified by a personal rags-to-riches story and by charitable gestures to mask guilt. The thematic pattern linking personal, psychological motives and an oppressive power already seen in Ostnia and Westland recurs. Here, though, capitalism becomes the deadly force, just as autocratic rule and nationalism had in Ostnia and Westland. Like a plague virus, the train carries invisible germs of human self-destruction everywhere it goes. It has struck in Ostnia and Westland; the train bears it across borders, spreading everywhere, even the romantic comedy world of Pressan Ambo.

The chorus picks up the theme that powerful social and psychological forces operate across borders as Alan enters Paradise Park, a land of distractions from reality, the "comely" places of refuge and the "tabernacles of [middle class man's] peace": books, playing-fields, romantic love, art, and music (241). All are diversions that pleasantly mask "the sigh of the most numerous and the most poor; the thud of their falling bodies" (241). There the self-absorbed dwell: a poet in a tree, lost in language; two fairy-tale lovers dressed in "nursery-teapot-Dutch costumes," and invalids in wheel chairs talking about their infirmities (241). The audience may laugh at a poet in a tree or invalids with ear trumpets wheeling about the stage, but the memory of the chorus's revelation that middle class pleasures mask the suffering of the poor lingers, unsettling the comic moment.

To drive the unsettling truth home, Auden and Isherwood end the Paradise Park episode with the mock-heroic death of Chimp Eagle, another lost son of Pressan Ambo who had quested for the lost Sir Francis Crewe. Though he has given up the quest, Chimp has knowledge of Sir Francis Crewe's whereabouts. Unlike Sorbo,

---

[6]Sidnell notes that Auden and Isherwood appropriated the theatricalist staging from this scene from Thornton Wilder's 1931 one-act play, "Pullman Car Hiawatha" (Sidnell, 162). Just as Wilder minimized stage set and props to generalize or universalize human experience, so too Auden and Isherwood in collaboration with Rupert Doone chose a theatricalist staging.

who has blocked out the human sorrow he encountered in Ostnia with a drug-induced fog, Chimp Eagle has been distracted in his quest by social activism to confront the cruel social reality. Alan and the dog discover Chimp Eagle among the invalids, gut-shot by police machine-gun fire at a dock strike. Unlike Sorbo, Chimp has not forgotten his mission, but as he relates to Alan while dying in an operating room, "for me was another destiny / Chance made it clear / My work was here / For me the single-handed / Search was ended" (252).[7]

While Chimp Eagle has made a noble sacrifice, Auden and Isherwood present his death in the style of scathing, absurd farce. Attended by an inept surgical staff with the dog assisting in a nurse's uniform, Chimp relates his love for Pressan Ambo and Iris in short rhymed couplets in a duet with Alan sung in "the style of Wagnerian opera" (251). While the audience may laugh at the parody of Wagnerian death duet, it must also be troubled by the sincerity of the socialist swan song done in dimmed stage lighting.[8] Troubled by the uncertainty of whatever laughter Chimp's death scene elicits, the audience is momentarily caught in a moment of cognitive dissonance, unable to decide how to value his self-sacrifice. Auden and Isherwood let the audience momentarily off the hook, bringing the stage lights back up and having the surgery room explode into vaudevillian chaos as the surgeon discovers that he is being assisted by a dog. The scene ends in "General dismay, confusion, screams, laughter, pursuit" (253) as all rush off the stage.

Manipulating dramatic rhythm masterfully, Auden and Isherwood have played variations on their humanistic themes.

---

[7]Auden and Isherwood's use of names is always intriguing. Unlike their frequent practice of alluding to historical characters or family members, Sorbo Lamb and Chimp Eagle seem much more direct. Lamb is a passive sacrifice to the false idyllic Britannia; Chimp Eagle seems to embody both the human being's earthbound animal nature as well as our ability to soar toward higher ideals.

[8]Here, I suppose, I am using something not textual to prove my point. It is not unusual for an actor to sense the significance of even the silliest stuff and bring the audience new insight, to operate against the literal text. A good example of what I am talking about can be found in many recent productions of *Midsummer Night's Dream* in which Bottom, as Pyramus, brings real emotion to the bombast and alliteration of the lines spoken at Thisbe's death.

Through a series of scenes culminating in Chimp Eagle's death, they bring the audience to the climax of the journey, to the brink of self-discovery, and to a transformed England. The chorus sets the last scene of the journey in the Nineveh Hotel, located in a city, "a center of culture" (256), which proves to be English. Suggesting extravagant decadence with an historical precedent, the Nineveh Hotel stands as a modern version of the doomed Babylonian empire and an indictment of the materialistic pleasures that amuse and distract the middle class from the social realities of cruelty and poverty. As if recognizing themselves caught in the large forces that affect the stage world, Auden and Isherwood objectify and bring themselves as the collaborative "writer" into the world of the play. The chorus shifts its focus from audience to exhort the "writer" to complete the task of closing the gap between theatrical reality and the audience's unreality:

Writer, be glib: please them with scenes of theatrical bliss and horror,
Whose own slight gestures tell their doom with a subtlety quite foreign to
          the stage.
For who dare patiently tell, tell of their sorrow
Without let or variation of season, streaming up in parallel from the little
          Houses
And unabsorbed by their ironic treasures
Exerts on the rigid dome of the unpierced sky its enormous pressures?
                                                                          (257)

Suddenly and unconventionally having the chorus address the author is one of two daring theatrical moves that Auden and Isherwood use to resolve the uncertainty of audience's laughter and their anxiety. The second is the deconstruction of the dog character, to be discussed shortly. Up to the arrival at the Nineveh Hotel, choral comments have been addressed to the audience, enjoining them, like Shakespeare's Chorus in *Henry V*, to use their imaginations to fill in what the theater scenery cannot provide and subtly encouraging them to make connections between the theatrical illusion and their own masked reality. Now, the chorus addresses the play's "writer," urging "him" to write so that the audience will find in the theater's scenes of "bliss and horror" a mirror of their own life and historical epoch, a reflection that may prove apocalyptic, exerting "enormous pressures" on the seeming solidity of their romantic comedy illusion of reality. This variation in address relocates the audience in relation to the play. Rather than being addressed directly, the audience now overhears the authoritative speaker talking to the maker of the play about them. Unusual and unsettling, this choral moment precedes the play's final movements in which Alan both succeeds and fails in his quest. While he returns Sir Francis home, the lost heir destroys the romantic comedy world of Pressan Ambo. By displacing the audience, the chorus builds a sense of curiosity and suspense; it gives them time for a critical pause, to see themselves as others do and to wonder and worry about how so slight a thing as a play can reveal their doom. Suddenly the gap between metaphor and life, the Nineveh Hotel and England, collapses. The play is playing for keeps.

The Nineveh Hotel scene, done in a crude and rowdy cabaret style, suggests all that is venal, gross, and inhumane about capitalist materialism. The Cabaret Announcer plays on the hotel audience's sentimental nationalism to connect this gross cabaret world with the idyllic Britain beloved by the middle class theater audience. Introducing Madam Bubbi, the cabaret's feature singer, the Announcer notes: "The romance of foreign lands has been celebrated by every song-writer. But we feel that insufficient justice has been done to our own country. We are presenting therefore to you to-night Madam Bubbi, in a new song entitled Rhondda Moon. When you have heard her, I'm sure you will be convinced, as we are, that, in the opportunities she offers to the Tender Passion, Britain is second to none!" (261). Madam Bubbi, an immense woman in a sequin dress, sings a song that further reinforces the connection: "I come with a message to the farmers and the cities; / I've a simple slogan, it's just: Love British! / British Romance, British joys, / British chorus girls and boys" (261).

Because they are grotesques, the Announcer and Madam Bubbi serve to mock the romantic illusions they endorse. Love becomes mere appetite and sexual pleasure an edible commodity; the Nineveh Girls perform crudely and are selected by the hotel audience for consumption. In another cabaret routine, Destructive Desmond gratuitously destroys Beauty in the form of a Rembrandt painting to the applause of the hotel audience. Finally, Alan is tempted and seduced into self-destructive consumption by the glitzy and glamorous Lou Vipond, "the star of whom the world is fond" (266).

The shift in choral address, the association of the cabaret with English self-aggrandizement, and the hero's diversion from the quest triply threaten the theater audience's nationalistic illusion of sanity, civility, and order represented by Pressan Ambo. Yet, Alan's wooing of Lou Vipond is presented comically. He is revealed as foolishly undressing a shop window dummy. To heighten the absurdity and the point that his fascination with the false Vipond is self-deception, Alan delivers his own love lines, then runs behind the dummy to answer himself in a falsetto voice (271–72). Auden and Isherwood underscore the world-shaking seriousness of Alan's comic self-seduction. When pledging the depth of his love Alan foolishly promises that "if she might live" he would "give the Netherlands with all their canals, / The earth of the Ukraine, the Niagara Falls, / The Eiffel Tower also and the Dome of St. Paul's" (271). To prove his love, he destroys Iris' picture, the last vestige of "one I thought I loved beyond measure" (271), his commitment to the Pressan Ambo idyll. Alan is so far in debt trying to please Lou Vipond's voracious tastes that he is threatened with arrest. Thus, in a poetic way, dramatic action turns metaphoric; false values prove bankrupting illusions.

To this point in the play, the chorus has functioned as an omniscient consciousness to close the gap between the audience's illusory reality and a theatrical but true unreality. Now that function shifts as Auden and Isherwood make their second unconventional theatrical move by deconstructing the dog as character. Using the non-realistic figure of an anthropomorphic dog, obviously an actor dressed as a ridiculous simulacrum of a dog, Auden and Isherwood both lull and unsettle the audience with a comic poetic symbol central to the play's resolution. The shaggy dog comically reinforces the romantic charm of Pressan Ambo, yet its human resemblance remains odd. It charms and lures the audience into a romantic comedy illusion and simultaneously though subconsciously signals its unreality. It is a shaggy dog joke waiting for a punch-line. Moreover, the audience develops plot expectations. Finding in the dog the faithful character who solves plot obstacles, expectations build that it is somehow central to the successful conclusion of the quest and the ultimate comic ending, the restoration of Pressan Ambo's social order and harmony. From the beginning the dog has been Alan's loyal, mute mutt, his comic sidekick and savior. He drinks whisky, plays cards, and dances with Alan; he also cleverly helps Alan escape from the Westland asylum, bites the poet's hand to protect Alan in Paradise Park, dresses as a nurse to prolong Chimp Eagle's life long enough to find out the secret that the lost heir has not left England, and tries to distract Alan from the allure of Lou Vipond. Thus, the audience expects a solution to the romantic comic quest from this familiar yet strange character. On the ideological level, of course, this anticipated plot resolution would also reinforce the myth of British potency or superiority enscripted in the traditional romantic comic form: tenacious Englishman, with the help of faithful dog, overcomes obstacles to complete his duty of rejuvenating Britannia.

With the hero distracted from his quest and the restoration of tradition and social order in theatrical limbo, Auden and Isherwood shatter the audience's expectations about character and plot. They make division between the dogskin and the character inside it. The audacity of fragmenting the dog into character and costume *as* character unsettles the audience in a number of ways. With the dogskin assuming a speaking role in the surreal, nighttime scene while Alan is lovemaking, Auden and Isherwood destroy any traditional concept of character. The stage is split: Alan and the dummy Vipond in a hotel room, the dog asleep in the adjacent corridor next to a grandfather's clock. The lights dim in Alan's room and the sleeping dog is brightly spotlighted.

With Alan and his critical faculties asleep under the influence of materialistic allure, the dogskin itself, an unsleeping historical and poetic perspective, speaks. While the dog does not move, the dogskin delivers a long monologue that halts all plot action, calling attention not to Sir Francis Crewe, the disguised runaway heir, but to the historical perspective of reality, formerly represented by the chorus. Having a literal dogskin speak is a "glib" piece of theatre intended to pierce "the rigid dome of the sky," the structuring myth of British superiority enscripted in a romantically comic nationalistic tradition. Destroying any vestige of conventional characterization, the authors simultaneously attack the British self-congratulatory self-perspective as a bastion of sanity in a 1930s Europe gone insane as well as a dominant tradition of British Theater. It is as if some subconscious recognition of reality emerges from below waking surfaces and conventional theatrical representation. With plot action stopped and the costume of a sleeping character speaking, Auden and Isherwood have arrested all conventional action and deconstructed conventional character, the most compelling features of theater, to present a highly theatrical moment in a seemingly anti-theatrical mode.[9]

---

[9]Jo-Anne Cappeluti, in her article "The Caliban Beneath the Skin: Abstract Drama in Auden's Favorite Poem,' provides a good deal of insight into the technique in her discussion of the dogskin's monologue as an experiment that prepared Auden for the creation of Caliban in *The Sea and the Mirror*.

When the dogskin speaks, one must imagine perplexity and perhaps bemused surprise among the audience. The expected plot solution is deferred for a very curious moment, one that compels attention if only to figure out what is going on in a now strange and unfamiliar theatrical representation. A mute character's costume speaking *must* signal significance. Fragmentation of the dog character creates cognitive dissonance and becomes an optimal "teaching moment." The audience now pays special attention to the content of the speech if only to re-orient itself. With heightened attention, the audience becomes conscious of their own complicity in the deathly substructure of their idyllic middle-class perspective of Britain. The theatrical shaggy dog joke becomes a Trojan horse, a subterfuge to destroy the foundations of the romantic illusions of Britain, as a demi-Edenic island of solid, middle-class sanity, order, and social harmony. As poetry of the theater, the dog acts allusively, too, playing on a variety of paradoxical meanings for the term *dog*. In this pawing over the meanings of the theatrical sign—as best friend to man, a sly fellow, and traitor—the audience is prepared for a transformed and complex ending to the romantic comic plot and world.

The fragmented character forces the audience back on their theatrical experience of the dog throughout the play, bringing to it and the play a self-consciousness of theatrical signs that leads to self-scrutiny and new social consciousness. From the dog's first entrance, other characters recognize its ambiguity as both aid to the hero and antagonist to Pressan Ambo. In Act 1, scene 1, as the romantic quest is about to begin with the ritual investiture of Alan Norman as hero, the dog enters. As Alan kneels to receive his commissioned duty as representative Englishman from the village Vicar and as the watching villagers bow their heads in prayer, the dog "begins sniffing around" (201). The dog immediately establishes itself as a comic and disruptive element in the ritual that involves the village's future. He is both familiar yet annoying as a critical presence, one who "sniffs around." "People surreptitiously kick it or pat it, but it refuses to stay quiet" (201). Faced with the village's institutional representatives, the Vicar and the General, the dog stands aloof. He runs away when the Vicar calls him and demonstrates "an almost human contempt" (203) for the General, who points to the curious nature of this theatrical sign:

> Most extraordinary animal I ever came across. Turns up on your doorstep one morning with his tongue hanging out, like the prodigal son; lets you feed him, slobber over him, pet him,

makes himself quite at home. In an hour or two he's one of the
family. And then, after a week or fortnight, he'll be off again,
cool as you please. Doesn't know you if you meet him on the
street. And he's played that trick on all of us. Confounded un-
grateful brute! It's his mongrel blood, of course. No loyalty; no
proper feeling. Though I'm bound to say, while he was with me
he was the best gun-dog I ever had. (203)

Despite his ambivalence toward the villagers, and in particular those who represent institutionalized power, the dog bonds
himself to Alan, fawning upon him and "wagging his tail" (203).

Thus, the dog functions as a poetic symbol from the start. It
simultaneously suggests cherished values of a bucolic England
and the opposite. It is loyal and dutiful while at the same time it
lacks loyalty. It plays on the British popular view of the dog as
repository of all that is best in humanity, most particularly loyalty
and duty, thus reinforcing the romantic idyll's potency. As the
dogskin will later relate, "I enter and the audience starts sighing,
thinking of spring, meadows and goodness knows what else"
(275). Simultaneously in the General's view the dog is contemptu-
ous and signals "not English," but have "mongrel blood" (203), a
sort of traitor.

While the audience may be charmed by this curious rustic
symbol and thus drawn into the romantic comedy world of Pressan Ambo, it remains aware that this dog is played by an actor.
What it is unaware of throughout most of the play is that the actor
inside the dogskin is playing the lost heir, Sir Francis Crewe. In the
end, it is the comic dog unmasked as the lost heir who dashes the
hope of renewing the old values and innocence by unmasking
England's own participation in the corruption of capitalism and
fascism. The audience first sees the dog as representative of English loyalty, duty, and common sense but must later re-see it as
the destroyer of those values. So, the dog comically undermines
romantic illusions even while seeming to support them initially. In
so doing, the dog transforms the comic ending by revealing his
insider knowledge and turning the romantic comedy world inside
out revealing its corruption.

Having displaced the plot solution from a human character
onto a dog, Auden and Isherwood make their revolutionary depiction of the dog character central to the play's action and the catalyst for an audience's epiphany. While Alan has seen the powerful
deflections, intoxicating substances, and substitute satisfactions
that have waylaid his questing predecessors in Ostnia's Red Light

District and Paradise Park, he himself had become hopelessly enamored of opulence and decadence. Clearly, to solve the plot ob-
stacle, he must be freed to find the heir and return home; otherwise, the comedy fails and he becomes another lost son like Sorbo
Lamb and Chimp Eagle.

At this critical point, the dog character deconstructs. While
Alan makes love to an artificial doll, the artificial dog takes on a
heightened reality, motionless in the spotlight. The dogskin takes
on a life of its own at once more fantastical yet more real than anything else in the play. It launches into a monologue presented as a
dialogue with Ticker, the non-speaking immobile grandfather's
clock. The clock's presence serves to reinforce the dogskin's
themes. It brings a history of human behavior, especially of human
self-aggrandizement and violence in the service of nationalism, to
the audience's attention. The behaviors attributed to the King of
Ostnia, Grabstein the Financier, and the Westland Leader are generalized, made familiar by associating them with an English poet
who had served as the dogskin's master when it was still a dog.

In discovering its own identity, the dogskin analyzes English
identity. Though not English, the dogskin points out that it has
appropriated an English accent and become "quite deracine, as
they say in Bloomsbury" (273). In the throes of "a romantic mood
... I decided to throw my lot in with theirs [the English] and sever
all ties with my past" (273). The dogskin discovered, however, that
trying to become English only called more attention to its non-
Englishness, its otherness. Clearly the audience must speculate on
what this curious theatrical being represents appearing English
but not being English. It must begin thinking. Rather than representing a specific set of values, the dogskin seems to have a poetic,
imaginative perspective. Indeed, it tells Ticker that in some phase
of its life, it had "composed poems that I imagined highly id-
iomatic" (273). The dogskin's imaginative vision collects human
experience not only from an adopted English perspective but that
of an outsider. The new identity seems much like that of the chorus, a transnational if not panoramic perspective, bound neither by
space nor time. Becoming English, then, becomes merely a disguise to cloak a wider identity. It is then, perhaps, that the English
audience members can begin to see themselves not as a superior
species but merely as disguised human beings.

To add authenticity to the broadly humanistic perspective, the
dogskin talks historically of "the old days, before I became a skin,"
in March 1918 during a particularly bloody World War I offensive.

At that time, it was "the pet of a very famous author" (273) who in a whisky-induced self-revelation reveals to the dumb dog that the writer recognizes his complicity and guilt in the bloodbath because he helped "conjure up all the vigours and the splendors, skillfully transformed our envy into an image of the universal mother, for which the lad of seventeen whom we have always sent and will send again against our terrors, gladly immolates himself" (273). Personal demons have promoted human carnage on a grand scale, yet the writer has been knighted for his "virile poetry" (273). After the drunken revelation, when sober, the writer must now protect his ego from self-abuse. Consequently, he commodifies and rids himself of the pet in whom he has invested his guilt: "He couldn't bear the sight of me after that evening and sold me as soon as he could" (274). The dog serves as alter ego and superego and must be gotten rid of because he has seen into the hidden springs of evil the man has found in himself. This is a perspective Sir Francis has absorbed in wearing the dogskin, and one that the audience, too, must now contemplate.

As the sequence ends, the lights come up and a character, soon to be revealed as Sir Francis Crewe, steps out of the dogskin. The stock comic recognition scene is at hand, and the audience is thrown back into the romantic comic form but with a new and disturbing consciousness that will transform the happy homecoming. Rejected by Vipond and deeply in debt, Alan sees a man putting the dogskin back on. When he reveals himself to be Sir Francis, Alan acts as if the romantic comic script will proceed to the inevitable happy ending. He exclaims: "Francis! At last! [They embrace.] Oh, this is the happiest moment of my life! Everything's all right now!" But Francis is skeptical: "I'm glad you think so" (277). The audience is uncertain again, smiling at the promise of the romantic comic ending but feeling their hope destabilized by the dogskin's monologue and Francis's own skepticism. Significantly, Alan escapes from the Hotel Nineveh by dressing in the dogskin. He and the audience are now prepared for a return to Pressan Ambo with new dogskin eyes. As Francis warns Alan: "Places sometimes look different when one comes back to them." And he invites him, and indirectly the audience, to "go there and you shall judge for yourself" (278).

Absent for several scenes, the chorus speaks again to frame the return to Pressan Ambo and add a serious note to the more comic ones raised in the recognition scene. This choral speech reveals the "unpleasant" beneath the "green lid" of romantic self-ideals as it had promised in its opening lines. In an ode to man, the chorus reveals the human being as "divided and restless always: afraid and unable to forgive," always "Afraid of the clock," and "Desperately anxious about his health," forever "caught in the trap of his terror destroying himself" (279–80). The speech dwells on the human condition and the self-deceptions used to cope with human suffering, but it also emphasizes individual consciousness. It is consciousness that enables humans to face the hard truths below our destructive illusions and provides hope for avoiding the cruelty caused by seeing one's self as different and therefore superior to others: "Beware of yourself: / Have you not heard your own heart whisper: 'I am the nicest person in this room?' / Asking to be introduced to someone 'real': someone unlike all those people over there?" (280). Auden and Isherwood put the burden for reform and a more truly civilized existence squarely in the consciousness of the individual and in the individual's determination to use "knowledge and your power" because they "are capable of infinite extension" (281). In the following sequence, Auden and Isherwood will make reality more complex. On returning home, Sir Francis will also blame human suffering on a social system that, by manipulating individuals' demons, perpetuates itself.

In the return to the romantic comedy world of Pressan Ambo the choral perspective now, rather than being separate from the dramatic action, colors the atmosphere. There is general anxiety the villagers see Pressan Ambo as "a dead-alive hole" as they commiserate about Iris' impending marriage to a politician and scion of an industrial capitalist. The deranged Mildred Luce enters and delivers a warning that the village cannot "order chaos with the common kiss" (284). The mood contrasts sharply with the wedding decorations festooning the stage, but the needs of the romantic comic form are fulfilled ironically with the return of Alan and Sir Francis.

Sir Francis, dogskin in hand, speaks as dog and man and reveals himself as both traitor and savior. When he reveals his identity as the village dog, all seem guilty and anxious about the knowledge he possesses. Made bold by the revelation of his dog wood and the wider knowledge of humanity gained on the continental journey, he attacks the villagers' illusions in a jeremiad First, he makes a general indictment, destroying self-protective illusions and then offering a humane hope: "I thought such obscene cruel, hypocritical, mean, vulgar creatures had never existed before in the history of the planet" but then tells the villagers that they are not different but part of an immense, ignorant army who "would probably die without knowing either what your leaders are really fighting for or even that you are fighting at all" (285). This knowledge that humans are generally prone to destructive self-delusions and manipulation by leaders prompts hope. If villagers know exactly what the dog knows about each of them, then overcoming fear and change are possible. Next, Sir Francis exposes the Vicar and the church as using religion to preserve the status quo that causes suffering by preaching love but failing to practice it. The solution is to destroy the existing "social system in which one man can only succeed at the expense of injury to another" (286). Then, he turns to the General to scourge those who falsely believe that wealth and class make them superior. Finally, he turns to the psychological roots of human cruelty by revealing Mildred Luce's hatred of Germans as an externalization of her own self-hatred, which is itself a manifestation of a "social system in which love is controlled by money" (287). Sir Francis at last reveals that Mildred has created an elaborate fantasy to mask the fact that she sacrificed her love for a young German cavalry officer to care for her mother. Thus, the dog has had his bite, and Sir Francis must die like a dog. Mildred stabs him with her hat-pin asserting that his unmasking of reality makes him a traitor.

The grotesquely comic mode of murder unsettles the audience again. Killed in a bizarre way by a certified loony, the strange and charming dog is dead. The lost heir cannot fulfill his romantic comic function. Yet, if seen rightly, from the dogskin's point of view, "from underneath" (285), Sir Francis has created hope for a new ending, one that has application in real life: a new social ideal with equality, justice, and compassion for all. In a scene reminiscent of his Wagnerian duet with the noble Chimp Eagle, though now stripped of the comic musical element, Alan and the dying Sir Francis comfort each other. Sir Francis offers Alan advice, metaphorically passing the dogskin to him by enjoining the now ineffectual romantic comedy hero to: "Remember when I am dead / The plain and the extraordinary / On our devious journey / Remember. No longer in ignorance / Of its significance ... Able more clearly to act / Man's history to fulfill" (288). As Sir Francis dies, the chorus again draws theatrical illusion and reality together, telling the audience: "Mourn not for these ... / Mourn rather yourselves; and your inability to make up your minds" and "Choose therefore that you may recover: both your charity and your place / Determining not this that we have lately witnessed: but another country" (289).

With the dogskin's perspective now shared by Francis, Alan, and the audience, the separation between life and art is gone. Alan escapes with his dogskin consciousness into the audience. So, it is little matter that the romantic comedy must be wrapped up and Sir Francis' body disposed of comically and without repercussion by being wrapped up in the dogskin and carried off. As we know from the strange monologue earlier, the dogskin has many lives and is likely, with Alan and the audience sharing its knowledge to be carried forward into the real world. So, though Iris is married amid fireworks, balloons, and bells to fulfill the romantic comic demands, the audience can only shake its head and laugh ruefully at the villagers' joyous song, "O day of Joy in happiness abounding." Laughter is no longer uncertain or insignificant.

With *Dog Beneath the Skin*, Auden and Isherwood produced a vibrant and theatrically revolutionary statement of how bold confrontation of the complex personal and social realities underlying a bourgeois culture of death can generate hope for transforming it. The pathetic romantic comic wedding in Pressan Ambo can be stopped if Alan and the audience—those with dogskin eyes—can rescue Iris. In the process, Auden and Isherwood have proven the potency of the poetry of the theater.

Works Cited

Auden, W.H. *W.H. Auden and Christopher Isherwood: Plays and Other Dramatic Writings by W.H. Auden, 1928–38.* Edited by Edward Mendelson. Princeton: Princeton UP, 1988.

Buell, Frederick. *W.H. Auden as Social Poet.* Ithaca: Cornell UP, 1973.

Cappeluti, Jo-Anne. "The Caliban Beneath the Skin: Abstract Drama in Auden's Favorite Poem." *Style* 33 (Spring 1999): 107–29. (The article may also be found at www.findarticle.com/cf_0/m2342/1_33/58055907/print.jhtml.)

Eliot, T.S. *The Sacred Wood: Essays on Poetry and Criticism.* London: Methuen & Co., 1969.

Fuller, John. *A Reader's Guide to W.H. Auden.* New York: Farrar, Straus, & Giroux, 1970.

McDiarmid, Lucy. *Saving Civilization: Yeats, Eliot, and Auden Between the Wars.* New York: Cambridge UP, 1984.

Sidnell, Michael J. *Dances of Death: The Group Theatre of London in the Thirties*. Boston: Faber and Faber, 1984.

Wright, George T. *W.H. Auden*. New York: Twayne Publishers, 1969.

Paid on Both Sides:
Auden and Yeats and the New Tragedy

Richard Londraville and Janis Londraville

Auden was certainly influenced by W.B. Yeats as concerns verse, and this relationship has been explored extensively by Auden scholars. Here one will see connections between Yeats and Auden (plus Isherwood) as dramatists. Richard and Janis Londraville are noted Yeats scholars, and here they share their knowledge of Yeats as applied to Auden.

Aristotle suggested distinctions among lyric, epic, and dramatic poetry, indicating that the first was an outpouring of personality; the second a melange of history, literature, and folklore; and the third a way in which certain actions in the epic were a prism through which human behavior could be presented with some hope of objectivity. Auden and Yeats experimented early with the lyric as a suitable vehicle for their personal utterances, but turned to drama when they wished to express truths which transcended the individual. As satisfying as the lyric expression can be, it did not often lead to more than an exhaustive—and at times exhausting—self-examination.

Other lyric poets have moved in a similar direction, the most notable of whom may be Shelley. There is no other poet for whom the lyric is more definitional; he is the man who wails, "I fall upon the thorns of life; I bleed." One may be forgiven at that point for feeling shock; it is as if the reader opened a psychic door and witnessed unprepared the intensity of the poet's emotion. It may be that Shelley turned to drama (although he certainly did not abandon the lyric) for the distance it provides. His plays, particularly *Prometheus Unbound*, allowed him that necessary dramatic separation so that he might discover data that the lyric does not furnish. To put it simply, there is no way in drama for the poet to speak other than through his characters. This extrication of the self from the work may be a necessary step in the development of the serious artist.

The drama of the early twentieth century, for the main relentlessly realistic after the overwhelming influence of Ibsen, did not provide a satisfactory model for Auden or Yeats. Reasonably enough, both wished to retain their successful poetic mode when they turned to the theatre, and they recognized that dramatization could make their work stronger. All of us can detect the collateral understanding that a good reader can add to a poem. Yeats has suggested that the written poem is a script, and that poetry is shaped by a living voice ("Four Lectures," 84). Unlike Auden, who knew what he wanted to impart, and made his plays, in good measure, polemics that he hoped would engage a general audience, Yeats wished for an "unpopular theatre." He believed that the very ambiguity and density of his verse could arouse meditative rhythms that would lead to discoveries about one's self and the *anima mundi.* Not surprisingly, the dramatic explorations of Yeats and Auden strengthened their poetry, and the reader can see the evidence in much of their subsequent work, such as Auden's long poem *Letter to Lord Byron* in *Letters From Iceland* as well as the volume *Look, Stranger* (American title: *On This Island*), and Yeats's "A Dialogue of Self and Soul."

Poets write in order to understand. As Yeats said, "out of the quarrel with ourselves we make poetry" ("Per Amica," 331). Serious poetry is not undertaken to interpret for others, but to attempt to understand, first ourselves, finally the universe. Thus a poem is an argument that hopes to be challenged, a thesis in search of an antithesis, the self quarreling with self. In drama, the poet has the added advantage of the interplay of characters, who come together to argue points that the poet may not comprehend until he puts two such characters into action.

For Yeats, his quarrel with himself dealt with his suspicion that the universe was indifferent to human action, but that humans could mitigate this indifference by coming together as a community, and he chose drama as a more appropriate investigative vehicle than lyric. Yeats was intrigued with drama from early in his career, and he experimented with several forms, but the most flexible for his purposes was his adaptation of the Japanese *Noh* of the Ghosts. In this drama, a soul is caught between incarnations because of its attachment to a former life, unable to do anything other than relive the past. It may feel guilt for an act committed or omitted—reasons are irrelevant; it suffers because it believes it should. An intercessor called a Waki, usually a traveling priest, is introduced into the play, recognizes the problem, performs a ritual prayer, and frees the soul to be reborn.[1] Many of Yeats's plays, from *The Dreaming of the Bones* in 1918 to *Purgatory* in 1939, explore this idea as did Auden in his verse preceding his plays with his theme of an ancestral curse.

Yeats was intrigued by the possibilities for such a supportive structure and hoped that a comparable community could be established in his modern, Western world. But what he discovered through the characters in his plays was that there is no such community in our fragmented society. (Whether such nurture existed in medieval Japan is moot.) In any event, Yeats concluded through a series of experiments in his plays that the individual has the responsibility to be his own judge and jury. He must decide for himself the boundaries of reality and discover ways in which he can transcend them.

Auden's quarrel with himself dealt with message, and he experimented with the dramatic mode as the vehicle through which he might best communicate that message. His plays, from *Paid on Both Sides* to the several he wrote in collaboration with Christopher Isherwood, are searches for truth. Truth is somewhere, and we *ought* to discover it; it is our job. Like Yeats, Auden also felt the force of a chaotic society, but his drama, with the exception of *The Ascent of F6*, ignores the idea of the individual as his own salvation. One might argue that Auden believed as Plato did, that truth is universal, not relative—that there is some sort of ideal form, some system, some Republic, that if set up properly will provide us creatures of chaos with ways to lead productive lives without destroying each other.

Auden, then, seemed to be a struggling student doing an algebra problem, and his incompleteness as a dramatist is that he didn't understand that a closed system can only be defined in terms of itself. His plays are replete with the sense that people can be taught and can be helped through the maze that is the twentieth century. But he isn't sure how that will happen; he hasn't quite gotten the answer and realizes it by the end of most of his dramas. So he tries another external force, and another. There must be *something* that we are not doing that would help us refrain

---

[1]A literary antecedent for the Waki may be seen in the Palmer, who assists the Red Crosse Knight with moral decisions in Spenser's *The Faerie Queene*.

from killing each other, so let's try love—or socialism—or ...
what? And so, even though their dramas may germinate from the
same philosophical concerns, the difference between Auden and
Yeats is profound. The former is didactic; the latter dialectic.

Nowhere is this clearer than in Yeats's 1918 and 1919 plays,
The Dreaming of the Bones and *The Only Jealously of Emer*, and Auden's early play, *Paid on Both Sides* (1927–28) and one written in
collaboration with Christopher Isherwood, *The Dog Beneath the
Skin* (1935).

Yeats's *The Dreaming of the Bones*, an obvious imitation of the
Japanese *Noh*, explores an idea that Yeats calls the Dreaming Back:

> The conception of the play is derived from the world-wide belief
> that the dead dream back, for a certain time, through the more
> personal thoughts and deeds of life.... The lovers in my play
> have lost themselves in a ... self-created winding of the labyrinth
> of conscience. *(Variorum Plays, 777)*

The setting is Ireland, 1916. A young man who "seems an Aran
fisher" (763) enters and converses with a Stranger and a Young
Girl. The young man was "in the Post Office, and if taken/ I shall
be put against a wall and shot" (764). The Stranger and the Young
Girl are actually the ghosts of Diarmuid and Dervorgilla, young
adulterous lovers who betrayed Ireland centuries earlier. They are
looking for forgiveness so that they can be released from their past
lives. When the Young Girl says "No, no" (772) at the young
man's suggestion that their sin was simple adultery, he questions
further:

> What crime can stay so in the memory?
> What crime can keep apart the lips of lovers
> Wandering and alone? (772)

The Young Girl provides enough information for the young man
to understand:

> You speak of Diarmuid and Dervorgilla
> Who brought the Norman in?
>
> O never, never
> Shall Diarmuid and Dervorgilla be forgiven.
> (772–73)

The Stranger and the Young Girl are rejected and spin again in
their endless guilt. They are so attached to their belief (a belief that
suggests there will be no release or union for them without forgiveness by one of their countrymen) that there will certainly be

no release unless they can dispel that very belief. They are unlike Yeats in his poem "Man and Echo" ("Did that play of mine send out/ Certain men the English shot?" [*Poems*, 345]), who discovers that neither forgiveness nor understanding can come from others. Yeats knows that only organization ("That all's arranged in one clear view") allows the individual the power to escape "man's dirty slate" (346).

The Stranger and the Young Woman in the Dreaming Back do not find resolution, only despair. They don't know that they need to define for themselves what their reality is and not rely on the help of another to "get them through," because unlike the Waki in the Japanese *Noh*, we in the West (according to Yeats) have no reliable attendant to help us discover our own truths.

The next play in which Yeats explores the possibility of outside aid in freeing a character from the "labyrinth of conscience" (*Variorum Plays*, 777) is *The Only Jealousy of Emer*, a work which examines the Buddhist concept of attachment. At the opening, Queen Emer, wife of Cuchulain, is sitting beside his apparently lifeless body. The action continues from *On Baile's Strand*, written in 1904. In that play Cuchulain, for the only time in his life, accepts the bidding of another, King Conchubar. As a result, he fights and kills a young challenger whom he then discovers to be his only son. When he learns what he has done, Cuchulain goes mad and fights the sea. He thus drowns and his body washes up upon the shore. In *The Only Jealousy of Emer*, Emer tends to the body and attempts to break what she believes is a spell under which Cuchulain has been placed. She enlists the aid of Eithne Inguba, Cuchulain's mistress, asking her to kiss the body to revive it. When Eithne Inguba asks why Emer does not do this herself, the Queen replies that she is "but his wife":

> ... but if you cry aloud
> With the sweet voice that is so dear to him
> He cannot help but listen.
> (*Collected Plays*, 187)

In this dramatic experiment, Yeats tests the premises of the Japanese *Noh* plays as they apply to a Western mode. Not only is there a mortal who is willing to help the soul through to the next incarnation, but there is even the semblance of a community with the two women who love Cuchulain. Unfortunately, the women are not alike. Eithne Inguba does as she is asked and kisses the corpse, but she is frightened by Bricriu, the god of mischief who has inhabited the body, and she runs away. Emer, though, stands up to the apparition and demands to know what he has done with the spirit of Cuchulain. Bricriu tells her that Cuchulain is now suspended between life and death, in the thrall of Fand, one of the Sidhe. (The Sidhe are the warrior women who have battled with Cuchulain throughout his life. It is one of these women who bore him Conlaoch, the son he recently killed.)

The complexity of this play is intense, for Fand wishes to transport Cuchulain to her spirit world and tempts him with the promise that he shall never again feel the grief and guilt that is human. But her attraction to him is the human vitality that he exudes, and she seems unaware that his energy might not transfer to her world.

Bricriu has another agenda. He wishes only to thwart Fand, and so he promises that he will release Cuchulain from the spell if Emer will renounce her only desire, which is to spend her old age with her husband. She had long ago reconciled to the fact that he was a warrior and a womanizer who would never cease such conduct until age slowed him. Her desire, her hope, is to spend their last years together. Bricriu demands that she renounce that hope, and although it nearly destroys her, she does so:

> *Bricriu.* There is still a moment left; cry out, cry out!
> Renounce him, and her power is at an end.
> Cuchulain's foot is on the chariot-step.
> Cry—
> *Emer.* I renounce Cuchulain's love forever. (193)

Cuchulain is immediately released, and he awakens as if from a dream. He does not see the wife who has rescued him, and turns instead to Eithne Inguba, who claims:

> ... it is I that won him from the sea,
> That brought him back to life (193).

Emer is left to spend the rest of her life alone.

In all of Yeats's plays Cuchulain is the only character who is retrieved from a spiritual limbo, and interestingly, he does not go to a new life but back to his old one. He is, however, helped by a mortal, his unselfish wife, although he credits his timorous mistress.

Emer's desire is modest, wifely, even commendable, but it is not the magnitude of the desire which stalls her, but the fact that she wants "what is not" so much that she destroys "what is." Certainly one's everyday life is full of transient longings. We want to be younger, brighter, more attractive; but only when one becomes fixated do these desires distort existence. Whatever end we hope for clouds the actuality of what is. Whenever we become attached to any outcome, our attempt to direct forces to that end distorts reality. We live, in that case, in the past or future while the present spills by us unheeded. Ironically, Emer's freeing of Cuchulain only exacerbates her own bondage to her idea of sharing a comfortable old age with her husband.

In Yeats's plays, characters are put in situations and the audience—and Yeats himself—watches. How will they respond? What will become of them? Conversely, most of Auden's characters offer opinions and do not possess that interconnectedness that is demanded by the very nature of drama. Yet both Yeats and Auden seem to recognize that their new world requires a new definition of tragedy.

Auden's first attempt at serious drama contains some of the same problems of attachment that confront the characters in Yeats's plays. Edward Mendelson explains that *Paid on Both Sides* grew out of several lyrics "conceived as separate poems" (Auden, 525) and that these poems "describe variation on a single theme: life is a constant state of isolation and stagnated desire" (Mendelson, 29).[2] David Garrett Izzo writes that

> ... this isolation was brought about by the alienating effects of the depersonalized industrial city-state. Even more was brought about by the Old School where the highbrow, unathletic Auden remembered that he had felt isolated from the general run of hearties. (Izzo, 81)

Paid on Both Sides examines a present trapped in the past, with feuding characters who are indistinguishable from one another and share inexorably in their communal fate. Auden seems satisfied to sacrifice characterization in order to focus on the play's message. As he will say later in "September 1, 1939," "We must love one another or die." Although he subsequently saw this solution as simplistic, in *Paid on Both Sides* he is content to present Ann Shaw and John Nower as manifestations of that message.

The play begins in the middle of the feud between the Lintzgarth (Nower) and Nattrass (Shaw) families. Joan Nower is told that her husband has been killed, and the shocking news brings on

---

[2]For the purposes of this essay, we refer to the second version of *Paid on Both Sides*, which was published by T.S. Eliot in the *Criterion*, 1930.

premature labor and the birth of her son, John. We meet the grown
John after the Chorus's interlude, where it laments the state of
humanity:

> O watcher in the dark, you wake
> Our dream of waking, we feel
> Your finger on the flesh that has been shunned
> By your bright day
> See clear what we were doing, that we were vile.
>
>   (Auden, 16)

John becomes the leader of the Lintzgarth clan and makes plans
with his men to kill another Nattrass, Red Shaw. While the am-
bush is being carried out, Trudy (a Lintzgarth) expresses his dismay. Like Shylock, he muses:

> He's trash, yet if I cut my finger it bleeds like his. (19)

Trudy sees no hope—only the evolution of a mutated human:

> But here no remedy
> Is to be thought of, no news but the new death;
>
> Last night at Hammergill
> A boy was born fanged like a weasel. (19)

Others enter, including John Nower. Functioning as a chorus,
they describe the killing of Red Shaw by the Lintzgarth clan. During the same fight one of John Nower's own men, Edward, is slain.
A Nattrass man is then found hiding in an outhouse and is taken
away to await his fate. John, whose very moment of birth was
caused by the feud, wonders about his position in this history of
violence. He is unable to free himself from the past:

> Always the following wind of history
> Of others' wisdom makes a buoyant air
> Till we come suddenly upon pockets where
> Is nothing loud but us. (21)

Although John wonders what his life might have been like if he
had not been born into this feud, he recognizes that he cannot escape. What he does not understand is that he can never be free because he has accepted the reality of the system. What he *does* testifies to his acceptance of his fate. Unlike Blake, who informs the
Angel in *A Memorable Fancy*, "All that we saw was owing to your
metaphysics" (Blake, 74) and thus rejects the hell created by another, John laments, "could I have been some simpleton that lived

/ Before disaster sent his runners here" (Auden, 21). The Chorus knows that John will never renounce his hell:

> Now the most solid wish he tries to keep
> His hands show through; he never will look up.
> Say "I am good." On him misfortune falls
> More than enough. (22)

The spy is brought in, and John knows the enemy must be killed and that it is "Better to get it over" (23). Before he does, though, the androgynous Man-Woman appears, a portrayal of conscience—or perhaps God, or love, or that essence in us that has been killed by our own betrayal of our species. Man-Woman, a prisoner of war who is stuck behind barbed wire and is standing in snow, reminds us of Yeats's Waki in *The Dreaming of the Bones*. Yet, in that play, the young man (the Waki figure) is not aware that his forgiveness will release Diarmuid and Dervorgilla from their torment, and, in any case, he is not willing to forgive. The lovers are doomed because they do not reject *his* hell. In *Paid on Both Sides*, Auden's Man-Woman knows what should be done but cannot get the people to listen:

> Love was not love for you but episodes.
>
> Nothing was any use; therefore I went
> Hearing you call for what you did not want. (23)

Paid on Both Sides is, of course, not patterned on the Japanese *Noh* of the Ghosts, but the Man-Woman shares qualities of a Waki who could help these lost souls caught between metaphorical incarnations because of their attachment to the feud. The souls of the community, though, are fragmented and blind to the possibility of release. They imprison Man-Woman and drive it away:

> Now I shall go. No, you, if you come,
> Will not enjoy yourself, for where I am
> All talking is forbidden.... (24)

Man-Woman will return to a place not unlike the place of the long-dead ancestors in Thornton Wilder's *Our Town*, an American *Noh* of the Ghosts.[3] These silent ones have escaped the attachment to life and to language. In our Western world, we equate this escape with a loss of personality rather than the way to experience

---

[3]See Richard Londraville, "*Our Town:* An American *Noh* of the Ghosts," *Thornton Wilder: New Essays*, eds. M. Blank, D.H. Brunauer, D.G. Izzo (West Cornwall, CT: Locust Hill Press, 1999): 365–78.

life most deeply. And so we return to the world of the Lintzgarths
and Nattrasses, unable or unwilling to reject its hell.

The spy is brought in, and John shoots him. The lights go out,
and when they are brought up again, John is in a burlesque
dream. A doctor is fetched who has pliers, a circular saw, and a
bicycle pump for instruments. He extracts an enormous tooth
from the spy ("This tooth was growing ninety-nine years before
his great grandmother was born" [25]), a message that we are
rooted to the past. The spy recovers and converses with John, who
in this dream understands that he and the spy share in the human
experience:

> *John.* Sametime sharers of the same house
> We know not the builder nor the name of his son.
>
> *Spy....*
> Sharers of the same house
> Attendants on the same machine
> Rarely a word, in silence understood. (26)

Auden gives the Lintzgarths and Nattrasses one more chance
to use the admonition that we must "love one another or die" as a
permanent solution. The announcer, like Thornton Wilder's Stage
Manager, arrives and informs the audience that

> There is a time for peace; too often we
> Have gone on cold marches, have taken life,
> Till wrongs are bred like flies....
>
> Now this shall end with marriage as it ought:
> Love turns the wind, brings up the salt smell,
> Shadow of gulls on the road to sea. (29)

Ann Shaw and John Nower have fallen in love, and their union
should terminate the feud. But, like Romeo and Juliet, they are
doomed. The announcer tells us that the play "shall end with
marriage as it ought," but we are not surprised when this traditional end to comedy, the mending of families and states, is replaced with the death of John Nower. Mendelson writes:

> The New Year that Nower hopes to inaugurate with his love is
> born in celebration and triumph, only to be destroyed by the ha-
> treds that persist in his society, unaltered by his cure. (Auden,
> xvi)

John has awakened from his dream in a state of reconciliation, and
is free to love Ann, the issue of his enemy. "But," Mendelson explains, "he is destroyed by the undiminished wrath of the feud

that continues around him, its origins lost in a past too distant to be probed by dreams" (xv).

Seth, a Nattrass, is ordered by his mother to kill John:

> I can't do that. There is peace now; besides he is a guest in our house. (32)

But Seth's mother will not forget the past:

> Have you forgotten your brother's death ... taken out and shot like a dog? (32)

Even though Seth tells her, "I don't want to," he reluctantly does her bidding:

> It shall be as you like. Though I think that much will come of this, chiefly harm. (33)

Seth murders John, and others are killed, and the warriors of both sides withdraw to prepare for more battles, leaving Ann to mourn the dead:

> The hands that were to help will not be lifted,
> And bad followed by worse leaves to us tears.... (33)

The chorus is the last to speak. There will be no escape from killing. The mother bade the son to murder a man who had slain her other son. She could not let go of the blood feud, and sons will continue to kill and to die, as ancestral hatreds are passed on to succeeding generations:

> But he is defeated; let the son
> Sell the farm lest the mountain fall:
> His mother and her mother won. (33)

A few months after *Paid on Both Sides* was published in 1930, William Empson wrote of it that the psychoanalysis, surrealism, and "all the irrationalist tendencies which are so essential a part of the machinery of present-day thought ... are made part of the normal and rational tragic form, and indeed what constitutes the tragic situation" (as quoted in Auden, xvi). The tragic situation is, in fact, John Nower's inability to reject the past, or, in Auden's words, "the Tyranny of the Dead"; and the message, love, is ineffective and even in its most positive form only temporary. In *Paid on Both Sides*, Auden provides his characters with only one way out of the maze; but this way doesn't work; he does not provide them with the understanding to achieve escape velocity on their own. The tragedy of this play is not that a great king has fallen and taken a nation with him, nor that a man has been blinded by his own pride. It is that since the characters cannot extricate themselves from history, they are doomed to repeat the errors of the past.

Seven years later, Auden explored the nature of this premise more fully in *The Dog Beneath the Skin*, a collaborative effort with Christopher Isherwood (The title is from a T.S. Eliot poem, "The Skull Beneath the Skin.) The Chorus opens *Dogskin* by asking the audience to picture an English village "wherever you were a child or had your first affair" (Auden, 191). But this village, we discover, has changed; its aristocracy has disintegrated:

> The great houses remain but only half are inhabited,
> Dusty the gunrooms and the stable clocks stationary. (191)

Man is not able to live in the moment. He is "changed by his living; but not fast enough." He cannot embrace the "now," and so he is always left behind:

> His concern to-day is for that which yesterday did not occur
> He tosses at night who at noonday found no truth. (192)

Act 1, scene 1 presents some of the representative people of the town. The vicar, who "labours" to expound the truth, is a false teacher. The general, who rules his house like a brigade, is the dictator. The general's wife, who must do her "utmost to advance," is the propagandist; and Iris Crewe, the daughter of the recently deceased village aristocrat, is the courtesan who charms the men around her "with fur and hat and things like that" (196).

The plot of the play is simple. The villagers seem unable to forget their past and to live in the present. Their "Master," the old aristocrat, has died and his son's whereabouts are not known. The villagers must locate him, for he is the fabric that will hold the community together:

> Without his face we don't know what to do,
> We're undone. (199)

The villagers believe they must call back the aristocracy that has abandoned them.

The atmosphere of a fairy tale is invoked when Iris Crewe promises to wed the man who finds her brother. Alan Norman is selected. To keep Alan warm, the curate gives him a package of undergarments made of high-grade Botany wool. The Botany Mills had been brought to trial in the 1920s as violators of the Trading with the Enemy Act, a fact certainly not lost on Auden.

Alan, like Beowulf or Roland, does not act for himself alone, but is an agent of his culture. A strange stray dog (one that has wandered the streets of Pressan Ambo for ten years) attaches itself to Alan, who heads off, as many a knight has before him, on his quest that is also a pilgrimage of self-discovery. He becomes involved in a series of escapades through foreign lands in search of the lost "Master."

The quest saga, a "metaphorical search for inner peace" (Izzo, 119), quickly turns into burlesque adventures that Auden uses to comment on the more serious issues which lie just "beneath the skin." Little distinguishes one place or one group from another. Ostnia, the first stop for Alan and the dog, is run by a gangster King:

> The Commander-in-Chief is no better than a bandit: he makes all the big stores pay for protection. (Auden, 209)

The Queen lectures the women of Ostnia whose husbands and sons have been taken prisoners and are not likely to be seen again. She identifies with their grief ("I too have borne the pangs of childbirth" [215]—hardly a comparison to their present loss to which she is oblivious) and tells them that their suffering is their greatest attribute, providing them with an opportunity:

> And remember that Suffering is Woman's fate and Woman's glory. By suffering we are ennobled; we rise to high things. (215)

Her commentary finished, the Master of Ceremonies announces that "The ladies of the Court will offer the bereaved some light refreshment" (215).

The peasants in Ostnia have their own set of problems, primarily poverty and disease, but like Mussolini's Italy, it isn't a bad place for tourists, who "only see the mountains and the Renaissance Palace" (209).

After a visit to the red light district of Ostnia, where they encounter an addict who does not want to be saved ("The light of your world would dazzle me and its noises offend my ears" [223]) and meet two journalists, Alan and the Dog find themselves in a lunatic asylum in a neighboring realm called Westland. The leader of the inmates, whom the audience knows only through a loud-speaker as The Voice of the Leader, paints the picture of an ideal land of simple old inns and "snow-capped peaks already flushed with the sunset glow" (228). Ostnia, the Voice says, plans to take all this away from Westlanders through military power. People will lose their homes, their inheritances, and their lives unless they can be prepared, and preparation means giving things up to the state so that the government will be able to build a mighty defense force. The Leader's speech dissolves into Fascist gibberish.

With the help of the journalists, Alan and the Dog escape Westland and hop a train on which they meet the stereotypical corrupt capitalist, who is a swindler and murderer. The capitalist suggests that Alan look for Sir Francis Crewe at a place called Paradise Park. Up to this point, Auden has not allowed Alan and the Dog to participate in a sense of discovery, but has instead concentrated on examining the wrongs of each society. A return to the old ways of aristocracy isn't going to work; fascism isn't going to work; capitalism isn't going to work. Auden imposes moral or political or philosophical dogma on his characters to show that intrusive ideologies fall sadly short of success. The audience has no sense of Alan and Dog learning anything in particular, except that nothing is going to work very well. The reader is reminded of a diametrically opposite situation in Henry James's *The Portrait of a Lady*. Ralph Touchett tells Isabel Archer that he is giving her the means, the money, to determine her own fate; he wants to sit back and watch what becomes of her. The audience of *Dogskin*, though, has no sense of Alan and the Dog changing through a gradual inner exploration. They are not moving forward though experiences, as Isabel Archer does when she learns the truth about Osmond, or as Yeats's Cuchulain does when he turns and fights the waves in *On Baile's Strand*. Auden's characters move in circles. Cuchulain may not always act rationally, but he is action incarnate; he always moves through the maze—more often cuts through it—no matter what the consequences.

It is not until Alan arrives in Paradise Park that Auden begins to explore the idea of a personal salvation. Alan and Francis, still disguised as the Dog, meet a Berkeleian poet who tells him where Francis is:

> Poet (tapping his forehead). Here. Everything's here. You're here. He's here. The park is here. If I shut my eyes they all disappear.
> Alan. And what happens if I shut *my* eyes? Do you disappear, too?
> Poet (crossly). No, of course not! I'm the only real person in the whole world. (243)

One must shape his own reality. But the poet does not understand that he cannot ignore his membership in the human community. He lives in isolation and denies his birth, not understanding that there is also a spiritual reality. Instead of saying, "Yes, I did that," and moving on, he drops out of life:

> Alan. Isn't your Father the famous financier?
> Poet. I used to think so. But I got tired of that and forgot him. Give me another cigarette.

After being bitten by the Dog, he cries, "Oh my poor hand!" Alan answers, "Never mind. Just shut your eyes and forget about us." But the poet ignores the flaws in his own philosophy: "Oh, I've forgotten *you* long ago! It's my hand I keep remembering! (243).

After meeting the poet, Alan and Dog get tangled in a farcical intrigue in Paradise Park, this time with invalids and an incompetent doctor. Other than the comment made on modern medicine as a placebo for society's ills, the scene adds little value to the play and only provides Alan and Dog with a reason to leave the park. On the Highroad, alone at night, the two fall asleep, and the chorus reminds the audience again that in sleep men are "all ... members upon one condition,/ That they forget their own importance ..." (254). There are no masks in sleep. The capitalist, the fascist, the poet all share in the same human experience. The "charades of self-deception," of "wearing their public masks in both public and private" (Izzo, 119), are stopped for a time, but sadly only when they temporarily give up their control over their consciousness.

One last important adventure befalls Alan and Dog, this one at the Nineveh Hotel, where a small stage is set for a cabaret show. Madame Bubbi, "an immense woman in a sequin dress" appears to proclaim that all things good are British: "Remember British Love is quite the best." The Nineveh girls, in their robot-like exploitation, "Come to excite you" (Auden, 261):

> We lift our legs for your masculine inspection,
> You can admire us without our correction, we
> Do this nightly. (262)

Finally, the feature performer appears, Destructive Desmond, who is carrying a Rembrandt and a knife: "I suppose I can do what I like with my own painting" (265), he proclaims over the protestations of an art expert in the audience. A drum roll sounds, and, to the cheers of the audience, he slashes the painting. The capitalist believes that possession of an art object is de facto ownership of the concept of art.

Alan, weakened by the onslaught of disturbing experiences, succumbs to the charms of an odd sort of harlot—a beautiful mannequin. He takes her to his bedroom and tears up his picture of

Iris Crewe, murmuring to his mannequin, "For, love, in your arms I find the only treasure" (271) Nearby, the dog skin, now absent of Francis, begins to speak. We are reminded again of Yeats's "Man and the Echo" when the dog skin observes that humanity has been unable to accept responsibility, to say "I did that," and move forward. Too often we are frozen, and lost in the spinning cycles of the Dreaming Back. The dog skin recalls the last time his owner, a famous author, spoke to him:

> *(Quoting the author):* I say to myself: You fired that shell. It isn't the cold general on his white horse, nor the owner of the huge factory, nor the luckless poor, but you.... We have conjured up all the vigours and all the splendors, skilfully transformed our envy into an image of the universal mother, for which the lad of seventeen whom we have always sent and will send again against our terrors, gladly immolates himself. *(Dog Skin):* It was the last talk I ever had with him. He couldn't bear the sight of me after that evening and sold me as soon as he could. (273–74)

Like Alan, who is spinning downward, the dog skin's owner sees only a repetition of what he and others before him have done. There is no possibility of change.

When Alan is unable to pay his bill at the hotel, Francis reveals his true identity and helps Alan escape. Before the final scene of the play, once again in Pressan Ambo, the Chorus defines the hopelessness of the human condition:

> Man divided always and restless always: afraid and unable to forgive:
> Unable to forgive his parents, or his first voluptuous rectal sins
>
> Seeing others only in reference to himself....
>
> Men will profess devotion to almost anything
>
> Unite.
> Your knowledge and your power are capable of infinite extension:
> Act. (279–80)

But Auden, although he hopes otherwise, believes that man will not act; he will only spin. He is not likely to change, and yet self-knowledge and self-power are the only paths to salvation. The stage is set for the final scene. Alan and Francis, at least, have a chance.

Pressan Ambo has found a new system to follow in the absence of their traditional leader. It is Iris's wedding day to another man, a political climber. Alan reveals himself and presents Francis to his community. When Francis confesses his disguise, the villagers grow uncomfortable because he has "had a dog's eye view" of them for ten years (285). He tells them:

> You are not the extraordinary monsters I thought. You are not individually important. You are just units in an immense army.... You are fighting your own nature, which is to learn and to choose. (285–86)

The Vicar retorts, "Don't listen to him. He is trying to destroy religion. Satan will destroy us all." Alan reminds the Vicar of the lessons taught about loving God and each other, and asks,

> Why is it you will not lift a finger to destroy a social system in which one man can only succeed at the expense of injury to another? (286)

Nothing has come from the quest except an understanding that nothing has come from the quest. There is no hope for community.

Dramatically, Auden and collaborator Isherwood were left with no effective solution, and so they provided two. In one ending of the play—when Francis dies after being stabbed by a hatpin—Alan leaves to save himself. When Iris arrives and asks, "Where's Alan?" a villager replies, "He's been away a long time and that's all over" (292). Memory of Alan and Francis will soon fade. In an earlier ending, Francis declares that he will become "a unit in the army of the other side" (xxiv). He departs with his first recruits, including Alan, and the Chorus concludes with a paraphrase of the communist dictum: "'To each his need: from each his power'" (595). In either case, the ending is anticlimactic. Alan (and in the original version, Alan and Francis) has missed the point. He leaves to do what? To be what? To be like the Poet in Paradise Park? Personal salvation is internal, and Alan (and Francis) could have found it anywhere—in Ostnia, in Westland, in Paradise Park, in Pressan Ambo. They are unable to construct their own validity, and are thus enslaved by others' reality. A man who heeds the precept can be destroyed by the inexorable forces of life, but he cannot be defeated by them. Yeats's Cuchulain intuits this; Alan and Francis do not.[4]

---

[4]Isherwood was largely responsible for writing the final scene in the original ending. Mendelson explains that Auden "wrote the new dialogue [for the version in which Francis dies] according to a scenario supplied by Isherwood" (Auden, xxiv).

Auden was uncertain about his own role in and his beliefs about the political world during this period in his life, and his uncertainly is evident in *Dogskin*. His vision was like a photographer's who did not yet have the skills to keep his figures in aesthetic balance. He still wished for absolute answers, and there were none to give. The fact that Auden and Isherwood found it necessary to supply two endings for *Dogskin* suggests that both writers were beginning to realize that a single solution for society's ills may be inadequate.

Two years later Auden's ideas were articulated more clearly in another venture with Christopher Isherwood, *The Ascent of F6*. When Michael Ransom says in his opening soliloquy, "One can picture Ulysses' audience: a crook speaking to crooks" (Auden, 295), we are immediately reminded of the false teachers in *Dogskin*. Only on the summits of mountains, far from the madding crowd, can Ransom find the unpolluted air:

> Here is no knowledge, no communication, no possession; nothing that a bishop could justify, a stockbroker purchase or an elderly scientist devote years to explaining.... (296)

Ransom's name, though, suggests that he is not as free from the human condition as he might wish. Like *Dogskin's* poet, he doesn't completely understand that retreating or removing himself from the Others may not work. Something more has to happen. Hidden in the road to this discovery are land mines that can defeat and destroy.

The plot of the play switches between Ransom's adventures and the complaints of Mr. and Mr. A., who epitomize the media-controlled general British public. Times are difficult, and they are discontent, unhappy, and restless—dangerous emotions, the seeds of rebellion: "When will they notice us? When will they help us? When there's a war!" (298). They plead, "Give us something to live for" (299). Mr. and Mrs. A. need something to "take us out of ourselves. Out of the oppression of this city ..." (298). This need is supplied by the government, represented in part by Sir James Ransom, Michael Ransom's twin brother and, symbolically, his alterego. He chooses British Sudoland as a way to deflect "problems raised by a great democratic electorate" (300). With nearby Ostnia threatening to claim the mountain "F6" and invade Sudoland, the British government needs to do something, as well, to protect its enormous financial investment in the tiny country. James Ransom's aristocratic colleague, Lord Stagmantle, explains:

> The truth … is that the natives of British Sudoland would like us
> to go to hell.… The truth is that we've got fifty millions invested
> in the country and we don't intend to budge—not if we have to
> shoot every nigger from one end of the land to the other. (301)

In order to cement the British hold on Sudoland, James wants
his brother to lead an expedition to F6. When he fails to convince
Michael, who responds, "Keep to your world. I will keep to mine"
(310), James solicits help from their mother, who, like Mrs. Shaw
in *Paid on Both Sides*, manipulates Michael's guilt. She convinces
him to climb the formidable peak. James knows that the expedition will provide opportunities for imperialistic propaganda. If his
brother can capture the summit, the British public (their passions
aroused by the media) will want to keep British Sudoland, the
colony F6 borders.

It works, at least at first. The newspaper reports excite the
public. The quest becomes symbolic: Michael's journey is their
own, to rid them of everything that seems wrong in their lives,
never understanding that the British are themselves the foreigners
in Sudoland:

> *Mrs. A.…* The foreigner everywhere,
> Competing in trade, competing in sport,
> Competing in science and abstract thought:
> And we just sit down and let them take
> The prizes! There's more than a mountain at stake. (332)

But the expedition is a disaster, and in the end all the climbers
die, including Michael Ransom. Filled with guilt or angst or
pride—probably all three—Ransom dies because he does
another's bidding and is defeated because he never understands
why he submitted.

In *F6*, Auden's idea of tragic drama comes close to Yeats's. Because Michael cannot "keep to his world," he dies; but different
from the bold Cuchulain, Michael created a world at least partially
from the feelings of guilt and resentment over his childhood. Long
before any request from James, when Michael was climbing mountains of his own choosing, he was already caught in the Dreaming
Back.

The old man in Yeats's *Purgatory* (published in the same year
as *F6)* is trapped by his family history as much as Michael Ransom
is, and decides that to end the corruptness of his lineage he must
kill his son. His aristocratic mother had married a groom from her
father's stables, and so began the destruction of order:

My father burned down the house when drunk.

I stuck him with a knife,
That knife that cuts my dinner now,
And after that I left him in the fire.
(Yeats, *Collected Plays*, 432)

The old man himself had a careless coupling with a tinker's daughter to produce his own son, who is untroubled by conscience:

What's right and wrong?
My grand-dad got the girl and the money.
(Yeats, *Variorum Plays*, 1043)

The question of right and wrong is irrelevant to him. Yeats demonstrates in the boy's speech the concerns of the class that democracy begot: lust and money. There is in the heritage of the grandfather, perpetuated in the old man and his son, a commonness that detests and fears all excellence. Instead of imitating the example of better people, this kind of man works to destroy and suppress that which he recognizes as greater than himself, but he can imagine no means of changing the order of things other than through more destruction. The blood of his mother and father have never mixed in his body, but have served only to make the contrary aspects of his nature more distinct.

The old man sees a young girl in a lighted window as the Dreaming Back, the spinning in history, begins. The boy sees "nothing but an empty gap in the wall" (Yeats, *Variorum Plays*, 1045). The old man watches, horror-stricken, as his drunken father stumbles from the stable to the marriage-chamber. The old man tries to warn his mother, but he cannot make himself known to the ghosts who must live through their torment again:

Do not let him touch you! It is not true
That drunken men cannot beget,
And if he touch he must beget
And you must bear his murderer.
Deaf! Both deaf! (1046)

They do not hear him; they are so wrapped in their Dreaming Back that they have lost touch with everything else. The old man's attempts to help have been fruitless. He is unable to assist the ghosts of his parents.

The son tries to sneak off with a bag of money belonging to them both. The father struggles with him and stabs him:

> My father and my son on the same jack-knife!
> That finishes—there—there—there—. (1048)

The old man believes that killing his son will set his mother free and let her be "in the light because / ... I killed that lad ..." (1049). But he is mistaken. Even as he speaks he hears the hoof beats that announce another round of the Dreaming Back. He is "Twice a murderer and all for nothing" (1049). The play ends with the old man's appeal:

> Release my mother's soul from its dream!
> Mankind can do no more. Appease
> The misery of the living and the remorse of the dead.
>
> (1049)

There is little hope that a spirit can be released from the Dreaming Back. Even though the old man believes that he has completed the ritual that will free his mother, she turns again to her torment. Freedom, then, does not consist of following some prescription, but in action which breaks the chain of cause and event. As Kant suggested, we may in fact be captives of determinism, but if we act as if we are free, we will be.

Yeats's final comment on the trauma of twentieth-century consciousness is contained in *The Death of Cuchulain*, also published in 1939. In this play the Irish hero has fought his last battle and, mortally wounded, straps himself to a tree in order that he may die on his feet, as befits a hero. He is confronted by a blind beggar who has been attracted by the twelve-penny reward promised for Cuchulain's head. The most powerful of men is now too weak to resist. The irony is unmistakable, and the situation arrests Cuchulain for a moment. "Twelve pennies!" he says. Then immediately, "What better reason for killing a man?" (Yeats, *Collected Plays*, 444). He recognizes that at any moment forces beyond his control can kill him, but he cannot be defeated unless he acknowledges another's power. He says,

> There floats out there
> The shape that I shall take when I am dead.
> My soul's first shape, a soft feathery shape,
> And is not that a strange shape for the soul
> Of a great fighting man? (444)

"The shape that I shall take when I am dead." With these words Yeats cuts through the concerns of this century. Whether or not we are controlled by mechanical or religious determinism, as long as we act as if we are independent agents, we are. We will no longer cower before the forces which loom over us, but by our actions obviate them. We will fight the fecund sea itself.

Both Auden and Yeats experimented within the framework of an evolving modern drama. In the final years before his death in early 1939, Yeats continued to be interested in a world spirit—*anima mundi*—that would reclaim our sense of a human community. After *F6*, Auden found his way, somewhat predictably, to yet another dogma, Christianity. Perhaps because of the difference in their ages—Yeats was in his last years and his "temptation was quiet," Auden was still young and politically involved—Auden felt more strongly than the older poet the effects of corruption on reason and power, and may have had more difficulty in letting go of the possibilities of an external fix. Richard Ellmann explains that if Yeats had spoken to Auden at the end of his life he could have "maintained that he was in his supernatural beliefs much less dogmatic than Auden, in his later phase of revived Christian feeling, has become. Auden would have sternly replied ... that there was no virtue in stickling [sic] at the wrong dogma" (Ellmann, 115).

But it is not only conception that separates the two playwrights. It is execution. In Yeats's drama there is a combination of lyric intensity and dramatic vitality that grows naturally out of the material. James Flannery writes of Yeats's "struggle between lyric instinct and histrionic temperament" and credits that struggle with the "unity that [Yeats] ultimately created out of the dialectic of opposites" (Flannery, 1–2). In other words, Yeats creates a tension in his plays between the dramatic and the lyric, which give them movement.

Perhaps in an attempt to appeal to the common man, much of Auden's drama is heavily infused with elements of farce or burlesque. With the exception of *F6*, his plays are static. Even in *Dogskin*, where the characters are physically mobile and more interconnected than in previous work, they are not really much more vital than the stiff figures in *Paid on Both Sides*. Their movement is more often frenetic than illuminating. There is minimal internal intensity even in Francis and Alan, who, after all, learn little on their journey.

The difference between Auden's and Yeats's tragic dramas is that the former comes to the conclusion that we must not accept another's reality, for if we do, we will face destruction. Yeats agrees, but takes the formula further. In his adaptation of the *Noh*, he explores the possibility that the drama, with its depiction of the

Dreaming Back, may be an instrument of release for those of us living in the West in the twentieth century. If we follow the pattern shown in the *Noh*, we may be able to break out of the cycle of endless repetition of guilt and reproach. Yeats explores the different requirements of the *Noh* in several plays, trying first one solution, then another, until *Purgatory* teaches him that even if all these stipulations are met, there is nothing that will free us from the burning wheel of earth-bound existence except our declaration that we "make the truth."

The fact that most of us will be unable to make that breakthrough is what constitutes the new tragedy. Many have admitted that old definitions don't adequately fit a modern world; and some, like Arthur Miller, for example, have recognized that tragedy can as well affect a "low" man as a king. But what Yeats showed us (and what Auden was reaching for) was that all tragedy, from the Greeks to the moderns, is predicated upon a character becoming fixated at a point in his life and being unable to move out of that position. Tragedy, then, depends less on Aristotelian models of hamartia and hubris than upon our recognition of and identification with characters who are stuck in their reality, unable to let go and return to the continuum that is life. We see an Emer or a Dervogilla, a John Nower or a Michael Ransom, and recognize how much of their obsession we share. Because life is movement, such characters are doomed to spin around such a vortex until they are sucked under and drowned.

Works Cited

Auden, W.H., and Isherwood, Christopher. *Plays and Other Dramatic Writings by W.H. Auden 1928–1938.* Edited by Edward Mendelson. Princeton: Princeton UP, 1988.

Blake, William. "A Memorable Fancy." In *English Romantic Writers*, edited by David Perkins. New York: Harcourt, Brace and World, 1967.

Ellmann, Richard. *Eminent Domain.* New York: Oxford UP, 1970.

Flannery, James. *W.B. Yeats and the Idea of a Theatre.* New Haven: Yale UP, 1976.

Izzo, David Garrett. *Christopher Isherwood: His Era, His Gang, and the Legacy of the Truly Strong Man.* Columbia: South Carolina University Press, 2001.

Mendelson, Edward. *Early Auden.* Cambridge: Harvard UP, 1981.

Yeats, W.B. "Four Lectures by W.B. Yeats 1902–4." In *Yeats Annual #8* (78–122), edited by Richard Londraville. London: Macmillan, 1991.

———. *The Collected Plays of W.B. Yeats.* New York: Macmillan, 1952.

———. *The Collected Poems of W.B. Yeats.* Edited by Richard Finneran. New York: Macmillan, 1989.

———. "Per Amica Silentia Lunae." In *Mythologies* (319–69). New York: Macmillan, 1959. 319–69

———. *The Variorum Edition of the Plays of W.B. Yeats.* Edited by Russell K. Alspach. London and New York: Macmillan, 1966. [Cited from the corrected 2nd printing (1966) or later printings.]

Letters and Iceland:
W.H. Auden and Generational Differences among Gay Modernists

Robert L. Caserio

Just when and where did Auden give thought to his relationships with gay writers alongside him and particularly with those who came before him? Here Robert L. Caserio traces a lineage that includes Edward Carpenter, Frederick Rolfe (Baron Corvo), W. Somerset Maugham, and T.E. Lawrence. He targets Letters from Iceland *as the verse in which Auden gives clues to his place in the history of gay Modernism.*

> "For no one thinks unless a complex makes him"
> *Letter to Lord Byron*, Part V

The first problem one wants to address is the always perplexing relation of Auden's published work to his homosexuality. Auden at times does outrightly own that relation, even though until recently critics have overlooked the fact and the impact of his avowals.[1] And when they do not overlook the fact, critics too frequently take Auden's comment in 1947 to Alan Ansen—"It's wrong to be queer"—as Auden's summary credo, rather than as a temporary speculation, or a passing remark, or a sign of the poet's negative capability. Still, there also is undoubted reticence and self-criticism in Auden's disclosures: far more than current taste and assumptions expect and indeed require. Does the reticence mean that Auden's work suffers from, and even is shaped by, self-censorship and cultural homophobia?[2]

---

[1] Richard Bozorth's full-scale corrective is now in print.

[2] The biographical enlistments of Auden's comment to Ansen (80) produce strikingly divergent analyses. Mendelson (1999) sees the comment as a definitive result of Auden's recent affair with Rhoda Jaffe. He

The answer is not simple. It must comprehend the possibility that expressions of homosexuality in Auden's work, or even criticisms and disavowals of it, are shaped by Auden's debate with writers who are, as it were, Auden's gay elders in the practice of loving and writing. What looks to us, from a long distance, as closeting and censorship is really the buried sign of a once-open conversation among gay modernists, and a generational conflict among them, too. If Auden doesn't speak up loudly about his homosexuality, or speak loudly for it, the cause might be his aim to speak differently from earlier gay ways of speaking up. The cause also might be an intention to extend a predecessor's reticence, even if Auden's motives are not the same as the predecessor's. In either case, it is time for critics to engage the hypothesis that multiple gay personalities and voices—not just Auden's own, but others'—inform his work. One can suggest that Auden's *Letters from Iceland* (1937), besides being a product of collaboration with his "heter" poet friend Louis MacNeice, also originates in, and expresses, Auden's inward conversations, collaborations, and conflicts with two, indeed with three, preceding generations of gay elders. The elders are represented by Edward Carpenter, Frederick Rolfe, W. Somerset Maugham, and T.E. Lawrence. Auden's characteristic reticences and utterances result as much from his relation to these writers as from his alliance with hetero-normality.[3]

---

suggests that the affair made Auden's "militant homosexuality harder to maintain" (268); in a footnote on the same page, he glosses what appears to be the comment's "implicit contrast" between the superiority of "heterosexual partners" and the inferiority of homosexual partners. Davenport-Hines emphasizes the factitiousness of some of Auden's feelings for Jaffe; he interprets the comment to Ansen as an expression of Auden's restless need for "comprehensive experience" (245), and immediately reminds readers that a year later Auden wrote "The Platonic Blow, by Miss Oral" and that Auden's passion for Ronald Firbank's homoerotic imagination of utopia was revived by visits to Fire Island during the time of the affair with Jaffe. Humphrey Carpenter, who appears to have no knowledge of Auden's comment to Ansen, treats the end of the relation with Jaffe by quoting Auden's remarks that the affair "was a sin" and "did not affect me at all. I felt I was cheating'" (349).

[3]In Mendelson's two volumes, Carpenter, Rolfe, and Maugham are not mentioned; a discussion of Auden's relation to T.E. Lawrence is fixated, as in other commentaries, on Auden's 1934 review of Liddell Hart's biography of Lawrence, rather than on Auden's relation to any specific text by Lawrence. Only Ronald Firbank receives attention from Mendel-

Within or alongside the problem of Auden's modes of avowing his homosexuality in print arises a second problem, one equally difficult to explore. It is the problem of the autonomy of poetry in relation to the culture in which any poet produces it. In *Letters from Iceland*, a so-called travel book that is a brilliant modernist collage, Auden includes a five-part verse epistle, *Letter to Lord Byron*. In the epistle Auden acknowledges that art is dependent on economic history and the artist's class situation. There is even a New Historical reading of Jane Austen: "Beside her," Auden writes, "Joyce seems innocent as grass./It makes me most uncomfortable to see/An English spinster of the middle class ... /Reveal so frankly and with such sobriety/The economic basis of society"(182). And the economic basis of literature. On this showing, Austen's novel gives the lie to all autonomous impulse, artistic or social. Only in the romantic era in England, according to Auden's literary history here, did artists aim for and achieve what (as Pierre Bourdieu would call it) "the conquest of autonomy"; but Auden admits that art's conquest of autonomy seems to have been more illusory than real. *Letter to Lord Byron* concedes context's defining relation for art. The poem, in spite of its jaunty tone, is legible as an act of resignation. Auden resigns himself and his poetry to dependence on everything external: on class ambitions and conflicts; on normality; on the mundane order of things; on "Capitalism in its later phases" (356). And yet *Letter to Lord Byron* addresses one of the conquerors of autonomy. The conquerors, according to the poem's Part III, created a "Poet's Party" (254), a political-aesthetic independence movement, in the name of the

---

son and other Auden scholars as a gay writer with whom Auden is in dialogue; but the attention is fleeting at best. There is one passing reference to Firbank in Mendelson 1981. Mendelson 1999 describes Auden's efforts in 1947 to secure a reprint of Firbank's "butterfly-like novels" (283), and characterizes Auden's postwar interest in Firbank as a "choosing [of] Firbank for a brief term as his literary master" (284). Auden's enduring intergenerational dialogue with Firbank deserves a full and separate study. I have not further burdened my essay with an attempt to include Firbank as another voice in the dialogue. The omission is regrettable; nevertheless, Auden's relation to the other writers has been even more ignored. I hope the present essay might initiate serious full-scale consideration of gay predecessors' influence on Auden; I also hope that this essay can be read profitably alongside the last chapter ("From This Island") of Mendelson 1981. The latter volume contains relatively few pages on *Letter to Lord Byron*, and fewer on *Letters from Iceland.*

special character, the singularity of art. Is the conquest only a delusion? If so, why is Auden writing to Byron in Byron's style, as if Auden were Byron's double, and Byron were writing to himself.

I think we must consider that the most important aim of *Letters from Iceland* is to meditate upon, rethink, and even to instance, the relations of art to its own autonomy as well as to its heteronomous contexts. For Auden a poet does yield or resign his independence but only thanks to art's capacity for discovering a measure of liberty from context, and only thanks as well to the singularity of the poet and the poet's work, which also marks a limit for context. The Iceland of *Letters from Iceland* is no less a real place than the English isle or MacNeice's native Ireland, but it is also an island of letters a literary place. In Iceland, we need to see, the two poets produce a book on literature's situation, its ground in the world. That ground is admitted to be unreal in the poem called "Journey to Iceland" "This is an island and therefore," Auden writes, "Unreal" (185) "But," MacNeice writes in an answering poem in the collection "we are not changing ground to escape from facts/But rather to find them" (192–94). "The crude/Embryo rummages every latitude/Looking for itself, its nature, its final pattern.... /We find our nature daily or try to find it,/We must keep moving to keep pace/Or else drop into Limbo, the dead place" (194). From such lines as these, we gather that the unreal, which includes art's phantasms, the litter of letters, is not Limbo; and even might save us from death.

The saving aspect is that literature opens a space in which we can rummage, looking for the final pattern that might be our nature. Of course the final pattern might only amount, disappointingly, to our context, rather than be a discovery of our singular selves. If nothing rummaged from the islanded autonomous literary space were to survive the journey home to context, we'd have to resign ourselves to autonomy's defeat. Nevertheless, even if hidden within a historical reality named Iceland, the island is there: a mystery, or an alter ego, out of which or for the sake of which one might shape a speech or a vision that reconciles us to where we are.

But what does Auden suggest the island place of letters has to do with homosexuality? If homosexuality's isolated place, its autonomy, cannot survive a return home, should its reconciliation to a censorious context be accepted or tolerated? In Part V of *Letter to Lord Byron*, Auden doubts if homosexuality, represented in one of Part V's stanzas by Hugo Wolf's art song about Ganymede, can nove us creatively away from that intractably real ground of our contexts: the political state and economic order. "The Great Utopia, free of all complexes,/the Withered State is, at the moment, such/A dream as that of being both the sexes./I like Wolf's Goethe-Lieder very much,/But doubt if Ganymede's appeal will touch/—That marvelous cry with its ascending phrases—/Capitalism in its later phases" (356). Ganymede can help neither the state nor its capitalist underpinnings wither away. And if Auden believes that, doesn't his resignation, coupled with his indirect avowal of homosexuality here, help the State flourish? What has happened to the power whereby a journey to a place of letters, a change of ground from fact to fantasy, can be a finding of new facts, rather than an escape from, or a capitulation to, facts at their old, oppressive worst? Wouldn't directly confrontational speech by Auden about sex and about Auden's homosexual kind wither the state more than Goethe and Hugo Wolf? Art song be damned!

We have to remember, however, that not just Auden is speaking. Directness of statement is limited by the poem's bi-textual voice: the side-by-sideness of Byron with Auden. A sideways rather than straightforward speech results from intergenerational talk. Besides, there is also intragenerational conversation in progress, since Auden and MacNeice are writing in company. The company disperses directness. But it can claim indirectness as an autonomous, state-withering force. For the authorial comradeship of *Letters from Iceland* serves notice of a straight-gay alliance. The writers seem to know in advance the strong hatred for the so-called Nancy poets which George Orwell, within a year *of Letters from Iceland*, will utter in *The Road to Wigan Pier*. It's MacNeice who contributes to the *Letters* a campy segment, composed of a long-winded epistolary chat by an ex-schoolteacher named Hetty, who writes vacation letters from Iceland to a correspondent named Nancy. The joke is that "Hetty" is code for "heter," as in heterosexual, so that the letters are a Hetty-Nancy boy line of communication and friendship.

Auden's reticence, then, is not censorship but resistance to censorship, a mark of autonomy; and the reticence also reflects in part MacNeice's pro-gay, third-party contribution to the Auden-Byron pair. Where more than one person is expressing himself, there is bound to be a knotting complication of speech. But there is even more complexity of conversation producing Auden's autonomizing reticence. Neither Auden's collaboration with a member of his own generation of writers, nor his doubling of Byron's ancient generation, matters more to his poetry's character and career than does Auden's implicit conversation with gay modernists in the era preceding his own.

In the letter to Byron, Auden describes his and MacNeice's generation in the following way: "We were the tail, a sort of poor relation/To that debauched, eccentric generation/That ... made new glosses on the noun *Amor*" (333). Thanks to those glosses made by an earlier generation, the 29-year-old Auden doesn't have to gloss over his own *Amor*. When in the *Letter* he jokingly allegorizes himself as Pure-in-Heart, Auden reports of his personification that "He's gay" (334). The report is complemented by the poem's acknowledgment of Gide as another inspiring influence, and it also is complemented by the poem's imagination that Byron, were he alive, would form a political United Front with Gide. The Gide-Byron coalition makes sense in terms of the poem's evocation of the current social prominence of homosexuality in England. Mother England, Auden says, "looks odd today dressed up in peers/Slums, aspidistras, shooting-sticks, and queers" (355). In that last diction there is, to be sure, a satiric or self-satiric aggression. But Auden permits himself a flippancy about homosexuality's established appearance, in order to suggest that homosexual *Amor* is open to flippancy, and open even to criticism and to contest, not only because of its vulnerable minority, but also because of its now (in 1936) recognized public place. The use of "queer" is part of *Letter to Lord Byron*'s conversational commonplace style. And queer was made conversationally commonplace because of that prior time when an eccentric generation found itself uniquely receptive to the strange variety of modes whereby *Amor vincit omnia*. Since we are told that the earlier eccentric generation "grew up with their fathers at the War," we can surmise that their fathers—the grandfathers of Auden's era—grew up because of their new glosses on Eros no less than because of combat. Auden and his fellows are the tail to at least a pair of generations.

To attend to the effects of generational alliances, differences or conflicts among gay modernists might help us resist the attractive temptation to simplify cultural history. We simplify when we assume that there is a post-Stonewall consciousness superior to its predecessors; and we simplify when we assume that a previous era is characterized by a uniform epistemology of the closet. In the era of that hypothetical epistemology, as Auden's poem attests, something distinctly un-closeted went on. And its having gone on across generations facilitated gay writers' speculations and argu ments about what constitutes a queer tradition or about what use one might make of such tradition.

Because a sideways rather than straightforward speech results from intergenerational talk, the tradition often is hard to get at. Because of the difficulty it is easy to mistake and underestimate Auden's important relation to one preeminent queer eccentric in the older generation, Frederick Rolfe, the pseudonymous Baron Corvo, who belongs among the grandfathers of Auden's cultural time. Auden has an impulse to resist Rolfe; and the resistance can look like Auden's phobic compromising of his own group label. A crabby foreword Auden wrote in 1953 for a re-issue *of The Desire and Pursuit of the Whole* (1909) intensifies one's unease. Auden's foreword stresses the unpleasant character of Rolfe's protagonist Nicholas Crabbe, and the likeness of Crabbe to the the real-life Rolfe, who for Auden epitomizes "a homosexual paranoid" (v). The phrase is unsettling: how narrow or how broad a specification is it? Does Auden want us to read Rolfe because it would purge us—even us homosexuals—of paranoia; or would reading him renew invidious reductions of homosexuality to a clinical condition? *The Desire and Pursuit of the Whole* manages to represent, against the odds of cultural censorship, male-male romance of the greatest intensity; so why is Auden edgy about this gloss on *Amor* from the eccentric generation he was celebrating in the mid-1930s? One answer is that the paranoid style stands in Auden's mind for elitist, neo-aristocratic ideas of heroism, and consequently for anti-democratic practices in love and politics. In his foreword Auden is not charmed by Rolfe's characterization of the male lovers in the novel, because one of the lovers is only the soothing submissive subordinate of the demanding, and paranoid, heiresiarch Crabbe. Yet Auden does pay his respects to Rolfe; so why? Auden recommends Rolfe's creative ability to turn watery Venice, an island city, into a utopia, "The Great Good Place, ... the perfect embodiment of ... beauty, tradition, grace and ease" (ix). In 1953 Rolfe's Venice perhaps resonates with Auden's memory of his own island journey to a Good Place two decades earlier. But to understand Auden's dialogue and differences with Rolfe, still more answers are necessary.

Rolfe belongs undoubtedly to the context in which *Letters from Iceland* was gestated. *The Desire and Pursuit of the Whole* was first published posthumously in 1935. In the preceding year appeared A.J.A. Symons' brilliant *The Quest for Corvo: An Experiment in Biography*. It is from Symons that Auden derives the diagnosis of

Rolfe as a homosexual paranoid. It also is notable that Symons' diagnosis, on which Auden's foreword relies, is subtle and generous; and a similar generous diagnosis (albeit more euphemistic about Rolfe's sexuality) would have been read by Auden a decade earlier. In 1925 D.H. Lawrence (whose work was consumed by young Auden) favorably reviewed a re-issue of Rolfe's greatest success, the novel *Hadrian the Seventh* (1904). If we judge solely from Auden's reaction to the paranoid protagonist of the Venetian novel, we might think that The Great Good Place is successfully imagined there only despite Rolfe and Crabbe's elitist and suspicious projections. But Crabbe is another version of the earlier novel's Hadrian, who also is aristocratic, homosexual, and paranoid, and who is the vehicle of another utopian imagination (a radically renewed and unworldly Catholic Church). Side by side the homoeroticized figures of Crabbe and Hadrian suggest a creative tie between exceedingly isolated (hence paranoia-prone) singular individuals and utopian places. Moreover, because Hadrian is a Pope, and because the character of Crabbe combines homosexual desire with priestly asceticism, what is continually refigured and kept vivid in Rolfe's work is homosexual shamanism. This shamanism has a compelling political as well as aesthetic interest for Auden. It signifies another layer of intergenerational exchanges and differences among gay modernists.

The great propounder of shamanism for English homosexual cultures is Edward Carpenter. In *Intermediate Types among Primitive Folk* (1914), Carpenter's shaman is the prophet or priest of all cultural advance, including an advance upon heterosexuality. (Carpenter associates the latter with arrested development.) Carpenter's shaman is at once a priest of love and an ascetic, for his eros inspires those sublimations—for example, religion and art—that build civilization. Both homosexuality and art in Carpenter are the vehicles of humanity's conquest of autonomy. But the Carpenter shaman-priest is no heiresiarch. What the shaman advances toward is democracy, Carpenter's greatest passion, with which Carpenter believed homosexuality had an innate affinity. He discovered this affinity partly through an experience he recounts in an afterword to poems he wrote in the 1880s about democracy. The experience was of an inward autonomous place or space, "transcending the ordinary bounds of personality" (410) and suggesting individuality to be an illusion. Carpenter understood the experience as a political vision, for the transcendence of personality spoke of a common mystery of being, which is shared by all without distinction or discrimination, and which hence guarantees our universal equality.

Auden could not but have been drawn to Carpenter's democratic vision and Carpenter's prestige among the generation of gay grandfathers. Yet he involved himself, and his versions of The Great Good Place, with Rolfe, who must be read as a gay artist creating shaman figures in order to contradict Carpenter's versions of homosexuality's importance for democracy. I suggest that, despite Rolfe's elitist bent, Auden was drawn to him as a far better writer than Carpenter, as a more powerfully creative artist—and therefore, whatever his biases, as a more trustworthy inspiration. Carpenter's writing characteristically sounds a note of Arnoldian sweetness and light. But the sweetness predominates—especially because Carpenter lacks Arnold's satiric edge—and this is at odds with Carpenter's weighty oppositional stance as a critic of heterosexuality. Carpenter himself describes his verse as airy and "yielding" (*Towards Democracy*, 415). *Intermediate Types* is a great poem, but it does not have the intransigence its doctrine needs and deserves, and whereby it might have been more attached to reality. And here is the probable nub of Auden's attraction to the Rolfe whom also he criticizes as paranoid. Rolfe's writing sentence by sentence instances the autonomy of homosexual spirit and craft in the face of a hostile world. However paranoid, Rolfe's masterful invectives against the world derive from a constant close attention he pays to it. His obsessive aggression against the prevailing social standards of normality, and the inventive gravity and hilarity with which his sentences grapple worldly contexts, maintain Rolfe's hold on reality even as his own shamanism, like that of his protagonists, makes him an island unto himself. Rolfe's books and his heroes model a structure of autonomous detachment from the world simultaneous with attachment to it that has a beautifully strange variant in *Letters from Iceland*.

I will set out the structure of the autonomy, because of the structure's relevance to the deep logic and to the multiple personae of *Letters from Iceland*. In *Hadrian the Seventh* an obscure Englishman named Rose is elected Pope, largely because of his decades-long fidelity to a priestly vocation, in which he continues to hope, in spite of cruel rebuffs by the Church. Rose believes in aristocracy and hates socialism; he wouldn't have had time for Carpenter's lib-lab gay circle. But at the same time Rose is what one character calls an "academic anarchist" (117)! And indeed, once he becomes Pope (the seventh to take the name Hadrian), he manages to maintain the Church hierarchy and, at the same time, by a kind of anarchist fiat, he disestablishes the church's worldliness, partly by selling off every one of the Vatican treasures. He then endows the Italian nation with the proceeds of the sale, and thus at one blow constitutes Italy as the century's first welfare state. An enraged socialist who cannot bear that the ends of a Labour party should be achieved by an heresiarch assassinates Rose-Hadrian; but the assassination is almost less awful than the tabloid press's assassination of the Pope's character prior to his death. The tabloids discover that before Rose became Hadrian he had invented for himself a set of alternative personalities, and pseudonyms to go with them; and the papers use the discovery to maintain that the Pope is a lying charlatan. Hadrian is coerced into confession. "In fact," he tells his cardinals, "I split up my personality.... There were four of me at least.... Most people have only half developed their single personalities. That a man should split his into four and more; and should develop each separately and perfectly, was so abnormal that many normals failed to understand it" (392).

Yet it is understandable, Rolfe and Rose, or Rolfe-Rose, explain; and it also is not insane. The splitting of personality is not a disorder, but an order; a disciplined way of response to material circumstance and necessity, a materialism, as it were. Each of Rose's personae was invented so that Rose, vocationally frustrated, could find employment, in lieu of a calling; and each employment exacted a different work, hence a different character for the sake of the disciplined, fully developed agency necessary to do the work. The very capitalism around which the Pope makes an end run is what exacted the Pope's multiple personality order. And what *Hadrian the Seventh* suggests is that economic and social modernity exact of each of us, as a pragmatistic and materialist disciplinary vocation, a similar order.

But in one's response to that exaction, a curious supplement is discovered. In the light of multiple personality the ego has no individual identity; at least it has no match with any ordinary bounds of personality (including bodily bounds), and the ego's individuation is illusory. What a unit of multiple personality order has, instead of individuality, is singularity—a singularity that is the sum of multiple personal co-consciousnesses. The place or space out of which multiple personality order unfolds is a mysterium tremendum. It is that region Carpenter spoke of: "transcending ... the ordinary bounds of personality" and suggesting that individuality is an illusion. This must be a radically autonomous region. Its freedom from determination convinced Carpenter that it was a fountain of democracy. But fountains need conduits. In Hadrian the Seventh's life as Rose, Rose knew this autonomous space or place could have no effectiveness in the world unless it were made over into one or another pseudonymous executive personality. To express and to enact itself the mystery must be repressed and disciplined even by the shaman, and certainly by those who—like Rose in his pre-papal life—must resign themselves to capitalism in its later phases. The condition whereby autonomous spirit gets to utter itself turns out to be a grinding servitude to one's servants—to those several personalities without which one's curiously singular spirit has no agency in the world, and can only submit to context. But inasmuch as one personality becomes the executive agent of the others, as Hadrian becomes the executive agent of Rose and of Rose's earlier distinct personalities, the mystery of multiple selves wins some measure of autonomy, even amidst service, and even when bound to context.

Multiple personality order is by now familiar to us, given the fact that we are imbued by the patternings of multiple personae invented by modernism, through exactly such figures as Rolfe-Rose. His "abnormal" endowment by *Amor* arguably helped him invent or consolidate those patternings; and Auden's early work seems a quest for those patterns' renewed instance in a younger gay generation. But Rolfe's attraction for Auden passed through persistent mediating stages. The mediations are burdened with conflict. Rolfe-Rose both negates and sublates Carpenter. Rose-Hadrian's queer aristocratic isolation, although it reacts against Carpenter's homoerotic egalitarianism, ends up as a comprehensive—and socialistic—benefit to the body politic. But an internal logic in Rolfe's imagination appears to dictate Hadrian's elimination from the world. He cannot endure, after all, the worldly contexts to which he is returned from his isolation of spirit. Auden might well have remembered D.H. Lawrence asking, in his review of Corvo, "What's the good of being Pope if you've got nothing but protest and aesthetics up your sleeve?" (329). The specter of Rolfe's persecution mania, and Auden's eagerness to move less indirectly than Rolfe to democracy, leads Auden to engage with another gay shaman: T.E. Lawrence. Auden's interest in this Lawrence has been much remarked; but there is more to say about it.

Compared to Carpenter and Rolfe, T.E. Lawrence was of an intermediate generation, as well as an intermediate type. His work
in the autonomizing of the Arab states, his very mode of transgressive dress, seems to spring out of Carpenter's pages about the
shaman's liberating political vocation. But unlike Carpenter's airy,
idealizing version of the public-minded homosexual hero,
Lawrence's version inhabits the world of real politics and embodied experience. The novelist Lawrence had answered his question
about protest and aesthetics by proposing that one should have
"up one's sleeve" not unworldy detachment and art but an un-
afraid intimacy with worldly power and with animal vitality. T.E.
Lawrence's career in Arabia and after had both. And in suiting the
novelist's proposal, Lawrence's career directs multiple personality
order toward universal democratic norms. To be sure, like Rolfe
Lawrence split up his personality. How many of him were there?
Overwhelmed by guilt because of his heroism in leading the Arabs
out of bondage to the Ottoman empire and back into bondage to
the British, in 1922 Lawrence created for himself the pseudonym
and the alter ego of J.H. Ross, in order to enlist in the ranks of the
RAF, as just one of the common mass of men in service. When this
strategy failed, he re-invented himself in 1925 as T.E. Shaw, and
enlisted all over again, finally with success. So we find that to the
Rolfe-Rose model of shamanistic agency, Ross-Shaw applies a corrective: his other personalities intend to be the agents of escape
from the rigors, terrors and paranoias of singularity and individu-
ated heroism. In Rolfe singularity results from the resolution of
multiple personalities into single identity; but Ross wants no identity. He wants to be merged in a collective rhythm. *The Mint*
(1935), the remarkable book which records his enlistments, and
which circulated in manuscript before its limited publication, ex-
ults that as "we gain attachment so we strip ourselves of personality"(248); we resolve "the mail and plate of our personality back
into the carbo-hydrate elements of being" (249). *The Mint* ends
when Ross-Shaw, having become an airman at last, feels
"everywhere a relationship: no loneliness any more" (250).

The path to "everywhere a relationship," a *ne plus ultra* of
democratic fusion, is harrowing. Radically undoing his own autonomy, Ross-Shaw commits himself to becoming a collective
technological enterprise: "the conquest of the air" by the RAF. The
enterprise is considered by Ross-Shaw to be "the first duty of our
generation" (218). He believes this in the spirit of anti-heroic, anti-
imperialist egalitarianism. To conquer the air, the men of the RAF

must be conquered daily, their bodies tortured by drill and training, by verbal beatings and demeaning commands. They are submitted to, penetrated by, an absolute hierarchy. Yet *The Mint*'s
author claims that aircraft technology turns the "technical men"
(233) on whom the flying machines depend into enemies of hierarchical soldiering. The conquest of the air is the end of plumed
wings, swords, eagles; the end of submission for everyone: that is
Lawrence's prophetic wager, and the purpose of his enlistment
and his personae. Indeed, the technological conquest will end the
British empire, in Lawrence's scheme; and at last will assuage his
bad conscience about Arabs.

Auden publically consummated his admiration for Lawrence
in his review, in 1934, of a biography by Basil Liddell Hart. The review couples Lawrence with Lenin as "the two whose lives ex-
emplify ... what is best and significant in our time, ... the most potent agents of freedom" (62). Yet two years later, on the brink of
departure for Iceland, Auden we know was at odds with the authority he had assigned Lawrence.[4] Was the cause of the change
The Mint, which likely was read in Auden's queer circle? Whether
or not Auden saw *The Mint* in manuscript between 1934 and its
ensuing publication, something disappointing in what it communicates about Lawrence seems to have penetrated to Auden. Ross-
Shaw, instead of solving the aesthetic and political tug of war
among autonomy, isolation, and worldly contexts, seems to have
become for Auden an inverted Rose-Rolfe. Rose-Rolfe figures an
excess of autonomy and isolation, but Ross-Shaw figures an opposite excess, a worldly attachment into which the singular mind and
will collapse altogether. Carpenter's shaman avatar of democracy
is dubiously incarnated in Lawrence.

Auden recalls the homosexual shaman priest's combination of
eros and asceticism when, in his review of Liddell Hart's biography, he refers questions of sexuality to Lawrence. "Personal love is
a neurotic symptom," Auden writes, "a bad answer to our real
wish to be united to ... life.... In our convalescence sexual relations
can ... but postpone our cure." The cure, Auden suggests, is "the
way back to real intimacy ... through a kind of asceticism" (62).
And Lawrence in 1934 appears to figure such curative asceticism.
But *The Mint*'s asceticism is indistinct from a quivering experience
of the flesh, an orgy of sensuousness which Ross-Shaw's writing
painstakingly evokes, even as it censors, or is squeamish about,

---

[4]See Mendelson, *Early Auden*, 248–51.

sense and sex. In the last stages of training, while the mechanics wait for a plane overdue to return to its hanger, Ross-Shaw describes the contentment of the workers as "drugged with ... absorption ... we lay there spread-eagled in a mesh of bodies, pillowed on one another and sighing in happy excess of relaxation" (249). The description does not square with Auden's claim that Lawrence illustrates how "sexual relations" will not cure isolation, how "the way back to real intimacy is through a kind of asceticism." Ross-Shaw's RAF democracy/technocracy radiates the heat of a long unconsummated or perhaps a perpetually blocked male-male rutting.

In Ross-Shaw sensuousness and asceticism fuse in a way that betrays the heroic shamanism which wanted to reshape the eros of "normals" by emphasizing the gaps between personal agency and mystical or mysterious abstraction, rather than by suppressing both in favor of "a mesh of bodies." Personality is unloaded by Ross-Shaw in exchange for collective flesh by merger, and democratic agency is identified by him with the material form of the best technology. Meanwhile, *The Mint*'s desire to accommodate the demos seems to require a drugged state so that Ross-Shaw's articulateness can be absorbed into the bodies of men whose sentences are, characteristically, "You bloody-fucking-cunting-syphilitic bastard'"(143) and whose democratic apotheosis is to become technological instruments. That model might be more congenial to our technological state than it is to Auden. In Auden's terms, Ross-Shaw does not gain autonomy, is not the most potent agent of freedom, after all. He loses his rank in Auden's imagination of predecessor gay allies, because Ross-Shaw refuses to give any place of honor in sexual or political considerations to the cultural and personal equivalents of Auden's figure for autonomy: islands.

Neither Rolfe, the father of the fathers at the war, nor Ross-Shaw, not quite old enough to be Auden's father, but of the war's generation, furnishes Auden the intergenerational alliance he appears to seek with gay modernists. Faced with the generational differences between the modernists Rolfe and Lawrence, Auden moves to an intermediate gay modernist—younger than Rolfe, older than Lawrence—W. Somerset Maugham.

Maugham must be read into *Letters from Iceland*, the *Letter to Lord Byron* included. However odd it is that Maugham be there, Auden tells us in "Letter to William Coldstream, Esq." that Maugham's stories, no less than Byron's poem, are being read on the Iceland trip (349). Now Byron has always been an idol for youth; but what is Maugham an idol of? In 1919, in *The Moon and Sixpence* Maugham writes into his novel's and his narrator's opening chapter the declaration that, where the post-war young are concerned, Maugham is "on the shelf" (7), out of date; that he, the novel's author who also is its I-narrator, was out of step already among the pre-war modernists. The painter Charles Strickland, who is the novelist-narrator's subject, was not out of step with his time; in contrast, Maugham confesses, he himself might best be compared to the poet George Crabbe's survival into the era of the Romantics, who were the Stricklands and the modernists of their age. Given the confession, it is all the more wonderful that Maugham should be in Auden's *Iceland*, from which letters get sent to the Romantic modernist Byron, and not to out-of-date Maugham-Crabbe.

Now that Maugham-Crabbe, yet another persona-complex, enters the queer hyphen-spliced characters in this foray into literary history, it is not surprising to notice that Maugham the narrator of Charles Strickland's tale becomes the artist's spokesman, his executive personality. In becoming that, almost against his will, in speaking for Strickland as well as about him, Maugham is perplexed by the contradictions that split personalities. "I'm reminded," he says of Strickland, "of those strange stories ... of another personality entering into a man and driving out the old one" (44). The Maugham-narrator would seem to be an impervious foil to such changes of personality: always the same phlegmatic observer, he is all consistency, whereas Strickland is indeed incoherent, in his passionate likes and dislikes, and in his way of acting them out. One moment the devoted friend of a man whose wife he is about to seduce, the next moment Strickland is throwing the cuckolded friend out of the cuckold's own house, as if the ejection were a reward for friendship. But, wonderfully, the narrator shows signs of inhabiting the same multiplicity. When Strickland incites a woman who loves him to commit suicide, the narrator discovers that his moral condemnation of Strickland feels hollow: "my disapprobation had in it already something of a pose" (105). The narrator is not the single, stable personality he himself expects to count on, especially when it comes to judging Strickland. Instead of maintaining disapprobation in Strickland's presence, the narrator has to prevent himself from laughing at Strickland's wit, or from laughing with Strickland at human absurdity: at the absurdity comprehended by Strickland's treachery and its fatal effects.

Maugham-Crabbe undergoes a split: "an interest in the singu
larities of human nature" is "so absorbing that ... moral sense is
powerless against it"(105). The older generation falls into mod
ernism. Strickland occasions the fall, but what encapsulates the fal
is less the artist than his art. Strickland's painting of the seduced
wife is discovered by the cuckold after his wife's suicide. The
painting nullifies all the man's personal attachments: Strickland's
victim, himself a painter, is "transported" by the painting "into a
world in which the values were changed" (101); and in effect he
describes the painting as the birth of art's autonomy alongside
Strickland's advent into multiple personality order—Strickland
can only have painted this way by having forged or discovered a
new executive self of his own.

But the executive self finds resources in isolating flight from
the world. Such a self cannot have executive power unless it has
pursued and experienced detachment. It goes off to an island, an
appropriate place for art's radical self-sufficiency. One of the formal aspects of *The Moon and Sixpence* is its daring compositional
slackness, the effect of its narrative's limping after its subject, who
disappears from the world of the Maugham-narrator, and becomes
an island ghost or a mysterium tremendum when the novel still
has a third of its length to go. Given Strickland's flight, the I-narrator (hitherto an eye-witness) must become a researcher into the
remainder of Strickland's life. The remainder resists, Maugham
confesses, the narrative shape and coherence one associates with
fiction. In fact, Maugham introduces the last third of his novel
with the re-assertion that the text is biography, not fiction; and that
Strickland resists even a biographer's requirements, which are less
exacting than a novelist's, for making one's subject intelligible.
One requirement for biography is context. In the journey Strickland takes to Tahiti, where as an artist-shaman he hides away and
also make autonomous his multiple personalities (keeping, as always, his "various activities in various compartments" [117]),
Strickland moves altogether out of context. With an appropriate-
ness that complements Strickland's piecemeal selves, the
"biography"'s closing chapters are separate stories, and the tellers
of these stories are emanations of Strickland, each in turn his executive agents. His autonomy is mysterious indeed: its witness,
Strickland's greatest art, is painted on the walls of his house; but
his dying wish, granted by his wife, is that the house be burned
down.

Strickland replicates Hadrian the Seventh's fierce and fatal detachments. But this new Hadrian has a mediator, Maugham-Crabbe, who uses *The Moon and Sixpence* to reattach to a worldly context the spectre of Strickland's independence. Loyal to the spectre despite his own worldliness, Maugham the narrator assumes the double, split character he had first recognized in Strickland, but not in himself. He had seen Strickland as both "a great idealist" and as "cruel, selfish, brutal, and sensual" (118). This double vision is translated in the narrative's last third into a divided allegiance. The tale and its teller submit to alliance with the mundane world (whose selfishness and sensuality have been intensified by the brutal cruelty of the Great War); yet the tale and its teller are compensated for the submission by their fidelity to Strickland's island home, another version of The Great Good Place. On the narrative's last pages Maugham-Crabbe is in touch with Strickland's abandoned first family, which includes a now-grown son, who is a pompous soldier-hero on leave from the front. The son, hearing from the narrator the story of his father's leprosy, draws from it a conventional, and vindictive, social and religious moral. In response the narrator is moved to envision Strickland's other son, whom the artist sired in Tahiti. Maugham sees him, in imagination, "on the schooner on which he worked, wearing nothing but ... dungarees," dancing "with another lad" (164). In a reticent way, Maugham-Crabbe identifies Strickland's island offspring as the ideal son. And in a reticent way, he identifies Strickland's ideal offspring with homosexuality.

Maugham is a multiple personality in real life as well as in *The Moon and Sixpence*. Auden's favorite among the Maugham stories he read in Iceland is from Maugham's *Ashenden* volume, where Maugham makes spy fiction out of his own real life as a World War I secret agent. The Maugham story most liked by Auden is "His Excellency," which recounts the eros-inspired double lives of two diplomats. One of the diplomats happens to be named Byring. Despite Byring's relevance to Auden, however, another Maugham production seems especially important to Auden's island/Iceland. This is Maugham's essay on El Greco, published in 1935 when Maugham was 61, in which Maugham debates the possibility of El Greco's homosexuality. It's with this essay in mind that one can hypothesize Auden's alliance with Maugham as one solution of Auden's intergenerational differences with Rolfe and Lawrence. The essay on El Greco makes a lightweight first impression, like so much of Maugham; and, once it broaches the topic of homosexuality, seems coarsely censorious as well as timid. But Maugham characteristically is weightier than his surface.

The essay admits Maugham's love for El Greco, who he thinks is one of "the greatest painters" (1205). And he is one of the greatest because he isolated his art, and thereby freed it, from references both to the world and to religion. Although El Greco paints religious subjects, he has, Maugham maintains, no emotional attachment to them. His art's detachment, its self-referring character, is what makes it compelling. And its self-referential quality Maugham also thinks is a mark of El Greco's homosexuality. Maugham believes that El Greco's artistic autonomy, whereby the world comes to seem an object to be regarded with "inane flippancy" or "sardonic humor" (1209), symptomizes the isolation and autonomy of homosexuality, when culture (and religion) have no avowed use for it. Yet while culture cannot use that erotic autonomy, culture can be used by it. In 1935 Maugham sees El Greco's painting as the prototype of Picasso, Braque and Leger, as the prototype of modernist abstraction's version of the conquest of autonomy.

Maugham is intrigued by this conquest, but he also makes—from within his Crabbe-y corner of modernism—a complaint about autonomy's modernist form and even about its queer prototype. By virtue of sardonic detachment, his version of island/Iceland, El Greco dismisses the content of art in favor of its form; he endorses "the heresy," as Maugham calls it, "that subject is of no consequence" (1216). Much as Maugham is entranced by the heretic, Maugham objects to the heresy because he believes that El Greco's detachment and abstraction dissolve personality altogether. The dissolution in itself is not objectionable, for it is the threshold to the mysterium which multiple personality order, in all of its exponents, takes to heart. But in El Greco the dissolution of personality did not issue in the multiple personae that, despite grave difficulty, utter the sublime mystery underlying personhood and loan the mystery agency and liberty. Instead, El Greco's dissolution of personality issued in a corrosive skepticism toward agency and liberty, as well as toward art. Because of El Greco's detachment, art in his hands became beautiful but impotent, an empty formalism. And this means that El Greco's proto-modernism, homosexual and autonomy-enciting though it is, became a political liability rather than a strength. The post-Renaissance state found no challenge to its coercive power in art's investments in those potential accompaniments of formalism, inane flippancy and sardonic humor. Maugham finds that modernism's incarnation of El Greco's proto-modernism makes the same mistaken investments. And when modernist artists, as Maugham says, make "technical devices the end and aim of their endeavor" (1216), one gathers that artists follow a trajectory like T.E. Lawrence's. Their rebellious detachment from the state or religion becomes submission to them.

Maugham himself is having a cross-generational discussion about homosexuality and art. The El Greco essay reproduces and yet also criticizes the figure of Strickland the modernist, with whose character Maugham seems to fuse the gay El Greco. Undoubtedly Maugham himself has a conflict of feeling about previous—vastly previous—generations of gay utterance. He loves El Greco, but he loves alternative possibilities of expression more. There are sentences in Maugham's essay that wound homosexual self-love as much as does Auden's remark about Rolfe the "paranoid homosexual." Homosexuality is "abnormal," homosexual Maugham declares; and declares as well that "it cannot be denied that the homosexual has a narrower outlook on the world than the normal man" (1208). For us now these are scarcely likeable assertions. But they might be plausible ones if their context is Maugham's intention to transform homosexual traditions, to bring them out of hermetic isolation and exclusiveness and into a state of wordly engagements. In the course of his cross-generational discussion, Maugham claims the cultural coming of age and the cultural aging of modernism and homosexuality, and claims even the aging of their conquest of autonomy. The motive for the claims is not self-censorship or a case of sleeping with the enemy; instead Maugham appears to be taking up—in the midst of the fascist era—a new political responsibility. In order to engage it, he seems to believe, homosexuality and its artistic heritage must transform themselves.

The new responsibility, as Maugham's literary practice as well as his essay imply, takes neither the form of Rolfe-Rose's paranoia-risking ascetic intransigence toward contexts nor the form of Ross-Shaw's over-fleshed solidarity with a national service. It takes a form aptly illustrated by *Letters from Iceland*'s purpose to evoke and embody states of literary and personal autonomy in order to return from those states to contexts. But with what prospects for future conduct, the multiple personality order of Auden-MacNeice wonders, should one return from the land of letters? In a collaborative eclogue, the poets are joined by the ghost of the saga hero

Grettir. His story is of the defeat of a colossal independence. His counsel to the poets is not to submit their autonomy to defeat. Yet he does not advise them to remain on the road of escape from attachments, lest the poets themselves become ghostly anonymities. As a visionary literary space Iceland cannot be over-praised, for "who can ever praise enough/The world of his belief?"(281). The unreal visionary place saves one from death paradoxically because it is an abstraction from the flesh, an askesis. The askesis is self-possessed, not secretly flesh-drugged, like Ross-Shaw's. Reacting away from T.E. Lawrence, the island space of letters also plays out the conflicts between Carpenter and Rolfe over the contrasting virtues of democratic merger and aristocratic singularity. In that mediating role, the island appears to be Utopia, the Great Good Place. But Utopia is as curiously faceless and anonymous as it is nowhere. Grettir directs the poets along lines that recapitulate Rose-Rolfe's return from mystic space and its anonymity to pseudonymous personalities that can grapple with contexts. But the return from the island will draw upon autonomy even as it curbs autonomy. Grettir's ghost advises the poets thus: "My friends, hounded like me, I tell you still/Go back to where you belong. I could have fled/To the Hebrides or Orkney, ... /Preferred to assert my rights in my own country,/Mine which were hers for every country stands/By the sanctity of the individual will" (276). The poets quail at this: the journey from the mysterious place of liberty, through multiple personality order, to effective singular individuation, is difficult. Could the poets do something less taxing, something less context-responsive and more island-centered? In answer Grettir moderates his diction: "Minute your gesture but it must be made—/Your hazard, your act of defiance and hymn of hate,/Hatred of hatred, assertion of human values/Which is now your only duty ... /And, it may be added, it is your only chance" (276). The only chance, it might also be added, is a blessing only the island can give.

In a well-received, much-cited literary history, *British Writers of the Thirties*, Valentine Cunningham argues that Auden and his friends celebrated themselves as "youthies," who above all admired protofascist heroes, and made a youth cult of sexual "immaturity" (150)—which, for Cunningham, means homosexuality. Cunningham concedes that Auden "grew up" under the impact of the Spanish Civil War; and that, once grown up, Auden moderated his arrogance, if not his "immature" eros (200, 207–8). Blatantly intolerant, Cunningham does not represent the sort of questioning of homosexuality from within that Maugham and Auden permit themselves. Not surprisingly, his intolerance is blind to Auden's absorbed relation to his gay fathers. The relation makes implausible the idea of Auden's exclusive hero-worship of contemporaries. It also makes makes clear that, in his engagements with Carpenter, Rolfe, and Shaw, Auden attempts to reduce their claims for homosexuality's heroism to the more modest scale of things recommended by Grettir. Maugham belongs to that modest scale.

It is not only patently intolerant critics who ignore Auden's alliances and differences with earlier gay modernists. Although the names sometimes are mentioned by biographers and critics who sympathize with Auden's eros, the mentions are never more than nominal. To be sure, Auden's review of T.E. Lawrence's biography invariably gets noticed. But the notice does not explore the review's meaning for any intergenerational gay dialogue. *Letters from Iceland* gives us such a dialogue even in the face of Auden's involvement with MacNeice. Grettir's last words are really the "heter" poet's. The eclogue dramatizes three voices: Grettir's, Ryan's (a persona for MacNeice), and Craven's (a persona for Auden). Auden allows his "heter" collaborator to speak for him and as him. His consent in Iceland to this way of ordering multiple personalities surely is facilitated by his simultaneous conversation with his gay seniors. They no less than others made the country of letters to which Auden belongs.

Works Cited

Ansen, Alan. *The Table Talk of W.H. Auden.* Edited by Nicholas Jenkins. Princeton: Ontario Review Press, 1990.

Auden, W.H. Foreword to *The Desire and Pursuit of the Whole: A Romance of Modern Venice,* by Frederick Rolfe [Baron Corvo, pseud.]. 1953. In *The Desire and Pursuit of the Whole: A Romance of Modern Venice.* New York: Da Capo Press, 1986. v–xi.

———. *Letters From Iceland.* 1937. In *The Complete Works of W.H. Auden: Prose, and Travel Books in Prose and Verse.* Vol. 1, 1926–1938. Edited by Edward Mendelson. Princeton: Princeton UP, 1996. 171–380.

———. "T.E. Lawrence." Rev. of *T.E. Lawrence,* by Liddell Hart. *Now and Then,* Spring 1934. Rpt. in *The Complete Works of W.H. Auden: Prose, and Travel Books in Prose and Verse*. Vol. 1, 1926–1938. Edited by Edward Mendelson. Princeton: Princeton UP, 1996. 61–62.

Bourdieu, Pierre. *The Rules of Art: Genesis and Structure of the Literary Field*. Translated by Susan Emanuel. Meridian: Crossing Aesthetics; Stanford: Stanford UP, 1995.

Bozorth, Richard. *Auden's Games of Knowledge: Poetry and the Meanings of Homosexuality*. New York: Columbia UP, 2001.

Carpenter, Edward. *Intermediate Types among Primitive Folk: A Study in Social Evolution*. 1912. New York: Mitchell Kennerley, 1914.

———. *Towards Democracy*. 1905. Gay Modern Classics. London: GMP Publishers Ltd, 1985.

Carpenter, Humphrey. *W.H. Auden: A Biography*. London: George Allen & Unwin, 1981.

Cunningham, Valentine. *British Writers of the Thirties*. Oxford: Oxford UP, 1989.

Davenport-Hines, Richard. *Auden*. London: William Heinemann, 1995.

Lawrence, D.H. Rev. of *Hadrian the Seventh*, by Baron Corvo [Frederick Rolfe]. *Adelphi*, December 1925. Rpt. in *Phoenix: The Posthumous Papers of D.H. Lawrence*. 1936. London: William Heinemann, 1961.

Lawrence, T.E. *The Mint*. 1935. New York: Norton, 1963.

Maugham, W. Somerset. *Ashenden: The British Agent*. 1927. Harmondsworth: Penguin, 1977.

———. "El Greco: An Essay." 1935. In *The Maugham Reader*. Garden City, NY: Doubleday, 1950. 1189–1217.

———. *The Moon and Sixpence*. 1919. New York: Dover, 1995.

Mendelson, Edward. *Early Auden*. New York: Viking, 1981.

———. *Later Auden*. New York: Farrar, Straus and Giroux, 1999.

Rolfe, Frederick [Baron Corvo, pseud.]. *Hadrian the Seventh*. 1904. London: Chatto & Windus, 1959.

Symons, A.J.A. *The Quest for Corvo: An Experiment in Biography*. 1934. Hopewell: Ecco, 1997.

Auden's *Journey to Iceland*

Rory McTurk

Auden was much intrigued by his father's assertion of their Norse heritage, and indeed read Icelandic sagas from which he and Christopher Isherwood, in their earliest work, were inspired to write their own pseudo-sagas of life at St. Edmund's preparatory School: Isherwood's short story "Gems of Belgian Architecture" and Auden's one-act play Paid on Both Sides. *(See Isherwood's* Lions and Shadows *for his account of how this came about.) In 1936, Auden visited Iceland with his friend and fellow poet Louis MacNeice to see the land of his ancestors (maybe). His poem* Journey to Iceland *was translated into Icelandic shortly after it appeared in English. Icelandic specialist Rory McTurk here looks at both the English and Icelandic versions of the poem and considers the linguistic components and historical references.*

The purpose of this paper is threefold: to print side by side W.H. Auden's poem "Journey to Iceland," as first published in English in 1936, and Magnus Ásgeirsson's Icelandic translation of the poem, also first published in 1936; to provide a close translation into English of the Icelandic translation, so that the semantic correspondences and differences between it and Auden's poem can be appreciated by an international audience; and to supplement John Fuller's recently published commentary on the poem[1] with some remarks about the poem's specifically Icelandic terms of reference.

The English and Icelandic texts of the poem are given below. The English text is taken from *The Listener*, 7 October 1936, p. 670,

---

[1]See John Fuller, *W.H. Auden: A Commentary* (London: Faber and Faber, 1998), 208–9.

where the poem first appeared in English;[2] and the Icelandic text
which in 1936 appeared in Magnús Ásgeirsson's *Þýdd ljóð* ("Trans
lated poems"), 6 vols. (Reykjavík: Bókadeild Menningarsjóðs
1928–41), V, 67–69, and is here quoted from Magnús Ásgeirsson
Ljóðasafn ("Collected poems"), 2 vols. (Reykjavík: Helgafell, 1975)
II, 100–101.[3] I have supplied stanza numbers for ease of reference.

Journey to Iceland

(1)   And the traveller hopes: "Let me be far from any
      Physician"; And the ports have names for the sea:
                The citiless, the corroding, the sorrow;
                And North means to all: "Reject!"

(2)   And the great plains are for ever where the cold fish is hunted,
      And everywhere; The light birds flicker and flaunt;
                Under the scolding flag the lover
                Of islands may see at last,

(3)   Faintly, his limited hope; and he nears the glitter
      Of glaciers, the sterile immature mountains intense
                In the abnormal day of this world, and a river's
                Fan-like polyp of sand.

(4)   Then let the good citizen here find natural marvels:
      The horse-shoe ravine, the issue of steam from a cleft
                In the rock, and rocks, and waterfalls brushing the
                Rocks, and among the rocks birds.

---

[2]See *The Listener*, vol. XVI, Wednesday, 7 October 1936, no. 404, p
670. The subsequent printing history of the poem (as published in English
may be traced in Fuller, 208.

[3]According to Edward Mendelson, in his edition of W.H. Auden
Prose and Travel Books in Prose and Verse, vol. I, 1926–1938 (Princeton, NJ
Princeton University Press, 1996), 772, this same translation also appeared
in 1936 in the annual literary magazine *Rauðir pennar* ("Red Pens"). Of the
two 1936 texts of the translation, I have seen only the one published in vol
V of Magnús Ásgeirsson's *Þýdd ljóð*, 6 vols. (Reykjavík: Bókadeild Menningarsjóðs, 1928–41), V, 67–69, and it is not clear to me at the time of writ
ing which of them appeared first in that year. The text printed here (from
Magnús Ásgeirsson, *Ljóðasafn*, 2 vols. (Reykjavík: Helgafell, 1975), II, 100-
101) is virtually identical with the one published in *Þýdd ljóð* V, except that
it corrects one misprint (changing *tálkrossa* to *tálkossa* in stanza 8), and
slightly adjusts the spelling and punctuation of stanza 6, l. 2 (by removing
a comma after *hlíðin* and supplying a second *r* in *kyrrt*).

Ferð til Íslands

(1) Og sæfarinn óskar: Æ, sé nú hver læknir mér fjarri!
     og sjávarnöfn skáldanna fylgjast með honum um borð:
          Borgleysa, Ótryggur, Svörfuður, Sorgin.
          Og synjun er Norðursins orð.

(2) Og ómælissléttur hins blóðkalda veiðifisks blika,
     Og brim er í lofti af vængjum svífandi flokks.
          Og undir þeim þjótandi, iðandi fána
          sér eyjavinurinn loks

(3) hilla undir von sína: og fannblikið nær honum færist,
     fjöllin, nakin og seiðsterk, um vornætur dag.
          Og undir þeim sandflæmi í ósum fljóta,
          Sem árskrímsl með blævængslag.

(4) Svo megi hinn ágæti borgari furður hér finna:
     fjöll eins og hófspor, eimgos, sem bergrifa spýr,
          gljúfur og fossa og hornbjargsins háu
          höll, þar sem sjófuglinn býr.

(5)   And the student of prose and conduct places to visit;
       The site of a church where a bishop was put in a bag,
               The bath of a great historian, the rock where
               An outlaw dreaded the dark.

(6)   Remember the doomed man thrown by his horse and crying;
       "Beautiful is the hillside, I will not go";
               The old woman confessing: "He that I loved the
               Best, to him I was worst."

(7)   For Europe is absent. This is an island and therefore
       Unreal. And the steadfast affections of its dead may be bought
               By those whose dreams accuse them of being
               Spitefully alive, and the pale

(8)   From too much passion of kissing feel pure in its deserts.
       Can they? For the world is, and the present, and the lie.
               And the narrow bridge over the torrent,
               And the small farm under the crag

(9)   Are the natural setting for the jealousies of a province;
       And the weak row[4] of fidelity is formed by the cairn;
               And within the indigenous figure on horseback
               On the bridle path down by the lake

(10)   The blood moves also by crooked and furtive inches,
       Asks all your questions: "Where is the homage? When
               Shall justice be done? O who is against me?
               Why am I always alone?"

(11)   Present then the world to the world with its mendicant shadow;
       Let the suits be flash, the Minister of Commerce insane;
               Let jazz be bestowed on the huts, and the beauty's
               Set cosmopolitan smile.

(12)   For our time has no favourite suburb; no local features
       Are those of the young for whom all wish to care;
               The promise is only a promise, the fabulous
               Country impartially far.

(13)   Tears fall in all the rivers. Again the driver
       Pulls on his gloves and in a blinding snowstorm starts
               Upon his deadly journey; and again the writer
               Runs howling to his art.

---

[4]Thus the text in *The Listener*, 7 October 1936, p. 670. This seems to be a misprint; it appears as *vow* in, for example, W.H. Auden and Louis Mac-Neice, *Letters from Iceland* (London: Faber and Faber, 1937), 26; and the word *sworn*, which appears in place of *formed* in the second edition of *Letters from Iceland* (London: Faber and Faber, 1967), 24, tends to suggest that *vow* was the original reading.

(5)   Og höfundur sá, er vill kynna sér kjör manna og háttu:
       kirkjustað biskups, sem troðið var niður í sekk,
              Laug mikils sagnfræðings, klettaey kappans,
              sem kvíða langnættið fékk.

(6)   Og munið hinn seka, er fákur hans féll og hann mælti:
       "Fögur er hlíðin og aftur um kyrrt ég sezt,"
              konuna gömlu, sem vitnaði: "Eg var þeim
              verst, er ég unni mest."

(7)   Því Evrópa er fjarri, og einnig þá raunveruleikinn.
       Við öræfa- og söguhefð landsins þeir kaupa sér dvöl,
              sem dreymir sitt líf vera í óþökk, til einskis,
              og andlitin fölu, sem böl

(8)   of heitra tálkossa tærði, á þess öræfum laugast.
       En tekst það? Því Heimur og Nútími og Lygi eru sterk.
              Og hin örmjóa brú yfir beljandi ána
              og bærinn í fjallsins kverk

(9)   eru eðlileg virki og herstöðvar héraðarígsins,
       sem hollustu þegnsins bindur við merkjastein.
              Og í bóndanum þarna, sem berst á hesti
              út bakkans vallgrónu hlein,

(10)   sig þumlungar líka blóðið á bugðóttum leiðum
       og biður um svör, eins og þitt: Finnst ei trúnaður neinn?
              Ó, hvað dvelur réttlætið? Hver er gegn mér?
              Ó, hví er ég stöðugt einn?

(11)   Svo kynnum þá heiminum eyna, hans eltandi skugga,
       með oflæti í búningi og versnandi fisksölukjör.
              Í afdal hvín jazzinn, og æskunnar fegurð
              Fær alþjóðlegt filmbros á vör.

(12)   Því hvergi á vor samtími vé þau, er allir unna.
       Vor æska ekki neina staðhelgi, verndaðan reit.
              Og fyrirheitið um ævintýraeyna
              er eingöngu fyrirheit.

(13)   Tár falla í allar elfur og ekillinn setur
       aftur upp glófa og bíl sinn á vegleysur knýr
              í æðandi blindhríð, og emjandi skáldið
              aftur að list sinni flýr.

This author's translation of the Icelandic text now follows.[5] Th
goal was to be as accurate as possible without producing a tex
that is so literal as to be unreadable:

(1) And the seafarer wishes: Ah, may every physician be far from me! An
the poets' names for the sea follow him on board: Citylessness, Faithles
Ruffian, Sorrow. And "rejection" is the North's message.

(2) And the measureless plains of the cold-blooded, hunted fish glitte
and the wave of a hovering flock's wings breaks in the air. And under tha
thrusting, fidgeting flag the friend of islands sees at last

(3) his hope heave into view; and the glitter of snowdrifts draws near t
him—the mountains, naked and spellbinding, in the daylight of a sprin
night. And at their feet (he sees) stretches of sand, like fan-shaped rive
monsters, in the mouths of rivers.

(4) May the good citizen then be able to find marvels here: mountains lik
hoofprints; gushes of steam which a rock-cleft spits out; chasms and wa
terfalls; and the jutting rock's lofty palace, where the seabird dwells.

(5) And (may) the author who wishes to study people's conditions an
customs (find here) the church precincts of a bishop who was stuffed int
a bag; the bath of a great historian; the rocky island of a hero whom th
long nights filled with apprehension.

(6) Remember the one found guilty, who, when his steed fell, said: "Fair i
the slope; I'm not leaving after all"; the old woman, who testified: "I wa
worst to the one I loved the most."

(7) For Europe is far away, and so too is reality. It is those who dream tha
their lives are thankless, to no purpose, who pay to live within this cour
try's tradition of deserts and history; and the pale faces, at which the evil

(8) of over-passionate, alluring kisses has eaten away, bathe in its desert
But does it work? For the World, the Present and the Lie are strong. An
the spindly bridge over the roaring river, and the farm nestling up to th
mountain

(9) are the natural strongholds and encampments of the provincial discor
which ties the citizen's loyalty to a boundary-marking stone; and in th
farmer there, who is borne on horseback along the (lake-)bank's grass
landing rock,

---

[5]I am grateful to my friends Bergljót S. Kristjánsdóttir and Guðni Elís
son, of the Departments of Icelandic and Literature, respectively, of th
University of Iceland, Reykjavík, for checking and commenting on m
translation.

(10) the blood also inches forward on winding paths, and asks, like yours, for answers: is there no trust? O what delays justice? O who is against me? O why am I always alone?

(11) Let us then present the island to the world as the shadow that chases it with ostentation in dress and declining fisheries. In a remote valley the jazz shrills, and the beauty of youth acquires an international, film-set smile.

(12) For nowhere does our time have those holy places which all hold dear; our youth has no sanctuary or protected plot. And the promise of the fairytale island is only a promise.

(13) Tears fall into all rivers, and the driver puts on his gloves again and forces his car onto trackless ways, into a raging, blinding snowstorm; and the howling writer flees again to his art.

Apart from the word *row* in the second line of stanza 9, which must surely be a misprint for *vow*, the English version of the poem printed in the left-hand column above is essentially the same as that printed at the beginning of the second chapter of the first edition of *Letters from Iceland* (1937);[6] the only other differences between the former and the latter version are very minor ones of punctuation. In *Letters from Iceland* this chapter is itself entitled "Journey to Iceland," with the sub-title "A Letter to Christopher Isherwood, Esq." The chapter begins with the text of the poem, immediately after which the letter (which is signed simply "W.") begins as follows:

> Dear Christopher,
>   Thank you for your letter. No, you were wrong. I did not write: 'the *ports* have names for the sea' but 'the *poets* have names for the sea'. However, as so often before, the mistake seems better than the original idea, so I'll leave it.[7]

In light of these remarks of Auden's, it is obviously of great interest that the Icelandic translation should render the line in question as "the poets' names for the sea follow him on board"; the translator seems to have had access to an earlier version of the poem than that reflected in its first published English version.[8] One reason,

---

[6]See Auden and MacNeice, *Letters from Iceland* (1937), 25–27.

[7]Ibid., 27.

[8]This is pointed out by Mendelson in his edition of W.H. Auden, *Prose and Travel Books* (1996), 772. Mendelson notes here that the manuscript of "Journey to Iceland" sent by Auden to Michael Roberts for

indeed, for making the Icelandic translation accessible to an inter national audience is that it may help to throw light on the early history of the poem. Certain of the poem's specifically Icelandic terms of reference may now be considered.

It will be noticed that, in stanza 1, Auden gives three epithets for the sea ("the citiless, the corroding, the sorrow") and that the translator gives four ("Citylessness, Faithless, Ruffian, Sorrow") Thus for "the sea," Auden supplies two adjectives and a noun (though each of the adjectives is given noun function in being pre ceded by the definite article), and the translator supplies three nouns and an adjective. In the Icelandic, the adjective *Ótryggu* "Faithless" is used in a form (the so-called "strong" form) and a syntactic context which preclude its being accompanied by the definite article[9]—hence my translation "Faithless" rather than "the Faithless One" (though the latter meaning is of course to be under stood). Of the three relevant nouns in the Icelandic (*Borgleys* "Citylessness," *Svörfuður* "Ruffian," and *Sorgin* "Sorrow") only the third is accompanied by the article (in the form of the suffix -*in* or the end of *Sorg* "Sorrow"). This has not been reproduced in my own translation, however, since it is not uncommon in Icelandic for the suffixed definite article to be used with nouns for which antonyms can readily be found (such as *sorg* "sorrow," of which *gleði* "joy" is an obvious antonym).[10]

---

inclusion in *Poetry*, January 1937 (where the poem was published in En glish for the second time, see Fuller, *W.H. Auden: A Commentary* (1998) 208), is now in the Berg Collection, and "is the only surviving English tex that has the original reading 'the poets have names for the sea.'" He fur ther comments that Magnús Ásgeirsson's translation of the poem "wa evidently based on a manuscript with the same original reading." Mendelson's remarks thus suggest that the manuscript sent to Michae Roberts is not identical with the one used by Magnús Ásgeirsson, and tha the latter manuscript no longer survives.

[9]Although the definite article may sometimes be used with the strong form of the adjective in Icelandic, it can only do so when the adjective i modifying a noun, as in a phrase such as *blátt hafið*, "the blue sea," which is not the case here. See further Stefán Einarsson, *Icelandic. Grammar, Texts Glossary* (Baltimore, MD: Johns Hopkins UP, 1949), 116.

[10]This is a somewhat simplified account of the matter. See further M Nygaard, *Norrøn syntax* (Kristiania: H. Aschehoug, 1905), 33, and cf. Jakob Jóh. Smári, *Íslenzk setningafræði* (Reykjavík: Bókaverzlun Ársæls Árna sonar, 1920), 44–45.

If it may be assumed that Auden had specifically *Icelandic* poets and ports in mind when he made the change from "poets" to "ports," he would have been on somewhat surer ground if he had stuck to "poets." While it can certainly be claimed that Icelandic poets "have names for the sea," it cannot easily be said that Icelandic ports do. Of the sixty-odd Icelandic ports, ancient and modern, listed and discussed by Einar Laxness in his dictionary of Icelandic history (under *hafnir* "harbours"), not a single one has a name that means "sea."[11] Of the very few that come at all near to doing so may be mentioned *Djúpivogur*, meaning "(the) deep cove," and *Ísafjörður*, meaning "fjord of ice-floes"; the words *vogur* "cove" and *fjörður* "fjord" are for obvious reasons not uncommon as endings in Icelandic coastal place-names. Another such ending is *-vík*, also meaning "cove" or "small bay," as in the name of the capital of Iceland, *Reykjavík*, the original form of which, *Reykjarvík*, means "bay of smoke" or "bay of steam," and which is thought to derive from the columns of steam rising from hot springs of the kind that are active in various parts of Iceland, including the southwest, where Reykjavík, itself a port, is located.[12] These examples will suffice to indicate that Icelandic ports tend to have, at least as the final elements in their names, words referring to features of the coast rather than to the sea itself.

Icelandic poets, on the other hand, do indeed "have names for the sea," as already hinted. The Icelandic term *heiti* "(poetic) appellation" may refer to a word or name that is used either exclusively in poetry, or, if used in ordinary speech or in prose, is used in poetry with a different meaning. *Heiti* are most often nouns, but may sometimes be adjectives used as nouns; examples of *heiti* for "sea" are the noun *salt* "salt" and the adjective *órór* "(the) rough (one)," "(the) agitated (one)."[13]

Another way in which persons or things may be referred to in Icelandic poetry is by the use of the circumlocutory expressions known as kennings. Whereas a *heiti* may and often does consist of

---

[11]See Einar Laxness, *Íslandssaga a-k*, second edition (Reykjavík: Bókaútgáfa Menningarsjóðs og Þjóðvinafélagsins, 1987), 170–72.

[12]See Preben Meulengracht Sørensen, *Saga and Society: An Introduction to Old Norse Literature*, trans. by John Tucker (Odense: Odense University Press, 1993), 6.

[13]See Einar Ól. Sveinsson, "Dróttkvæða þáttur," in Einar Ól. Sveinsson, *Við uppspretturnar: greinasafn* (Reykjavík: Helgafell, 1956), 34–63, esp. 37–42.

a simplex word, a kenning always consists of two elements, known as the "basic word" and the "determinant." In its simplest manifestations, a kenning consists either of a compound noun or of two nouns. In the case of a kenning consisting of a compound noun, the second element in the compound is the basic word, and the first element, which has the effect of qualifying the sense of the second, is the determinant. An example of a kenning of this type for "sea" is *brimslóð*, in which the first element, *brim*, means "surf" and the second element, *slóð*, means "track"; the determinant, *brim*, qualifies the sense of the basic word *slóð*, showing what kind of "track" is meant in this case, i.e., a surfy one, the sea; the sea is here thought of as a route by which to travel.

In the case of a kenning consisting of two nouns, the determinant is always a noun in the genitive case, qualifying the sense of the other noun, the basic word, which may be in whatever case its syntactic context requires. An example of a kenning of this type for "sea" is *svana fold* "swans' land," i.e., "sea," in which *fold* "land" is the basic word and *svana*, genitive plural of *svanr* "swan" is the determinant.[14]

What has been said here about Icelandic poetry is particularly true of the type of poetry known as skaldic, an essentially occasional type of poetry (i.e., composed most often in response to specific situations) which flourished from the ninth to the fourteenth century.[15] *Heiti* and kennings are however also found, to a greater or lesser extent, in the work of other poets contemporary with and subsequent to that of the skalds.[16]

It will be clear from the foregoing that, if viewed in terms of Icelandic poetry, Auden's "names for the sea" in stanza 1 ("the citiless, the corroding, the sorrow") are *heiti* rather than kennings; the first two of them are adjectives used as nouns; the third is a simplex noun; and all three of them, in referring here to the sea, are being used in a meaning different from the meanings they would have in prose or in ordinary speech. The translator's four terms for Auden's three are also *heiti* rather than kennings. The one adjective

---

[14]See E.O.G. Turville-Petre, *Scaldic Poetry* (Oxford: Clarendon Press, 1976), xlv–lix, 65; and Snorri Sturluson, *Edda: Skáldskaparmál*, ed. by Anthony Faulkes, 2 vols. (London: Viking Society for Northern Research, 1998), I:97, and II:251

[15]For a discussion of skaldic poetry in relation to other Old Icelandic literary forms, see Sørensen, *Saga and Society* (1993), 74–132, esp. pp. 87–91.

[16]See Einar Ól. Sveinsson, "Dróttkvæða þáttur," 34–63.

among them, Ótryggur "Faithless," which, with its negative prefix Ó-, essentially means "unfaithful," may be compared with the adjective órór "rough," which has this same negative prefix, means literally "un-calm," and is given above as an example of a *heiti*. Of the three nouns used by the translator in this context, only the first, *Borgleysa* "Citylessness," with its obviously compound character, looks on the face of it more like a kenning than a *heiti*; its second element, *-leysa* "-lessness," however, is rather more abstract than the basic word in a kenning would normally be expected to be,[17] and while *Borgleysa* is indeed a noun, its second element carries with it such strong associations of the adjective *laus* "free (of)," "lacking (in)," to which it is related etymologically, and which is also used as an adjectival suffix meaning "-less," that it would, I believe, be hard for an Icelandic reader or listener to encounter the noun *Borgleysa* without mentally conjuring up an adjective *borglaus* "cityless"—a consideration which tends to reinforce the noun's status as a *heiti* rather than a kenning.

Once all this has been said, however, it must be pointed out that none of the four words used by the translator for "sea" in this context is recorded in that sense in any of the dictionaries that cover Icelandic poetic usage.[18] The translator has done his best with the "names for the sea" that he has found in Auden's text, throwing in an extra one (*Ótryggur* "Faithless") for good measure, and can indeed be credited, as a result, with introducing new *heiti* for "sea" into the Icelandic poetic tradition. Auden obviously deserves some of the credit for this as well. It can hardly be said, however, that his own *heiti* for the sea ("the cityless, the corroding, the sorrow") reflect Icelandic poetic usage with full accuracy, if it was indeed Icelandic poets that he was referring to in writing, as

---

[17]See Rudolf Meissner, *Die Kenningar der Skalden: Ein Beitrag zur skaldischen Poetik* (Bonn: Kurt Schroeder, 1921), 20–21.

[18]E.g., *Ordbog til de af Samfund til udg. af gml. nord. litteratur udgivne rímur samt til de af Dr. O. Jiriczek udgivne Bósarímur*, by Finnur Jónsson (København: J. Jørgensen, 1926–28); *Lexicon poeticum antiquæ linguæ septentrionalis: ordbog over det norsk-islandske skjaldesprog*, by Sveinbjörn Egilsson, second edition by Finnur Jónsson (København: n.p., 1931, rpt. 1966); *An Icelandic-English Dictionary* [...]by Richard Cleasby [...] and [...] Gudbrand Vigfusson, M.A., second edition [...] by Sir Willaim A. Craigie [...] (Oxford: Clarendon Press, 1957, rpt. 1962); *Íslensk orðabók handa skólum og almenningi*, ed. by Árni Böðvarsson, second edition (Reykjavík: Bókaútgáfa Menningarsjóðs, 1983, rpt. 1985).

he claims to Christopher Isherwood to have done, "the *poets* have names for the sea." If he had kept "poets," and had meant by this "Icelandic poets," in the published version of the poem, he would have been on somewhat surer ground than with "ports" (as indicated above) in attributing to the poets in question (as opposed to the ports) such "names for the sea" as "the cityless, the corroding, the sorrow." Only *somewhat* surer, however, since while his use of such terms for the sea is not seriously at variance with Icelandic poetic usage, there is no evidence that I can find that equivalents of these particular terms were ever used for the sea by any Icelandic poet until the poem here under discussion was itself translated into Icelandic.

Before leaving the "names for the sea" we may note that one of them, "the corroding," is rendered in Icelandic as *Svörfuður*, which in turn is rendered in my translation as "Ruffian." The Icelandic term, which occurs as a nickname in the anonymous *Landnámabók* "Book of Settlements," thought to date originally from the twelfth century,[19] does indeed mean "ruffian," "one who wreaks havoc," and the word *ruffian*, with its echo of the adjective *rough*, seems a suitable enough English rendering of the term when it is being used as a name for the sea. It may be asked, however, why the Icelandic translator should choose the term *svörfuður* "ruffian" as an Icelandic rendering of "the corroding." The answer seems to be that he has associated this term with the verb *sverfa* "to file," "to wear away (at)," from which the Icelandic word for "erosion," *svörfun*, derives. The word *svörfuður* "ruffian" is perhaps more readily associable, etymologically, with the verb *svarfa*, meaning essentially "to dislodge," "to overturn," and hence coming to have connotations of causing trouble or wreaking havoc. The translator is hardly guilty of a serious mistake here, however, since the two verbs, *sverfa* and *svarfa*, are themselves etymologically related.[20]

The Icelandic translation of Auden's poem is, in fact, a remarkable achievement. What may not be immediately obvious to

---

[19]See *Íslendingabók. Landnámabók*, ed. by Jakob Benediktsson, 2 vols. (Reykjavík: Hið íslenska fornritafélag, 1968), I:cvi–cxx; II:237, 252, 268, n. 2; cf. *The Book of Settlements: Landnámabók*, trans. with introduction and notes by Hermann Pálsson and Paul Edwards (Winnipeg: University of Manitoba Press, 1972), 4–5, 97.

[20]See the entries under *svarfa*, *sverfa*, and *svörfuður* in the Icelandic etymological dictionary *Íslensk orðsifjabók*, by Ásgeir Blöndal Magnússon (Reykjavík: Orðabók Háskólans, 1989), 993, 998, 1008.

readers who do not know Icelandic, however, is the fact that the translation not only preserves the stanza form and stress patterns of the original, but also supplies end rhyme in the second and fourth line of each four-line stanza. Furthermore, each even-numbered line of the poem in the translation is linked to its immediate odd-numbered predecessor by alliteration, in the manner of traditional Icelandic poetry. The first stressed syllable of each even-numbered line regularly alliterates with two stressed syllables in the immediately preceding odd-numbered line. Thus, in the first stanza of the translation, the first stressed syllable of the second line is the initial one of *sjávarnöfn* "names for the sea," beginning with *s*; and *s* is found to be the initial letter of two stressed syllables in the first line: the initial syllable of *sæfarinn* "the seafarer" and the word *sé* "may [...] be." In the fourth line of this same stanza the first stressed syllable, that of *synjun* "rejection," also begins with *s*; and this word, it will be noticed, alliterates with *Svörfuður* "Ruffian" and *Sorgin* "Sorrow" in the third line of the stanza. In the second line of the second stanza the first stressed syllable, *brim* "surf," "breaking wave," with its initial *b*, is found to alliterate with *blóðkalda* "cold-blooded" and *blika* "glitter" in the first line of the stanza. The lines alliterate in pairs, and there is no requirement that the same alliterating sound should be carried on from one pair to the next; the fact that *s* is the alliterating consonant in the third and fourth lines of the translation as well as the first and second is coincidental. When consonants carry the alliteration, the consonant in each case alliterates with itself; thus *s* alliterates with *s*, *b* with *b*, and so on, as in the examples so far given. When vowels carry the alliteration, however, it is common for one vowel to alliterate with another, rather than with itself. This is illustrated in the third and fourth lines of the second stanza of the translation, where the initial *e* of the first stressed syllable of the fourth line, that of *eyjavinurinn* "the friend of islands," alliterates with the *u* of *undir* "under" and the initial *i* in *iðandi* "fidgeting" in the preceding line.[21]

In stanzas 4–6 there are some allusions to Icelandic topography, history and literature. Fuller correctly identifies the "horseshoe ravine," referred to in stanza 4, as Ásbyrgi, but can hardly be said to be correct in describing it as "a rock island." It is in fact on

---

[21]See Turville-Petre, *Scaldic Poetry*, xviii–xxi, and Ph. Schweitzer, "Um stuðla setning og höfuðstafs í íslenzku," *Tímarit Hins íslenzka bókmentafélags* 8 (1887): 316–18.

mainland Iceland in Öxarfjörður (also known as Axarfjörður) i
the north, and is some way inland. It is a gully three-and-ha
kilometers in length, shaped somewhat like the hoofprint of
horse, and is enclosed on all sides except the north by cliffs reacl
ing to a height of 100 metres. To the north it splits into two on e
ther side of a cliff called Eyjan ("The island"), which was once, bu
is no longer, an island in the river Jökulsá—hence, possibl*
Fuller's idea that Ásbyrgi itself is an island. According to legen
Ásbyrgi is a hoofprint left by Sleipnir, the eight-legged steed of th
god Óðinn.[22] It is noteworthy that Magnús Ásgeirsson render
Auden's "horse-shoe ravine" as *fjöll eins og hófspor* "mountains lik
hoofprints," since it is cliffs, as already shown, rather than mou
tains, that are characteristic of Ásbyrgi. It would seem that th
translator (as opposed to Auden) was thinking not especially (
Ásbyrgi here, but rather in general terms of mountain and valle
formations in Iceland which might be thought to resemble th
hoofprints of gigantic horses.

The bishop who "was put in a bag" (see stanza 5) was Jón Ge
reksson, who, as Fuller correctly states, was drowned in a sack i
the river Brúará near Skálholt in 1433. He was of Danish nationa
ity and was bishop of Skálholt from 1426 until his death. Icelan
had come under Danish rule in 1380, and its two bishoprics, Hól
in the north and Skálholt in the south, had many foreign incun
bents in the fifteenth century. When Jón Gerreksson's illegitimat
son Magnús, spurned by a certain Margrét Vigfúsdóttir whom h
had wished to marry, killed Margrét's brother, she vowed t
marry the man who would avenge him. One Þorvarður Loftsso
came forward as her champion, and together with, among other
Teitur Gunnlaugsson, who like Þorvarður had earlier escaped fro
imprisonment by the bishop and had a score to settle with hir
seized him at Skálholt and drowned him in Brúará in a sac
weighed down with stones. Margrét and Þorvarður subsequentl
married.[23]

[22]See Guðmundur Páll Ólafsson, *Iceland the Enchanted* (Reykjavík: M
og menning, 1995), 262–63; cf Fuller, *W.H. Auden: A Commentary* (1998
208.

[23]See John C.F. Hood, D.D., *Icelandic Church Saga* (London: Society f
Promoting Christian Knowledge, 1946), 135–38. In my own account of tl
events in question I have ventured to correct one or two slight errors i
Hood's, mainly involving the spelling of names. Cf. Fuller, *W.H. Auden:
Commentary* (1998), 208.

The "great historian" whose bath is referred to in stanza 5 is Snorri Sturluson (d. 1241), the author of the encyclopedic history of the kings of Norway known as *Heimskringla* and also of the handbook for poets known as the Prose Edda. His bath is the circular stone-lined pool, nearly four metres in diameter, called *Snorralaug* "Snorri's bath," which can still be seen at Reykholt (formerly Reykjaholt) in the west of Iceland. Snorri, who had been brought up at Oddi in the south, moved from there in 1198 to Borg on the west coast, and later, in 1206, to Reykholt, some forty kilometers inland from Borg. The bath is referred to in the thirteenth-century *Íslendinga saga* "The saga of the Icelanders," an account of contemporary Icelandic history by Snorri's nephew Sturla Þórðarson (1214–84). Fuller's phrase, referring to Snorri, "whose bath may be seen at Snorralaug," should perhaps be corrected to: "whose bath, known as Snorralaug, may be seen at Reykholt."[24]

The "outlaw who dreaded the dark," also mentioned in stanza 5, is, as Fuller rightly states, Grettir, that is, Grettir Ásmundarson, also known as Grettir the Strong, the hero of the anonymous *Grettis saga Ásmundarsonar* which, it has recently been argued, may not have been written before 1400; it was earlier thought to have been written in the early decades of the fourteenth century.[25] Grettir's fear of the dark begins in earnest after he has fought with and beheaded the ghost of the shepherd Glámr in ch. 35 of the saga; the ghost prophesies that Grettir will be outlawed and will find it difficult to be alone. Grettir does indeed become outlawed, on dubious grounds, in ch. 46, and frequent mention is made of Grettir's fear of the dark from ch. 35 onwards. As for the rock mentioned in this context in Auden's poem, Fuller refers to chs. 55 and 59 of the saga, suggesting that the rock in question "is perhaps Grettishof."[26] Ch. 55 certainly refers to Grettir's fear of the dark, but makes no mention of a rock; ch. 59, on the other hand, mentions a rock called *Grettishaf* (as opposed to *Grettishof*), but does not refer to Grettir's fear of the dark. The name *Grettishaf*, meaning "Grettir's lift" is used three times in *Grettis saga* for a rock, referring to a different rock each time. In this instance (in ch. 59) it

---

[24]See Magnus Magnusson, *Iceland Saga* (London: The Bodley Head, 1987), 188–200, esp. 192; and cf. Fuller, 208.

[25]See *The Saga of Grettir the Strong*, trans. by Bernard Scudder with introduction by Örnólfur Thorsson (Reykjavík: Leifur Eiríksson, 1998), xxv–vi.

[26]See Fuller, 209.

refers to a rock from which Grettir defends himself against some
attackers; in each of the first two instances, in chs. 16 and 30, it
refers to a rock which he lifts and tries to lift respectively. None of
these three instances occurs in a context of Grettir's fear of the
dark; the first two of them, indeed, occur before the saga's accounts of his fight with Glámr and his outlawry. It seems most
likely that the rock referred to in Auden's poem is the cliff island
of Drangey in Skagafjörður in the north of Iceland, where Grettir,
according to the saga (chs. 69–82), spent his last days and met his
death. This is how the translator appears to have understood the
reference. The first element in the island's name, *Drang-*, derives
from the noun *drangr* "pillar of rock"; the second, *ey*, means
"island." It is true that Grettir's fear of the dark is not mentioned in
the parts of the saga describing his time on Drangey (where, however, he has other problems to contend with, notably the sorcery
which weakens him to the extent that he becomes an easy target
for his killers), but it is emphasized at the beginning of ch. 69,
shortly before his departure for the island (by moonlight) is described.[27] In this respect the translator has covered himself better
than Auden has, in not specifying, as Auden does, that the rock in
question was *where* the outlaw "dreaded the dark."

Fuller is correct in identifying "the doomed man thrown by his
horse" in stanza 6 as Gunnarr,[28] i.e., Gunnarr Hámundarson of
Hlíðarendi in the south of Iceland, who is one of the two main
characters of the anonymous *Njáls saga*, dating from the late thirteenth century; the other main character is the eponymous hero of
the saga, Njáll. Gunnarr is doomed because, at the stage in the
events of the saga to which reference is here being made, he has
been compelled by circumstances largely beyond his control to
disregard Njáll's advice never to kill twice in the same family; the
prescient Njáll had indicated, in ch. 55 of the saga, that, if Gunnarr
did not take this advice, he would not have long to live. As a result
of his killings, Gunnarr is "found guilty" (cf. my translation of the
Icelandic translation, stanza 6) at a meeting of the Alþingi, the Icelandic General Assembly, and condemned to three years' banish-
ment from Iceland (chs. 73–74). The reference in Auden's poem is

[27]Reference may be made to the relevant chapters in *Grettis saga Ásmundarsonar* [...], ed. by Guðni Jónsson (Reykjavík: Hið íslenska fornritafélag, 1936), and in the translation by Bernard Scudder referred to in
note 25 above.

[28]See Fuller, 209.

:o what is described in ch. 75 of the saga: as Gunnarr is riding to
:he ship on which he intends to leave Iceland, his horse stumbles
ind he leaps from the saddle. He happens to look toward the slope
of the hillside near his home, Hlíðarendi (the name means "the end
of the slope"), and famously remarks: "Fögur er hlíðin" ("Beautiful
.s the hillside"). He goes on to declare that the slope has never
seemed to him so beautiful, and that he will ride home and not
.eave after all. His decision to stay proves fatal to him; his enemies
:atch up with him and kill him soon afterward (ch. 77), thus fulfill-
ng Njáll's prophecy. Magnús Ásgeirsson reproduces "Fögur er
nlíðin" word for word (as will be evident), but otherwise rephrases
ind shortens Gunnarr's statement.[29]

The old woman mentioned in this same stanza (6) is, as Fuller
:orrectly notes, Guðrún, i.e., Guðrún Ósvífrsdóttir, the heroine of
:he anonymous *Laxdæla saga*, dating most probably from early in
:he second half of the thirteenth century. In the part of the saga
here referred to, ch. 78, the final chapter, Guðrún is indeed speaking, as Fuller says, "to young Bolli,"[30] i.e., to her son by her third
husband, Bolli Þorleiksson, after whom he is named. The likeli-
hood is that, as Fuller claims, she is referring to Kjartan in saying,
as Auden has it, "He that I loved the / Best, to him I was worst."
This is Kjartan Ólafsson, to whom she was never married, with
whom she had had an intimate and intense relationship between
the second and third of her four marriages, and whom her third
husband, Bolli, Kjartan's kinsman and close friend, had killed at
her instigation after Kjartan's marriage to another woman (chs. 39–
49). In the scene referred to here, Guðrún as an old woman is being
pressed by her son, well after the death of her fourth husband, to
reveal which man she loved the most. Her reply in the saga, "Þeim
var ek verst, er ek unna mest"[31] ("I was worst to the one I loved

---

[29]See *Brennu-Njáls Saga*, ed. by Einar Ól. Sveinsson (Reykjavík: Hið
íslenska fornritafélag, 1954), 182. Reference may be made to the relevant
chapters in this edition, and in *Njal's saga*, trans. with an introduction by
Magnus Magnusson and Hermann Pálsson (Harmondsworth, Middlesex:
Penguin, 1960).

[30]See Fuller, 209.

[31]See *Laxdæla saga* [...], ed. by Einar Ól. Sveinsson (Reykjavík: Hið
íslenska fornritafélag, 1934), 228. Reference may be made to the relevant
chapters in this edition, and in *Laxdæla saga*, trans. with an introduction by
Magnus Magnusson and Hermann Pálsson (Harmondsworth, Middlesex:
Penguin, 1969).

the most"), is reproduced practically word for word in Magnús Ásgeirsson's translation; the only differences are the reversed order of the first three words, and the modern spellings of *Eg/ég* "I" and *unni* "loved." It may be noted that the word *þeim*, found in both the saga and the translation, is more accurately translated as "to the one," "to the person," than as "to him" (as Auden has it); although the grammatical gender of this Icelandic pronoun is masculine, it can in fact refer to either a male or a female person. Fuller is certainly not alone in thinking that Guðrún is referring to Kjartan here, and it is indeed highly likely that this is the case. It may be noted, however, that it has recently been suggested (by Svava Jakobsdóttir) that Guðrún is here referring to herself.[32] It is clear that, in not specifying, as Auden does, the sex of the person referred to, Magnús Ásgeirsson has had the advantage over Auden of being a native speaker of Icelandic and fully understanding the implications of the saga's phrasing.

In this essay I have concentrated on the distinctively Icelandic stylistic and metrical features of Magnús Ásgeirsson's translation of Auden's "Journey to Iceland," as well as on the specifically Icelandic allusions in Auden's text, and their treatment by the translator. In doing so, and in providing a close English rendering of the Icelandic translation, I hope to have laid the basis for the use of this translation as an aid to the study of Auden's poem. The Icelandic translation, which, with its reference to poets (rather than ports) in the opening stanza, clearly reflects an earlier version of the poem than any of its published English versions, is of great potential value to students of the poem as an early, considered, poetic response to it.[33] For those encountering the Icelandic translation after first becoming acquainted with the original, the translation, with the questions it raises as to the extent of its accuracy, is bound to stimulate reexamination of the original, and of what precisely is the meaning of Auden's poem. With the increased accessibility which this essay has aimed to provide for it, Magnús

---

[32]See Svava Jakobsdóttir, "Skáldskapur og fræði," *Tímarit Máls og menningar* 60:4 (1999), 52–61, esp. 60–61.

[33]Magnús Ásgeirsson (1901–55) is regarded in Iceland as a poet in his own right—mainly on the basis of his verse translations of poems composed by non-Icelandic poets from many different countries, but also on the basis of a small number of original poems. These are printed together with his verse translations in the two volumes of his collected poems *Ljóðasafn* (1975), taking up just over thirty pages of the first volume.

Ásgeirsson's "Ferð til Íslands" may, I hope, now be acknowledged as an important early landmark in the internal and external history of Auden's "Journey to Iceland"; that is to say, in the history of both the composition and the reception of Auden's poem.

Auden, "Spain," and the Crisis of Literary Popular Frontism

Peter C. Grosvenor

The travesty of the Spanish Civil War became the turning point for what Auden would later call the "low dishonest decade" of the 1930s. Auden and his peers were greatly affected by this first battle, in effect, between democracy and fascism, and were caught up in its desperate importance. Political scientist Peter Grosvenor depicts the background of the Spanish Civil War and places Auden front and center of the conflict that caused him to write the best poem he wished he'd never written, "Spain 1937."

Auden's 1937 poem "Spain" occupies a central place in a flawed orthodoxy in Auden studies. That orthodoxy is that there is a dichotomy between the poet's political phase during the 1930s, which represents the height of his imaginative powers and literary influence, and the apolitical remainder of his life, which is characterized by artistic decline and marginalization.[1] "Spain," the poem that he wrote upon his return to England after a visit to the Spanish Civil War, is frequently taken to mark the transition. The poem has also been invoked to illustrate the shallowness and insincerity of Auden's Marxism. Certainly, his experiences in Spain are held to be crucial in marking his break with the left, his gradual depoliticization, and his return to Christianity.

There are obvious truths in such an interpretation. Auden's centrality to the British literary intelligentsia in the 1930s is largely undisputed, and was never matched subsequently. His literary influence therefore did indeed coincide with his most politically engaged period. It is also true that "Spain" is a problematical part of

---

[1]The orthodoxy referred to here is discussed by Perrie in "Auden's Political Vision."

239

the Auden canon, and he himself grappled with the difficulties it posed, rewriting some lines and deleting others, openly repudiating some of the sentiments contained in the original version, and eventually excluding it from anthologies of his work. Nor should it be denied that Auden's Marxism had always been blended with other intellectual and spiritual interests, producing an esoteric and idiosyncratic ideological concoction—and one that was certainly unsatisfactory to the more orthodox Plekanovite materialists of the period. And Auden's exposure to the Spanish Civil War undoubtedly figured prominently in his religious development.

At the same time, this interpretation contains a number of questionable assumptions and misleading overstatements. To begin with, it is not clear that Auden is best interpreted as a political poet, in the conventional sense of writing in the service of a given political movement or ideology, even in his 1930s phase. A preoccupation with morality, and the exploration of moral choice, constitutes a continuity in Auden's work, predating and outlasting his Marxist phase. In fact, it is an error to conclude from his use of the fashionable language of the decade that he was ever in any meaningful sense a Marxist at all. Auden seems to have been a moderate in both political and religious terms, temperamentally suited to social liberalism and Anglicanism at a time when liberalism appeared spent and the Church of England was part of the larger English establishment that had been discredited by the trauma of the Great War. Much the same can be said of the rest of the Auden group, who were seeking to articulate what were to all intents and purposes liberal ideas, while freeing themselves from what in the context of the time they believed to be the feeble vocabulary of the liberal creed. The Marxism of the Auden group always had a veneer quality to it, concealing underneath their cooler political disposition, and their inconfident and embarrassed subscription to political values that no longer seemed relevant or durable in the context of the time.

Auden's brief and mysterious Spanish interlude is significant because it forced his ultimately inevitable confrontation of uncertainties and contradictions that were inherent in his already complex and eclectic world view. It was a demonstrably painful experience, but its effect was to accelerate a process of evolution, rather than to occasion an abrupt discontinuity in his political and religious development. But another justification for studying this aspect of Auden's life is that his post-Spain intellectual crisis was a personification of the crisis of a moment in British literary history, namely literary Popular Frontism. Auden's ideological convictions moved him to try to make a practical contribution to the defense of Republican Spain, but his experiences there helped to undermine precisely those convictions. In much the same way, the Spanish Civil War was the *cause célèbre* for a British left intelligentsia that coalesced around the anti-fascist Popular Front. Yet the war also exposed the irreconcilable differences of opinion within the Front, which became more of a forum for conflict than for co-operation.

The preoccupation of British writers with events in Spain between 1936 and 1939 illustrates the political radicalization of the literary community during what F.R. Leavis called the "Red Decade." Though it can be qualified and elaborated upon, the view that the Auden group was central to British literary developments during the period remains a defensible orthodoxy. The group is usually taken to comprise, in addition to Auden himself, Stephen Spender, Cecil Day Lewis, and Louis MacNeice—"Macspaunday" in the sobriquet coined by Roy Campbell. Christopher Isherwood, though socially integral to the group, and a literary collaborator with Auden in drama, is usually excluded, presumably on the grounds that he was not a poet. The group was informal, resting on nothing more than ties of personal friendship, though Auden appears to have been the dominant personality.

With the exception of MacNeice, whose essentially liberal politics could plausibly be said to be those of the rest of the group minus the Marxist inflection, all of the Audenites expressed sympathy to one degree or another for communism. Auden and Isherwood themselves never joined the Communist Party. Spender did so, but only briefly. Day Lewis was the most committed communist and was an active party member from 1933 to 1938. But the group clearly had unifying political themes, such as a contempt for their own social class, anti-capitalism, opposition to dictators, and a determination to seek alternatives to war. They were regarded as a movement in British poetry, and their extensive literary influence also contributed greatly to the rise of left-wing ideas to the level of orthodoxy in literary circles.

This is not to suggest that the left was unchallenged among the literary elite. T.S. Eliot, W.B. Yeats, Ezra Pound, and Wyndham Lewis all took up positions on the right, while Hilaire Belloc and G.K. Chesterton (until the latter's death in 1936) moved increasingly rightward from their earlier liberal philosophy of distributism. But there was less ideological unity among the right-wing intellectuals than on the left, and they were less likely to be connected to organized political movements.

The relationship between the left and right wings of the British literary intelligentsia was a complex one. The political polarity had no corresponding division on the question of literary form. The Auden group looked to writers such as Eliot, Yeats, and Pound as pioneers of the modernist movement in literature, to which they were grateful heirs, and the emphatically apolitical nature of modernism was endorsed by Auden and his Oxford friends in the 1920s. As Spender explained in his reflections on the decade, it was the crisis atmosphere of the 1930s that made this modernist schism between literature and politics untenable: the Auden group, under extreme pressure of circumstance, were "putting the subject back into poetry" (Spender, *Thirties and After*, 14).

As students during the 1920s they had wrestled with the legacy of the Great War, debating the merits of pacifism and sharing in the widespread disillusionment with the political establishment. But it was not until the early 1930s that their interest in varieties of socialism and communism matured and their poetry and plays began to address directly issues of domestic and international politics. Samuel Hynes has pointed out that the relationship between literature and its historical context is likely to be at its most direct during times of crisis, and Auden himself, writing in mid-decade, described the 1930s as "this hour of crisis and dismay" (quoted in Hynes, 12). The Wall Street Crash of October 1929 and the onset of the Depression appeared to Auden as the final crisis of the capitalist system:

> The prospects for the future aren't alluring;
> No one believes Prosperity enduring.[2]

Britain was in the grip of mass unemployment by 1931. In the political crisis of that year, the Labour Party imploded and was reduced to an ineffectual rump in the October election. On the far right of politics Oswald Mosley, impressed by his visit to Mussolini's Italy, formed the British Union of Fascists in 1932. Authoritarian regimes proliferated and came to be seen by democrats as variants on a generic fascism, one characteristic feature of which was an aggressive and expansionist foreign policy which threatened the prospect of a second global conflagration: the Japanese

---

[2]Quote from "Letter to Lord Byron"; see Cunningham, *British Writers*, 39.

occupied Manchuria in 1931; Mussolini invaded Haile Sellasie's Abyssinia in pursuit of the New Roman Empire in 1935; and in 1936 Hitler re-militarized the Rhineland.

Against this background, the Soviet Union presented itself as a demonstrably viable alternative to mass unemployment, fascism, and war. The apparent success of the Soviet Five Year Plans, and the Soviet Union's insulation from the global economic crisis, legitimized the communist experiment in the eyes of many western intellectuals. In 1935, Sidney and Beatrice Webb published their two-volume study *Soviet Communism: A New Civilization?*, which famously appeared in a 1937 second edition with the question mark omitted. The book became one of the most influential works in Britain and did more than any other to boost the prestige of the Soviet Union among left-wing intellectuals (Wood, 45). Fears that Russia was in reality an oppressive dictatorship were fueled by the Moscow trials, but at least partially allayed by the new Soviet Constitution of 1936.

Viewing the situation at home and abroad, the British literary leftists felt a heavy burden of responsibility arising from their perception of an impending disaster to which the British political establishment seemed oblivious. As Spender put it in his reflections on the decade, "If a small but vociferous and talented minority of what was called the 'intellectuals' ... was almost hypnotically aware of the Nazi nightmare, the vast majority of people, and the government and members of the ruling class, seemed determined to ignore or deny it. One had the sense of belonging to a small group who could see terrible things which no one else saw" (*Thirties and After*, 12). This is no doubt a sincere expression of the frustration felt at the time, but Spender's assessment ignores the large numbers of politicians, political activists, trade unionists and others who shared the Auden group's concerns. Nonetheless, the "small but vociferous and talented minority" must be credited with having presciently warned of fascism's impending dangers. Auden's compelling "Ballad" (1932), despite its implied Jacobite subject matter, can be read as an indictment of the rising political repression in Europe.[3] Spender's long poem *Vienna* (1934) roundly condemned the Dollfuss regime for its ruthless suppression of the Austrian left in February 1934. Isherwood's two Berlin novel-

---

[3]Alternative title: "O What Is That Sound" (Auden, *Collected Shorter Poems*, 72–73). The eighteenth-century setting and its possible application to 1930s authoritarianism is plausibly suggested by Fuller, 153–54.

memoirs, *Mr. Norris Changes Trains* (1935) and *Goodbye to Berlin* (1938), based on his experiences in Germany between 1929 and 1933, drew a vivid picture of the impending Nazi threat.

The British literary leftists were galvanized into anti-fascist writing and political campaigning by the substantial political realignment made possible by a strategic change on the part of the Communist Third International, or Comintern. At its Seventh Congress in 1935 the Comintern abandoned its earlier denunciation of European social democratic and labor parties as "social fascists" and called for a "Popular Front" of progressive political forces united against the common enemy of fascism. In Britain, the immediate effect of this change of policy was the Communist Party's emergence from its sectarian isolationism and anti-intellectual "workerism," and its engagement with sympathetic elements in the progressive intelligentsia in general. This produced a major change of political tenor on the left as a broader and more open interpretation of Marxism emerged, enabling a wider array of leftists to associate themselves with it.

A Popular Front government came to power in France in 1936, under the leadership of the socialist Leon Blum. Though the French communists did not formally enter the government, they supported it in the Chamber of Deputies. In the same year, a Popular Front government was formed in Chile to counter the influence of the military. But it was in Spain that the Popular Front idea was to have its most significant political impact. The Spanish Popular Front government was elected in February 1936 and, despite real tensions within the coalition, it pressed ahead with the collectivist economic program and secularist social agenda that was to provoke the nationalist rebellion of 18 July.

By contrast to all this, Popular Frontism in Britain never entered the political mainstream. The National Government formed by Labour apostate Ramsay MacDonald in August 1931 was given a resounding landslide in the election of the following October, and became a Conservative administration in all but name after its re-election under Stanley Baldwin in 1935. Beneath this right-wing government a vibrant left culture of protest and demonstration flourished, manifesting itself, often spectacularly, in hugely symbolic hunger marches and in street confrontations with the Mosleyites. It also produced a proliferating literary counter-culture. In fact, it is not an exaggeration to say that in Britain the Popular Front was substantially a literary phenomenon, finding its most tangible and enduring expression in the Left Book Club founded in May 1936 by the former Liberal-turned-Christian-socialist, Victor Gollancz.

The cohesion of this literary Popular Frontism benefited greatly from the outbreak of the Spanish Civil War, and defense of the Second Republic against General Franco's forces became the focus of the left's energies and the high point of the literary left's political engagement. The Labour Party in Parliament had been reduced to an ineffectual rump since 1931. The Independent Labour Party (ILP), one of its key constituent units, had seceded from it in 1932 and suffered a catastrophic fall in membership. The Popular Front therefore provided an opening for the Communist Party, led by Harry Pollitt. The party had been formed in 1920, with only 2,500 members at its foundation. Unable to supplant the Labour Party, its membership remained small in comparison to its counterparts in continental Europe and the United States, and by the mid-1930s it was still in the region of a meager 11,000. Yet it effectively seized the leadership of the Spanish aid movement, securing in the process a prominence on the British left that it would never enjoy again. It was during this era of Communist Party prestige that prominent left-wing writers found their way to party membership. Internationally, there was a concerted effort, mainly communist-driven, to enlist artistic and academic support for the Madrid government. It was the German communist activist Willi Meunzenberg, who had directed some of Arthur Koestler's party activities, who coined the Spanish Civil War slogan "We must organize the intellectuals" (quoted in Davenport-Hines, 162).

The success with which British intellectuals were mobilized was revealed when the measure of support for the Spanish Republic was taken by the *Left Review*. This journal, which was founded in October 1934 and ran until May 1938, was edited by Communist Party members but, in keeping with the spirit of the Popular Front, opened its pages to non-communist left-sympathizers, including Auden. Under the auspices of the *Left Review*, the writer Nancy Cunard conducted a questionnaire survey of prominent British writers and their attitudes to the Spanish situation. The results were published in *Authors Take Sides on the Spanish War* (1937). Out of 149 responses, 127 names appeared for the Republic, including Auden's. Only sixteen declared themselves to be neutral, though these included some extremely influential figures, such as Eliot, Pound, H.G. Wells, and Vita Sackville-West. Eliot felt that "it is best that at least a few men of letters should remain isolated, and take no part in these collective activities" (Cunningham,

Spanish Front, 56). The handful of respondents declaring themselves for the Nationalists included Evelyn Waugh, who wrote that
"If I were a Spaniard I should be fighting for General Franco"
(Cunningham, *Spanish Front*, 57). Others who may have been expected to offer a view did not reply to the questionnaire, one being
Graham Greene. Another was George Orwell, who actually fought
in Spain and angrily dismissed the survey, which he later described as "bloody rot" (letter to Stephen Spender, 2 April 1938;
Collected Essays, 1:311–12).

There is some evidence of manipulation, with some pro-na-
tionalist responses being excluded from the final publication, and
the questionnaire itself was loaded: "Are you for, or against, the
legal Government and the People of Republican Spain?"
(Cunningham, *Spanish Front*, 51). Nonetheless, the document remains an important indicator of both the left-wing orientation of
the literary elite and the importance attached to Spain. It must be
remembered that the lopsided division of opinion among intellectuals was not at all representative of the state of British public
opinion overall. Mass Observation[4] developed for the first time in
1937, but there was no scientific public opinion polling. By "public
opinion" in the 1930s what was usually meant was the state of
play among the various opinion-forming organs, which is to say
newspaper and periodical editorials. Among the leader writers,
the balance of opinion was much more evenly divided, but
nonetheless equally polarized. On the right of the newspaper spectrum the Rothermere-owned *Daily Mail* and *Evening News* were
joined by the *Catholic Herald* and the *Catholic Times* in protesting
against Republican atrocities. Papers approximating to neutrality
included the *Daily Telegraph*, the *Evening News*, and the *London
Times*. On the left, the *Manchester Guardian* and the *News Chronicle*
supported the Republican government. Among the political week-

---

[4]Mass Observation was founded in 1937 by the anthropologist Tom
Harrison, the poet Charles Madge, and the documentary film maker
Humphrey Jennings. Its purpose was to conduct social surveys of the
British population and to report the findings widely. The project did not
confine itself to statistical studies and included diaries and interviews.
The scope of the research was extremely broad, encompassing politics, the
family, unions, strikes, public health, housing, crime and policing, leisure
and entertainment. Though its research methods are considered primitive
today, Mass Observation studies continue to provide invaluable historical
data on social change in Britain before and during World War II.

lies, the *Saturday Review* strongly supported the Nationalists, the *Spectator* took a neutral and non-interventionist line, and the *New Statesman and Nation*, under the editorship of Kingsley Martin, strongly supported the Republicans.

Whatever it seemed to be to the outside world, the Spanish Civil War was first and foremost a momentous clash between two profoundly irreconcilable visions of Spanish nationhood—one resolutely traditionalist, the other aggressively modernist. It was also a revolution within a civil war, a situation of immense complexity and dynamism that was only ever partially understood by its foreign observers. But at the same time, it was the testing ground for all the major contending ideologies in 1930s Europe: fascism, communism, anarchism, and liberal democracy. As George Orwell said, "It was above all things a political war" (*Homage to Catalonia*, 46).[5] The conflict of ideas in Spain drew the attention of leading European intellectuals from across the political spectrum, all of whom saw the outcome of the war as a potential historical turning point.

For the minority of pro-Franco right-wing writers, a nationalist victory was a preferable alternative to the increasingly communist direction of the Republic. Evelyn Waugh, who with some justification protested at the left's often indiscriminate use of the "fascist" label to describe all its critics, protested that "I am not a Fascist nor shall I become one unless it were the only alternative to Marxism" (Cunningham, *Spanish Front*, 57, 70). For the leftist majority, on the other hand, the outbreak of the Civil War represented the first sign that the dangers of fascism, about which they felt themselves to be voices in the wilderness, had finally been recognized and confronted. In *Homage to Catalonia* (1938), Orwell wrote: "When the fighting broke out on 18 July it is probable that every anti-Fascist in Europe felt a thrill of hope. For here at last, apparently, was democracy standing up to Fascism. For years past the so-called democratic countries had been surrendering to Fascism at every step.... But when Franco tried to overthrow a mildly Left-wing Government the Spanish people, against all expectation, had risen against him. It seemed—possibly it was—the turning of the tide" (48). In similar terms, the young Philip Toynbee believed that "the gloves were off in the struggle against fascism" (quoted in

---

[5]For a survey of Spain in the pre-Civil War period, see Brenan. Standard works on the Civil War are Thomas, *The Spanish Civil War*; Preston, *The Spanish Civil War*; and Carr, *The Spanish Tragedy*.

Thomas, 347). Auden, in his contribution to *Authors Take Sides*, also located the Spanish situation in the context of the wider European crisis, arguing that the defeat of the Spanish government "would make a European war more probable" and spread "Fascist Ideology and practice to countries as yet comparatively free from them" (Cunningham, *Spanish Front*, 52).

But resistance to the spread of fascism is not in itself enough to explain why the left became so emotive in the Spanish cause. A recent study by Tom Buchanan has increased the emphasis on the positive appeal of Republican Spain as a social experiment: "The campaigns in solidarity with the Spanish Republic were not only defensive, but were inspired by the passionately held belief that a new and better society was being created in Spain.... Thus, the Republic was worth fighting for not because it was the equivalent of British democracy, but because in many respects it seemed to be superior to it" (4). This more positive support for the Republican political project almost certainly has been understated in the literature. But among intellectuals specifically, the anti-fascist struggle, and the defense of a legal government against an illegal army rebellion, appear to have been the most prevalent motives for Spanish solidarity. If *Authors Take Sides* is the indicator, only a few of the pro-Republican statements referred directly to the domestic record of the Madrid government.

The remarkable interest taken in Spain by British left-wing writers must also be understood in terms of how they, specifically as writers, saw fascism. As Margot Heinemann has expressed it, the "'pull' of Spain ... was not, for most writers, a blind flight into action, but a lucidly accepted chance to save European civilisation and culture" (129–32). Franco's uprising was not another in a succession of *pronunciamentos* but a calculated assault on all the values that the left-wing literary community held dear. Fascism presented itself to the left-wing writers of Europe as barbarism incarnate, and nothing could have reinforced this interpretation more strongly than the Nationalists' murder of the distinguished Spanish poet and playwright Federico Garcia Lorca in the early part of the hostilities. Auden, for example, would offer readings of Lorca's poems when speaking for the Spanish cause.[6] While Auden once half-seriously attributed his own understanding of, and opposition to, fascism in terms of having attended an English boarding school, it

---

[6]See, for example, a lecture given at Shrewsbury School, 30 October 1938 (*Complete Works* 1:716–26).

is clear that like many other writers he saw in fascism a repudiation of the artist's place in the world. In his contribution to *Authors Take Sides*, he wrote that the continued expansion of fascism "would create an atmosphere in which the creative artist and all who care for justice, liberty and culture would find it impossible to work or even exist" (Cunningham, *Spanish Front*, 52).

As John Lehmann, editor of *New Writing*—a major vehicle for literary leftism launched only months before the outbreak of the Spanish conflict—recalled it: "The pull was terrific: the pull of an international crusade to the ideals and aims of which all intellectuals ... who had been stirred by the fascist danger, felt they could, in that hour of apocalypse, whole-heartedly assent" (274–75). The John Donne lines "And therefore never send to know for whom the *bell* tolls; It tolls for *thee*" perfectly encapsulate the idea of the defence of the Spanish government as an inescapable responsibility, and were used to such good effect in the title of the Spanish Civil War's most famous novel.

As stated earlier, the intellectuals were by no means the only ones to hear the call of Spain. With international organizations, and established charities, reluctant to involve themselves in so explicitly political a situation, there was a spontaneous proliferation of *ad hoc* humanitarian aid committees under no clear political direction, though without doubt the overwhelming majority of them favored the Republican side.[7] A prominent and representative example was the Spanish Medical Aid Committee, founded in July 1936, under whose auspices Auden traveled to Spain. There was also an impressive groundswell of specifically working class support for what was seen as a workers' government under siege. Historian Hwyel Francis has attributed this to an animating spirit of "proletarian internationalism"—ordinarily a largely vacuous Marxist-Leninist phrase, describing an elusive condition of political consciousness to be achieved through agitation, rather than an actually existing phenomenon. But in the context of the ideologically charged 1930s it is a meaningful term, as Francis's study of solidarity action in Wales amply demonstrates.

The ultimate act of solidarity was, of course, to volunteer to fight on the Republic's behalf. This remarkable course of action was undertaken by over 2,500 British people. The official government policy of non-intervention meant that the volunteers ran afoul of the authorities, sometimes having to travel covertly on

---

[7]See Fyrth.

false papers, and often having to hike across the Pyrenees to join the International Brigades. It remains a story of genuine heroism that is hard to rival, and Auden paid tribute to the volunteers in his Spanish Civil War poem:

> They clung like birds to the long expresses that lurch
> > Through the unjust lands, through the night, through the
> alpine tunnel;
> > They floated over the oceans;
> They walked the passes. All presented their lives.
> > (61–64)[8]

Most of the British pro-Republican writers showed their support by plying their craft. Short stories began to appear in left-wing literary magazines before the close of 1936, and in March 1937 the *Left Theatre Review* included a short play about the international volunteers in Spain (Osborne, 131). The writers spoke at solidarity meetings, fund-raisers, and demonstrations against the government's non-intervention policy. They also joined with their foreign counterparts at morale-boosting events in Spain itself, such as the Second International Writers Congress, which was opened by the Spanish prime minister Juan Negrín in Valencia on 4 July 1937. Created as a unity forum for writers of various political views opposed to fascism, this was the largest single demonstration of international literary Popular Frontism. The literary guests were frequently greeted by crowds shouting *"Viva los intellectuales!"* and visits and tours of this kind seem to have been welcome and effective demonstrations of solidarity. Another way in which writers, as writers, could help the Republic was to contribute to anti-fascist anthologies, which became something of a literary feature of the war. Several were produced by Spanish poets early in the conflict. In 1939, when the Republic was substantially lost, *Poems for Spain* appeared. The volume was edited by Stephen Spender and John Lehmann and contained fifty-three poems written over the course of the war, mainly by British poets.

But other writers felt an inescapable duty to volunteer to fight. "For some authors," Stanley Weintraub has explained, "writing was an insufficient commitment to the fight against Fascism: the final test was action—to expose the body to danger and discomfort and to offer it, if necessary, in sacrifice. Only then would the ideals

---

[8]All quotations from "Spain" are from Cunningham, *The Penguin Book of Spanish Civil War Verse* (97–100).

about which one wrote be put to the ultimate test of sincerity" (13). It was the French novelist André Malraux who most closely approximated in reality the individualist military heroism of Hemingway's explosives man, Robert Jordan (himself an intellectual—a university professor of Spanish), and his service as a squadron commander in the Republican air force provided a counterweight to the airman-as-reactionary stereotype, demonstrated in real life by the pro-Axis aviator Charles Lindbergh, and by the arguably fascistic airman in Auden's *The Orators* (1932), or, indeed, the pro-Franco "charming young English aviators" he would mention in his "Impressions of Valencia" (in Cunningham, *Spanish Civil War Verse*, 100–102). But even without the opportunity for individual gallantry afforded to pilots, some of the British writers served with unquestionable distinction and valor in Spain. Tom Wintringham, a veteran of the Great War, was valued for his military experience. George Orwell served with the revolutionary leftist, though anticommunist, POUM militia and was dangerously wounded in the throat. The poet and painter Clive Branson was captured and held prisoner by the Nationalists for eight months. And talented writers, many of whom were only beginning to realize their talent while on military service in Spain, lost their lives in the Republican cause. They included the communist journalist and novelist Ralph Fox; John Cornford, who had recently graduated from Cambridge, and only just begun to write poetry; the novelist and poet turned Marxist literary theorist, Christopher Caudwell; the Irish poet Charles Donnelly; and Virginia Woolf's nephew (and John Lehmann's best friend) Julian Bell.

Having said this, the role of the literary combatants, from Britain and elsewhere, has certainly been exaggerated, not least by the intellectuals themselves. The Spanish Civil War was not the "poets' war" Stephen Spender famously claimed it to be, and in the region of 80% of British volunteers were of working class origin. The disproportionate attention paid to the writer-volunteers is easily explained (*God That Failed*, 244). To begin with, they were heavily represented in the initial wave of recruits. The departure of literary celebrities for Spain, in any capacity, was also widely publicized in the left-wing press, which understood very well the considerable propaganda of martyred poets. The historian Hugh Thomas, for example, recounts the story of Harry Pollitt urging Spender to go to Spain and get killed because the movement needed a Byron (491, n.2). Furthermore, it was the writers who provided the historians with the written records of their activities.

The criticism that has been leveled at Spender's notorious overclaim is understandable, conjuring up as it does an absurd image of the "small but vociferous and talented minority" charging to the rescue of the Republic. But in all fairness, this was probably not Spender's intent. A fairer interpretation is that he was alluding to the grip of the Spanish Civil War on the minds of his peers, and to the immense poetic potential of the war's Spanish setting, at least in terms of English preconceptions and stereotypes: "The peculiar Spanish passion, idealism and violence of temperament, and even the Spanish landscape, colored the struggle and gave it intensity and a kind of poetic purity which it scarcely had before or afterward." The Spanish theater, he explained, took on a double meaning as both a theater of war and a dramatization of European ideological conflicts (*God That Failed*, 244). In the same vein, Charles Osborne has suggested that the appeal of Spain to British writers was that forces of reaction and liberation, so often juxtaposed in their poetry and drama, had now moved into the realm of reality (131).

Writers were also drawn to Spain by a simple desire for adventure. In a decade of mass unemployment and the increasing threat of war, politically conscious artists felt a powerful impulse to engage, to bridge, as C. Day Lewis put it, "the old romantic chasm between the artist and the man of action, the poet and the ordinary man" (quoted in Ford, 18). The pervasive influence of Marxist ideology among the left literary intelligentsia at the time was an additional imperative to break down the dichotomy of thought and action. And there were the historical precedents of poets putting themselves in harm's way for a noble cause.

Of course, these motives were vulnerable to criticism and mockery. Indeed, there was no shortage of either, and it came thick and fast from within the literary community itself. To begin with, it was alleged that the literary champions of Spain were reneging on the primary social responsibility of intellectuals to contemplate and reflect. Instead, they were caught up in an uncritical groundswell of bias and sentiment. T.S. Eliot, for example, wrote that the polarization of British intellectual opinion by the Spanish conflict had resulted in "a deterioration of political thinking, with a pressure on everyone, which has to be stubbornly resisted, to accept one extreme philosophy or another" (Cunningham, *Spanish Front*, 60). Ezra Pound went further and accused the pro-Republicans of irresponsible and self-indulgent romanticism.

Spain was, in his view, "an emotional luxury to a gang of sap-headed dilettantes" (Cunningham, *Spanish Front*, 57).

This notion that even the British writers who went over to Spain were striking a pose, and enjoying a kind of *avant-garde* political tourism, was developed by Graham Greene, in an ingenious but mischievous historical parallel published in the *Spectator* in December 1937. In "Alfred Tennyson Intervenes," Greene compared the support of the 1930s poets for the Spanish Republic to the support of Tennyson and the Apostles for the exiled Spanish liberals just over a century earlier. Tennyson, and Hallam, ventured into Spain to take money and dispatches to the liberal rebels, though they returned home without having witnessed any military engagement. The Apostles who had traveled to Gibraltar, in anticipation of supporting a liberal rebellion, "tired of the long wait" and "scattered through Spain with guidebooks, examining churches and Moorish remains." Nonetheless, Greene conceded that the 1930s poets—"hysterical partisans," as he termed them—were much more serious-minded than their nineteenth-century predecessors, who would have disapproved of Tennyson's motives because "there is every reason to suppose that he went for the fun of it" (Cunningham, *Spanish Front*, 67–69). Similarly, in Arthur Koestler's assessment, the typical writer's tour of warring Spain amounted to a "a revolutionary junket" (326).

The charge of poserism was often coupled with anti-homosexual bigotry and the allegation that support for "Red Spain" was just another example of transgressive politics as an accompaniment to transgressive sex. The most accomplished dispenser of this vitriol was Roy Campbell, the Spanish Civil War's only reactionary British poet. Campbell, an obsessive anti-Semite and a contributor to British fascist publications, claimed to have fought on the side of the nationalist rebels, and liked to describe himself as "a Catholic soldier of Spain." Yet it appears that the nearest he actually got to the fighting was in his capacity as a war correspondent for *The Tablet*. In one of his poems, "Hard Lines, Azana," he jeered at the Republicans: "The Sodomites are on your side, / The cowards and the cranks" (quoted in Cunningham, *Spanish Civil War Verse*, 53). His *Flowering Rifle* is also punctuated by homophobic military puns about "fronts" and "rears."

The Auden group's engagement with Spain contains stories of serious political commitment, but is also rich in bathos for their contemporary and subsequent detractors to exploit. Louis MacNeice emerges unscathed. Characteristically, he approached the

Spanish situation with circumspection and caution, though he certainly supported the Spanish government and visited Catalonia toward the end of the conflict. Upon his return to Britain he wrote a report for the *Spectator* ("Today in Barcelona") in which he sought to depict a healthy society surviving in defiance of fractious politics and the privations of war. He reproduced the same picture in poetic form as part of his *Autumn Journal* (1939).[9] Cecil Day Lewis felt impelled to fight in Spain, but he never did bridge that gap between the poet and the man of action. "I believed I ought to volunteer for it," he wrote, "but I lacked the courage to do so" (quoted in Ford, 129). He attempted to compensate for this considerable burden on his conscience by continuing to appear as a valuable public speaker on the home front, even though he was never particularly comfortable in that role.

It was Spender who made the greatest personal commitment to Spain, though the experience complicated both his political and his personal life, and intertwined the two. Spain was the reason he joined the Communist Party, and the reason he left. The party's leading role in organizing Spanish aid drew him into it in February 1937. Shortly afterward, he was dispatched to Spain on a curious Communist Party errand. Over several visits, he toured the front, attended the Writers' Congress, and made some English-language propaganda broadcasts. During this time he broke with the communists over their imperious direction of the Republican war effort. He also became embroiled in the problems of T.A.R. Hyndman, who appears as "Jimmy Younger" in *World Within World*. Spender had left Hyndman in 1936 and subsequently married a woman he had met at a Spanish aid meeting. Hyndman, more out of pique than anything else, had then enlisted in the International Brigades. When Spender met up with him in Spain, Hyndman declared his conversion to pacifism and implored Spender to extricate him from the Brigades. This Spender eventually managed to do, after the compromise solution of a non-combatant assignment broke down.

Auden himself was in Iceland, where he had been joined by MacNeice, when he first received news of the Franco rebellion. Shortly before Christmas 1936 he confirmed for Christopher Isherwood the rumors that had been spreading about his intentions of volunteering in Spain, "either ambulance-driving or fighting. I

---

[9]MacNeice's works are reprinted in Cunningham, *Spanish Civil War Verse*, 142–45 and 453–56.

hope the former" (quoted in Isherwood, 261).[10] Isherwood claimed
a readiness to overcome personal timidity and to follow Auden to
Spain were it not for his absorbing commitment to protect his homosexual companion, Heinz, from the Nazi authorities. He did,
however, feel himself to be missing out on an important experience by remaining behind (263).

Greene had mocked Tennyson for seeing out a Cambridge
term before leaving for the Spanish struggle, so he presumably
would have made something of Auden's delaying his departure
for Spain in order to complete a book (Davenport-Hines, 163). The
left-wing press marked his departure for Spain on 11 January with
a great fanfare that embarrassed him. The *Daily Worker* realized the
publicity value of what it termed "the most famous of the younger
English poets" and "a leading figure in the anti-Fascist movement
in literature" committing himself to the Republic (Hynes, 251). But
Auden saw himself as no Byron, and showed no concern to live up
to the expectations of his excited admirers among political activists
and readers of "movement" poetry. It is not clear whether his
poem "Danse Macabre," written shortly before he left for Spain
(with its voice of a crazed dictator and a view of history as random
madness), was intended to deflate these expectations, or to pre-
empt the sneering of his critics. In Isherwood's interpretation, it
was "a dazzling explosion of ironic fireworks and a send-up of the
Warrior-Hero which seemed to poke fun at Wystan himself" (263).
When the two met in Paris before Auden crossed into Spain, Isherwood assured himself that the prospects that his indispensable
companion would get into harm's way were pretty remote, and
that he would be put to work in some sort of propagandist capacity, though with Byron and Rupert Brooke in mind, he feared the
possibility of disease (263).

As it transpired, Isherwood was right. Though it is frustratingly difficult to reconstruct what is the least well-documented
episode of his adult life, we can be confident about what Auden
did not do in Spain. He never fought, though he does seem to have
visited the front. Despite his Medical Aid for Spain credentials, he
never drove an ambulance. Nor did he get to Madrid, though he
spent time in Valencia and Barcelona. He did make some propa-

---

[10]Davenport-Hines has plausibly suggested that Auden's preference
for driving an ambulance stemmed from his father's having been a successful physician, his mother's experience as a nurse, and his own abiding
interests in things medical.

ganda broadcasts but, as Charles Osborne has pointed out, these would have been in English and transmitted over a radius in which they would have been heard by predominantly monolingual Spanish people who were already loyal to the government (133). It is hard to avoid the conclusion that Auden made an ineffectual and inglorious contribution to the Spanish Civil War. In the recollections of communist journalist Claud Cockburn, Auden cuts a ludicrous figure:

> ... of course, what we really wanted him for was to go to the front, write some pieces saying hurrah for the Republic, and then go away and write some poems, also saying hurrah for the Republic; and that would be his job in the war—and bloody important at that. Instead of which, unfortunately, he took the whole thing terribly seriously; he wanted to *do* something.... When Auden came out we got a car laid on for him and everything. We thought we'd whisk him to Madrid and that the whole thing would be a matter of a week before the end-product started firing. But not at all: the bloody man went off and got a donkey, a mule really, and announced that he was going to walk through Spain with this creature. From Valencia to the front. He got six miles from Valencia before the mule kicked him or something and only then did he return and get in the car and do his proper job. (Osborne, 134)

But this story should not be taken at face value. Cockburn related it nearly thirty years later, and it is almost certainly a caricature of the real events. It is, after all, difficult to square this picture of Auden as a quixotic buffoon with the Auden of "Danse Macabre." There is, however, one confirmed comic episode, in which Auden was arrested by the Republican authorities for public urination in the Monjuich gardens. Of course, this story survives in large part because of its value to Auden's right-wing detractors, such as the journalist and historian Paul Johnson (315).

Comedy aside, the Spanish interlude remains an important, if obscure, part of Auden's life, and it is important to try to draw the right lessons from it. The principal reason we have so few facts at our disposal is that Auden, like Tennyson before him, would not discuss his Spanish experiences publicly once he returned to England, and Spender recorded that he refused to be drawn even in private (*World Within World*, 225). No doubt this can be explained to some degree by his embarrassment at not having been allowed to do what he considered useful, and his sense that the expedition had been a resounding failure in terms of the goals he had set himself. But for the most part, his virtual silence on the matter was a symptom of doubt and re-evaluation. It was nearly twenty years before he would be forthcoming about his true impressions of Spain. In 1937, his meager writings from or about Spain were the only clues as to his thoughts.

Auden offered only one dispatch from Spain—an article entitled "Impressions of Valencia"—which appeared in the *New Statesman* on 30 January 1937. The eagerly awaited article was something of a disappointment to its readers, many of whom were unsettled by its flippant tone and its detailing of trivia, such as the stimulant the war had provided to poster artists. But the piece must be judged to be unequivocally pro-Republican in its insistence that "a revolution is really taking place, not an odd shuffle or two in cabinet appointments," and in its mockery of the right-wing caricature of Spain as a "bloodthirsty and unshaven Anarchy." It also conveys Auden's internalization of the super-abundant Republican morale at that early stage of the Civil War, in its assertion that "General Franco has already lost two professional armies and is in the process of losing a third" (Cunningham, *Spanish Civil War Verse*, 101–2).

"Impressions of Valencia" was written within a couple of weeks of Auden's arrival in Spain, and therefore makes no mention of the factors that would later cause him anxiety. There were two such factors, namely communist culpability in the internecine conflicts on the Spanish left, and the evidence of anti-clericalism on the part of the Republican government. In private correspondence in 1962, Auden wrote that "I did not wish to talk about Spain when I returned because I was upset by many things I saw or heard about. Some of them were described better than I could ever have done by George Orwell in *Homage to Catalonia*. Others were what I learned about the treatment of priests" (letter to H. Ford; quoted in Osborne, 134).

This wording implies that political and religious factors contributed equally to his Spanish dilemma. The reference to Orwell is very significant because Orwell's civil war memoir was a damning indictment of the Moscow-directed Spanish communists for their domination of the Republican government, and for their brutal purge of the anarchists and Trotskyists, despite the military value of their frontline units at the opening of the war. In fact, Orwell's account of the Soviet Union's manipulation of the Spanish situation for Stalinist goals was so uncongenial to the British left that the Left Book Club actually turned down *Homage to*

Catalonia for publication. There is good reason to believe that
Auden and Orwell had reached similar conclusions about the
political unviability of the Republican coalition. In October 1938,
Auden favorably reviewed André Malraux's Spanish Civil War
novel *Days of Hope*, and specifically credited Malraux with having
honestly confronted the "Inefficiencies, cruelties, intrigues, the
conflict between Anarchists and Communists, between those who
want to *be* something and those who want to do something," the
clear implication being that these problems were commonly elided
in most left-wing writing on the war.[11]

Every bit as real as the ferocious political in-fighting was the
violent Republican suppression of the Church. José M. Sánchez
claims that the anti-clerical violence of the early years of the Spanish Civil War was greater than that of the French, Mexican, or Russian revolutions in terms of the total number of clerics killed, or
the percentage of clerics in the overall fatalities (8). Antonio Mon-
tero Moreno has calculated that 6,832 priests were killed between
1936 and 1939, to which must be added an incalculable number of
laymen (cited in Sánchez, 9). At the beginning of the Second Republic in 1931, a legislative offensive against the powers of the
Church proved to be a politically valuable source of unity among
the liberals and socialists in the governing coalition. The abolition
of the monarchy served to release pent-up antagonisms toward
Spain's feudal political and economic structures, of which the
Church was deemed to be a part, and triggered a wave of anti-clerical violence, including church burnings. In 1934, attempts by the
Catholic Party CEDA to secure a place in the government resulted
in an abortive leftist rebellion and attacks on the clergy. But it was
the outbreak of civil war in 1936 that led to an explosion of anti-
clerical violence, as the Church was held to be complicit in the
army uprising.

Auden's objections to Republican anti-clericalism were part of
his awakening to disagreeable Spanish political realities, because it
reminded him of the authoritarianism he had gone there to resist.
But there was also an undeniable religious dimension to his reaction, as he made clear in his contribution to James Pike's edited
volume *Modern Canterbury Pilgrims* (1956), in which he recounted
his thoughts about a walk around Barcelona:

---

[11]"Men of Thought and Action," a review of T. Mann's *The Coming
Victory of Democracy* and A. Malraux's *Days of Hope*, in *The Town Crier*
(Birmingham), 14 October 1938 (*Complete Works*, 1:458–60).

... I found as I walked through the city that all the churches were closed and there was not a priest to be seen. To my astonishment, this discovery left me profoundly shocked and disturbed. The feeling was far too intense to be the result of a mere liberal dislike of intolerance, the notion that it is wrong to stop people from doing what they like, even if it is something silly like going to church. I could not escape acknowledging that, however I had consciously ignored and rejected the Church for sixteen years, the existence of churches and what went on in them had all the time been very important to me. (41)

Obviously, his time in Spain contributed significantly to Auden's religious reawakening. But if he was "profoundly shocked and disturbed" by what he saw of anti-clericalism, it is reasonable to wonder why he did not speak out against it at the time, or upon his return. One explanation may be that he seems to have encountered the phenomenon only in its milder forms. Orwell, for example, recorded a much grimmer reality in the same Barcelona, at around the same time:

Actually churches were pillaged everywhere and as a matter of course, because it was perfectly well understood that the Spanish Church was part of the capitalist racket. In six months in Spain I only saw two undamaged churches, and until about July 1937 no churches were allowed to reopen and hold services, except for one or two Protestant churches in Madrid. (*Homage to Catalonia*, 52)

Another reason is that wars are necessarily polarizing events in which there is little room for ambiguity of affiliation. If Auden had defended the Church against the government in 1937 it would have meant effectively changing sides, or at least incurring the disapprobation, even disavowal, of his political and intellectual associates. Auden's discomfort with Republican anti-clericalism may have collided with his idealization of the Republic, but it had also to co-exist with it. Across the political spectrum, the Spanish Civil War reduced the ideological conflicts of the 1930s to a Manichaean struggle. It would have been inconceivable for Auden simply to have jettisoned his preconceptions on account of the Church question. Like Graham Greene, who as a result of his firsthand experiences of Mexican politics, was no stranger to left-wing anti-clericalism, Auden could continue to support the Republic, despite its offenses against religion. Greene toured Tabasco and Chiapas in 1938 and chronicled the religious persecution he witnessed there in *The Lawless Roads* (1939). But he also made his Republican sympathies clear in his thriller *The Confidential Agent* (1939), for which the Spanish Civil War provides a thinly-veiled backdrop. And, as his depiction of the nameless fugitive "whiskey priest" in *The Power and the Glory* (1940) shows, Greene appreciated that an at least partially degenerate Church could be the architect of many of its own problems. This suggests a further similarity between Greene and Auden, because Auden conceded that churches in Spain were often burned not under political direction but spontaneously by the people, who were acting out of a hatred of the Church as a wealthy landlord.[12]

Though he would not address his own Spanish experiences directly, Auden continued to write and speak in sympathy with the Republican cause for the remainder of the war. It is important, therefore, not to overstate the impact of Spain on his political reorientation. Similarly, it is tempting to exaggerate its role in his religious development, and Auden has been compared to Simone Weil in this regard. As Auden himself made clear in his essay in *Modern Canterbury Pilgrims*, the closed churches of Barcelona helped him to realize that religion had, in reality, never ceased to be important to him. He had thought of himself as having lost his religious convictions as early as 1922, when he was fifteen years old. But his agnostic phase was compromised by the strange mystical experience that he reported sharing with friends in the summer of 1933, so it seems likely that his religious propensities subsisted beneath the surface the whole time. (Auden wrote a poem about his mystical experience, "A Summer Night," and one can read his own account of that night at the end of this volume's "The Student and the Master.") If there was a pivotal moment in his return to Christianity it was not Spain but a chance encounter, shortly after his return, with an impressive Anglican layman in a publisher's office. (This was author Charles Williams.[13]) It was

---

[12]Lecture given at Shrewsbury School, 30 October 1938 (*Complete Works*, 1:715–16).

[13]*Editor's note:* Charles Williams (1895–1945) was as much an influence on Auden in the late 1930s as Gerald Heard had been earlier in the decade. Williams was a devout Anglican as Auden had been in his youth and would later become again. He was a writer of poetry, novels, and of great theological importance to Auden, especially, is his *The Descent of the Dove: The History of the Holy Spirit in the Church*. Williams was also an editor, teacher, and lecturer. Of him, Auden wrote: "When I met Charles Williams I had read none of his books; our meetings were few and on

then that he began reading his way back to Christianity, via the works of Kierkegaard (Pike, 41).

The difficulties of assessing the significance to Auden of the brief Spanish period are exemplified in his poem "Spain," which he wrote between January and April 1937. Though it is widely regarded as the most accomplished poem of the Civil War, "Spain" should be seen not only as a literary product but also as a political intervention in its own right. Whatever reservations he had begun to nurture did not prevent Auden from producing a powerful call to arms for the Republic. The poem was published as a sixteen-page pamphlet by Faber and Faber in May 1937, priced at one shilling, and its proceeds went to the Spanish Medical Aid Committee. If, as Stanley Weintraub suggests, "Spain" can be read as having a "strangely elegiac tone of an already-lost cause," that is not how it was received at the time, when it was read aloud at pro-Republican rallies (67). However reluctantly and ineffectually Auden had played the role of propagandist in Spain, his Spanish Civil War poem was a propaganda success.

Even so, "Spain" remains one of the most controversial and enigmatic poems in the Auden canon. As Edward Mendelson has written, if it is the best of the substantial corpus of Spanish Civil War poems it is also "the one that expresses the least sympathy for the Republic and its defenders" (316). Auden never believed, with Shelley, that poets could or should legislate for the world. That is why "Spain" is not a didactic but a parabolic poem, to use Hynes's distinction: its purpose is not to prescribe action but to highlight the moral choices that make action more urgent (14–15). It is detached and impersonal, containing no vivid details of the war, and could conceivably have been written without having left England. It is a highly ambiguous poem, lending itself to a range of interpretations, some of them demonstrably contrary to the author's intentions. It also reveals contradictions in Auden's

---

business, yet I count them among my most unforgettable and precious experiences. I have met great and good men in whose presence one was conscious of one's own littleness; Charles Williams' effect on me and others with whom I have spoken was quite different: in his company one felt twice as intelligent and infinitely nicer than, out of it, one knew oneself to be.... [M]ore than anyone else I have ever known, he gave himself completely to the company he was in." ("Introduction," *The Descent of the Dove* [New York: Meridian Books, 1956, v]).

thinking that, while they by no means appear for the first time in "Spain," are rendered there in a stark and concentrated form.

In particular, "Spain" makes us confront the complex problem of Auden's Marxism. It is certainly possible to sustain a Marxist reading of the poem. To begin with, its temporal movement and historical analysis have been used to support Spender's view that it was an attempt "to interpret the Marxist dialectic into the Spanish conflict" (*Thirties and After*, 14). Quite clearly, Auden offers a progressive and linear interpretation of history:

> Yesterday all the past. The language of size
> Spreading to China along the trade-routes; the diffusion
>   Of the counting-frame and the cromlech;
> Yesterday the shadow-reckoning in the sunny climates.
>
> Yesterday the assessment of insurance by cards,
> The divination of water; yesterday the invention
>   Of cartwheels and clocks, the taming of
> Horses. Yesterday the bustling world of the navigators.
>
> Yesterday the abolition of fairies and giants,
> The fortress like a motionless eagle eyeing the valley,
>   The chapel built in the forest;
> Yesterday the carving of angels and alarming gargoyles.
>
> The trial of heretics among the columns of stone;
> Yesterday the theological feuds in the taverns
>   And the miraculous cure at the fountain;
> Yesterday the Sabbath of Witches....
>
>   (*ll.* 1–16)

History here is characterized by humankind's emancipation by knowledge from the confines of myth and superstition. So far, the historical philosophy is as Whig as it is Marxist, but then Auden focuses on the imperial spread of industrial capitalism:

> Yesterday the installation of dynamos and turbines,
> The construction of railways in the colonial desert....
>
>   (*ll.* 17–18)

The poem also has a Marxist emphasis on struggle. The poem's famous refrain, "But to-day the struggle," invokes both the 1930s proletarian emphasis on class struggle and the centrality allotted to the Spanish conflict in the European-wide Manichaean ideological confrontation. It depicts struggle as the unavoidable phase through which history must pass in order to secure Tomorrow for the full realization of human potential. And it is in this aspect that the poem's major controversy lies. Peter Collier, for example, finds in "Spain" an implicit endorsement of Bolshevik revolutionary ethics (143):

> Today the deliberate increase in the chances of death,
> The conscious acceptance of guilt in the necessary murder....
>
> (*ll.* 93–94)

These lines are clearly open to the interpretation that murder is justifiable in the achievement of socialism. Such a reading was the basis of Orwell's fierce attack on Auden in "Inside the Whale" (1940). Orwell believed that "Spain" was the work of "a good party man" and he interpreted "necessary murder" in the cold-blooded sense of, for example, assassination, rather than the inevitable and commonplace business of killing the enemy in time of war. With obvious bitterness, Orwell drew on his own traumatic experiences as a witness to murder to accuse Auden of a "brand of amoralism" that is "only possible if you are the kind of person who is always somewhere else when the trigger is pulled." In going on to say that "So much of left-wing thought is a kind of playing with fire by people who don't even know that fire is hot," Orwell was echoing the charges of self-indulgence and political tourism leveled by Pound, Greene, and others (*Collected Essays*, 1:516).

Auden felt the injustice of Orwell's attack and in May 1963 directly repudiated any such interpretation, insisting that he had meant only to strip away euphemisms that diminish the seriousness of killing and to acknowledge the reality that killing is an inescapable feature of warfare:

> I was *not* excusing totalitarian crimes but only trying to say what, surely, every decent person thinks if he finds himself unable to adopt the absolute pacifist position. (1) To kill another human being is always murder and should never be called anything else. (2) In a war, the members of two rival groups try to murder their opponents. (3) *If* there is such a thing as a just war, then murder can be necessary for the sake of justice. (quoted in Davenport-Hines, 167)

He should be taken at his word: the Auden who told Spender that political expediency could never be the justification for telling lies is an unlikely proponent of ideologically necessary murder (Spender, *World Within World*, 225). He was acutely aware of the potential for misinterpretation, and two years after its publication he revised the poem as "Spain 1937," in which the offending lines were modified:

> To-day the inevitable increase in the chances of death;
> The conscious acceptance of guilt in the fact of murder; ...
> (ll. 81–82)[14]

Auden's bigger problem with the original poem was not one of public misinterpretation but his own personal interpretation of the final stanza:

> The stars are dead. The animals will not look.
> We are left alone with our day, and the time is short, and
>   History to the defeated
> May say Alas but cannot help nor pardon.
> (ll. 101–4)

In excluding even the revised poem from a 1966 collection of shorter verse, Auden explained that to write in such terms "is to equate goodness with success. It would have been bad enough if I had ever held this wicked doctrine, but that I should have stated it simply because it sounded to me rhetorically effective is quite inexcusable" (Foreword, *Collected Shorter Poems*, 15). In an often repeated story, he stumbled upon the poem in Cyril Connolly's library and scratched out the final two lines, writing in the margins "This is a lie."

But this is a recantation of Machiavellianism, not Marxism. What Auden wanted to distance himself from was the poem's implied consequentialist ethics, which are by no means confined to the Marxist sphere. There is no reason to believe that Auden thought that violence was legitimate in the service of some objective law of historical progress, and to interpret the poem's closing lines in those terms is to stretch the Marxist reading beyond its sustainable limits. As Edward Mendelson has argued, Auden's philosophy of history in "Spain" is far from clear, and the poem's central tension is between determinism and voluntarism, between a directional history, and a history that is made in a series of human choices. It celebrates, for example, the voluntary rallying of Republican supporters to oppose the nationalist rebels as individual acts of goodness solidifying into a formidable force:

> Madrid is the heart. Our moments of tenderness blossom
>   As the ambulance and the sandbag;
> Our hours of friendship into a people's army.
> (ll. 74–76)

---

[14]"Spain 1937" is reprinted in *The Norton Anthology of English Literature*, 7th ed. (New York: Norton, 2000), 2:2502–5.

The importance of personal choices—even personal sacrifices—in determining political outcomes, and the centrality of Spain in the choice of Europe's future, are both clearly present in the poem:

> 'What's your proposal? To build the just city? I will.
> I agree. Or is it the suicide pact, the romantic
> > Death? Very well, I accept, for
> I am your choice, your decision. Yes, I am Spain.'
> > > > (*ll.* 53–56)

Hugh Ford wrote that "Spain" was Auden's last and "most ambitious Marxist poem, being a kind of projection of what a successful socialist revolution might accomplish" (206–7). But its vision of Tomorrow is probably the least ambiguous aspect of "Spain," and it does not support the Marxist reading. Marxist literature in general is vague and elusive about the shape of the future society. Marx and Engels themselves wrote little about it, with the exception of the endlessly mined passages in *The Critique of the Gotha Programme* (1875) and the *German Ideology* (1846). But there is no withering away of the state in Auden's Tomorrow; no reorganization of society upon the basis of "from each according to his capacity, to each according to his needs"; and no hunting, fishing, shepherding, and criticizing without ever becoming a hunter, a fisherman, a shepherd, or a critic. There is no hint, even, of a collectivist and egalitarian Spain. Instead Auden offers a romantic and pastoral vision perfectly compatible with Stanley Baldwin's idealization of England:

> To-morrow the rediscovery of romantic love,
> The photographing of ravens; all the fun under
> > Liberty's masterful shadow;
> To-morrow the hour of the pageant-master and the musician,
>
> The beautiful roar of the chorus under the dome;
> To-morrow the exchanging of tips on the breeding of terriers,
> > The eager election of chairmen
> By the sudden forest of hands. But to-day the struggle.
>
> To-morrow for the young the poets exploding like bombs,
> The walks by the lake, the winter of perfect communion;
> > To-morrow the bicycle races
> Through the suburbs on summer evenings. But to-day the struggle.
> > > > (*ll.* 81–92)

As Edward Mendelson has said, even at his most ideological, Auden's political vision "had less to do with the class struggle than with the visionary hopes to build Jerusalem in England's green and pleasant land" (305)—Blake, not Marx.

The desired future in "Spain" is a liberal one of freedom of expression and movement. And it was that liberalism that formed the basis of Auden's support for the Republic. Orwell, as a socialist (albeit a fiercely independent one), looked at revolutionary Barcelona and saw for the first time "a town where the working class was in the saddle," and where "Human beings were trying to behave as human beings and not as cogs in the capitalist machine" (*Homage to Catalonia*, 4–6). By contrast Auden, in Valencia, was inspired by the Spanish people's embrace of liberty:

> In the past six months these people have been learning what it is to inherit their own country, and once a man has tasted freedom he will not lightly give it up; freedom to choose for himself and to organize his life, freedom not to depend for good fortune on a clever and outrageous piece of overcharging or a windfall of drunken charity.[15]

The difference in language is significant. While Auden's description celebrates Republican egalitarianism, the focus is on liberal and democratic freedoms. The Spanish people had chosen freedom, and Auden wished to support them in their fight to defend it. It was when he discovered that those freedoms were being consumed in that very fight that he reluctantly settled into a partially formed disillusionment. Perhaps the most significant impact that the Spanish conflict can be said to have had upon Auden was the explosion of any utopian dimension to his politics. His poem "The Voyage," which forms part of *Journey to a War* (1939), reflects his post-Spain conviction that it is simply futile to seek to find the good society in a given place:

> And, alone with his heart at last, does the traveller find
> In the vaguer touch of the wind and the fickle flash of the sea
> Proofs that somewhere there exists, really, the Good Place,
> As certain as those the children find in stones and holes?
>
> No, he discovers nothing....   (*ll*.5–9)[16]

Instead, the good society is something we are all perpetually obliged to make in our unending moral choices. Yet it would be futile to argue that "Spain" is devoid of Marxism. In fact, it may be

---

[15]"Impressions of Valencia"; reprinted in Cunningham, *Spanish Civil War Verse*, 102.

[16]W.H. Auden and C. Isherwood, *Journey to a War* (Auden, *Complete Works*, 1:497).

that the poem's contradictions derive at least in part from the contradictions between voluntarism and determinism within Marxism itself. But it remains significant that Auden is less able, or less inclined, than many 1930s Marxists to rein in the voluntarist aspect.

While it would be a mistake to entirely dismiss the Marxism of "Spain," it would be another to allow the presence of contradictions in the poem to lead us to dismiss Auden as a political thinker. As Walt Whitman, a poet who actually did serve in a medical capacity in another civil war, wrote in *Song of Myself*:

> Do I contradict myself?
> Very well then I contradict myself,
> (I am large, I contain multitudes.)
>
> (*st.* 51)

The contradictions in Auden's thought require not resolution but navigation. Despite drawing attention to some perceived commonalities between psychoanalysis and dialectical materialism in his essay "The Good Life" (1935), Auden never synthesized the two into a coherent system of thought as did, for example, Erich Fromm and other Freudian-Marxists.[17] Furthermore, as the visit to Spain demonstrated, Auden's psychological and political interests had to co-exist with religion on some level. And always in the background was the middle-class liberalism with which he grew up.

Many former Marxists rebounded into other totalizing narratives, as in the case of Simone Weil and Roman Catholicism. After Spain, however, Auden drifted back to a mild Anglo-Catholicism and English liberalism. That he was able to do so speaks volumes about the nature of his Marxism. There was a common pacifist saying during and after the Great War about going to war with Rupert Brooke and coming home with Siegfried Sassoon. In similar fashion it could be said that Auden and Spender went to Spain with Karl Marx and came home with John Stuart Mill. And they were far from alone in having their essential liberalism exposed by Spanish Civil War realities. As Spender commented, "the best books of the War—those by Malraux, Hemingway, Koestler and Orwell—describe the Spanish tragedy from the liberal point of view, and they bear witness against the Communists" (*God That Failed*, 248). In a similar vein, Auden wrote in 1955 that "Nobody I

---

[17]For example, see Eric Fromm, *Beyond the Chains of Illusion* (London: Abacus, 1962).

know who went to Spain during the Civil War who was not a dyed-in-the-wool Stalinist came back with his illusions intact" (quoted in Davenport-Hines, 164).

The perfect representative of the essentially liberal intellectual volunteer who is expediently prepared to accept the leadership provided by the Soviets and the Spanish Communist Party in the resistance to Franco is Hemingway's Robert Jordan in *For Whom the Bell Tolls* (1940). In reflecting on his acquiescence to Marxist materialism, Jordan asks himself:

> Since when did you ever have any such conception? ... Never. And you never could have. You're not a real Marxist and you know it. You believe in Liberty, Equality and Fraternity. You believe in Life, Liberty and the Pursuit of Happiness. Don't ever kid yourself with too much dialectics. They are for some but not for you. You have to know them in order not to be a sucker. You have put many things in abeyance to win a war. If this war is lost all of those things are lost. (305)

By contrast, Auden and Spender were liberal intellectuals convinced of the bankruptcy of liberalism, studiously trying to learn a new political language—and in the context of the time that language was Marxism. Spender once protested that the so-called "movement" poets were no such thing, because movements "have meetings, issue manifestoes, have aims in common," whereas this was never true of the Auden group (*Thirties and After*, 8). The point is well taken, but there may have been more political than literary unity among the group, it did have a serviceable manifesto, and Spender was its author. In January 1937, Gollancz published Spender's *Forward from Liberalism*. Like many Left Book Club titles, the book shows signs of having been hurriedly written. Nonetheless, it is a serious and relatively neglected work that more than any other theorizes the politics of literary Popular Frontism, at least as it was interpreted by the Auden group. Nothing could better demonstrate that the agenda of significant literary leftists was essentially liberal in character, even if expressed in the prevailing Marxist idiom of 1930s progressive politics. Auden's January 1939 article "Democracy's Reply to the Challenge of Dictators," for example, clearly displays the influence of *Forward from Liberalism*.[18]

---

[18]See "Democracy's Reply to the Challenge of Dictators" (*Complete Works*, 1:463–66).

Spender's book attempted to explain his paradoxical statement that "I am a communist because I am a liberal" (*Forward from Liberalism*, 189). In his analysis, liberalism and communism shared the goal of a classless society and that it was these commonalities that enabled them to combine in the resistance to fascism. But drawing on the Marxism of Harold Laski's *The Rise of European Liberalism* (1936), Spender went on to argue that liberal ideals were negligent of the economic basis of power (52).[19] He drew on literary examples to illustrate that, in a capitalist society, liberal individualism was restricted to the wealthy classes. Virginia Woolf, for example, in her feminist tract *A Room of One's Own* (1929), had gone so far as to put a money price of £300 a year on a writer's creative freedom. Though he later dismissed the enterprise as absurd, Spender also attempted a Marxist reading of Henry James, whose characters "recognize that there is a contrast between the freedom their money will enable them to enjoy and the brutal background of competition which enabled them to gain that freedom" (52).[20]

The perception that individualism was a bourgeois privilege led many socialists and communists to reject individualism itself. Spender saw this as a fundamental analytical error and tried to construct the case that communism was not the negation of individualism, but the means of its generalization:

> The communist seeks to destroy bourgeois individuality, bourgeois freedom, bourgeois culture, because he wants to establish the individuality that everyone may hope to achieve within a classless society—economic freedom, and a culture whose traditions and inventions are not confined to one class. (93)

In Spender's view, the goal of communism could be achieved by "a united front of all the forces opposed to the great capitalist interests." The revolution would take place "within the democratic system," and liberal-democratic freedoms would be suspended for a minimal amount of time (124). Following this very British revolution, the model of development would be the Soviet Union. Working from the Webbs's study, Spender seems genuinely to

---

[19]It has been convincingly argued that Laski himself, despite his status as a leading Marxist intellectual in the 1930s, remained a liberal pluralist and was merely expressing his ideas in the fashionable ideological language of the period. See Greenleaf.

[20]Spender repudiated his Marxist reading of James in *The Thirties and After*, 13.

have believed that the Soviets were in the process of realizing the goals of liberal individualism in practice—rather oddly, considering the Webbs's general disregard for individualism.

There can be precious few political outlooks developed at book length that have been so quickly and thoroughly repudiated. In fairness, there is evidence of doubt in *Forward from Liberalism* itself, in the sense that Spender expressed real concern over the Moscow show trials and the execution of Zinoviev, and went on to suggest that the Soviet Union would degenerate into an oppressive state unless political opposition was legalized. But, as in the case of Auden, it was experiences in Spain that forced Spender to confront what had been a series of self-deceptions. For Spender, the most important lesson learned from Spain was that the Popular Front was not a genuine attempt to unite anti-fascist forces from across the political spectrum, but an instrument through which the Moscow-directed communist parties sought to control other progressive movements.

A significant impetus to Spender's rethink was his reaction to the tirades against André Gide at the International Writers' Congress in 1937. Gide had recently published his *Retour de l'URSS*, in which he chronicled his political disappointments during his Russian tour. Gide had gone to Russia as a declared admirer of its revolutionary achievements. He was also prepared to praise its international literary impact and, in the early stages of his tour, he spoke at the funeral of Maxim Gorky, a principal theorist and practitioner of socialist realism. At first impressed with the welcome he received, Gide quickly became disillusioned through a succession of experiences. He was alarmed at the queues and at the poor quality of consumer goods available in Moscow. He remarked on the indolence and lethargy he detected in the workers he met. And he was appalled at the depersonalizing effects of Soviet housing. Above all, he was repelled by the powerful pressures of conformity that he encountered everywhere.

Gide had encountered at first hand what many left-wing writers were content to dismiss as capitalist propaganda. What had perturbed Gide the most was the threat posed by Soviet orthodoxy to the freedom of expression that must always be the concern of the artist. "Culture is in danger," he wrote, "when criticism is not free" (55). The closed-mindedness of the Soviet officials at the Congress served to legitimize Gide's claims in the eyes of Spender, who then began to adopt a similar position. He later joined Gide as a contributor to *The God That Failed* (1949), a volume of essays, edited by the British socialist Richard Crossman, containing anti-communist testimonies from former believers.

At least in the experience of the Auden group, the crisis of literary Popular Frontism was a crisis of liberal Popular Frontism: the inescapable realization that precisely those liberal values that had taken various anti-fascists into an alliance with the communists were threatened by the nature of communism itself. As Tom Buchanan has argued, many of the Republic's British supporters interpreted the Spanish struggle in the light of the great liberal causes of the nineteenth century, such as Greek independence, the First Carlist War in Spain, Italian unification, the "Bulgarian atrocities," and even the American Civil War (5). The Spanish Civil War "offered the twentieth century an 1848," as Spender put it (*World Within World*, 170). When personal experience dictated that such a liberal interpretation could not be sustained, the support inevitably withered.

Katherine Hoskins records that, politically speaking, Auden was often seen as a "puzzled liberal, seeking solutions but skeptical of all those being offered" (193), and it is difficult to improve on that assessment. After Spain Auden was profoundly skeptical of any totalizing theory, as he and Isherwood demonstrated in their reactions to Chiang Kai Shek's New Life movement in China only a year later.[21] Auden's predisposition was to think in moral, rather than political, terms. But in the context of the 1930s that scarcely seemed to be an option: as Thomas Mann wrote, "In our time the destiny of man presents its meaning in political terms."[22] But for Auden Marxism was an available political language, not an ideological straightjacket. Many ideological communists who went to Spain were resolutely loyal to the Soviet Union and were sincere apologists for the conduct of Soviet policy in the Civil War, while others who were less committed were able to shelve their reservations for the expedient purposes of simply defeating Franco. As an equivocal Marxist who had never fully shed his religious nature, Auden could not assume the role of communist advocate, and as a liberal idealist he could not with any conviction rationalize illiberalism in the name of expediency. In fact, nothing could better illustrate his quintessentially English liberal naiveté than his expec-

---

[21]Auden and Isherwood, *Journey to a War* (*Complete Works*, 1:522–25).

[22]Quoted in W.B. Yeats, "Politics" (Cunningham, *Spanish Front*, 66).

tation that the Spanish Republic could preserve its ideals intact in the face of the exigencies of war, or that the preponderance of Soviet power on the Republican side would not manifest itself in an attempt to direct Spanish domestic politics.

Auden and Isherwood arrived in New York to begin the American phase of their lives just as the Republic was falling. Shortly thereafter, Auden withdrew from active politics altogether, rendering the 1930s as an aberrant departure from his reticence about the political engagement of intellectuals. Nearly thirty years later, in 1967, he contributed to a selection of literary opinion on the war in Vietnam, published under the title *Authors Take Sides on Vietnam*. In his response, he reiterated his contra-Shelley skepticism about the presumed political insights of writers and went on to argue for a negotiated peace, claiming that simply to call for the withdrawal of American troops was in reality to call for a communist victory. The following year, he broke his post-Spain moratorium on explicitly political poetry to write "August 1968," a condemnation of the Soviet offensive against Alexander Dubcek's liberal communist experiment in Czechoslovakia. The skeptical liberal communist, turned anti-communist liberal, therefore remains the most suitable description of Auden's political odyssey: the transformation from Byronic radical to Wordsworthian conservative simply does not fit.

Auden's critics will continue to exploit the more bathetic aspects of his Spanish interlude. His role there was at least partially comic, and he is not totally immune to the charge of political tourism—even Isherwood flippantly conceded that he and Auden left for China upon the outbreak of the Sino-Japanese War at least in part because the Spanish Civil War was overcrowded with literary celebrities: "We'll have a war all of our very own," Auden is claimed to have said (Isherwood, 189). But Spain was also an occasion for a solemn re-evaluation of politics and theology. While it is a mistake to see the Spanish experiences as seminal, this is not to deny that they brought into sharp relief doubts and contradictions that lay beneath the surface. For these reasons, Auden scholars will continue to revisit "Spain" and to seek to distill from it the balance of ideas in its author's mind at the time.

Works Cited

Auden, W.H. *Collected Shorter Poems, 1927–1957*. London: Faber & Faber, 1966.

———. *The Complete Works. Vol. 1: Prose.* Edited by Edward Mendelson. Princeton: Princeton UP, 1996.

Brenan, G. *The Spanish Labyrinth.* Cambridge: Cambridge UP, 1990.

Buchanan, T. *Britain and the Spanish Civil War.* Cambridge: Cambridge UP, 1997.

Carr, R. *The Spanish Tragedy: The Civil War in Perspective.* London: Weidenfeld & Nicolson, 1977.

Collier, P. "The Poetry of Protest: Auden, Aragon and Eluard." In *Visions and Blueprints: Avant-Garde Culture and Radical Politics in Early Twentieth-Century Europe,* edited by E. Timms and P. Collier. Manchester: Manchester UP, 1988. 137–58.

Cunningham, V. *British Writers of the Thirties.* Oxford: Oxford UP, 1988.

———, ed. *The Penguin Book of Spanish Civil War Verse.* London: Penguin, 1980.

———, ed. *Spanish Front.* Oxford: Oxford UP, 1986.

Davenport-Hines, R. *Auden.* New York: Vintage, 1999.

Ford, H. *A Poets' War: British Poets and the Spanish Civil War.* Philadelphia: U of Pennsylvania P, 1965.

Francis, H. *Miners Against Fascism.* London: Lawrence & Wishart, 1984.

Fuller, J. *W.H. Auden: A Commentary.* Princeton: Princeton UP, 1998.

Fyrth, J. *The Signal Was Spain: The Spanish Aid Movement in Britain, 1936–39.* New York: St. Martin's, 1986.

Gide, A. *Back from the U.S.S.R..* London: Secker & Warburg, 1937.

Greenleaf, W.H. "Laski and British Socialism." *History of Political Thought* 2.3 (Nov. 1981): 573–90.

Heinemann, M. "*Left Review, New Writing* and the Broad Alliance Against Fascism." In *Visions and Blueprints: Avant-garde Culture and Radical Politics in Early Twentieth-Century Europe,* edited by E. Timms and P. Collier. Manchester: Manchester UP, 1988. 113–36.

Hemingway, E. *For Whom the Bell Tolls.* New York: Scribner, 1995.

Hoskins, K.B. *Today the Struggle.* Austin: U of Texas P, 1969.

Hynes, S. *The Auden Generation: Literature and Politics in England in the 1930s.* London: Bodley Head, 1976.

Isherwood, C. *Christopher and His Kind.* New York: North Point Press, 1976.

Johnson, P. *Intellectuals.* London: Weidenfeld & Nicolson, 1989.

Koestler, A. *The Invisible Writing.* Boston: Beacon, 1955.

Lehmann, J. *The Whispering Gallery.* New York: Harcourt, 1954.

Mendelson, E. *Early Auden.* New York: Viking, 1981.

Orwell, G. *The Collected Essays, Journalism and Letters of George Orwell.* Edited by S. Orwell and I. Angus. *Vol. 1. An Age Like This: 1920–1940.* New York: Harcourt, 1968.

———. *Homage to Catalonia.* San Diego: Harcourt, 1952.

Osborne, C. *W.H. Auden: The Life of a Poet.* New York: Harcourt, 1979.

Perrie, W. "Auden's Political Vision." In *W.H. Auden: The Far Interior,* edited by A. Bold. London: Vision, 1985. 47–72.

Pike, J.A., ed. *Modern Canterbury Pilgrims.* London: A.R. Mowbray, 1956.

Preston, P. *The Spanish Civil War, 1936–39.* New York: Grove, 1986.

Sánchez, J.M. *The Spanish Civil War as a Religious Tragedy.* Notre Dame: U of Notre Dame P, 1987.

Spender, S. *Forward from Liberalism.* New York: Random House, 1937.

———. *The God That Failed.* Edited by R. Crossman. New York: Harper, 1949. 229–73.

———. *The Thirties and After.* New York: Random House, 1967.

———. *World Within World.* New York: Harcourt, 1952.

Thomas, H. *The Spanish Civil War.* New York: Harper, 1961.

Weintraub, S. *The Last Great Cause: The Intellectuals and the Spanish Civil War.* New York: Weybright & Talley, 1968.

Whitman, W. "Song of Myself." *Complete Poetry and Selected Prose.* Edited by J.E. Miller. Boston: Houghton Mifflin, 1959. 25–68.

Wood, N. *Communism and British Intellectuals.* New York: Columbia UP, 1959.

Journey to a War:
"a test for men from Europe"
Douglas Kerr

Auden and Isherwood's collaboration on a "travel book" about China turned out to be almost an "anti-travel" book in its departure from the other popular books of the period in this genre. Kerr is well-suited to the task of analyzing a China venture, as he is a Professor of English at the University of Hong Kong.

"The Ship," Auden's sonnet describing his sea voyage to China at the beginning of 1938, ends on an apprehensive note:

> Slowly our Western culture in full pomp progresses
> Over the barren plains of a sea; somewhere ahead
> A septic East, odd fowl and flowers, odder dresses:
>
> Somewhere a strange and shrewd To-morrow goes to bed,
> Planning a test for men from Europe; no one guesses
> Who will be most ashamed, who richer, and who dead.

The generalization, whereby the ship becomes a metonym for all Western culture, is typical, and so is the apprehension. In the 1930s Auden was disposed to regard almost any experience as a "Test," with its several implications of ordeal, examination, and authentication. The nature of the test (in the first published version it is indeed "the" test) in store for these men from Europe was certainly multiple. For the ocean-going voyagers it was their destination, the comprehensively alien culture of Asia: what would they make of it? For Auden and his fellow-traveler Christopher Isherwood, it was also the war they were going to witness as they had missed seeing any conflict in the Spanish Civil War: how would they react, and what might it reveal of their true nature? For the test for men from Europe was also a test for men. Further, it was clear to Auden as to many Europeans early in 1938 that tomorrow, or the

275

next day, would confront them with a war much closer to home, a
European war. This anxiety, too, informs the poem, as it informs
most of Auden's earlier work in a way that would cause Philip
Larkin to declare that "Europe and the fear of war" were Auden's
"key subject and emotion"—both to be lost in 1939, with depress-
ing consequences, Larkin argued, for the later poetry (Larkin, 125).
Any voyage in 1938 was a stage in a journey to a war.

In the summer of 1937, Faber and Faber and Random House
had offered a contract to W.H. Auden and Christopher Isherwood
to collaborate on a travel book (a fashionable genre in the 1930s),
and the outbreak of the Sino-Japanese war that August determined
them to go to China.[1] For left-wing intellectuals, solidarity with
China's resistance to invasion was an obligation similar to support
for the Republican cause in the Spanish Civil War. By the time he
came to write up his part of the book, in the dangerous summer of
1938, Isherwood was in a mood to grumble about the political
pressures—or expectations—under which he wrote, but not to
challenge them. "Besides, the 'line' I have to take—united front,
resistance to the Japanese, etc., etc.,—has lost whatever meaning it
ever had for me. These are only slogans now" (*Down There on a
Visit*, 133).[2] But the journey to the Chinese war had been an exciting prospect a year earlier. Many young European and American
writers had flocked to Spain—Auden had made his own brief excursion there in the spring of 1937 although not to the front—but
China by contrast was not already "crowded with star literary observers," and this made it professionally attractive: "We'll have a
war all of our very own," Auden said (qtd. in *Christopher and His
Kind*, 289).

Auden was by this time the acknowledged leader of his poetic
generation. Isherwood had made a name for himself as a novelist,
and especially with his Berlin stories. They were old friends and
occasional sex partners. They left England in January 1938, returning at the end of July. Their book *Journey to a War* was published in

---

[1]For discussions of the continuing travel-writing boom of the 1930s,
see Fussell, Dodd, and Cunningham, chs. 11, 12. For an account of political reportage in English from the Russian Revolution to the Spanish Civil
War, see Williams.

[2]The words quoted occur in a diary entry for 31 August 1938, reproduced in the autobiographical *Down There on a Visit*, which was first published in 1962. I enter the usual caution about the fictionality of Isherwood's autobiographical writings.

March 1939.[3] Auden and Isherwood's China book, like Auden and MacNeice's *Letters from Iceland* (1937), is eccentrically shaped. It starts with six poems by Auden on themes arising from the journey from London to Hong Kong. Then comes the "Travel-Diary," a substantial prose narrative by Isherwood relating their China journey from its beginning at Hong Kong to its end in Shanghai. This is followed by the "Picture Commentary"—thirty-two pages of photographs, mostly by Auden—and finally by Auden's "In Time of War," which consists of a sequence of twenty-seven sonnets and a thirteen-page "Verse Commentary." At the end of the book there is a map. *Journey to a War* is one of Auden's collaborations that is not just structural, but textural: Isherwood drew on Auden's notes as well as on his own for the Travel-Diary, and there seems to be plenty of Isherwood's brand of observation in Auden's verse. It would be a futile exercise to try to disentangle their dialogic embrace within the pages of their book, and in fact the relation between them is an important generator of its meanings. Still, simply in structural terms Isherwood's travels come enclosed in Auden's journey, and one of the questions to be raised in this essay is whether the traveling companions were at one about where they were going and, later, where they thought they had been.

A discourse of European travel—particularly in the colonial period, especially travel to the east, and above all to an east represented as in some intrinsic way disadvantaged, dangerous or insufficient—is bound to be subject today to a critical gaze sharpened by Edward Said's account of Orientalism. Said reaccentuated this term to indicate, famously, "a Western style for dominating, restructuring, and having authority over the Orient" (3), a set of language and perception habits arguably so embedded in the collective enterprise of Western speech as to be inescapable, so that any Western representation of the East is bound within the dominating and coercive system of knowledge that is the discourse of Orientalism. Subsequent readings of Said have often been concerned to qualify what can seem a too deterministic homogenizing

---

[3]Page numbers in the text refer to W.H. Auden and Christopher Isherwood, *Journey to a War*, rev. ed. (London: Faber, 1973). For this edition Auden made some substantial alterations, dropping a passage of the verse commentary and several of the sonnets, and revising the wording and the order of others. I have used the revised versions, and drawn attention to these changes where relevant. Isherwood made no revisions.

in the original thesis of *Orientalism*. It remains, however, a productive and challenging idea, and a reading of the Western writing of Asia—even in scholarly and aesthetic genres—as exercises in domination and authority can provide a starting point for thinking about Auden's and Isherwood's China, texts in which the issue of authority is particularly vexed, indeed tested.

For the travel writer as for the traveler, the first problem is to find one's bearings. Dennis Porter, in his *Haunted Journeys*, explains what this can entail.

> From the beginning, writers of travel have more or less unconsciously made it their purpose to take a fix on and thereby fix the world in which they found themselves; they are engaged in a form of cultural cartography that is impelled by an anxiety to map the globe, centre it on a certain point, produce explanatory narratives, and assign fixed identities to regions and the races that inhabit them. Such representations are always concerned with the question of place and of placing, of situating oneself once and for all vis-à-vis an Other or others. (20)

This finding and situating of oneself, and of others in relation to oneself, is a process of orientation—a term that sets up useful reverberations in the direction of the critique of "Orientalism." The point is—to anticipate a bit—that while Auden's orientations really are global, so that China interests him only as a sort of epitome of the world itself, the more prosaic and down-to-earth Isherwood never does really find his bearings in China, and eventually gives up looking for them. He never achieves that stable orientation that would enable him to experience and write about China with any authority. He produces an ironic narrative of disorientations, which is bound together with Auden's epic orientations, to produce this strange binocular book.

Their journey to a war took Isherwood and Auden first by sea from England to Hong Kong, from the metropolis of empire to its extreme edge in the "Far" East. Hong Kong was doubly marginal, of course, being peripheral both to the West and to China, and Isherwood's narrative starts with the travelers' impatience to get away from this outpost and penetrate the "real" China. The word "real" chimes increasingly forlornly through Isherwood's prose, and is also much invoked in Auden's verse in the book. It occurs, with its relatives "really" and "unreal," seven times in "Whither?," the opening five-stanza poem. But though the tone of that first poem is gloomy and anxious, and though the perpetual hurry of their few days in Hong Kong was a distraction, the beginning of the "real" journey—the journey in China—was an exciting prospect. "'Well,' Auden said, 'here we are. Now it's going to start'" (*Journey*, 18).

The real East was what they were after, and they had come properly equipped with the instrument of realism, a camera, to capture it—perhaps the same camera Auden had taken to Iceland on his travels a couple of years before, declaring photography "*the* democratic art," purely content-oriented and rendering the question of the practitioner's skill irrelevant, for "artistic quality depends only on the choice of subject" (Auden and MacNeice, 137); it seemed the observer needed only to point the camera at a piece of reality and press the button. (But finding the piece of reality was to be the problem. There will be more to say about these photographs later.) It was Isherwood who famously likened himself to a camera, on the first page of *Goodbye to Berlin*: "I am a camera with its shutter open, quite passive, recording, not thinking. Recording the man shaving at the window opposite and the woman in the kimono washing her hair. Some day, all this will have to be developed, carefully printed, fixed" (1). But on the China journey, Auden was the one who played the camera-man, occasionally to irritating effect. Years later, Isherwood remembered sometimes "really hating him—hating his pedantic insistence on 'objectivity'" (*Christopher and His Kind*, 304). Isherwood, the slightly older man by three years, was less confident of his own abilities to capture in a snap or a phrase the subject they had chosen, or to be sure it was really there, even once they had passed over from colonial Hong Kong into real China. Already the reality of Asia was starting to seem elusive. Was their journey really real, for one thing—and were they real travelers? The literary travelers of the 1930s were always aware of their ghostly *Doppelgänger*, the tourist, breathing down their neck. "I question whether the reactions of the tourist are of much value," Auden had written blithely in *Letters from Iceland*. "At the best he only observes what the inhabitants know already; at the worst he is guilty of glib generalizations based on inadequate and often incorrect data" (209). This startling candor is a characteristically Audenesque gambit. But to anticipate such criticism was not really to answer it: after all, something more was expected of the commissioned travel writer.

Meanwhile, the circumstances of the sea journey itself—its artificial sociabilities, its seeming suspension of the passage of time—had induced a sense of unreality in the travelers. Shipboard life had been like a monotonous dream. "At Hongkong, we had said to each other, we shall wake up, everything will come true" (*Journey*, 18), but it had not. Now, traveling upriver from coast to hinterland (and thus incidentally recapitulating the history of imperial travel writing[4]), things somehow fail to get much better. Isherwood feels adrift: no anchor, no orientation; he is *in* but disconcertingly still not *inside* China. In Canton, during a tea party, he experiences his first air raid, while incongruously surrounded by the imagery and rituals of English expatriate civility and culture:

> My eyes moved over this charming room, taking in the tea-cups, the dish of scones, the book-case with Chesterton's essays and Kipling's poems, the framed photograph of an Oxford college. My brain tried to relate these images to the sounds outside; the whine of the power-diving bomber, the distant thump of the explosions. Understand, I told myself, that those noises, these objects are part of a single, integrated scene. Wake up. It's all quite real. And, at that moment, I really did wake up. At that moment, suddenly, I arrived in China. (*Journey*, 22)

His sense of arrival—his ability to comprehend his surroundings and his place in them, in other words his orientation—depends on his ability to make the link between the familiar and the unfamiliar, the known and the unknown, and to apprehend them as "a single integrated scene." He negotiates this cognitive frontier; he arrives. But the integration, and the arrival, are temporary. He has to keep trying to arrive; and meanwhile his narrative is haunted by a trope of disintegration. China continues to baffle him, and the further the travelers move inland, toward where they hope the action is, the more any center or real China seems to recede and elude Isherwood. He travels toward a series of destinations of discovery, only to find once again his fingers close on thin air. In Isherwood's part of *Journey to a War* there is a failure—a conscious, if not a deliberate failure—to write a travel book. It is a failure of arrival, comprehension, integration, and closure. He cannot domesticate and appropriate China to his own system of manners and meanings, as his hosts in Canton had done, in their charming room with its reassuringly recognizable English amenities. He fails, in other words, to put China into English to his own satisfaction, and this after all was one form of the test for men from Europe.

---

[4]See Pratt, 15–37.

Traditional forms of travel writing are acts of observation and explanation. It is a genre in which, says Dennis Porter, "there is typically an indecent rush to assign meaning to the manifold phenomena of alien cultures" (289). The gradient of China travel writing slopes down invitingly toward authoritative generic pronouncements about China and the Chinese, but Isherwood, although one of the most acute observers of his generation, does not find himself carried toward such confident or easy discourse. He finds too much resistance in the surface of his China experience, and falls back again and again on doubts of his own authority. He is just a "tripper," not a real reporter, and still less a war correspondent; in fact—he confesses—he is a coward, and he does not much enjoy travel for that matter, and what is more he can't really make sense of the country he travels through. He can see things happen, but he is unable to see quite why they happen. The real is now invoked—"really"!—in exasperation:

> Really, the proceedings of the Chinese are so mysterious as to fill one, ultimately, with a kind of despair. During the morning Auden heard an explosion and ran out into the road to see what had happened. All he could see was an officer haranguing his men, and a group of peasants who were burning an old book. Then a woman rushed up and prostrated herself before the officer, wailing and sobbing. The officer raised her to her feet and, immediately, the two of them began talking quite naturally, as though nothing whatever had occurred. (*Journey*, 81–82)

Here is action but no plot, a story without a syntax. It seems to be controlled by no grammar of causality, but merely to happen— perhaps like those Chinese meals which, to Isherwood's observation, were "served in no recognizable order of progression (*Journey*, 30). From some angle, doubtless, these elements would add up to what Isherwood was groping for in the air raid, "a single, integrated scene." They must presumably make sense to the participants, the woman and the officer and the peasants, but they make none to the disoriented and estranged narrator. Kipling, whose entire career was an exhibition of expertise, would have provided a knowing teleology for this incident, and done the voices, too. But for Isherwood the only sure meaning of the event is his own ignorance.

The role of interpreter of the foreign scene, supplier of explanatory narratives, is a generic obligation of the travel writer. "What an anonymous country this is!," thinks Isherwood, watching, from his train window, peasants laboring in the fields (*Journey*,

64). Yet the peasants certainly had names. It is not that the country is anonymous, but rather that it is illegible, and Isherwood knows he is not doing very well at giving it an authoritative reading, possessing it in knowledge and expertise. Isherwood's China is no Baedeker's. The traditional expectations of the travel writer are made more burdensome in Isherwood's case since his is a journey to a war. There are many kinds of war reporting, but the first test of a war reporter is that he or she should find the war, and then report it. This is more easily said than done.[5] Hardly have the travelers left Hong Kong, than they meet an American reporter who warns them gloomily that there is no "real story" (that word again) in China (*Journey*, 20), and he turns out to be right. Just as Isherwood was not able to find the story in the incident of the burning book, so on a wider scale they travel through a country at war, without ever quite finding the war. Neither the country nor the war has a center. Maps turn out to be unreliable. Haunted like the rest of their generation by the European Great War of their childhood, they had learned from Wilfred Owen and the others that it was a writer's duty to tell the truth about war,[6] and furthermore that that truth was only to be found at "the front," where the trenches are. But when their Chinese hosts reluctantly take them there, this moment of destination—the narrative climax and center of the travel-book form, with its parabola of preparation, ordeal, discovery and return—this arrival is an anti-climax which Isherwood cannot disguise.

> Our own route was the same as yesterday evening. There were the same semi-farcical precautions: the advance in single file across the fields and some dramatic dodging along communica-tion trenches, only to emerge from them right on the crest of the sky-line as brilliantly illuminated targets. Finally we reached the canal bank itself. But this part of the front—as one of the officers, who spoke a little English, had to admit—was only occupied by

---

[5] *Journey to a War* can instructively be read alongside Evelyn Waugh's farcical novel about war reporting, *Scoop* (1938), a product of Waugh's own spell as a war correspondent in Africa, and published in the year Auden and Isherwood went to China. Waugh's African journey to a war is recounted in non-fictional form in *Waugh in Abyssinia* (1936).

[6]"My subject is War, and the pity of War.... All a poet can do today is warn. That is why the true poets must be truthful." Owen's famous draft preface was quoted in full in Edmund Blunden's influential 1931 edition of *The Poems of Wilfred Owen*, 40–41.

the Japanese at night, when almost all the real fighting and raid-ing takes place. During the daytime the Japs retire into Han Chwang village. (*Journey*, 103)

Theirs was a journey *to* a war, but the scene of their arrival is not powerfully textualized, as such scenes of penetration usually are in traditional travel narrative (or traditional war or other ad-venture stories, which typically move toward and through the climax of a baptism of fire). There is no center to their journey; or the center must be sought elsewhere. Here, the "real fighting" takes place only at night. Once again they have arrived at the wrong place, or the wrong time, for their encounter with the real object of their journey. At the front, rituals of solidarity (or is it tourism?) are performed, they pose for group-photographs and exchange visiting-cards with the Chinese commander. "Your fami-lies," he tells them, "will be very pleased to know that you have been so brave" (*Journey*, 104). There is some noisy but distant shelling, an enemy plane passes harmlessly overhead, and the visi-tors are ushered back to a village behind the lines in time for lunch. Isherwood has come to this place in search of self-testing sensation and journalistic copy. His account of this non-event—in its dry manner one of the funniest parts of his story—scrupulously reveals a certain pompous and self-regarding quality about his own nervousness and his own curiosity, sincere though they both are. The "front," meanwhile, is drab, confusing, and not even par-ticularly dangerous. It is undramatic and epistemologically thin. No revelations attend it. There is no story here.

But a story was taking place somewhere else. For while Au-den, as a character in the travel-diary, shared the bewilderments and boredoms and disorientations that Isherwood records, the sonnet sequence "In Time of War" was to place the Sino-Japanese war confidently within the frame of a story—a *grand récit*, in-deed—as big as human history itself. The first ten poems (in the original 1939 version they are twelve) tell the story of humankind's continuing struggle, a history of the world in a handful of sonnets, largely through a series of paradigm or parable careers—the farm-er, the tyrant, the poet, the money-man. (It is an exclusively male history.) The rest of the poems settle on the subject of the present Chinese war, and its implications in that world history.

This sonnet sequence deserves more attention than it has had. It is one of Auden's most impressive productions, as John Fuller has argued: "'In Time of War' represents a new scope of historical understanding and new powers of generalization and condensation in Auden's work…. In its discussion of evil, of human nature and society, [it] is Auden's *Essay on Man*, a seriously secular theodicy" (234, 235). Auden's management of the sonnet form—and a generally very simple syntax and vocabulary—for narrative is extraordinary. The story moves from the beginnings of life to the evolution of our own species, the "childish creature" who stumbles out of a natural paradise into freedom and grief, and the invention of language, agriculture, cities, political organization, and science. The sonnet on the poet is a good example of this sort of poetic historiography by paradigm.

> He was their servant (some say he was blind),
> Who moved among their faces and their things:
> Their feeling gathered in him like a wind
> And sang. They cried 'It is a God that sings',
>
> And honoured him, a person set apart,
> Till he grew vain, mistook for personal song
> The petty tremors of his mind or heart
> At each domestic wrong.

The tribal shaman, or Homeric bard (some say he was blind), has no personality. Though credited with divinity, in fact he speaks with the voice not of a god but of the community, as the medium of the hopes and fears he shares with them through his easy familiarity with their lives. For this he is honored and "set apart," but this apartness feeds his egotism; the divine (or communal) afflatus now abandons him.

> Lines came to him no more; he had to make them
> (With what precision was each strophe planned):
> Hugging his gloom as peasants hug their land,
>
> He stalked like an assassin through the town,
> And glared at men because he did not like them,
> But trembled if one passed him with a frown.

The sonnet describes a single exemplary career, but something like the whole history of the poet's relations with society is inscribed in it. Poetry began as a kind of priesthood, even a divine possession, but the rapt singer becomes the conscious writer, a craftsman, a professional, and the poet's own unhappiness becomes his romantic topic. Finally the modern alienated bourgeois writer, speaking only for himself, neurotically guarding his privacy and his depression, is now an antagonist of his fellow citizens, whom he regards with suspicion and fear. Auden's poet began as servant and spokesman of his community, but he ends up severed from it, misunderstanding and misunderstood, an alien in his own city. The sonnet travels from the *Iliad* to Baudelaire (or *The Waste Land*) in fourteen lines, three sentences, and no footnotes.

It is a remarkable poem in its own right, but what is it doing in a sequence that follows a narrative of travels in China in 1938? The answer is that it is part of an orientation. *Journey to a War* is a book about history, and to find out where he is, Auden needs to remind himself where he has been. Very likely he had in mind the brilliant catalogues of imagery—attached to Yesterday, Tomorrow and To-day—of his poem of the previous year, "Spain 1937" (*The English Auden*, 210). Thus after the great transitional sonnet "Certainly praise: let song mount again and again," the sequence moves smoothly into the present as it becomes geographically specific, coming literally down to earth in the here and now, China, 1938; the Chinese war is the here and now of all our history.

Here, now, are sonnets on an air raid, a military hospital, headquarters—and this, sonnet XIII (XVIII in the earlier version).

> Far from a cultural centre he was used:
> Abandoned by his general and his lice,
> Under a padded quilt he turned to ice
> And vanished. He will never be perused
>
> When this campaign is tidied into books:
> No vital knowledge perished in that skull;
> His jokes were stale; like wartime, he was dull;
> His name is lost for ever like his looks.
>
> Though runeless, to instructions from headquarters
> He added meaning like a comma when
> He joined the dust of China, that our daughters
>
> Might keep their upright carriage, not again
> Be shamed before the dogs, that, where are waters,
> Mountains, and houses, may be also men.

This faceless soldier is a marginal figure, his life expended far from the center of things, yet in him Auden is claiming to have found, as it were, the dead center of the war. His passivity and his mute ordinariness have been learned from Owen and Sassoon, but this sonnet restores some of the public meaning that Owen had drained from the death of soldiers in such poems as "Futility." For while the octave denies this man discourse—he is unnamed, uno-riginal, uninteresting and unremembered—the sestet restores him to signification. His death helps you to read what this war means—what it's all about—as the humblest punctuation point may determine the meaning of a sentence. He confers a meaning which is lacking in the epical discourse of commanders;[7] indeed he is the most important person in the war, which makes him, in the scheme of the sequence, the most important person in the world here and now. From the lowest depths of the ironic mode, the unknown soldier is rescued into epic, the making of history. And this moment of discovery is also a moment of triumphant orientation, where Auden arrives so conclusively as to arrogate to himself the right to speak *as a Chinese* ("our" daughters)—an identification all the more extraordinary, when you consider the cultural context of the utterance. For while the "upright carriage" of Chinese women is a symbol deriving real political weight from the notorious fact that in the occupied areas they were forced to bow to Japanese soldiers in the street, the disgrace "before the dogs" which the next line was bound to evoke was the legendary notice erected by the *British* colonial authorities in a park in Shanghai, which allegedly read: "No Dogs, No Chinese." Does that pronoun "our" represent a generous gesture of united-front sympathy, or an insulting colonialist appropriation and incorporation?[8] It is easy to see how "your daughters," though discursively the more obvious option, might have seemed politically infelicitous in drawing attention to the distance between poetic voice and political subject. It would simply look patronizing. With the bold choice of "our daughters," the pronoun becomes the "single, integrated scene" where poetic voice and political subject are the same thing. The British poet belongs to China, and China to the British poet.

Auden's "In Time of War" is authoritatively historicist, telling a story in which the Japanese attack on China is understood as the latest catastrophe in the long struggle of the species to fulfill its human potential and become what it might be. And meanwhile in the China poems we can watch a historical discourse of Marxist

---

[7]The "instructions from headquarters" were an afterthought. The original version reads: "He neither knew nor chose the Good, but taught us, / And added meaning like a comma, etc."

[8]The poem was well received in China, and immediately translated into Chinese and published in the Chinese press, though the translator amended the line "Abandoned by his generals and his lice" to the more morale-boosting "The rich and the poor are combining to fight" (*Journey*, 151).

determinism beginning to mutate into one that looks something like Christian providence. History itself was, of course, the big game stalked by so much of the serious European writing of the 1930s. Isherwood was after it, too. He had got close to it in Berlin earlier in the decade. Now in Hangkow—"the real capital of wartime China" (*Journey*, 40)—he felt he was hot on its trail again. But what seemed to disclose itself so clearly to the poet's olympian view, ranging across the global dimensions of history and geography, was not so visible to the grounded Isherwood, perusing the Chinese city with the scrupulous eye of the novelist. If Auden sees China as a hawk might, or a helmeted airman (his distanced objective vision of his early poems)—and hence the monologic and aloof authority of his privileged vision—Isherwood is that other 1930s myth, the baffled detective. "Hidden here are all the clues which would enable an expert, if he could only find them, to predict the events of the next fifty years" (*Journey*, 40). *Journey to a War* does not score highly for prediction—for one thing, it seriously underestimates Mao and the Communists—and the real problem, it seemed, was indeed expertise. Hangkow was full of experts— the Nationalist military and political authorities, foreign diplomats and missionaries, old China hands and veteran journalists; it sometimes seems Auden and Isherwood are the only amateurs in the place. And Isherwood was distinctly more of an amateur even than Auden, who had already made and reported on a journey to a war (in Spain), and had already published a travel book (on Iceland, with MacNeice). Isherwood offers a droll portrait of himself decked out in "beret, turtleneck sweater, and oversized ridingboots which gave him blisters," but he was really only "in masquerade as a war correspondent" (*Christopher and His Kind*, 224). Just as he is dwarfed by his subject—and how could anyone write a book big enough to be about China?—he stands in a relation of ironic belatedness to people he sees as real travelers in and writers about the East.

Two such in particular cross their path, each in a way a reproachful image of what Auden and Isherwood themselves might have been. The American journalist Agnes Smedley ("not unlike Bismarck" in appearance [*Journey*, 50]), is a model of the politically committed writer. Her *China's Red Army Marches* had appeared in 1934, and in that year, 1938, her *China Fights Back: An American Woman with the Eighth Route Army* was to be published in London. She is portrayed as full of single-minded zeal, passionately de-

voted to the Revolution and particularly to the Red Army. "'Wher
I was with them,' she told us, 'for the first time I felt at one with
the universe'" (*Journey*, 56). No problems of orientation for her
Equally at home, though in a different way, is the seasoned English explorer and war correspondent Peter Fleming, a real professional and already author of two travel books about China
One's Company (1934) and *News from Tartary* (1936), as well as o
Brazilian Adventure (1933) with which he had made his name at the
age of twenty-four. *One's Company*—its very title seeming like a
well-bred proleptic put-down to the dual-authored *Journey to a*
War, which Evelyn Waugh, reviewing it for the *Spectator*, was to
liken to the hind and front legs of a pantomime horse (*Essays*
251)—begins with a canny disclaimer of authority, a "Warning to
the Reader":

> The recorded history of Chinese civilization covers a period of
> four thousand years. The population of China is estimated at 450
> millions. China is larger than Europe.
> The author of this book is twenty-six years old. He has spent,
> altogether, about seven months in China. He does not speak
> Chinese. (i)

But amateur status for Fleming is a gambit; the narrative o
One's Company shows him a gentleman adventurer, modest but re-
sourceful and well informed, and full of the traveler's *savoir-fair*
that Isherwood portrays himself as lacking. Fleming always knows
exactly where he is, in relation both to his material and to his readers. He had traveled longer and further in China, including at least
two visits to Peking, though he was cool enough to forego a
description of the capital—"You will be spared the pen-picture
which you had good reason to dread," he told his readers suavely
(175).[9] *Noblesse oblige*. He was an Etonian and well connected. Auden and Isherwood make much of an interview they secured with
Mme Chiang Kai-shek, who rather overawed them ("certainly a
great heroic figure" [*Journey*, 59]). But Fleming had interviewed the
Generalissimo himself, *and* the emperor Pu Yi, on his first journey
to China, in which he had also made the first visit by a foreigner to
the anti-communist front: at the end of the journey he and his
companion Gerald Yorke were de-briefed by the British authorities
in Hong Kong and, later, in Shanghai. "We had become—or at any
rate we had no difficulty in passing ourselves off as—the Greatest

---

[9]Even so, he goes on to give a stylish sketch of the city.

Living Authorities on a subject" (301). And in the journey from Peking to Kashmir, for all the self-deprecation with which it is described in *News from Tartary*, Fleming had undergone hardships beyond the dreams of riding-booted Isherwood and carpet-slippered Auden. Here was a real traveler, with an authority he had earned for himself. (The metaphor of the real traveler's *earned* authority is not a casual one. Being a tourist, by contrast, was something to feel rather ashamed of, like having an unearned income; Auden says that the tourist always looks with the eye of a *rentier* [Auden and MacNeice, 209].) As writer and gentleman-adventurer, Fleming occupies an intertextual niche in the travels of Auden and Isherwood in China similar to that assigned to Byron in the equally belated travels of Auden and MacNeice in Iceland.

So when their paths cross for a few days in *Journey to a War*, Isherwood and Auden defer to Fleming's travel expertise, and half-mockingly entitle him the Chief. Their initial reaction of anti-Etonianism and professional jealousy quickly gives way to admiration. As a traveler, he is tried and tested. They recognize him as a strong precursor; they would follow him anywhere. "Laughing and perspiring we scrambled uphill; the Fleming Legend accompanying us like a distorted shadow" (*Journey*, 204). They amuse themselves by improvising passages from an imaginary travel book called *With Fleming to the Front* (*Journey*, 204). The formula of the title is that of many historical adventure stories by G.A. Henty, often about boys whose path crosses that of some hero of imperial destiny—*With Wolfe in Canada*, *With Kitchener in the Soudan*, *With the Allies to Pekin*, etc. But this ghostly intertext is just what the narrative of *Journey to a War* can never be. Isherwood cannot emulate the confident authority of Fleming's Asia discourse, but nor can he escape its genre. So his travel book implodes, turning its own inadequacies into comedy.

For the belated travelers, then, it is a different story, or hardly a story at all. Isherwood's narrative, like the journey itself, wanders about, unsure of direction, its report characterized by the sort of odd discontinuities which we can recognize as the faultlines which the experience of foreignness and dislocation scored into the landscape of literary modernism. At its best, Isherwood's diary resembles a series of brilliant snapshots.

> A pause. Then, far off, the hollow, approaching roar of the bombers, boring their way invisibly through the dark. The dull, punching thud of bombs falling, near the air-field, out in the suburbs. The search-lights criss-crossed, plotting points, like di-

viders; and suddenly there they were, six of them, flying close
together and high up. It was as if a microscope had brought
dramatically into focus the bacilli of a fatal disease. They passed,
bright, tiny, and deadly, infecting the night. (*Journey*, 60–61)

This is an unforgettable image, but it is the work of a highly subjective and uncertain vision, and far from the simple and objective
photographic record that Auden had spoken for in his Iceland
book.

Auden's photographs in *Journey to a War* comprise a narrative
of their own. There are sixty-three of them, the great majority being portraits, most of them head-and-shoulders, almost all of men.
Three women are portrayed—a doctor, a beggar, and the photo-
genic Mme Chiang. The sequence begins with "United Front," six
portraits of leaders including Chiang Kai-shek and Chou En-lai.
These people are identified by name, but the rest of the portraits
gloss their subjects by rank, function (like missionaries, or doctors)
or type, such as "Railway Engineer," "Press Bureau," "Shanghai
Businessman"; when names are given it is seemingly as an afterthought, as with "Intellectual (C.C. Yeh)" and even "Special
Correspondent (Peter Fleming)." This pattern continues with the
photographs from the "War Zone," which include pictures of the
wounded and the dead, allegorized as "The Innocent" and "The
Guilty," and even "Train Parasites" (a beggar woman at the carriage window). Even in this most particular and naturalistic of
media Auden seems to be drawn toward generalization, allegory
and myth. The images are not unmoving, but they are subject to an
eerie depersonalization. A photograph of cheery children, perhaps
refugees, is given Malraux's title *La Condition Humaine*: its subjects
are made to stand for something beyond themselves. Toward the
end of the sequence (its actual end is a portrait of a young Chinese
in uniform, perhaps inevitably entitled "Unknown Soldier"), as if
finally surrendering any ambition to render actual particular experience, Auden prints two stills from *Fight to the Last*, a Nationalist
propaganda film made at the Hangkow Film Studios. The meaning of propaganda images is public and, if anything, overdeter-
mined. These pictures are at the far end of the epistemological
scale from Isherwood's inability to process the story of the officer
and the burning book (his inability to "get the picture").

The photographs themselves serve Auden's urge to generalization and the global view. In contrast to Isherwood, not once
does Auden speak in the first-person singular in this book. The

generalized vision that enables him to survey from the beginning of evolution to the end of history, and from China to Peru and beyond, also enables and indeed obliges him to see the orient and oriental people as generic, representative, exemplary. For Auden, Chinese experience always stands for something else, as it must as he lifts further and further away from particularity.

> Night falls on China; and the great arc of travelling shadow
> Moves over land and ocean, altering life.
> Thibet already silent, the packed Indias cooling....
>
> *(Journey, 270)*

Thrilling as this is, it is a view of the orient available only from space.[10] And it is not surprising that, from that olympian vantage, all Auden hears arising from Shanghai in the last verses in the book is a generic "human cry"—"the voice of Man," in the original version—or that what it has to say is a series of airy generalized banalities.

> It's better to be sane than mad, or liked than dreaded;
> It's better to sit down to nice meals than to nasty;
> It's better to sleep two than single; it's better to be happy....
>
> *(Journey, 271)*

In the sonnet "He was their servant (some say he was blind)," the first poet was credited with giving voice to the feeling of his community. Here Auden is rehearsing, perhaps rather clumsily, for the role of global village poet.

Auden's Chinese poems, needless to say, are about a great deal more than China. Indeed they are not about China at all, in the way that Isherwood's narrative is. It is by taking an extremely long-range view that Auden is able to claim the authority to comprehend Chinese experience in an embracing and integrated vision of human solidarity, that has simply blurred the specific differences of particular history, nation, ethnicity, and the rest. The poet's is a generous vision, but not a sharp one. But the prose realist works under a different set of obligations, as Auden's poem "The Novelist" acknowledges (*The English Auden*, 238). Time and again, what Isherwood has to report is estrangement, failures of contact or comprehension, the way China and the Chinese remain beyond a western reach, or grasp—even with the best will in the world on

---

[10]See Cunningham, ch. 6, for a full discussion of the tropes of looking up and looking down in the writing of the period.

both sides, as for example when Isherwood and Auden are invited
to a tea party to meet Chinese intellectuals in Hankow.

> We both find functions of this sort extremely tiring. There is no
> lack of goodwill on either side—indeed, the air positively vi-
> brates with Anglo-Chinese *rapprochement*—but are we really
> communicating with each other at all? Beaming at our hosts we
> exchange words: "England", "China", "Poetry", "Culture",
> "Shakespeare", "International Understanding", "Bernard Shaw"
> —but the words merely mean, "We are pleased to see you."
> They are just symbols of mutual confidence, like swapping blank
> cheques. Never mind. It is all in a good cause. So we move from
> table to table, trying to say something to everybody, and our
> faces ache with smiling. (*Journey*, 144–45)

Journey to a War is dedicated to E.M. Forster, and I would guess
that this withering little essay of Isherwood's on the inadequacy of
"goodwill" carries a memory of the ladies at the Bridge Party in *A
Passage to India*, exchanging useless tokens of cultural recognition—"Eastbourne, Piccadilly, High Park Corner" (Forster, 62).
The problem, in other words, is not simply one of language difference. A willingness to trade the names of cultural landmarks does
not necessarily bring the east within the protocols and genres of
western understanding.

   Thus far, one has used the names "Auden" and "Isherwood"
in a way that could suggest that the difference between the writing
of these two men was simply personal and temperamental. There
were of course such differences, but, while acknowledging them,
one should point out that what interests one more here is a distinction of medium, between poetry and prose. It is less clumsy to
write "Auden" than to write "those parts of the book that are written in poetry." As a matter of fact Isherwood drew on Auden's
(prose) travel notes as well as his own, to write up the "Travel Diary," and Auden for his part was famously ready to incorporate
his friends' ideas and even phrases into his verse: the similar imagery in Isherwood's description of the Japanese bombers, quoted
above, and Auden's sonnet on the same subject later in the book, is
an example of this two-way creative traffic. So the personal distinction can sometimes become blurred; but the distinction of
medium remains sharp. Auden as a character in Isherwood's narrative is slightly clownish, but his own verse never once loses its
poise. The verse parts of *Journey to a War* are authoritative, assured, and fluent of movement. The prose part in contrast often
seems uneasy, provisional, ready to admit interruption and quali-

fication by voices that are native or more expert or authentic-sounding or mocking (in the last case, including its own). That possessive pronoun, in "our daughters," marked a spot where the discourse of the other, China, was smoothly incorporated into that of the poetry. But the prose part—or "Isherwood"—lacks this facility, and will not or cannot stake a claim to singular authority.

There is a case here for invoking the distinction (never a quite satisfactory one) Bakhtin tried to make between literary prose, which always avails itself of the internal dialogism of discourse, and poetry, which tends to behave—as language—as if it were single-minded and single-voiced. "The world of poetry," says Bakhtin, "no matter how many contradictions and insoluble conflicts the poet develops within it, is always illumined by one unitary and indisputable discourse. Contradictions, conflicts and doubts remain in the object, in thoughts, in living experiences—in short, in the subject-matter—but they do not enter into the language itself. In poetry, even discourse about doubts must be cast in a discourse that cannot be doubted" (Bakhtin, 286). It would also be worth adducing the distinction between the poet and the prose man which is elaborated in Auden's sonnet "The Novelist," mentioned above, and written for Isherwood in the year of their collaboration on *Journey to a War*. In this book the contrast is not a contradiction but a complementarity—a true collaboration—as the verse, however monologic and mandarin, is always in dialogue with the self-mocking, hesitant, bourgeois prose.

As Auden (or "Auden"), from his hesitant beginnings, becomes more authoritatively vatic as the book progresses, Isherwood ("Isherwood") chooses to flounder ever deeper in the viscous particularity of China. It is in this sense that the two voices of the book move in different directions. In "The Ship," Auden had imagined the east preparing a "test for men from Europe." China certainly seems to offer a test for European literary modes, and it is one which Isherwood's descriptive realism was finding very difficult, since China did not seem to confirm even the minimal assumptions on which the mode was based. Isherwood was unable to speak with any of the expert-sounding authority that attends the conclusions that Auden's poems are forever drawing in and from China: he found it hard to see through it to the typical, or beyond it to the universal. In the travel-diary, China continues not to yield itself up to Western explanations and categories, and Isherwood seems ready to admit defeat, the realist surrealized.

> The journey was uneventful. T.Y. Liu, in wonderful spirits, told
> us: "I am never sorry." He spoke too soon, for presently he was
> sick. We stopped to get petrol near a restaurant where they were
> cooking bamboo in all its forms—including the strips used for
> making chairs. That, I thought, is so typical of this country.
> Nothing is specifically either eatable or uneatable. You could
> begin munching a hat, or bite a mouthful out of a wall; equally,
> you could build a hut with the food provided at lunch.
> Everything is everything. (*Journey*, 220–21)

China will not surrender to even the primary tools of anthropological description, or exhibit the basic stable differences that
make language itself possible. "Everything is everything"—this
rueful admission of defeat has a more tragic relative in the insight
of that other traveler in search of the "real" Orient, Forster's Mrs
Moore in the Marabar Caves: "Everything exists, nothing has
value" (Forster, 146); where we may wish to take "value" in the
Saussurean sense, a function of difference. In both moments, the
east treats western realism to a demonstration of its own limits
Isherwood's China eludes the categories and distinctions with
which these kinds of Western meanings are built.

There is, then, a fascinating contrast in *Journey to a War* between Isherwood's underauthoritative prose and the characteristic
breezy omniscience of Auden's verse, especially on the subject of
history. The east fits comfortably within the frame of Auden's
panoptic vision, with its olympian orientation. But on the closer
inspection of Isherwood's realist prose it is forever receding in its
alterity, escaping, overflowing, or just slipping away. One should
not think the implosion of the travel-book form in Isherwood's
hands means that he has written a bad book, as Paul Fussell seems
to judge it (219–10)—on the contrary; but that in these circumstances China precipitates a kind of crisis of representation for the
genre, mode and authority of Isherwood's writing, a crisis which
that writing is too scrupulous not to admit, and from which it sal-
vages its distinct tone of ironic comedy.

Isherwood the realist enacts and thematizes a kind of failure of
the "Test" which their journey to a war had set these two writers
Auden in contrast seems to have succeeded in comprehending
China in a different kind of discourse, though he does so by not
paying too close attention to its individual features. Maps could
indeed "point to places / Where life is evil now," and poetry could
name them: "Nanking. Dachau" (*Journey*, 253). But in another

sense history itself, seen from the right orientation, could present to the view a "single, integrated scene," so that Auden in China saw himself as reporting from "one sector and one movement of the general war / Between the Dead and the Unborn, the Real and the Pretended," a war that was not only global but also eternal:

> Now in a world that has no localized events,
> Where not a tribe exists without its dossier,
> And the machine has taught us how, to the Non-Human,
>
> That unprogressive blind society that knows
> No argument except the absolute and violent veto,
> Our colours, creeds and sexes are identical,
>
> The issue is the same. Some uniforms are new,
> Some have changed sides; but the campaign continues:
> Still unachieved is *Jen*, the Truly Human.
>
> *(Journey*, 263)

Works Cited

This essay is a revised and expanded version of "Disorientations: Auden and Isherwood's China." Literature and History, *3rd series. 5:2 (Autumn 1996): 53–67*

Auden, W.H. *The English Auden: Poems, Essays and Dramatic Writings 1927– 1939*. Edited by Edward Mendelson. London: Faber, 1977.

———, and Christopher Isherwood. *Journey to a War*. Rev. ed. London: Faber, 1973.

———, and Louis MacNeice. *Letters from Iceland*. London: Faber, 1937.

Bakhtin, M.M. *The Dialogic Imagination: Four Essays*. Edited by Michael Holquist. Translated by Caryl Emerson and Michael Holquist. Austin: U of Texas P, 1981.

Cunningham, Valentine. *British Writers of the Thirties*. Oxford: Oxford UP, 1988.

Dodd, Philip. "The Views of Travellers: Travel Writing in the 1930s." In *The Art of Travel: Essays on Travel Writing*, edited by Philip Dodd. London: Frank Cass, 1982. 127–38.

Fleming, Peter. *News from Tartary: A Journey from Peking to Kashmir*. London: Cape, 1936.

———. *One's Company: A Journey to China*. London: Cape, 1934.

Forster, E.M. *A Passage to India*. Abinger edition. Harmondsworth: Penguin, 1985.

Fuller, John. *W.H. Auden: A Commentary*. London: Faber, 1998.

Fussell, Paul. *Abroad: British Literary Traveling Between the Wars*. New York and London: Oxford UP, 1980.

Isherwood, Christopher. *Christopher and His Kind*. New York: Farrar Straus, Giroux, 1976.

———. *Down There on a Visit*. London: Methuen, 1985.

———. *Exhumations*. London: Methuen, 1966.

———. *Goodbye to Berlin*. London: Hogarth Press, 1939.

Larkin, Philip. *Required Writing: Miscellaneous Pieces 1955–1982*. London and Boston: Faber, 1983.

Owen, Wilfred. *The Poems of Wilfred Owen*. Edited by Edmund Blunden. London: Chatto and Windus, 1931.

Porter, Dennis. *Haunted Journeys: Desire and Transgression in European Travel Writing*. Princeton: Princeton UP, 1991.

Pratt, Mary Louise. *Imperial Eyes: Travel Writing and Transculturation*. London: Routledge, 1992.

Said, Edward W. *Orientalism*. London: Routledge and Kegan Paul, 1978.

Smedley, Agnes. *China Fights Back: An American Woman with the Eighth Route Army*. London: Victor Gollancz, 1938.

———. *China's Red Army Marches*. London: Lawrence and Wishart, 1934.

Waugh, Evelyn. *The Essays, Articles, and Reviews of Evelyn Waugh*. Edited by Donat Gallagher. London: Methuen, 1983.

———. *Waugh in Abyssinia*. London: Longmans Green, 1936.

Williams, K.B. "'History as I saw it': Interwar new reportage." *Literature and History*, 3rd series 1/2 (Autumn 1992): 39–54.

Answering Herod:
W.H. Auden, Paul Tillich, Ernst Toller, and the Demonic

Brian Conniff

There has always been much talk of Auden's "conversion" to Christianity after he arrived in America. More emphasis should be placed on this as a "re-conversion," as the younger Auden—pre-Oxford—was quite devout and even by the mid 1930s was accompanying his preparatory school students to church where he sang in the choir. (See "The Student and the Master," above.) Then in Spain he was gravely dismayed at the burning of churches and the mistreatment of priests. (See Peter Grosvenor's article in this volume.) Hence, his arrival in America was not a sudden return to the church but a reaffirmation of an Auden whose spirituality had never really left him.

Perhaps no day has acquired more significance, among readers of W.H. Auden's poetry, than January 26, 1939. By most ways of looking at it, through the combined lenses of literature and history, it appears to have been a day of desolation, even despair. In New York City, as Humphrey Carpenter notes, it was the coldest day of the winter, with snow falling and blocks of ice floating in the Hudson River (253). For the rest of his life, Christopher Isherwood would remember standing in that snow. He and Auden had arrived that morning in New York harbor aboard the *Champlain*, which looked "like a wedding cake" after passing through a blizzard off the coast of Newfoundland (*Christopher and His Kind*, 338). Standing on the shore, Isherwood paused, just as one might expect, to look at "the made-in-France Giantess with her liberty torch" (339). To his famously camera-like eye, the "nervous New World" seemed determined to flaunt its "rude steel nudity." "We're Americans here," she told him, "and we keep at it, twenty-four hours a day, *being* Americans.... Don't you come snooting us with your European traditions—we know the mess they've got you into. Do things our way or take the next boat back—back to your Europe that's falling apart at the seams" (339). Even the Statue of Liberty herself "seemed to threaten, not welcome, the newcomer" (339). This atmosphere must have seemed all the more foreboding when, early in the afternoon, the news arrived that Franco's forces had captured Barcelona, effectively ending the Spanish Civil War and, many observers assumed, hastening Great Britain's inevitable entry into a widening struggle against fascism in the heart of Europe.

That morning, Isherwood and Auden set out to begin their new lives in this "nervous New World." For more than decades since then, Auden's critics, biographers and assorted literary observers have recorded the moment of emigration with accounts that are sometimes adulatory, sometime bitter, but always highly dramatic. The British novelist Michael Nelson would recall a former student, soon to be killed in the War, weeping when he heard the news. The American poet Guy Davenport would see Auden's arrival as a heroic attempt "to ensure that he was among humanity at its worst in this century" (quoted in Davenport-Hines, 181). For its part, the British literary establishment, like the British Parliament, would be quick and savage in its condemnation. Evelyn Waugh, Kingsley Amis, and Anthony Powell were among those eager to accuse Auden of cowardice and desertion, as if the presence of poets on English soil were somehow a matter of national security. More than thirty years later, reading his morning paper, Powell would spot Auden's obituary. "No more Auden," he would joyfully proclaim, "I'm delighted that shit is gone.... It should have happened years ago ... scuttling off to America in 1939 with his boyfriend like a ... like a ..." at which point he became too excited to finish his sentence (quoted in Davenport-Hines, 180).

These reactions to Auden's arrival on the shore of America were not merely hero worship, on the one hand, or merely reactionary politics and homophobia on the other. In the literary politics of the time, played out against the backdrop of the European crisis, this otherwise minor event could be treated as though it were momentous, even historic. As Richard Davenport-Hines has written, for much of the English-speaking world, Auden's change of residence would become the most visible sign of an irreversible transformation in national identity and cultural authority:

> It was hard for some English to forgive Auden for settling in the USA on the eve of war because that war so firmly settled Britain's pretensions to cultural and political hegemony of the English-speaking world. Those who considered him to be a military deserter were often those who resented Britain's eclipse as a world power after 1945, and were most reluctant to admit that the greatest English-language novelists and poets in the 1950's were not British-born or British-resident. (180)

As Auden himself had put it so compellingly in his poetry of the early 1930s, the "old life" had just about come to an end, at least in a literary sense. Now, he was discovering that he could dramatize this moment of transformation more powerfully by moving to New York, and reinventing himself, than by staying in Europe and continuing, as he had done for more than a decade, to prophesy a vaguely political apocalypse.

At the same time, the rather excessive reactions of Auden's large audience show how firmly his reputation had been established, by the time he was 31 years old, as the engaged, engaging, prophetic, outrageous, innovative, infuriating, camp young poet of the British left. It was a cultural construction of the poet's role so persuasive that he would never be able to escape it, particularly in England. For the vast majority of his readers, anything Auden wrote after crossing the Great Divide of January 26, 1939, would have to be anticlimactic. Worse yet, to the extent that his later work could be seen as a decline, it would be viewed as some sort of punishment for his unforgivable act of betrayal. James Fenton has accurately described this peculiar logic:

> Auden the man tended, in the years soon after his death, to be remembered for what he had become in the depression of his last days, rather than for what he had been. As for the poems, there lingered a common English view, pioneered by Philip Larkin and writers of his generation, that dated a decline from Auden's move to the States at the end of the thirties. Auden had one decade as a poet, and that was that. Implicit in this view was the suggestion that the decline of the poetry was a punishment for a sort of treachery. (ix)

Fenton does not deny—nor does this author—that Auden's work declined significantly in his later years. But I believe it is highly misleading to mark this decline, as tradition now has it, from his arrival on the shore of America. To accept the conventional view is to submit to the national, political, and literary biases of Auden's contemporaries. It is also an act of disregard for

some of the greatest poetry of the century and for the remarkable
intellectual life that made it possible.

In other words, there is much more to the various accounts of
Auden's change of residence than a collective anxiety about national and imperial identity, or a nostalgia for the poetics and literary politics of the "Auden generation." A central idea here posited
is that the reactions to Auden's emigration also suggest the difficulty his various readers would have understanding the kind of
poet he was about to become. For that matter, when he arrived in
America, Auden himself did not have a very clear understanding
of his new poetics or his new identity. He had decided, by then,
that he no longer wanted to play his familiar role as the leading
literary synthesizer of Marx and Freud, the healer who would release his generation—at least his generation of British writers—
from the interlocking shackles of psychosexual repression and political oppression. In the same passages of *Christopher and His Kind*
in which Isherwood recounts his journey with Auden to New
York, he describes their frustration with "the Popular Front, the
party line, the anti-Fascist struggle" (334). "I simply cannot swal-
low another mouthful," Isherwood says at one point, to which
Auden replies "Neither can I" (334). In *The Prolific and the Devourer*,
the highly revealing Mandarin-style *"pensées"* Auden wrote in the
summer and autumn of 1939, he confessed that "[f]ew of the artists
who round about 1931 began taking up politics as an exciting new
subject to write about had the faintest idea what they were letting
themselves in for" (18). He believed that his already famous
generation had been "carried along on a wave which is travelling
too fast to let them think"; as a result, they had managed little
more than eight years of "follies." "As far as the course of political
events is concerned," he concluded, "they might just as well have
done nothing. As regards their own work, a few had profited, but
how few" (18). Though Auden does not admit that he considers
himself one of the "few" who "has profited," I think it is clear that
he does, and that his own success has left him feeling hypocritical
and guilty. In the context of the European crisis, no merely literary
profit seems to have been worth the potential cost, in human
suffering, of misguided political views.

Of Auden's many dramatic assertions in "The Prolific and the
Devourer," perhaps the most dramatic is that he is no longer willing to give priority to the "material" over the "spiritual." He is
particularly and openly distrustful of "the man who says, 'First
things first! First let us raise the material standard of living among

the Masses, and then we will see what we can do about the spiritual problems'" (17).

By January 26, 1939, Auden had prepared himself to approach his new situation, and his new sense of vocation, on several fronts: in his *pensées*, book reviews, and various other short prose pieces; in the remarkable transitional poetry he would continue to write for the next two or three years; and in his initially hesitant religious practice. In all of these ways Auden was beginning to arrive at a new language, and a new system of belief, with which his poetry could speak more convincingly to the moral and spiritual needs of his very troubled historical moment.

Of course, at the heart of these literary developments was Auden's decision to return to the Anglican Communion in which he had been raised.[1] His biographers and critics have generally agreed that his move to America occurred near the mid-point of a period in which Auden was profoundly questioning what he himself described as "laws"—"call them for convenience divine laws" ("The Prolific and the Devourer," 23). In fact, Auden scholars have reached a high degree of consensus on the most salient moments in this biographical narrative: Auden's journey to the Spanish Civil War early in 1937, where he learned that communist factions were torturing and murdering priests, saw churches that had been closed and burned, and from which he returned, in a few weeks, largely disillusioned with his prospects for uniting his poetry with the causes of leftist politics (Carpenter, 214–25; Ford, 288); his meeting later that year in Oxford with Charles Williams, who impressed him, he would later claim, in a way that made him aware for the first time of the "presence of personal sanctity" ("W.H. Auden," 41); a night in Manhattan in 1939 when he was watching a film on the Nazi invasion of Poland and, as Poles appeared on the screen, heard members of the audience shout "Kill them!"—an experience that led him to react "against the denial of every humanistic value" by going "back to the Church" (quoted in Carpenter, 282).

Auden's literary life might have been easier—or at least more easily understood—if he had viewed his return to religious prac-

---

[1]Carpenter provides a succinct summary of some of the denominational issues involved in Auden's decision to join the Episcopalian Church as an American equivalent of the Church of England: e.g., his affinities with Roman Catholicism, "Neo-Calvinist (i.e., Barthian)" theology, and Anglo-Catholic ritual (301).

tice as a "private" matter separate from his writing. But he assumed that his religious belief required that he commit himself to
a "vocation"; and so, if he were going to continue as a writer, he
would need to understand this practice, day by day, as a religious
activity. In this respect and others, his understanding of Christianity was similar to that of Søren Kierkegaard, the theologian for
whom his affinities would eventually be most apparent and enduring. Like Kierkegaard, Auden did not see himself *as a Christian* so
much as he saw himself as a person striving *to become a Christian*.
And he had to undertake this struggle in a time and a place, like
Kierkegaard's "Christendom," in which such a task was likely to
be unpredictable, isolating, and anxiety-ridden. Late in his life, in
one of his two major essays on Kierkegaard, Auden still described
his own situation in the terms he had established in the first few
years after his move to America:

> Today, in our part of the world, society could not care less what
> one believes; to be a Christian is regarded by the majority as a
> rather silly but quite harmless eccentricity, like being a Baconian
> or a flat-earth man. But there are large areas elsewhere where
> Christianity is taken seriously, where a Christian is debarred
> from all but the lowliest jobs and may even lose his life. What
> would Kierkegaard say to all this? ("Knight," *Forewords & After-
> words*, 194–95)

Even in this late essay, Auden never directly answers his own
question, but he is convinced that the Anglo-Irish literary world
has become one of those places in which religious belief is viewed,
at best, as a harmless eccentricity. He has come to believe that
"Kierkegaard speaks with absolute authority" on the one problem
that has plagued him since he arrived in America, and that would
continue to plague him until the end of his life: "No person of talent who has read him can fail to realize that the talented man, even
more than the millionaire, is the rich man for whom it is so difficult to enter the Kingdom of Heaven" (197).

Just as Auden struggled in his "private life" to come to terms
with the question of how to use his own talent—or, as he more often put it, his "gift"—to become a Christian poet, in a modern
world in which such a feat had not been accomplished in any way
that seemed to him sufficient, in the early 1940s the problem of
becoming a Christian emerged as the most compelling and pro-

ductive theme of his poetry.[2] For a period of just about five years, from his move to the United States until his completion of *The Sea and the Mirror* around the start of 1944, Auden would succeed brilliantly in his efforts to give poetic expression to this theme, writing much of his most powerful poetry and demonstrating some of the vast possibilities of a contemporary Christian poetics. To put it in a slightly different way, it was largely because the act of becoming a Christian was for Auden one of considerable personal difficulty— and seemingly limitless intellectual complexity—that it drove his poetry, for this brief time, to heightened innovation and accomplishment. By the same token, Auden's later decline was not the result of any religious complacency, as many of his critics have assumed; rather, this decline, too, was directly related to the difficulty and complexity of his religious struggle.

In other words, the central point about the "later Auden" is that the development of his poetry throughout this period of his career—its rapid rise in the early 1940s and, shortly afterward, its gradual fall—can best be explained as a result of his deliberate at-

---

[2]Of course, in his return to Christianity, Auden was well aware of T.S. Eliot's "conversion" more than a decade earlier. But despite Auden's more or less official statements of admiration for Eliot, there are telling suggestions, in the development of Auden's own Christian poetics, that he did not see Eliot as a satisfactory example. In one of the odes near the end of *The Orators*, he asks "Where is Eliot?" and answers "Dreaming of nuns" (*English Auden*, 105). Considering possible titles for the volume that would be published in England as *Look Stranger!* and in the U.S. as *On This Island*, Auden suggested that "On the analogy of *Burnt Norton* I might call it *Piddle-in-the-hole* (quoted in Carpenter, 199). Most significantly, I think, he includes in *For the Time Being* a reference to Eliot's notorious comment, in *After Strange Gods*, to "free thinking Jews" (*Collected Poems*, 373) and begins Herod's speech with a parody of Eliot's *Ash Wednesday*: "Because I am bewildered, because I must decide," etc. (390). As Nicholas Jenkins has recently written, Auden was certainly willing to come to Eliot's defense when, in the middle of the war years, critics like Archibald MacLeish and Van Wyck Brooks attacked Eliot and other modernists for "defeatism" and "coterie" writing (7). In a January 1943 talk at Swarthmore College on "Vocation and Society," which Jenkins describes as "a rousing, polemical lecture" (1), Auden referred to Eliot as "the greatest poet now living, one in whom America and England may well rejoice, one whose personal and professional example are to every other and lesser writer at once an inspiration and a reproach," and then concluded with a quotation from the recently published "Little Gidding" (30).

tempt to reinvent himself as a Christian poet. Auden articulated his struggle for faith, especially its relationship to his poetic gift, through a rich and sometimes idiosyncratic encounter with modern theology. The enormous gap between the critical reception of Auden's later work, on the one hand, and his poetic accomplishments of this period, on the other, is primarily the result of a refusal on the part of his most influential readers to take this encounter seriously. In an essay of 1941, Auden described the attitude of literary intellectuals toward theology as "the final prudery" (quoted by Davenport-Hines, 226)—a phrase that acutely suggests his critical audience's fundamental dismissal of, and its vague embarrassment about, matters of religious belief, even on the most literary or intellectual level.

One of the central problems with the conventional view of Auden—as evident in the melodramatic accounts of his emigration—is that this view obscures, and in most cases completely erases, the remarkable public world in which Auden found himself. As soon as he arrived on its shore, the "New World" of America began to play as significant a role in his poetry of the early 1940s as the more recognized British setting of the "Auden generation" had played in his poetry of the early 1930s. The nexus around Union Theological Seminary, where Reinhold Niebuhr was on the faculty, and the New School for Social Research, where Auden sometimes lectured, was an especially challenging and exciting "scene," most of all for a poet with Auden's concerns and interests. A remarkably active group of Protestant theologians had set out to define and organize itself as a "generation," partly through the Theological Discussion Group and international organizations like Faith and Order. Still in the early stages of their careers, many of them had recently settled into colleges, universities and seminaries between New Haven and New York—Niebuhr and Henry Van Dusen at Union, John Bennett and Georgia Harkness at Auburn Seminary and Elmira College, Francis P. Miller and H. Richard Niebuhr at Yale. They considered it their moral and professional obligation to oppose nationalism and the rise of fascism (Warren, 34), and the escalating European War invested even their most intellectual debates with a heightened sense of human and historical consequence.

The war also provided these debates with some of their most notable participants. Of special significance for Auden, the major schools in the area were, in Ursula Niebuhr's words, "very full of émigrés from Germany and France; the members of the Institute for Social Research from Frankfurt, Jacques Maritain, Jean Wahl, and the Swiss Denis de Rougemont and many others" (107). Also among the recent arrivals were Albert Einstein, Bertolt Brecht, Kurt Weill (whose music Auden fondly associated with his early days in Berlin), and Igor Stravinsky (for whom Auden, with Chester Kallman, would later write libretti). After the fall of France in June of 1940, the émigré community would include André Breton, Salvador Dali, and Max Ernst (Callan, 164). Among the recent arrivals, Auden's closest acquaintances included the Gestalt psychologist Wolfgang Köhler, whom Auden came to know when he taught at Swarthmore and whom he described as "one of the greatest men" he had ever met (quoted in Carpenter, 254), and Auden's "in-laws" of the Mann family, especially Klaus and Thomas.[3]

One of Auden's closest friends throughout this period, James Stern, has described "the electrifying atmosphere of pre-war New York," where he and Auden often spoke to each other in German, "the language of our friends, the refugees," and where they discovered "the sense of solidarity common to self-imposed exiles" (123, 126). In fact, as far as the ongoing development of Auden's poetry is concerned, an argument might be made that he could not have been in a better place. Contrary to popular belief—which Auden himself did much to encourage, along the lines of that notorious phrase, "poetry makes nothing happen"—Auden found, in New York, a place in which poetry could matter a great deal. At the same time, however, this vital intellectual "scene" would force him to arrive at a new understanding of the *kind* of poetry that would matter, at this particular historical moment, and the *way* it would matter. His vaguely political notions of the early 1930s, for which he had already become famous, could no longer go unexamined.

I think that any specific account of the "electrifying" atmosphere in Auden's New York will make it clear that neither Auden nor any of the other major émigré intellectuals minimized the catastrophic reality of the European crisis. The constant influx of exiles from Europe made any simplistic "escapism" untenable. For

---

[3]Auden's biographers consistently tell the irresistible story of his marriage to Erik Mann. Still, Auden's critics have failed to consider how his continuing friendship with the Mann circle helped him to negotiate an intellectual productive sense of himself as an émigré and border intellectual.

the rest of his life, in fact, Auden remained highly conscious of his status as a "self-imposed exile"—or, to put it in the terms borrowed, in part, from Paul Tillich, as a "boundary" intellectual. He remained sharply aware of the persecution of Jews and the daily reports of the war, and at times he was hurt by suggestions in the British press, and even in the British Parliament, that by coming to America he and Isherwood had deserted their country in its time of need (Davenport-Hines, 205–6). Even as Auden found in his New World a chance to reformulate his enduring moral preoccupations in light of religious practice and modern theology, and despite his recent disavowal of British partisan politics, his new understanding of the poet's vocation, much like his earlier one, was largely a response to the fascist threat to European culture and common humanity. In particular, Auden's attraction to the Christian realism and neo-orthodox theology of Reinhold Niebuhr and Paul Tillich is a logical response—and a distinctly non-escapist response—to the heightened sense of the human capacity for evil that he, like many other European intellectuals of his day, had developed largely by witnessing the rise of fascism.

As Heather Warren has recently demonstrated, Christian realism was preeminently a theology of international engagement. Like Auden's poetry, it had deep roots in the European reaction to World War I, especially the sense among theologians of Niebuhr's "circle" that the previous generation's progressive Christianity and social gospel could not account for, or ameliorate, the forces of evil manifest in both European fascism and communist totalitarianism (18). Moreover, the difficulties Auden faced in his efforts to restore his religious faith, and reconcile it with his poetry, were compounded by his recognition—one he shared with many of these same intellectuals—that the source of greatest human evil, the heart of darkness, could be found at the center of civilization as he knew it. Of course, it might be argued that such a view is Eurocentric, to the extent that it tends to project onto events in Europe the "end of civilization." But this limitation does not negate either the moral urgency of the questions Auden poses in his poetry of this period or the compelling force—and at times the sheer poetic brilliance—of his efforts to answer them.

Of all the European émigrés Auden met in his early years in New York, the one who would eventually have the most profound influence on his poetry was Paul Tillich. Tillich had come to America under circumstances that seem to have been designed to capture Auden's sympathy and interest. In 1932, when he was dean of the philosophy faculty at the University of Frankfurt, Nazi students rioted on the campus, attacking leftist and Jewish students. Near the end of that year, Tillich published *The Socialist Decision*, in which he argued that a socialism with "religious roots" was necessary to counteract the current trend toward "warlike nationalism" and thus rescue Europe from "a return to barbarism" (xxxvi, 161). When these lines were quoted by Nazi journalists, the book was banned, along with a socialist journal with which Tillich was affiliated. A few months later, while Hitler was consolidating his power as chancellor of the coalition government and inciting efforts to purge the German Universities of Jewish and Communist influences, Tillich's name appeared on the first list of suspended faculty. By the next year, when the number of suspensions would reach nearly 1,700, Tillich decided, after considerable deliberation, to leave for the United States.[4] For the rest of his life he would often remark, with a pride some considered inordinate, that he "had the honor to be the first non-Jewish professor dismissed from a German university" (quoted in Pauck and Pauck, 198).[5]

While Tillich was struggling with the fascist assault on German universities, his fate was already being played out, more than he knew, in New York City. As the suspensions of German scholars began, Columbia University formed a committee to arrange for the employment of those who could be brought to the United States. A list of "deposed professors" was circulated. Henry Sloane Coffin, President of Union Theological Seminary, attended the committee's initial meeting and, seeing Tillich's name on the list, began negotiations to provide him with a position. The Union faculty voted to accept a salary reduction of five percent to create a stipend for Tillich's first year. Reinhold Niebuhr, who with his brother had translated Tillich's *The Religious Situation*, joined in the

---

[4]See Ringer, 436–40. From 1929, when Auden first went to Berlin, the National Socialists made inroads in German universities, beginning with efforts to take control of the National Student Union. When Hitler's followers gained positions in the state government of Thuringia, in 1930, "they promptly created a new professorship at University of Jena for the 'race scientist' F.K. Gunther" (436). By 1930, the National Socialists attained a majority in student elections at many universities.

[5]As the Paucks demonstrate in some detail, through mid-1934 Tillich did try to convince the Nazi Ministry for Science, Art and Education to allow him to retain his post in Frankfurt (148–50). By 1946, the University of Halle had reinstated his academic credentials (218).

effort, and before long he played a crucial role by gathering information and convincing Tillich to leave Germany. Eventually, long-
term provisions were made, with Columbia agreeing to provide a
joint appointment in their philosophy department and with Ger-
man-speaking students volunteering to help Tillich improve his
English. A few years later, when Auden entered the Niebuhrs'
circle, Reinhold would also bring Tillich's writing to the poet. In
particular, the Niebuhrs loaned Auden a copy of *The Interpretation
of History*, along with mimeographs of the "propositions" for a
systematic theology that Tillich was using in his classes (U.
Niebuhr, 106).

These "propositions" were not your average lecture notes.
They contained, and often expanded in considerable complexity,
the central principles of Tillich's life's work. He had written his
first outlines of a systematic theology shortly after completing his
doctoral studies, as he prepared to serve as a chaplain in World
War I; he revised them fairly consistently throughout the course of
his academic career, providing and expanding drafts for courses
he taught in the United States; later, along with detailed notes
maintained (and typed) by his students, they provided the basis of
his *magnum opus*, the *Systematic Theology* he published in three volumes between 1951 and 1963 (Pauck and Pauck, 232–45; Coffin,
139).

As for *The Interpretation of History*, Tillich thought of it as a
general introduction to his work for an American audience. Toward this end, it did not succeed (Pauck and Pauck, 175). In the
first place, Tillich's writing of this period tended to be exception-
ally murky—eventually his transition to English, along with
decades of reiterating some of his central concepts, would help
considerably. But Auden immediately brought to his reading of
Tillich the same breadth and tenacity of intellect that led him to
read and review books on subjects like theoretical biology and
(worse yet) educational methods. To the Niebuhrs, he quickly reported that he found Tillich's work "exciting" (U. Niebuhr, 106).

Considering his New York friendships, Auden would have
known Tillich's story in detail. And considering Auden's sense of
crisis, both personal and historical, he would also have been pre-
disposed to look to Tillich's work in the hope of healing the psychic and spiritual wounds he had been steadily developing for
more than a decade. From the very beginning of their careers, as
Samuel Hynes has meticulously demonstrated, Auden had shared
with many of the British writers of his generation dark premoni-

tions of the coming of the second world war and the continuing spread of European fascism (41–64). His witnessing of the early rise of the Brown Shirts in Berlin, when he and Isherwood were living there in 1929, proved to be a formative experience for such early works as Isherwood's *Goodbye to Berlin* and *Mister Norris Changes Trains* as well as Auden's "It was Easter as I walked in the public gardens" and *The Orators*.[6] In 1935 Auden had agreed to marry Erika Mann, whom he would not meet until a few days before their wedding, so she could escape likely arrest after her anti-fascist cabaret review had become an irritation to Nazi authorities (Carpenter, 175–77). His 1937 trip to Spain not only contributed to his disaffection with politics; even more, it brought him to the recognition that religion was his only hope for a sufficient answer to the problem of human evil. In the course of his disoriented effort to aid the loyalists in the war against Franco, Auden was deeply disturbed not only by the fascists' continued success but also by reports that communist factions were torturing priests— one bishop was murdered before two thousand witnesses (Carpenter, 214). As for the Valencia government, though Auden still thought it was far preferable to Franco, he could not view it uncritically, as so many other poets did, as a force of justice (Mendelson, *Early Auden*, 319–20). To his surprise, when he saw churches that had been destroyed, he was shocked to feel that something terribly important had been missing in his life. By the time he moved to America, he was ready to consider the possibility that history might be shaped, somehow, by forces not taken into account by the distinctly secular ideologies from which he had fashioned his early poetry.

Enter Tillich. On a couple of levels, Auden's initial reading of Tillich's theology was similar to his initial reading, a year or so earlier, of Reinhold Niebuhr's.[7] Once again, Auden found an intel-

---

[6]In Berlin in May 1929, Auden saw the fighting in the streets between the Communists and the police—the "anxiety at night, / Shooting and barricade in street"—that generated much of the atmosphere of "It was Easter as I walked in the public gardens" (Carpenter, 102; *English Auden*, 38).

[7]Edward Mendelson notes that Auden had been "peripherally aware of radical Protestant theology since around 1933," when he seems to have read the work of Karl Barth, perhaps the recently published translation of Barth's 1919 commentary on Paul's Epistle to the Romans (*Later Auden*, 149).

lectual deeply ingrained in European cultural traditions who could reconcile Christian faith and doctrine with the political realities, as he understood them, of the contemporary crisis. And on a more personal level, Auden seems to have experienced, once again, a shock of recognition on finding key concepts of his poetics—concepts his literary critics have typically considered idiosyncratic—echoed, occasionally anticipated, and often expanded, in specifically theological terms.

On a distinctly poetic level, however, there was a clear difference. Whereas Auden's reading of Niebuhr basically crystallized elements of his early poetics within a moral framework of neo-orthodox Christianity, his reading of Tillich would provide a more compelling impetus for poetic innovation. Niebuhr led Auden to the conviction that he could re-conceive his vocation as a modern poet in traditional Christian terms; Tillich convinced him that the historical moment called for, even tragically demanded, highly ambitious poems grounded in theology and made possible by faith.[8]

Before long, as Edward Callan has noted, a number of Tillich's "special terms"—including the Abyss, the Void, the Demonic, and *Kairos*—"began to appear" in Auden's writing (181–82). Especially in times of crisis, Auden was increasingly inclined to turn to Tillich's category of "the demonic." Faced with Chester Kallman's initial infidelities, for instance, he came to realize that sexual jealousy could make him act as if he were "the prey of demons in both the Greek and Christian sense, stripped of self-control and self-respect, behaving like a ham actor in a Strindberg play" ("W.H. Auden," 41). Eventually, "the demonic" would become his preferred term for most any especially dangerous personal excess, as in his essay "Kierkegaard," in which he writes that "the sufferer by fate" is tempted into "demonic defiance" and "demonic despair" (*Forewords & Afterwords*, 169). Yet his most powerful applications of this particular term involve his efforts to confront, as a Christian poet, the political and social forces most destructive of the human spirit.

---

[8]For Auden's encounter with Reinhold Niebuhr and its influence on his sense of the poet's vocation see my essays, "Auden, Niebuhr, and the Vocation of Poetry" (*Religion and Literature* 25.3 [Autumn 1993]: 45–65), and "What Really Became of Wystan? Auden, Niebuhr and *For the Time Being*" (*Christianity and Literature* 44.2 [Winter 1995]: 133–44).

Tillich devotes the second part of *The Interpretation of History* to the "demonic." It is one of several terms—others include "the boundary," "theonomy," "Kairos," "the Protestant principle," and "ultimate concern"—he "reintroduced into theological language" in the early 1920s (*Systematic Theology*, III:102), partly because he believed that the clarity and relevance of Christian thought had been diminished by decades, even centuries, of careless interpretation and application (Adams, "Introduction," 5), and partly because he believed a new theological language was necessary to address and ameliorate the unprecedented crisis of modern civilization (Shinn, 51; Adams, *Paul Tillich's Philosophy of Culture*, 229). Tillich shared with many of the artistic and literary modernists of his time—Picasso, Stravinsky, Joyce, and Eliot, to mention a few— a sense that traditional language and subjects needed to be revived through formal innovation and methodological complexity; and he shared their tenuous hope that such approaches might provide, as Eliot famously wrote of Joyce's *Ulysses*, "a way of controlling, of ordering, of giving a shape and a significance to the immense panorama of futility and anarchy which is contemporary history" (177). At the same time, like Auden in particular, Tillich had eagerly appropriated central ideas, language, and metaphors from modernism's intellectual precursors of the late 19th and early 20th centuries, especially Marx, Freud and, increasingly through the 1930s, Nietzsche. This powerfully ambivalent approach to modernity, which had made Auden's poetry so compelling for the English writers who began their careers between the two world wars—including Graham Greene, Cecil Day-Lewis, Stephen Spender, and George Orwell—now made Tillich's theology just as compelling for Auden.

Tillich's treatment of the demonic in *The Interpretation of History* is one of his most extensive and richly suggestive. Often, it is also one of his most impenetrable. He defines the demonic variously, positively and negatively, sometimes explicitly, more often implicitly, and almost always vaguely. He refers to it as "the unity of form-creating and form-destroying strength" (81); the separation in existence of "form of being and inexhaustibility of being ... the relatively independent eruption of the 'abyss' in things" (84); "the actual uprising of the abyss against the form" (85); "the reign of a superindividual, sacred form which supports life, which at the same time contains the force of destruction in such a way that the destructive power is essentially connected with its creative power" (91); "the perversion of the creative" (93); and so on. Later in his

career, especially in his *Systematic Theology*, Tillich would more often identify the demonic as a danger, and a potentially destructive
force, in the religious life itself (I:140, 222, 227; III:174). But in *The
Interpretation of History*, his view is more expansive: his primary interest is to demonstrate that the demonic can be a useful conceptual tool for the interpretation of (among other things) visual art,
the history of religion, individual personality, mysticism, spirituality, sin, myth, history, and oppressive social and political organization. By approaching the topic in this multidisciplinary, pris-
matic way, Tillich suggests that, at least in certain historical periods, the demonic can be pervasive: at one point he states that there
is a "particular demonry at every point of society" (116). The present, he strongly implies, is one such moment. Because the demonic
seems to be everywhere, artists and intellectuals must summon all
available resources to discern it and oppose it.

Wide-ranging as these comments are, they share a central
principle, both with each other and with Tillich's various applications of the term throughout his career. He consistently characterizes the demonic as the inflation of a finite quality, perhaps an individual personality trait that is presumed to be more than merely
human, or an aspect of social organization that it is treated as more
than a historical product. As Tillich succinctly puts it in *The Protestant Era*, the demonic is "an absolute claim made for a relative reality" (163). Or, to use the terms he would prefer in the *Systematic
Theology*, it is "the elevation of something conditional to unconditional significance" (I:140).

Because of this "relative" or "conditional" quality, the demonic is never found in a pure form. Its destructive power is always merged, inextricably, with creative or productive energy. On
a personal level, the demonic might appear when a human being,
faced with "the elimination of all sacramental mediation," turns
toward God, only to see Him as an "absolute claim" and "rejecting
wrath" (95). On a political or historical level, Tillich writes—with
his own recent experiences clearly in mind—the demonic can be
found when the "national impulses of the bourgeois era," which
contain at their best "the strength to offer resistance to the
technical economization of the whole of Occidental existence,"
develop into "the last great demonry of the present," imperialistic
nationalism (120).

By the same token, in *The Interpretation of History* Tillich suggests that the demonic can be a driving force of social conservatism or social progress. Yet even in its more apparently pro-

gressive forms, its promise is deceptive and dangerous: it devalues human life in the temporal world by obscuring its relationship to the eternal. In a language that anticipates the "Christian Realism" with which he would later be associated—a language highly attractive for a writer like Auden who was so deeply influenced by modernist poetics—Tillich's discussion of the demonic often amounts to a deep suspicion of "revolutionary" or "utopian" social schemes. Even a seemingly innocuous concept like "progress" must be treated with suspicion: it is often merely another name for "revolutionary Utopianism that has become tame," and as such it "devaluates every moment of history in favor of the ideal that lies in infinity instead of in eternity" (97).

This account of the demonic provided Auden with direct access to Tillich's theological system. For instance, early in the second part of *The Interpretation of History*, in a passage on "The picture of the demonic," Tillich discusses one of his favorite topics, the visual arts. Central to this discussion is an assertion that, even though the demonic has recently come to pervade Western culture, it has become in this same period especially difficult to recognize. Accordingly, Tillich turns to the art of "primitive peoples and Asiatics"—including statues of Gods, fetishes, crafts, and dance masks—where he finds traces of the demonic that have been "long inaccessible to our Occidental consciousness" (77). In this art, Tillich believes, "destructive elements" often "break forth" in ways that defy "natural proportion" and "classical esthetics": "The organs of the will for power, such as hands, feet, teeth, eyes, and the organs of procreation, such as breasts, thighs, sex organs, are given a strength of expression" (77–78).

When applied to art of this kind, Tillich believes, developments of the 1920s and 1930s in the study of religion, art history—and most of all "the new psychology of the subconscious" (77)—provide modern intellectuals with the means of recognizing the "destructive elements" so often disguised by creative energy. In this way, Tillich arrives at an idea of artistic form that accounts for the modernism of his own favorite example, Picasso's *Guernica*. At the same time, he anticipates some of the more striking features of Auden's later Christian poetics, especially its method of imbedding destructive energy in the various guises of modern sophistication.

Within a very short period—roughly two years—Tillich's theology of culture would complement, in Auden's poetics, Søren Kierkegaard's critique of aesthetics and Reinhold Niebuhr's more distinctly moral and political version of Christian Realism. Auden certainly would have understood that, in Tillich's system, the poet could have a powerful social role. Throughout his first year and a half or so in America, Auden recorded the constant vicissitudes of his own search for faith in letters, diaries, poems, essays, reviews—on just about every scrap of paper, it seems, that came his way. Nonetheless, Auden's critics and biographers have often floundered in their efforts to trace his thinking through this period. Humphrey Carpenter, who does better than most, resorts to the overly general and misleading terms of a "search for ideology." He eventually decides that Auden "was in a muddle—or at least he gave different reasons on different occasions, with no apparent consistency" (293). Yet even in this difficult transitional period, Auden's thinking about religion was never as muddled as Carpenter and many of Auden's critics like to suggest. For a while, Auden experimented with various moral and religious propositions, until he finally set out to work toward a more systematic understanding of his religious commitment. Most notably, in the summer and fall of 1939—that is, the midpoint between his move to America and his meeting with the Niebuhrs, he recorded many of the nuances of his search for faith in a series of prose meditations he often called his "pensées."

Though it would not be published until nearly a decade after his death, "The Prolific and the Devourer" provides the most significant and extended documentation of Auden's return to Christianity. Auden takes his title from a passage in William Blake's *The Marriage of Heaven and Hell* in which Blake refers to "two classes of men" who are "always upon earth" and always enemies. He begins with a quote from Blake that asserts the perpetual opposition of these two figures, and their mutual interdependence: "Whoever tries to reconcile them seeks to destroy existence" (quoted by Auden, 7). In the course of his pensées, Auden seldom refers to Blake's formulation. At one point he does directly associate the Prolific with the Artist and the Devourer with the Politician, yet here too he is interested primarily in their "complementary" qualities:

> The Prolific and the Devourer: the Artist and the Politician. Let them realize that they are enemies, i.e., that each has a vision of the world which must remain incomprehensible to the other. But let them also realize that they are both necessary and complementary, and further, that there are good and bad politicians,

good and bad artists, and that the good must learn to recognize
and to respect the good. (20)

Even in this passage, Auden's main concern is not Blake. Rather,
he is more concerned with reconceptualizing his own vocation as a
poet in terms that are, from the start, less political—and then increasingly theological.

Most notably, Auden's account of Blake's Devourer directly
anticipates his encounter with Tillich's "demonic," especially the
kind of self-inflation—the "absolute claim for a relative reality"—
that Tillich considers one of the demonic's most persistent features: "To the Devourer it seems as if the producer was in his
chains but it is not so, he only takes portions of existence and fan-
cies it the whole." Central to Auden's crisis of vocation, in fact, is
his fear that the writer, like the politician, might be particularly
susceptible to this temptation: "The Dictator who says "'My People': the Writer who says 'My Public'" (8). For Auden, it was not a
new problem. In earlier works like *The Orators* and "Here on the
cropped grass of the narrow ridge I stand," he had considered the
seductions and perils of the writer's profession in the modern
world. As a poet who had been highly acclaimed since the early
stages of his career—and thus highly "public"—he had come to
understand that public proclamations are always at risk of becoming the language demagogues:

> And over the Cotswolds now the thunder mutters:
> "What little of the truth your seers saw
> They dared not tell you plainly but combined
> Assertion and refuge
> In the common language of collective lying."
> (Early Auden, 143)

But now, more than ever before, Auden needed to understand the
destructive forces of history—that is, the power of Blake's Devourer—in terms more compelling and explanatory than
"collective lying." Even though he maintained his long-standing
suspicion about any human claim to universal truth, he needed to
believe in a divine law. The result was a combination of faith and
skepticism that he would soon find echoed in Tillich's theology. In
"The Prolific and the Devourer," Auden wrote:

> Human law rests upon Force and Belief, belief in its rightness.
> The Way rests upon Faith and Scepticism. Faith that the divine
> law exists, and that our knowledge of it can improve; and scepti-
> cism that our knowledge of these laws can never be perfect. (24)

Particularly in the powerful elegies he wrote in this period, Auden was able to generate compelling poetry not so much out of any particular theological explanation for modern destruction as out of his sense of the need for such an explanation.

The most telling example is one of the best poems his critics have chosen to ignore, "In Memory of Ernst Toller." Though nearly forgotten today, Toller was arguably the most recognized German dramatist of the 1920s and 1930s (Dove, 1–4). Prior to his literary successes, he had established a national reputation as a socialist activist and orator. In late 1918 and early 1919, he was one of the most visible participants in the leftist uprising in Munich—an attempt to establish a Bavarian Socialist Republic. Arrested and convicted for this revolutionary effort, he was then, for five years, the most famous political prisoner of the Weimar Republic, an experience out of which he produced a handful of plays, two books of poetry, and a volume of "prison letters." As early as 1923, in one of the comedies he wrote in prison, *Der entfesselte Wotan (Wotan Unchained)*, he anticipated the rise of a fascistic National Socialism.

Auden came to know Toller as one of the most famous exiles of 1933. Forced to leave Germany, Toller spent more than two years in England, where he acquired a considerable reputation for his plays and anti-fascist speeches. During this period his collected plays, prison letters, and autobiography appeared in English translation, accompanied by reviews in publications like the *Times Literary Supplement*, *New Statesman*, and *Spectator*. Many of his personal appearances drew large and enthusiastic crowds (Furness, 180–87). At the same time Tillich was beginning to establish himself in the United States, Toller became a powerful "symbol of German opposition in exile" (Dove, 212).[9]

---

[9]Isherwood records his impressions of Toller and Toller's reputation in the essay "The Head of a Leader" (*Exhumations*, 125–32). Another of Auden's closest friends, Stephen Spender, translated Toller's *Pastor Hall* in 1938, though rather reluctantly and not very successfully (Dove, 248, 263). Later that year, when Isherwood agreed to help Toller by contacting President Roosevelt to request his support for the Spanish Relief Plan, Auden and Spender were among those who signed his telegram (Dove, 256). Considering the poems of the late 1930s, Anthony Hecht notes that Auden "had a very alert sense of what 'exile' meant," as shown not only in the Toller Elegy but also in "Refugee Blues and "Roman Wall Blues" (136). Taking a longer view of Auden's career, Hecht also observes that he "was not only himself largely an exile, and often lonely, but he knew and celebrated a good number of others (like Freud, Toller, Hannah Arendt,

Auden met Toller briefly in 1936 when he and Isherwood were living in Portugal and writing *The Ascent of F6*. Seventeen years later, Isherwood remembered Toller talking through dinner like a general "entertaining his troops" and "building up their morale on the night before a desperate battle" (*Exhumations*, 127). The younger writers listened, mostly, with a reverence that might seem excessive in retrospect, but was probably genuine enough at the time:

> [T]hroughout supper it was he who did most of the talking—and I was glad, like the others, merely to sit and listen; to follow with amused, willing admiration, his every gesture and word. He was all that I had hoped for—more brilliant, more convincing than his books, more daring than his most epic deeds. It was easy enough to see him on that cinema platform, years ago, when he told the workers: "You must occupy the factories. You must resist." I could picture him at the magnificent moment of defeat, crying out to his judges: "You can silence me. You can never silence history." I watched him pace his cell, five years long, in the mountain fortress, aloof and dangerous as the untamed tiger. (125–26)

It was probably at this same meeting that Auden agreed to translate songs from Toller's play, *Nie Wieder Friede!*, which was performed in English as *No More Peace!* a month later at London's Gate Theatre. For better and for worse, this play has many similarities—in subject, tone, plot, and formal experimentation—with Auden's dramatic work of the mid-1930s, especially *The Ascent of F6*. Toller's title mocks the familiar slogan, "No More War," of the pacifist movement, which Toller had endorsed in his youth but had later come to view as inadequate in the face of fascist expansion. Three years later, reading Niebuhr and considering his return to Christianity, Auden would employ a nearly identical logic in his own rejection of pacifism.

Toller's later lyric drama shares a leftist stance and stylized irreverence with much of the literature, "high" and "low," that had shaped Auden's thinking about poetry since the late 1920s, when he first visited Berlin after graduating from Oxford. Like Brecht's drama, popular German cabaret songs, Erika Mann's musical satires, Edward Upward and Christopher Isherwood's Mortmere stories, and Isherwood's early fiction, Toller's later work satirizes

---

Isaiah Berlin, Elizabeth Drew, Igor Stravinsky, Neil Little, Teckla Clark, and Joseph Brodsky) who also were displaced persons (356).

bourgeois complacency and political oppression in a manner that is often manic, sometimes brilliant, and occasionally merely adolescent. For instance, *No More Peace!* alternates scenes between two settings: Olympus, where St. Francis wagers with Napoleon that men desire peace on earth; and Dunkelstein, a country where a barber named Cain has become a fascist dictator, thanks to the efforts of a rich industrialist. War breaks out, of course, thanks mostly to the industrialists who see it as a good business opportunity. When Auden "adapted" the songs from *No More Peace!* for the English translation, he dealt loosely with Toller's text, applying his own light verse style and some of his familiar preoccupations:

> Spies in the bedroom, spies on the roof,
> Spies in the bathroom, we've got proof. (73)[10]

Poetically, Auden was momentarily backsliding: as early as his 1935 birthday poem to Isherwood, he had looked back, critically, on an earlier period in which "Our hopes were still set on the spies career" (*English Auden*, 156). As the Toller translations suggest, Auden could still feel a deep nostalgia for those earlier days, only now he was more inclined to mourn the youthful spirit of wild innovation he associated with German culture and Berlin.

When Toller visited Republican Spain in 1938, his status in Auden's circles could only have risen further. Toller witnessed the fascist air-raids, addressed the International Brigades, and took up the cause of a civilian population that was slowly starving as a result of blockades, bombings, and the influx of refugees into areas under Republican control (Dove, 250–52). After moving to New York later that year, Toller spent the last few months of his life organizing and seeking support for a Spanish Relief Plan intended to provide food to civilians on both sides of the lines.

Though Toller's compassion and personal commitment were truly impressive—very near the end of his life, he would still confide to friends, "I can never forget the faces of those starving Spanish children" (quoted in Dove, 253)—many of those who knew him best also considered him difficult and egocentric. In more recent terminology, he was pretty clearly manic-depressive, and after his move to New York he slid into a deeply depressive phase, tormented by an unrelenting insomnia.

---

[10]Auden's lyrics received more favorable reviews than the play itself, which was not published in its original German during Toller's lifetime (Dove, 227, 294).

Nonetheless, it was not hard for a writer like Auden to see Toller as a victim of political and historical circumstances. His campaign against European fascism had been hindered by the climate of appeasement in England and the United States; the Popular Front, which he had long supported, remained disorganized and ineffective to the end; his hopes for socialism in the Soviet Union had been irreparably disillusioned by the Moscow show trials; and, perhaps most painful of all, the Spanish Republic soon fell, ending his last hopes for his relief project (Dove, 263–64). At the same time, since he could write only in German, Toller had to face, like many other émigré writers, the loss of his once adoring audience, and having spent his money on his efforts for Spain, he was now unable to support himself.

Suddenly Toller seemed to have outlived his time and place. When he visited for the last time at Toller's New York apartment, Isherwood suggested that he write a novel about the city. "No," Toller replied, "I should never write about this country. I have come here too late" (Isherwood, *Exhumations*, 132). In May of 1939, as Auden was beginning "The Prolific and the Devourer," Toller hanged himself.

Soon after Toller's death, Auden's "father-in-law," Thomas Mann, was among those who referred to Toller as a symbol of the resistance to Hitler—and more generally as a martyr to the destructive forces of modernity (Prater, 297). Auden knew Toller just well enough, personally and professionally, to see in the story of this anti-fascist exile certain features of his own earlier career that, under different circumstances, might have led him to a similar tragedy; equally important for his poetry, he also found in Toller a figure of the collective life of his generation of European writers. As the "low dishonest decade" of the 1930s came to an end—to borrow a phrase from the better-known poem he would write a few months later on the occasion of England's entry into the war— Auden saw in Toller's suicide much of the artistic and ideological foundation of his own past now brought to destruction, somehow persuaded to destroy itself, as he stood idly by in the nervous new world, trying to find a way to rebuild his own life and beliefs.

Largely because Auden was now inclined toward this tragic sense of history, the elegiac mode came easily to him. On a personal level, "In Memory of Ernst Toller" is a lament, in the face of the "European crisis," for the conception of the engaged intellectual life Auden had famously tried to cultivate in the early and mid-1930s—a conception which, ironically, Toller came to represent just as Auden was preparing to abandon it. In this particular sense, "In Memory of Ernst Toller" is a precursor to Prospero's farewell to Ariel in *The Sea and the Mirror*, another of Auden's elegies to his own poetic past and another of his greatest poems. "In Memory of Ernst Toller" should also be considered as part of the series of elegies—including those for W.B. Yeats, Sigmund Freud, and Henry James—that Auden wrote, on and off, through this transitional period of his career. Viewed collectively, these poems address his current condition through what he would call, decades later in "Thanksgiving for a Habitat," "the companionship of our good dead" (*Collected Poems*, 694). Together, they constitute one of Auden's most remarkable accomplishments: a transformation of a conventional elegiac tension—between the private experience of loss and the public expression of mourning—into a moving commentary on the social condition of the creative intellectual in a world that seems increasingly dependent on collective thought and raw political power.

"In Memory of Ernst Toller" is also a crucial poem in the development of Auden's career, because in it he tries to confront the demonic at a point in his life when he is nearly ready to commit himself to Christian faith and practice. The elegy begins as an effort to find a voice that can express emotions of grief, ask for forgiveness, and still demand the kind of public moral judgment for which Toller had come to be known. As such, the poem is a moving testimony not so much to Toller's life as to Auden's belief that his culture is in need of a richly symbolic, even ritualistic, poetic language:

> The shining neutral summer has no voice
> To judge America, or ask how a man dies;
> And the friends who are sad and the enemies who rejoice
>
> Are chased by their shadows lightly away from the grave
> Of one who was egotistical and brave,
> Lest they should learn without suffering how to forgive.
> (*Collected Poems*, 249)

Five months after his move to America, Auden still imagines his "New World" as an atmosphere of undeniable, almost oppressive brilliance. Yet it has no voice of judgment. The bright light of America's possibilities—its "shining neutral summer"—is not enough to banish the "shadows" surrounding the grave of the wounded and self-destructive exile.

Again, Auden looks back, briefly, to some of the preoccupations of his earlier career. Not long ago, he would have found the forces that drove Toller to suicide in a repressed childhood memory or an oppressive social order. In this poem, he still recognizes that such forces take their toll on human lives, but he assigns them a secondary role. The audacious self-assurance that had characterized his earliest poetry gives way to a tone that is genuinely searching:

> What was it, Ernst, that your shadow unwittingly said?
> Did the small child see something horrid in the woodshed
> Long ago? Or had the Europe which took refuge in your head
>
> Already been too injured to get well?

By turning some of the most fundamental assertions of his earlier system of thought into a series of questions, Auden suggests that his familiar approaches will no longer suffice—not even his famous fusion of Marx and Freud, with its conflation of psychological repression and political oppression, with its amplification of psychosomatic illness into a cultural death wish. The ideas most responsible for giving his earlier poems their characteristic and disturbing "modernity" now seem inadequate to combat the forces that have driven Toller to his destruction.

At the same time, Auden has abandoned the "clinical detachment" so often praised by his early critics—or as he himself had recently put it, "the surgeon's idea of pain." He has arrived at a more reverent sensibility:

> Dear Ernst, lie shadowless at last among
> The other war-horses who existed till they'd done
> Something that was an example to the young.
>
> We are lived by powers we pretend to understand:
> They arrange our loves; it is they who direct at the end
> The enemy bullet, the sickness, or even our hand.
>
> It is their to-morrow hangs over the earth of the living
> And all we wish for our friends: but existence is believing
> We know for whom we mourn and who is grieving.

Auden no longer even imagines that he might reasonably view a man like Toller merely as a psychological case study or as a product of historical circumstances. Existence itself—not just artistic production or political action but the very act of being in the world—depends upon belief.

The poem's most striking feature is the passive construction of the penultimate sentence: "We are lived by powers." Later that year, Auden would repeat this formulation, and elaborate on it, in a review of Walter de la Mare's *Behold the Dreamer*. In doing so, he would indicate the sources of the Toller elegy in Tillich's conception of the demonic:

> We are confronted today by the spectacle, not of a utilitarian rationalism that dismisses all that cannot be expressed in prose and statistics as childish stuff, but rather by an ecstatic and morbid abdication of the free-willing and individual before the collective and daemonic. We have become obscene night worshippers who, having discovered that we cannot live exactly as we will, deny the possibility of willing anything and are content masochistically *to be lived*, a betrayal that betrays not only us but our daemon itself. ("Jacob and the Angel," 292)

In this essay, Auden proposes an alternative to the kind of passive suffering that overcame Toller at the end of his life. The alternative is not an escape from suffering. Rather, it is an acceptance, by conscious choice, of a kind of suffering that is more personal and more meaningful: "After a labyrinth of false moves and losses, you come at last to the place that you know is for you, unfortunately—the place you must learn to suffer" (292).

Here is the answer that Auden anticipated at the start of "In Memory of Ernst Toller," when he called upon Toller's memory, lest the shadows gathered around Toller's grave "should learn without suffering how to forgive." In one of his essays on Kierkegaard, Auden would propose the same answer to the twin temptations of "demonic defiance" and "demonic despair":

> For, while ultimately the Christian message is the good news: "Glory to God in the highest and on earth peace, good-will towards men—" "Come unto me all that travail and are heavy laden and I will refresh you"; it is proximately to man's self-love the worst possible news—"Take up thy cross and follow me." (*Forewords and Afterwords*, 169)

This acceptance of suffering only makes sense if one believes that one's suffering is an inescapable consequence of bearing the cross—that is, as Auden suggests with the final line break of "In Memory of Ernst Toller," that "existence is believing." Even though the language of "In Memory of Ernst Toller" is never specifically religious, the poem concludes with a powerful statement of one of the central concerns of Auden's later career: his growing need for a community of faith—the "we" of the poem's closing lines—to confront the demonic forces, the "powers we pretend to understand," that will live our lives if we let them.

"In Memory of Ernst Toller" is one of the greatest of Auden's poems that no one seems to read. Like Auden's other great elegies of this period—and like several of his other poems of the period, including "Voltaire at Ferney," "Rimbaud," and "Pascal"—it considers the figure of the intellectual struggling to articulate a system of belief commensurate to the horrors—as Tillich would say, the "demonry"—of the twentieth century. To put it another way, these poems are a response to the problem posed by Auden's "New Year Letter," his conscious farewell to the "low dishonest decade" of the 1930s:

> Twelve months ago in Brussels, I
> Heard the same wishful-thinking sigh
> As round me, trembling on their beds,
> Or taut with apprehensive dreads,
> The sleepless ghosts of Europe lay
> Wishing the centuries away,
> And the low mutter of their vows
> Went echoing through her haunted house,
> As on the verge of happening
> There crouched the presence of The Thing.[11] (199)

Throughout his early years in America, Auden's poetry would consider this "presence" in one complex manifestation after another. Tillich's concept of the demonic informs Caliban's speech in *The Sea and the Mirror*, in which primitive energy and anarchic impulse are nearly—but not quite—concealed by the refined prose of Henry James. The same concept influences the narrative movement of *The Age of Anxiety*—the poem Tillich cited as the perfect expression of the modern condition—in which the familiar social gestures of men and women who meet in a New York bar give way, in the course of a night, to deep associations, psychological

---

[11]*Editor's Note:* Here Auden says "The Thing" to refer to the indefinable God. See the earlier essay on Gerald Heard where he refers in a similar manner to "This Thing" for the same purpose. Heard persuaded Auden in the early 1930s that "This Thing" was the true purpose of man's evolving consciousness. See Izzo's *Christopher Isherwood, His Era, His Gang, and the Legacy of the Truly Strong Man* for an explication of Auden's search for "This Thing" even in his earliest poems and throughout the 1930s. See also Mendelson's *Later Auden* for more on Heard's influence.

projections, and inarticulate fears. And in another very different setting, in the most powerful of Auden's later lyric poems, "The Shield of Achilles," the goddess Thetis comes to realize, when she takes her son to the underworld to receive a new shield from Hephaestos, that the "Iron-hearted man-slaying Achilles" is no more noble than a "ragged urchin," wandering about a vacant lot, throwing stones at birds:[12]

> That girls are raped, that two boys knife a third,
> Were axioms to him, who'd never heard
> Of any world where promises are kept,
> Or one could weep because another wept.
>   (*Collected Poems*, 598)

The poem's elegant interplay of ballad and rime royale stanzas, and its narrative "frame" of classical myth, eventually reveal a "modern condition" of extreme brutality and discompassion. Again and again, in its most compelling expressions, Auden's Christian poetics depends upon this particular theological understanding of humanity: whatever seems most cultivated, or most civilized, or most courageous, is likely to mask the demonic as these are all expressions of willfulness.

So it is just about inevitable that Auden's fullest and most effective depiction of the demonic is found in his most explicitly Christian poem—and in the guise of a cultivated, thoroughly modern man. When he finally appears near the end of *For the Time Being*, Herod is a model civic administrator. He presides over the Rational City where there is no visible sign of disorder, no crime. The coastal highway "goes straight up over the mountains" (391). The price of soft drinks and sandwiches is reasonable. After twenty years of work, he can boast that there are children in his province "who have never seen a louse, shopkeepers who have never handled a counterfeit coin, women of forty who have never hidden in a ditch except for fun" (391). Now, he can look down condescendingly at those who live in the outlying regions, where many still believe in witches and a good bookstore still cannot turn a decent profit. Considering all he has accomplished, he tells him-

---

[12]*Editor's Note:* Achilles is, in fact, an ego-absorbed Truly Weak Man, a figure developed in the late 1920s by Isherwood and Auden and a precursor to the image of Tillich's demonic man. The Truly Weak Man's opposite is the ego-less Truly Strong Man who only aspires to abnegate his will and merge into the collective good of Heard's evolving consciousness.

elf that, perhaps, after all, "nothing could be more innocent than he birth of an artisan's son" (391).

Still, there is something about this particular child that makes him anxious. After all, despite his efforts, Herod must admit that he Empire is only "a tiny patch of light compared with those immense areas of barbaric night that surround it on all sides"— where superstition reigns, "where the best cuts of meat are preserved for the dead" (391). And even within "the little civilized patch" he has cultivated with such devotion, there arises a "wild prayer of longing" against which even the most carefully calculated legislation remains helpless. On this level, which he does not understand, the anonymous Kierkegaardian Public simply refuses to be reasonable. He knows that the time has come when he can no longer rely on the "Poetic Compromise," all the "lovely fairy tales in which Zeus, disguising himself as a swan or a bull or a shower of rain or what-have-you, lay with some beautiful woman and begot a hero" (392). The Public senses that, behind such myths of origins, there must be a "real human excellence that is a reproach to its own baseness" (392). If he is not careful, Herod fears, this peculiar need to worship "will be driven into totally unsocial channels where no education can reach it" (393). Beneath his appearance of self-assurance, he suspects that the Rational Law, which has had such a difficult time of it all along, might prove to be helpless when confronted with Prophecy and Revelation. So, with impeccable logic, he orders the massacre of the innocents.

Of course, Herod claims he has no choice. For all his faith in progress, he understands, as Tillich would, that "the appearance of the New Being overcomes the ultimate power of the demonic structures of destruction'" (Tillich, *Systematic Theology*, III 173). But Herod does not realize that he has drawn his power from the same surrender of humanity that led Toller to his destruction— what Auden called, elsewhere, the "abdication of the free-willing and individual before the collective and daemonic." Just as much as the suicidal playwright, Herod is being lived by demonic powers; but rather than succumbing to "demonic despair," he chooses to act out of "demonic defiance."

For Auden's part, by the time he wrote *For the Time Being*, he had come to understand his vocation as a poet much as Tillich had imagined the social role of the creative artist: to counteract Toller's "demonic despair" and Herod's "demonic defiance." That was why, for Auden, to become a Christian poet was not to abandon social responsibility, and it was not to surrender to forces beyond his control. Rather, to become a Christian poet was to perform an essential act designed to protect the creative mind and the innocent life from the demonic forces that seemed to dominate his troubled historical moment. His "conversion" was an effort to resist the forces that he—and Tillich, and Toller, and so many in the community of exiles he discovered in the "nervous New World"— found trying to live every life.

Works Cited

Adams, James Luther. *Paul Tillich's Philosophy of Culture, Science, and Religion.* New York: Harper & Row, 1965.

———. "Introduction." In Adams, Pauck, and Shinn. 1–29.

———, Wilhelm Pauck, and Roger Lincoln Shinn, eds. *The Thought of Paul Tillich.* San Francisco: Harper & Row, 1985.

Auden, W.H. *Collected Poems.* Edited by Edward Mendelson. New York: Random House, 1976.

———. *The English Auden.* Edited by Edward Mendelson. New York, Random House, 1977.

———. *Forewords and Afterwords.* Edited by Edward Mendelson. New York: Random House, 1973.

———. "Jacob and the Angel." *New Republic* 101 (December 27, 1939): 292.

———. "The Prolific and the Devourer." *Anteus* 41 (1981): 4–65.

———. "W.H. Auden." *Modern Canterbury Pilgrims.* Edited by James A. Pike. London: A.R. Mowbray, 1956. 7–43.

Callan, Edward. *Auden: A Carnival of Intellect.* New York: Oxford UP, 1983.

Carpenter, Humphrey. *Auden: A Biography.* Boston: Houghton Mifflin, 1981.

Coffin, Henry Sloane. *A Half Century of Union Theological Seminary.* New York: Scribner, 1954.

Conniff, Brian. "Auden, Niebuhr, and the Vocation of Poetry." *Religion and Literature* 25.3 (Autumn 1993): 45–65.

———. "What Really Became of Wystan? Auden, Niebuhr, and *For the Time Being. Christianity and Literature* 44.2 (Winter 1995): 133–44.

Davenport-Hines, Richard. *Auden.* New York: Pantheon, 1995.

Dove, Richard. *He Was a German: A Biography of Ernst Toller.* London: Libris, 1990.

Eliot, T.S. "*Ulysses*, Order, and Myth." In *Selected Prose of T.S. Eliot*. Edited by Frank Kermode. New York: Harcourt Brace Jovanovich, 1975. 175–78.

Fenton, James. "Introduction" to Thekla Clarke, *Wystan and Chester: A Personal Memoir of W.H. Auden and Chester Kallman*. New York: Columbia UP, 1995. ix–xii.

Ford, Hugh D. *A Poet's War: British Poets and the Spanish Civil War*. Philadelphia: U of Pennsylvania P, 1965.

Furness, N. A. "The Reception of Ernst Toller and His Works in Britain." In *Expressionism in Focus: Proceedings of the First UNE Symposium on German Studies*, edited by Richard Sheppard. Blagowrie, Scotland: Lochee, 1987. 173–97.

Hecht, Anthony. *The Hidden Law: The Poetry of W.H. Auden*. Cambridge, MA: Harvard UP, 1993.

Hynes, Samuel. *The Auden Generation: Literature and Politics in England in the 1930's*. New York: Viking, 1977.

Isherwood, Christopher. *Christopher and His Kind, 1929–1939*. New York: Avon, 1977.

———. *Exhumations: Stories, Articles, Verses*. London: Methuen, 1984.

Jenkins, Nicholas. "Introduction" to W.H. Auden's "Vocation and Society." In *"In Solitude for Company": W.H. Auden after 1940*, edited by Katerine Bucknell and Nicholas Jenkins. Oxford: Oxford UP, 1995. 1–14.

Mendelson, Edward. *Early Auden*. New York: Viking, 1981.

———. *Later Auden*. New York: Farrar, Straus and Giroux, 1999.

Niebuhr, Ursula. "Memories of the 1940's." In Spender, 104–18.

Pauck, Wilhelm, and Marion Pauck. *Paul Tillich, His Life and Thought*. San Francisco: Harper & Row, 1989.

Prater, Donald. *Thomas Mann: A Life*. New York: Oxford UP, 1995.

Ringer, Fritz K. *The Decline of the German Mandarins: The German Academic Community, 1890–1933*. Cambridge, MA: Harvard UP, 1972.

Shinn, Roger. "Tillich as Interpreter and Disturber of Contemporary Civilization." In Adams, Pauck, and Shinn. 44–62.

Spender, Stephen, ed. *W.H. Auden: A Tribute*. New York: Macmillan, 1975.

Stern, James. "The Indispensable Presence." In Spender, 123–27.

Tillich, Paul. "Existentialist Aspects of Modern Art." In *Christianity and the Existentialists*, edited by Carl Michalson. New York: Scribner, 1956. 128–47.

———. *The Interpretation of History*. Translated by N.A. Rasetzki and Elsa L. Talmey. New York: Scribner, 1936.

———. *The Protestant Era*. Translated by James Luther Adams. Chicago: U of Chicago P, 1948.

———. *The Socialist Decision*. 1933. Translated by Franklin Sherman. New York: Harper & Row, 1977.

———. *Systematic Theology*. Chicago: U of Chicago P, 1967.

Toller, Ernst. *No More Peace! A Thoughtful Comedy*. Translated by Edward Crankshaw. Lyrics adapted by W.H. Auden. London: Merrill, 1937.

Warren, Heather. *Theologians of a New World Order: Reinhold Niebuhr and the Christian Realists*. New York: Oxford UP, 1997.

"Spiritual Sunburn": Dramatic Journeys from the Auden-Isherwood Plays to *A Meeting by the River*

James Fisher

James Fisher is a theater scholar and has written before on gay drama-tists, particularly Tony Kushner. This essay establishes the basic themes of Auden and Isherwood in dramatic collaboration and then considers this influence on the writing of the Isherwood-Don Bachardy play, A Meeting by the River. *Fisher saw the play in 1972 and here gives, with an assist from an interview with Bachardy, perhaps, the fullest explica-tion of its transition from the Isherwood-Auden plays to its version as a novel in 1967, and its transformation to a drama and even screenplay in 1972 and after.*

> "What unites us is the one and only thing that matters."
> (Isherwood, *A Meeting by the River*, 120)

A Meeting by the River, Christopher Isherwood's final novel, is a quest saga about two brothers in search of fulfillment found, fi-nally, in visions of natural and symbolic brotherhood. Shortly after the publication of the novel, Isherwood, along with his longtime partner Don Bachardy, adapted this tale of two brothers into a play. Logically proceeding from the three plays Isherwood co-wrote with W.H. Auden in the mid-1930s, the play *A Meeting by the River* provides interesting parallels in the recurring themes of both writers, as well as the progression of Isherwood's conception of a modern hero, The Truly Weak Man, who aspires, but does not always succeed, to be Truly Strong. The process of artistic collabo-ration between two men, seen first in the Auden-Isherwood plays and later in Isherwood's collaboration with Bachardy, is mirrored in the connections between the men prominent in the works themselves. Tied to each other in various ways—by bloodlines, work, artistic collaboration, and sexuality—the complex intersections of the male characters, as well as those of their collaborating authors, is illuminating. All present a broadly conceived definition of brotherhood shown in various guises along difficult personal journeys toward spiritual fulfillment.

In the case of *A Meeting by the River*, this journey is made by two British brothers, Patrick and Oliver. Oliver abandons his work with the Red Cross to become the disciple of an aging Hindu Swami residing in Munich. When the Swami, who profoundly influences Oliver, dies, Oliver believes the old man has chosen his exact moment of departure. Moved by this, Oliver travels to India to spread the Swami's ashes in the Ganges and stays on to continue studying Hindu precepts and, eventually, to take *sannyas* (final monastic vows). Patrick, traveling to Thailand on business, detours to India to persuade Oliver to abandon his plans. Despite the fact that he has a wife (Penelope) and two daughters, Patrick has recently embarked on a homosexual relationship with a young man named Tom. The situation is further complicated by Oliver's feelings for Penelope and the intrusions of Mother, a formidable presence who shares concerns about her sons' well-being. Manipulating Oliver in both subtle and obvious ways, Patrick attempts to shake his commitment to becoming a Swami. He only succeeds briefly when he compels Oliver to recognize that within him is a powerful will and ambition counter to his Hindu beliefs, aspects of his persona that presumably must die as Oliver is reborn as a Swami. Temporarily thrown by Patrick's assault, Oliver has a startling revelation while seated on his Hindu mentor's favorite bench; his resolve is restored and he takes his vows as Patrick decides to break off his relationship with Tom and return to his wife. With some humor about their individual dilemmas, the brothers move to a greater awareness of their connections and differences.

Both brothers fall comfortably within the range of Isherwood's Truly Weak Man, a recurrent figure in Isherwood's œuvre evolving from the central characters in his collaboration with Auden. The Truly Weak Man "is doomed always to fail or to elude The Test, even when he appears to have succeeded" (Summers, 45), and is coupled with The Evil Mother, a "domineering mother, a Freudian carnivore who destroys her child by arresting his maturity" (Summers, 45). Embryonic versions of these character types appear in Isherwood's earliest novels, *All the Conspirators* (1928) and *The Memorial* (1932), but evolved further through his collaboration with Auden. By *A Meeting by the River*, the Truly Weak Man, as exemplified in different ways by both Oliver, a creature of the spirit, and Patrick, a confirmed hedonist, had become stronger through a spiritual journey. Also, The Evil Mother had been defanged—no less potentially malignant in her way, she becomes *in A Meeting by the River* more comic, sad, and ineffective at damaging her son(s) beyond their initial development. The son(s) have largely grown past their Mother's hold, with only the remnants of her dominance fading with each passing year. Perhaps, Isherwood seems to suggest, The Evil Mother can only be vanquished by the separation of years, continents, and by plunging into another culture, a new spirituality, and as complete a cutting loose from the past as is possible.

The influence of Auden on Isherwood's later writing is important as it demonstrates a striving toward perfecting recurring themes and characters. As a charter member of the Auden generation of writers—a group of "angry young men" of the 1930s including Stephen Spender, Cecil Day-Lewis, and Louis MacNeice—Isherwood found himself part of a well-educated, politically inspired group of British writers who, in various and individual styles and genres, gave voice to their generation's feelings of betrayal and disillusionment. Whether a result of the carnage of World War I and the decline of the pre-war class system, or their rejection of the social and familial mores of the world in which they were raised, these writers altered the course of mid-twentieth-century literature and art. Sharing these literary, social, and cultural roots, Auden and Isherwood embarked on a journey of literary and personal brotherhood beginning in boyhood at St. Edmunds School in Surrey and continuing through a brief sexual relationship and on to one of literary peers. The quality of their dramatic collaborations (as well as their volume of reportage on the Chinese-Japanese War in the late 1930s) does not obscure the fact that Auden and Isherwood were far too singular as artists to work together effectively for very long. Wise enough not to collaborate in areas of one or the other's specialties, they found within the realm of drama, in which both were essentially beginners, a forum for experimentation with neither emerging as a too-dominant force.

Auden and Isherwood were drawn to the theatre with the zeal of reformers of what they viewed as an exhausted medium. Firmly rejecting the popular commercial stage as well as the prevalent style and techniques of modern realistic drama, they looked instead toward inventing a lyrical, satiric dramatic style owing to Bertolt Brecht and Kurt Weill, but much more to their own original experimentation. By the time they began to collaborate in earnest, Auden had already written about the possibility of a modern English poetic drama and worked to produce theatre in that vein while teaching at the Downs School. What truly connects Auden and Isherwood is their conception of the moral conundrums of the modern world—an increasingly technological society that invites a moral corruption resisted, with various degrees of success, by central characters who are humane rebels battling against this corruption and the outmoded and hypocritical values of the immediate past.

The Auden-Isherwood plays, which include their first, *The Enemies of a Bishop or Die When I Say* (1929), a morality drama in four acts, inspired Auden to write a "dramatic and psychological manifesto," revised by Isherwood, which seems to have been planned as a preface for the play. This manifesto proposes that "Dramatic action is ritual" while stressing the importance of realistic art, which is something that "has happened to myself" (Auden, 459). Other ideas include the notion that "Dramatic plot is the assertion that God could not exist without Satan" and that characters "are always abstractions" (Auden, 459); these concepts are central to the Auden-Isherwood plays and the Isherwood-Bachardy adaptation of *A Meeting by the River*. There are also connections in theme and character—the central male figures are often extensions of the personalities of Auden and Isherwood themselves and exemplars of Isherwood's Truly Weak Man. In *A Meeting by the River*, Isherwood draws on these prototypical characters, making the two brothers seem, at times, to be two sides of the same persona.

A brief examination of the three major Auden-Isherwood plays is valuable in illuminating aspects of *A Meeting by the River*. From 1932 until its disbanding in 1939 (the same year Auden and Isherwood departed London to report on the Chinese-Japanese War), Auden and Isherwood were involved with the Group Theatre, a leftist propagandist theatre troupe for whom Auden was a factor articulating its founding concepts. He also supplied plays, among these, *The Dance of Death*, as well as other solo efforts including *Paid on Both Sides* (1928), *The Chase* (1934), several documentary films, a cabaret entertainment (*Alfred* [1936]), and a radio play (*Hadrian's Wall* [1937]).

Most scholars and critics regard the 1935 Auden-Isherwood play, *The Dog Beneath the Skin or Where Is Francis?*, as their outstanding stage collaboration. Auden hoped for powerful results, feeling that "a realistic writer like Christopher and a parabolic writer life myself" (cited in Davenport-Hines, 137) could produce challenging new works.

Jonathan Fryer describes the collaboration of Auden and Isherwood as "the occasion for much ribald banter, criticism and insult. Yet they worked extremely fast, both of them having a considerable facility with words" (Fryer, 149). For *The Dog Beneath the Skin*, Auden led the way and did much of the writing—in fact, Auden's publishers wished not to credit Isherwood at all, although Auden insisted despite the fact that Isherwood himself felt he had contributed comparatively little. Scholars have fully explored the Auden-Isherwood collaboration, and the complexities of their personal relationship, but not always in complete agreement. What emerges is that despite the fact that Auden was three years younger than Isherwood, he was his literary and artistic mentor in ways that mirror Isherwood's later mentoring of Don Bachardy, his collaborator on the stage adaptation of *A Meeting by the River*.

The nature of the Auden-Isherwood collaboration has been described in many different ways, but never more succinctly than by Isherwood himself. As he recalled, "I have always thought of myself as a librettist to some extent with a composer, his verse being the music; and I would say, 'Now we have to have a big speech here', you know, and he would write it" (Poss, 51). In his own works, Auden explores the textures of human experience, and this binds him to Isherwood who similarly pursues the same goal with different tools. After World War II, Isherwood's writing becomes less overtly lyrical as he reaches beyond Auden's influence to discover a pared-down, sparse lucidity matching the smaller and more personal probings of his work and his incisive skill at character revelation.

Most critics seem to believe that the Auden-Isherwood plays only partly succeed. More experimental than assured dramaturgy, these works are more interesting in the context of their solo efforts. Joseph Warren Beach asserts that "Isherwood was evidently more interested in the satirical and comic modes of propagandist drama, whereas Auden wished to emphasize the moral and affirmative elements in their social faith" (Beach, 167). while John Fuller finds *The Dog Beneath the Skin* "a happy balance between suggestive symbolism and myth, and direct caricature and propaganda; between doggerel, knockabout and pastiche, and some of Auden's finest lyrical and analytic poetry" (cited in Bahlke, 54). Mirko Jurak notes that in these politico-poetic dramas, "Auden and Isherwood have difficulty in moving from the abstractness of their didacticism to the need for action on the part of the spectators" (Jurak, 345), a difficulty Isherwood continued to grapple with in the depiction of The Truly Weak Man.

Auden and Isherwood depended to a great extent on their desire to break free from the conventions of early twentieth-century British drama. *The Dog Beneath the Skin* is, on first glance, a satiric rejection of the pretenses of early twentieth-century upper-class British values and the society's illusions about its predominance in world affairs, but it is more than mere satire. The play's protagonist, Alan Norman, "moves through a disturbing and oppressive dream-world which represents the nightmare into which the society is lapsing" (Jurak, 345), but he does not simply reject a set of values—he is neither a reformer nor a moralist in any traditional sense. He is, instead, striving to cut loose from any bounds or known values. The play has surrealist qualities, a looseness of structure and freedom from the unities that matches the striving of Alan to break free from social constraints—as such, its structure is an especially effective mode of depicting the moral abstractions Auden and Isherwood wish to explore.

The Dog Beneath the Skin surrealistically deals with Alan and a dog (within whom a lost baronet is concealed) embarking on a journey through the modern world, which they come to see as a corrupted system which permits humanity to avoid facing harsh realities and truths—or taking action to correct social problems. The corrupt idols of the mid-twentieth century world are attacked by Auden and Isherwood in scenes depicting fascist dictators, the press, scientists, and wealthy businessmen, as well as scenes mocking human modes of escape, including everything from art and religious faith to sex.

The Dog Beneath the Skin is very much a play of the 1930s, as Fryer notes, "urgent in its anti-fascism and aggressive in its overt suggestion that such things might also take place in England" (Fryer, 149). Calling its audience to take positions in opposition to the rise of fascism, the play suggests that Auden and Isherwood were collaborators with different goals. Auden engaged himself in "making propaganda," while Isherwood "was fascinated by the satirical and comic possibilities" (Fryer, 149) as well as the more personal struggles of Alan Norman. Decades later, in *A Meeting by the River*—and especially its stage version—Isherwood similarly uses satire to explore the spiritual strivings of his characters in juxtaposition with the remnants of early twentieth-century British society.

Stephen Spender considered that in *The Dog Beneath the Skin*, Auden and Isherwood's "preoccupation with the values and behavior of English upperclass education gives the play a juvenile air" (Spender, 16) which undermines the most valuable aspect of the play—an account of "the modern young hero [Alan] in search for his soul in the circumstances of an England putrescent with retired colonels, vicars, schoolmasters and politicians—all adding up to a smaller evil confronted by the much vaster one of Hitler" (Spender, 16). Norman Page is more appreciative of this first major Auden-Isherwood collaboration, stressing that their "rejection of traditional forms and modes, and the collaborative nature of their art," led them to create "pastiches of ballads, cabaret songs or graffiti drawn zestfully on popular sources in defiance of traditional hierarchies of the 'serious' and the 'light'" (Page, 83) inspired, in part, by Kurt Weill and Bertolt Brecht.

The effective blend of parable and didacticism in *The Dog Beneath the Skin*—and in the subsequent Auden-Isherwood plays—establishes Isherwood's intent to view all aspects of humanity and nature as profoundly and irrevocably connected. Alan Norman is, like Michael Ransom of Auden-Isherwood's *The Ascent of F6*, an even more fully drawn prototype of The Truly Weak Man. Applauding Ransom's first monologue as Auden's writing at its very best, Spender also found Ransom to have "the makings of a character in a real play. Modelled on T.E. Lawrence, he is divided between conscience-stricken, cruelly self-critical self-abnegation and the passion to act and be a leader" (Spender, 16), and these are tensions that, in their individual ways, Patrick, and especially Oliver, struggle with in *A Meeting by the River*.

How much Isherwood contributed to the most shattering central conceit of *The Ascent of F6* is not clear, but when Ransom, described by Richard Davenport-Hines as a Peer Gynt figure, reaches the top of F6 (a previously unscaled mountain peak), he has a vision of his oppressive mother and dies. Spender condemns Auden and Isherwood for using this "most stifling piece of psychological machinery ... the mother fixation" (Spender, 16), but, in fact, such figures as The Evil Mother—and all she represents—are critical to understanding the joint and individual work of Auden and Isherwood. In exorcising their own mothers and the social values inscribed in them, they find the source of their art. Isherwood would continue to grapple with maternal images in other writings—whether in overtly autobiographical works or fiction, including *A Meeting by the River*. As Francis King sees it, under the spur of "his domineering mother's ambition for him, and his guilty feeling that he could never win her wholehearted approbation" (King, 11), Isherwood continued to attempt to reinvent her until she becomes, as in *A Meeting by the River*, a harmless and sadly comic bastion of dead proprieties. The Truly Weak Man is also critical here; in his collaborations with Auden, and in his own early novels, Isherwood created heroes in Sisyphian battles against the outmoded social and political constraints of their time while also striving for a spiritual fulfillment they may never achieve. By *A Meeting by the River*, the struggle had become less Sisyphian. The political and social elements fade to some extent (glimpsed only in Patrick's hedonistic bent, in Mother's emptily cozy world of vicars and kitty cats, and in Penelope's marital proprieties), while the struggle becomes more intimately personal for its two heroes. There are no more mountains to climb; each character must conquer the demons in his own heart.

This particular variation of The Truly Weak Man is found in Isherwood's least successful late novel, *The World in the Evening* (1954), a coming-of-age story of a mature man in a struggle against values that have shaped him (and that he has accepted without question). Stephen Monk is a true modern hero not unlike Larry Darrell, the central character of Somerset Maugham's *The Razor's Edge* (Maugham is thought to have used aspects of Isherwood's persona for the character, although Isherwood himself denied it[1]), who, having returned from World War I, is not satisfied to return to the conventional expectations of the life he lived before the war. He embarks on a spiritual quest which may or may not ever pro-

---

[1]*Editor's note:* Isherwood denied being Maugham's Larry Darrell in *The Razor's Edge* because, in fact, Darrell was truly based on their mutual friend and inspiration, Gerald Heard. (See the essays on Heard in this volume.) There is a letter from Maugham to Heard in the Heard Collection at UCLA that makes this very clear. Isherwood did, however, let Maugham see his diaries in which he had recorded lectures by Heard that are, in part, spoken by Darrell in the novel. Nonetheless, Isherwood was in total agreement with Heard—and Darrell—with the Vedantic beliefs they were both learning from Swami Prabhavananda at the Vedanta Society of Southern California.

vide him with the answers he seeks. Similarly bound to a spiritual odyssey that seems a precursor of achieving a sort of maturity that may be indistinguishable from sainthood, Stephen Monk in *World*, and to some degree Oliver in *A Meeting by the River*, seem to be in preparation for achieving sainthood—or at least a thorough acceptance of the outcome of their spiritual quests.

Despite Isherwood's close collaboration with Auden in the 1930s, King sees Maugham as Isherwood's closest literary ally, noting that "the style of both novelists is notable not for poetic grandeur, but for the more modest virtues of lucidity, simplicity and an almost conversational relaxation" (King, 23). The influence of Maugham becomes more evident in Isherwood's post-war central characters, or personas, as King calls them. In *A Meeting by the River*, elements of Isherwood's own personality are present in Oliver's spiritual search and in Patrick's rational and sensual reality.[2] Isherwood also began to evolve more fully as a literary ethicist, with a focus on the moral dilemmas of characters increasingly moved to challenge the strictures of traditional social norms.

The final Auden-Isherwood play, *On the Frontier* (1937–38), a melodrama in three acts about the conflict between a democracy and a totalitarian state, is "made up of political satire and a minor descant on Love, and is the dullest work which the collaboration produced" (Williams, 206), according to socialist critic Raymond Williams. The play continues to explore the drift from spiritual struggle to politics in the three Auden-Isherwood dramas. The totalitarian ruler was obviously inspired by Hitler—and the play's fictional countries represented war-torn Europe of the period—but Auden and Isherwood seem more interested, as Richard Davenport-Hines writes, in disinterring "the human experiences that had been buried under the debris of slogans and false description" (Davenport-Hines, 171).

Page writes of the importance of frontiers in the Auden-Isherwood collaboration, stressing that a "frontier is both a barrier, a restraint on freedom and movement, and an invitation or challenge to step across into a new world, and it seems likely that residence in Germany, where the frontiers drawn by the Versailles Treaty were still of passionate concern, added contemporary force to

---

[2]*Editor's note:* See a discussion of just how much Isherwood is both Oliver and Patrick in *Christopher Isherwood, His Era, His Gang, and the Legacy of the Truly Strong Man* (Izzo). Patrick and Oliver are versions of Isherwood as two halves of his own persona: saint and sinner.

what may have originated as a more personal metaphor" (Page, 181). Of this third and final dramatic collaboration, *On the Frontier*, Isherwood felt that "Auden was writing more than I, although it was still definitely a collaboration. The first play we wrote more or less by correspondence, sending each other pages. But on the second and third plays we worked together, in Portugal and elsewhere" (Scobie, "The Art of Fiction," 170). When critics and friends, including Virginia Woolf, were not approving of *On the Frontier*, Auden and Isherwood collaborated on no more plays and embarked on new frontiers together and separately.

Shortly after *Frontier's* initial performances, Auden and Isherwood departed for China, a remarkable trip that led to their "travel" book *Journey to a War*. (See Kerr in this volume.) Following their emigration to the United States, Auden and Isherwood increasingly went their separate ways. The Auden-Isherwood plays, Stephen Spender believed, "inadvertently throw a good deal of light on Auden's and Isherwood's reasons for becoming American citizens: impatience and disgust with the England of Baldwin and Ramsay MacDonald provides for the most effective satire in a volume whose final scene offers bitterly the toast "England, England, England" (Spender, 16), after which Auden "makes his intellectual way from liberal humanism to Kierkegaardian Christianity" (Wright, 64). (See Conniff in this volume.) Perhaps this was the obvious point for a professional parting of ways between Auden and Isherwood, as Auden's work became "more removed from ordinary sensuous existence" (Wright, 90).

Isherwood became increasingly engaged with issues of gay rights from the 1940s forward. When Auden and Isherwood became sexual partners in the mid-1920s, it was not an ultimately satisfactory experience. As Brian Finney writes, Isherwood "soon found Auden too much like himself to provide the sexual frisson which only his opposite in type could give him" (Finney, 64), but Finney credits Auden with helping Isherwood to "begin the long and difficult task of detaching himself from the deeply implanted beliefs of an older generation" (Finney, 34), and by becoming much more of an "out" gay man than Auden, Isherwood was certainly bluntly severing his connection to the social proprieties of his world. Auden and Isherwood's joint vision of literature and their homosexual inclinations certainly drew them together; both, in some ways, felt a freedom in their collaboration not always evident in their individual efforts, which, in many cases, are superior works of art. Auden brought Isherwood into contact with other lit-

erary forces, including Spender, with whom Auden and Isherwood lived in Berlin in the years of the collapse of the Weimar Republic and the rise of Hitler, a time that inspired Isherwood's most
celebrated works, particularly his *Berlin Stories*, made up of *The
Last of Mr. Norris* (1935), *Sally Bowles* (1937), and *Goodbye to Berlin*
(1939).

It is important to more fully address the issue of homosexuality, both in the personal relationship of Auden and Isherwood—
and, subsequently, Isherwood and Bachardy—but more significantly in the ways in which sexuality emerges in Isherwood's
work from the time of his collaboration with Auden, when it was
heavily veiled, through the end of Isherwood's life, by which time
he had become an outspoken gay rights activist. He had also written several works in which homosexuality is prominently featured—most effectively in *A Single Man* (1964), his own favorite
novel, and in both the novel and play versions of *A Meeting by the
River*.

Variant homosexual figures appear in Isherwood's work, some
more conventional than others. In *A Meeting by the River*, Patrick is,
in fact, bisexual—or perhaps a deeply closeted gay man whose relationship with Tom results, at least in part, from his attempts to
repress his urges through his proper marriage to Penelope. How
many other such encounters, if any, there have been in his life is
not made clear. Patrick frees himself from the constraints of his
conventional life in his actual relationship with Tom and can
imagine what will very likely be impossible—a breaking away
permanently from his conventional life to enter into a committed
homosexual relationship. Here Isherwood seems to arrive at the
summit of his Truly Weak Man's struggle with conventional life,
although it is interesting to note that in the final analysis, Patrick
breaks off his relationship with Tom and returns to his marriage
(although he writes to Penelope that he will return and will be a
better husband if she would sanction his occasional need for
extramarital adventures).

Isherwood's rebellion against the values and conventions of
upper class British life in the twentieth century serve as a metaphor for a central theme in his work—the struggle of each individual to realize what he or she wants (and needs) in life, but
have been taught by social strictures, family, and religion to conceal or to deny. The satiric elements of the plays can obscure the
serious undertone of the Auden-Isherwood collaboration and the
importance of the characters as "real" and "metaphorical." For ex-

ample, Ransom, a defining character for the Auden-Isherwood generation, and his twin brother James seem, at times, two halves of the same persona, which is a recurring theme in both Isherwood's art and in his diaries. The metaphor of twinship repeats itself in *A Meeting by the River*; although Patrick and Oliver are not twins in the literal sense, they can be viewed as two halves of the same persona. As Paul Piazza writes, the creation of the Auden-Isherwood hero, and Isherwood's Truly Weak Man, grew out of their own doubts about "their iconoclastic bravura and impatient anticipation of the brave new world" which "left many young rebels disaffected and spiritually destitute" (Piazza, 137). Although the themes of the Auden-Isherwood plays are very much alive in Isherwood's solo work, especially in his depiction of a hero corrupted through the act of ruling and leading—or by merely being born to privilege—an emphasis is placed on an individual's journey toward spiritual fulfillment.

Auden and Isherwood began to move in their own highly individual separate directions when they landed in America to stay in 1939. In reflecting on their plays, Spender considered their work "not so much a collaboration as a pooling of talents" (Spender, 17) and as "half brave attempts, half cynical exercises" (Spender, 16). Insisting that the plays in the hands of either author individually would have emerged as more fully realized works, Spender believes "Isherwood alone would have grappled to create vivid characters, Auden alone would have given imaginative life to his situations instead of relying on Isherwood's great gifts as a scenario-writer to carry through incompletely imagined ideas" (Spender, 17). Socialist critic Raymond Williams found instead that "What is most interesting in the three main plays is the use of existing conventions of popular entertainment" (despite attempts to create a new form of dramatic art) (Williams, 199). Thematically, Williams stresses that the plays suggest that "Individual salvation, at the end of the quest, was at least conceivable to Auden and Isherwood; and according to the rules of their attitude this would imply social salvation also" (Williams, 205). Grasping at ways of expressing the struggle toward individual salvation explored in the Auden-Isherwood plays, Isherwood continued to strive for it and, as such, his own art reaches its apotheosis in *A Meeting by the River*.

In a discussion with Auden before they came to America, Isherwood angrily, and at length, assailed religious conversions, to which Auden replied, "Be careful my dear, if you carry on like that, one day you'll have such a conversion" (cited in Scobie, "Art of Fiction," 143). Auden's prophetic statement took some time to come to fruition. Once in America, Isherwood arrived in Hollywood as a dialogue writer for Metro-Goldwyn-Mayer and involved himself in war relief work. During this time, he became a naturalized United States citizen and a resident student of the Vedanta Society of Southern California, working from 1943 to 1945 with Swami Prabhavananda as co-editor of the society's journal, *Vedanta and the West*. As Isherwood's teacher, friend, and mentor, Swami Prabhavananda powerfully influenced Isherwood in the study of Vedanta, a religion based on ancient Hindu scriptures, which is about, as Isherwood explained, "meditation and serving your fellow man" (Lawson, C2). Auden was skeptical of Isherwood's Hindu mentor, but ultimately concluded that the Swami was saintly because his innocent and humble faith was so genuine and, as such, inspiring. At one point, Isherwood even "thought I might become a monk myself" (cited in Scobie, "Art of Fiction," 143). Instead, he wrote about his spiritual journey in many of his post-World War II works. Reviewing Isherwood's *My Guru and His Disciple* in the *New York Times* in 1980, Edmund White found it:

> a record of a religious adventure that would have delighted Kierkegaard, for Isherwood rejects conventional piety—all the humdrum apparatus of worship—in favor of a direct, even jaunty appreciation of how preposterous, certainly precarious, spirituality can be today. No other writer I'm aware of has so accurately rendered what it would be like to sit down one day on the floor to meditate—to be a clever, upper-class Englishman, a socialist and skeptic, a handsome party-boy, a celebrated novelist who sits down and begins to meditate for the very first time. (White, 9)

Squaring his homosexuality with his religious belief might seem a tremendous leap, but in discussing issues of celibacy as related to his Hindu beliefs, Isherwood insisted that the Hindus are "the first to agree that all love is related, and that one can go a very long way through genuine devotion to another human being" (Scobie, "Art of Fiction, 145).

Isherwood's homosexuality, like Auden's, is an important element in understanding their literature. During and following World War II, Isherwood's screenwriting, his involvement with the Quakers (in a refugee camp in Haverford, PA), interest in pacifism, and his crusading for gay rights began to radically alter his approach to his work. At the same time, these trends were evident from the beginning of his life. "With me, everything starts with autobiography" (cited in King, 3). Isherwood asserted that among the first and most devastating biographical developments was the death of his father, Frank, a British soldier in World War I. Isherwood credited his father with creating a sense in him that writing was "play rather than work" (Scobie, "Art of Fiction," 173), and his style emerged from building on genuine experiences of his own, embroidering on the reality of incidence and character, and imagining developments beyond the reality and the inner life of characters both based on himself and those he knew. Grounded in elements of truth and imagination, Isherwood's writings are especially powerful in the incisive probing into character that is his hallmark. *A Meeting by the River* especially profits from Isherwood's gifts at finding, as Gavin Lambert notes, "his own life his best subject. He wrote with complete honesty and with a clarity of style that few of us possess" (Braun, 1).

It must certainly have been a burden for Isherwood to contend with the image of a heroic father and, perhaps somewhat more importantly, with a mother, Kathleen, who came from a more "solidly bourgeois background" (Fryer, 17) than her husband who by name, if not with money, was an aristocrat. Fryer describes Kathleen as "an unrepentant snob, immature in her appreciation of the world, spoilt, apron-clinging and blighted by a patronising attitude towards her fellow human beings that was far more typical of the nineteenth than the twentieth century" (Fryer, 19). Fryer describes Kathleen Isherwood, in fictionalized dramatic terms, as Oliver and Patrick's otherwise unnamed "Mother" in *A Meeting by the River*, a lonely widow "carefully lied to" (Heilbrun, 44) by her sons and exuding, as Brian Finney writes of Kathleen, a "complex combination of love and hypocrisy" that "confused and infuriated" (Finney, 59) her son in his youth. (Mother also connects to Isherwood's time with Auden—the old woman of Auden's cabaret sketch *Alfred*, who talks with a white gander she keeps in a cage, may have suggested Mother's serio-comic speech in *A Meeting by the River* when she expresses her fears, interspersed with inane chatter with her three cats.)

Finney also suggests that Isherwood's homosexuality was "heavily motivated by his need to rebel against the conventional majority epitomized by his mother" (Finney, 59) who, Isherwood believed, attempted by force of will and the pressure of calling on British tradition, toward a more conventional life as perhaps, a Don at Cambridge, and certainly a husband and father. In *Christo-*

pher and His Kind, however, Isherwood makes clear that this was never in the cards for him: "If boys didn't exist, I should have to invent them" (Isherwood, *Christopher and His Kind*, 17). The importance of Isherwood's mother as the inspiration for Mother in *A Meeting by the River* stems from Finney's assertion that Isherwood acquired much of his personality—especially willfulness—from his need to "withstand the despotic side" (Finney, 22) of his mother's personality. In fact, much of Isherwood's obstinacy was a trait inherited from his mother. The matriarchal despot of *A Meeting by the River* is more comically harmless, a woman whose loneliness is acknowledged and who is seen through somewhat more understanding eyes, by Isherwood, if not entirely by Mother's two sons, Patrick and Oliver. Patrick retains an emotional detachment by treating her dismissively as a benevolent dictator, which she recognizes and despises while Oliver has gone half a world away to escape both Mother as well as his yearnings for Penelope (developed previously to her marriage with Patrick), and his striving for what he certainly believes to be a potentially more valuable life as a monk.

Isherwood's sexuality was part of his rebellion, but it was much more. In a 1975 interview with the gay magazine *The Advocate*, Isherwood discussed the relationship of his homosexuality to his literary achievements: "Being gay has given me an oblique angle of vision on the world. Without it, I might never have been a writer" (Scobie, "A Lively Exchange," 6–8). Isherwood felt his taking up the cause of homosexual rights was tantamount to speaking out for all minorities. Of the sort of Whitmanesque homosexuality of Isherwood's works—and as exemplified in his life and by his relationships, especially those with Auden and Bachardy—Isherwood believed in "the concept of two men going off together, living a life that is in many ways not confined by the sense that recognized heterosexual marriage is confined. It's a way of life that disturbs some people—quite needlessly, in my view—because there is at the back of their minds this illogical fear that *something* [bad] *will happen*" (Scobie, "Art of Fiction," 160).

Auden was less overtly comfortable with dealing with public expressions of sexuality than Isherwood who, in 1984, said "Homosexuality suited me, and I have always felt at home with it. I don't doubt that I have a certain streak of heterosexuality in my nature, but it hasn't been my particular wish to pursue that" ("Novelist Isherwood Dead at 81," A-3). Particularly from the 1950s—tellingly, not long after he began his long relationship with

Bachardy in 1953—Isherwood became an increasingly frank spokesman for gay issues. He became "quite a cult figure in 'gay' circles, though he loathed that adjective, much preferring the more brutal word 'queer.' He had never hidden his own homosexuality from his friends—indeed, they were obliged to accept it, if they were to become or remain friends" (Fryer, 285). Isherwood was interviewed widely on the subject, particularly in the last two decades of his life, and, along with Bachardy, spoke to college teachers about teaching homosexual literature and found other ways to support the cause of homosexual rights and even defended promiscuity.

Gay characters frequently appeared in Isherwood's writings from the beginning, although tacitly rather than explicitly until *World in the Evening* in 1954, and more so after this. Prior to *A Meeting by the River*, Isherwood's *A Single Man* dealt with a middle-aged British college professor bereaved by the death of his homosexual partner—a work more about the ravages of loneliness than about the pros and cons of sexual difference. Following Isherwood's death, director James Bridges, who staged a 1972 Mark Taper Forum production of *A Meeting by the River*, said, "He was very open about his life, and a long time before it became easy to do so" (Braun, 1). In *Christopher and His Kind*, Isherwood focused on his homosexual experiences with a frankness rare at that time in discussions of the subject. He stressed that "I think that kind of political action [speaking out for gays] is one of the functions of old age. I feel it's the duty of people like me to get in the act. It seems sort of contemptible for old people not to speak up. When the hell are you going to speak out?" (Pearson, B5). Bachardy shared this view, adding that Isherwood "never felt ashamed of being gay. He never worried what other people thought of him as a gay man" (cited in Mendez, 9). Bachardy also discussed the complexities of a gay relationship that described his with Isherwood and, perhaps, Isherwood's with Auden, explaining that Isherwood "doubled as my lover, mentor, father, and adviser. I think it made it easier for us. From the beginning it established an unconventionality. We were not like other pairs of men we knew who lived together. And there wasn't that natural competition that two men of the same age living together naturally feel. We didn't compete because we didn't have to" (cited in Mendez, 9). Indeed, Isherwood was thirty years older than Bachardy.

Isherwood's sexuality, along with his spiritual studies, are essential elements in fully appreciating his later work—and especially in understanding his final foray into the dramatic medium. Aside from the plays with Auden, Isherwood's dramatic contributions were comparatively few and his reputation is based on his novels and translations of Brecht, Baudelaire, and Indian literature, as well as poems, autobiographical works, and essays on Europe during World War II, on his international travels, and on Vedanta and other aspects of Indian religion and life. Isherwood's work in film—and his avid interest in cinema—is of importance in understanding him as a writer. In speaking of film director Stanley Kubrick, Isherwood pointed to Kubrick's ability to recognize "the great archetypes that govern life to an extraordinary extent" (Scobie, "Art of Fiction," 164), something he sought to achieve with his own work. The dramatic version of *A Meeting by the River* demonstrates cinema techniques in its short, episodic scenes, overlapping and intercut in the style of much mid-to-late twentieth-century film.

In the aftermath of the great success of the stage and screen productions of *Cabaret*, a Broadway musical drawn from Isherwood's *Berlin Stories* (as well as John Van Druten's *I Am a Camera*, also adapted from Isherwood's stories), Isherwood seemed increasingly inclined to work in the theatrical medium. Despite the nearly thirty years that had elapsed since his dramatic collaborations with Auden, Isherwood seemed undaunted by this challenge, especially since he involved Bachardy as his collaborator. Bachardy, who was only eighteen when he and Isherwood began their relationship in 1953 (a relationship that continued until Isherwood's death in 1986), studied Theater at UCLA in the mid-1950s and developed into a fine artist, capturing Isherwood and other celebrated figures of the literary world, the stage, and the screen during their years together and since, but he also had little experience in drama. Prior to *A Meeting by the River*, there had been some discussion of the possibility of Isherwood adapting Frank Wedekind's two "Lulu" plays, *Earth Spirit* and *Pandora's Box*, for London production. This was another pull back toward the theatre (despite the fact that the deal fell through), as was his adaptation of George Bernard Shaw's novella, *The Adventures of the Black Girl in Her Search for God*, staged in 1969 at Los Angeles's Mark Taper Forum.

The dramatization of *A Meeting by the River* (1972; revised 1978), is by far Isherwood's most interesting post-Auden dramatic achievement in that it is based on his own novel and, like his work with Auden, it benefits from a collaboration. It is also interesting in that he chose to dramatize a novel that seems, at least on the surface, to be a decidedly non-dramatic source, and that the novel itself had not been especially well received by critics. Before the war, writers like Somerset Maugham and Virginia Woolf believed Isherwood to be the great hope of the British novel, but Isherwood's post-war novels, written after he settled in California, are often viewed by critics as lacking "the clear-eyed confidence" (Weatherby) of his pre-war work. There can be little doubt that some of the critical ambivalence toward Isherwood's later writings resulted from the inclusion of overtly homosexual characters and themes, but there was also a significant shift in his literary goals. Isherwood's writings became more intimately personal, less overtly political, and, generally speaking, more delicate and spare in language, structure, and overall style. Some critics felt this shift caused his writing to lose some of its power to a kind of vulnerability. Francis King sees this as a strength, stressing that in the novel version of *A Meeting by the River* Isherwood "writes yet again—and writes more convincingly than ever before—of the first steps that a man takes on the road to spiritual enlightenment" (King, 20). Others were less convinced. Carolyn G. Heilbrun calls *A Meeting by the River* a "failure," an ineffective "attempt to use insufficiently digested material gathered on a visit to a monastery in India" (Heilbrun, 44), and that the use of letters and the diary as the framing device for telling the story is "unsuccessful on even the most superficial level" (Heilbrun, 44) because "connections and repercussions between the two men are insufficiently dramatized" (Heilbrun, 44). On examination, *A Meeting by the River*, both novel and play, does not support Heilbrun's view. What Isherwood achieves in the novel—and is carried through into the play—is a depiction of the social structures of two worlds, the space between them, and the emotions and drives of characters belonging to those worlds, but not completely encompassed by them. The use of letters and diary entries may seem, at first, to be a cumbersome narrative device, belonging more to the eighteenth or nineteenth centuries, but as in Alice Walker's *The Color Purple*, in which this device is similarly employed, it serves to create an intimacy available in a poem. The private emotional realms of both Oliver and Patrick are examined uniquely, with the cumulative effect of greater intimacy achieved.

With Bachardy, Isherwood commenced work on adapting *A Meeting by the River* into a stage drama within a year of its publication as a novel. In November 1968, Isherwood wrote to Edward

Upward that the process of adapting the novel "is very instructive work," providing a chance to learn "over again those truths we used to preach about the dangers of describing your effects instead of creating them. And then one falls in love with a bit of literary dialogue and has to admit painfully that it isn't dramatic dialogue" (Fryer, 280).

Through a relationship with director Tony Richardson, an initial plan involved staging *A Meeting by the River* at the Royal Court Theatre with ballet dancer Christopher Gable as Oliver. However, this production did not materialize, leaving Isherwood and Bachardy to continue revising the script while also working on other projects.

In an October 20, 2000, interview, Bachardy recalled that Isherwood had been approached in the early 1970s by director Jim Bridges, who wanted to adapt *A Meeting by the River* for either stage or screen. Bachardy recalls that he and Isherwood decided to try writing "a preliminary version" which evolved into *"our* writing project," with Bridges consulting with them. Bridges succeeded in arranging a workshop production scheduled as part of the New Theatre for Now program at Los Angeles' Mark Taper Forum in 1972, with a cast including Sam Waterston, Lawrence Luckinbill, and Michael Ontkean. As the production was being prepared, Isherwood told a reporter for the *San Francisco Sunday Examiner and Chronicle* that *"A Meeting by the River* is a secret little book, but when I write for the stage I immediately become bold and want broad effects. My instinct is, if there's music, it ought to be louder! It's rather like painting with a broom" (May 21, 1972). Looking ahead at future production possibilities, Isherwood considered Michael York as a possibility for the play, but when the film version of *Cabaret* was released, Isherwood was so disappointed and angry about the liberties director Bob Fosse had taken with his characters and themes, especially in the depiction of the bisexuality of Cliff (played by York), that York became, in Isherwood's view, tainted by his association with the film. Following the Forum staging, most of its cast appeared in one performance of the play at New York's Phoenix Repertory "Sideshow" series in December 1972. *New York Times* critic Richard F. Shepard appreciatively focused on the interest of Isherwood and Bachardy in "relationships among people, between the two brothers, the wife, the mother, the boy, the swamis in the monastery. A layer of hypocrisy is peeled off to find a layer of honesty, which turns out to be a another layer of insincerity (or confusion) and so on"

(Shepard, 54). Shepard also found that these "constantly shifting triangles and relationships make an over-all interesting but wordy evening, one that slumps in troughs of tedium" (Shepard, 54). Structurally, Shepard applauded the use of a stage "shorn of props" (Shepard, 54) and the ways Isherwood and Bachardy had found to bring together characters physically separated by continents "in such a way that a personal touch seemed never to be absent" (Shepard, 54). Following the Forum and Phoenix stagings, Isherwood and Bachardy continued revisions on the play during 1973, this time transforming it into a screenplay. They had no luck in getting it made as a film and, at about this time, Auden's death shocked Isherwood, who spent some time re-reading his old friend's work.

The death of Auden must certainly have seemed a trifle ironic to Isherwood as he continued to work with Bachardy on the stage adaptation of *A Meeting by the River*. Thirty years earlier, Auden had been his only significant collaborator. Now, late in his life, he was collaborating again. Bachardy and Isherwood's attempts to dramatize Isherwood's work actually extend back to the late 1950s when they worked on a stage adaptation of Isherwood's 1954 novel, *The World in the Evening*. Bachardy describes it as an experiment and, upon completing it and before proceeding further, "we made up our minds to show it to two people only—Dodie Smith and Cecil Beaton. Neither liked it, so we put it away" (Fisher). However, that was not the end of their dramatic ambitions, as Bachardy recalls, "we always had it in the back of our minds to do another collaboration on a play. We didn't learn much out of *The World in the Evening*, a novel that was impossible to turn into a stage play—it was a good screenplay instead" (Fisher). Isherwood's working relationship with Bachardy was strikingly similar to his *modus operandi* with Auden. Bachardy stresses that the words were all Isherwood's, adding that "I often had suggestions and he would incorporate them" (Fisher). Isherwood himself underscored that Bachardy's involvement was important, pointing out that there are "a tremendous lot of his suggestions, of all kinds" (cited in Kaplan, 273). They had lengthy discussions and made endless notes—as Auden and Isherwood had—until they gradually constructed a framework, at which point, Bachardy says, "I took my place at the typewriter and Chris dictated." As Bachardy viewed it in an interview with Niladri R. Chatterjee, he and Isherwood "had a very symbiotic relationship" (cited in Chatterjee, 106–7).

Moving from novel to stage play, Isherwood was pleased to discover that, as Bachardy explains, "our reworking of the material brought out things only hinted at in the book" and that "Chris milked aspects more effectively in the play" (Fisher) than he had been able to do in the novel. Bachardy adds that Isherwood was centrally aware of the difficulty of adapting a novel employing the device of telling its story exclusively through diary entries and letters. Mother, Penelope, Tom, and the various Swamis were characters only referred to in the novel; the shift to a stage play meant fleshing out these figures and inventing new ones. Bachardy describes Isherwood's pleasure in writing "wonderful soliloquies"— especially for Oliver—and "luxuriated" (Fisher) in the writing of these speeches. Out of the expansion of the shadow characters, Isherwood created some of the strongest moments in the play, as when the Mother laments her circumstances while scolding her cats.

It was for this production (produced by Terry Allen Kramer and Harry Rigby) that Isherwood and Bachardy sharpened up the 1972 version of *A Meeting by the River*. This Broadway-bound production started at the Clarence Brown Theatre on the campus of the University of Tennessee at Knoxville, where it opened for a short run on February 19, 1979 (where this author saw a performance), followed by a two-week run at the Colonial Theatre in Boston beginning on March 12, 1979. It opened at New York's Palace Theatre on March 28, 1979, with an impressive cast featuring Simon Ward (who had played the title role in the 1972 film *Young Winston*) as Oliver, Keith Baxter (who had recently appeared in the Anthony Shaffer play *Sleuth*) as Patrick, Meg Wynn-Owen (of the popular British TV series *Upstairs Downstairs*) as Penelope, Sam Jaffe (the veteran stage and screen character actor) as Tarun Maharaj, Gilbert Cole as Asim, Paul Collins as Rafferty, Ronald Bishop as the Head Swami, Tom McDermott as Tom, and Siobhan McKenna, the distinguished Irish stage actress, as Mother. Albert Marre, best known for his staging of the original production of *Man of La Mancha*, directed. In preparation for the production, Marre, along with Ward and scene designer Robert Mitchell, spent five days in a Hindu monastery a few months before beginning work on the production in Tennessee on January 29, 1979.

The outstanding cast resulted from one of the major shifts required in moving *A Meeting by the River* from novel to play. The invention and expansion of supporting characters brought out different values in the overall tone of the work. The play more boldly exploits the delicate comic elements in the novel, especially those regarding familial relationships. It brings out the tensions in the marriage of Patrick and Penelope, as well as Mother's relationships with Oliver and Patrick—and their tensions with each other—in ways not possible in the novel. Bachardy stresses that one of the exciting aspects of the project for him had to do with the reinvention of the novel for the stage—and, later, for the screen. The "variety of forms," Bachardy notes, did not reveal a definitive version, but he hopes to see either the stage or screen versions produced in the future.

As a play, *A Meeting by the River* is a work of great potential waiting to be fulfilled by a strong production. In the years since its 1979 production, audiences in the United States have become increasingly familiar with Eastern religions, as many seeking new routes on their own spiritual odysseys have looked toward these traditions. At the same time, there has been an explosion of gay-themed plays that have rendered this previously "controversial" aspect of the play moot. Finally, American playwrights have ventured further from the entrenched traditions of dramatic realism, suggesting that the Brechtian-inspired cinematic structure of *A Meeting by the River*, resulting in part from experiments Auden and Isherwood made in their 1930s collaborations, would be more fully appreciated by today's audiences.

A Meeting by the River, as well as Isherwood's other post-World War II work, suggests that he had learned what Auden had discovered in the 1930s: traveling to faraway places allows one to "reflect on one's past and one's culture from the outside" (cited in Davenport-Hines, 147). Isherwood and Bachardy carry this notion through in the play's themes and in its structure. From the start, they strip away realistic stage elements, noting in the stage directions that the only necessary scenic element is "The Seat," a backless marble garden bench which was the favorite place of Oliver's Hindu mentor, Tarun Maharaj, whose inspiration has brought him to the banks of the Ganges and the possible end of his spiritual quest.

Midway through the play, Oliver explains that before meeting Maharaj, life's choices "seemed awfully simple," a choice "between public service and private selfishness—which, in my mind, included every kind of mysticism"(p. 1-41). Maharaj, Oliver explains, "didn't believe in persuasion or conversion. That's such a western attitude. The Christians are all car salesman at heart...." (p. 1-42). Oliver was also drawn to Maharaj because "he wasn't some sort of unearthly being, he was definitely human. He made me feel: If he can know God, I can" (p. 1-42), which led Oliver to despise "mystics who tried to save their own souls while their neighbors were hungry" (p. 1-43) and to realize that "you can't save your own soul without helping other people—I mean helping them basically, in the only way that really matters" (p. 1-43). In a flashback, Maharaj explains to Oliver that "You resolve to be pure in thought, word and deed, but you only resolve to *try*. (with a giggle) If you fail, you will not go to Hell. And this is not a legal trap, like marriage!" (p. 1-44). As their relationship grows, Oliver worries about the ailing Maharaj's well–being; he doesn't want to leave to go to work, but Maharaj insists, saying, "Don't you know that the guru can never run away from his disciple—even if he should want to? Not in this life. Not in any other" (p. 1-45). Paul Piazza finds Maharaj is the most "convincing" among Isherwood's attempts to create guru figures in his work and that this character is "gifted with both the irresistible genius of Bergmann [from the novel *Prater Violet* (1945)], and the other-worldliness of Parr [*Down There on a Visit* (1962]" (Piazza, 73). The Maharaj's effectiveness, both as he is described in the novel and as he appears in the play (and as performed by Sam Jaffe in the Broadway production), re-sults from Isherwood's actual relationship with his guru, Swami Prabhavananda. In *My Guru and His Disciple*, a 1980 memoir of their thirty-three year relationship, Isherwood chronicles his en-counters with the Swami over four decades, from their first in 1939 and continuing to the Swami's death in 1976. Yet, while elements of their encounters are fictionalized in *A Meeting by the River*, Ish-erwood is more interested in depicting the struggle for serenity and the essential element of humility in achieving a faith. Oliver has vanity and ego he is trying to erase, and he was raised in a British culture that felt itself superior; he struggles, not always successfully, to destroy those aspects of his persona in order to be spiritually reborn, as represented by his taking *sannyas*, the vows of conversion to a monk. From Swami Prabhavananda, Isherwood came to an understanding that "there is such a thing as a mystical experience. That was what seemed to me extraordinary—the thing I had completely dismissed," (cited in Scobie, "Art of Fiction," 143), and it is this revelation he attempts to capture in *A Meeting by the River*.

It is interesting to note that Isherwood called the stage adapta-tion of *A Meeting by the River* a "religious comedy" (Drake, 39), but hastened to add that "it does not make fun of religion: it is just that comedy is possible in a monastery. It's about serious matters, but a comedy nevertheless—an all's-well-that-ends-well situation" (Drake, 39). The satire, if indeed that is what it should be called, is focused on the intense, often contradictory conflicts within his characters, a perspective derived directly from Isherwood's collaborations with Auden. The attitudes of the characters, which are frequently at cross purposes with their reality, and their feelings of discordance with the world around them, is the essence of Isherwood's work, but such internal struggles are, by their very nature, difficult to dramatize. Drama is inherently action, it is inherently external—staging the intimate interior complexities of character and revelations of the spirit are problems solved by Isherwood and Bachardy through enhancing the battle of wills between the two brothers, Oliver and Patrick, who are at once very different and very similar beings. Supporting this, critics Stanley Kauffman and Francis King view *A Meeting by the River* as a monodrama in which Oliver and Patrick indeed represent two sides of one man: Patrick, the strong, materialistic, hedonistic, sensual, and manipulative; Oliver, the spiritual seeker of knowledge, more emotionally fragile and reactive. Isherwood certainly intended this connection, but perhaps somewhat less literally—his goal was a work about brotherhood in its broadest definition. Each brother is in search of a full understanding of their connection—Patrick confesses to a lifelong search for his brother while Oliver finds new "brothers" among the Hindu monks and achieving a greater understanding of his biological brother.

Adapting the novel into a play "made it something very different" (Drake, 39), Isherwood believed, and that adapting it "was extremely difficult. The novel has many letters and phone calls that had to be adapted into scenes. Actually it lends a fluidity to the play. We jump about freely in both time and place—from India, to England, to California. Even a brief moment in Tokyo" (Drake, 39). Critics reviewing the novel felt that the use of letters and diary entries as a mode of telling the story was a failed and antiquated device, while others regarded this device as an effective approach for revealing the inner thoughts of Oliver and Patrick. Isherwood applies particular delicacy in implanting the differences between the brothers in the way they write, contrasting the amusing wit and charm of Patrick's at times flowery letters with the intimate, spare, and terse diary entries of Oliver. Isherwood's sense of the need for fluidity is only the most obvious difficulty of connecting different cultures, an inherent issue in the novel and play—and, more so, in connecting two such different brothers who both started life in the same culture, but are now separated by continents. Isherwood strives to avoid final judgment on either brother—or either culture; the flaws of both brothers emerge fully, as do the pros and cons of living in Eastern or Western cultures. For Isherwood, *A Meeting by the River* is "really quite different from any of my other works" because "there is no real point of view. It's just as I always say: it's like a trial where both sides give evidence. But there's no judgment, no verdict, no summing up, nothing. You just hear all of the evidence" (cited in Kaplan, 261). Despite this, Isherwood's sympathies seem to lie more fully with Oliver and, to an extent, Isherwood acknowledged that what Oliver

> is pushing is much more practical than what Patrick is pushing. But I wouldn't say that they're weighted otherwise. As a matter of fact, one's sympathy and the sympathy of most readers goes strongly to Patrick, I find.... You see, I have now approached this material three times, and every time the two characters change very subtly in certain ways. When we made the play, Oliver luckily was played by a very good actor, Sam Waterston, who gave it great energy and a kind of conviction and even a sort of sexiness, so that he held his end up very well. But otherwise, it's uphill work for Oliver, because onstage all that sort of skullduggery [of Patrick's] is very charming. It has a kind of eighteenth-century appeal, this villainy. Anyway, then you see more and more that one comes to something else in the material, which is that Patrick is doing this in a very sincere way, that's to say he is genuinely horrified by the monastery. (cited in Kaplan, 261–62)

The play essentially begins at the monastery. When Maharaj dies, Oliver goes to India to spread his mentor's ashes in the Ganges and explains that right from the start, his "decision to become a monk is of long standing, made after careful deliberations and absolutely final" (Isherwood and Bachardy, 1-2). The importance of setting the scene at the monastery beside the Ganges was important to Isherwood in its inherent explication of the "inwardness" (cited in Kaplan, 262) of the story; the setting is a representation of "a place that Oliver lives in" both physically and spiritually, and "it represents a problem of Patrick's" (cited in Kaplan, 263)—a problem that was there even before his arrival in India. Isherwood describes Patrick's presence as not only an attempt to persuade Oliver to leave, but as a result of his curiosity with what might happen to him, as well as Oliver, if he went there. Both

Patrick and Oliver find it is "terribly, terribly hard to do anything
that is against the usual concepts of your culture. It is very, very
painful and embarrassing, and doubts come—always" (cited in
Kaplan, 263).

Isherwood's own experiences in India inspired the novel and
the play, and began to codify his sense that within him were two
distinct personas; *A Meeting by the River* is Isherwood's last great
internal debate, one carried out more in understanding and reflection than in the angrier debates of his earlier novels and, in fact,
his collaborations with Auden. This internal debate is essentially
one of Isherwood arguing with himself. At the time he was working on the adaptation, Isherwood discussed his reasons for writing
A Meeting by the River with W.I. Scobie, stressing that for a long
time he had been interested in writing a "confrontation story,
where the representative of something meets the representative of
something else, and quite suddenly it came to me that this was the
way to do it" (cited in Scobie, "Art of Fiction," 142). Seeking a
mode to make this confrontation dramatic, Isherwood explained
that the idea was

> what if a worldly person—which I consider myself to be—had a
> brother who went into a monastery. How would he feel? In the
> play, the worldly brother visits the other one just before he takes
> his final vows. He wants to see if he can get his brother out of the
> monastery. That's the whole ballgame—the confrontation and
> conflict between the two brothers. (Lawson, C2)

Isherwood carefully constructed the play much as he had the
novel, emphasizing the difficulty Oliver has in truly entering his
newfound faith. His British reserve, his ego and background of
privilege make his full commitment especially problematic, a problem resolved by the final revelation which comes, as Isherwood
stresses, "when he sits on the stone bench in the monastery and he
feels that Swami has been sitting beside him" (cited in Scobie, "Art
of Fiction," 147). In that moment, Oliver achieved a joy counter to
his typically reserved persona and his doubts about his faith are
overcome as he realizes with "a terrific sense of relief" that "after
all the whole thing is true!" through this astounding, but
inherently undramatic, revelation (cited in Scobie, "Art of Fiction,"
147). This is a central difficulty of this play or any other play that
attempts to convey an inner conversion. Oliver's revelation must
be taken on faith by the audience as there is not the option of
narrative available to fiction. Isherwood's literary works are
frequently praised for their unique blend of reality and

imagination, but such internal transitions are problematic for the stage. (Wilder's *Our Town* is the notable exception with his use of the Stage Manager to "narrate" the play.)

The stage adaptation of *A Meeting by the River* allows Isherwood to explore new tools to resolve problems like the revelation. The mixing up of fact and fiction, or the real and the illusory, gives his writings a pseudo-documentary style, while at the same time retaining the inherent freedom of a work of fiction. The melding together of life and art seems to have pleased Isherwood, who regarded the stage version of *A Meeting by the River* to be "far more realised than the book: it plays out the undecided duel between the two brothers more intensely, and so the nature of the comedy comes out more clearly" (cited in Scobie, "Art of Fiction," 146).

Bringing out the conflict between the brothers—and their internal struggles—was not the only problem facing Isherwood and Bachardy in adapting the novel into dramatic form. The development of secondary characters (Mother, Penelope, Tom, Tarun Maharaj, the various swamis) only referred to in the novel, proved "a challenge," Isherwood felt, because they were "all elsewhere—except for the two principals," forcing an imposed technique "which was fun: the people are there, and yet they're not there, just as they are in life" (cited in Scobie, "Art of Fiction," 146). On stage, Isherwood and Bachardy allow the characters—continents apart in some cases—to move freely in and out of each other's realities.

The tensions between the brothers provide much of the action and conflict in the play. There is a grudging respect between them, as when Patrick acknowledges that Oliver "always does exactly what he wants to do. And I must say, I find that inspiring" (Isherwood and Bachardy, 1-3). However, he cynically adds, "what in the world is going to become of him when he runs out of causes to embrace and prophets to sit at the feet of?" (Isherwood and Bachardy, 1-4). Claude J. Summers calls Patrick the "most unpleasant" character in Isherwood's fiction (Summers, 129), but he is a necessary counterbalance to the borderline saintliness of Oliver. Some of the tension between the brothers grows out of Patrick's awareness of the strong bond between Oliver and Penelope, which is implied when he rather maliciously says to her, "I ought to know by now—understanding Oliver is your department" (Isherwood and Bachardy, 1-4). Penelope comes to realize that rebuffing Oliver to marry Patrick has been the central mistake of her life, but her feelings extend beyond jealousy and regret, as when she asks Patrick to "Tell him I'm glad he's found something he can believe in" (1-5). Penelope and Mother are aware that Patrick's trip to India provides him a chance to manipulate Oliver for his own amusement: "If Olly's new found faith can't bear a little friendly inspection, it isn't worth much" (1-6). Patrick's friendliness is, of course, suspect, as Oliver realizes from the start. "You smell mischief, that's all," he notes when he learns of Patrick's imminent arrival, but Oliver confesses to himself that he constructed the letter informing Patrick of his intentions in such a way as to peak his interest: "curt, mysterious, with 'keep out' signs all over it" (1-7).

Even before Patrick arrives, he is dealing with his own crisis: a passionate involvement with a young man named Tom, despite the fact that he has no intention of ending his marriage. Oliver is struggling, too, with his feelings about Patrick, admitting "what a terrific problem you still are for me" and appreciating Patrick's "boldness in demanding enjoyment for yourself, and the get-away-with-murder impudence with which you accept the best as your absolute right" (Isherwood and Bachardy, 1-11). Their relationship is not exclusively one of grudging admiration, however, but a deeper bond. Oliver sees that "At moments I can actually feel and think like you, and that scares me, of course" (1-11). Patrick is central to Oliver's past life, and he is struggling to obliterate his past and what it has created in him, especially "the ego, the Oliver in me, never will and never can be anything but a vain little monkey," and he realizes that within the concepts of his new religion, "the monkey is methodically starved to death" (1-18).

Patrick, for his part, feels that Oliver is wasting his life, telling Penelope that when Oliver worked for the Red Cross in Africa it was "like a great general pretending to be a private soldier" (Isherwood and Bachardy, 1-20), and Oliver's Hinduism is, for Patrick, an even more horrifying abdication of his brother's true persona. Patrick's admiration for Oliver is sometimes grudging, sometimes genuine, as when he explains that Oliver always "seemed so strong and self-sufficient. He made no compromises. He didn't even seem to know there were any compromises one could make! As I watched him, I couldn't help feeling awfully corrupt and shop-soiled, because I was so different" (1-22). The Truly Weak Man recognizes his own weaknesses and strengths.

In the middle of the first act, the play flashes back to establish Oliver's love for Penelope by showing their first meeting. The intensity of their feeling is obvious from the beginning, but Penelope chooses Patrick because he offers a conventional marriage and children, despite her awareness that Patrick "likes to play games" (Isherwood and Bachardy, 1-20) and that she has a far stronger sexual attraction to Oliver. Patrick will be her husband, she realizes, whereas what Oliver wants is "a kind of marvelous incest—a brother and sister who share every thought, who read each other's moods, and who go to bed together" (1-23). Penelope worries that she is responsible for Oliver's choices, but Oliver not-too-convincingly replies, "You think I'm in this monastery because I couldn't have you? Don't flatter yourself" (2-11).

Oliver's struggle for serenity is tested by Patrick in many ways, as when he goes to Patrick's room to find him exercising in his briefs. In the novel, this scene is far more homoerotic—Patrick is exercising in the nude. (Isherwood, in his biography of his parents, *Kathleen and Frank*, recalls the sight of his father exercising in his shorts and that it was, indeed, erotic.) As he jogs in place, Oliver notices Patrick's large penis slapping against his flat stomach. Oliver understands that it is a test devised "to see if I'd risen above the flesh, and was so pure I wouldn't even notice if you were naked or not! You are just like a woman, sometimes! It was like a scene in a Russian novel, where the woman tries to seduce the young monk ..."; Patrick's flirtatiousness, he recognizes, "is just a nervous habit you've gotten into. You try it on all ages and both sexes" (Isherwood and Bachardy, 1-26).

Oliver is also tested by Patrick when a pushy reporter, Rafferty, hounds Patrick for access to Oliver. This dramatic device, despite its obviousness, adds pressure to the situation. Patrick succeeds in securing Rafferty's interview by ingratiating himself with the Head Swami, who makes it clear he wishes Oliver to give the interview. Oliver is furious with Patrick, aware that Rafferty's crass assault is no more than an attempt to create a "comic picture," a depiction of "the Englishman in Hindu drag" (Isherwood and Bachardy, 2-15). It is through the presence of Rafferty, and Patrick's lack of knowledge of the practices of Hinduism, that Isherwood and Bachardy efficiently provide the audience with the necessary background on Hinduism as Patrick asks questions that allow answers that explain Hindu terms. Final vows are called *sannyas*, a *namaskar* is a deep bow with the palms of the hands pressed together as in prayer ("It means you're saluting the Eternal in the other person"), a *pranams* is "taking the dust off someone's feet," and *darshan* is "exposing yourself to the spiritual radiations of a holy man," a mentor figure that Oliver found in Maharaj and, in reality, as Bachardy found with Isherwood and, earlier,

Isherwood found with Auden, and ultimately, as Isherwood found with Swami Prabhavananda. Penelope describes *darshan* as a sort of "spiritual sunburn" (1-28–1-29), an experience both mystical and painful, which, near the end of the play, Patrick experiences as well as Oliver.

Angered by Patrick's intrusions and attempted manipulations, Oliver frustratingly notes that "All the filth out of the past keeps backing up on me," and Patrick acknowledges that "I know it's childish, but I can't help provoking you" while privately resolving, as the play's first act ends, to pull Oliver away from his newfound faith.

> This languid supercilious oriental negativism—it's an anti-life. It turns all values upside down and inside out.... If they can do this to you, then anything is possible. But I'm going to fight this place and get you out of it, whether you like it or not. (Isherwood and Bachardy, 1-51)

This lifelong battle between the two brothers wearies Mother, who demonstrates a surprising lack of affection for Patrick: "Does he seriously believe I believe he has a *heart*?," she grumbles at one point and is hurt by the distance Oliver has put between them (Isherwood and Bachardy, 2-3). One of the most affecting additions to the play is Mother's speech, at the beginning of Act Two, in which she expresses her exasperation with her sons and about her own situation, while bantering with her three (invisible to the audience) cats. Frustrated that her sons expect her to "play the Frantic Fusspot," she is angered by Patrick's glib assessment of her having found happiness: "How *dare* he talk to me about happiness! I'm full of hate, and I'm old and I'm lonely" (2-4). She resents Penelope's presence, dislikes her grandchildren, and fears death, which causes her to assail Oliver: "If this new religion of yours is any good, why don't you use it to help me? The Vicar can't help me. He doesn't believe a word he says. I sit there in church, knowing its all lies and that I'm going to die" (2-4). All of this is juxtaposed with intrusions by the cats, who are circling her for their treat: "You don't understand love, do you, my Darlings. You understand fish and cream and mice and baby birds that you drag out of the nest, alive and twittering" (2-4). She departs to feed her cats, leaving Patrick and Oliver to play out their "precious duet" (2-5).

Patrick's at-times almost malicious interference in Oliver's life masks his hurt over the alienation that has grown up between them. It also partly explains Patrick's relationship with Tom, to whom he says, "I've tried to love my brother. But he doesn't need me. Tommy, I want *you* to be my brother—and the one I've been searching for all these years" (Isherwood and Bachardy, 2-8). Patrick uses Tom as a provocation with Oliver, claiming that they can "share everything, in the spirit *and* in the body. A life without fear" (2-8). Here Isherwood implants his gay rights activism, while also demonstrating Patrick's joy in sexuality which leads him to suggest that Oliver is "missing all the fun!" (2-10). Is Patrick's relationship with Tom merely a fling, an escape from his responsibilities, or is this truly a possible life change for him? His eventual break with Tom, and his seemingly renewed commitment to his marriage, like Oliver's renewed commitment to his spiritual life, suggests a major change in Patrick that may or may not be permanent.

Oliver's presence when Patrick receives a drunken phone call from Tom gives Oliver the upper hand rather suddenly and unexpectedly. Patrick is forced to confess his relationship with Tom in a moving passage in which he confronts some of his own needs, especially the invigorating aspects of his sexual relationship with the younger man who, he explains, "wanted to make me as alive as he is—to bring me back to life" (Isherwood and Bachardy, 2-20). Patrick describes them in their first encounter as "ravenous naked cannibals" devouring each other in a cove near a trailer park where they might be discovered at any moment. This, too, is invigorating for Patrick, who claims, "I wanted them all to see what it's like—the real thing—shameless and brutal and glorious" (2-20). Oliver criticizes Patrick not for this homosexual confession, but because it means Patrick is living a lie with Penelope and his children. As he says, "to *live* with them out of duty, that's heartless" (2-22).

As the two brothers hash out their pained but loving relationship, certain hard truths emerge, including Oliver's confession that "When I was going through my Freudian phase, I used to wonder if I wasn't actually in love with you, romantically, even physically" (Isherwood and Bachardy, 2-23). Patrick seizes the opportunity to use Oliver's vulnerability to convince him that "what you've *got* to admit to yourself is that you have powers you absolutely refuse and *fear* to make use of" (2-25). Patrick, insisting that Oliver is horrified by his own ambition, has "the power to lead people—no, far more than that—the power to turn people into people who are worth leading" (2-25). Patrick continues to drive the point home—even suggesting that Oliver work for the United Nations—and succeeds in temporarily shaking Oliver's resolve: "One moment, everything that you said seems utterly idiotic and laughable. The next, it seems terribly, insidiously true" (2-28). Oliver considers asking Patrick for a loan to return to England, seeing "it as the only thinkable act which wouldn't have even the least taint of falseness in it. All other ways of mortifying Oliver seem like self-cheating. But this one would really strike Oliver's pride at its roots and bring him down grovelling to the ground" (2-28). Oliver prays to Maharaj for guidance. "Maharaj, I'm praying to you as I've never prayed before. Show me what I must do" (2-28). This is followed by a moment of spiritual fulfillment which leaves Oliver "radiant with joy" (2-29) as the transition is accomplished through a stage direction that has the stage go to darkness followed by a slow flooding in of light and a "long pause of absolute silence" ended by Oliver's tearful acknowledgment that despite the fact that Maharaj is dead, "we can't ever be separated. He is with me always, wherever I am" (2-28–2-29). Patrick's connection is also revealed at this point, as Oliver explains:

> Patrick wasn't with us [Oliver and the Swami] but I knew that he was very close to us. And I was aware that he was an established part of our life—the three of us belonged together intimately and I accepted this as a matter of course. There was no question of feeling any jealousy or hostility towards him—in that situation, such feelings would have been unimaginable. He even had his own special place on the Seat, on Maharaj's right hand.... Maharaj seemed gravely concerned about Patrick—and yet, despite his concern, he was amused. My general impression was that Patrick had got himself into a spiritual condition which was very serious and at the same time ridiculous. Maharaj could laugh at it indulgently because Patrick was in his care and would be all right. (a pause) When I think of us two, sitting there with Maharaj—(OLIVER begins to sob, then checks himself and smiles) But I'll only think about that when I'm alone or I'll embarrass everybody. (Isherwood and Bachardy, 2-29)

As Oliver goes forth to his spiritual rebirth, Patrick acknowledges that "I find this act of his, the sheer courage of it, terribly moving. He's so utterly, almost unimaginably alone in what he's doing— far more than any lone hero on a battlefield." (Isherwood and Bachardy, 2-32) Patrick, too, receives a benediction; he is, as Oliver privately notes, "in a state of grace and you don't know it!" (2-35) Some scholars, like Claude J. Summers, see that the satire rests in the play's sense that life—and life's choices—are one great joke, as suggested by the end of both the novel and the play when Patrick says, "Well Olly, you've really gone and torn it now!" and Oliver replies, "Looks like I'm stuck with it, doesn't it?" (2-36).

The commercial and critical failure of the 1979 Broadway production of *A Meeting by the River* had less to do with what happened on stage than off. Isherwood and Bachardy had doubts about Marre as the director of this delicate "chamber" play. Much of Marre's experience was in musical theater, and the intricacies and delicacies of the play were largely ignored while Marre staged a lavish *sannyas* scene which, in its realistic visual spectacle, seemed inappropriate to the play's more intimate tone and suggestive style. And although the play was produced in Knoxville closer to the intentions of Isherwood and Bachardy, when it reached New York Marre made some disturbing deletions. As Bachardy remembers, "he jollied us along in Tennessee, but we came to believe he always intended to make deep cuts" (Fisher). These involved the elimination of a major scene between Patrick and Tom, truncating the homosexual aspects of the play and, in Bachardy's words, "cutting Tom's role severely—down to nothing" (Fisher). Bachardy stresses, correctly, that the "queer thing built into" *A Meeting by the River* was "basic" and to skimp on it "unbalanced" the play's structure (Fisher). Marre undoubtedly feared critical censure over the gay aspects of the play on a Broadway that in the late 1970s was not especially welcoming to the subject. This was a mere ten years after Mart Crowley's *The Boys in the Band* had presented a serious exploration of gay-related issues and characters, and well before writers from Harvey Fierstein and Larry Kramer to Terrence McNally and Tony Kushner would break through to offer dramas exploring a full range of gay issues. For Bachardy, it was simply the fact that Marre was the "wrong director, he was completely in charge, an autocrat" and, coupled with the bizarre choice of the cavernous Palace Theatre for this rather intimate and character-centered drama, Bachardy laments the "great difficulties" with Marre and the "severe" cuts that significantly damaged the play's effectiveness (Fisher).

Critics were predominantly negative in their response to *A Meeting by the River*, both in its 1972 Mark Taper Forum production and when it reached Broadway in 1979. Brendan Gill found it a "wordy, not to say preachy, account of certain anguished transformations in the life of two upper-class English brothers" (Gill, 97), but *New York Times* reviewer Richard Eder set the general tone of condemnation, calling the play an "exercise in High Twaddle" (Eder, C15). Eder found the play's sensibility dated and felt it suffered from two problems: (1) a disconnection between the play's spiritual scenes and those driven by character conflict, and (2) that Oliver's conversion—his transformation into a swami—is invisible, therefore undramatic. However, W.I. Scobie, reviewing the Forum production, sensed the connection between the Isherwood-Bachardy adaptation and the earlier Auden-Isherwood plays, finding it an "excellent" work, "a comedy of gay, quasi-Mozartian surfaces, beneath which lies a passionate questioning of some no less passionately held Western values" (Scobie, "England in Los Angeles," 859). Bachardy recalls that he and Isherwood "liked that production [Forum] much better than the one in New York, and it was much closer to the original play" (cited in Chatterjee, 107), which, thanks to Marre's last-minute cuts, had been obscured. Bachardy also felt that Isherwood found the play more effective than the novel, and found the subsequent screenplay they worked on even more effective. As Bachardy notes, "All very different from each other, all written expressly for the particular medium" (cited in Chatterjee, 107). Isherwood, as Piazza explains, "could not revise whole novels, once published, as Auden boldly amended lines and entire poems in light of his Christianity," but through adaptation, Isherwood continued to revise *A Meeting by the River*, confirming Piazza's notion that throughout his career, "Isherwood wrote one novel which he constantly amended, incorporating new, original insights so that the final copy is a palimpsest recording of the results of his modified interpretation of the anti-myth; or that he actually wrote a Proustian remembrance of things past" (Piazza, 196–97).

Interestingly, Bachardy compares his collaboration with Isherwood on *A Meeting by the River* with Isherwood's prior collaborations with Auden. Bachardy believes that Auden and Isherwood "both felt themselves to be novices as dramatists. Playwriting for them was a game they were learning together. The three plays they collaborated on were experimental—they were not sure what would work and what wouldn't. It was fun" (Fisher). That spirit carried over to Bachardy's work with Isherwood, an experience he enjoyed and which led to their work together on five subsequent screenplays. *A Meeting by the River* turned out to be, as Bachardy points out, "a warmup for our screenplays. We were encouraged by our work on *Meeting*, feeling we'd gotten something we were quite pleased with." When some commissions for screenplays

came up, "Chris proposed me as his collaborator. He didn't want
to work on screenplays alone." The screenplay version of *A
Meeting by the River*, one of these collaborations, expanded on
relationships—bringing Patrick's amour, Tom, to India, along with
his wife, Penelope, creating some interesting tensions, as well as a
scene in which Penelope tells Oliver to stay in the monastery "and
not come out" (cited in Kaplan, 262).

Certainly, Isherwood was on a highly personal journey toward
spiritual fulfillment which finds full voice in *A Meeting by the River*,
a work that in both its narrative and dramatic forms results from
Isherwood's reasons for writing: "I write because I am trying to
study my life in retrospect and find out what it is, what it is made
of, what it is all about. The attempt to do this is ultimately frustrat-
ing, of course, but nevertheless the most fascinating occupation I
can imagine" (Braun, 1). *A Meeting by the River*, in which Isherwood imagines regeneration (and reconciliation)—of two individuals (who are, perhaps, one) and two societies (East and West)—is
"the logical completion of Isherwood's long road to self-under-
standing" (Faraone, 256), although Isherwood frequently es-
chewed the notion that he was attempting to make any sort of final
philosophical statement. In both the novel and the play, he avoids
making any final judgment on the personal philosophies of either
Patrick or Oliver. Emphasis lies with his statement of the need for
the individual to journey toward spiritual fulfillment, a journey
that for Isherwood was one begun in earnest in his collaboration
with Auden and concluded in his collaboration with Bachardy.

Works Cited

Auden, W.H. *The Complete Works of W.H. Auden. Plays. 1928–1938.* Edited
    by Edward Mendelson. Princeton, NJ: Princeton UP, 1988.

Bahlke, George W., ed. *Critical Essays on W.H. Auden.* New York: G.K. Hall
    & Co., 1991.

Beach, Joseph Warren. *The Making of the Auden Canon.* Minneapolis: U of
    Minnesota P, 1957.

Braun, Stephen. "Christopher Isherwood, Whose Tales Inspired *Cabaret*,
    Dies." *Los Angeles Times*, January 6, 1986, Metro section, 1.

Chatterjee, Niladri R. "Portrait of the Artist as Companion. Interviews
    with Don Bachardy." In *The Isherwood Century. Essays on the Life and
    Work of Christopher Isherwood.* edited by James J. Berg and Chris

Freeman. With a Foreword by Armistead Maupin. Madison: U of Wisconsin P, 2000. 97–107.

Davenport-Hines, Richard. *Auden.* New York: Vintage Books, 1999.

Drake, Sylvie. "'River' Bill at the Mark Taper." *Los Angeles Times,* April 23, 1972, Sunday Calendar Section, p. 39.

Earle, Anita. "Writing for the Stage Is 'Like Painting with a Broom'." *San Francisco Sunday Examiner and Chronicle,* May 21, 1972, 7–8.

Eder, Richard. "Stage: *A Meeting by the River.*" *New York Times,* March 29, 1979, C15.

Faraone, Mario. "The Path That Leads to Safety. Spiritual Renewal and Autobiographical Narrative." In *The Isherwood Century. Essays on the Life and Work of Christopher Isherwood,* edited by James J. Berg and Chris Freeman. With a Foreword by Armistead Maupin. Madison: U of Wisconsin P, 2000. 247–58.

Finney, Brian. *Christopher Isherwood. A Critical Biography.* New York: Oxford UP, 1979.

Fisher, James. "Interview with Don Bachardy." October 20, 2000.

Fryer, Jonathan. *Isherwood.* Garden City, NY: Doubleday & Company, Inc., 1979.

Gill, Brendan. "The Theatre: No Good Deed Goes Unpunished." *New Yorker,* April 9, 1979, 97.

Heilbrun, Carolyn G. *Christopher Isherwood.* New York & London: Columbia UP, 1970.

Isherwood, Christopher. *Christopher and His Kind. 1929–1939.* New York: North Point Press/Farrar, Straus and Giroux, 1976.

———. *A Meeting by the River.* Minneapolis: U of Minnesota P, 1967.

———, and Don Bachardy. *A Meeting by the River.* A Play in Two Acts. Manuscript dated November 28, 1977.

Jurak, Mirko. "Commitment and Character Portrayal in the British Politico-Poetic Drama of the 1930s." *Educational Theatre Journal* 26 (October 1974): 342–51.

Kaplan, Carola M. "'The Wandering Stopped': An Interview with Christopher Isherwood." In *The Isherwood Century. Essays on the Life and Work of Christopher Isherwood,* edited by James J. Berg and Chris Freeman. With a Foreword by Armistead Maupin. Madison: U of Wisconsin P, 2000. 259–72.

King, Francis. *Christopher Isherwood.* Edited by Ian Scott-Kilvert. Essex, England: Published for The British Council by Longman Group Ltd., 1976.

Lawson, Carol. "Broadway: Two Cultures Clash in New Play by Isherwood." *New York Times,* January 26, 1979, C2.

Mendez, Carlos. "Isherwood and Bachardy on Each Other. The Diaries Are Published; Don Bachardy Is Interviewed." *Harvard Gay & Lesbian Review* 4:2 (Spring 1997): 9.

"Novelist Isherwood Dead at 81; Musical *Cabaret* Inspired by Book of Short Stories." *San Diego Union-Tribune,* January 6, 1986, A-3.

Page, Norman. *Auden and Isherwood. The Berlin Years.* New York: St. Martin's Press, 1998.

Pearson, Richard. "Writer Christopher Isherwood Dead at 81." *The Washington Post,* January 6, 1986, B5.

Piazza, Paul. *Christopher Isherwood: Myth and Anti-Myth.* New York: Columbia UP, 1978.

Poss, Stanley. "A Conversation on Tape." *London Magazine,* June 1961, 41–58.

Scobie, W.I. "The Art of Fiction: Interview with Christopher Isherwood." *Paris Review,* 14 (Spring 1974): 138–82.

———. "England in Los Angeles." *National Review* 24 (August 4, 1972): 859–60.

———. "A Lively Exchange with One of Our Greatest Living Writers." *The Advocate,* December 17, 1975, 6–8.

———. "Theatre: Fat Hollywood in Hungry Bengal." *London Magazine,* n.s. 13 (April/May 1973): 137–44.

Shepard, Richard F. "Stage: A Series Begins." *New York Times,* December 20, 1972, 54.

Spender, Stephen. "The Auden-Isherwood Collaboration." *The New Republic,* November 23, 1959, 16–17.

Stoop, Norma McLain. "Christopher Isherwood: A Meeting by Another River." *After Dark* 7 (April 1975): 60–65.

Summers, Claude J. *Christopher Isherwood.* New York: Frederick Ungar Publishing Co., 1980.

Weatherby, W.J. "Disciple Who Became a Guru." *The Guardian,* January 6, 1968.

White, Edmund. "A Sensual Man with a Spiritual Quest." *New York Times,* June 1, 1980, Section 7, 9.

Williams, Raymond. *Drama. From Ibsen to Brecht.* New York: Oxford UP, 1969.

Wright, George T. *W.H. Auden.* New York: Twayne, 1969.

W.H. Auden as Librettist/Translator of Mozart's *The Magic Flute*

Robert Stanley

Who better to consider the Auden-Kallman libretto of The Magic Flute *than a professor of German and French who is also an opera fan?*

Auden wrote several opera libretti, many of them in collaboration with Chester Kallman (1921–1975). One of his first was a mythical version of *Paul Bunyan*, set to music by Benjamin Britten. *The Rake's Progress* (1947–1948), set to music by Igor Stravinsky, was the first collaboration on a libretto by Auden and Kallman. Next came *Delia or A Masque of Night* (suggested by George Peele's play *The Old Wives' Tale*), a collaboration by Auden and Kallman done in 1952. From 1955 comes *The Magic Flute*, which was rather more a rewriting than just a translation of the Mozart-Schikaneder opera from 1791.

This libretto for *The Magic Flute* was as much a reworking of the original libretto as it was a translation. In the introduction to their version of the libretto of Mozart's beloved last opera, Messieurs Auden and Kallman go to the trouble of explaining why they took such liberties in the translation. They felt themselves obliged to correct some of the idiosyncrasies and sources of confusion inherent in the original libretto. This is particularly true in regard to the Queen of the Night, with whom the audience tends to empathize in the first act (since she is portrayed as the grief-stricken mother wrongfully robbed of her beloved daughter Pamina), and whom the audience regards with a mixture of fascination and horror in the second act, since she astoundingly threatens her daughter with all sorts of unpleasant things if the daughter does not kill Sarastro, the Queen's deadly enemy. It is a known fact that Mozart's original librettists (Schikaneder and Giesecke) shifted their treatment of the Queen of the Night between the first and second acts. As Auden and Kallman write:

> [...] to allow the Night [i.e., the irrational and the unconscious] a creative role is very untypical of the Enlightenment doctrines for which they [the librettists Schikaneder and Giesecke] stood and, had they denied it to the Queen, they would have spared themselves the most obvious criticism which is always brought against them, namely, that without any warning the audience has to switch its sympathies at the end of the First Act. (*Libretti*, 130)

This basic "flaw" in the structure of *The Magic Flute* is one of the features which Auden and Kallman attempted to correct in their version. Although the Queen of the Night is unnamed in the Schikaneder-Giesecke libretto, Auden and Kallman call her Astrafiammante ("flaming star"), a name, moreover, which could well have been suggested by Papageno's reference to her rather early in the first act as "die sternflammende Königin."

It must be made clear from the outset that the translation of Mozart's *Die Zauberflöte* made by Auden and Kallman was more than just a translation: it was, in certain aspects, a reworking and a "clarification" of various points that the two translators regarded as muddled and confused. Mention has already been made of the inconsistencies in the original treatment of the Queen of the Night. But the translators of the libretto also took it upon themselves to re-arrange certain scenes of the second and final act of the opera.

In addition, they also saw fit to add three pieces of poetry that were most definitely not a part of the original. They added a prologue or "proem," as they called it, that consists of nine strophes of four lines apiece; a "metalogue" of considerable length which they positioned between the two acts of the opera and which is supposedly spoken by the singer who plays the rôle of Sarastro; and an epilogue or, to use their term, a postscript, that contains exactly 12 strophes of 3 lines, all 3 lines of which rhyme throughout each individual strophe. The last word in each of the 3 lines, respectively, of the first strophe are "throne," "own," and "known." Moreover, this postscript is presumably addressed to the two translators by Astrafiammante, the name they arbitrarily assigned to the Queen of the Night. All three of these poems are intentionally humorous, presumably in keeping with the humor that is to be found in some parts, though by no means in all parts, of the opera. One begins by considering briefly the so-called Proem or Prologue.

The Proem or Prologue consists of nine quatrains which serve as a sort of humorous summary of the opera's plot. The first quatrain refers to the Queen of the Night as Queen Astrafiammante, though in the original German libretto she is never named as such. The rhyme scheme of the Proem is quite ingenious. The rhyme scheme of the first three quatrains is as follows: *abcb; defe; ghih;* etc. Moreover, the first and third lines of each strophe count six syllables to a line. But that is by no means all. In each first line and in each third line, the poets have succeeded in making the fourth syllable rhyme with the eighth syllable, in addition to achieving a rhyme between the last syllables of the second and fourth lines respectively. Thus we see the first three strophes:

> Queen Astrafiammante, she
>> Long ruled the primal Night,
> In realms of dream had reigned supreme,
>> Until there came the Light.
>
> But she defied that civil guide,
>> Refused to share her throne,
> With the High Gods became at odds
>> And fled to dwell alone,
>
> Deep underground a refuge found,
>> Hating all love and joy,
> And, plotting there in her despair
>> Sarastro to destroy.
>> > (*Libretti*, 135)

One can ask why the poets/translators elected to add this Proem, which was not a part of Schikaneder's original German libretto. First of all, the Proem summarizes in a succinct manner the basic plot of the opera. Moreover, it does so in a sprightly, somewhat humorous manner that is abetted by the rather sing-song rhyme scheme. As a case in point, here is the fifth and middle strophe:

> A daughter she [i.e., the Queen] bore to her paramour,
>> Pamina was her name,
> Gentle and fair beyond compare
>> Despite her birth in shame.
>> > (*Libretti*, 135)

The Proem does not exactly make fun of the opera, but it points to those humorous elements, as well as to the serious elements that make up this marvelous musical piece. The rhyme scheme and the rhythm of the Proem are perhaps an indication to the reader/spectator to enjoy the work and not to take it as being overly solemn, although there are some solemn moments, particularly in the second act.

It is obviously neither possible nor even necessary to comment upon every detail in every scene of the opera. One can concentrate on certain scenes where the translators have dealt in one way or another with a particularly challenging scene or situation. Let's take, as a case in point, the first strophe of Papageno's famous entry aria "Der Vogelfänger bin ich ja." This is an excellent introduction to an important character in the opera, the one who for the original librettist represented the *Naturmensch* or child of nature. Papageno will be the somewhat reluctant travel companion of Tamino as the latter makes his voyage toward self-knowledge and full maturity. The first strophe is as follows in the original libretto:

> Der Vogelfänger bin ich ja,
> Stets lustig, heisa, hopsasa!
> Ich Vogelfänger bin bekannt
> Bei Alt und Jung im ganzen Land.
> Weiß mit dem Locken umzugehn
> Und mich aufs Pfeifen zu versteh'n.
> Drum kann ich froh und lustig sein,
> Denn alle Vögel sind ja mein.
> (Schikaneder, 1–2)

Auden and Kallman render this strophe as follows:

> The lark, the ruddock and the willow-wren
> And the jolly nightingale I ken;
> In vain do all the pretty little creatures fly
> When they the tall bird-catcher spy.
> With a whistle I their ears decoy
> And many a cunning snare employ,
> So that I can merry merry-hearted be,
> For all the birds belong to me.
> (*Libretti*, 135)

Although this is a very free translation, it is a successful translation. Schikaneder's original text, of course, refers to "alle Vögel" ("all birds") but Auden and Kallman have somewhat arbitrarily chosen four specific species: lark, ruddock, willow-wren and nightingale. Most readers are probably unfamiliar with the word "ruddock"; it is simply a rather obscure word for "robin," a reference no doubt to the bird's red breast. The choice of "wren" was no doubt made to rhyme with the verb "ken." Whereas Auden and Kallman's penultimate line "So that I can merry merry-hearted be" is a faithful rendition of "Drum kann ich froh und lustig sein," it also takes into consideration the second line of the original German. "Stets lustig, heisa, hopsasa!" ("Always happy, heisa, hopsasa!"—the last five syllables being essentially filler.) This well conveys the happy-go-lucky nature and world-view of Papageno.

In the next major aria, we see and hear Tamino react with what can best be described as rapture upon seeing the portrait of Pamina which the three ladies, attendants of Astrafiammante, have given him. The German original consists of fourteen lines of poetry, of which the first four lines have 8 syllables apiece and of which the second group of four lines have 9 syllables in lines 5 and 6 and then back to 8 syllables in lines 7 and 8. These facts, perhaps not so remarkable in themselves, are interesting insofar as the two English translators have respected the original number of syllables in these first 8 lines, with one slight exception: Auden and Kallman have given 10 syllables (instead of 9) to the sixth line. The first 8 lines of the German text read:

> Dies Bildnis ist bezaubernd schön,
> Wie noch kein Auge je gesehn!
> Ich fühl' es wie dies Götterbild
> Mein Herz mit neuer Regung füllt.
> Dies Etwas kann ich zwar nicht nennen.
> Doch fühl' ich's hier wie Feuer brennen.
> Soll die Empfindung Liebe sein?
> Ja, ja, die Liebe ist's allein.
> (Schikaneder, 4)

The rhyme scheme of the German version is, of course, *abcdeeff*. On the other hand, the rhyme scheme of the English translation is *aabbccdd*. Auden and Kallman have rendered the first eight lines into English thus:

> True image of enchanting grace!
> O rare perfection's dwelling place
> Where beauty is with virtue shown
> More noble than itself alone.
>
> Is she the dream to which I waken,
> The pursuit where I am overtaken,
> Body and mind and heart and soul?
> She is! To love her is my goal.
> (*Libretti*, 140)

The first quatrain is noted as much as anything for language that has strongly religious associations: "True image," "grace," "perfection's dwelling-place," "virtue," and "noble." This is in keeping, one could say, with the German original, where one of the most striking words is "Götterbild" at the end of the third line. "Götterbild," meaning literally "portrait of the gods" or more freely "divine portrait," shows the reverence with which Tamino regards the young lady who is the object of his affection. Although the English translators do not literally render "Götterbild" into English, they are nonetheless faithful to the idea when they write "Where beauty is with virtue shown."

In the second quatrain, Tamino asks himself whether his emotion is really love. After all, it could be something else that moves him deeply, something other than love. But he answers his own question affirmatively: "She is! To love her is my goal." Although Tamino seems to hesitate when he asks himself what he would do, in the final tercet, which is not quoted above, he affirms that he will press her to his chest—and she will be eternally his. Interestingly, both the last word in the German original and the last word in the Auden-Kallman version are the same: "mein" = "mine."

Another aria is that of the Queen of the Night in Act I. This is one of the highlights of the opera, as the Queen both recounts to Tamina the details of her daughter's abduction and tells him that he will be her rescuer. That Mozart's music for the Queen's aria is incredibly complex and vocally demanding makes this piece all the more compelling. There is a 4-line recitative that precedes the actual aria. The German text for the recitative is:

> O zitt're nicht, mein lieber Sohn!
> Du bist unschuldig, weise, fromm.
> Ein Jüngling, so wie du, vermag am besten,
> Dies tiefbetrübte Mutter herz zu trösten.
> (Schikaneder, 4)

Although the rhyme scheme is essentially *aabb*, one notes that "Sohn" and "fromm" are not perfect rhymes, but this would scarcely be noticed in an actual performance. Moreover, the first two lines have 8 syllables apiece, while the 3rd and 4th lines have 11 apiece. Auden and Kallman have rendered the recitative thus:

> Brave Prince, approach: we welcome you.
> We know you gentle, courteous, true,
> A young knight born for deeds of love and glory;
> My son, hear now a mother's doleful story.
> (140–41)

Again, what we have is not a literal translation but rather a free translation which is very true to the spirit of the original text.

The last two lines of the German text say, literally, "A youth like yourself can best console this deeply grieved mother's heart." The translators have, so to speak, changed this to "hear now a mother's doleful story." This is a new twist, to be sure, but it remains essentially true to the story.

Following the recitative is the actual aria, which itself one may divide into two parts: the first 12 lines detail the Queen's grief and recount her daughter's abduction, and the last four lines encourage the young prince to be Pamina's savior. Musically, this was very skillfully handled by Mozart, because the 12th line of the lament ("For my help was too weak") ends almost on the musical equivalent of a whisper, as the Queen expresses her despair at being helpless to prevent the abduction. The translators, who use 14 lines to render the original German text of 12 lines, conclude this section thus: "My protestation all in vain, / My frantic weeping all in vain." The phrase "in vain" picks up on the German adverb "vergebens," the second word of the 11th line of the German text.

After the gloom-laden melancholy of this 12-line section comes the sprightly—and vocally thrilling—final quatrain in which the Queen exhorts in the strongest possible terms Tamino to free her daughter. In the first line of the quatrain, she sings, "Du, du, du wirst sie zu befreien gehen," even though the printed text contains but one "du." Auden and Kallman have picked up on this by writing "You, you, you / Are the hero, her predestined saviour!" (141). The last two lines of the quatrain read in the German original: "Und werd' ich dich als Sieger sehen, / So sei sie dann auf ewig dein." For these lines the English translators have given: "To the victorious hero I will give her, / And you shall take her for your bride" (141). The words "victorious hero" are obviously suggested by the noun "Sieger." And while the German text does not use the word for "bride," nevertheless "So sei sie dann auf ewig dein" certainly implies the sanctity of holy matrimony. The recitative and the aria are translated in a manner that is fully in keeping with the spirit of the Schikaneder text.

Another personage to consider, and indeed one of the stranger aspects of the opera, is the man known as Monostatos. Monostatos is a Moor, and his name seems to imply that he is locked in a single psychological state, indeed a state of arrested development. He is obsessed with Pamina's beauty and seems determined to possess her physically, both in the first act and later in the second act. In both cases, however, his plans are thwarted by the arrival of another party: in the first case, by Pagageno, in the second, by Pamina's mother, the Queen of the Night.

One can also concentrate on the trio (Monostatos, Pamino, and Papageno) that occurs in Act I, scene 2. The music here moves very quickly, as it usually does when Monostatos is on the stage. There is what one could describe as a "fluttering anxiety" in the music that corresponds wonderfully to the agitated mental state typical of Monostatos. Since his designs are usually malevolent, he is usually in a nervous temperament and eager to complete his putative misdeed. Even for this unsympathetic character, Mozart has provided some glorious music.

The musical exchange between Monostatos and Pamina (this is the first time we've seen Pamina onstage, though, a little earlier, Tamino had sung rapturously to her portrait) lasts for only ten lines, after which she faints. These ten lines, that are Monostatos' threats and Pamina's reactions, go by very quickly. The rhyme scheme of these ten lines is *aabbccdeed*. For purposes of illustration, here is the German text:

Monostatos:	Du feines Täubchen, nur herein!
Pamina:	O welche Marter, welche Pein!
Monostatos:	Verloren ist dein Leben!
Pamina:	Der Tod macht mich nicht beben,
	Nur meine Mutter dauert mich;
	Sie stirbt vor Gram ganz sicherlich.
Monostatos:	He, Sklaven, legt ihr Fesseln an!
	Mein Hass soll dich verderben.
Pamina:	Lass mich lieber sterben
	Weil nichts, Barbar, dich rühren kann.

(Schikaneder, 7)

A few comments are in order here. The only line not a part of the Monostatos-Pamina exchange is the 7th line, which Monostatos sings to his slaves; yet this 7th line rhymes with the last line sung by Pamina before she faints. The 8th line ("Mein Hass soll dich verderben.") is an odd thought to be expressed by a man to a woman whose love he supposedly wishes to win.

The Auden-Kallman translation renders these ten lines in an interesting manner. The number of syllables of lines 1 through 8 is the same in both the German original and the English version; in lines 9 and 10, the translators have increased by one syllable, respectively, the syllable count per line. Their translation of "Du feines Täubchen, nur herein!" ("Ah, pretty bird, so white and pure!") is doubtless influenced by information contained in

Monostatos' second-act aria to the effect that he finds white women appealing. There is, of course, no mention of color in the ten lines under discussion here. In a similar vein, the translators' rendition of "Verloren ist dein Leben!" as "Prepare to die or love me!" is influenced by an exchange between the two that occurs in the second act, in which Monostatos offers to help Pamina in exchange for her love. Again, the knowledge possessed by the translators of information in Act II has influenced their translation here. The remainder of the translation is quite faithful to the original text.

Between the end of Act I and the start of Act II, Auden and Kallman have placed a somewhat lengthy poem they have styled a "Metalogue." In his Introduction to *Libretti and Other Dramatic Writings by W.H. Auden (1939–1973)*, Edward Mendelson has this to say apropos the "Metalogue":

> The metalogue, written as a bicentennial celebration of Mozart's birth, lamented on his behalf, and on Auden's, the pestilence of operatic production in which the words and music are forced to endure the "small vanities" of the stage director ("who with ingenious wit/Places the wretched singers in the pit/While dancers mime their roles") and the designer ("Who sets the whole thing on an ocean liner,/The girls in shorts, the men in yachting caps"). (*Libretti*, xxvi)

The tone of this "Metalogue" is both humorous and occasionally sarcastic. As Mendelson mentions, this was a tribute to Mozart, just as the commissioning of a new translation was for a 1956 production of *The Magic Flute*, scheduled to coincide with the 200th anniversary of Mozart's birth (in January 1756).

In spite of the fact that the metalogue is written in a tongue-in-cheek style, it does have some serious points to make:

> *Relax, Maestro, put your baton down:*
>   *Only the fogiest of the old will frown*
>   *If you the trials of the* Prince *prorogue*
>   *To let* Sarastro *speak the Metalogue,*
>   *A form acceptable to use, although*
>   *Unclassed by* Aristotle *or* Boileau.
>   (*Libretti*, 152–53)

The injunction to the Maestro to stop the beginning of the second act is the start of the Metalogue and also explains why the metalogue is necessary in the first place. Auden (it was, after all, probably Auden who penned the Metalogue) has shown the elasticity of the English language. For example, he has taken the noun "fogey" (as in "old fogey") and turned it into an adjective in the superlative degree ("the fogiest of the old"). His poetic cleverness is demonstrated by the fact that he even thought of rhyming the conjunction "although" with the name of the French critic Boileau, who, like Aristotle, wrote his own *Ars poetica*. Later in the early part of the Metalogue we read (lines 16–20):

> I come to praise but not to sell Mozart,
> Who came into this world of war and woe
> At Salzburg just two centuries ago,
> When kings were many and machines were few
> And open Atheism something new.
>
> (*Libretti*, 153)

Line 16 is a humorous variant on Marc Antony's "I come to bury Caesar, not to praise him" from Shakespeare's *Julius Caesar*. Line 18 is a reminder, in case one were needed, that this translation is being made for a production of the opera to honor the bicentennial of Mozart's birth. Line 20, with its reference to "open Atheism," is a bit ambiguous. Perhaps it refers to the fact that Mozart himself was a Mason and something of a freethinker, though scarcely an atheist. It may also be a reference to the fact that the Enlightenment had certain strains of atheism among some, though by no means all, of its adherents. And it has been said that *Die Zauberflöte* was Austria's only contribution to the Enlightenment.

Mozart's steadily rising stock among music critics and intellectuals is the inspiration for these lines (31–38) that are humorous and true:

> We know the Mozart of our fathers' time
> Was gay, rococo, sweet, but not sublime,
> A Viennese Italian: that is changed
> Since music-critics learned to feel "estranged":
> Now it's the Germans he is classed amongst,
> A Geist whose music was composed from Angst,
> At International Festivals enjoys
> An equal status with the Twelve-Tone Boys [...]
>
> (*Libretti*, 153)

This is probably an accurate albeit humorous assessment of Mozart's position among the critics; no longer is he "merely" "gay, rococo, sweet, but not sublime"; rather, he is an artist whose profundity and seriousness are almost universally acknowledged.

Since Germans are often jocularly referred to as having *Angst*, this gives elevated status to the composer whose music is associated therewith. Of course, "the Twelve-Tone Boys" are Arnold Schönberg, Anton von Webern, and company, whose musical achievements Mozart equaled and even surpassed.

Also in a humorous vein are Auden's lines about what the various characters might be doing, were they alive in the year of grace 1956.

> *In Nineteen Fifty-Six we find the* Queen
> *A highly paid and most efficient Dean*
> *(Who, as we all know, really runs the College),*
> Sarastro, *tolerated for his knowledge,*
> *Teaching the History of Ancient Myth*
> *At* Bryn Mawr, Vassar, Bennington *or* Smith;
> Pamina *may a* Time *researcher be*
> *To let* Tamino *take his Ph.D.,*
> *Acquiring manly wisdom as he wishes*
> *While changing diapers and doing dishes;*
> *Sweet* Papagena, *when she's time to spare,*
> *Listens to* Mozart *operas on the air,*
> *Though* Papegeno, *one is sad to feel,*
> *Prefers the juke-box to the glockenspiel* [...]
> (*Libretti*, 154)

This is how, as seen through Auden's humorous perspective, the characters would react to "modern life." Sarastro would function well as a (somewhat pedantic) college professor. The four colleges cited are all prestigious and, at least at the time, they were predominantly women's colleges. Pamina, the lovely and gracious woman, is working to help put her husband through graduate school. On the other hand, Papageno's aspirations to "high culture" have certainly not increased; on the contrary, he has, so to speak, "gone to seed," as evidenced by his preference for the jukebox, the coin-operated purveyor of pop music, over the glockenspiel, the 18th-century instrument that he so skillfully played in this very opera.

In the last section of the metalogue, Auden praises Mozart for his creative genius and for his gentle approach to life.

> *How seemly, then, to celebrate the birth*
> *Of one who did no harm to our poor earth,*
> *Created masterpieces by the dozen,*
> *Indulged in toilet humor with his cousin,*

> *And had a pauper's funeral in the rain,*
> *The like of whom we shall not see again [...]*
> (*Libretti*, 155)

The cousin, with whom Mozart indulged in off-color jokes, was Mozart's Augsburg cousin (often called in German the *Augsburger Bäsle*). Mozart's father Leopold was born in Augsburg in 1719. It has been argued that Mozart's burial in a common grave was not really unusual, that is, was typical of burial customs in the Vienna of his day. In any event, Auden's genuine admiration for Mozart's genius in general and for the delightful beauty of *The Magic Flute* in particular is evident from this Metalogue.

The most far-reaching changes made by Auden and Kallman in the whole opera are changes in the numbers or set-pieces of Act II of *The Magic Flute*. They made these changes to remove ambiguities and to clarify certain points that were confusing. Chief among the ambiguities to be removed is that regarding what befalls Pamina. In their preface to the translation, Auden and Kallman make this statement:

> In Act Two, as written, Pamina's troubles with Monostatos and the Queen precede the trial of Tamino's silence and departure. We have reversed this order for the following reasons. It does not seem natural that, having seen her fall into Tamino's arms at the end of Act One, she should appear, when we see her next, to have forgotten his existence. (*Libretti*, 131)

Auden and Kallman have decided to place the trio (sung by the three boys) beginning with the words "Seid uns zum zweiten Mal willkommen" before the priests of Sarastro's order place upon Tamino and Papageno an order of silence. This period of silence observed by Tamino in the face of the pleading of Pamina causes the latter to sing her moving aria "Ach, ich fühl's." This is the point of the opera where Pamina is at her point of deepest despair. The translators go on in their preface to say:

> Secondly, the effect of Monostatos and her mother upon her would be a much greater temptation to suicidal despair if she had to endure them after she imagines her lover has deserted her rather than before, when she could console herself with the thought of him and even call on him for help and guidance. Thirdly, we wished to make her appearance in the Finale with a dagger more plausible and more dramatic. (*Libretti*, 131)

What the translators refer to here is the attempt by the evil Monostatos to seduce Pamino—an attempt fortunately thwarted by the unexpected arrival of the Queen of the Night—and the attempt made by the Queen to force Pamina to kill Sarastro. This attempt, too, is unsuccessful. The psychological pressure exerted upon Pamina by her beloved's apparent rejection, by Monostatos' evil designs, and by her mother's inexplicable demand that she kill a man who is obviously beneficent: all this places her in a particularly vulnerable position.

In the original Schikaneder version of the libretto, the arias "Alles fühlt der Liebe Freuden" (sung by Monostatos), "Der Hölle Rache kocht in meinem Herzen" (sung by the Queen of the Night), and "In diesen heil'gen Hallen" (sung by Sarastro) *precede* the trio "Seid uns zum zweiten Mal willkommen" (sung by the three boys) and "Ach, ich fühl's" (sung by Pamina). In the Auden/Kallman version, however, the last two numbers mentioned in the previous sentence are placed ahead of the first three numbers mentioned, with the trio "Soll ich dich, Teurer, nicht mehr sehen?" placed after "Ach, ich fühl's" by Auden and Kallman. In both the Schikaneder original version and the Auden/Kallman version, Papageno's delightful aria "Ein Mädchen oder Weibchen" precedes the finale. All this is done to make the psychological states of the characters, especially that of Pamina, more realistic and more true-to-life.

One must also consider the deeply moving aria "Ach, ich fühl's," which Auden and Kallman list as the fifth number of Act II. As mentioned earlier, this is the moving response of Pamina to the silence (and, to her way of thinking, the apparent indifference) of Tamino. This is the nadir of the opera from the viewpoint of Pamina. The aria in its original German version has only eight lines:

> Ach, ich fühl's, es ist verschwunden,
> Ewig hin der Liebe Glück!
> Nimmer kommt ihr, Wonnestunden,
> Meinem Herzen mehr zurück.
> Sieh, Tamino, diese Tränen,
> Fliessen, Trauter, dir allein!
> Fühlst du nicht der Liebe Sehnen,
> So wird Ruhe im Tode sein.
> (Schikaneder, 19)

This is a relatively brief aria, full of pathos and grief. It comes at a time when Pamina believes that her true love has abandoned her. She feels that the severity of her pain and grief are such that it can be assuaged only in death. Auden and Kallman accept this basic premise, but their 14-line rendition of the original 8-line aria is obviously an expansion of the original. The two translators have Pamina sing:

> Hearts may break though grief be silent,
> True hearts make their love their lives,
> Silence love with ended lives:
> Love that dies in one false lover
> Kills the heart where love survives.
>
> O Tamino, see the silence
> Of my tears betray my grief,
> Faithful grief: if you flee
> My love in silence, in faithless silence,
> Let my sorrow die with me.
>
> If you can betray Pamina,
> If you love me not, Tamino,
> Let my sorrow die with me,
>   And silent be.
>   (*Libretti*, 163–64)

That the two translators have expanded the 8-line aria is evident. How successfully they have handled this is another matter. The first 5-line strophe is a bit confusing on first reading, especially the second and third lines. One has to read two or three times to realize that what the translators want to say is:

> True hearts make their love [become] their lives,
> [And two hearts] [s]ilence love with ended lives [...]

This is somewhat confusing at best. What it seems to be saying is that "true love" comes to an end, that is, it is silenced, only when one or both parties die. The next two lines ("Love that dies in one false lover/Kills the heart where love survives") seem to imply that if one of the pair loses love, that is enough to ruin the situation for the party no longer blessed by being loved. This may be psychologically true and very realistic, but it is far more than Pamina really sings in the original.

The translators have used their second strophe to translate or, better, to paraphrase the last four lines of the original aria. The last four lines of the aria translate literally as: "See, Tamino, these tears/ flow, beloved, for you alone! / If you do not feel love's yearning, / then [my] peace will be in death." Again, what one observes here is an expansion and a paraphrase of the original. The German word "Ruhe" in the 8th line of the aria is doubtless the word which inspires the word "silence" that is used thrice in the translators' version, while the words "Let my sorrow die with me" are basically a paraphrase of "So wird [meine] Ruhe im Tode sein." The last four lines of the paraphrase are an expansion by the translators, although the third line of the last quatrain is merely a repetition of the 10th line of the aria. The paraphrase is basically true to the original, although it is considerably longer than the original text in German.

The next aria to be considered is the second and final aria of the Queen of the Night or, as Auden and Kallman call her, Astra-fiammante. This aria, let us recall, is the 6th number in the original Schikaneder version of the opera, whereas Auden and Kallman's version has it as the 8th number. In any event, it a vocal *pièce de résistance* that requires tremendous ability to execute and usually produces an electrifying impression on the audience. It also demonstrates vocally and psychologically the different way in which the Queen is portrayed in the first act from the way she is portrayed here: from being a grief-stricken mother who laments her only daughter's abduction in Act I, she is now shown to be a fire-breathing virago, hell-bent on the destruction of Sarastro and insistent that Pamina be the one to do the murderous deed.

The original German text in the first four lines is as follows:

> Der Hölle Rache kocht in meinem Herzen,
> Tod und Verzweiflung flammet um mich her!
> Fühlt nicht durch dich Sarastro Todesschmerzen,
> So bist du meine Tochter nimmermehr!
> (Schikaneder, 17)

The German text is noteworthy for the presence of what one could call "harsh words," that is, words that connote unpleasant realities that the Queen wishes to stress to Pamina: "[d]er Hölle Rache," "Tod und Verzweiflung," "Todesschmerzen," "nimmer-mehr" and these mean, respectively, "hell's revenge," "death and despair," "the pains of death," "never more." Let's consider how these four lines are handled by Auden and Kallman:

> Avenging fury lacerates my spirit,
> Rage at Sarastro darkly throbs and wild
> Blood cries for blood, O may my own blood hear it!
> Impale his heart or you are not my child.
> (*Libretti*, 68)

A literal translation this is not, but it is faithful to the thought of the original. The translators have also respected the original rhyme scheme of *abab*. (To achieve this, however, they have had to resort to what the French call *enjambement*: the descriptive adjective "wild" at the end of the second line modifies the word "Blood' at the start of the third line.) Auden and Kallman's fourth line neatly sums up the essential thought of the original third and fourth lines.

And here are the last six lines of the aria in German:

> Verstossen sei auf ewig,
> Verlassen sei auf ewig,
> Zertrümmert sei auf ewig
> Alle Bände der Natur,
> Wenn nicht durch dich Sarastro wird erblassen!
> Hört, Rachegötter, hört der Mutter Schwur!
>
> (Schikaneder, 17)

Auden and Kallman render these 6 lines thus:

> Sarastro has betrayed me! Tamino now betrays me:
> My daughter would betray me and a mother's love deny.
> Tormented, impassioned Nature sways me
> As the heartless I defy!
> My pain is deep, Sarastro's blood allays me:
> Swear! Swear! Swear to avenge me! Or accursèd die!
>
> (*Libretti*, 68)

This is an interesting rendition of the German text. The three-fold use of forms of the English "betray" reflects the three "destructive" past participles ("verstossen," "verlassen," "zertrümmert") of the German, although the German does not use the verb "betray" at all. At first glance, the line "As the heartless I defy!" is difficult to grasp, but a closer reading determines that "the heartless" refers to those three persons (Sarastro, Tamino, Pamina) who have betrayed, are betraying, or would seek to betray the Queen. The use of the imperative "Swear!" corresponds to the use of "Hört!" while the English *verb* "swear" is a cognate of the German *noun* "Schwur" (meaning "oath"). And, appropriately, the verb "avenge" picks up on the first element of the compound noun "Rachegötter" (meaning "gods of revenge"). In other words, Auden and Kallman have shown their keen sensitivity to the nuances of the German text, without, for all that, having given a literal translation.

Little mention has been made thus far of the chorus, but there is indeed a chorus in *The Magic Flute*. It functions as a mouthpiece for Sarastro and his exalted brotherhood; it appeals to Isis and Osiris to bestow aid and assistance to Tamino; it expresses gratitude to Sarastro for his fairness in dispensing justice (esp. at the end of Act I); and it praises Isis and Osiris for bringing Tamino and Pamina to a successful and happy end of their trials. The music Mozart composed for the chorus is noble and uplifting and sometimes jubilant. I would like to consider one chorus sung by the chorus in Act II, scene 3 of the Auden/Kallman version of the opera. The German text for this chorus reads thus:

> O Isis und Osiris, welche Wonne!
> Die düst're Nacht verscheucht der Glanz der Sonne.
> Bald fühlt der edle Jüngling neues Leben,
> Bald ist er unserm Dienste ganz ergeben.
> Sein Geist ist kühn, sein Herz ist rein,
> Bald wird er unser würdig sein.
>
> (Schikaneder, 19)

The German text is remarkable for a number of things. First of all, as is fitting, the chorus is addressed to Isis and Osiris, the Egyptian gods whose "wisdom" informs Sarastro's brotherhood. The second line demonstrates the dichotomy of darkness and light, a dichotomy that the opera exploits on several occasions. Equally remarkable is the three-fold use of the adverb "Bald" ("soon"), that begins the 3rd, 4th, and 6th lines. The last four lines of the chorus refer to Tamino—what he is/feels and what he will be. The words "der edle Jüngling" refer to Tamino whom the chorus goes on to describe as "ergeben," "kühn," "rein," and "würdig" (meaning, respectively, "devoted," "bold," "pure," and "worthy").

The 6-line chorus is rendered by Auden and Kallman thus:

> O Isis and Osiris, great and gracious,
> The pathless shade inform with light sagacious
> When all the unchecked elements deride him,
> Down through their realm of hostile chaos guide him:
>   Inspire his heart, instruct his youth,
>   Soon, soon,
>   May he be soon reborn in truth,
>   Light and truth.
>
> (*Libretti*, 170–71)

As it does so often, the chorus begins by invoking Isis and Osiris. But while the second line of the German original says "The glory of the sun disperses the gloomy night," the translators make of this second line an imperative (addressed to the Egyptian gods) "The pathless shade inform with light sagacious." A second imperative, also addressed to the same gods, is contained in the fourth line: "Down through their realm of hostile chaos guide him [...]" Although the original German version contains no impera-

tives, the translators' version employs no fewer than four impera-
tives. As mentioned above, the adverb "Bald" ("soon") begins the
3rd, 4th, and 6th lines. The translators use the adverb "soon" three
times, but not in the same position as the German text has it.
Whereas the original German text consists of four lines of 11 syllables followed by two lines of 8 syllables, the new version by Auden and Kallman has four lines of 11 syllables followed by one line
of 10 syllables and by a final line of 11 syllables. Even more interesting is the fact that our 20th-century translators have basically
managed to retain the original rhyme scheme of *aabbcc*. (I say
"basically" because the last two lines have been broken in such a
way that "youth" and "truth" rhyme, even though the word
"soon" does not fit into the rhyme scheme. This is, however, relatively minor.)

There is another example not strictly speaking of a chorus but
of a chorus-like chorale sung by the Two Men in Armor just before
Tamino and Pamina undergo the trials of fire and water. This
chorale is said to be a good example of Mozart's composing in a
contrapuntal style similar to that of Bach. The solemnity of the
musical style is fitting for the occasion, that is, the final rites of
testing for both Tamino and Pamina. The German text reads:

> Der, welcher wandert diese Strasse voll Beschwerden,
> Wird rein durch Feuer, Wasser, Luft and Erden:
> Wenn er des Todes Schrecken überwinden kann,
> Schwingt er sich aus der Erde himmel an:
> Erleuchtet wird er dann im Stande sein,
> Sich den Mysterien der Isis ganz zu weih'n.
>
> (Schikaneder, 23)

Like the music composed to accompany them, the words of
this chorale are both noble and solemn. At the precise moment
when they are sung by the Men in Armor, Pamina and the Three
Spirits have just exited the stage and Tamino presumably is about
to appear. Thus the Two Men in Armor are singing ostensibly to
the audience, explaining, so to speak, the rites of purification that
the young couple will undergo. This is one of the key passages of
the opera. Here is a literal translation of the first four lines.

> He who wanders along this path [literally, "street"] full of grief,
> Becomes pure through fire, water, air and earth:
> If he can overcome death's fright,
> He swings himself out of the Earth toward heaven [...]

The classical four elements of fire, water, air, and earth are mentioned as being the purifying elements through which one becomes pure and is enabled to rise above earthly cares and woes. Once this purification is achieved, the initiate is then free to dedicate himself to other, higher activities; as the last two lines put it:

> Enlightened he will be then in a position
> To dedicate himself completely to the mysteries of Isis.

In other words, as in so many religious and spiritual systems, only when one has been in some way purified can one go on to achieve spiritual progress. This is probably true of Christian, Buddhist, and other spiritual traditions. Let us examine how Auden and Kallman have rendered these six essential lines.

> Now shall the pilgrim tread a valley dark and dire,
> Face death by air and water, earth and fire.
> Who shall this dreadful passage to the end endure,
> He his salvation shall thereby secure,
> In mansions of the Light forever dwell;
> Isis her mysteries to him shall full tell [...]
>
> (*Libretti*, 177)

In observing the difference between the German original and the Auden-Kallman rendition, one is struck by the way in which the two versions handle the four elements of fire, water, air, and earth. Whereas the German version speaks of the searcher's becoming "pure through fire, water, air and earth," the new translation speaks of a "pilgrim" who will "[f]ace death by air and water, earth and fire." The German version, for its part, refers to death only in the 3rd line where we read "Wenn er des Todes Schrecken überwinden kann," literally, "If he can overcome death's terrors." Those who have seen an actual staging of the opera know that the trial by fire and the trial by water are not without danger to Tamino and Pamina. Were it not for their steadfast resolve, they could be overwhelmed, even killed by the primal elements. The position of the past participle "erleuchtet" at the beginning of the 5th line is significant. It means "enlightened" and refers to the state of the initiate after his purification rites are behind him: it is then (and only then) that the initiate will be in a position (e.g., intellectually and morally) to "devote himself completely to the mysteries of Isis." As mentioned above, the solemnity of Mozart's music for this chorale is appropriate to the importance of the ideals which the text champions.

After the end of the opera has put all things aright—the Queen of the Night and her retinue are plunged into the bowels of the earth, Tamino and Pamina are united in love and triumph at the end of their trials, and Papageno and Pagagena have found joy in their supposedly unending connubial bliss—the two translators have placed a 12-strophe Postscript that consists of rhymed tercets. This Postscript, humorous to a high degree, is pronounced by the Queen of the Night herself to the translators, as a way of "putting them in their place."

Astrafiammante, the name the translators have given the Queen of the Night, begins her tirade by mockingly quoting the last line of the chorus at the end of the opera itself: "For Wisdom and Beauty have mounted the throne." To this she adds:

> May be *your* parting words, but the last is Our own:
> It is We who dismiss, as you ought to have known.
> *(Libretti, 182)*

The use of the royal "we" is befitting the Queen of the Night, as is the fact that the pronouns "we" and "us" and the possessive adjective "our" are capitalized. The authors of the Postscript poke gentle fun at themselves, particularly their re-arrangement of certain scenes in Act II, as we saw above. This change is supposedly displeasing to Astrafiammante who says:

> In Act Two, We observed, you saw fit to contrive
> A later appearance for Us and deprive
> Our rage of its dialogue. We shall survive
>
> To laugh, unimpressed, at your liberal correction
> Of conservative views about women's subjection;
> Male vanity's always been Our best protection.
> *(Libretti, 182–83)*

This represents, of course, the Queen's slap not only at the male translators but also at her enemies in the persons of Sarastro and his male brotherhood. Her next two strophes are further criticisms of men and their ridiculous ways. She says here:

> You may think, if you will, your New Order excuses
> Putting Us in Our place, but it merely amuses:
> Little men, have you any idea who your Muse is?
>
> As for Wisdom and Beauty in heart-warming bliss,
> Upon whom do they call every time that they kiss
> But the blood-curdling Queen of the Kingdom of Dis?
> *(Libretti, 183)*

Who but Auden would ever conceive of making rhymes out of "amuses" and "Muse is"? Again, at the beginning of the fifth strophe, we note another mocking reference to "Wisdom and Beauty." Somewhat cryptic is the question "Upon whom do they call every time that they kiss/But the blood-curdling Queen of the Kingdom of Dis?" The Kingdom of Dis is the Kingdom of Pluto, that is, a realm of Stygian darkness. Less clear, however, is why Wisdom and Beauty, that is, Pamina and Tamino, would ever call upon Astrafiammante as Queen of the Underworld. Is it because it was the Queen who, through her own three ladies, first gave Tamino a portrait of the lovely Pamina? Perhaps, but this hardly seems to be reason enough for the young couple to "evoke" the Queen on every occasion of their sharing a kiss. The Queen may have lost her position of authority in the play, but the "little men," as she disparagingly addresses the translators, are still dependent on her for their poetic inspiration.

Astrafiammante affirms that, contrary to what the original librettists (Schikaneder and Giesecke) may have hoped for, the fact remains that she will survive. She says, in the seventh tercet:

> Schikaneder and Giesecke clung to the hope a
> Stage trap-door would bury this dark interloper,
> But we'll never lack friends back in Mittel-Europa.
> (*Libretti*, 183)

The reference to the trap-door is explained by the Queen's and her retinue's disappearance through such an aperture toward the end of the opera. More problematic is the line "But we'll never lack friends back in Mittel-Europa." Perhaps this is a reference to central Europe's association with political absolutism, either monarchist or fascist. Perhaps it is a reference to the fact that *The Magic Flute* is a product of Central Europe. In any case, it seems a sly put-down of the emphasis on Enlightenment values that the opera upholds. The next tercet continues with an enumeration of the Queen's fellows in "dark" activities in other eras and in other situations.

> We were Goethe's *Die Mütter*, an understage chorus,
> Then for Wagner We half-rose as Erda, now for Us
> Freud adds a blunt synonym to the thesaurus.
> (*Libretti*, 183)

This tercet is also a little difficult to analyze. The reference to "Goethe's *Die Mütter*" is somewhat obscure, but a friend who knows Goethe well pointed out to me that it is a reference to sub-

terranean goddesses/phantoms that are mentioned in *Faust II*, Act
I, scene v, called "A Dark Gallery" in English translation. Faust
wants to learn from them. Mephistopheles gives Faust a key that
will supposedly take him into the Mothers' presence. Mephisto,
however, points out to Faust that a visit to the dark realm of the
Mothers is not without danger. In Wagner's cycle *Der Ring des Ni-
belungen*, Erda is a goddess who rises halfway from the earth to
predict future events. Though not "malevolent" as Queen Astrafiammante is, Erda nevertheless represents a realm of darkness and
mystery. She arises partially from the earth and, after predicting
the future, sinks back into the realm, presumably the Queen's
realm, from whence she came. As to Freud's "blunt synonym," one
cannot be sure what the authors of the Postscript have in mind.

The Queen goes on to criticize the translators as being dull and
misguided. She says, in essence, that, in spite of what they have
done, she retains her power and influence. The tenth tercet reads:

> Let the Press laud your language as sharper and purer
> Than the German can boast: when We strike in Our furor,
> You won't hear a word in Our high tessitura. (183)

The Queen will retain her power to dazzle the listeners to her
enthralling tessitura; she will carry them off, so to speak, with her
bravura performances. That she will do, regardless of whether she
sings in German or English. Her disdain for the translators continues in the eleventh and penultimate tercet.

> And it won't be with diction, industrialized dull sirs,
> Who with graph, daylight-saving and stop-watch repulse Us,
> That We strike, but with hangover, sinus and ulcers. (183)

Apparently Astrafiammante believes that she can wreak her
revenge, but it will be achieved through physical maladies rather
than through musical devices. And the Postscript concludes with a
certain triumphalism.

> Though translated to Hell, We still govern, a light
> That wanes but to wax; whether shrouded or bright,
> We are always Queen Astrafiammante:—Good night! (183)

Did Auden and Kallman have any "political" objectives in
their project of translating/reworking the libretto of *The Magic
Flute* ? The answer is yes, according to Edward Mendelson, Auden's literary executor and author of *Later Auden* (New York: Farrar, Straus, and Giroux, 1999). We have seen that the two translators intentionally strove to remove some of the ambiguities and

confusion from Act II, by re-arranging some of the scenes. But, according to Mendelson, the translating team wanted to remove some of the elements that smack of what might be called "male triumphalism." One reads:

> He and Kallman [...] threw out everything in the original libretto that celebrated the triumph of masculine reason over feminine passion. The eighteenth-century text, in Auden's view, was an example of history written by the victors. As if to address an old wrong, Auden's Sarastro explains, in a newly written soliloquy, that he too must die when the Queen of the Night is defeated. (Mendelson, *Later Auden*, 398)

There is little doubt that Auden wanted not only to translate but also to "improve" the libretto of this wonderful opera. Whether he actually did improve on the original text by making these alterations is open to question.

By and large, the improvements made by Auden and Kallman are genuine. The attitude taken by the Queen of the Night is more understandable if we follow the sequence of the second act as structured by Auden and Kallman. Pamina's emotions, too, are more understandable in the Auden-Kallman version. As for the translation itself, it is a very successful translation, certainly true to the spirit of the original German text. One can argue, if one is so inclined, about the necessity of the Metalogue and the Postscript, both of which are inventions of Auden and Kallman. But they are humorous and do give insight into the attributes of the main characters. Perhaps the most significant aspect of the Postscript is the ultimate triumph of the Queen of the Night. (In the German libretto, of course, the Queen and her retinue are plunged into the depths of the earth, supposedly destroyed.) In the Auden-Kallman Postscript, however, the Queen has survived triumphantly and will doubtless continue to do so. Certainly an English-speaking reader who knows no German could approach *The Magic Flute* admirably and profitably thanks to the translation/adaptation of Auden and Kallman.

Works Cited

Auden, W.H., and Chester Kallman. *Libretti and Other Dramatic Writings by W.H. Auden, 1939–1973*. (Part of *The Complete Works of W.H. Auden*.) Edited by Edward Mendelson. Princeton: Princeton UP, 1993.

————. *The Magic Flute. An Opera in Two Acts. Music by W.A. Mozart. English Version after the Libretto of Schikaneder and Giesecke*. New York: Random House, 1956.

Schikaneder, Emanuel [sic]. *The Magic Flute*. English version by Ruth and Thomas Martin. New York: G. Schirmer, 1941.

Mendelson, Edward. *Later Auden*. New York: Farrar, Straus and Giroux, 1999.

Search Conditions:
Find "Auden" & "Modernism"

Jay Ladin

This search consists of two moving targets: Auden *and* Modernism. *For one to say that Auden is a modernist (along with Eliot, Pound, Williams, et al.)—and the term "modernism" here certainly applies to Auden mainly from 1930 through the early 1940s—one must locate on the twentieth-century map that sometimes elusive place where "modernism" is and then go about defining it. Then one must follow Auden around his own poetic perambulations to see if, and how often, he made stops at this particular location.*

"To what extent is Auden a modernist?" Lynn Keller asked in a 1987 study, *Re-making It New: Contemporary American Poetry and the Modernist Tradition* (184). Though *Re-making It New* never answers that question, Keller is one of few critics who bother to ask it.[1]

W.H. Auden was one of the twentieth century's most influential poets, and modernism was the century's most influential poetic movement. Auden's first books were published under the enthusiastic editorial auspices of T.S. Eliot, and prominent poets on both sides of the Atlantic, including Philip Larkin, John Ashbery and James Merrill (see Gwiazda in this volume), have

---

[1]Keller, whose focus is not Auden but James Merrill, makes a rather casual distinction between Auden's early English poems, which "have much in common with modernist works of the preceding decades," and those written after his emigration to the United States in 1939, which "reacted against modernism ... [by] using traditional poetic forms and a conversational, discursive manner" (185–86). This bifurcation of Auden's career follows Mendelson's influential account, which, as I shall argue, begs important questions.

looked to Auden for lessons in how to survive, thrive and individuate in the shadow of High Modernism.

Yet despite such richly tangled lines of influence, for the most part, scholars have ignored the question of Auden's relation to modernism. Hugh Kenner's *The Pound Era*, for example, which remains one of the most definitive histories of modernist poetry, contains only a few passing references to Auden. By the same token, the index of George W. Bahlke's 1991 collection of *Critical Essays on W.H. Auden* lists three citations for "Vulcan" and one each for "Mediocrity," "Ma Tong-na" and "Double deconstruction," but none, no mention at all, of "Modernism." Little has changed in the past ten years. A 2001 computer search of the MLA's index of books and periodicals returned 4,399 entries for "Modernism" and 876 for "Auden," but yielded a mere 11 items when the search conditions included both.[2]

For many critics the question of Auden and modernism was settled conclusively by Edward Mendelson, Auden's literary executor, who saw scuttling the notion that there is any significant link between Auden and modernism as a prerequisite for rehabilitating Auden's sagging reputation. "Most critics of twentieth-century poetry still judge poems by their conformity to modernist norms; consequently, a myth has grown up around Auden to the effect that he fell into a decline almost as soon as he began writing" ("Auden's Revision of Modernism," 112).

Mendelson's rebuttal of this "myth," here and in his 1983 landmark study *Early Auden*, opened many eyes to Auden's less-fashionable virtues. But in order to sever the Auden-modernism connection, Mendelson is forced into misleading and contradictory assertions that obscure the nature of both.

In "Auden's Revision of Modernism," for example, Mendelson writes that in his earliest published poems, Auden's "voice retained something of the modernist accent he had learned from Eliot," and that "the turn away from this early style, and from the manner and subjects of modernism, can be dated precisely" to

---

[2]Those eleven items included two versions of the same essay, one unpublished dissertation, and Rainer Emig's book-length argument that Auden should be read as a pre-post-modernist whose "poetics demonstrate a breaking away from the norms set up by the classical modernism of Yeats Eliot and Pound" (204). Computer searches, of course, are notoriously unreliable. A subsequent search using the same conditions yielded only one "hit."

1933 (113). In *Early Auden*, however, Mendelson declares that, "When Auden set out to write in a different [i.e., non-modernist] tradition, his goal was a poetry that reflected the formal and linguistic lessons of modernism yet could still serve the public good," and that "in the 1930s Auden kept trying to adapt the techniques of modernism to contexts unsuited for them" (205). Was modernism an "accent" Auden picked up during his poetic apprenticeship and shed by the early 1930s, or was it a set of techniques that the mature Auden struggled to "adapt" throughout the decade, which many still point to as his finest? Both accounts are plausible, but both cannot be right. The fact that these contradictory claims seem equally persuasive suggests how many questions about Auden and modernism Mendelson left unanswered.

But the issue of when Auden stopped writing in ways that might be considered modernist is less important than what one has to do to the term "modernism" in order to prove that Auden did, sooner or later, make a clean break from it. The vagary of "modernism" as an aesthetic and historical category has become a critical cliché; but if it is true that "Except in his very earliest and latest poems, there is virtually nothing modernist about [Auden]," it should be easy enough to define the modernism that Auden had so little to do with ("Auden's Revision," 112).

In fact, however, Mendelson offers a blizzard of contradictory descriptions. In the opening paragraphs of "Auden's Revision of Modernism," for example, Mendelson characterizes modernism as (1) a nostalgic "turn ... away from a flawed present to some lost illusory Eden where life was unified, hierarchy secure, and the grand style a natural extension of the vernacular" (111); (2) "disenfranchised from the past by its own sense of isolated 'modernity'" (111); (3) "tend[ing] to look back toward the lost reigns of a native aristocracy"; and (4) seeing "the reflected glory of ancient 'tradition' in [contemporary] political leaders" (112). Each of these claims is true for some modernist writers, but it would be difficult for any one of them, much less all, to simultaneously turn away from the present and idolize Fascist strongmen, or to feel 'disenfranchised from the past" and to "look back toward the lost reigns of a native aristocracy."

Part of the problem is one that dogs modernist studies: the conflation of roughly contemporary but radically different "modern" writers under the same banner. Here, for example, Mendelson names Yeats, Lawrence, Eliot and Pound as modernist exemplars. While it might be argued that Yeats sees—or tries to see—in "the grand style a natural extension of the vernacular," Eliot wrinkles his nose at colloquialisms, Pound proudly flaunts them, while for Lawrence, the vernacular has socio-economic connotations that render it the very antithesis of "the grand style."

In *Early Auden*, still the most authoritative account of Auden and modernism, Mendelson goes even further in his efforts to sunder Auden from "the manner and subjects of modernism."[3] Historical accounts tend to portray modernism as a development of either English Romanticism or French Symbolism; a few argue for an indigenous American modernist tradition. Mendelson collapses English Romantics, French Symbolists and American modernists into a single lineage:

> Despite all the claims to the contrary made by Eliot and Pound, the modernist poetic had its origins in romanticism.... [However, this] genealogy ... is obscure because its descent from romanticism is not by direct lineal transmission through the native line ... but collaterally, through the French line that crossed the Channel and intermarried early in the twentieth century. Eliot traced his poetic ancestry to Laforgue, not Shelley, but all three were scions of the same clan. (203)

According to Mendelson, Romantics, Symbolists and modernists are all vatic poets, whose "first law is the law of their genius ... who live in voluntary or psychological exile, at home only in their art.... When they address an audience, it is no finite class or existing category of readers. It is either ... the universe or all mankind or things that don't listen, like mountains or skylarks; or ... the poet himself [sic], or someone like a sister whom he treasures as a version of himself, or the ideal reader imagined by W.B. Yeats, 'A man who does not exist,/A man who is but a dream" (xv–xvi). Auden, by contrast, represents a "civil" tradition which includes "all poets who write as citizens, whose purpose is to entertain and instruct, and who choose subjects that would interest an audience even if a poet were not there to transform them into art" (xv).

The distinction between modernist vaticism and Auden's civil-minded poetry seems clear enough at first, but in order to maintain it, Mendelson is forced to severely distort the nature of mod-

---

[3]*Early Auden* is so authoritative that in *Later Auden*, the recently published sequel, Mendelson seems to consider the Auden/modernism issue settled. Between "'Model, The'" and "Monod, Jacques," the index of *Later Auden* pointedly omits any entry for "Modernism."

ernism by insisting that modernist literature completely divorces itself from the social realm. Mendelson asserts, for example, that "The frontier between private perception and public fact ... remained unchallenged by modernism" (205). Marianne Moore made "challenging" that "frontier" her life's work; Virginia Woolf devoted one of her finest modernist achievements, *Mrs. Dalloway*, to exploring it; "Hugh Selwyn Mauberly" and "The Love Song of J. Alfred Prufrock" frontally assault the boundary between "private perception and public fact," as does Yeats's "Leda and the Swan," with its disconcerting glimpse into the sexual fantasies a group of school children awaken in a "smiling public man."

If Jane Austen's novels had been written during the same period that Auden's were, it would surely not be necessary to rewrite the history of the novel to distinguish her work from that of her modernist contemporaries. The fact that Mendelson has to rewrite the history of poetry to dissociate Auden from modernism testifies to just how intimately the two are connected.

Paradoxically, in order to clarify that connection, one wants to complicate the single Auden/modernism link that everyone seems to recognize: i.e., the modernism of the earliest Auden. Stan Smith reports that Auden, while still a student at Oxford, declared to his tutor, "I've been reading Eliot. I now see the way I want to write," and the doomy intonations of *The Waste Land* certainly reverberate through Auden's first collection (53). But on close examination, Auden's modernist "accent" becomes harder to place. Though many of those early poems present the resonant non sequiturs, baffling shifts of perspective and syntactical dislocations that had become High Modernist trademarks, there is little of the collage-style cutting-and-pasting, decontextualized quotations, idiosyncratic linebreaks, or swerves of situation, persona and tone one finds in Eliot & Co.:

> Yet there's no peace in this assaulted city
> But speeches at the corners, hope for news,
> Outside the watchfires of a stronger army.
>
> And all emotions to expression come,
> Recovering the archaic imagery:
> This longing for assurance takes the form
>
> Of a hawk's vertical stooping from the sky;
> These tears, salt for a disobedient dream,
> The lunatic agitation of the sea;

> While this despair with hardened eyeballs cries
> 'A Golden Age, a Silver ... rather this,
> Massive and taciturn years, the Age of Ice.'
> (from XVII, "The strings' excitement,
> the applauding drum")

At twenty-two, Auden, always the technical whiz-kid, was already a master of the High Modernist technique Donald Davie calls "phantom syntax": seemingly grammatical statements which do not in fact perform the coordinating functions of syntax. But Eliot and Pound tend to use phantom syntax as a cover for radical shifts in frame of reference. Auden does the opposite. Though we can never tell exactly what they are pointing to, his earliest poems are marked by an almost obsessive metonymic insistence (*"this* assaulted city," *"This* longing," *"These* tears," *"this* despair"). The feeling that we know, or ought to know, what all the "this"es and "these"s mean is heightened by Auden's penchant (a trademark throughout his career) for sociological detail and psychological diagnosis. Instead of *The Waste Land's* patently symbolic "red rocks," or Williams' inscrutably Imagist "red wheel barrows," Auden gives us "speeches at the corners" and "stronger armies." Rather than going in fear of abstractions, presenting ideas in things, or establishing objective correlatives, Auden waxes poetic over "emotions to expression come,/Recovering the archaic imagery." Moreover, interspersed amidst what Mendelson calls early Auden's "gnomic fragments" are poems that pointedly turn their backs on modernist technique altogether. Poem XXI, for example, begins, "The silly fool, the silly fool,/Was sillier in school/But beat the bully as a rule," introducing the nursery rhyme rhythms and educational settings that became staples of Auden's mature repertoire *(English Auden,* 34). Similarly, poem XXVI makes a crude stab at the ventriloquism-as-social-commentary—"It's no use raising a shout./No, Honey, you can cut that right out"—that later became the precisely calibrated mimicry of poems such as "Fleet Visit": "They are not here because/But only just-in-case"(*English Auden,* 42; *Collected Poems,* 550). Indeed, according to John Haffenden, reviewers tended to see Auden's early work as a reaction against rather than a continuation of High Modernism. "The consensus of positive criticism [when Auden's first collection, *Poems,* came out] ... greeted Auden as the harbinger of a long-awaited poetry which might surmount the unsatisfying views of T.S. Eliot, D.H. Lawrence and the Georgians" (4–5).

Auden's most patently "modernist" poetic effort, *The Orators*, published in 1932, splices together immaculately formal verse and audaciously non-"poetic" materials such as diary entries, a Mendelian heredity chart and a list of military commands with the same gusto that the later Auden lavishes on difficult feats of prosody. However, unlike sprawling High Modernist collages such as Pound's *Cantos* and W.C. Williams' *Paterson*, the centrifugal force of *The Orators'* juxtapositions is firmly contained within contextualizing frames—the Airman's journal, the post-public-school moping of "The Initiates." *The Orators* is cryptic and paranoid, but, as its subtitle tells us, it is at every moment "An English Study," a fractured social portrait obscured by but never quite lost among the hodge-podge of modes and materials. There is simply too much *there* there for *The Orators* to fit in with the High Modernist "project" in which, as William Carlos Williams put it, meaning "appears, it disappears, a sheen of it comes up, when as its shattering implications affront us, all the gnomes hurry to cover up its traces" (287).

But if early Auden is not as modernist as most accounts make out, it is equally true that later Auden is more modernist than critical gospel has it. Keller, for example, writes that "Auden's American work was not markedly modernist, either in prosody or attitude: not formally innovative, not compressed and economical, not taking the impersonal hawk's eye view" (186). Mendelson put it more bluntly in *Early Auden*: "The augustan literary tradition ... unmistakably—in the rhymed octosyllabic couplets of "New Year Letter" [written in 1940, after Auden left England for America]— bec[a]me [Auden's] real home" (176).

But having won *Early Auden*'s battle to free Auden from the clutches of modernism, in *Later Auden* Mendelson argues that "'New Year Letter' is sinuous, various, and far more elusive than its formal style suggests" (103). Indeed, Mendelson claims that "New Year Letter" is "the poem that Ezra Pound, after much self-advertisement, had failed to write in *The Cantos*" (104):

> Rhymed octosyllabic couplets give it the air of a patterned, rational argument, but this eighteenth-century manner ... masks a restless idiosyncratic exploration of vast historical changes and uncertainties. Phrases from a half-dozen languages, and quotations from Plato, Augustine, Wagner, Eliot, and dozens of others, fall neatly into metrical step at Auden's command, but the poem cannot contain his thought or allusions.... (101)

Gone is the absolute distinction between the modernist "vatic" tradition and the neo-Augustan "civil" tradition: Mendelson now sees Auden and Pound as playing the same game, and Auden as playing it better.

Whatever the relative merits of "New Year Letter" and *The Cantos*, many of the modernist qualities and concerns Auden was supposedly free of by the 1940s are evident just beneath—and sometimes in—the highly polished surfaces of his later poems. For example, lines such as "Not to lose time, not to get caught,/Not to be left behind, not, please! To resemble/The beasts who repeat themselves, or a thing like water …" marry the colloquial and the "grand style" as successfully as any poem by Williams in lines such as ("In Praise of Limestone," *Collected Poems*, 542), and these lines, "The Fall of Rome's Unendowed with wealth or pity,/Little birds with scarlet legs,/Sitting on their speckled eggs,/Eye each flu-infected city," offer as "impersonal [a] hawk's eye view" as any stanza of Pound or Eliot (*Collected Poems*, 333). "The Sea and the Mirror" as well, with its dazzling panoply of verse forms and voices, is nothing if not "formally innovative."

In other words, much of Auden either prosecutes modernist ends by non-modernist means (like "New Year Letter"), or non-modernist ends by modernist means (like "Journal of an Airman"). But if the most modernist Auden is not as modernist as supposed, and the most anti-modernist Auden is often more so, where, oh where, can we locate "Auden" and "modernism"?

One of the benefits of Mendelson's account of Auden's relation to modernism is that it resolves one of the most dazzlingly varied oeuvres in English literature into manageably periodized form. The earliest Auden, speaking with a modernist lisp, grows into the conflicted, activist Auden of the 1930s, who struggles to either free himself from modernism's shadow or wrestle modernism into a posture of social responsibility; he, in turn, is succeeded by the wise (or wizened, depended on your tastes) Auden of the 1940s and beyond, who embraces eighteenth-century poetics and the Anglican Church with equally disconcerting sincerity.

Once we acknowledge that modernism, for Auden, was not a passing phase, this neat sequence collapses. Early, middle and late, we find Auden fusing modernist technique and content with what seems to be its opposite, the mode he called "light verse":

> When the things in which the poet is interested, the things which he sees about him, are much the same as those of his audience, and that audience is a fairly general one, he will not be con-

> scious of himself as an unusual person, and his language will be
> straightforward and close to ordinary speech ... [and] his poetry
> will be "light" ...
>
> Lightness is a great virtue, but light verse tends to be conven-
> tional, to accept the attitudes of the society in which it is written.
> The more homogenous a society, the closer the artist is to the ev-
> eryday life of his time, the easier it is for him to communicate
> what he perceives, but the harder for him to see honestly and
> truthfully, unbiased by the conventional responses of his time.
> The more unstable a society, and the more detached from it the
> artist, the clearer he can see, but the harder it is for him to
> convey it to others. ("Light Verse," *English Auden*, 363, 364)

For Auden, light verse's conversational clarity connotes a
"homogenous society" in which the poet is "closer ... to the everyday life of his time." The "vatic" difficulties of modernist poetry
reflect an "unstable" society from which the poets, Cassandra-like,
are so alienated that they cannot communicate their truths. Auden
was well aware that he lived in an "unstable" society—his apparent embrace of the "augustan literary tradition" coincided with
World War II. For Auden, then, the adoption of the light-verse
mode constitutes a sort of magical thinking, as though poetic
"lightness" could create the kind of world in which it naturally
arises. In this sense, Auden, like Mendelson's vatic modernists,
"turn[s] nostalgically away from a flawed present to some lost illusory Eden where life was unified, hierarchy secure, and the
grand style a natural extension of the vernacular."

But Auden's nostalgic wish for unalienated community is
qualified by his sense that "the closer the artist is to the everyday
life of his time ... the harder [it is] for him to see honestly and
truthfully, unbiased by the conventional responses of his time,"
while the more "detached" and obscure [i.e., vatic] the artist, the
clearer he can see." Auden, double-man extraordinaire, wanted
it—and often had it—both ways, marrying the clear-sighted anti-
conventional honesty of the alienated modernist to the ingratiating, communally identified manner of the light-verse author of
simpler, and perhaps imaginary, times.

One of the truisms about modernist writing is that it is
"difficult," i.e., it presents us with complicated surfaces that resist
our efforts to interpret—or even read. According to Richard Poirier's essay "The Difficulties of Modernism and the Modernism of
Difficulty," for example, the defining mark of modernist literature
is "textual intimidation felt in the act of reading" (105). This notion
is clearly wrong. Reams of poetry that are generally considered

"modernist"—including Eliot's "Preludes," Pound's "In a Station of the Metro," a good bit of Williams, and individual poems by Stevens and Moore—hardly register on the "textual intimidation" scale. But there is a truth beneath the truism. All the works crammed beneath modernism's overcrowded umbrella imply, in one way or another, that life is too evanescent and complex to be comprehended by or expressed in terms of any stable perspective.

This is not a definition of modernism; it is rather a sort of lowest common denominator, a necessary but distinctly insufficient condition for literature to qualify as "modernist."[4] It is useful to spell this condition out, because it helps distinguish between two aspects of modernism that are often confused: complexity of vision and complexity of presentation. Auden's commitment to writing "light" verse under distinctly non-light-verse conditions did not reflect his commitment to anachronistically Augustan clarity. Rather, it reflected his recognition that a modernist sense of the mind- and language-boggling complexity of life did not necessitate a commitment to mind-and language-boggling poetics. As Mendelson notes of "New Year Letter," Auden's vision in his "light versified" poems can be just as fluctuating, contradiction-riddled and otherwise convoluted as that of the highest of High Modernist works.

Take Auden's 1936 *Letter to Lord Byron.* Mendelson sees *Letter to Lord Byron* as an early symptom of Auden's commitment to "civil poetry": "Auden had spoken *ex cathedra* in his plays and redemptive poems; now he is a citizen among citizens" (287). Edward Neill calls the poem "a deliberate attempt to be what one might call the 'obverse' of modernism ... an unbuttoned, expansive, continuous, formally organized, discursive, chatty, comic, perhaps slightly middle-brow antithesis" (83, 84). Certainly, no poem could look less "modernist" than this amusing—or at least straining to be amusing—rhyme-royal commentary on life, art, the rigors of travel, and any other topic the speaker cares to sound off on. But though the tone is light-verse, the technique—a sort of discursive collage—is quintessentially modernist:

---

[4]For example, though this definition of modernism would not keep Chaucer out of the club, it does, I would argue, exclude Yeats from the modernist canon, though he is indubitably central to *modern* poetry in English.

> The Great Utopia, free of all complexes,
>   The Withered State is, at the moment, such
> A dream as that of being of both sexes.
>   I like Wolf's *Goethe-Lieder* very much
>   But doubt if *Ganymede's* appeal will touch
> —That marvellous cry in ascending phrases—
> Capitalism in its later phases.
>
> (*English Auden*, 199)

This passage reads like a rhetorical jumble sale. Beneath a snippet of editorial ("Great Utopia"), we find a snatch of psychoanalysis ("free of all complexes"); beneath that, a left-wing slogan ("Withered State"); and beneath that, a veritable ragbag of discourses: bourgeois cultural consumption ("I like Wolf's *Goethe-Lieder* very much"), newspaper criticism ("But doubt if *Ganymede's* appeal will touch"), musicology ("That marvellous cry in ascending phrases"), economic theory ("Capitalism in its later phases"). Do any seven lines of *The Waste Land* cover more cultural ground?

The stanza bubbles cheerily and self-deprecatingly ("I like Wolf's *Goethe-Lieder* very much") along, carrying us through drastic shifts of perspective with hardly an intellectual bump, its puckishly self-conscious rhymes, like "phrases" and "phases," subliminally suggesting that incommensurate realms of discourse mesh as easily (and pleasurably) as limerick rhymes. The soufflé-light syntax enables us to feel that we have effortlessly grasped the significance of each discourse, what it means to this particular speaker and how it reflects the general human condition. The "Withered State" reference, for example, simultaneously communicates a certain perspective on government, a political critique of that perspective (its "utopian" impossibility), and a psychological diagnosis of it as an irrational "dream" of escaping an inescapable human condition. It tells us that the speaker considers this perspective admirable but naive, that he once believed it and wishes he still could, and sums up with a condescending but heartfelt sigh over the effort to find in history some progressive motion.

But smart as the light-verse manner may make us feel, the poem never resolves the contradictions between the discourses it invokes. It would be difficult to determine, for example, whether Auden considers the psychoanalytic perspective represented by "free of all complexes" more or less enlightened than the political-economic perspective of "Capitalism in its later phases." The authorial viewpoint—intellectual, moral, temporal—changes from line to line, as does the speaker, who morphs before our eyes from the post-historical sophistication of "The Great Utopia, free of all complexes" to the gee-whiz disingenuousness of "I like Wolf's *Goethe-Lieder* very much" and back again.

Some critics, such as Rainer Emig, have suggested that Auden should be read as a proto-post-modernist poet.[5] That's certainly what John Ashbery made of him. But such critical assessments overread Auden's "vatic" complexities as much as Mendelson underreads them. When it comes to understanding Auden's relation to modernism, Auden is better served by one of his attackers than by his defenders.

In "Changes of Attitude and Rhetoric in Auden's Poetry," an essay that did much to establish the myth of near-instantaneous poetic decline Mendelson has worked so hard to dispel, Randall Jarrell argues that what he calls "Perspective by Incongruity" is the definitive effect of Auden's poetry. According to Jarrell, by yoking together incongruous words, phrases, list-items and images, Auden's poems "make us see ... what we could not possibly see without [incongruity]. [Auden made] his poems depend on perspective by incongruity very much more than other modern poetry does; and he made them depend very much less on violence, forced intensity, emotional heightening, etc." (142–43).

Jarrell likes this effect in the early poems and finds it "bureaucratized" to the point of self-parody in what, in 1941, he termed the "later" poems. But questions of quality aside, there is no question that in great poems and mediocre ones, early and late, Auden's signature move is the juxtaposition, not just of incongruities, but of incongruous perspectives. In the oblique early poems Jarrell is so fond of, these juxtapositions tend to be created by syntactical deficiencies which suggest conflicting readings. The syntactical ambiguity of Auden's famous opening line, "Who stands, the crux left of the watershed," for example, makes it sound simultaneously like a statement about a person, an abandoned crossroads and an unresolved problem in the hermeneutics of landscape (*English Auden*, 22).

---

[5]For example, in a chapter entitled "Auden's Postmodernism," Emig asserts that "Auden's writings ... develop some modernist premises, anxieties and even contradictions ... until they reach a poetic ground that leaves the label 'modernist' behind. His poetry continually pushes itself forward into territory that becomes unstable for traditional concepts of thought and in which traditional poetic techniques become lost" (204).

In the "later"—or rather, "lighter"—poems, Auden generally follows the opposite procedure, using strong syntactical structures to weld words and phrases representing "incongruous" viewpoints into grammatically complete but semantically unstable phrases and sentences. In "Pliocene Friday," for example, the geological eons connoted by the adjective collide head-on with the noun's work-week temporality, while, as we have seen, in the "threat Utopia" sentence from *Letter to Lord Byron*, each subclause connotes a different point of view ("Bucolics I: Winds," *Collected Poems*, 556). Auden was so enamored of this effect that he turned it into a formal principle, organizing stanzas, poems and even long cycles like "The Sea and the Mirror" as paratactic sequences of incongruous perspectives.

At their best, as Joseph Brodsky claimed in one of his apologia for Auden, "These juxtapositions ... are effective and memorable because of [the] merciless light—or rather dark—their parts ... cast on one another" (349). For example, "Musée des Beaux Arts"'s splicing of magi "reverently, passionately waiting/For the miraculous birth," with ice-skating children, "dreadful martyrdom," and the "innocent" anus of "the torturer's horse," limns the futility of human efforts to grasp the whole of life through individual moments, whether of joy, revelation, or horror (*Collected Poems*, 179). "The Fall of Rome"'s famous finale cuts from "Caesar's double-bed" to "an unimportant clerk" to the afore-mentioned scarlet-legged birds to an "Altogether elsewhere," where "Herds of reindeer move across/Miles and miles of golden moss,/Silently and very fast," the miraculous glimpse of luminously indifferent motion rendering its witty evocations of social decay rendered both more sordid and less solid (333).

Auden's juxtapositions enable us to "see ... what we could not possibly see without" them not because of the originality of their constituent elements—there is little originality in the details of "Musée des Beaux Arts," for example—but because the disorientation generated by the "incongruities" pushes us into brief but telling identifications with each of the contiguous perspectives. When Auden leaps from a glimpse of "muscle-bound Marines" who "mutiny for food and pay" to Caesar's "warm" double-bed, for example, the shift from generalized group portrait to intimate tactile detail seems, for an instant, to land between the sheets.

Even when these glimpses are proffered in an ironic tone that seems to judge and invite us to judge the lives they represent from some Pope-esque pinnacle of omniscience, Auden withholds the means to form such judgments. Despite the elaborate syntax, each perspective is merely juxtaposed, rather than being subordinated to larger structures of meaning. As a result, despite their disarming fluency and anachronistic prosodic élan, the poems skip and slide from viewpoint to viewpoint, posing each as an implicit commentary on the others without adjudicating their quarrels and contradictions—a maddeningly non-committal procedure which prompted a paradoxical combination of praise for "complete self-identification with every human need or perplexity" and complaints that "the disparity between insights and poetic feeling has reached disastrous proportions" (Haffenden, 361, 43).[6]

Poems such as "The Fall of Rome" are proof positive that neither Auden's light-verse manner nor what Jarrell terms his shift from the "strong language" of the earliest work to the "strong rhetoric" of the later necessarily diminish either their complexity or their capacity to cast "merciless light—or rather dark" on the perspectives they represent. But the same habits of mind, language and vision could also produce entertainingly erudite irrelevance:

> ... Here is a windmill whence an emperor saw
> His right wing crumple; across these cabbage fields
> A pretender's Light Horse made their final charge.
>
> If I were a plainsman I should hate us all,
>   From the mechanic rioting for a cheap loaf
> To the fastidious palate, hate the painter
>   Who steals my wrinkles for his Twelve Apostles,
> Hate the priest who cannot even make it shower.
>   What could I smile at as I trudged behind my harrow
> But bloodshot images of rivers screaming,
>   Marbles in panic, and Don't-Care made to care?
>
> As it is, though, I know them personally
>   Only as a landscape common to two nightmares:
> Across them, spotted by spiders from afar,
>   I have tried to run....
>   (from "Bucolics VI: Plains,"
>   *Collected Poems*, 566–67)

This is a prime example of what Jarrell calls the "Bureaucratization of Perspective by Incongruity." The "windmill" of the first line is

---

[6]The first opinion was proffered by John Van Druten in a 1945 *Kenyon Review* essay; the second by David Daiches in the *Virginia Quarterly Review* the same year.

automatically linked to "an emperor"'s vantage point, the cabbage fields of the second to "a pretender's." Then the speaker, in the guise of imagining (yet another perspectival hop) the disdain of an ancient "plainsman," evokes in quick succession the viewpoints of starving rioters, aristocratic epicures, and a painter of religious scenes. The speaker cannot even describe a bad dream without telling us how the scene appeared to the distantly menacing spiders who terrified him. Yet even Auden's most augustan "Bucolics" exhibit the flash-card approach to history, obsessive conflation of past and present, and predilection for telling the Mind of Europe what it thought and ought to think, which are often cited as defining High Modernist characteristics of Eliot and Pound. If Auden scholars have found it convenient to detour around the question of modernism, modernist scholars have found it equally advantageous to make a wide swerve around Auden, and for the same reason: at the intersection of Auden and modernism, definitions that seem perfectly workable elsewhere no longer work at all.

The question "To what extent is Auden a modernist?" presents us with two choices. We can try to gerrymander the boundaries of modernism so that the term excludes Auden while including the usual transatlantic suspects. Or, we can abandon the notion that the contemporaneity of English and American modernists implies the existence of a transatlantic, "Anglo-American" modernism, and consider the possibility that Anglo and American writers developed modernisms as different, and as closely related, as those of, say, the French and Spanish Surrealists.[7]

There is certainly historical evidence for such a view. The most prominent "Anglo" literary modernists—Woolf, Joyce, Lawrence, Forster and Ford—made their marks in fiction.[8] (Yeats, after closeting himself with Ezra Pound, was modernized, but never, one

---

[7]Though he doesn't mention Auden, Robert Pinsky hints at such an idea in *The Situation of Poetry*'s description of the distinct reactions of American and British poets against what he calls "Tennysonian language." More recently, Edward Neill came close to a similar suggestion in his ruminations on "Modernism and Englishness."

[8]The modernism of D.H. Lawrence's poetry is debatable, but its secondary importance is not. The dust has not yet settled on the debates over Mina Loy's status as a major modernist poet, but my hunch is that the unevenness of her work and the brevity of her prominence will keep her on the edges of the modernist canons that emerge in the twenty-first century.

would argue, a modernist.) Expatriations and international influences like Symbolisme, T.E. Hulme and Ford Maddox Hueffer notwithstanding, the standard-bearers of poetic modernism—e.e. cummings (once considered an epitome of modernist poetry), H.D., Eliot, Robert Frost, Langston Hughes (an intermittent modernist), Marianne Moore, Pound, the Gertrude Stein of *Tender Buttons*, Wallace Stevens, Williams—were all American, born and bred.[9] In fact, Mina Loy, one of the few British candidates for admission into the early modernist poetic canon, stated unequivocally in her essay "Modern Poetry" that "The new poetry in English has proceeded out of America" (157).

Of course, the term "Anglo-American modernism" is a convenient shorthand for thinking conditions and characteristics that American modernist poets and British modernist fiction writers shared. But though these writers were certainly aware of and involved with each other, the modernism of the British novelists has too little in common with that of the American poets for "Anglo-American modernism" to constitute a literary classification. For example, in modernist American poetry, there is little concern with the major technical issue which fueled the innovations of modernist British novels: the need to extend the technical resources of realism to reflect modern conceptions of subjectivity and intersubjectivity. By the same token, modernist British novelists were far less preoccupied with "making it new"—i.e., overthrowing the language and rhetoric of their nineteenth-century predecessors— than their American poetic counterparts.

Once we cut the Gordian hyphen and entertain the notion that contemporaneous, mutually influential but distinctly different modernisms arose on either side of the Atlantic, Auden becomes much easier to place. Rather than appearing as an anachronistic Augustan or premature post-modernist, Auden emerges as the first and still central exponent of a late-blooming but long-lasting British modernist poetics which has its roots in Byron and Hardy and extends through Philip Larkin to contemporary poets such as Geoffrey Hill.

------

[9]Eliot, to be sure, was an Anglo-American modernist in the literal sense of the word. But even William Carlos Williams, who certainly wished he could expunge Eliot from his "American Grain," admitted that, "in spite of everything ... Eliot's experiments in the '[Four] Quartets' ... show him to be more American in the [modernist] sense I seek than, sad to relate, Auden, with his English ears, will ever be able to be" (289).

It would take much more than a single essay to detail this poetics and fill out its genealogy—not to mention considering its cultural and historical context. One can only sketch its outlines through examples from Auden and Larkin. Rather than seeking to "break the pentameter" like their American cousins, modernist British poets tend to marry the direct, conversational manner Auden associated with light verse to patently artificial—and sometimes extremely intricate—verse forms. This fusion produces an astonishing flexible medium for social portraiture, ventriloquism, and parody, and enables British modernists to maintain a "light verse" discursive intimacy with their audiences without sacrificing modernist distance and complexity.

For example, when Larkin's sad sack persona confesses in "Annus Mirabilis" that he lost his virginity "In nineteen sixty-three/(Which was rather late for me)—/Between the end of the *Chatterly* ban/And the Beatles' first LP," the amusingly sing-song versification tunes us in to three distinctly different viewpoints on this historic sexual act, that of the repressive prudes of the 1950s, the libidinous rockers of the 1960s, and the nostalgia of the adult speaker for a quite obviously lost youth (167). And should one refer to the complete poem, one can hear a diverse set of tones and attitudes that cheerfully recall to the reader the chase after lust that was often disguised as a quest for romance that was a kind of "bargaining" and "a wrangle for a ring" that began for Larkin at sixteen and then consumed "everything."

In a few transparent lines, Larkin presents the first flush of sexual gratification as a life-changing triumph and a long-faded illusion, as a vision of equality and abundance and a threat to the social economy of desire, as a kind of universal communion and as the ultimate form of cheating at solitaire. Moreover, the poem x-rays not only the boy's feelings but the conflicting attitudes toward them. We seem to see them, and see through them, from some ironic, all-comprehending perspective which transcends the languages of youthful romance and of adult disenchantment, of repressive social convention and wanton rebellion, of hard-headed realism and utopian hope that the poem invokes. But like the authorial viewpoint of *Letter to Lord Byron*, "Annus Mirabilis"'s has a shifty, ephemeral quality. It seems clear enough while we are reading any given line, but turns out to be quite elusive when we try to pin down exactly what the poet thinks of his speaker's brief sexual revolution. The vantage the poem seems to offer us dissolves in our grasp, leaving us—and the poet—enmeshed in a web of discredited attitudes we can disdain but cannot escape.

American modernists tend to create complexity through radical fragmentation, enigmatic imagism, inexplicable shifts in diction and tone, and patent non sequitur. British modernists like Larkin and Auden generate complexity by juxtaposing incongruous glimpses of contrasting viewpoints within stable formal and contextual frames, such as "Annus Mirabilis"'s confessional reverie, and the claustrophobic cityscape of Auden's "The strings' excitement, the applauding drum." American modernist complexity often leaves readers baffled or "textually intimidated"; British modernist complexity reminds us at every moment of how much we know about our world, metonymically invoking readily recognizable viewpoints—while at the same time leading us ever deeper into thickets of irreconcilable difference.

In *Letter to Lord Byron*, the speaker complains that Byron's "sense of other people's very hazy" (171). This is certainly true of most American modernist verse, though there are notable exceptions.[10] But no one could ever accuse Auden or Larkin of "haziness" regarding "other people." Indeed, one of the major effects of British modernist perspective by incongruity is to heighten our sense of other people—both of their otherness and their humanness.

Take the clash between the "Arcadian" and the "Utopian" in the "Vespers" section of Auden's "Horae Canonicae." The poem is written in the voice of the Arcadian, but unlike, say, "The Love Song of J. Alfred Prufrock," the first-person perspective only sharpens the portrayal of the speaker's interlocutor:

> He would like to see me cleaning latrines: I would like to see him removed to some other planet...
> Glancing at a lampshade in a store window, I observe it is too hideous for anyone in their senses to buy: He observes it is too expensive for a peasant to buy.
>
> (*Collected Poems*, 637)

Though we see through the Arcadian's eyes, "Vespers" does not side with him; the speaker himself pointedly refuses to dismiss

---

[10]Williams, for example, created a number of fine portraits; Eliot and Pound produced some acid social satires; and Frost's early dialogues are masterpieces of characterization.

his *bête noir*'s opinions. Rather than resolving their disagreements, "Vespers" emphasizes them, counting on their collision (Bakhtin, ever the optimist, would call it "dialogue") to point the way toward some perspective that comprehends both viewpoints, though it cannot be comprehended through either:

> Was it ... simply a fortuitous intersection of life-paths, loyal to different fibs,
>
> or also a rendezvous between accomplices who, in spite of themselves, cannot resist meeting
>
> to remind the other (do both, at bottom, desire truth?) of that half of their secret which he would most like to forget,
>
> forcing us both, for a fraction of a second, to remember our victim (but for him I could forget the blood, but for me he could forget the innocence)
>
> on whose immolation (call him Abel, Remus, whom you will, it is one Sin Offering) arcadias, utopians, our dear old bag of a democracy, are alike founded ... (639)

This strategy of limning the elusive yet moral, clearly articulated yet unparaphraseable truth of life through the juxtaposition of mutually unintelligible perspectives is also characteristic of modernist British fiction. We see it, for example, in D.H. Lawrence's peculiar (for such a didactic author) insistence on satirizing *Women in Love*'s hero, Birkin, even as he measures the other characters against him; in E.M. Forster's transformation in *Howards End* of the traditional comic-novel marital resolution into a permanent yoking of incongruous value systems; and especially (for all that Auden was pitted against her in the critical and political discourse of the 1930s) in Virginia Woolf's extraordinarily fluid indirect discourse, which soars and somersaults among perspectives as effortlessly as "The Fall of Rome" or "Annus Mirabilis."

But there is a crucial difference between the "perspective by incongruity" we find in British modernist poetry and fiction. Joyce, Woolf, Forster and Lawrence embrace the stance of third-person omniscience they inherit from nineteenth-century novels; indeed, their indirect discursive rendition of individual viewpoints tends to enhance rather than compromise the sense of their omniscient detachment. But no matter how absolute their pronouncements or Olympian their vantage points seems, Auden's and Larkin's speakers remain umbilically tied to the ironizing fluxes of the social milieus they evoke, inescapably—and often comically—conscious of their entanglement in the mess of incongruous perspectives.

As Brodsky noted of Auden, British modernist poets' critiques of others are always self-critiques as well. We have already seen the unsparing self-characterizations of the speakers of "Annus Mirabilis" and "Vespers." Larkin is famous for comic self-deprecation, but we find the trait throughout Auden's oeuvre as well. The speaker of "At the Grave of Henry James," for example, refers to "the awkward footsteps of my apprehension"; Auden's elegy for Yeats proclaims "You were silly like us"; the speaker of "September 1, 1939" introduces himself as "Uncertain and afraid"; and Auden's "Thanksgiving for a Habitat" opens with the speaker remarking that for him "already it is millions of heartbeats ago/back to the Bicycle Age,/before which is no *After* for me to measure,/just a still prehistoric *Once* ..." (*Selected Poems*, 252).

Such self-references ensure that what would otherwise seem like omniscient, or at least authoritative, authorial perspectives become themselves subjects of scrutiny, exposed by the same process of perspective by incongruity which they enact. And the more closely we scrutinize these speakers' viewpoints, the less defined they become, until, as we saw in "Annus Mirabilis," what seems a transcendent vantage from which all others can be judged is revealed as the unstable sum of the poem's perspectival parts.

This distinctly British version of modernist poetic self-reflexivity is showcased in "Caliban to the Audience," the penultimate section of Auden's *The Sea and the Mirror*:

> If now, having dismissed your hired impersonators with verdicts ranging from the laudatory orchid to the disgusted and disgusting egg, you ask and, of course, notwithstanding the conscious fact of his irrevocable absence, you instinctively *do* ask for our so good, so great, so dead author to stand before the finally lowered curtain and take his shyly responsible bow for this, his latest, ripest production, it is I—my reluctance is, I assure you, co-equal with your dismay—who will always loom thus wretchedly into your confused picture, for, in default of the all-wise, all-explaining master you would speak *to*, who else at least can, who else indeed must respond to your bewildered cry, but its very echo, the begged question you would speak to him *about*. (*Collected Poems*, 422)

Auden's Caliban embodies the unbearably distilled quintessence of modernist British poetry. Though unquestionably prose, this sentence—and the entire piece—represents the dark side of the light-verse virtuosity Auden prized. The interminably subject-deferring elaborations patently parody themselves and their acknowledged model, Henry James, yet the syntax never loosens its grip on the proliferating subclauses, never releases us from the deeply conditioned need to find out how the maze of subjects and predicates will ultimately be coordinated—and what this monstrously verbal Caliban is saying to, and about, us. Auden's Caliban has gained something more profitable from language than the ability to curse. He has gained the power to use our own yearning for words to make sense against us, both by keeping us dangling from his syntactical cliffs for lengths of time that strain our language-processing capabilities to their limits, and by gratifying our need with a series of precisely observed, impeccably articulated, indelibly nasty observations about ourselves.

Yet this hyperverbal Caliban's mastery is inseparable from his involvement with his interlocutors' consciousnesses, which he cannot separate from his own ("my reluctance is, I assure you, co-equal with your dismay"). Indeed, after this opening paragraph, Caliban submerges himself in the first-person plural, with the nervously italicized comment that *"for the present I speak as your echo"* (423). This echo, it seems, knows everything about the audience Caliban addresses with such contempt—its wishes, its fears, its shames and aspirations, the struggles of the would-be artists in its midst, the personal, social and existential quagmires in which its members, who are less individuals than symptoms of a diseased culture he gleefully diagnoses, are hopelessly enmired.

Like Auden's archetypal light-verse author, Caliban is so "close"—so excruciatingly close—to "the everyday life of his time" that he readily expresses any aspect of it which concerns him. And like that of Auden's archetypal light-verse "community," this "everyday life" is so extraordinarily "homogenous" that Caliban's sweeping generalizations—"you instinctively *do* ask for our so good, so great, so dead author"—apply equally and ineluctably to every member of it. At the same time, Caliban has no difficulty (far from it) "see[ing] honestly and truthfully, unbiased by the conventional responses of his time"; his intimacy with "the attitudes of the society in which [he] is written" only fuels his furiously alienated assessment of it. Yet Caliban's omniscience is not a sign of transcendence, but of its opposite: as a representation of a representation of a repressed sin of civilization, he is inextricably, intestinally implicated in the minds he disdainfully reads. "

412   Jay Ladin

The Sea and the Mirror ends with Caliban's declaration that he and Ariel are "swaying out on the ultimate whip-whipped cornice that overhands the unabiding void," and Ariel's wistful confession that he is "helplessly in love" with Caliban (444, 445). This homoerotic romance between the sub- and super-human seems willfully naughty in relation to "The Tempest"; but it is almost too accurate a depiction of modernist British poetry's marriage of Ariel-ite lightness and virtuosity and Calibanesque misanthropic intimacy to be called a metaphor. And if the progeny of this incongruous union sometimes veer toward the fatalistic sighing of Auden's Ariel ("This was long ago decided,/Both of us know why,/Can, alas, foretell,/When our falsehoods are divided,/What we shall become,/One evaporating sigh"), more often they lead us toward Caliban's tough-minded revelation:

> There is no way out. There never was,—it is at this moment that for the first time in our lives we hear, not the sounds which, as born actors, we have hitherto condescended to use as an excellent vehicle for displaying our personalities and looks, but the real Word which is our only *raison d'être*. Not that we have improved; everything, the massacres, the whippings, the lies, the twaddle ... are still present, more obviously than ever ... our shame, our fear, our incorrigible staginess, all wish and no resolve, are still, and more intensely than ever, all we have: only now it is not in spite of them but with them that we are blessed by that Wholly Other Life.... It is just here, among the ruins and the bones, that we may rejoice in the perfected Work which is not ours. (444)

Works Cited

Auden, W.H. *Collected Poems*. Edited by Edward Mendelson. New York: Vintage Books, 1991.

———. *The English Auden: Poems, Essays, and Dramatic Writings, 1927–1939*. Edited by Edward Mendelson. New York: Random House, 1977.

———. *Selected Poems*. Edited by Edward Mendelson. New York: Vintage Books, 1979.

Bahlke, George W., ed. *Critical Essays on W.H. Auden*. New York: G.K. Hall, 1991.

Brodsky, Joseph. *Less Than One: Selected Essays*. New York: Farrar, Straus & Giroux, 1986.

Emig, Rainer. *W.H. Auden: Towards a Postmodern Poetics*. New York: St. Martin's Press, 2000.

Haffenden, John. *W.H. Auden: The Critical Heritage*. London: Routledge & Kegan Paul, 1983.

Jarrell, Randall. "Changes in Attitude and Rhetoric in Auden's Poetry." *The Southern Review* 7 (1941): 326–49.

Keller, Lynn. *Re-making It New: Contemporary American Poetry and the Modernist Tradition*. Cambridge: Cambridge UP, 1987.

Kenner, Hugh. *The Pound Era*. Berkeley: U of California P, 1973.

Larkin, Philip. *Collected Poems*. Edited by Anthony Thwaite. New York: Noonday Press, 1993.

Levenson, Michael H. *A Genealogy of Modernism: A Study of English Literary Doctrine 1908–1922*. New York: Cambridge UP, 1984.

Loy, Mina. *The Lost Lunar Baedeker: Poems of Mina Loy*. Edited by Roger L. Conover. New York: Farrar, Straus and Giroux, 1996.

Mendelson, Edward. "Auden's Revision of Modernism." In *W.H. Auden*, edited by Harold Bloom. New York: Chelsea House, 1986.

———. *Early Auden*. Cambridge: Harvard UP, 1983.

———. *Later Auden*. New York: Farrar, Straus and Giroux, 1999.

Neill, Edward. "Modernism and Englishness: Reflections on Auden and Larkin." In *Essays & Studies 1983*, edited by Beatrice White. London: John Murray, 1983.

Pinsky, Robert. *The Situation of Poetry: Contemporary Poetry and Its Traditions*. Princeton: Princeton UP, 1976.

Poirier, Richard. "The Difficulties of Modernism and the Modernism of Difficulty." In *Critical Essays on American Modernism*, edited by Michael J. Hoffmann and Patrick D. Murphy. New York: G.K. Hall, 1992.

Smith, Stan. "Remembering Bryden's Bill: Modernism from Eliot to Auden." In *Rewriting the Thirties: Modernism and After*, edited by Keith Williams and Steven Matthews. London: Longman, 1997.

Williams, William Carlos. *Selected Essays of William Carlos Williams*. New York: New Directions, 1969.

W.H. Auden on Fairy-Tales, Quests, and Sagas

David Garrett Izzo

This author has made much in previous writings about Auden (and Isherwood, Spender, et al.) that the poet Auden was truly a child—in the best sense—who reluctantly endured adulthood while still playing at his child-like inclinations and predilections. Among these was an abiding interest in children's literature even when it was also adult literature in the various so-called children's genres (The Grimms, Anderson, George MacDonald, Tolkien). He wrote essays on the nature of this literature, and much of what he says also accounts for Auden's ideas on the role of language and literature as the mirrors that reflect back upon the child and the later child in his adult disguise.

The image one has of W.H. Auden is usually of the later Auden: the deeply furrowed visage lined with Martian canals, the sleepy-tired eyes, the rumpled clothes, a face looking older than his actual years. Those who knew the later Auden recounted that his demeanor gruffly matched his appearance, and curmudgeon was not an altogether inappropriate appellation. Nonetheless, within the exterior image was another Auden, the inner-child who never grew up, and this child, having been disappointed in the trials of adulthood, had retreated into a misanthropic pose as a defense mechanism. Still, the child Auden, the early Auden of the 1930s, and the inner-child Auden of old age retained a deep love for fantasies, marvels, and tales. For Auden, they were a sacred secondary world, which, to him, had a more meaningful reality than the profane primary world. Auden escaped into these secondary worlds of, among others, the Grimms, Anderson, Icelandic sagas, Camelot, George MacDonald, Naomi Mitchison (see Hopkins in this volume), and Tolkien, of whom Auden was one of the first champions (see Jellema in this volume). Auden read these works (as well as detective novels that he believed were a modern extension of marvels, tales, and quests), and also did translations of some of his favorites including *The Elder Edda*, and Jean Cocteau's *The Knights of the Round Table*. Auden (and Chester Kallmann) also wrote libretti, most notably one for Stravinsky's *The Rake's Progress*—itself an adult fable. More importantly, Auden wrote essays about marvels and tales, quests and sagas, and in doing so explained their archetypically mythological importance to the human psyche as being inextricably coordinated with the evolution of human consciousness (see the Izzo and Eros essays on Heard in this volume). In Auden's purview the need for marvels and tales equated to a secular theology. Auden made his explanations with a delightful enthusiasm and originality that matched his zeal for the genres he was describing. Auden the critic-as-essayist had a coherent theory of literature that was also a metaphysical theory of existence and, if one wishes to do the correlating, a consistent epistemology.[1] He believed literary art "involves the whole past" by making certain congruent particulars into a universal view of life and art, with art being the mirror into which humans see themselves in analogous parables ("Making ...," 34).

Auden thought that the child's literature became the basis for the adult's literature, and his theories are based in how a child's awe continues to reside in the adult's psyche and thus motivates the adult's adult reading—if he remains a reader—or a movie and TV viewer, or a sports enthusiast, etc. Consequently, the nature of marvels and tales, and a child's relation to them, is the basis for the development of all literature including screenwriting. A summary overview of Auden's literary metaphysic will enhance the consideration of his thoughts on marvels and fairytales that follows. Indeed, in his manner, Auden believed all language, and particularly the language of art, is by definition supernatural—that is, analogous to effable natural experience, which in the instance after the experience becomes history, immediately becomes ineffable and can never be reproduced, only intimated through imitation.

---

[1]See the Editor's evaluation of Auden-as-philosopher in his study *Aldous Huxley and W.H. Auden: On Language* (West Cornwall, CT: Locust Hill Press; 1998).

The Universal as Perpetual Continuum

The earliest Auden was a child nurtured by doting, upper-middle-class parents who were socially progressive and encouraged their son to read copiously of marvels and tales. This nurturing led to a precocity of daring invention that would manifest itself later as Auden the poet/dramatist/essayist. The adult Auden clung to childhood, saying in old age that being doted on as a child had the effect of having him believe "that in any gathering, I was the youngest person present. It was not that I imagined myself younger in years than I actually was.... I simply thought of others as older" ("Aging," 5). Auden, near the end of his life, credited the beginning of his life with giving him the fantastical imagination that dominated all of his life in between. In Auden's 1970 anthology *A Certain World: a Commonplace Book*, he has a section called "Nursery Library," in which he lists the favorites among his childhood reading (292):

Beatrix Potter	All her books
Hans Anderson	*The Snow Queen*
Morris and Magnuson	*Icelandic Stories*
Lewis Carroll	The two *Alice* books
George MacDonald	*The Princess and the Goblin*
Jules Verne	*The Child of the Cavern,*
	Journey to the Center of the Earth
H. Rider Haggard	*King's Solomon's Mines*
	She
Dean Farrar	*Eric, or Little by Little*
Ballantyne	*The Cruise of the Camelot*
Conan Doyle	The *Sherlock Holmes* Stories

Of the nursery state, Auden said in his preface to his list:

> As readers, we remain in the nursery stage so long as we cannot distinguish between taste and judgment, so long, that is, as the only possible verdicts we can pass on a book are two: this I like; this I don't like.
>
> For an adult reader, the possible verdicts are five: I can see this is good and I like it; I can see this is good but I don't like it; I can see this is good and, through perseverance, I shall come to like it; I can see this is trash but I like it; I can see this is trash and I don't like it. (291–92)

The differences Auden makes between taste and judgment, child and adult, are based in his distinctions of what constitutes the engendering factors that become the game of life. Principally, these are differences between the primary and secondary imaginations, the definitions of which he adapts from Coleridge (and Tolkien) while adding his own unique formulation.

> A clear distinction is made between certain actions which are regarded as sacred rites of great importance to the well-being of society, and everyday profane behavior. The concern of the primary imagination is with sacred beings and sacred objects. The sacred is that to which it is obliged to respond.... The profane is known to other faculties of the mind, but not to the primary imagination. The impression made upon the imagination by any sacred being is of overwhelming, but undefinable importance.... The response to the imagination to such a presence or significance is passion or awe.... This condition is absolute. That it arouse awe.
>
> The secondary imagination is of another character and at another mental level. It is active, not passive, and its characters are not the sacred and profane but the beautiful and ugly. Beauty and ugliness pertain to form not to being. The primary imagination only recognizes one kind of being, the sacred, but the secondary imagination recognizes both beautiful and ugly forms.
>
> The impulse to create a work of art is felt when, in certain persons, the passive awe provoked by sacred beings or events is transformed into a desire to express that awe in a rite of worship or homage, and to be homage, this rite must be beautiful. In poetry the rite is verbal, it pays homage by naming. A child looks [at the moon] and for him this is a sacred encounter. In his mind "moon" is not a name of a sacred object but one of its important properties and, therefore, *numinous*.
>
> The value of a profane thing lies in what it usefully does; the apt name for a profane being, therefore, is the word or words that describe his function—a Mr. Smith.... The apt name for a sacred being is the word or words which worthily express his importance—Son of Thunder, The Well-Wishing one.... Every poem [marvel or tale] is rooted in imaginative awe. ("Making ...," 34–62)

For Auden, all art is supernatural fantasy as it, even when it is about tragic reality, is only intimating and imitating that reality, never duplicating it. Art cannot recreate immediate experience; art can only intimate experiences analogously as parable by taking the particular and making it universal. The artist, in Auden's terms, plays the game of art to satisfy himself and win the approval of others.

> The writing of art is gratuitous, i.e. play.... Natural man hates nature and the only act, which can really satisfy him is the *acte gratuite*. His ego resents every desire of his natural self for food, sex, pleasure, logical coherence, because desires are given, not chosen, and his ego seeks constantly to assert its autonomy by doing something of which the requiredness is not given.
>
> In addition to wanting to feel free, man wants to feel important.... The rules of a game give it importance by making it difficult to play, a test of skill. In this, however, they betray that their importance is really frivolous, because it means that they are only important to those who have the physical or mental gifts to play them, and that is a matter of chance....
>
> If the fall made man conscious of the difference between good and evil, then the Incarnation made him conscious of the difference between seriousness and frivolity. Before that, one might say that only children, i.e those in whom the consciousness of good and evil was not fully developed, could play games. The adult had to take the frivolity seriously, i.e. turn games into magic, and in consequence could never wholeheartedly enjoy them because necessarily he was always anxious as to whether the magic would work this time. ("Squares and Oblongs," 166–71)

The literary-art game is played by writers who create secondary worlds for like-minded readers who also wish to enter a secondary world. When Auden calls art magic, he means white magic as opposed to black magic and notes the difference in this manner:

> Like the White Magic of poetry, Black Magic is concerned with enchantment. But while the poet is himself enchanted by the subjects and only wishes to share his enchantment with others, the Black Magician is perfectly cold.... He uses enchantment [i.e. advertising and propaganda] as a means of securing domination over others and compelling them to do his will. ("Review," 30)

(When Auden herein refers to poetry, he is using the term more broadly to include all of the literary arts.)

To be enchanted by white magic is what writers and readers of marvels and tales are seeking by escaping into a secondary world as a retreat from the primary world. The secondary world, for Auden, is a psychic Eden where writers and readers can be eternal children, free from the "real world" knowledge of good and evil and the responsibility of having to know the difference. As a form of escape, Auden said, "We want a poem to be a beautiful object, a verbal Garden of Eden which by its formal perfection, keeps alive in us the hope that there exists a state of joy without evil or suffering which it can be our destiny to attain. At the same time we look to a poem for some kind of illumination about our present wandering condition, since, without self-insight and knowledge of the world, we must err blindly ("Walter de la Mare," 389). Contained within this definition are the two essential aspects of Auden's literary theory: art is escapism for the child or child-as-adult; art is parable that teaches indirectly rather than didactically.

The actual child escapes into secondary worlds with intuitive innocence undiluted by the adult's need for rationalization. Hence, as Auden said, the child either likes or dislikes. The adult corrupted by knowledge (i.e., that Santa Claus is not real) further rationalizes his opinions of literature with Auden's five additional forms of judgment or, in a manner of speaking, these more astute judgments reflect the adult's greater knowledge of good and evil that renders what were once the child's "game" into the adult's "work." Ultimately, for the actual child or the child-in-the-adult, the need for escape into secondary worlds is an opportunity to frivolously play a game and assert the right to be frivolous as a form of autonomy. The child plays with *Awe*—the adult also plays with awe and it's still fun, but there is a greater awareness of one's ego in relation to other egos.

Games are a form of escape, and the need for escapism begins in childhood. The game of art is only one type of escape. Religion, sports, nationalism, drugs, etc., are others. The highbrow is inclined toward art, science, and mystical theology; the lowbrow seeks the other escapes. Moreover, the distinction of highbrow or lowbrow is not based on intellectual ability per se, or affluence per se, but on a combination of intellectual ability and the sensitive, sympathetic desire to interact actively within the symbiotic environment of mind with nature. Anyone who is active toward his environment by trying to make discoveries about it, rather than be passive in it, is a highbrow. This includes the scientist, mystic, and artist who create white magic for children young and old.

The child who appreciates the artist can be highbrow or lowbrow, and he is not only enchanted by white magic, but derives from it, aided by an intuitive power of wonder, an intimation of primeval awe. Marvels and tales inspire *Awe*-sociations such as those that were first felt by the primeval tribe in encountering inexplicable natural phenomena such as lightning, thunder, rainbows, snow, stars, moon, fire. Art is the attempt to recapture natural awe, and literary art becomes a verbal artifact because if it is good art, its particulars transcend a particular time and place to be understood universally in any time or place.

The best awe is the child's first awe, experienced for the first time. The second time is not quite the same. The adult loses innocence when he loses childhood; but awe, second-hand, or understood as such or not, is chased after by children and adults enduringly. And although the adult can no longer accept the fantasy he once believed in as a child can, his knowledge of the thrill of disbelief in his childhood creates an everlasting regret that it can't be retained in the same ways as an adult. Nonetheless, even though adults may no longer believe in the details of marvels and tales, they still remember the *Awe*-sociations engendered by them and never really let go of these pure emotions. (Hence, the compulsive efforts for vicarious awe in various forms of fanaticism.) One of Auden's goals as an adult poet, and the goal of any adult who seeks escape into a secondary world, was to allow himself to see again with the eyes of a child and make, he said, "The transition from the child's 'We believe still' to the adult's 'I believe again'" ("As It Seemed to Us," 187). This remark implies that long after the child's naïve innocence is lost because he has learned, as an adult, how to rationalize (the ability to rationalize is the end of innocence), the adult's memory of his childhood awe still resides in his unconscious, waiting for an intimation, natural or artistic, to arouse it from dormancy. Indeed, for child and adult, this is the Power of Wonder, or the "ah" effect, which is the feeling of intuitive awe unmediated by antecedent rationalization. For Auden, if this awe can be aroused through parable-art, the emotional impact will indirectly "teach" with greater meaning. (Fables are the prototype of parable-art.) Auden said, "You cannot tell people what to do, you can only tell them parables; and that is what art really is, particular stories of particular people and experiences, from which each according to his immediate and peculiar needs may draw his own conclusions. There must be two kinds of art: escape-art, for man needs to escape as he needs food and sleep, and parable-art, that art which shall teach man to unlearn hatred and learn love" ("Psychology ...," 341). By Auden's definition, the best art would be that which one could escape into and learn from as well, and the more awesome the better.

Awe is, indeed, awesome, and humans since the primeval tribe to the present have attempted to recapture their sense of awe by intimating or having intimated to them, *Awe*-sociations. Awe is mysterious, and the tribe's *Teller* told stories so as to re-intimate the original awe through analogous parable that gave his tribe an identity that could be preserved as myth and ritual. The teller's role as recorder, historian, ritualist, theologian, teacher, and entertainer was enhanced by his gift of doing the *Telling* with imaginative verve. The Telling—and all art—becomes a mirror into which one asks his reflection the two questions that Auden said parable-art should inspire:

> *Who am I?* What is the difference between man and all other creatures? What relations are possible between them? What is man's status in the universe? What conditions of his existence which he must accept as his fate which no wishing can alter?
>
> *Whom ought I to become?* What are the characteristics of the hero, the authentic man whom everybody should admire and try to become? Vice versa, what are the characteristics of the churl, the unauthentic man whom everybody should try to avoid becoming? ("Robert Frost," 344–45)

Auden said we are analogy-drawing beings who reflexively compare ourselves to others. This is what the child or adult does when meeting a story, just as when meeting a person. Marvels and tales recreate awe and also serve as the mirror in which one can compare himself to the hero or heroine who already exists in our wishes and dreams. Art is an extrapolated aggrandizement of reality, and Auden believed that no matter how beautiful and/or complex his or any other poetry or literature was, at bottom, the literary artist was really a "mixture of spy and gossip" and that the story's inner truth was paramount ("Poets ...," 360). In other words, the *Telling* must have something to say that listeners want to hear while intimating to both artist and listener an identification of someone else's particulars which they can relate to their own particulars thus making both sets of particulars become a commonly identifiable universal. Hence, marvels and tales, however fantastic, are an Awe-associated hyperbolization of man's reality that is timelessly transcendent of that reality and connects man to the mysteries of inner existence in whatever context he consciously or unconsciously chooses to fit them in.

The inner mind and the *World Mind* of the collective unconscious were paramount to Auden when he was a young man in the 1920s and 1930s, during which the ascension of psychoanalysis was taking form. Thus, Auden's interpretations of literature react to the needs of the inner man and to the archetypal stories and myths that constitute the subliminal relationship of man to art. From this basis, Auden interprets marvels and tales as being a means to the subconscious wish-fulfillment that serves certain ends in the universal psyche.

The Wish Game

Auden said, while acknowledging Tolkien: "The state of enchantment is one of certainty. When enchanted, we neither believe, nor doubt, nor deny: we *know*, even if, as in the case of a false enchantment, our knowledge is self-deception. All folk tales recognize that there are false enchantments as well as true ones. When we are truly enchanted we desire nothing for ourselves, only that the enchanting object or person shall continue to exist" ("Enchantment," 149). For Auden, fairytales and fantasies are about enchantment first; also for Auden, they are the first lessons that all art is about enchantment, and adults learn to appreciate art and the awe-sociations that art engenders by first having been enchanted in childhood by the fantasies and fairytales they heard or read. The cause-and-effect psychic connection from the child's fairytale to Beethoven, or Picasso, or Ibsen, is palpably real to Auden, who sees the former as precursor to the latter. The oral tradition and nursery library teaches children to appreciate that the marvels and tales are created to be enchanting but not *just* enchanting. Fairytales are parable-art through which the actual child and the child-in-the-adult learn the differences between right and wrong, good and evil, hero and villain, awe and human frailty. The judgments of childhood—"I like it," or "I don't like it,"—are learned first, and from these judgments will develop the five more subtle judgments that Auden defined for the adult.

For Auden, in his essay "The Wish Game," there is a distinction between the folk or fairytale and other forms of literature. He writes, "The difficulty of judging fairly a printed folk tale, still more a collection of tales[2] [is] that [they] were never intended to be grasped through the eye.... To begin with, both the occasion of the telling and the voice and the gestures of the teller are important elements in the effect ..." (209). Moreover, Auden said, "Folk tales have suffered from certain preconceived ideas on the part of the

---

[2]Auden here refers to *The Borzoi Book of French Folk Tales*, edited by Paul Delarue.

general public. They are commonly thought of as being entertainment for children or documents for adult anthropologists and students of comparative religion. Children enjoy them, it is true, but
that is no reason why grownups, for which they are primarily intended, should assume that they are childish. They undoubtedly
contain elements drawn from ancient rituals and myths." But unlike the underlying rituals and myths themselves, which are intended to pose serious questions, an extrapolated "tale that is
drawn from them," Auden said, "is to be told only if some one
wishes to hear it, and one question it presupposes is, 'How are we
to spend a pleasant evening?' As the soldier-narrator of the 'John-
of-the-Bear' says,"

> I go through a forest where there is no woods, through a river
> where there is no water, through a village where there is no
> house. I knock at a door and everybody answers me. The more I
> tell you, the more I shall lie to you. I'm not paid to tell the truth.
> (209–10)

Auden then gives an example of his belief that tales are
derivations extrapolated from rituals and myths: "'The Doctor and
His Pupil' contains a motif common to many folk tales—of one
character pursuing another through a series of metamorphoses.
The hunted turns into a hare, whereupon the hunter turns into a
dog, whereupon the hare turns into a lark, whereupon the dog
becomes an eagle, and so on." Auden then imagines the possible
rite from which this folk tale might have emerged:

> The primal source of this idea is probably a ritual fertility dance
> in which the twelve months were symbolically mimed. In such a
> rite, if it existed, the symbolical animals would be fixed in
> number and kind and the worshipers would know in advance
> what they were, but a tale that makes use of that notion can use
> any beasts, and any number of them it pleases, provided the
> pairs logically match. If the story makes the hunted a hare, he
> cannot make the hunter a donkey.... The pleasure of the audience
> is that of suspense, pattern and surprise, so that at each
> transformation it wonders, "How will the hunted get out of that
> one?" (210–11)

While other tales may have mythical sources—for example,
Auden says, "the motif of the virgin and the seven-headed dragon
in 'Three Dogs and the Dragon' may well be derived from the
myth of Perseus and Andromeda—there is no apparent effort to
relate these tales to any historical person or event" (211). When
they are being told, the tales stand or fall, not based on any asso-

ciations to myth or history, but of themselves as entertainment as compared to the entertainment value of other tales, and other literature. "One characteristic," Auden said, "that clearly differentiates the fairy tale from other kinds of narrative is the nature of the fairy-tale hero. The epic hero is one who, thanks to his exceptional gifts, is able to perform great deeds of which the average man is incapable. He is of noble (often divine) descent, stronger, braver, better looking, more skillful than everybody else" (211). Conversely, the fairytale hero is not a superman, but *Everyman*. He resembles the epic hero in words and deeds, but is usually of more humble origin with a humble demeanor to match. Auden says, "he may be a prince by birth, but, if so, he is a prince of the first generation, for he never possesses, as the epic hero does, a genealogical tree."

> More commonly, however, he is the child of poor parents and starts life at the very bottom of the social scale. He is not recognizable as a hero except in the negative sense—in that he is the one to the outward eye appears, of all people, the least likely to succeed. [An Arthur before he pulled Excalibur from the stone.] Often he is a child, lacking even the strength of an ordinary adult.... The virtue by which he succeeds when others fail is the very unmilitant virtue of humble good nature. (211–12)

In other words, "humble good nature" is a virtue that anyone—including the tale's listener—can cultivate. And, of course, the fairy-tale hero with his humble good nature always stops to help the helpless on the way to his heroic quest, "thereby securing magical aid," while his rivals pass by without offering aid and in consequence come to grief (212). For Auden, the fairy-story world is one of a Calvinist pre-destination. The hero's adventures are not so much his doing, as he would be helpless without magical assistance. "Officially, he is a lover, not a warrior" (212) who seeks fame or fortune only if they help him win the hand of the fair maiden (i.e., princess), and he will win herewith a chasteness completely devoid of any eroticism (The Vision of Eros—love without sex). "Fairy-tale love," Auden says, "is not an emotion, but a formal principle, one of the rules by which the game is played.... As a character, [the hero] is the same person at the end as he was at the beginning; all that has changed is his status.... his awareness of himself has not altered" (212). Meaning the awareness of his success doesn't include a swelled ego that would change his humble nature.

The fairy-story is a game told to a child or child-in-the-adult about a fictional child or child-like hero who himself is an Everyman instead of a superman. Thus, the child-listener can identify with this "normal" hero. The hero is chaste, just as the pre-pubescent child-listener is unaware of sexual angst, and thus enjoys a form of parable-art with fewer complications or confusion. This art is objective, clearly defined, and unambiguously black and white, eschewing the shades of gray that come with the adult's rationalization. Consequently, according to Auden, "since the characters in a fairy story are either good or bad, benevolent or malevolent—it is rare for a bad character to repent and unknown for a good one to become bad—they cannot be said to be tempted. There are occasions when the hero (or heroine) though warned not to do something—not to pick up a wig or enter a particular room—ignores the warning and gets into trouble, but the prohibited act is never, in itself immoral" (212).[3]

For other types of fiction, plots develop through the conflict of chance or fate on one hand and desire on the other; conversely, "the fairy story is peculiar in that the main cause of any event is a wish" (213). Auden then explains the difference between desire and a wish:

> A desire is real and given experience of a human individual in a particular historical context. I am not free to choose what desire I shall feel, nor can I choose the goal that will satisfy it; if the desire is real, it proposes to remain its own satisfaction. When I desire, I know what I want. I am then free to wish anything I choose, but the cause of all wishes is the same—that which is should not be. If I say, "I desire to eat," I do not mean, "I desire not to be hungry," for if I was not hungry I should not desire to eat.... When a scolded child says to a parent, " I wish you were dead," he does not mean what he actually says; he only means,

---

[3]Auden adds: "There is only one fairy-tale motif, to my knowledge, that contains an element of inner conflict: the theme of Grimm's 'Faithful John' and M. Delarue's 'Father Roquelaire.' The prince's loyal servant learns by chance that, in order to serve his master, he must do things which will appear to be evil, and if he explains the reason he will be turned to stone. He does them--under threat of death or because he cannot bear his master's displeasure--he tells and is turned to stone. The prince then discovers that to restore his faithful servant he must sacrifice his own child" (212). Are not variations of this general theme a staple of modern fantasy and pseudoscience fiction such as the Star Wars trilogy?

"I wish I were not what I am a child being scolded by you...."
(213)

On the other hand, if the heir to an aunt's fortune says, "I wish my aunt were dead," this is what he may say, but what he really means is that he desires his aunt's money and her death would allow him to get it, or as Auden put it, "I wish that my conscience and the law did not, as they do, forbid murder" (213). He then continues, "We can wish anything we choose precisely because all wishes are equally impossible, for all substitute an imaginary present for the real one. A world in which all wishes were magically granted would be a world without desire or will, for every moment of time would be disjunct and there would be no way of distinguishing between animate and inanimate beings, animals or men" (213).

And while wishing is not the only factor prompting action in a fairy story, it allows a great deal of latitude to tell the story without the concomitant strong emotions that are essential to other types of stories. The fairy story has the advantage of depicting the most alluring maidens without sexual tension and/or the most horrible monsters that would otherwise cause nightmares; it can describe terrible fates for the wicked "which in real life would be acts of sadism, and make them all *playful*" (213). (Does this not bear truth in the way pre-pubescent children laugh at the violence in Saturday morning cartoons or The Three Stooges?) However, regardless of how playful the fairy story appears, there must be an internal logic—rules—that are consistent and easily understood by the child as being proper. "Characters in the fairy tale must have a 'fate' to which even their wishes must submit" (214). Language used may ask for or describe something of pure invention, but the rules of language, the grammar, must be conventional so as to be understood by the child-listener. Auden gives this example:

"What are you doing there good woman?" he asked.
"I'd like to take some sunshine home, a whole wheelbarrow-ful, but it's difficult, for as soon as I get in the shade it vanishes."
"What do you want a wheelbarrowful of sunshine for?"
"It's to warm my little boy who is at home half dead from the cold." (214)

For Auden, another law of the fairy story is the law of the numbered sequence. If three tasks are given to the hero, then three tasks cannot become two or four. Auden posits that one should not confuse the fantastic in the fairy story as solely being escapist in nature. That is, mindlessly escapist without any value as parable-art: "A World may justly be condemned as escapist only if it claims to portray the real world when in fact its portrait is false. But the fairy story never pretends to be a picture of the real world" (214). The audience knows that this is a make-believe world where one can visit, but never actually move to. One can fantasize about it, but in a different way than one, if hearing a story that takes place in Paris, desires that some day visiting Paris will become a reality, and the dream of escape to Paris remains while the story is forgotten. (While one cannot truly expect to book airfare to Middle Earth, one remembers what happens there.)

Auden then compares French folk tales to versions that can be found in Grimm in order to point out differences that he believes show the qualities to be looked for in determining how one tale may be superior to another. Comparing *The Lost Children* to *Hansel and Gretel*, Auden considers the latter to have the better opening in terms of detail and setting up dramatic suspense. The former dispenses with the conflict of the "kind but weak father" versus the "bad mother," thus omitting a source of tension that a child-listener could relate to. Another problem is that the French story has the children see, among other things, a white house which is never explained or referred to again. "This," Auden said, "is a violation of one of the laws of storytelling, namely, that everything introduced must be accounted for" (215). The French version, however, improves as it continues in the middle, by having the devil and his wife on a farm thus replacing the witch and her edible house of the German account. In the French account, the children kill the devil's wife when the devil is away. Auden believes that this element gives the French tale greater character interest and leads to an ending that is "much superior" (215). In the French version, Auden says, "the devil pursues the runaways and this pursuit is punctuated by a ritual verse dialogue between him and those he meets. They all fool him and finally cause him to be drowned in a river that he is told the children have crossed, though in fact they have simply gone home" (215).

Next, Auden compares *The Godchild of the Fairy in the Tower* with *Rapunzel*. In the latter, the girl tells the witch about the prince; in the former, the witch learns about the prince from a talking dog who watches the girl. This, Auden says, "is more interesting than logical" (215). Yet, Auden also says, "The unhappy ending of the French—the witch turns the girl into a frog and grows a pig's snout on the prince—seems to me an artistic mistake

In the playful world of the fairy story, all problems, including that of moral justice must be solved. When a fairy story ends unhappily, we do not feel that we have told an unpleasant truth, we merely feel that the story has been broken off in the middle" (215).

For his third pair for comparison, Auden says that the French tale, *The Story of Grandmother*,[4] is superior to *Little Red Riding Hood* and is "the model of what a folk tale should be" (216).

> There was once a woman who had some bread, and she said to her daughter: "You are going to carry a hot loaf and a bottle of milk to your grandmother."
>
> The little girl departed. At the crossroads she met *bzou* [the wolf], who said to her: "Where are you going?"
>
> "I'm taking a hot loaf and a bottle of milk to grandmother."
>
> "What road are you talking," said the *bzou*, "the Needles Road or the Pins Road?"
>
> "Well, I shall take the Pins Road."
>
> The little girl enjoyed herself, picking up needles.
>
> Meanwhile the *bzou* arrived at her grandmother's, killed her, put some of her flesh in the pantry and a bottle of her blood on the shelf. The girl arrived and knocked at the door.
>
> "Push the door," said the *bzou*, "it's closed with wet straw."
>
> "Hello, grandmother; I'm bringing you a hot loaf and a bottle of milk.
>
> "Put them in the pantry. You eat the meat that's in it and drink a bottle of wine that is on the shelf."
>
> As she ate, there was a little cat that said: "a slut is she who eats the flesh and drinks the blood of her grandmother!"
>
> "Undress my child," said the *bzou*, "and come and sleep beside me."
>
> "Where should I put my apron?"
>
> "Throw it in the fire, my child: you don't need it any more."
>
> And she asked where to put all the other garments ..., and the wolf replied: "throw them into the fire my child; you will need them no more."
>
> "Oh, Grandmother, how hairy you are!"
>
> "It's to keep me warmer, my child."
>
> "Oh, Grandmother, those big shoulders you have!"
>
> "All the better to carry kindling from the woods, my child."
>
> "Oh, Grandmother, those big ears you have!'
>
> "All the better to hear with, my child."

---

[4]Auden says "M. Delarue tells us in his notes that the Grimm story is ꞁrgely derived from Perrault. The French oral version he prints is in-꜀nitely superior to either.

"Oh, grandmother, that big mouth you have!'

"All the better to eat you with, my child."

"Oh Grandmother, I need to go outside to relieve myself."

"Do it in bed, my child."

"No, Grandmother, I want to go outside."

"All right, but don't stay long."

The *bzou* tied a woolen thread to her feet and let her go out, and when the little girl was outside she tied the end of the string to a big plum tree in the yard. The *bzou* got impatient and said "Are you making cables?"

When he became aware that no one answered him, he jumped out of bed and saw that the little girl had escaped. He followed her, but arrived at the house just at the moment she was safely inside. (216–17)

What Auden admired here is that the French version of the tale was a combination of parable-art-as-morality play, and as such was the child-listener's precursor to both adult comedy and tragedy. (Comedy in the sense that the comic is contained in the building up to the possible tragedy, which is unfulfilled because the girl gets away.) The comedy herein is led up to by the titillating suspense of having the little girl "eat" her grandmother while seeming to fall for the wolf's "game." She turns out to be cleverer than the wolf, just as the storyteller hopes the child-listener would be clever enough not to be fooled by a stranger in real life.

The role of fairy tales is that they are told as the earliest form of parable-art that begins to influence children to think for themselves about those areas in life that require their critical faculties: personal security, morality, aesthetics. The dichotomy therein is the enormous divide of Awe juxtaposed to frailty. The fairy tale intimates natural awe by referring to magic and enchantment; the fairy tale also emphasizes that Everyman, or the common man, can overcome frailty to become Truly Strong, if he is virtuous.

The Grimms and Anderson

In his essay "Grimm and Anderson," Auden states that fairy tales were/are a means for parents to educate their children, and he debunks the idea that these tales "are not viable in modern culture." His test of their viability is this: "If a tale is enjoyed by the reader or audience, it is viable; if he finds it boring or incomprehensible, it is not" (199). Auden finds Grimm and Anderson viable. Referring to himself "as a child who [was] pleased with tales" (200), Auden says that he liked tales to be *told* rather than read, meaning even if they were read, they should be acted out. Auden also refutes those who would dismiss fairy tales as being frightening or sadistic or silly because they are not, in fact, true. He said that he found "such people so unsympathetic and peculiar that I do not know how to argue with them" (200). The only danger Auden can see from a fairy tale is the same danger that is possible with any art, which is that one may not be able to distinguish that the art is meant only as a parable for life and is not life itself.

A fairy story is a story about virtues that are clearly defined: "In many cases," Auden said, "indeed, [the hero] would fail were he not assisted by friendly powers who give him instructions or perform tasks for him which he cannot do himself; that is, in addition to his own powers, he needs luck, but this luck is not fortuitous but dependent upon his character and his actions. [Good things happen to good people; therefore the lesson is that one should be good in order to find happiness.] The tale ends with the establishment of justice; not only are the good rewarded but also the evil are punished."

> Broadly speaking, the fairy tale is a dramatic projection in symbolic images of the life of the psyche, and it can travel from one country to another, one culture to another culture whenever what it has to say holds good for human nature in both, despite their differences. Insofar as the [tale] is valid, the events of the story and its basic images appeal irrespective to the artistic value of their narrative; a genuine [tale] can always be recognized by the fact that its appeal cuts across all differences between highbrow and lowbrow tastes. (203)

Auden credits the Grimms as "the first men to attempt to record folk tales exactly as they were told by the folk themselves," and he credits Anderson as "the first man to take the fairy tale as a literary form and invent new [tales] deliberately." Further he says that Anderson's tales, compared to the Grimms's tales, "have the virtues and defects of conscious literary art" (204). That is, Anderson elevates the language and in his role as omniscient narrator analyzes the symbols therein as no genuine folk tale would. Auden gives this example:

> Little Kay was blue with cold—but he did not know it, for the Snow Queen had kissed away the icy shiverings.... He went about dragging some pieces which he placed in patterns, trying to make something of them, just as when we at home have little

tablets of wood, with which we make patterns and call them a "Chinese Puzzle."

Kay's puzzles were the most ingenious because they were "Ice Puzzles of Reason." In his eyes they were excellent and of the greatest importance: he made many patterns forming words, but could never find the right way to place them for one particular word, a word he was most anxious to make. It was "eternity." The Snow Queen had said to him that if he could find out his word he should be his own master, and she would give him the whole world and a new pair of skates. But he could never discover it. (204–5)

Of this passage, Auden said, it "could never occur in a folk tale. Firstly, because the human situation with which it is concerned is an historical one created by Descartes, Newton, and their successors, and, secondly, because no folk tale would analyze its own symbols and explain that the game of ice-splinters was the game of reason" (205). Further, the subtlety of Anderson writing, "the whole world and a new pair of skates," is such that Anderson is recognizable as the author, and Auden thinks it would be difficult to retell Anderson's story in one's own words. The difference, Auden says, between Grimm and Anderson "is one that distinguishes all primitive literature, that is, in attitude, from modern" (207). In Anderson, "the action is subordinate to the actors, providing them with a suitable occasion to display their characters which are individual" (207). Or, in other words, the stories and characters are somewhat less universal and somewhat more particular, which makes them more subject to a "distancing" from the listener's own sensibilities. The folk tale retains a generically understood universality precisely because it is not too particular. Auden further distinguishes the folk tale from modern stories in this passage:

In the folk tale, as in the Greek epic and tragedy, situation and character are hardly separable; a man reveals what he is in what he does, or what happens to him is a revelation of what he is. In modern literature, what a man is includes all the possibilities of what he may become, so what he actually does is never a complete revelation. The defect of primitive literature is the defect of primitive man, a fatalistic lack of hope which is akin to a lack of imagination. The danger for modern literature and modern man is paralysis of action through an excess of imagination, an imprisonment in the void of endless possibilities. (207)

And these "endless possibilities' are exemplified as the crux of the Auden-named *Age of Anxiety*. The folk and fairy tale are not about endless possibilities, but just a few choice timeless ones.

The Quest Hero

In Auden's essay "The Quest Hero," he says, "The Quest is one of the oldest, hardiest, and most popular of literary genres.... the persistent appeal of the Quest as a literary form is due to its validity as a symbolic description of our subjective personal experience of existence as historical" (42). Auden then gives six elements that are integrally systemic to the typical Quest story:

(1) A precious Object and/or person to be found and possessed or married.
(2) A long journey to find it, for its whereabouts are not originally known to seekers.
(3) A hero. The precious object cannot be found by anybody, but only by one person who possesses the right qualities of breeding or character.
(4) A Test or series of Tests by which the unworthy are screened out, and the hero revealed.
(5) The Guardians of the Object who must be overcome before it can be won. They may be simply a further test of the hero's *arete*, or they may be malignant in themselves.
(6) The Helpers who with their knowledge and magical powers assist the hero and but for which he would never succeed.
Does not each of these elements correspond to an aspect of our subjective experience of life?

Then Auden goes on to answer his own question by relating these elements to conditions universally prevalent in the human psyche. In summary: (1) man in various ways or "quests" seeks happiness in some ideal or substitute: art, theology, romantic love, hero worship, state worship; (2) time is a process of irreversible change which is the metaphorical quest journey; (3) each person is unique, a new *Adam*, who, like Adam, will be tested; (4) man understands, consciously or unconsciously, the duality of contradictory forces within him of which he must judge what is either good or evil "and either yield to desire or resist it" (45).

Often the quest is not only to the benefit of the questor, but ultimately a benefit to his society: i.e., Arthur becomes King and establishes the Knights of the Round Table, itself a symbol of circularity or time without beginning or end.

There are two types of quest hero: "One resembles the hero of the epic; his superior *arete* is manifest to all. Jason is instantly recognizable as the kind of man who can win the Golden Fleece. The other type, so common in fairy tales, is the hero whose *arete* is concealed.... [The] least likely to succeed turns out to be the hero when his manifest betters have failed" (46). The hero benefits from out-side help through magic means, and he gets it, not for outward bravado, but for his humble virtues shown by his good will to-wards others. Within the two types of Quest hero are numerous variations, just as, for Auden, there are variants of the Quest story such as the detective novel, the adventure story, Moby Dick, and Kafka's novels. Within each type, Auden's six elements prevail in many configurations. Some are timeless dream states which are imaginary, and others have recognizable socio-historical settings. Auden turns now to an example of the former, which creates its own complex socio-historical context such as Tolkien's *Lord of the Rings*. Tolkien's world is imaginary, but this world is consistent within itself with its own history, which appeals to the modern reader "who has been exposed to the realistic novel and scientific research" (50).

> A dream world may be full of inexplicable gaps and logical in-consistencies; an imaginary world may not, for it is a world of law, not of wish. Its laws may be different from those which may govern our own, but they must be as intelligible and inviolable. Its history may be unusual but it must not contradict our notion of what history is, an interplay of Fate, Choice, and Chance. Lastly, it must not violate our moral experience.... Good and evil are to be incarnated in individuals and societies [so that] we must be convinced that the evil side is what every man would acknowledge as evil. (50–51)

Conversely, every sane man should also recognize what is good. In Tolkien's world, the internal logic is bolstered by the au-thor's extensively layered construction of the "imagined" societies and their histories. Auden praises Tolkien's ability to maintain not just an internal logic that readers, notwithstanding the overall complexity of this imaginary world, see and identify within the imaginary world that retains Auden's six quest elements. Auden says, "If there is any Quest Tale which, while primarily concerned with the subjective life of the individual person as all such stories must be, and manages to do more justice to our experience of so-cio-historic realities than *Lord of the Rings*, I should be glad to hear of it" (61).

The World of Sagas

In 1927, W.H. Auden and his good friend Christopher Isherwood became examples of art-influencing-life-influencing-art. Auden, as seen from his nursery library, was intrigued by Norse sagas, particularly Icelandic sagas. (Auden believed he had Icelandic ancestors and in 1936 would go there, resulting in his book, with Louis MacNeice, *Letters from Iceland*.) That Auden truly admired these sagas was clear in his enthusiastic telling of them to Isherwood, who then also embraced them. Auden, then age twenty, and Isherwood, twenty-three, were young adults with child-like imaginations. Isherwood said of this time:

> On [Auden's] recommendation, I now began for the first time to read *Grettir* and *Burnt Njal*. These warriors, with their feuds, their practical jokes, their dark threats conveyed in puns and riddles and deliberate understatements ("I think this day will end unluckily for some, but chiefly for those who least expect harm"): they seemed so familiar—where had I met them before? Yes, I recognized them now; they were the boys at our preparatory school. [Auden] was pleased at the idea; we discussed it a good deal, wondering which of our schoolfellows best corresponded to the saga characters.... About a year later, I actually tried the experiment of writing a school story in what was a kind of hybrid language composed of saga phraseology and schoolboy slang. [Auden] produced a short verse play in which the two worlds are so confused that it is impossible to say whether the characters are epic heroes or members of a school OTC. (*Lions and Shadows*, 192–93)

(The story was "Gems of Belgian Architecture"; the verse play was *Paid on Both Sides.)*

In 1930, Auden's first volume of poems appeared, making him an instant sensation on a par with Eliot a decade before. *Paid on Both Sides* was included in this volume along with poems with secret agents, spies, borders, feuds, frontiers, etc. Much it was interpreted as forecasting fascism. This was not the case. Auden, as Isherwood said, had combined Norse sagas with the "old school," which he, Isherwood, and hundreds of their peers despised. Eventually, in 1934, Auden would himself see the comparison, saying, "the best reason I have for opposing Fascism is that at school I lived in a Fascist state" ("The Liberal Fascist," 321). Nonetheless, the fact that the sagas, the old school, Germany, Italy, and Spain seems to have had similar resonance, says more about the consistency of human nature in a perpetual continuum than of sagas, schools, and fascism separately.

In his essay "The World of the Sagas," Auden considered that there were two urges that compel works of literature: "the will-to-truth as historian, and the will-to-recreation as the poet. The historian cannot function without some assistance from the poet, nor the poet without some assistance from the historian, but, as in any marriage, the question who is to command and who to obey, is the source of constant quarrels" (49). Even the most outré fantasy, which seems to not have any historical basis, in fact, does, because if the language is recognizable, this is because language itself is a history, even if the plot or characters seem not to be. Language is both historical and an implied philosophy of the society it represents. Hence the poet is de facto historian-philosopher regardless of his possible conscious resistance to history-philosophy, which he must, through the use of language, concede to unconsciously.

The saga can be historical or entirely fiction, but it has the aspect of "history" in either case, such as *The Lord of the Rings.* The actual historian can never be totally objective because "any history is already a secondary world in that it can only be written or told in words, [and] language must be abstract and select" (50). Moreover, Auden believed, "for us, certain beings are of more concern to us than others ... and appeal to our imagination" which is subjective (51).

> No historian, however dispassionate he tries to be, can omit this fact without falsifying his picture of the human past. On the other hand, if he did not experience such feelings of awe, wonder, enchantment, in the primary world, I very much doubt if the poet would desire or believe it possible to create secondary worlds. Being a man, not God, a poet cannot create *ex nihilo.* If our desire to create secondary worlds arises at least in part from our dissatisfaction with this primary world, the latter must first be there before we can be dissatisfied with it. (51)

A major "dissatisfaction" is that evil and suffering are an insoluble problem and while the secondary worlds artists create may include them, they do so in a simplified more comprehensible form that doesn't quite hurt so much.

> In fairy tales, instead of encountering as we do in the primary world, human beings who are potentially good and evil, everyone we meet is either good or evil, except when under a spell. We cannot mistake one for the other, since the good are beautiful and speak finely, and the evil ugly and coarse of speech. Further,

> while in the primary world, evil so often appears to triumph
> over good, in the fairy-tale, good is ultimately victorious; the
> nice guys rewarded, the bad guys punished. (52)

Auden turns to Icelandic sagas to amplify his idea of the poet-historian/historian-poet. In them, he believes the historian is predominant over the poet because the narratives "seem" very realistic as "histories," even though, in fact, they are not. (As an example, Auden notes, "Icelandic writers had so mastered the art of realistic narrative that it was only in 1949 that the Hrafnkels sagas was discovered to be purely fictitious; till then all scholars believed it to have a historical basis" (60). The implication is that this saga was such a good example of the literature of social realism that it was mistaken for realism period. This type of saga is different than the typical ancient saga or neo-classical saga prevalent since Tolkien. Auden's point about each and the concept of the poet-historian/historian-poet is that the actual distinctions are only so in the matter of degree as to who will take charge of the writer's inner partnership, the poet or the historian. Based on realism, or imagined as fancy, either type of saga is still a reflection of man in his world—the child, youth, or one who has not traveled from a small-town or rural milieu—the realistic saga, with its greater variations, may be more intriguing; conversely, to the reader who knows too much of the world, and wants a respite from it, the fantasy saga may be just as appealing. Both work, and Auden goes on to examine each in much detail.

Art derives from human nature within nature as a totality. The difference between art and science is that the latter measures nature while the former "metaphorizes" nature; hence, literary realism may be more measured metaphor and literary fancy a purer metaphor, which is still, nonetheless, adapted from the same original source, that is the known world, no matter how removed from this world the newly formed world becomes. Marvels and tales reflect humanity's wish to give and receive explanations for sensory experience that arouses emotions of both a visceral—that is, external—and supersensory—that is, internal—basis. For example, lightning and thunder can arouse tangible fear that can be observed by another but then becomes linked to intangible, indefinable, yet still quite palpable, feelings related to transcendent questions as to what causes these awesome events. These feelings, when subjectively collectivized in the tribe or group become myths, theology, religion, and, over time, various secular substitutes: art, romantic love, nationalism, etc.

333

438 | David Garrett Izzo

"There are certain art forms," Auden said, referring to sagas, quest, and fairy-tales, "which by their intrinsic nature ... continue to exist so long as people exist to whom the concepts of the sacred, the heroic, freedom, personal freedom and responsibility have real meaning" (84). Adults identify these needs, even if on a subconscious level, as being important enough to pass on to their children. Hence, fables, marvels, and tales answer the adult's wish to have certain beliefs and values and share them with the next generation. The tribe's continuity and security depend on this. Not only is art derived from human nature; art is derivative from itself to accommodate the changing nuances of new generations. Clearly, however, the nuances do not supersede the basic human needs that allow tribal stories to become tales, then sagas, then the old school, and even actual historical movements such as fascism. The trail from tale to fascist seems extreme, but is it? The tales with their mock, cartoon sadism are tragedies unfulfilled. They warn of the possibility of tragedy so that listeners can learn to ask themselves how to avoid their own tragedies. Listeners and readers can ask themselves if they wish to be like the humble hero or the cruel villain; they can recognize traits to imitate or to avoid imitating. Ultimately, they can see their reflection in the mirror of Awe-sociations and ask themselves: Who am I? Whom ought I to become? For W.H. Auden, lover of fairy-tales, quests, and sagas, this is what we really want from enjoying them: answers to these two paramount questions.

Works Cited

Auden, W.H., "Aging." *A Certain World, A Commonplace Book*, New York: Viking, 1970.

———. "As It Seemed to Us." *New Yorker*, 3 April 1965, 159–92.

———. "Enchantment." In *A Certain World*, pp. 149–50.

———. "Grimm and Anderson." In *Forewords and Afterwords*, edited by Edward Mendelson. New York: Random House, 1977. 198–208.

———. "The Liberal Fascist." In *The English Auden*, edited by Edward Mendelson. New York: Random House, 1977. 321–26.

———. "Making, Knowing and Judging." *The Dyer's Hand*. New York: Random House, 1962. 31–60.

―――. "Paid on Both Sides." *Collected Poems.* New York: Random House, 1976. 19–37.

―――. "Poets, Poetry, and Taste." In *The English Auden*, pp. 358–59.

―――. "Psychology and Art Today." In *The English Auden*, pp. 332–41.

―――. "The Quest Hero." *Tolkien and the Critics.* Edited by Neil David Isaacs. South Bend, IN: Notre Dame UP, 1968. 40–64.

―――. "Review of *Open House*." *Saturday Review of Literature*, 5 April 1941, 30–31.

―――. "Robert Frost." In *The Dyer's Hand*, pp. 337–53.

―――. "Squares & Oblongs." *Poets at Work.* New York: Harcourt Brace and Company, 1948.

―――. "Walter de la Mare." In *Forewords and Afterwords*, pp. 384–93.

―――. "The Wish Game." In *The Dyer's Hand*, pp. 209–17.

―――. "The World of the Sagas." *Secondary Worlds.* New York: Random House, 1968. 47–84.

Isherwood, Christopher, "Gems of Belgian Architecture." In his *Exhumations.* New York: Simon and Schuster, 1968. 176–99.

―――. *Lions and Shadows.* London: Hogarth Press, 1938.

Merrill's Auden: "Wystan" Turned into Character and Myth

Piotr Gwiazda

The poet James Merrill revered Auden as The Poet *of his lifetime, so much so that Auden, as "Wystan," became the central figure in Merrill's epic poems. Yet Merrill's Auden is not entirely placed on a sacrosanct pedestal. Far from it. "Wystan" is both character and myth, and Merrill's Auden is both a study of the "real" Auden and a study of the Auden that Merrill might have wanted Auden to be. Consequently, these epics make continual references to Auden's life, work, and philosophy. Sometimes "Wystan" argues with himself, and this is a vehicle for Merrill to give his views on Auden, pro and con. Finally, in this comprehensive essay, a reader will learn a great deal about* our *Auden through Gwiazda's interpretation of* Merrill's *Auden.*

> Only those poets can leave us
> whom we have never possessed.
> —Richard Howard, "Again for Hephaistos, the Last Time"

I

At the conclusion of Edmund White's *Farewell Symphony*, the narrator—a young, aspiring novelist—attains a sudden insight about his famous acquaintance Eddie:

> Now I understand why Eddie had invented his dress-up party version of the afterlife with its amusing social introductions across the centuries and its continuing revelations. It was a normal way of keeping the dead alive. I remember that a graduate student researching a thesis interviewed Eddie about Auden and finally asked, rather peevishly, "Did Mr. Auden say that *before* or *after* he died?" (414)

One has no idea whether this incident actually took place or not; one has an inkling, though, that many readers have asked themselves similar questions in the course of their encounters with James Merrill's unreferenced and by all accounts unverifiable poem *The Changing Light at Sandover*. Yes, constructing a dress-up party version of the afterlife is for Eddie, a character modeled on Merrill, a way of keeping the dead alive. And, yes, several of the notable people kept artificially alive in the poem sometimes say things they would never have said in their lifetimes. What W.H. Auden says in the poem does not always correspond to what he said, at least on the record, in "this" life. Is the discrepancy, then, between the "real" Auden and the "invented" one? And if so, invented by whom? What happens when one poet composes a work that features other writers, especially *dead* writers? What if these mighty predecessors prove to be not only the poem's characters but also its active speakers? What does their presence mean to the poet who positioned them in his work in the first place? And then, what are the attributes of this invention that set it apart from other literary constructions of this sort and make us reconsider, with Merrill rather than Auden as the object of inquiry, the questions of literary authority and allegiance, tradition and influence? As long as we keep the focus on Merrill rather than on Auden, the presence of Wystan (as he is often called in the poem) has essentially two purposes. It symbolizes how one late twentieth-century American poet already conscious of his poetic abilities comes into his own by undergoing, with a generous assistance of a dead poet, a ritual of initiation into a company of masters of verse. But the presence of Wystan in the poem also does violence to the "real" Auden by disowning some of his views while imputing various others. On the one hand, the poem pays homage to Auden as a person and a writer. On the other hand, it transforms Auden into the kind of person and writer Merrill would rather like him to have been— which means that the graduate student's peevish question merits, after all, some longer reflection.

Composed from numerous transcripts of his and his partner David Jackson's "conversations" with dead souls and otherworldly spirits via a Ouija board, Merrill's magnum opus revises universally accepted facts and fables concerning earth's distant past and imminent future. The poem consists of three parts: "The Book of Ephraim," initially included in *Divine Comedies* (1976), *Mirabell: Books of Number* (1978), and *Scripts for the Pageant* (1980), as well as "Coda: The Higher Keys," which first appeared in the

complete edition. Ethics, politics, religion, and science harmoniously complement one another on the pages of the trilogy, but
Sandover is predominantly a work about past and present literature
or, more specifically, about becoming or wanting to become a
modern epic poet. The driving mechanism behind the trilogy is
not Merrill's desire to retell the past and foretell the future, but his
aspiration to be admitted into a select company of literary masters;
it is, for the most part, a resolute, self-confident, triumphant performance describing the poet's advancement from the incon-
testable merit of such volumes as *Nights and Days* and *Braving the
Elements* to what might be considered literary excellence of Popean
proportions.

And this is where things become somewhat more complicated.
Since Merrill consistently denies any responsibility for deliberately
composing his characters' speeches ("I didn't deliberately bring in
anything," he declares to a disbelieving C.A. Buckley in 1992), the
more particular or literal readers of the poem face a number of in-
terpretative obstacles. First of all, they must accept the fact that, at
least in terms of certain opinions and sentiments, the figure of
Wystan that dominates the latter parts of the trilogy considerably
differs from his prototype in the earthly life. All right then, our
meticulous readers say, the persona of Wystan in *Sandover* is simply a creative reconstruction of the "real" Auden resulting from
Merrill's lifelong immersion in his work; it is a token of respect
combined, perhaps, with a wish for more intellectual exchange
and personal familiarity than actually took place when the older
poet was still alive. The instrument that facilitates this intertextual
project is the Ouija board, an eccentric departure on Merrill's part
from more conventional mechanisms of dream vision and automatic writing.

But this is where the second difficulty of reading the poem,
let's say, skeptically arises. The interpretation of the poem as a
form of intertextual engagement with the now safely deceased poetic forerunner respects its method but ignores half of its subject
matter. In other words, reading the poem as Merrill's ironic exposition of the unreliability of the concepts of authorship and originality leaves out the main subject of *The Changing Light*: how James
Merrill became a major poet. Notwithstanding the polyphonic and
self-effacing aspects of his inspirational device, Merrill continuously reflects upon his own artistic legacy in the poem and measures his ongoing achievement against those of his masters, especially Auden. As in so many of his earlier and later poems, life be-

comes literature in the epic that portrays, among other things, its own triumphant origin and progression from under Merrill's inspired pen or, more precisely, transcriber's pencil.[1] The method of its composition ties in with its content, and vice versa.

The appearances, at least in the beginning, are to the contrary. Merrill is never "in charge" of composition; the characters he and his companion David Jackson summon to the board are, similarly, out of their reach. And the poem is just about that: the freedom with which Auden, and all the dead for that matter, are able to retain even after they have technically ceased talking. In numerous interviews, as well as in *Sandover* itself, Merrill distances himself from the real author or authors (whoever they are) of the poem, assuming instead the role of one of its characters, JM or the Scribe, in addition to DJ or the Hand, Maria Mitsotáki, Auden, other dead friends, and a fantastic assembly of otherworldly creatures. The hapless readers of *The Changing Light* must thus either dismiss the whole poem as a kind of joke or suspend their disbelief and acknowledge the dictation-based method of its composition along with all of the revelations it has to offer. Here "acknowledge" does not mean to read literally (Merrill himself does not advise such a reading), but to interpret the poem on its own terms: like Poe's *Eureka*, *The Changing Light* is a poem too beautiful to be false.[2] Wystan also should be read on his own terms as a figure too beautiful not to be true. The Auden of *Sandover* is not a representation of the older poet constructed or controlled by Merrill. Instead, this "virtual" Auden is the target of the younger poet's subconscious projections of what he has meant to him as a person and a writer. Wystan is a necessary by-product of Merrill's reflections on his own art, its merits and its flaws, what in his poems needs to be preserved and what expurgated. He is the voice of conscience in Merrill's mind.[3] The real and the imagined, the conscious and the

---

[1]For the interdependence of life and literature, see especially the last stanza of "For Proust" in *Water Street* (19).

[2]Merrill describes the poem as such in his conversation with Helen Vendler (*Recitative*, 51).

[3]In 1964, Auden conveys a similar sentiment in his own poem on the death of Louis MacNeice, "The Cave of Making" (*Collected Poems*, 692):

> the dead we miss are easier
> to talk to: with those no longer
> tensed by problems one cannot feel shy and, anyway,
> when playing cards or drinking

subconscious, intersect in this necessarily distorted, but nonetheless fascinating portrait of Auden we receive in *Sandover*. What is he? A close-to-accurate version of the "real" Auden or a wholly invented literary character? A projection of what Merrill semi-consciously wishes the older poet to have been or a representation of the precursor poetic figure, whether benevolent or threatening, guiding ahead or leading astray? Wystan is partially each of these, but none exclusively.

Many of Merrill's dead friends and acquaintances (Maria Mitsotáki, Maya Deren, George Cotzias, Robert Morse, among others) reappear in the imaginative world of the Ouija board as voices of the lost time: the poet keeps them alive out of the human need of grief and love. They behave in the way we wish all the dead would behave. They say what we would like all the dead to say, enough to convince us it is the living who continue leading their lives and confront their futures. This is possible only because, in his engagement with the past, Merrill makes no attempt to readjust to it or reinvent himself in respect of the dead. He does the opposite: he allows the past to reinvent or readjust itself according to his own memory of the past imaginatively enriched by present experiences. Subscribing to a Proustian view of memory as time recaptured, Merrill lets the past become a part of the continuing life—and vice versa. This is what John Hollander has in mind when he talks about Merrill's peculiar Muse, "Memory Imagined/Imagined Memory": "James's pictures of what is were always shadowed by what was, what was being, what has and had been; and the wonder of it all is how these shadows are not deadening but quickening, affording flat tale-telling the truth of roundness" (345–46). Life, in other words, is at all times sacrificed to art. Memories, always so few and always the same, become enhanced, refined, and animated by the poet's creative act of remembering. In his villanelle "Dead Center" (*Inner Room*, 50), Merrill calls memory a "supreme equestrienne" that leaps through hoops of fire (16–17). The beginning of this villanelle says all there is to say about the poet's view of the past, as it is filtered through these mystifying processes of imaginative recollection:

---

or pulling faces are out of the question, what else is there
   to do but talk to the voices
of conscience they have become? (55–61)

Upon reflection, as I dip my pen
Tonight, forth ripple messages in code.
In Now's black waters burn the stars of Then. (1–3)

Within the intimate world of the Ouija board, Merrill and his dead friends encounter a future in which secrets are revealed and all ambitions find their fulfillment. Thus, when the figures of poetic authority like W.H. Auden, Wallace Stevens, and William Butler Yeats also surface in the poem, a sense of wanting to belong in their company replaces the sense of personal loss; the poet himself advances into the world of the dead instead of summoning the dead to the world of the living. The private past becomes a literary one. As far as Auden is concerned, the literary aspect of his relationship with Merrill intersects with the personal one, since the two poets also knew each other, though not intimately, in "this" life. Merrill's personal, but not very personal acquaintance with the older poet affords him a special status in the trilogy: first, as a person Merrill wishes he had known better and talked with more often in "this" life; secondly, as a literary model he simultaneously regrets and rejoices in never having lived up to, a poet he both admires and, in a misleadingly benign manner, continues to amend.

Early in the poem Merrill calls Wystan "father of forms" (135), a just epithet for someone without whom, in Karl Shapiro's phrase, "many of us would have never happened."[4] But calling the predecessor a poetic father means to accept all rewards and dangers such a relationship might entail. At first sight, Merrill's relationship with Auden could be perceived as similar to that he had with his own father, Charles E. Merrill, the founder of the brokerage firm Merrill Lynch, Pierce, Fenner and Smith. It was never close (the poet's parents divorced when he was only thirteen), but difficult and complex. "Father by son / Lives on and on," said Auden in an early poem (*Collected Poems*, 51). The presence, or rather the absence of the father in his life frequently makes Merrill reinvent him as a character in his poetry, now as a threatening shadow ("Scenes of Childhood") or a Wall Street broker he really was ("The Broken Home"), now disguised as Ali Pasha ("Yánnina") or a Sheik with beard and sword ("Lost in Translation"). Merrill's fa-

---

[4]"For W.H.A" in *The Wild Card* (172). Many other poets, including Anthony Hecht, John Hollander, Richard Howard, and Richard Wilbur paid tribute to Auden by dedicating or addressing their poems to him. For a recent examination of these poems, see Aidan Wasley's essay in *Raritan.*

ther is also the model for the sultan-like Benjamin Tanning in his first novel, *The Seraglio*. Merrill's portrayals of his father always inspire a certain amount of awe and trepidation; he is a man whom the poet owes much, fears much, but above all feels an overwhelming desire to come to terms with, if not altogether put to rest. Something of this sort takes place in the post-*Sandover* poem "Arabian Night," where the poet, while gazing in the mirror and musing on his deepening wrinkles, discovers in his own reflected face the countenance of his father (*Inner Room*, 14). In the trilogy, however, there seems to be little opportunity for Oedipal fixations. The dead, yet articulate souls of Wystan and Maria seem to have the same need of JM and DJ as the two mediums have of them; as the mediums imagine their symbolic dead parents, the parents in turn imagine the mediums. In the interview with Helen Vendler, Merrill says:

> *Strange about parents. We have such easy access to them and such daunting problems of communication. Over the Ouija board it was just the other way. A certain apparatus was needed to get in touch—but then! Affection, understanding, tact, surprises, laughter, tears.* (*Recitative*, 51)

As *The Changing Light* progresses and as Wystan liberally applauds and commends JM for his ongoing achievement, the generational difference between the two poets begins to diminish. After the initial display of father-and-son dynamics, Wystan becomes more of an uncle or older brother to JM. Instead of the literary competition, a literary fellowship is established. Just before the contact between them breaks off for good, the senior poet calls JM "OLD CONFRERE & FRIEND" and urges him to continue his life's work (516). No matter that Auden and Merrill were never on particularly close terms—in *Sandover* they are. No matter that Auden's public concerns as a poet clashed with Merrill's professed ignorance of all matters political—in *Sandover* Wystan appropriately adjusts his viewpoints. Not the other way around.

One of Merrill's reasons for this special treatment of Auden during Ouija board sessions is his reluctance to distinguish—or inability to reconcile—the poet and the man. Meeting an author one admires can be a confusing, and often disconcerting, experience. The following is what Edmund White's narrator has to say about his experience of meeting Eddie, the fictional version of Merrill, in person:

> I came to realize that meeting a writer, knowing him up close, in
> the hope of better understanding his work, was a useless, even
> destructive exercise [...] In Eddie the man I detected a perversity
> and snobbishness that he radiated in spite of himself, qualities
> he'd entirely transformed in his writing into impishness and
> humor. In life he had an age, a pear-shaped body, a maddening
> drawl; on the page he was eternally youthful, a charged field of
> particles, a polyphony of voices. Whilst nothing that showed up
> on the page was unintended and everything was a pure product
> of the will, Eddie, like everyone else, sagged after lunch, gener-
> ated a body heat, created an impression (of nervousness and ef-
> feminacy, in his case) that he himself was unaware of and that
> might not have been interpreted that way by someone who
> avoided appearing nervous and effeminate less strenuously than
> I. (241)

The contrast that White so perfectly outlines in this passage is that
between living and writing, biography and literature. The wistful
disappointment with which the novel's protagonist perceives the
rift between Eddie the man and Eddie the writer reflects Merrill's
own experience of reading Auden's poetry and knowing him, in
his old age, in person. His portrayal of Wystan in his own poem
minimizes the disparity that inevitably arises on such occasions.
"Real artists are not nice people; all their best feelings go into their
work, and life has the residue," wrote Auden to his brother in 1927
(qtd. in Davenport-Hines, 65). But in the world of the dead, where
one no longer sags after lunch or generates a body heat, the categories of "young" and "old," "nice" and "nasty" count little and
usually do not influence congenial communication with the living.
The Changing Light contains a very particular "version" of Wystan;
he is not the irritable, depressed, heavily-drinking Auden whom
Merrill came to know in the late 1960s, but the inquisitive, brilliant,
energy-driven Auden of, say, twenty years before, which is almost
exactly Merrill's age during the composition of his trilogy. If we
look at the inside cover of the 1982 edition of the poem, we discover that, in addition to photographs of the other participants of
Ouija board sessions, it contains a picture of Auden; judging by
the still rather shallow wrinkles and creases on his face, the photo
was taken in either the 1940s or 1950s. The choice of this photo is
critical to the understanding of Wystan's character in the poem.
This is the Auden whom Merrill read and admired but never knew
personally, the author of *For the Time Being*, *The Sea and the Mirror*
and *The Age of Anxiety*. This Auden differs from the Auden whom
Merrill eventually came to know in person, the author o

innumerable "Shorts" and poems like "Doggerel by a Senior Citizen." But as Wystan grows more and more youthful in the pages of *The Changing Light*, JM of course grows older; at many points in the poem we sense an effort to diminish the age gap and, by the time we reach *Scripts*, something like a perfect balance is achieved—the two poets become symbolic brothers. Wystan is the person Merrill would rather have known in "this" life: always gracious, always offering priority assistance and attention, always a supportive guide making place for him next to his elbow. Or, rather, it is JM that allows Wystan into his company and makes place for him next to his own elbow: after all, it is he who makes the decision to allow the older poet to participate in the seminar at the Ouija board (128). Auden's admission into the imaginative space of the poem requires some amount of give-and-take. Unburdened of his Christian doctrine, extolling the beauty of Merrill's experiment even at the cost of its truthfulness, and, above all, eager to place artistic fable above historical fact—such is the subjective portrait of Wystan in *The Changing Light at Sandover*.

In the "No" section of *Scripts for the Pageant*, the two mediums JM and DJ receive a chance to communicate with several religious prophets, with Jesus and Mohammed among them, but remain somewhat disappointed with the unimpressive performance of the latter. Several pages later Wystan informs JM and DJ that they did not actually hear the "real" Mohammed, but spoke with a mere parody of the prophet "GLEEFULLY REHEARSED / OF ATTITUDES EMBODIED BY HIS FAITHFUL" (472). Wystan, as we know him in *Sandover*, is also a parody of himself that is embodied by his loyal, and sometimes not so loyal, scribe. The portrayal of Auden in the trilogy is a literary parody, in part as it is rather narrowly defined by the English poet himself in his "Notes on the Comic":

> Literary parody presupposes a) that every authentic writer has a unique perspective on life and b) that his literary style accurately expresses that perspective.... It is only possible to caricature an author one admires because, in the case of an author one dislikes, his own work will seem a better parody than one could hope to write oneself. (*Dyer's Hand*, 382)

Parody is a mode of imitation, with alterations made deliberately for either critical or comic (or both) purposes. It is, literally, a mode of singing beside, in another voice, in another key or simply off key. To parody means to reproduce someone else's speaking or writing style in a context that is not appropriate for that style. In our case, we are dealing with a benign form of parody, an innocuous and well-meaning portrayal of the "Great Man" with an occasional combative urge to rectify or ridicule some of his views. Although many facets of Auden's "unique perspective" undergo revision in the poem, Merrill retains and imitates the elements of the older poet's style. The ghost of Auden literally speaks in his own voice, but what he says does not sound like the "real" Auden at all. And, conversely, whenever Wystan says something the "real" Auden would be likely to say, he sounds oddly out of context as far as the entire trilogy is concerned.

The vast parodic possibilities of formal poetry first put Merrill on this course, as he realized that forms "breed echoes. There's always a lurking air of pastiche which, consciously or unconsciously, gets into your diction" (*Recitative*, 80). Pastiche, however, is a rather neutral form of parody; in *Sandover*, this purposeless imitation of another poet's style gives way to full-blown parody, in which not only that poet's style but also the content of his work are made subject to good-natured yet decisive ridicule.[5] Literary parody implies literary competition. The portrait of Auden we receive in *The Changing Light* is a perfect caricature of Auden, in which some of the older poet's features are exaggerated for a comic as well as censorious effect. Admiration is here also: Wystan is by no means the poem's villain, but he is not its noble hero either. In Richard Sáez's view, to caricature does not necessarily mean to express a value judgment (219); the real joke may ultimately be on Merrill, as he naively aspires to take up Auden's poetic mantle. *Sandover*, therefore, does not truly mock, even if at times it appears to do so; it is comic, parodic, but ultimately Wystan is the shadow by which Merrill measures his own shortcomings and achievements. In this respect, Auden is closer to Blake's Milton than to Dante's Virgil; the only reason why the second or third part of the trilogy is not called *Auden* is because Merrill is, even more than Blake, interested in his own poet-making experiment than in rectifying the errors of his predecessor.

---

[5]Lynn Keller talks about the epic as pastiche (258). In *Languages of Liberation*, Walter Kalaidjian also sees it as a "dialogic satire" and "postmodern pastiche" (118–19).

II

Merrill never claimed to have known Auden well in "this" life. When J.D. McClatchy asked him "Did working on the poem *change* your feelings about [Maria Mitsotáki and Auden]?," Merrill answered:

> In a way, yes. The friendships, which had been merely "real" on earth—subject to interruption, mutual convenience, states of health, like events that have to be scheduled "weather permitting"—became ideal. Nothing was hazed over by reticence or put off by a cold snap. (*Recitative*, 63)

Although Auden knew and appreciated his work, Merrill could never overcome his timidity when talking to the much older poet. "It took the poem, and the almost jubilant youthfulness he recovers after death, to get me over my shyness," Merrill continues in the same interview (64). Despite the fact that in 1967 Auden was one of the judges who awarded Merrill the National Book Award (a distinction that gave the poet a "pleasurable shock"[6]), his relationship with Merrill never rose to the level of mentorship, not to mention companionship. In his biography of Auden, Richard Davenport-Hines writes that many younger poets like Merrill were simply overwhelmed by the older man's formidable presence (292). Merrill's friend and fellow poet Elizabeth Bishop thought that Auden looked nice but too scary to make her want to approach him (177). Not until later in his life did Auden begin to acknowledge Merrill as a poet in his own right, but the two never became as intimate as in the pages of the *Sandover* trilogy, where the scribe, as Merrill is frequently called, freely converses with his now oddly "youthful" master, a feature painfully missing from their rather infrequent interactions in the "real" life.

In his memoir *A Different Person*, Merrill recollects his rare encounters with the older poet with a curious and unvarying note of regret or self-reproach, as if wishing the events had taken a different turn than they did in actuality. Recalling his visit to Venice in 1951 for the premiere of Stravinsky's opera *The Rake's Progress* (to which Auden and Chester Kallman wrote the libretto), he wryly remarks:

---

[6]National Book Award Acceptance Speech, 1967. The other judges included poets James Dickey and Howard Nemerov.

> I'd met them both in New York through Kimon [Friar, Greek-
> American poet, teacher, and translator], once at the Algonquin
> bar and again at the Gotham Book Mart party for the Sitwells,
> whose famous group photograph has Auden perched on top of a
> ladder. (Chester, Kimon, and I, along with the dozens as yet un-
> published in book form, were herded without apology into a
> back room.) But those long-ago meetings I suffered through
> mute with shyness weren't to be presumed upon in Venice. (120)

In one of his numerous revisitings of the past in *The Changing Light*, Merrill returns to this occasion, recalling how he cheered the composer and the librettists bowing to the audience from the stage of La Fenice (481). In another chapter of his memoir, Merrill recalls his visit to Ischia, where Auden was spending summer months every year between 1948 and 1957. "In those years, W.H. Auden was that island's Prospero—invisible to us ..." (226), writes Merrill with the same tone of regret and self-reproach that marks most of the descriptions of his interactions with the older poet. Although an opportunity arises to visit Auden in his summer retreat, Merrill and his companions eventually decide not to disturb the great man. The two poets did not really begin their acquaintance until the mid-1960s. In 1964, the Ingram Merrill Foundation awarded Auden its Annual Award for Literature, which carried a monetary as well as honorary value.[7] Another passage *in A Different Person* describes a party in Athens given for Auden soon after T.S. Eliot's death in January of 1965. The older poet now approves of Merrill's work and moderation. Merrill introduces him to Maria Mitsotáki, the closest, he says, he'll ever get to having a Muse. The two begin to interact wonderfully and soon seem like accomplices to the elated poet (230–31). Many years later he revisits the scene in *Sandover*: "Father of forms and matter-of-fact mother / Saying what on Earth to one another ..." (135)—to the effect that their earthly encounter, given the roles they play in the epic, acquires even more symbolic qualities.

Merrill was on much closer terms with the older poet's companion Chester Kallman. Kallman admired Merrill's work and often recited passages from his poems to his friends (Clark, 56). Auden himself viewed Merrill as a person with useful contacts in the American publishing world. In one letter to Merrill, he asks him to intervene on Kallman's behalf at the Wesleyan University Press, to

---

[7]Letter to Ford, Jan. 16, 1964.

which Kallman submitted his poetry manuscript.[8] In 1968, Merrill visited Kallman and Auden in their house in Austria. What seems to have made on him the greatest impression is not as much the "Great Man"'s conversation as his behavior, conditioned on the strength and amount of his late-afternoon drinks:

> The evenings followed a predictable course. At 6:15 WHA began to fidget. At 6:30 the Greek butler-chauffeur brought him the first of two dry martinis made from ingredients kept in the deep-freeze—undiluted dynamite. During the hours in which he drinks these he blossoms by visible stages (like trick-photography movies of a flower) and repeats with real charm + vivacity [sic] things he has said a hundred times before. At table his chair isn't high enough so he sits on the vocal score of his + Chester's most recent opera, and drinks a good deal of wine. And then the flower begins to close. By 8:30 he is off to bed and Chester + I listen to records until midnight.[9]

Like the rest of the world's literary community, Merrill was shocked and saddened by Auden's death in September 1973; he had been kept well-informed about the poet's final years through Kallman, who resided part of the year in Athens. As Kallman's close friend, in 1979 he was summoned to make a deposition over the question whether Kallman had intended to give Auden's papers to the Berg Collection before he died.[10] On October 18, 1983, Merrill and a number of other distinguished poets participated in the poetry reading in New York City commemorating the tenth anniversary of Auden's death. Merrill chose to read from Part IV of *Letter to Lord Byron*—and for a good reason, it seems, since that section of the poem happens to be most autobiographical, tracing Auden's childhood, youth, early adulthood, as well as his chief poetic principles and influences.[11] By then, Merrill's technical skill and poetic style had made him Auden's foremost descendant in the eyes of many critics and poets—and he was to remain being perceived as Auden's heir for the rest of his life. "Merrill, for all the poignancy of his work, was a comic poet in the line of Pope and Byron and Auden," commented Helen Vendler after the poet's

---

[8]Letter to Merrill, Oct. 8 (undated).

[9]Letter to Moffett, Aug. 24, 1968.

[10]For this information I am indebted to Edward Mendelson.

[11]See Keller, 184.

death in 1995 (46). "He is the obvious immediate heir of W.H. Auden," echoed W.S. Merwin in the same year (73).

The Changing Light at Sandover is James Merrill's ideal opportunity to pay homage to his predecessor. It is also his best chance to situate himself with regard to Auden's poetic legacy. An artistic affinity between the two poets is established on the pages of the trilogy, where Auden's wit and wisdom perfectly match Merrill's subtlety and sensitivity, while his civil or communal manner harmoniously supplements the younger poet's more personal or confessional style. In *Sandover*, JM and Wystan find themselves speaking side by side; they frequently finish each other's thoughts and even, on a few occasions, each other's poems. Which doesn't mean, of course, that they ever sound *like* each other. After all, the trilogy concerns only one poet—and that poet is James Merrill. Early in his career Merrill learned from Wallace Stevens that the thing imagined is the imaginer; in *The Changing Light* he extends this proposition even further, implying that the *person* imagined can also be the imaginer. Figuratively speaking, Wystan *is* JM insofar as he is a projection of everything the younger poet wishes Auden to have been and realizes he himself is not. Wystan is a part of the revelation JM both receives and becomes; he is no more imaginatively alive than JM is factually dead. *Sandover* relates a story of the scribe and his master, but it also dramatizes the master's slow yet continuous undoing and the scribe's steadfast advancement toward the "rosebrick manor" of literary tradition, Merrill's idealized if idiosyncratic vision of Parnassus. Wystan's downfall in the trilogy, in the sense of being both in and out of the game that has become something more than just a parlor entertainment, makes it clear there is something more to the poem than a polite and respectful passing-of-the-torch between the older poet and Merrill. The younger poet pays his respects to Auden as his master, but he does so for reasons other than simply to turn for his assistance in the matters of literature, philosophy, religion, and science. There is a palpable tension between the two poets, as JM bravely rebukes Wystan for his shortcomings, heroically recognizes his own limitations as a poet and, in the process, becomes the poet he has always been but could never quite acknowledge in himself prior to this point.

In his essay "Elemental Bravery," David Lehman remarks:

> The apocalyptic epic as a genre allows for huge chunks of personal history, and so it must have seemed especially attractive to Merrill as he entered mid-career ... preparing to come to terms

> with Auden's eclipsed generation.... As a familiar spirit, a histor-
> ical personage filtered through Merrill's myth-making prism, a
> friend among the newly dead whose beneficent good cheer robs
> death of its terror if not of its sting, Auden is the wise guy and
> the wise man in one, no less sagacious for his foppery; it is his
> genius to convert seemingly contradictory impulses into com-
> plementary ones, to embody the spiritual and to sanctify the pro-
> fane. (49)

In one of her essays on Merrill and Auden in *Re-making It New*,
Lynn Keller argues on a similar note that the poem "gloriously
commemorates the ways in which Auden's theatricality, his humor, and his conversational voice have enabled Merrill to handle
personal material with a decorum that doesn't sacrifice warmth"
(214). I quote from these two critics in order to show how easy it is
to take for granted Merrill's ostensible congeniality or affability,
his seemingly unconditional, open-arms attitude toward his dead
predecessor. Most critics view the relationship between Auden
and Merrill in this way, swayed no doubt by Merrill's apparently
gentle and respectful treatment of the old poet in the trilogy. And
yet there is something aggressive about Merrill's portrayal of Auden in *Sandover*; now and then a competitive streak shows beneath
the appearance of congeniality. The players assembled around the
Ouija board are a very selective society. But they are not a particularly peaceful company: misunderstandings, disagreements, and
conflicts of opinion arise and are usually resolved to the advantage
of their presiding scribe, JM. No matter how loyal and devoted to
Wystan JM tries to appear, sooner or later we perceive a faint yet
firm determination to transform the older poet and his legacy from
dregs of fact into palatable wine of fable. This change aims at making Wystan a more acceptable participant of Ouija board sessions.
Again, this metamorphosis takes place on an almost unspoken
level under the general appearance of reverence and amicability,
which can easily be misinterpreted for the primary tenor of Merrill's engagement with literary tradition. It seems that the problem
lies not in our failure to notice the scribe's implicitly combative attitude toward his master, but in our deliberate refusal to draw
conclusions from it. One may refuse to believe that the imaginative
reemergence of Auden as witnessed in *The Changing Light* does not
generate (or is not generated by) a desire for some kind of literary
confrontation on Merrill's part. The best tribute one can give to
other writers is to read their work and be silent, not to resurrect
and change them according to one's personal liking and agenda.

When in 1972 Peter H. Salus asked Merrill, along with a group of
other writers and friends, to contribute something to a Festschrift
for Auden on the occasion of his sixty-fifth birthday, the poet
replied with a postcard: "I'm afraid I'm not gifted in this direction—experience has told me, 'Love and be silent.' But I'm pleased
to have been asked." Eventually, however, Merrill did contribute a
rather inconsequential poem dedicated to Auden called "Table
Talk."[12] Only two years later Auden was dead and, simultaneously, alive and talking as a participant in the younger poet's
Ouija board experiment! One has already observed a rather tense
personal and literary relationship between Auden and Merrill arising not only from the age gap, but also from their temperamental,
artistic, and philosophical differences. Why couldn't this uneasi-
ness or competitiveness continue into the imaginative sphere created by Merrill's Ouija board experiment, no matter how much he
would like to conceal it? Merrill's resurrection of the ghost of Auden in *Sandover* has both personal and literary reasons. It allows
Merrill to communicate, in a way, what he never had an opportunity to say to Auden in the "real" life. It also allows him to creatively reread though not exactly misread his predecessor's work.
Merrill's portrayal of Auden functions on the basis of willful mis-
representation, not misinterpretation. Throughout the poem, Merrill engages with Auden's work on several intertextual levels,
ranging from allusion and echoing to parody and a kind of revisionary ghostwriting that allows him to put strangely un-Aude-
nesque words in his mouth. All of these techniques not only put
into question the notion of poetic originality, but also operate as
forms of imitation. For Merrill, imitation ultimately proves to be a
technique of creative engagement with his own work as well, as
Auden's poetic undoing coincides with the advent of Merrill's self-
consciousness as a modern epic poet. Auden's presence in the
poem serves mainly to highlight Merrill's poetic advancement into
the company of such poetic "high climbers" as Pope and Byron.
Auden's transformation into a poet he never was assists Merrill in
becoming a poet he wants to be.

---

[12]Postcard to Salus, Nov. 1, 1971. The last two lines of "Table Talk"
(Salus and Taylor, 73) read: "If only Wystan, like a jolly priest, / Were
here to tell me: Go ahead, my son, enjoy the feast" (53–54).

III

Apart from a short episode in "The Book of Ephraim," Wystan appears early in the trilogy's second volume, *Mirabell: Books of Number*, and remains as an inseparable and garrulous presence for something like the next 400 pages—almost until the very end of the poem. At first, Auden's official admission into the Ouija board's sequestered circle comes as something of a surprise. "The Book of Ephraim" required anyone but the famous poet to look over Merrill's shoulder and separate the real from the imagined or the personal from the public. But the more we delve into *Mirabell*, the faster the initial surprise turns into epiphany as we discover what subject or subjects the poem, contrary to all expectations, seems to be taking on. The increasingly civil and public character of otherworldly revelations makes Wystan an indispensable presence in *Mirabell*. For Merrill, who rarely glanced at a newspaper and never bothered to vote, Auden is exactly the type of poet he needs in order to secure enough earnestness and resourcefulness for his unpredictably expanding poem. In *Mirabell*, Merrill transcends personal concerns and advances toward more public questions, history and science (or pseudo-history and pseudo-science) making uneasy entrance into his transcription notebooks. Mythical history and quasi-apocalyptic prophecy unexpectedly replace the nuances of private reflection and inner experience, which have heretofore occupied Merrill almost exclusively. Without Wystan's vast intellect, Merrill, who had never claimed any interest in the world of ideas, would simply have been lost in the simultaneously abstract and concrete, rigidly scientific and ebulliently poetic language of the heavenly revelations he receives via the board.[13] Wystan is there, for the most part, to help JM make sense of this difficult, uncomfortable material. Politics and environmental problems also emerge as the poem's urgent concerns, as if to highlight Merrill's former reluctance to handle overtly public issues; accordingly, after the poet-making experiment of *Sandover*, Merrill will tend to more eagerly address political, social, and environmental topics in such poems as "Little Fallacy," "Snow Jobs," "Spell," and "Self-Portrait in Tyvek(™) Windbreaker." Meanwhile, the trilogy intends to amuse, amaze, and instruct, at least according to Wystan's interpretation of it (324). Intending, or rather being forced, to

---

[13]To learn more about Merrill's notion of "ideas," see his poem under that title in *Late Settings* (31).

produce his own equivalent of Pope's "Essay on Man" and Auden's *The Age of Anxiety*, Merrill resorts to the older poet's intellectual astuteness and temporarily frees himself from his earlier preoccupations with life lived and time lost.

Or at least this is what we are led to believe at the outset of *Mirabell*. "The Book of Ephraim" had taken Merrill twenty years to compose. Much had happened during that period: the poet mislaid the manuscript of the novel originally intended to relate his experiences at the Ouija board (cf. "The Will"), lost his enthusiasm for combining and elaborating hundreds of pages of random notes and transcripts, and of course kept busy composing other poems. But although "Ephraim" took so long to gestate, it took the poet only a year to complete. Between January and December of 1974, Merrill combined old drafts and manuscripts with Ouija board transcripts, interweaved them with lyrical commentaries of his own, and prepared the poem for publication in *Divine Comedies*. The effort cost him not only physically, but also psychologically. At the beginning of *Mirabell*, Merrill gives an expression to his weariness by pleading "No more spirits please / No statelier mansions. No wanting to be Pope" (99). Yet no sooner the poet utters these words, several deaths among friends and family call him and his companion to the board. We learn of the deaths of David Jackson's ailing parents, his Greek friend Maria Mitsotáki (whose role will steadily increase in the poem), and Auden's long-time lover and companion, Chester Kallman (whose own presence, his "earthly" friendship with Merrill notwithstanding, will remain oddly peripheral). Merrill's appeal for "no more spirits" turns into the poet's worst nightmare as the chatty, frivolous Ephraim is now replaced by a different kind of spirits altogether, a group of batlike fallen angels claiming their origin in the earth's mythical past. One of them, at first designated by the number 741 and then by the name Mirabell, will become JM and DJ's guide and informant in a much different version of the afterlife than the one portrayed by his predecessor Ephraim. And Mirabell has a potent message to tell. Long sections of mythical prehistory and quasi-scientific formulas soon begin to emerge from under JM's transcribing pencil. In Book 1, JM relates how, months before, he and Jackson received orders from an unnamed spirit to compose a poem of science. A mysterious, antiquated-sounding voice spoke:

UNHEEDFUL ONE 3 OF YOUR YEARES MORE WE WANT   WE MUST HAVE
POEMS OF SCIENCE THE WEORK FINISHT IS BUT A PROLOGUE
ABSOLUTES ARE NOW NEEDED YOU MUST MAKE GOD OF SCIENCE

TELL OF POWER MANS IGNORANCE FEARES THE POWER WE ARE
THAT FEAR STOPS PARADISE WE SPEAK FROM WITHIN THE ATOM (113)

When he first hears the sonorous order, JM refuses to comply, arguing that for him science means only obfuscation and boredom (109). After all, Merrill prides himself on having a mind that (like Henry James's) has never been violated by an idea: he is a perfect aesthete, writing semi-confessional lyrics, "chronicles of love and loss" as he calls them, without ever bothering to read even the daily paper, not to mention scientific books and journals. Yet after even the ordinarily frivolous Ephraim alludes to some grander project awaiting the mediums, JM resigns himself to inspiration and then, experiencing no success, duly decides to brush up on his so far overneglected knowledge of science.

It is interesting to observe how Merrill approaches the problem of science, or the problem of having to write a poem that has science for its subject matter. Subsequent interviews with the poet indicate that among the books he opens is Isaac Asimov's two-volume *Guide to Science*, first published in 1960. One of the most exhaustive, informative, and at the same time easy-to-read popularizations of science, Asimov's book covers almost everything a lay person needs to know about science, from the structure of the universe to elements, molecules, particles, the atom bomb, radioactivity, metabolism, microorganisms, and the human brain. The wealth of unfamiliar concepts and inscrutable theorems at first terrifies the poet; he sees no reason for attempting to write a poem about what he cannot even understand. But Asimov's opening sentence, "Almost in the beginning was curiosity" (3), arouses JM's curiosity as well. Gradually, he begins to perceive the strange beauty of scientific terminology and realizes that even through "Wave, Ring, Bond, through Spectral Lines / And Resonances blows a breath of life" (110). More epiphanies arrive:

> Proton and Neutron
> Under a plane tree by the stream repeat
> Their eclogue, orbited by twinkling flocks.
> And on the dimmest shore of consciousness
> Polypeptides—in primeval thrall
> To what new moon I wonder—rise and fall. (110)

But a simple incorporation of scientific terminology into a poem is, as Hart Crane used to say, merely like painting a photograph (219). At last JM resolves to try his hand at writing a more sophisticated "POEM OF SCIENCE," as it is dictated to him and DJ by the bat-like spirits (or fallen angels) by means of the Ouija board. His reluctant decision to compose a didactic poem concerned primarily with absolutes rather than specifics has much in common with Auden's curiosity and courage to write from different perspectives and varieties of human knowledge and experience. Although in the course of the poem JM never sheds doubts about this part of his undertaking, we can observe how Wystan's presence allows him to keep up with the increasingly scientific nature of the poem. Through resorting to this most didactic of twentieth-century poets, Merrill himself becomes a poet of instruction.[14]

Although Auden entered Oxford with a scholarship in the natural sciences, his fascination with verse-making quickly took precedence over his other nonliterary interests. Relying on C.P. Snow's theory of "two cultures," Auden argued that the natural sciences and the humanities speak in different languages (*Certain World*, 92). Although he claimed that scientists are the true heroes of our time, he maintained that poets cannot celebrate their deeds, since scientists usually concern themselves with things rather than persons (*Dyer's Hand*, 81). Many of his most important poems, like "New Year Letter" and *For the Time Being*, point out differences between poetic and scientific perspective and underline the limits of each. His "History of Science" emphasizes the element of chance, intuition, and error in all scientific discovery. Science is not a methodical progression from ignorance to knowledge, but mainly a result of accidental discoveries capable of improving our common lot, but also leading to unanticipated disasters. In the poem called "After Reading a Child's Guide to Modern Physics" (not by Asimov, this time, by G. Gamov's *Mr. Tompkins in Wonderland* and *Mr. Tompkins Explores the Atom*) we see the same appropriation of scientific vocabulary Merrill resorts to early in *Mirabell*, but we also sense a dissatisfaction with the view of the world offered by science. According to Auden, human curiosity, this "passion of our kind / For the process of finding out" (33–34), is boundless, but no one has ever asked what we want the scientific knowledge for (*Collected Poems*, 741). The poem alludes to the dangers of the atomic bomb in a manner that is much amplified by Merrill and his heavenly interlocutors in *Sandover*. Auden's concern with the risks of the unbounded human desire to know shows best in his "Ode to Terminus" (*Collected Poems*, 811), where he addresses the god of walls, doors, and reticence with a plea to

---

[14]For a discussion of Merrill as a didactic poet, see Spiegelman's *The Didactic Muse*.

save the human race from intellectual excesses. Scientists "to be truthful / must remind us to take all they say as a / tall story" (60–62). And this should also work in reverse, as "[s]elf-proclaimed poets" must not "to wow an / audience, utter some resonant lie" (63–64), but stress subjectivity of all knowledge, imperfectibility of intellect, and anthropocentrism of the human mind. Auden has no doubts that science can answer our questions about the world in a way that is different from poetry, but he is also convinced that science cannot answer questions independently of the subjective human perspective.

Merrill's professed ignorance of science signaled at the beginning of *Mirabell* and his difficulty in accepting it as the subject matter of his poetry remind us of Auden's simultaneous fascination and distrust of scientific knowledge. By the end of his trilogy Merrill must have come to cherish Auden's ideas about science, but his own poem of science eventually surpasses even the Auden of "Ode to Terminus." Merrill also must have relished some of the quotations under the heading "Science" Auden included in *A Certain World*, his intellectual autobiography and anthology of selections by others with his own commentary, especially the one by Werner Heisenberg (the German physicist best known for defining the uncertainty principle):

> When we speak of the picture of nature in the exact science of our age, we do not mean a picture of nature so much as a picture of our relationship with nature. Science no longer confronts nature as an objective observer, but sees himself as an actor in this interplay between man and nature. The scientific method of analysing, explaining and classifying has become conscious of its human limitations, which arise out of the fact that by its intervention science alters and refashions the object of its investigation. In other words, method and object can no longer be separated. *The scientific world view has ceased to be a scientific view in the true sense of the word.* (emphasis in original, 333)

But unlike Auden, the younger poet also brings opinions like Heisenberg's to their logical conclusions. In his new guise as an expounder of quasi-scientific reality, JM consistently avoids viewing what he receives through the Ouija board as legitimate science. He also refuses to consider it exclusively as metaphors, because they, he fears, would inevitably relegate his poem to the status of Spenserian allegories, Stevensian fictions, or I.A. Richards' pseudo-statements. Truthfulness in the objective scientific sense or truthfulness in the subjective poetic sense is not what his other-

worldly informants are after, but of course it takes JM some time
to realize the full extent of his creative freedom. When one of the
angels emphatically asks: "HOW SHD I SPEAK COMMAND ME O
S C R I B E" (122), JM, still mistaking the role of scribe for that of scientist, replies:

> How should you speak? Speak without metaphor.
> Help me to drown the double-entry book
> I've kept these fifty years. You want from me
> Science at last, instead of tapestry—
> Then tell round what brass tacks the old silk frays.
> Stop trying to have everything both ways. (122)

The double-entry book is allegory, the tool used most dramatically
by poets like Dante and Milton in their own poetic approximations
of contemporary scientific and religious orthodoxies. Since in the
late twentieth century science has effectively replaced religion as
the instrument of knowledge, JM wants to hear only "straight" answers. But although the events of the world's prehistory come
down to JM under the guise of symbols, archetypes, and
metaphors, the body of knowledge thus created differs in form but
not in kind from the body of knowledge produced by scientists. In
other words, *all* knowledge is metaphor. The forces that speak to
him are, as they claim, both subatomic particles *and* fallen angels.
Thanks to its "crystalline / Reversibility" (174), the poem is an
ambitious attempt to unify two remote and seemingly incompati-
ble disciplines, to bring the evolution of human knowledge to a
higher stage realizable only when all science becomes poetry and
all poetry science. In his memoir *A Different Person*, Merrill admits
he has always tended to flee from ideas, especially scientific concepts, "as from the sight of a nude grandparent, not presentable,
indeed taboo, until robed in images" (84). Now, this is exactly
what happens in *The Changing Light*. Merrill aptly clothes what in
his view is science in literary images. If the Ouija board gives him
a chance to explore a "whole further realm of language" (265), his
acceptance of this language as a valid means of communication
and transmission of knowledge also involves an acceptance of the
poem's doctrine that for every question concerning reality there is
not one, but two answers: Yes *and* No. Does Merrill separate or
unify two different disciplines? The question should be put in another way. One cannot unite what has never been separated. While
Merrill's skeptical side continually questions his involvement in
the experiment, his other, more adventurous part absorbs the
knowledge that is on the surface both scientific and poetic. As

Lynn Keller suggests, "if science and poetry represent two evolving sides of knowledge, both are true, and consideration of either leads us to the paradoxically double nature of reality as something both created and discovered" (241). Although in his memoir Merrill contrasts "the sunset glow of fable" with "the poor lamp of fact" (181), he is less interested in showing that both methods are valid though distinct than in suggesting that one supplements the other, one depends on the other. There is no reality to be matched and approximated by either science or poetry; neither science nor poetry can offer a version of reality that is "out there," behind the corner, past the next slope. Merrill views reality as constructed, just as science and poetry are subjective constructions.

Merrill's extension of the possibilities of science and poetry also indirectly contradicts Auden's allegiance to efficiency at the cost of ornament. Auden was famous for insisting that it was his moral duty to sacrifice his aesthetic preferences to reality or truth (*Certain World*, 424). When JM refers to this very precept in *Sandover*, however, Wystan reverses his previous stance by admitting that, at least as far as the trilogy is concerned, "EFFICIENCY IS WELDED HERE TO BEAUTY" (345). The revision of his long-standing position on truth and beauty in the poem is only a logical extension of his earlier, no less astounding conclusion that "FACT IS IS IS FABLE" (263).[15] The radical nature of these two statements, which run exactly opposite to what the "real" Auden had made the pillars of his poetic and philosophical perspective, display the method of Merrill's revisionary approach to his predecessor's work. As if to put an end to the ancient division between beauty and truth, Merrill aims not at exposing the weak foundations of what passes for scientific knowledge as much as to suggest that poetry and science may in fact pursue the same objectives. Merrill writes a poem that is partially literature, partially science, and at the same time both. If there is any kind of distinction between scientific and poetic viewpoint, it might be this: while science tries to answer our questions about reality, poetry poses them. The poem challenges the epistemological basis underlying our claims to knowledge and, at the same time, takes a big step backward to the very beginnings, to the first questions, which are least likely to

---

[15]Robert Mazzocco argues this phrase is "unwisely" put in Auden's mouth (Polito, 219). However, Wystan's radical revision of his old belief and his difficulty in announcing it to JM seems to be exactly the point of the passage.

yield answers and most likely to confound. The absurdity of the Ouija board as a mechanism for transfer of knowledge has, as the poet himself realizes, a saving aspect to it. We do not *have to* accept its revelations at face value, since doing so would simply invalidate them. So, we do not—and thus we remain perpetually of two minds in a world where questioning matters more than understanding.

If Auden's interest in science warrants his presence in *Mirabell*, how to reconcile his religious principles with the bizarre doctrine of God Biology and his cohorts propagated by the Ouija board's informants? In the "real" life Auden scorned Merrill's experiments with the board for the sake of his High Anglican dogma "rooted like a social tooth / In some Philistine-destroying jaw" (87). Early in *Mirabell*, after the first revelations from the bat-angels have been uttered, Ephraim refers to the chosen dead of JM's inner circle as the audience of the poem and encourages them to continue: "U ARE BIG BOYS NOW" (128). As one of that audience is the newly dead Auden, the unsettled JM panics and inquires whether his and DJ's talks with spirits and bat-angels repel the great master. But here Wystan throws his first bombshell:

> GREEN
> MY DEARS WITH ENVY I   COULD CURSE MY HIGH
> ANGLICAN PRINCIPLES   IN OXFORD DAYS
> THE TABLES TAPPED OUT MANY A SMART OR EERIE
> RHYTHM UNTIL OUR POLITICS TOOK OVER
> THEN THE ABSORBING LOVES & THEN THE DREARY
> WASH   CONFESSION DONT U SEE   THE CHURCH
> MY DEARS THE DREARY DREARY DEAD BANG WRONG
> CHURCH & ALL THOSE YEARS I COULD HAVE HELD
> HANDS ON TEACUPS. (128)

Having apparently forgotten his previous opinion of Merrill's folderol (87), Wystan renounces Christianity which, in the "real" life, set serious limits on his artistic output. As with his views on efficiency and beauty, Wystan converts to the world of the Ouija board in order to find a place for himself within the circle. His resurrection in the imaginative space of Merrill's poem is conditioned, in other words, on *his own* renunciation of what Merrill's poem suggests was a kind of religious error: he is not only a spirit reborn, but also a spirit reformed. It bears notice that instead of simply assuming a new point of view in the poem that requires such a modification, Wystan first renounces his earthly errors and only then becomes a part of Merrill's selective assembly. He joins the "WIDE CHARMED CIRCLE" that surrounds the mediums to protect them from apocalyptic fire, but only after his full and very vocal rejection of Christian doctrine is he admitted into this utterly un-Christian company. Auden's rejection of his faith is one of his most serious transformations in *Sandover*, especially since he continues to censure his former doctrine as the poem progresses: "I LOOKED FOR INSPIRATION TO / RITUAL & DIFFY MORAL STRICTURES / SO WRONG" (164). Auden renounces Christianity so frequently in order to avoid the paradox of participating in a private ritual, which through its very nature subverts organized religion.

But he also converts so unconditionally to the Ouija board's doctrine in order to avoid another paradox. During his life Auden limited the influence of poetry to the sphere of art only, arguing that although poetry can show the audience a way to live, it is not ultimately responsible for ethical choices. His orthodox religious perspective negated the capacity of poetry to effect spiritual rebirth. Although Auden's religious beliefs shifted from the Protestant existentialism of the 1940s to a more communal, ritualized Catholicism of his later life, in both cases the strength of religious principle signified a conflict between spirituality and poetic expression, between belief and art. No "magic charm," for example, can lead human beings to the divinity in the final prayer of "New Year Letter." Even though Auden seeks to identify that divinity through resorting to various images ("O Unicorn among the cedars," "O dove of science and of light," "O Ichthus," "O sudden Wind," etc.), he finally settles on the enigmatic and essentially anti-poetic "It without image" (1669), as if to conclude the divinity cannot be represented in verbal terms (*Collected Poems*, 242). Similarly, in *The Dyer's Hand* Auden claims that there can no more be a "Christian" art than there can be a Christian science or a Christian diet (458). Following this contradiction in his "real" life (after all, he continued being a prolific writer despite his religious orthodoxy), in *Sandover* Wystan reconciles his religious and poetic views by rejecting the Christian doctrine and acknowledging that "LANGUAGE IS THE POET'S CHURCH" (252). His conflation of religion and art with all the implications of this claim—that poetry can effectively replace spirituality—contradicts his former views, but also painlessly resolves the conflict to which they were previously subjected.

The final result is one of Wystan's most memorable speeches in the third volume of *The Changing Light*. The central ethical conflict of *Scripts* takes place between Michael, the angel of light and day, the master of ideas, and Gabriel, the angel of fire and destruction, destroyer of two previous worlds still threatening to destroy the third; he is the forever swinging gate between life and heaven (316). Like the two influential twins from Auden's poem "The Watchers," these two twins and their less powerful brothers Emmanuel and Raphael watch over human race and report to their father, God Biology. One of the pivotal sections of *Scripts* is Wystan's emphatic address to Gabriel attempting to persuade the Shy Brother not to destroy the earth:

> SIRS, LORDS, LOVES, LET ME FIRST FALL ON MY KNEES.
> O SPARE, SPARE OUR WORLD! IMPERFECT, WASTEFUL,
> CRUEL THOUGH IT BE, YET THINK ON THE GOOD IN IT:
> THERE HAVE BEEN POETS WHOLLY GIVEN OVER,
> YES, TO CELEBRATING YOU, LORD LIGHT
> AND YOU LORD EARTH, AND YOU O THUNDERER.
> AND THERE ARE SINGERS, THERE ARE GENERATIONS
> BEHIND US, EXTOLLING IT ALL. TRUE, WE HAVE STRAYED
> FAR FROM SOME DIMLY CHARTED ROAD, BUT, LORDS
> WAS IT NOT FROM WONDER AT YOUR WORKS
> CATCHING OUR SORRY HUMAN FANCY THAT
> WE MISSED THE TURNING? SPARE US, I PRAY, WHO MAY NEVER
> HAVE ANOTHER GLORIOUS CHANCE TO FAIL. (328–29)

Again, it is important that Wystan himself proclaims this radically un-Christian view, because it further removes him from the "real" Auden, perpetually torn between belief and poetic expression. The speech reminds one of the aforementioned litany to the divinity at the close of "New Year Letter," but here instead of asking for strength, humility, and instruction, the poet seeks Gabriel's understanding of the human failure of self-perfection. Wystan's prayer validates the role of language as the instrument of our continuous though erratic progress toward that perfection. It is precisely the poet's urge to represent, to express the divinity with images, that Wystan considers humanity's saving aspect. Human beings cannot help but wonder at their surroundings and express their reactions verbally. Earth's survival lies in the hands of the poet, as the poet's art literally replaces every other mode of praising the world and its maker.[16]

---

[16]For more on Auden's Christianity and Merrill's imaginative reaction to it, see Kevin McManus' unpublished dissertation "W.H. Auden: The Poetry of Betrayal."

Though a latecomer to the Ouija board circle, Wystan possesses more knowledge of the afterlife than our earthly mediums, because he himself now inhabits the "other" side of the mirror through which he and Maria can observe the "real" world. Yet in spite of his interest in science and renunciation of Christianity, Wystan doesn't feel entirely comfortable in the afterlife. Often he seems to be disturbingly out of place; but it is frequently what he has to say that sounds alarmingly out of context. JM considers Wystan an intellectual authority, while the older poet encourages the younger one to pursue certain topics and discourages him from pursuing others. He remains equally inquisitive before and after it becomes clear that knowledge in itself is not the object of JM's quest. In his essay "Psychology and Art To-day" Auden speaks of development, in any form of artistic creation, "from elementary uncontrolled phantasy, to deliberate phantasy directed toward understanding" (*Prose*, 99). Although *Sandover* continually shifts between being an uncontrolled and deliberate fantasy, it also refuses to be fully understood. More than any other character in the poem, Wystan seeks to *understand* what comes through to him, Maria, and the mediums, to the effect that he often appears incongruous when he tries to make rational sense out of the angels' irrational revelations.

In Book 2, Mirabell explains how Dante came to write his *Paradiso* and how important for him was the "FIERCE CREDULITY" of his time and audience, when "DREAM, FACT & EXPERIENCE WERE ONE" (133). The implication of this statement is that the audience for which Merrill is writing will not "buy" the revelations as they stand, but seek figurative meanings to interpret the poem's "message" as far as their credulity and reason will allow. With regard to the fallen angel's lesson, Wystan comments:

> IT IS THEIR LANGUAGE I ADORE THEY SPEAK
> ONLY TO U WE PEEK OVER THEIR SHOULDERS.
> THEY QUIVER TO DICTATE A RATIONAL MESSAGE
> JM: I wish they would! NO EARTHLY USE
> TO THE LIKES OF US OUR BROADEST AVENUES
> THEY SEE AS MERE GOATPATHS TO & FROM CHAOS.
> THEY THINK IN FLASHING TRIGONOMETRIES
> WHAT SAVES U IS YR OWN FLAWED SENSE OF THESE
> BUT DO U NOT BEGIN TO SEE OUTLINES
> PRICKED OUT AS BY THE STARS THEMSELVES: ETERNAL
> ICECOLD BARELY LEGIBLE THRU TEARS?
> I DO JM DJ I DO MY DEARS (136)

Wystan is more receptive to messages the bat-like angels are striving to make rational; no wonder he is the first to perceive, through tears nevertheless, its outlines. Later in the poem, he and Maria will admit to converting angelic pronouncements into language in order to make them more comprehensible to JM and his partner (414). In his "real" life, Auden always viewed himself as a "thinking" type; in his letter to Stephen Spender commenting on the symbolic aspects of the four characters in *The Age of Anxiety*, he writes: "As you know my dominant faculties are intellect and intuition, my weak ones feeling and sensation. This means that I have to approach life via the former; I must have knowledge and a great deal of it before I can feel anything" (qtd. in Fuller, 371). Although in the poem Wystan tries to do as much thinking as possible, it will soon become clear to both him and the younger scribe that too much "thinking"—precisely that lack of credulity that Mirabell talks about—can bar one from understanding the otherworldly message. As Wystan himself points out, JM's flawed sense of flashing trigonometries makes him a perfect instrument in the angels' hands. He also adds another comment in Book 4: "HAS IT NOT STRUCK YOU THAT YR DOUBT MY DEARS / MAY BE THE KEY THAT OPENS THOSE GREAT DOORS?" (175), again as if to underscore the futility of comprehending the divine message unless it is through abandoning his own inquisitive, intellectual stance and doubting the legitimacy of the experiment itself. "You cannot have poetry unless you have a certain amount of faith in something," Auden said in his 1938 lecture at the Sorbonne, "but faith is never unalloyed with doubts and requires prose to act as an ironic antidote" (*Prose*, 724). Poetry or prose, in *The Changing Light* faith and doubt go hand in hand, but it gradually becomes clear that doubt alone can become the necessary factor in the continuation of Merrill's poetic undertaking: "DO NOTHING FORCD," advises JM's first otherworldly interlocutor (113).

And yet Wystan is always eager to theorize, urging JM, MM, and DJ to "PUT ON OUR THINKING CAPS" (159). On many occasions Wystan's relentless emphasis on reason leads to clashes with the younger scribe. When Mirabell discusses the bat-angels' friendly rivalry with Nature, Wystan asks "DOES IT BEAR THINKING OF?," to which JM responds: "Dear Wystan, who / Has time for thinking? (196). Elsewhere, as Wystan indefatigably inquires "IS TIME THEN THE SOIL OF FEELING?," JM replies with impatience: "Stop talking, Wystan, can't you please?" (209). Indeed, Wystan becomes increasingly distracting as JM and DJ learn more facts, or fables, from under the moving cup (Moffett, 195). All these snubs on JM's part dramatize the incongruity between Wystan's cerebral attitude and the overall anti-intellectual tendency of the poem. There is simply no place for Wystan's relentless search for dogma in Merrill's intoxicating exploration of uncertainty. "Too much understanding petrifies," says the narrator in Merrill's poem "From the Cupola" (*Nights and Days*, 38). Because *Sandover* does not call for an intellectual stance, the exclusionary aspect of Merrill's undertaking affects Wystan to a greater degree than we could have anticipated.

Wystan continues to sound tragically off key for the rest of the poem. In *Scripts*, his natural inquisitiveness remains as strong, but it becomes even less useful than it was in the previous volume. Wystan and Maria "see" what takes place in the imaginative heaven of Merrill's poem and communicate it to the mediums through language. After Michael and the other three archangels deliver their initial speeches, it is the dead mortals who provide Merrill and Jackson with their descriptions. Though he succeeds in depicting Michael as a cloud, Wystan admits the archangel seems to be beyond language, beyond thought, and even beyond curiosity (287). He remarks that the encounter he has just experienced could have rescued him from adopting wrong religious doctrines while he was alive (287). After this self-critical and self-humbling moment, however, Wystan continues asking provocative questions, even though JM and DJ prefer to sample the messages as they stand without further interrogations.

The theme of the first lesson in *Scripts* is innocence and how it can be destroyed by ideas. Wystan, naturally, misses its point: he demands answers the archangels do not want to disclose too quickly. He observes that his intellectual astuteness makes him more conversant with the angels' lore, while the other three mortals are often confused by their oblique pronouncements (at one point, JM even admits of having no ideas, as he is constantly busied transcribing the ideas of others). Lesson 2 of the same section is devoted to human thought, and here again Wystan seems to want to shine as the most indefatigable of the human "THINK TANKS" (327). When JM admits that without Wystan and Maria's help he could not have managed the poem on his own and confesses "Alone, I'm such a fool!," Wystan replies:

> YES PARSIFAL, IN ONE SENSE I AGREE
> U'VE ON YR SIDE UTTER NEUTRALITY
> NO MADE TO ORDER PREJUDICES NO

BACKTALK JUST THE LISTENER'S PURE O!
NULL ZERO CRYING OUT TO BE FILLED IN: (328)

This state of affairs will not, Wystan assures him, last long. And yet it continues to mark JM's performance at the board and soon leads to more misunderstandings with his poetic mentor. Following this episode, Gabriel passionately rejects the human plea for survival. Wystan is offended by Gabriel's censure of ideas and his recourse to feelings, arguing that "THAT WAY LIES NEMESIS" (331). When Wystan attempts to convince JM that feeling may yet "PROVE AN ELECTRIC CHAIR" for those who rely on it too much, the younger poet responds with a simple "*Don't*" and then embarks on an investigation of shortcomings of mere "thinking" (332). Indeed, JM's ability to receive ideas without having to comprehend or systematize them works against Wystan's persistent search for unequivocal answers. For *The Changing Light* argues for neither life nor death, survival nor destruction of the planet: it merely weighs both possibilities. Wystan's positive, affirmative outlook puts him on the side of "life," makes him a natural ally to Raphael and bitter foe to Gabriel. Wystan distrusts Gabriel because while his first nature is destruction, his second nature is thought: the intimation that thought can be destructive frightens Wystan as it frightened the poet Auden in "Ode to Terminus." Merrill's attitude toward Michael and Gabriel, the creative and the destructive principle respectively, is more complicated: he remains torn between two answers, "Yes" and "No," between "life" and "death," and lastly between "mind" and "feeling." Wystan does not see any affirmation in Gabriel's poignant speech; JM is drawn to its almost human aspects.

Similarly, Wystan's distrust of feeling and emphasis on "thinking" bars him from an opportunity to hear God B's no less human-like song at the end of the "Yes" section of *Scripts*: even after he is shown the transcript of the song, he cannot make any sense of it (360). Before he delivers his "TEXT" in the second Middle Lesson, Raphael encourages him to shed the unnecessary baggage of knowledge: "POET, I YOUR FATHER SAY, UNBURDEN YOUR EARTHLY WISDOM" (391). Constantly overstepping as to what he is allowed to say and what he wants to say, Wystan indeed unburdens his wisdom by challenging the angels, especially Gabriel, to defend themselves and their actions in anticipation of their intended destruction of the earth. His curiosity now changes into impatience, as he asks for concrete answers, concrete information (392–93). But this is also Wystan's last heroic moment in the whole poem. Although he remains a vocal presence for the next one hundred pages, much of him fades from view in the "No" section of *Scripts*, as it argues for the importance of mutability he so vehemently opposes and counteracts. The final verdict on his performance in the poem is devastating, as JM wonders on the detrimental effect of Wystan's "THINKING MIND" (527) on the trilogy in the "Coda." This occurs long after Wystan joined his natural ally, Raphael or the Earth Angel. For once relieved of Wystan's overbearing company and feeling as if he is to begin "The Book of Ephraim" all over again, Merrill alone conducts the final ceremonies and brings the poem to a close.

IV

Wystan is both an insider and an outsider in the poem's proceedings, a dead soul and yet a naive, uncomprehending mortal, a poet of considerable merit but also of serious shortcomings. He is variously lauded as "SENIOR SCRIBE," "ESTEEMED POETIC SHADE," and "WIZARD WIT." But, as is the case with his science, Christianity, and analytical thinking, when it comes to poetic art the ghost of Auden has to renounce his former beliefs in order to participate in the Ouija board sessions. This poetic renunciation takes place relatively early in the poem. As yet unnamed Mirabell first tells the gathering:

OUR PLATINUM PUPIL HERE DID WONDERS
IN HIS DAY HIS SINGLE FLAW HE NOW KNOWS: THE MISMARRIAGE
OF LYRIC TO BALD FARCE SO THAT WORK BECAME A PASTIME. (143)

The reference here is to Auden's four final poetry collections, *About the House, City Without Walls, Epistle to a Godson*, and *Thank You, Fog*, none of which produced the great poems his readers had grown accustomed to in previous decades, and many of which exasperate with their thematic self-indulgence and banality interspersed with mere charm and wit. This artistic lowering of the stakes has to do with the fact that, as Auden grew older, he became convinced of the essential frivolousness of art for human affairs; consequently, many of his poems from the late period are thematically deflated, epigrammatic, occasional. On account of its conversational tone if not garrulity, Merrill's work has been most often compared to Auden's late verse, but with one serious difference. Already in the 1950s Auden claimed that he was a poet only when he was actually writing a poem (*Dyer's Hand*, 41). Many of his late poems indeed sound like insignificant diversions from more profound acts of life. The belief that creative work is a pastime goes opposite to Merrill's assertions of the indeterminacy and continuity of the writing process, which has no proper beginning and no proper end and therefore can never become a form of pleasurable but inconsequential distraction. In the interview with J.D. McClatchy, Merrill maintains that life with all of its aspects—people, places, the exterior and the interior existence—is at all times a potential subject matter for a poet. There is a "constant eddy" in the poet's mind, a perpetual operation of creativity regardless of where one finds oneself or what one finds oneself doing (*Recitative*, 82). With few exceptions, there is no such thing as occasional verse for Merrill. In *Sandover*, a contrite Wystan readily agrees with Mirabell by acknowledging his mistake: "MY DEARS I CAN ONLY NOD IN ABSOLUTE / FASCINATED IF HUMILIATED AGREEMENT" (143). Later in the poem he adds:

> MY MINERALS MINED OUT EARLY,
> I SPENT SLOW DECADES COVERING THE SCARS.
> HAD I SUNK SHAFTS INTO MY NATURE OR
> UPWARDS TO THE DEAD I WD HAVE FOUND RICH VEINS (164)

The mining metaphor, apart from its overall significance in *Sandover*, is most appropriate here, as even while he is making this confession, Wystan knows he will not be granted another poetic reincarnation, nor any form of reincarnation, but join the elements as sand or stone, something Mirabell calls a "NEAR MIRACULOUS REPLENISHMENT" (309). Since a part of his labor will actually include causing bad crops and earthquakes in order to eliminate superfluous population, Wystan is not yet quite reconciled to this prospect. Later in *Scripts*, this "LAUGHING POET" who "SANG AND SINGS" will become most closely associated with Elijah or Raphael, the Earth Angel, his "CONFRERE IN WIT" (317–18). After hearing Raphael's speech that is as witty as some of Auden's worst compositions, Wystan again admits his mistakes:

> THE VOICE
> RANG ROUND ME & (IF I MAY BE IMMODEST)
> I UNDERSTOOD MY OWN LAST DECADES' WORK:
> SUSTAINED BY WIT AS BY A WRY YOUNG FRIEND
> AS I LIMPED FORWARD GRITTY TO THE END.
> FOR IS IT NOT OUR LESSON THAT WE COME
> EACH TO HIS NATURE? NOT TO ANY VAST
> UNIVERSAL ELEVATION, JUST
> EACH TO HIS NATURE PRECIOUS IF BANAL (308)

Wystan's self-humbling concessions and breast-beating assurances intend to highlight poetic wit, of which Merrill is also guilty. Just as Merrill's professed ignorance of ideas paradoxically allows him to better comprehend his progressing poem of science, so does his wit assist him in becoming the kind of scribe the bat-angels and the archangels require for the experiment. Wit, it appears, is something necessary to the poem. Wystan's account of his late years dominated by excessive wit indicates that Merrill himself finds himself susceptible to a similar charge. Merrill's wit is even more excessive than Auden's; his love of pun and double entendre, his propensity to find new meanings in clichés (see "The Broken Home") signify that he is not innocent of that particular if powerful mode of irony. Indeed, JM cannot even resist punning on the word "wit" as he fears that Gabriel's revelations might be "Dire enough to leave us witless": that would in turn make it "impossible to write / This poem they all want" (327). What this statement possibly indicates is that Auden's flaws should not be viewed solely through the prism of Merrill's achievements. Conversational tone and mere wit characterize his own work as well. As David Bromwich suggests:

> [Merrill] is in fact everything he calls Auden, and derides him for (less gently than he evidently supposed). He reveals *sub specie aeternitatis* that Auden's besetting flaw was "THE MISMARRIAGE / OF LYRIC TO BALD FARCE." No patron was required to tell us this—yet before passing it on, Merrill should have heeded the admonitions of an *un*familiar ghost, named Tu Quoque. (54–55)

The Changing Light is a poem about Merrill, not about Auden, even if they seem to perform in tandem. Wystan eventually begins to refer to the younger poet as his "CONFRERE," all previous pretenses to a possible father-and-son relationship having conveniently disappeared. In *Scripts*, Gabriel designates the two poets as "TWIN SCRIBES" (438). Indeed, Wystan seems to be familiar with Merrill's work as much as Merrill is familiar with his. A significant moment occurs when Mirabell somehow mischievously announces "HENCEFORTH LET OUR BRIGHTEST SCHOLAR CALL THE TUNES" and neither poet knows to whom the spirit is referring: "WHO, ME? Do you mean Wystan, Mirabell?" (239). The scene ends with the two poets coming to an agreement on the choice of meter for human and nonhuman voices, but the implication is that by now the scribe may no longer need his master. There can only be one brightest scholar.

But does our scribe ever need his master? According to the poem's version of literary history as depicted by Wystan in *Mirabell*, great poets harmoniously co-inhabit the imaginary "rosebrick manor" of literary tradition constructed from elements of poetic language: "ALL TOPIARY FORMS & METRICAL MOAT," "HERB GARDEN OF CLICHES," "ROOTSYSTEMS UNDERFOOT," "SNOW-CAPPED ABSTRACTIONS," etc. (262). The picture seems too beautiful not to be true. It is reminiscent of the "Parnassus" stanza of *Letter to Lord Byron* (*Collected Poems*, 85) in which a young Auden humbly asks to "pasture my few silly sheep with Dyer / And picnic on the lower slopes with Prior" (1, 167–68). There is something submissive and conciliatory about the poet's plea for space on the literary peak, something humbling about his petition for his own mansion among genuine, though second-rate poets. But there is also something contrived about it, even in his choice of the poets he would like to share eternity with in a letter which is, after all, addressed to a true "high climber," Lord Byron. Auden's irony is palpable here. His early compositions, such as his charade *Paid on Both Sides*, portray a struggle of the young generation with the ancestral curse in the form of frightening family ghosts preserving their tyranny over the living. His early poems abound in tricky fathers who lock their towers before their sons, gaitered gatekeepers shouting to turn back, and the air that is buoyant with others' wisdom. In one of his 1929 poems he speaks about the difficult work of mourning. Despite all these obstacles, Auden managed to create a niche for himself within the existent tradition by overcoming the pressure of immediate modernist influence of Hardy, Yeats, and Eliot and turning first to Anglo-Saxon, then to neoclassical models. Part I of "New Year Letter" features a tough encounter with a tribunal of literary masters, and even in his late essay "Reading," Auden frankly observes: "No poet or novelist wishes he were the only one who ever lived, but most of them wish they were the only one alive" (*Dyer's Hand*, 14).

Merrill's relationship with his own family ghosts is, at least on the surface, conciliatory rather than competitive, as he views poets like Eliot, Stevens, and Auden as "very much their own men" (*Recitative*, 41). In other words, Merrill implies his predecessors speak in their own voices, just as he always has spoken without much difficulty or anxiety in his own. And yet as he is writing the poem alarmingly slipping out of his control, Merrill reaches the famous crisis point at the end of *Mirabell*. After Wystan encourages

him "ON WITH THE WORK! THRILLING FOR YOU JM," an uneasy
JM replies:

> And maddening—it's all by someone else!
> In your voice, Wystan, or in Mirabell's.
>   [...] Very pretty, but I'd set
> My whole heart, after "Ephraim," on returning
> To private life, to my own words. (261)

Wystan's "rosebrick manor" speech that follows JM's complaint
ridicules the need of having one's "own words," trivializes his desire to return to the poetry of private experience, and de-empha-
sizes the element of competitiveness in poetry. It hypostasizes an
imaginary space where literature, so to speak, gets written. It attempts to convince JM that the self plays a relatively minor part in
a work of art. In short, it sounds very much like the historical W.H.
Auden. "Parnassus has many mansions" says Auden in his essay
on D.H. Lawrence (*Dyer's Hand*, 295). In his essay on American
poetry, he observes a characteristic peculiarity of every American
poet, the conviction that "the whole responsibility for contemporary poetry has fallen upon his shoulders, that he is a literary aristocracy of one." This conviction makes the poet demand approval
for his work "not simply because it is good but be because it is *his*"
(emphasis in original, *Dyer's Hand*, 366). Is Merrill making the
same mistake? Does he insist on the poem being his own, just as all
the poetry he has written prior to this moment is exclusively his
own? Yes, according to Wystan, as he upbraids JM for putting too
much stress on his personal voice. He evokes the image of a manor
adorned with shades of meaning and poetic figures and then concludes: "IT WAS THE GREATEST PRIVILEGE TO HAVE HAD / A
BARE LOWCEILINGED MAID'S ROOM AT THE TOP" (262).

But Wystan's speech sounds as contrived as Auden's false desire to be identified with Prior and Dyer. It also depicts literary
tradition in the same slightly caricatured manner in which Merrill
portrays other poets and writers in the trilogy. In fact, the speech
reveals the extent to which he uses Wystan to highlight his own
poetic elevation to "THE TOP." Those who suspect Merrill's more-
than-usual involvement with this speech will not be surprised
when they learn what the poet disclosed in his conversation with
Robert Polito:

> There are only a few places where I presume to pass "my own
> words" off as a message from the other world. The showiest is
> Wystan's evocation of the manor house (*Mirabell*, 9.1). It came

welling up from me one afternoon, instead of from the Board. I
never again felt so "possessed." (11)

If for Merrill to be "possessed" meant to speak his own words, in
his own voice, precisely at the point when he is complaining that
he cannot do so, his poem could have ended with Book 9 of
Mirabell. But the scribe, after all, still needs his master. JM enacts a
number of roles in the remainder of the epic in respect of his literary predecessor: he depicts himself as an apprentice who copies
and reinscribes the master's poems, an ephebe immersed in the
master's work, but also a mature poet asserting his literary independence from the master. Merrill did not suffer from the anxiety
of influence with regard to Auden. Arguing that Merrill's consistent parody of Auden is solely a form of distancing himself from
the poetic and philosophical principles of his master would probably lead us nowhere, as would the opposite argument that Auden's presence in the poem exclusively highlights Merrill's more
communal or public concerns. Merrill needs Auden because,
though he is already a mature poet, his poet-making experiment
has not yet been completed.

To illustrate the process of "becoming" a poet, one turns to
Auden's first Oxford lecture, "Making, Knowing and Judging"
(delivered in June of 1956 and subsequently published in *The Dyer's Hand*), whose subject matter is the acquisition of the Censor, or
poetic self-consciousness, necessary for poetic development from
apprenticeship to mastery, from imitating other poets to imitating
oneself. The belief that the process of poetic maturation inevitably
culminates in imitation of one's own poetic style indicates that
emulation is, at all times, the predominant mode of writing: although its object changes, it can never entirely disappear. The critical stage in this process is the birth of what Auden calls the Censor. Once the Censor is born, it will assist the poet in writing poems that can for once seem real. It will become the poet's first and
only audience. But before this intrinsic voice can be acquired, the
young poet can only imitate other poets and model his work on
those written in the past. He has no right to self-identity. The
novice poet "has to pretend to be somebody else; he has to get a
literary transference upon some poet in particular" (37). At this
point, Auden indulges in a kind of idealistic speculation about
perfect poetry workshops in which young poets could substantially better their skills:

> I can imagine a system under which an established poet would
> take on a small number of apprentices who would begin by

changing his blotting paper, advance to typing his manuscripts and end up by ghostwriting poems for him which he was too busy to start or finish. The apprentices might really learn something for, knowing that he would get the blame as well as the credit for their work, the Master would be extremely choosy about his apprentices and do his best to teach them all he knew. (37)

Of course this is not what really happens in today's creative writing workshops, but Auden's point is that, in very early stages of their poetic development, the apprentices faithfully copy the style of their master or even contribute to his output, but do not necessarily receive any credit for their labors. The apprentices take their ignorance of poetic craft for granted, while the master allows his pupils varied degrees of independence. The master's signature on a piece written by the pupils is a sign of his validation of their imitative skill, his approval of their emulative craft. The obvious analogy here is to Renaissance painting workshops, where apprentice painters improved their skills by making exact copies of their master's works.

Poetic apprenticeship of this sort, or at least an illusion of it, takes place to some extent in the trilogy. In several instances Wystan advises the younger poet on the matters of style and content. But the dynamics of this master/apprentice relationship is drastically different. After he has been familiarized with the contents of God Biology's song in *Scripts*, Wystan asks JM to finish the poem he has just composed in a tone that, indeed, makes it seem as if the younger poet served as his apprentice: "WORK ON IT FOR ME IT NEEDS POLISHING" (365). But earlier in the trilogy Wystan himself completes JM's poem on the union of the elements and then laments over his inability to revise it (160–61). Perhaps because Wystan has been and continues to be a target of what in the poem's lexicon is called the stripping process, the short poems Wystan composes during the proceedings are far from even more average productions of his "earthly" self. Wystan is continually being stripped in the poem. He loses not only his poetic faculties, but also much of his characteristic versatility. His poetic days are over; he is quickly becoming an empty vessel. JM, therefore, can only make polite comments like "Enchanting, Wystan," "Very nice, Wystan," or "Thank you, Wystan," while it is the older poet who has unqualified praise for the younger poet's skill, either commending him for his use of form (352), weeping at hearing his verses (348) or asserting the angels "CHOSE WELL IN YOU" (363).

Merrill's responses to the master's lyrics (this and others) are almost uniformly polite but reserved. One reason for this is that Merrill is, after all, in his fifties during the Ouija board transcriptions; his work had been lauded for its craft for more than two decades. As the poem progresses, the scribe excels in everything he puts his hand to, while his master continually fails to produce poetry of note.

Sandover, therefore, is not precisely a poetry workshop. Since the kind of workshop he imagined in his lecture is also impossible, Auden admits the best form of apprenticeship takes place in a library:

> This has its advantages. Though the Master is deaf and dumb and gives neither instruction nor criticism, the apprentice can choose any Master he likes, living or dead, the Master is available at any hour of the day or night, lessons are all for free, and his passionate admiration of his Master will ensure that he work hard to please him. (37–38)

Again, we see a partial analogy in what happens in *Sandover* to the process of poetic education. The last section of *Mirabell* contains a mention of Wystan's book opened face up to Miranda's villanelle (273). This is just a partial analogy, however, mostly because the master is not as deaf and dumb as he must or should be, nor does he withhold instruction, criticism, and frequently approbation of the apprentice's undertaking. In fact, it is the mediums that at times feel as if *they* were part of the afterlife: "We two are deaf and dumb; they see, they hear. / They suffer; we feel nothing. We're the dead ..." (361). But if Wystan serves in the poem as a metonymic representation of what constitutes the Auden œuvre, if he is a representation of his own books in the library, the primary form of Merrill's intertextual engagement with the dead master would have been through allusion. And there are all kinds of allusions to Auden's work in Merrill's poem, ranging from oper quotations and references to Auden's poems to subtle manipulations of phrase and vocabulary. Section "Q" of "The Book of Ephraim" opens with a stanza from Auden's "As I Walked Out One Evening" that uncannily prefigures Merrill's epic Merrill's allusions to Auden's work include references to *For th Time Being*, "In Memory of W.B. Yeats," "In Praise of Limestone," and "Law Like Love," among others. *Scripts* ends in an imaginar fete and performance of *The Rake's Progress* (and so does th "Coda"); from the poem's revisionary perspective, the story of th opera itself is viewed as an implicit warning against the danger of nuclear disaster (485).

   The question might be asked why Merrill alludes to Auden's work so much and, more importantly, how and when he does it. Some of the allusions are no doubt habitual, as Merrill absorbed so much of Auden's verse in his early formative years that it became impossible for him to forget, or ignore, or permanently shut out the master's inimitable but also incessant voice. Auden remained at the peripheries of Merrill's poetic consciousness neither as a source nor a barrier to inspiration, but rather as a witness to the younger poet's burgeoning creativity. And we see Auden's presence everywhere. Merrill's letters abound in references to Auden's poetry and prose. In essays and interviews, Merrill likewise refers to the older poet as if seeking to endorse his own views with the views of some indisputable authority.[17] Literary allusions imply intrinsic value of what is being alluded to; they also presuppose that readers possess a certain amount of literary knowledge that allows them to recognize a particular allusion. In either case, one poet alludes to another in a gesture of tribute, unless, of course, he or she chooses to parody the other poet. This broad definition of allusion oddly matches Auden's narrow definition of parody. Indeed, we could argue that the act of recreating a literary predecessor in one's poem is in itself a form of allusion, except that in his poem Merrill turns this kind of allusion into parody almost without seeming to do so. Insofar as they are voluntary and deliberate, Merrill's allusions to Auden's work signify that he has mastered the older poet's *œuvre*, accepted its authority, and now incorporates it into his own work in a sign of poetic allegiance. But, again, there is something strange about these allusions. First of all, JM tends to refer to Auden's poems as if to show how they prefigure his own poem in progress. When Wystan paints himself as a

---

[17]Merrill's references to Auden range from frivolous:

> Back to workshops—Auden used to say that he didn't believe in them, except that one might learn at an age young enough for it to take how to keep a tidy desk, and from then on everything would follow. (*Recitative*, 10)

o profound:

> For myself, I by and large put my faith in forms. The attention they require at once frees and channels the unconscious, as Auden kept reminding us. Even if your poem turns out badly, you've learned something about proportion and concision and selflessness. (*Recitative*, 61)

"CHANCERY JUDGE," in Book 8 of *Mirabell*, Merrill innocently asks "'Is law / like love' in Heaven, Wystan?" (252), referring to Auden's poem in which he compares the two on account of their changefulness and uncontrollability. Subsequently, chaos will be associated with feelings in the trilogy. After learning about Wystan's imminent transformation into earth crust, JM cannot help alluding to Auden's "In Praise of Limestone" (310), at the end of which the poet imagines life to come in the form of a limestone landscape. As they discuss possible destruction of large parts of human population in *Scripts* Wystan remarks: "COURAGE: GABRIEL / KNOWS WHAT HE'S UP TO & (LIKE TIME) WILL TELL" (442), no reader can miss the allusion to Auden's villanelle that begins with the words "Time will say nothing but I told you so" (*Collected Poems*, 314). Consequently, Gabriel will remain oblique about his apocalyptic designs.

At other instances JM alludes to Auden's work precisely at the moments when the older poet's poetic beliefs and principles are being questioned. The best example of this can be found in the exchange between the two poets following Gabriel's tearful plea for a plausible argument against another destruction of human civilization. Gabriel's passionate speech moves JM to observe "how much feeling / Is in the air! Such limpid bel / Canto phrases— raptures of distress" (331). But JM's reference to "In Memory of W.B. Yeats" visibly unnerves Wystan, who denies the angel the right to rapture or distress, accuses him of feigning his anguish, and insists on the power of the intellect in countering his destructive designs. Merrill's canzone "Samos" that begins the "&" section of *Scripts* is a formal allusion to Auden's own "Canzone," and it contains a textual allusion—"the world's enchanted fire"—to Auden's and Kallman's libretto to Stravinsky's opera *The Rake's Progress*. We should notice, however, the exact placement of Merrill's canzone. It immediately follows the poem on God B's song that Wystan asks the younger scribe to polish for him. Wystan's short piece describes a young sailor (presumably God B himself) looking for the green shores of land among dangerous spatial gales of the universe. Since Wystan's poem refers to the first act of *Tristan und Isolde* and the fifth act of *Les Troyens* (both of which take place on shipboard and at night), "Samos" can also be seen as a continuation of Wystan's poem, judging by its opening line "And still at sea all night …" (369). And JM quickly manages to "polish" Wystan's poem: in "Samos," darkness soon turns into dawn, and the speaker and his companion easily find the shore that Wystan's young sailor unsuccessfully awaits through the night. Through the affirmation of feeling that Wystan has refused to recognize in Gabriel's speech and in God B's plaintive song, JM and DJ are able to reach the shore on which they will continue trying to make sense of further heavenly revelations.

But there is more to the poem than just allusions. *Sandover* is not the kind of poem that Auden's *Letter to Lord Byron* is, for example, a hallmark of his indiscriminatingly allusive poetic method. Auden's poem contains allusions not only to Byron, but also to Pope, Housman, Henry James, Milton, and Shakespeare. The allusions in this poem do exactly what they ought to do: they give the poet a sense of validation from the figures of authority. Exuberant in substance, buoyant in diction, it is perhaps the best longer light-verse poem Auden ever wrote. It offers a commentary on the manners, life, and literature of the late 1930s, discusses the role of an artist in modern society, and gives an account of Auden's own poetic influences. Above all, Auden's address to Byron aims at establishing his own reputation as a poet. Auden ostensibly writes his letter to Byron in order to "chat about your poetry or mine" (1, 30) and, despite a consistent tone of self-deprecation, he hopes that Byron will have "all eternity to read it" (4, 308). Auden's epistle to Lord Byron is one-sided; the addressee never answers the younger poet from the "eternity" he inhabits.

In *Sandover*, however, Auden continuously answers Merrill who in turn answers back to Auden. Of course the reason for this phenomenon is that Merrill does not contact the spirit of Auden by letter, but through the Ouija board. Merrill's poem is not, therefore, merely a reverberation from a much stronger and louder source, or a belated sounding of an original voice, but a form of dialogue, a conversation between equals. Jeffery Donaldson interprets the patterns of correspondence between the two poets as an example of the poetics of echo. What could have been reverent allusions to the dead poet's work is transformed into constant echoing of one side by the other. Merrill's poem is not a one-sided letter, but a tête-à-tête with his literary exemplar. The poem downplays the need of an organized authority or source, and emphasizes interaction, no matter how unstable it may appear. This interaction with Wystan is only symptomatic, Donaldson suggests, of the "dialogic relationship that the poet experiences with literary history" (51). The voice of the great original becomes so internalized that it can hardly be distinguished from its source. Merrill echoes Auden and Auden in turn echoes Merrill.[18]

Both allusion and echo are nevertheless forms of imitation. According to Auden, for every poet there comes a moment when, for the first time, the inner critic inside the poet will be looking at the poems yet to be written, rather than those that have already been written. This is the moment when the poet begins to perceive differences between his and others' work. In his Oxford lecture, Auden continues:

> To please means to imitate and it is impossible to do a recogniz-able imitation of a poet without attending to every detail of his diction, rhythms and habits of sensibility. In imitating his Master, the apprentice acquires a Censor, for he learns that, no matter how he finds it, by inspiration, by potluck or after hours of laborious search, there is only one word or rhythm or form that is the *right* one. The right one is still not yet the *real* one, for the apprentice is ventriloquizing, but he has got away from poetry-in general; he is learning how *a* poem is written. (emphases in original, *Dyer's Hand*, 38)

The process of acquiring the internal Censor is also dramatized in *The Changing Light*. One of the strangest revelations in the poem is the so-called mining of intellectual resources from exceptional minds in a constant effort to create a perfect race of artists and in-tellectuals that will one day inhabit the earth. Conducted by the bat-like angels in otherworldly research laboratories, the process of mining can occur either while a person is still alive or while he or she is languishing between lives. This same mining accounts for the poverty of Wystan's poetic performances in the trilogy; but the angels also reveal that Wystan's mind was exploited even during his life, which perhaps accounts for the relative meritlessness of his late work. In the trilogy, Wystan attempts to describe the pro-cess of being mined as "AN ODD SENSATION LIKE MISSING NOT ONLY MY SPECS / BUT THE MEMORY OF WHAT IT WAS I MISSED" (189). That odd sensation is given another dimension moments later when we learn that what poets usually call inspiration is precisely accessing resources of one poet by another, a conclusion particularly pertinent to JM since Wystan also tells him: "U JM HAVE GOT / MY SPECS ON" (190). What normally would have

---

[18]Donaldson anchors his understanding of poetic echo on Hollander's definition as "[l]anguage answering language [...]—questions returned to questions [...] or answers to answers or even texts answering texts" (21).

seemed a manifestation of poetic exchange or transmission (one poet mines the other, one wears the other's specs, and therefore inherits the other's wisdom) acquires an even more dramatic meaning in the light of the passage from *The Dyer's Hand* that follows Auden's description of the Censor. In talking about the birth of his own Censor, Auden refers to the influence of Thomas Hardy he felt in his early years, but at one point found artistically constraining: "If I looked through his spectacles, at least I was conscious of a certain eyestrain" (38). Does Merrill look through Auden's spectacles? Yes, or at least this is what both he and Wystan seem to admit. But does he suffer from an eyestrain? Yes, and I believe it is quite a serious form of eyestrain which has caused him to perceive or picture Wystan, precisely as he is, in his own poem. The two poets appear to be equals throughout the trilogy, but WHA always delegates ultimate authority to JM with the unvarying words "U ARE THE SCRIBE" (340, 430, 461). In *Scripts*, the ghost of Yeats gives "WYSTAN AUDEN" and "JAMES MEREL" equal praise for their poetic endeavors (486), but the fact remains that Wystan's continual humbling coincides with JM's gradual elevation, and his authority diminishes as the younger poet's increases (Spiegelman, 240); which is another way of saying that Merrill is already writing on his own, with his own Censor in mind.

Conclusion

After his first entrance into the poem in *Mirabell*, Wystan seems to be a figure JM must by all means please or appease; he is a guardian poet, one of the silent tribunal that can so terrify a poetic newcomer in "New Year Letter." But very soon we notice that Wystan is extraordinarily easy to please. He assists the young scribe in his work and continually praises the results. We also notice that Auden's staunchest opinions and principles undergo radical, in many cases, transformation; in provocative gestures of self-humbling and self-criticism, he acknowledges his shortcomings and flaws as a thinker, a Christian, and a poet. The Auden of *Sandover* is still the poet who has seen more, read more, thought more, and written more than Merrill ever could, but all that proves useless to the poem's unfolding events. Wystan is still capable of wisdom and helpful insights, but his experience and knowledge illumine the way as often as they obscure it: gradually, his intellect simply "increases vertigo" (as he puts it in his own poem "The

Summons") rather than paves the way to understanding. Merrill's precarious innocence makes him a better vessel for the heavenly revelations; Wystan is intellectually more astute, but he admits that his intelligence most often works to his disadvantage. Auden's didacticism gives way to conceptual uncertainty and his world of boundaries proves to be a world of flux. Merrill's fusion of the real and the imagined makes Auden into a character who is both tall and small, profound and silly, admirable and ridiculous, capable of judicious insights and at the same time of foolish remarks. And, as Merrill's position as the scribe in the poem becomes stronger, Wystan eventually starts sounding hollow. Does he still deserve to be called a master? If to write poetry means to imitate *someone*, couldn't we talk about imitation of a different kind, which now becomes the dominant tenor of the poem? Auden continues in his lecture:

> Having spent twenty years learning to be himself, he finds that he must now start learning not to be himself. At first he may think this means no more than keeping a sharper look out for obsessive rhythms, tics of expression, privately numinous words, but presently he discovers that the command not to imitate himself can mean something harder than that. It can mean that he should refrain from writing a poem which might turn out to be a good one, and even an admired one. He learns that, if on finishing a poem he is convinced it is good, the chances are that the poem is a self-imitation. (52)

Auden himself reached this stage relatively early in his career with *The Age of Anxiety*. I cannot tell when Merrill wrote his first real poem, but by the time he composed the poems for *Divine Comedies* we could readily observe certain self-imitative features in his work. Ultimately, in *Sandover*, Merrill alludes to, echoes, or simply imitates himself more than any other poet we can imagine, including Auden. He continuously falls back on his own work. References to his own poems, including "The Broken Home," "A Tenancy," "Voices from the Other World," and "The Will," are scattered throughout the trilogy. Merrill soon ceases to imagine he has to write *like* Auden to become his own master, and he realizes that in order to achieve artistic independence he must stop trying not to imitate himself. He must undertake a quest to become the author of his own poem (Adams, 118). And this means that despite the pseudo-scientific subject of *Mirabell* and the operatic magnitude of *Scripts*, Merrill all along has been writing a poem only he could write, a chronicle of love and loss expanded to epic-like proportions. Has he also in the process fallen victim to what Auden saw as the danger for the American poet of writing "a parody of his own manner" (*Dyer's Hand*, 366)? Probably yes, but this is also a part of the poem's comic spirit. Comedy, Auden once said, differs from tragedy in that while at the beginning the characters are aware of the lack of freedom, at the end of the play they discover they were freer than they thought (*Prose*, 721). *The Changing Light at Sandover* is a comedy, because after its completion Merrill also realizes he is freer than he thought. As he says to J.D. McClatchy, he reached a self "much stranger and freer and more farseeing than the one [I] thought [I] knew" (*Recitative*, 66). Having successfully misrepresented his predecessor's views on life, art, science, and religion, Merrill causes Auden to renounce his late work, which is closest to the kind of poetry he himself had been writing before *Sandover* and was to continue writing afterward. Thus, a form of literary transference or transmission takes place as Merrill changes the literary past, and changes it considerably, in a lengthy ritual of poetic initiation, promotion, and final elevation. Wystan is conspicuously absent from the crowd of literary masters who attend the final reading of the poem and congratulate JM on his achievement. It is so not only because by now he has become a part of earth's crust, but also because the consummated drama of the scribe and his master has allowed Merrill to find justification for his art.

Works Cited

Adams, Don. *James Merrill's Poetic Quest*. Westport, CT, and London: Greenwood Press, 1997.

Asimov, Isaac. *Asimov's Guide to Science*. New York: Basic Books, 1960.

Auden, W.H. *A Certain World*. New York: The Viking Press, 1970.

———. *Collected Poems*. Edited by Edward Mendelson. New York: Vintage International, 1976.

———. *The Dyer's Hand and Other Essays*. New York: Random House, 1956.

———. Letter to Harry Ford. January 16, 1964. James Merrill Collection. Washington University Libraries, St. Louis, MO.

———. Letter to James Merrill. October 8. James Merrill Collection. Washington University Libraries, St. Louis, MO.

————. *Prose*. In *The Complete Works of W.H. Auden*. Edited by Edward Mendelson. Princeton, NJ: Princeton UP, 1996.

Bishop, Elizabeth. *One Art. Letters Selected and Edited*. Edited by Robert Giroux. New York: Farrar, Straus, and Giroux, 1994.

Bromwich, David. "Answer, Heavenly Muse, Yes or No." In Rotella, pp. 50–56.

Buckley, Christopher. "Exploring *The Changing Light at Sandover*: An Interview with James Merrill." *Twentieth Century Literature* 38.4 (Winter 1992): 415–35.

Clark, Thekla. *Wystan and Chester. A Personal Memoir of W.H. Auden and Chester Kallman*. New York: Columbia UP, 1996.

Crane, Hart. *The Complete Poems and Selected Letters and Prose of Hart Crane*. Edited by Brom Weber. Garden City, NY: Anchor Books, 1966.

Davenport-Hines, Richard. *Auden*. London: William Heinemann, 1995.

Donaldson, Jeffery. "The Company Poets Keep: Allusion, Echo, and the Question of Who Is Listening in W.H. Auden and James Merrill." *Contemporary Literature* 36.1 (1997): 35–57.

Fuller, John. *W.H. Auden. A Commentary*. Princeton, NJ: Princeton UP, 1998.

Hollander, John. *The Figure of Echo: A Mode of Allusion in Milton and After*. Berkeley: U of California P, 1981.

————. "Memorial Tribute." *Poetry* 166.6 (1995): 341–48.

Howard, Richard. "Again for Hephaistos, the Last Time." *Fellow Feelings*. New York: Atheneum, 1976.

Kalaidjian, Walter. *Languages of Liberation. The Social Text in Contemporary American Poetry*. New York: Columbia UP, 1989.

Keller, Lynn. *Re-making It New. Contemporary American Poetry and the Modernist Tradition*. Cambridge: Cambridge UP, 1987.

Lehman, David. "Elemental Bravery." In Lehman and Berger, pp. 23–60.

————, and Charles Berger, eds. *James Merrill: Essays in Criticism*. Ithaca and London: Cornell UP, 1983.

McManus, Kevin. "W.H. Auden: The Poetry of Betrayal." Diss., Cornell U., 1983.

Mazzocco, Robert. "The Right Stuff." In Polito, *A Reader's Guide*, pp. 208–21.

Merrill, James. *The Changing Light at Sandover*. New York: Knopf, 1982.

————. *A Different Person: A Memoir*. San Francisco: Harper San Francisco, 1993.

————. *The Inner Room*. New York: Knopf, 1988.

————. *Late Settings*. New York: Atheneum, 1985.

————. Letter to Judith Moffett. August 24, 1968. Berg Collection. New York Public Library, New York.

————. National Book Award Acceptance Speech. 1967. Berg Collection. New York Public Library, New York.

————. *Nights and Days.* New York: Atheneum, 1966.

————. Postcard to Peter Salus. November 1, 1971. Berg Collection. New York Public Library, New York.

————. *Recitative. Prose by James Merrill.* Edited by J.D. McClatchy. San Francisco: North Point Press, 1986.

————. *Water Street.* New York: Atheneum, 1962.

Merwin, W.S. "The End of More Than Just a Book." In Rotella, pp. 70–73.

Moffett, Judith. *James Merrill. An Introduction to the Poetry.* New York: Columbia UP, 1984.

Polito, Robert. "*The Changing Light at Sandover*: A Conversation with James Merrill." *Pequod* 31 (1990): 10–13.

————. *A Reader's Guide to James Merrill's The Changing Light at Sandover.* Ann Arbor: Michigan UP, 1994.

Rotella, Guy, ed. *Critical Essays on James Merrill.* New York: G.K. Hall & Co., 1996.

Sáez, Richard. "'At the Salon Level': Merrill's Apocalyptic Epic." In Lehman and Berger, pp. 211–45.

Salus, Peter, and Paul B. Taylor, eds. *For W.H. Auden. Felicitations to Wystan Hugh Auden on the Occasion of His Sixty-fifth Birthday.* New York: Random House, 1972.

Shapiro, Karl. *The Wild Card. Selected Poems Early and Late.* Urbana and Chicago: U of Illinois P, 1998.

Spiegelman, Willard. *The Didactic Muse. Scenes of Instruction in Contemporary American Poetry.* Princeton, NJ: Princeton UP, 1989.

Vendler, Helen. Rev. of *A Scattering of Salts*, by James Merrill. *New York Review of Books*, 11 May 1995, 46.

Wasley, Aidan. "Auden: The Poetic Inheritance." *Raritan* 19.2 (Fall 1999): 128–57.

White, Edmund. *The Farewell Symphony.* New York: Knopf, 1997.

Auden's Legacy:
A Temporarily Last Word

Roger Lathbury

In his essay on Robert Frost, reprinted in *The Dyer's Hand*, W.H. Auden distinguishes between Ariel- and Prospero-dominated writers. Acknowledging that in practice the categories are not pure, Auden defines the former as writers whose aim is primarily to produce self-contained works of verbal beauty, without necessarily affecting the way a reader lives—Auden cites George Peele and Edward Lear. The latter consists of writers who strive to speak to our "condition," to write about serious matters: e.g., Wordsworth and Robert Frost. Plainly, Auden would have identified himself with this group.

As the essays in *W.H. Auden: A Legacy* demonstrate (though such is not their intent), Auden brought to the practice of Prospero poetry the twentieth century's need for certainty and guidance and at the same the impossibility of finding them.

This is not surprising. Splits run throughout Auden's life. His mother was artistic, his father scientific. He was born in England but became an American citizen, yet he told Dick Cavett, "I don't think of myself as an American, but I am a New Yorker." (Cavett: "What's a New Yorker?" Auden: "I don't know.") As a New Yorker, he lived part of the year in Europe. A homosexual, he had affairs with at least two women. He wrote poetry but thought that to be a novelist was a higher calling. He found Lent and Carnival mutually necessary.

These splits multiply in his thinking and his poetry; the Ariel-Prospero division is only one division. Except for the supreme masters, writers are either Alices or Mabels. One of his essays is titled "Hic et Ille." Our wants, he explains in an analysis of Nathanael West, are either "wishes" or "desires." In another essay, "A is a good loser when, holding good cards, he makes a fatal error.... With B it is the other way round.... A's God—Zeus-Jehovah: B's God—The Unmoved Mover." "Whom do I read with the utmost pleasure?," he asks, and starts dividing and contrasting; "Not Dante, to my mind the greatest of poets, but Ronald Firbank." "Dichtung und Wahrheit" speaks of the "I-feeling" and the "You-feeling." How many of his lectures, reviews and notices begin by categorizing and classifying: "The major writer is of two kinds...." "I can recognize three species of the novel...." "*Measure for Measure* is about three things...." He loved crossword puzzles and found that any clue was helpful to get started on a solution.

This, after all, is the man who defined poetry as "the clear expression of opposites." Once again, he is right. He almost never wrote a poem without contradictory impulses and allegiances. *The Double Man* applies not only to the nature of humanity but also to the author who singlemindedly explored, for tragic and then comic purposes, the rifts between Ariel and Prospero, or, to shift terms, between the ordinary and the ideal life (see Peter Grosvenor's essay on "Auden, 'Spain,' and the Crisis of Literary Popular Frontism," and David Garrett Izzo's "W.H. Auden on Fairy-Tales, Quests, and Sagas"), between freedom and necessity (Paul Eros on "A Prevision of Agape ..."), between hope and fear (James Young on Lawrence and Auden), self and other (the Londravilles' essay on *Paid on Both Sides*). Take any poem from Auden's forty-five-year writing career—sometimes it can be done with a single line—and you find that the vitality and immediacy come from the author's use of and awareness of division. That awareness is in his first poems and his last. One effort of March 1922 speaks of a moon "like Stilton cheese" and talks about gathering stars like strawberries on "England land." The title over these images? "California."

In the first poem in the legendary 1928 *Poems*, the sprinkler waters the lawn, promising life and sexual fulfillment, but the boy vanishes into the darkness (I, 1928). In 1973, even as he wishes the good Lord would take him, he loves life. The final line of the title poem of his posthumous volume is: "Thank you, thank you, thank you, fog," a masterpiece of aural opposition.

The unexpectedness of Auden's opposed categories, their surprising qualities, their insightfulness, and their infectiousness give Auden's work intellectual and dramatic liveliness. What sheer fun! What energy!

Owen Brady's study of *The Dog Beneath the Skin* responds to these oppositions: the play is a joke, but the joke is serious, even i what seems serious is a joke. The oppositions are also Auden's way of making order, making sense and of thinking about what actions would be appropriate in different circumstances. A middle period masterpiece of categorization, "Horae Canonicae," is based upon sanctioned compartments: the canonical hours (themselves based upon the events of the crucifixion). And yet this most serious work is indebted to that Ariel-like poet George Peele.

It is the depth and integration of his awareness that enabled Auden, despite his sense of separateness, of removal from the ideal, to produce unified and instantly distinctive poetry. For notwithstanding its apparent transmutations and its jackdaw pluckings from Freud, Karl Marx, Tillich, Tolkien, Homer, Horace, Karl Kraus, Laura Riding, Montaigne, Lewis Carroll, Blake, the Bible, Frost, William Barnes, Rosenstock-Huessy, Plato, St. Augustine, Shakespeare, fairy tales, Spengler, Homer Lane, and a host of other books and writers so numerous that to mention them all would be to recapitulate the history of western culture, Auden's poetic world is Auden's. Its answers are couched in hesitation; it finds its surest assertions not in brash skepticism but in qualification. (Auden's philosophical uncle is not David Hume but Bishop Berkeley.)

If to view Auden's career as shifting from the recondite "modernism" of the late 1920s through the activism of the 1930s to the Christian perspectives affirmed in the remaining decades of the poet's life is to recapitulate the aesthetic trends of the twentieth century, it is equally true that no matter what his focus, Auden's words were always afraid to say more than they meant. As a consequence, they often undercut what on the surface they seem to say. Thus Jay Ladin writes in "Search Conditions: Find 'Auden' & 'Modernism,'" the early Auden is not quite as avant-garde as he appears to be, nor the later Auden quite as après. Both within and without the tradition, he speaks to us warmly and engagingly, the double man who insists upon unity within the poles of Prospero and Ariel, become flexibly constant to a self that sees within nature's flux a variety just as various as the other selves who read and inhabit his world, and pausing, he is aware that he may be passing the crucifixion itself.

It was his hesitation before the poem-as-propaganda that led him to exclude from his approved *œuvre* works such as "Sir, No Man's Enemy," "September 1st 1939," and "Spain." The compass, formal deftness, and rhetorical sweep of these poems would have made the career of poetic pygmies. "For all I know it may be quite a good poem," he said of one of these, "but it should not have been written by me." Prospero chastises Ariel!

This resolute—would the perverse say perverse?—fidelity to himself makes Auden one of the few writers of the twentieth century whom one reads with the utmost seriousness. Not simply admiration, which legions of Ariel writers command (Wallace Stevens is the current darling of the Ariel set), but seriousness; and not solemnity, for almost all the poems, from "This Lunar Beauty" and "It Was Easter as I Walked in the Public Gardens" and, to anyone with an ear, the later "prose-y" ones—"The Cave of Making," or "Thanksgiving for a Habitat"—as well as the "light verse," e.g., "The Truest Poetry Is the Most Feigning" or "Song of the Devil," possess an immediate surface delight whatever the subject. But they also—*au fond*—have that fundamental seriousness: for the poems speak about love, transcendence, death—issues that matter. Now any preacher, politician, neighbor, or person could do as much, but Auden connects his private concern of these with the public area informed by a seemingly casual allusiveness that can only come from earned wisdom. Without the integrity to "scrap" (a favorite Auden word) accomplished poems that are wrong, the poems that are right cannot be written. Even if the reader knows nothing of the context, the force of the past comes through, in ways felt though not made explicit.

Such wisdom characterizes the poems from mid-career onwards. Moreover, if Auden's moral force places him in the high company of others with the same quality (is this not implied in Adrienne Hacker-Daniels' presentation of "Ciceronian Rhetorical" tropes in *The Orators*?), it is still a respectful tone. A reader never feels as though Auden is talking down.

"He belongs to none yet gives to all," wrote Stephen Spender in "Auden at Milwaukee." What the earnest poetry of witness would *be*, even an Auden limerick *is*; Prospero must be disinterested. Such genuine impartiality—whether filtered through feeling as in the poems of the 1930s or intellect, as in the later poems (Brian Conniff in "Answering Herod ..." is not alone in preferring the earlier work), is perhaps the highest virtue a Prospero poet can attain. Paradoxically it leads, in Auden, to an Ariel-like property: wit. The danger of it is that it may lead a writer to say something clever simply for the sake of sounding "smart."

In *Secondary Worlds*, Auden resists (yet includes) a quip about the inability of actors to master speech rhythms. Auden's wit comes out of his divided allegiances. Both comic and lyric poems can exhibit this quality. His verse about speech-giving for hire, "On the Circuit," chides the speaker—and who else could the speaker be but Auden?—for, among much else, talking of poetry as though it were "the gospel." Movingly, in his lyric "The Song," the wit is a counterpoint to the loveliness to which the poem alludes, as acts to efface, change, and ultimately intensify feeling in its description of the way art betrays its own initial vision (a constant theme in Auden).

Complexities are one way Auden's work refuses to be used, to be less than fully human, for if he himself is classifier, the aim of his classifications is enlightenment and pleasure, never manipulation. Resistance to treating a person as a statistic or a number is central to Auden. More than one poem, most notably "Memorial for the City," turns upon it.

Although a homosexual, Auden resisted all attempts to present himself as a gay icon. Although he is, as Robert L. Caserio argues, different from other gay modernists, not the least reason is that his work appeals beyond such a coterie, even to heterosexual (or bisexual) readers. The work is so incidentally homosexual, like *The Aeneid* or *The Importance of Being Earnest*, that a love poem such as "Lullaby," which is certainly homosexually based, loses none of its conscious beauty when applied to heterosexual love. Even "The Platonic Blow," which never loses its grounding in male homosexuality, goes beyond the merely pornographic. Its language suggests ritual, so that its celebration of climax transcends its erotic particulars; like his other work, the private merges with the public.

In the early 1930s, critics were in the habit of speaking of "the Auden group," as though Auden's poems were something read by and relevant to a small group; yet this group soon included more than Auden's friends and schoolmates. Forty years later, when Samuel Hynes wrote a literary account of the decade, he called it *The Auden Generation*.

Universality, with Auden's clarity and aphoristic concision, accounts for the undiminished citations from Auden's work over the past several years. Indeed, except for Philip Larkin, no poet of recent times has been so quoted. The day before this was being written, George Will, in a column in *The Washington Post*, cited the poem "Under Which Lyre." Behind this writer on his bookshelf is John Le Carré's *The Honourable Schoolboy*; its epigraph comes from Auden's elegy on Yeats. Precisely when Auden became a recognized cultural landmark whose authority could be cited is anyone's guess, but it seems noteworthy that even that harsh dis-

approver of Auden's later work, Randall Jarrell, makes the fraudu-
lent Mr. Daudier in his *Pictures from an Institution* (1954) try to
palm off an Auden aphorism (that the ideal education is manual
labor and Greek) as his own. Nor does this trend show signs of
stopping, as Piotr Gwiazda's "Merrill's Auden: 'Wystan' Turned
into Character and Myth" illustrates.

    As Auden himself might ask: why is it so? "What does it pe-
riod? What does it *osse*?" My dear, I know nothing of either, but
the disappearance of poetry from the lives of the ordinary reading
public and its relegation, by and large, to the academy, does mark
a debasement in the way we connect, a lessening of something
unique that modern culture has lost. This writer does not believe
that he is alone in believing that the way to be most fully human is
through humanity's greatest achievement: language. This does not
mean the programmatic schema of artless propaganda, whether
masquerading as poetry or not, nor an extension of the romantic
impulses begun at the end of eighteenth century and that the
nonce-sense world of Yeats extended these impulses further, but
through a Horatian middle ground, true to Prospero and Ariel, yet
without being false to either, and speaking of a truth and beauty,
most likely found in the "embusqué havens" of the kind of poetry
that W.H. Auden wrote.

Index

The Locust Hill Literary Studies Series

1. *Blake and His Bibles*. Edited by David V. Erdman. ISBN 0-933951-29-9. LC 89-14052.

*2. *Faulkner, Sut, and Other Southerners*. M. Thomas Inge. ISBN 0-933951-31-0. LC 91-40016.

3. *Essays of a Book Collector: Reminiscences on Some Old Books and Their Authors*. Claude A. Prance. ISBN 0-933951-30-2. LC 89-12734.

4. *Vision and Revisions: Essays on Faulkner*. John E. Bassett. ISBN 0-933951-32-9. LC 89-14046.

5. *A Rose by Another Name: A Survey of Literary Flora from Shakespeare to Eco*. Robert F. Fleissner. ISBN 0-933951-33-7. LC 89-12804.

7. *Blake's Milton Designs: The Dynamics of Meaning*. J.M.Q. Davies. ISBN 0-933951-40-X. LC 92–32678.

8. *The Slaughter-House of Mammon: An Anthology of Victorian Social Protest Literature*. Edited by Sharon A. Winn and Lynn M. Alexander. ISBN 0-933951-41-8. LC 92-7269.

9. *"A Heart of Ideality in My Realism" and Other Essays on Howells and Twain*. John E. Bassett. ISBN 0-933951-36-1. LC 90-46908.

10. *Imagining Romanticism: Essays on English and Australian Romanticisms*. Edited by Deirdre Coleman and Peter Otto. ISBN 0-933951-42-6. LC 91-36509.

*11. *Learning the Trade: Essays on W.B. Yeats and Contemporary Poetry*. Edited by Deborah Fleming. ISBN 0-933951-43-4. LC 92–39290.

12. *"All Nature is but Art": The Coincidence of Opposites in English Romantic Literature*. Mark Trevor Smith. ISBN 0-933951-44-2. LC 93–27166.

13. *Essays on Henry David Thoreau: Rhetoric, Style, and Audience*. Richard Dillman. ISBN 0-933951-50-7. LC 92–39960.

*14. *Author-ity and Textuality: Current Views of Collaborative Writing*. Edited by James S. Leonard. ISBN 0-933951-57-4. LC 94-15111.

15. **Women's Work: Essays in Cultural Studies.** Shelley Armitage. ISBN 0-933951-58-2. LC 95-6180.

16. **Perspectives on American Culture: Essays on Humor, Literature, and the Popular Arts.** M. Thomas Inge. ISBN 0-933951-59-0. LC 94-14908.

17. **Bridging the Gap: Literary Theory in the Classroom.** Edited by J.M.Q. Davies. ISBN 0-933951-60-4. LC 94–17926.

18. **Juan Benet: A Critical Reappraisal of His Fiction.** Edited by John B. Margenot III. ISBN 0-933951-61-2. LC 96–51479.

19. **The American Trilogy, 1900–1937: Norris, Dreiser, Dos Passos and the History of Mammon.** John C. Waldmeir. ISBN 0-933951-64-7. LC 94-48837.

20. **"The Muses Females Are": Martha Moulsworth and Other Women Writers of the English Renaissance.** Ed. by Robert C. Evans and Anne C. Little. ISBN 0-933951-63-9. LC 95-22413.

21. **Henry James in the Periodicals.** Arthur Sherbo. ISBN 0-933951-74-4. LC 97-11720.

22. **"Miss Tina Did It" and Other Fresh Looks at Modern Fiction.** Joseph J. Waldmeir. ISBN 0-933951-76-0. LC 97-28923.

*23. **Frank O'Connor: New Perspectives.** Ed. by Robert C. Evans and Richard Harp. ISBN 0-933951-79-5. LC 97-32626.

24. **Aldous Huxley & W.H. Auden: On Language.** David Garrett Izzo. ISBN 0-933951-80-9. LC 98-11922.

25. **Studies in the Johnson Circle.** Arthur Sherbo. ISBN 0-933951-81-7. LC 98-35292.

26. **Thornton Wilder: New Essays.** Ed. by Martin Blank, Dalma Hunyadi Brunauer, and David Garrett Izzo. ISBN 0-933951-83-3. LC 98-48986.

27. **Tragedy's Insights: Identity, Polity, Theodicy.** Ed. by Luis R. Gámez. ISBN 0-933951-85-X.

28. **Denise Levertov: New Perspectives.** Edited by Anne Colclough Little and Susie Paul. ISBN 0-933951-87-6. LC 00-035705.

29. **W.B. Yeats and Postcolonialism.** Edited by Deborah Fleming. ISBN 0-933951-88-4. LC 00-059801.

30. **John Quinn: Selected Irish Writers from His Library.** Ed. by Janis and Richard Londraville. ISBN 0-933951-93-0. LC 2001029303.

31. **W.H. Auden: A Legacy.** Ed. by David Garrett Izzo. ISBN 0-933951-94-9. LC 2001050308.

*Denotes out-of-print title